EVANS'
AMERICAN BIBLIOGRAPHY

1639 - - 1820 A. D.

AMERICAN BIBLIOGRAPHY

BY

CHARLES EVANS

———————

A CHRONOLOGICAL DICTIONARY

OF ALL

BOOKS PAMPHLETS AND PERIODICAL PUBLICATIONS

PRINTED IN THE

UNITED STATES OF AMERICA

FROM THE GENESIS OF PRINTING IN 1639
DOWN TO AND INCLUDING THE YEAR 1820

WITH BIBLIOGRAPHICAL AND BIOGRAPHICAL NOTES

VOLUME 11
1796-1797

" What is hit is history — what is missed is mystery."

" Bibliography is the handmaid of History."

NEW YORK
PETER SMITH
1942

FIRST PUBLISHED 1931
REPRINTED 1942

PRINTED IN THE UNITED STATES OF AMERICA

TO

JOSIAH QUINCY, 1772-1864

SCHOLAR PATRIOT STATESMAN

— THE CATO OF NEW ENGLAND —

BUILDER AND DEFENDER OF ITS INSTITUTIONS

WHO ADDED THE WORDS "THE GREAT" TO EACH

POSITION IN PUBLIC LIFE HE FILLED

This Volume is Dedicated

BY THE AUTHOR

"WHILE PASSING DOWN THE SERIES OF SUCCEEDING YEARS, AS THROUGH THE INTERIOR OF SOME ANCIENT TEMPLE, WHICH DISPLAYS ON EITHER HAND THE STATUES OF DISTINGUISHED FRIENDS AND BENEFACTORS, WE SHOULD STAY FOR A MOMENT IN THE PRESENCE OF EACH, DOING JUSTICE TO THE HUMBLE, ILLUSTRATING THE OBSCURE, PLACING IN A TRUE LIGHT THE MODEST, AND NOTING RAPIDLY THE MORAL AND INTELLECTUAL TRAITS WHICH TIME HAS SPARED; TO THE END THAT INGRATITUDE, THE PROVERBIAL SIN OF REPUBLICS, MAY NOT ATTACH TO THE REPUBLIC OF LETTERS; AND THAT WHOEVER FEEDS THE LAMP OF SCIENCE, HOWEVER OBSCURELY, HOWEVER SCANTILY, MAY KNOW, THAT SOONER OR LATER, HIS NAME AND VIRTUES SHALL BE MADE CONSPIC-UOUS BY ITS LIGHT, AND THROUGHOUT ALL TIME ACCOMPANY ITS LUSTRE."

JOSIAH QUINCY'S *History of Harvard University*, I:6.

AMERICAN BIBLIOGRAPHY

1639 - - 1820 A. D.

1796

CONTINUED

30833   NANCREDE, PAUL JOSEPH GUERARD DE   1760–1841
JOSEPH NANCREDE'S CATALOGUE OF BOOKS IN THE VARIOUS BRANCHES OF LITERA-
TURE; LATELY IMPORTED FROM LONDON, DUBLIN, PARIS, AND OTHER CAPITALS
OF EUROPE; FOR SALE, WHOLESALE AND RETAIL, AT HIS BOOKSTORE, No. 49
MARLBRO' STREET, BOSTON: CONSISTING PRINCIPALLY OF A VARIETY OF PUBLI-
CATIONS IN DIVINITY, LAW, PHYSIC, CHEMISTRY, BIOGRAPHY, VOYAGES, MISCEL-
LANIES, NOVELS, ARTS AND SCIENCES, GEOGRAPHY, UNIVERSAL HISTORY, NAVIGA-
TION, ASTRONOMY, MATHEMATICKS, TRADE AND MANUFACTURES, BOOK KEEPING,
&c. [Thirteen lines.]
     [Boston: Printed for Joseph Nancrede, 1796.] pp. (2), [46.] 12mo.   AAS.

30834   NEALE, SAMUEL   1729–1792
SOME ACCOUNT OF THE LIFE AND RELIGIOUS EXERCISES OF MARY NEALE, FORMERLY
MARY PEISLEY. PRINCIPALLY COMPILED FROM HER OWN WRITINGS.
     *Dublin—Printed: Philadelphia: Re-printed for and sold by Joseph Cruk-
shank, No. 87, High-Street.* 1796. pp. [118.] 12mo.   AAS. WIPL.

30835   NECKER, JACQUES   1732–1804
OF THE IMPORTANCE OF RELIGIOUS OPINIONS. TRANSLATED FROM THE FRENCH OF
MR. NECKER.
     *Boston: From the Press of Thomas Hall: sold by Thomas and Andrews, Wil-
liam P. Blake, David West, and John West.* 1796. pp. 230, (2). 12mo.
           BU. HC. JCB. NYPL.

30836   NETLEY ABBEY, A GOTHIC STORY.
     Philadelphia: 1796. 12mo.

30837   DER NEUE, GEMEINNÜTZIGES LANDWIRTHSCHAFTS CALENDAR, AUF DAS JAHR, NACH
DER HEILBRINGENDEN GEBURT UNSERS HERRN JESU CHRISTI, 1797. WELCHES
EIN GEMEINES JAHR VON 365 TAGEN IST. [Nine lines.] ZUM ZEHNTENMAL HER-
AUSGEGEBEN.
     *Lancaster, Gedruckt und zu haben bey Johann Albrecht und Comp. in der
neuen Buchdruckerey in der Prinz-strasse, das 2te Haus, nordlich vom Gesangniss.*
[1796.] pp. (44.) 4to.   AAS. LOC.
     The cover has a full page cut of a farming scene, and title as: Neuen
Lancästerscher Calender, 1797.

30838 DER NEUE Hoch Deutsche Americanische Calender, auf das Jahr Christi 1797, welches ein Gemein Jahr von 365 Tagen ist. Darin enthalten die Wochen-Monats-und merkwürdige Tage, des Monder Auf-und Untergang; seine Zeichen, Grade, und Viertel; die Aspecten der Planeten, samt der Witterung; des Siebengestirns Aufgang, Südplatz und Uhtergang; Auf-und Untergang der Sonne &c. Eingerichtet vor 40 Gred Norder-Brute, sonderlich vor Pennsylvanien; jedoch in den angrenzenden Staaten ohne merklichen Unterschied zu gebrauchen. Zum Siebenten-mal her-ausgegeben.

> *Baltimore, gedruckt und zu finden bey Samuel Saur. Auch Konnen die auswartigen Kramer solche bekommen, in Philadelphia, bey denen Herren Becker und Comp. David Saur und Daniel Brautigam; in Lancaster, bey hrn. Laumann, Zanzinger und Grundacker; in Autztaun, bey Hrn. Herman; in Libanon, bey Hrn. Stover; in Tulpehacken, bey Hrn. Spicker; in Reading, bey Hrn. Hahn, Dundas, Jungmann und andern; in Millerstaun, bey Hrn. Schlauch; in Bethlehem, bey Hrn. Reich; in Easton, bey Herrn Opp; in Neu-Germantaun, bey Hrn. Miller; in Virginien, bey Hrn. Stauffer; in Baltimore, bey Hrn. Tschudy und Schultz; in Neu-York, bey Hrn. Leuthauer und Feineuer; und fals bey allen Buchhandlern. zu Stadt und auf dem Land.* [1796.] pp. (40). 4to. AAS.

The cover has a full page view of Baltimore, with the motto: Biel leichter ist das Glük zu finden, Als zu behalten und zu binden. Samuel Saur's Calendar auf das Jahr 1797.

30839 DER NEUE Unpartheyische Baltimore [cut] Bote und Märylånder Staats-Register. Num. 42. Mitwochs den 6 Januar. [—Num. 93. Mitwochs den 28 Dezember, 1796.]

> *Diese Zeitung wird erstlich alle Mitwochen heraus gegeben, von Samuel Saur Buchdrucker in der Fayettestrasse zu Baltimore fur zehn Schilling des Jahrs wovon die Halfte beym Einschreiben bezahlte wird.* 1796. fol.

30840 NEUE, Unpartheyische Lancäster Zeitung und Anzeigs-Nachrichten. Num. 440. Mitwoch, den 6 Januar, —Num. 492. Mitwoch, den 28 Dezember, 1796.]

> *Lancaster: Gedruckt bey Johann Albrecht & Comp.* 1796. fol.

30841 NEUE Unpartheyische Readinger Zeitung und Anzeigs-Nachrichten. Mit-woch, den 6 Januar, [—Mitwoch, den 28 Dezember, 1796.]

> *Reading: Gedruckt bey Gottlob Jungmann und Co.* 1796. fol.

30842 NEUER, Erfahrner, Amerikanischer Haus-und Stall-Arzt, mit den natür-lichsten und leichtesten Mitteln, wider alle Krankheiten und Schwach-heiten der Menschen und Viehe. Zum nützen der Deutschen Nation in den Vereinigten Staaten. Mit einem Privilegio, in Gemassheit einer Act des Congresses, dem Verleger dieses Buchs sein Eigenthum vor Nach-druck zu beschützen.

> *Frederick-Town, gedruckt bey Matthias Bartgis.* 1796.

30843 NEÜER Unpartheyisches Eastoner Bothe, und Northamptoner Kundschafter. Num. 122. Mitwochs den 6 Januar, [— Num. 173. Mitwochs den 28 Dezem-ber, 1796.]

> *Diese Zeitung wird alle Mitwoch morgens herausgegeben von Jacob Weygandt und Sohn, in der Neuen Buchdruckerey zu Easton . . .* 1796. fol.

30844 A NEW drawing book, from the best masters. Price, 1 d. 25 cts.

> *Philadelphia: Printed for, and sold by, William Cobbett, opposite Christ Church.* 1796.

30845   THE NEW-ENGLAND PRIMER, IMPROVED, FOR THE MORE EASY ATTAINING THE TRUE READING OF ENGLISH. TO WHICH IS ADDED, THE ASSEMBLY OF DIVINES CATECHISM.
> *Boston: Printed and sold by Joseph White, next to the Swan Tavern.* [1796.] pp. (64), 32mo.   NYSL.

30846   —— THE NEW-ENGLAND PRIMER, OR AN EASY AND PLEASANT GUIDE TO THE ART OF READING. ADORNED WITH CUTS. TO WHICH IS ADDED, THE ASSEMBLY OF DIVINES' CATECHISM.
> *Boston: Printed for William P. Blake, at the Boston Book-Store, No.* 59 *Cornhill.* 1796.

"By the gross, dozen or single."

30847   —— THE NEW-ENGLAND PRIMER: MUCH IMPROVED. CONTAINING A VARIETY OF EASY LESSONS, FOR ATTAINING THE TRUE READING OF ENGLISH.
> *Germantown: Printed in the year* 1796. pp. (80). 32mo.

30848   —— THE NEWENGLAND PRIMER, MUCH ENLARGED, AND BETTER ADAPTED TO THE USE OF CHILDREN. TO WHICH IS ADDED, THE ASSEMBLY'S CATECHISM.
> *Lancaster, Printed and sold by W. & R. Dickson, in Kingstreet.* 1796. pp. (80). 32mo.

30849   —— THE NEW ENGLAND PRIMER, OR AN EASY AND PLEASANT GUIDE TO THE ART OF READING. ADORNED WITH CUTS. TO WHICH IS ADDED, THE ASSEMBLY OF DIVINES' CATECHISM.
> *Printed for Edmund M. Blunt, at the Newburyport Book-Store.* 1796.

"By the groce, dozen or single."

30850   NEW HAMPSHIRE. STATE.
THE CONSTITUTION OF NEW HAMPSHIRE, AS ALTERED AND AMENDED BY A CONVENTION OF DELEGATES HELD AT CONCORD, IN SAID STATE, BY ADJOURNMENT, ON THE SECOND WEDNESDAY OF FEBRUARY, M.DCC.XCVI.
> *Printed at Concord by George Hough, for the Convention.* [1796.] pp. 59. 12mo.   JCB.

30851   —— *Half-title:* PROCEEDINGS OF THE HOUSE OF REPRESENTATIVES.
Title: A JOURNAL OF THE PROCEEDINGS OF THE HON. HOUSE OF REPRESENTATIVES, OF THE STATE OF NEW-HAMPSHIRE, AT A SESSION OF THE GENERAL-COURT' HOLDEN AT EXETER, ON WEDNESDAY THE 1ST OF JUNE, 1796. [— 17 JUNE' 1796.] [Arms.]
> *State of New-Hampshire, Portsmouth: Printed by John Melcher, Printer to the State.* 1796. pp. 90. 8vo.   AAS. LOC.

30852   —— THE LAWS OF THE STATE OF NEW-HAMPSHIRE, PASSED AT A SESSION OF THE HONORABLE GENERAL-COURT, BEGUN AND HOLDEN AT CONCORD, DECEMBER, 1795. PRINTED FROM ATTESTED COPIES.
> *Portsmouth—New-Hampshire: Printed by John Melcher, Printer to the State,* 1796. pp. (2), 530–535. 8vo.   AAS. LOC.

30853   —— —— THE LAWS OF THE STATE OF NEW-HAMPSHIRE, PASSED AT A SESSION OF THE HONORABLE GENERAL-COURT, BEGUN AND HOLDEN AT EXETER, JUNE, 1796. PRINTED FROM ATTESTED COPIES.
> *Portsmouth—New-Hampshire: Printed by John Melcher, Printer to the State.* 1796. pp. (2), 538–550. 8vo.   AAS.

NEW HAMPSHIRE. STATE, continued.

30854 —— BY HIS EXCELLENCY JOHN TAYLOR GILMAN, GOVERNOR OF THE STATE OF NEW-HAMPSHIRE. A PROCLAMATION . . . APPOINT THURSDAY THE SEVENTH DAY OF APRIL NEXT TO BE OBSERVED AS A DAY OF PUBLIC FASTING AND PRAYER THROUGH-OUT THIS STATE. . . . GIVEN AT THE COUNCIL CHAMBER IN EXETER, THIS TWENTY-FOURTH DAY OF FEBRUARY, ONE THOUSAND, SEVEN HUNDRED AND NINETY-SIX, AND OF THE INDEPENDENCE OF THE UNITED STATES OF AMERICA THE TWENTIETH. JOHN T. GILMAN. BY HIS EXCELLENCY'S COMMAND, WITH THE ADVICE OF COUNCIL. JOSEPH PEARSON, SECRETARY.
Exeter: Printed by Henry Ranlet. 1796. Broadside.

30855 —— STATE OF NEW-HAMPSHIRE. BY THE GOVERNOR. A PROCLAMATION FOR A PUBLIC THANKSGIVING . . . THURSDAY THE SEVENTEENTH DAY OF NOVEMBER NEXT . . . GIVEN AT THE COUNCIL-CHAMBER, IN EXETER, THIS SEVENTEENTH DAY OF OCTOBER, ONE THOUSAND, SEVEN HUNDRED AND NINETY-SIX, AND OF THE INDEPENDENCE OF THE UNITED STATES OF AMERICA THE TWENTY-FIRST. JOHN TAYLOR GILMAN. BY HIS EXCELLENCY'S COMMAND, WITH ADVICE OF COUNCIL. J. PEARSON, SECRETARY.
Exeter: Printed by Henry Ranlet. 1796. Broadside.

30856 THE NEWHAMPSHIRE AND VERMONT JOURNAL: OR, THE FARMER'S WEEKLY MUSEUM. [Mottos]. VOL. III. NO. 144. TUESDAY, JANUARY 5, [— VOL. IV. NO. 195. TUESDAY, DECEMBER 27, 1796.]
Printed at Walpole, Newhampshire, by Isaiah Thomas and David Carlisle, jun. in the Main Street. . . . 1796. fol.   AAS.

With the issue for April 5th, Isaiah Thomas temporarily withdrew his name, and David Carlisle, junior, became, nominally, the sole proprietor. At about this time Joseph Dennie's connection, as Editor, gave the paper a degree of popularity beyond that of any village newspaper in the country. With the change the motto was changed to "Ho, every one that thirsteth for novelty—come!"

30857 THE NEW-HAMPSHIRE DIARY; OR ALMANACK: FOR THE YEAR OF OUR LORD 1797. BEING THE FIRST AFTER BISSEXTILE OR LEAP-YEAR, AND THE TWENTY-FIRST OF THE AMERICAN INDEPENDENCE. CALCULATED FOR THE MERIDIAN OF BOSTON, LAT 42 DEG. 25 M. N. BUT WILL SERVE FOR THE ADJACENT STATES WITH LITTLE VARIATION. CONTAINING A VARIETY OF USEFUL AND ENTERTAINING MATTER, SUITABLE FOR SUCH WORK. [Cut.]
Printed at Exeter. by H. Ranlet, and sold at his Book-store, by the groce, dozen, or single. [1796.] pp. (40). 8vo.   AAS. BA. BM. LOC. NHHS. NYPL.

Contains, The Romish priest. A tale. By Peter Pindar, esq. And, An Account of the plague in London—in the year 1665. Account of the plague in Marseilles, in the year 1720. Extract from the Account of the malignant fever, prevalent in the city of Philadelphia, in the year 1793. Of the yellow fever in Charleston, (S. C.) 1796. And, a sketch of the malignant fever which appeared in Newburyport in the year 1796.

30858 THE NEW HAMPSHIRE GAZETTE. [Motto.] VOL. XL. NUMB. 2040. SATURDAY, JANUARY 2. [— VOL. XLI. NUMB. 2092. SATURDAY, DECEMBER 31, 1796.]
Portsmouth: (New-Hampshire)—Published every Saturday morning by John Melcher, Printer to the State, at his office, corner of Market Street. . . . 1796. fol.   AAS.

In January this motto was added: Here Truth is welcome—Candour guides the way.

30859   THE NEW-HAMPSHIRE SPY. VOL. I. NO. I. SATURDAY, SEPTEMBER 24, [—NO. 15. SATURDAY, DECEMBER 31, 1796.]
     Exeter, (New-Hampshire) Published on Saturdays by Henry Ranlet, in Main-Street, . . . 1796. fol.   AAS.
     Established, as a weekly, by Henry Ranlet, and continued by him to the issue for March 18, 1797, when it was discontinued.

30860   NEW JERSEY. STATE.
     ACTS OF THE TWENTIETH GENERAL ASSEMBLY OF THE STATE OF NEW-JERSEY. AT A SESSION BEGUN AT TRENTON ON THE 27TH DAY OF OCTOBER, 1795, AND CONTINUED BY ADJOURNMENTS. BEING THE SECOND SITTING. [Arms.]
     Trenton: Printed by Matthias Day. M.DCC.XCVI. pp. (2), (25)–114. fol.
                               LOC.

30861   —— — ACTS OF THE TWENTY-FIRST GENERAL ASSEMBLY OF THE STATE OF NEW-JERSEY. AT A SESSION BEGUN AT TRENTON. BEING THE FIRST SITTING. [Arms.]
     Trenton: Printed by Matthias Day. M,DCC,XCVI. pp. (2), 107–127. fol.

30862   —— JOURNAL OF THE HOUSE OF ASSEMBLY. NEW JERSEY. WITH MINUTES AND PROCEEDINGS OF THE JOINT MEETING. [30 OCTOBER, 1795, — 18 MARCH, 1796.]
     [Trenton: Printed by Matthias Day. 1796.] pp. 5–61, 63–69. fol.

30863   NEW JERSEY. COLLEGE OF, NOW PRINCETON UNIVERSITY.
     [CIRCULAR.] PRINCETON, 179–. SIR, AS COMPLAINTS HAVE SOMETIMES BEEN MADE OF THE EXPENSES INCURRED BY A YOUNG MAN IN OBTAINING AN EDUCATION AT THIS PLACE, I HAVE THOUGHT IT PROPER, FOR THE INFORMATION OF PARENTS, TO MAKE A STATEMENT OF THOSE THAT ARE STRICTLY NECESSARY. THEY ARE– [totalling 171,21¼ cents. Urging economy by parents – purchase of clothing, and other necessaries at home. "Horses and barbers are utterly unnecessary to students; . . . the allowance for private expenses need not, at the utmost, exceed two dollars per month." Signed in ms. Sam'l S. Smith.]
     [Trenton: Printed by Matthias Day. 1796.] Broadside. 4to.   LOC.

30864   —— TO THE HONOURABLE THE LEGISLATIVE COUNCIL AND GENERAL ASSEMBLY OF THE STATE OF NEW-JERSEY. THE MEMORIAL AND PETITION OF THE TRUSTEES OF THE COLLEGE OF NEW-JERSEY HUMBLY SHEWETH, [The need of public appropriation of funds for its support.] SAMUEL S. SMITH, [and six others.] FEBRUARY 9, 1796.
     [Trenton: Printed by Matthias Day. 1796.] Broadside. fol.   LCP.

30865   THE NEW-JERSEY AND PENNSYLVANIA ALMANAC, FOR THE YEAR OF OUR LORD 1797; BEING THE FIRST AFTER BISSEXTILE, OR LEAP YEAR, AND THE TWENTY-SECOND OF AMERICAN INDEPENDENCE, AFTER THE FOURTH OF JULY. CONTAINING BESIDES THE USUAL REQUISITES OF AN ALMANAC, A VARIETY OF ENTERTAINING MATTER, IN PROSE AND VERSE.
     Trenton: Printed and sold, wholesale and retail, by Matthias Day. [1796.] pp. (40). 12mo.   LOC. NJSL. NYHS. NYPL.

30866   THE NEW-JERSEY JOURNAL. VOL. XIII. NO. 639. WEDNESDAY, JANUARY 6, [— VOL. XIV. NO. 690. WEDNESDAY, DECEMBER 28, 1796.]
     Elizabeth-Town: Printed and published by Shepard Kollock, every Wednesday, . . . 1796. fol.   AAS.

30867   NEW-JERSEY STATE GAZETTE. INDEPENDENCE 20TH YEAR. FEDERAL GOVERNMENT, 7TH YEAR. VOL. IV. NO. 18. WHOLE NO. 174. TUESDAY, JANUARY 5, [— VOL. IV. NO. 44. WHOLE NO. 200. TUESDAY, JULY 5, 1796.]
     Printed by Matthias Day, Trenton. 1796. fol.   AAS.
     Continued as *The State Gazette & New Jersey Advertiser.*

30868   NEW MILFORD. CONNECTICUT. UNION LIBRARY.
CONSTITUTION AND BYE-LAWS OF THE UNION LIBRARY, NEW MILFORD. [With Cata-
logue of books, and names of members.]
[Danbury: Printed by Douglas and Nichols. 1796.] pp. 16. 16mo.

30869   NEW STAR. [No. 1.] TUESDAY, FEBRUARY 2, 1796.
Hartford: Printed by Apollos Kinsley. 1796. 16mo.   AAS.

> Apparently but one issue of this curious little paper was made. It
> contains the following announcement: "This small paper is printed
> for the purpose of making experiments with a model of a Printing
> Press, on a new plan, lately invented by the Printer hereof. Though
> the Press is by no means complicated, it puts the ink on the types,
> carries in the papers and prints two sheets at a time, and will deliver
> them well printed at the rate of more than two thousand sheets in an
> hour, by the labor of one person only."

30870   THE NEW WORLD: OR, THE MORNING AND EVENING GAZETTE. VOL. 1. No. 1.
MONDAY, AUGUST 15 ? [— No. 170. SATURDAY, DECEMBER 31, 1796.]
*Philadelphia: Printed by Samuel Harrison Smith, No. 118 Chesnut Street.
1796.* 4to.   AAS, LCP. WHS.

> Established, as a twice a day paper, in royal quarto, by Samuel Harri-
> son Smith. With the issue for October 24, 1796, the paper was enlarged
> to folio, with a once a day issue, under the title of *The New World*.
> With the issue for August 16, 1797, Smith discontinued its publica-
> tion; and, in November, established in continuation *The Universal
> Gazette*.

30871   NEW YORK. STATE.
JOURNAL OF THE SENATE OF THE STATE OF NEW-YORK. AT THEIR NINETEENTH
SESSION, BEGUN AND HELD AT THE CITY-HALL, OF THE CITY OF NEW-YORK, ON
WEDNESDAY, THE SIXTH OF JANUARY, ONE THOUSAND SEVEN HUNDRED AND
NINETY-SIX. [—11 APRIL, 1796.] [Arms.]
New-York: Printed by John Childs, for the Printer to the State. M,DCC,-
XCVI. pp. [110.] fol.   NYHS. NYPL.

30872   —— SIXTEENTH SESSION, OF THE LAWS OF THE STATE OF NEW-YORK. [Arms.]
[GREENLEAF'S EDITION.] NUMBER I.—VOLUME III.
New-York—Printed by Thomas Greenleaf—M,DCC,XCIII. pp. (2), 100, (2).
8vo.   AAS.

30873   —— — SEVENTEENTH SESSION, OF THE LAWS OF THE STATE OF NEW-YORK,
[Arms.] [GREENLEAF'S EDITION.] NUMBER II.—VOLUME III.
New-York—Printed by Thomas Greenleaf—M,DCC,XCIV. pp. (2), 101–
158. 8vo.

30874   —— — EIGHTEENTH SESSION, OF THE LAWS OF THE STATE OF NEW-YORK.
[Arms.] [GREENLEAF'S EDITION.] NUMBER III.—VOLUME III.
New-York—Printed by Thomas Greenleaf—M,DCC,XCV. pp. (2), 159–258,
(3). 8vo.   AAS.

30875   —— — NINETEENTH SESSION, OF THE LAWS OF THE STATE OF NEW-YORK.
[Arms.] [GREENLEAF'S EDITION.] NUMBER IV.—VOLUME III.
New-York—Printed by Thomas Greenleaf—M,DCC,XCVI. pp. (2), 259–
354, (2). 8vo.   AAS.

30876　NEW YORK. STATE, continued.
—— — LAWS OF THE STATE OF NEW-YORK. NINETEENTH SESSION. [9 JAN-
UARY,—11 APRIL, 1796.] [Arms.]
New-York: Printed by John Childs, for the Printer to the State. 1796. pp.
54, (2). fol.　　　　　　　　　　　　　　　　　　　　　　NYHS. NYPL.

30877　—— THE MILITIA ACT. WITH LATEST AMENDMENTS.
Poughkeepsie: Printed by Nicholas Power. 1796.

30878　—— THE TEN POUND ACT. WITH THE AMENDMENT.
Poughkeepsie: Printed by Nicholas Power. 1796.

30879　NEW YORK. CITY. BAPTIST ASSOCIATION.
MINUTES OF THE NEW YORK BAPTIST ASSOCIATION.
[*New-York:* 1796.] 4to.

30880　NEW YORK. CITY. CABINET AND CHAIR MAKERS.
THE JOURNEYMEN CABINET AND CHAIR-MAKER'S NEW-YORK BOOK OF PRICES.
New-York: 1796.

30881　NEW YORK. CITY. CHAMBER OF COMMERCE.
BYE-LAWS, RESOLUTIONS, AND ORDERS, ADOPTED BY THE NEW-YORK CHAMBER OF
COMMERCE, AT A SPECIAL MEETING HELD MAY 10TH, 1796.
New-York: Printed by Archibald M'Lean. M,DCC,XCVI. pp. 12. 12mo.

30882　NEW YORK. CITY. MARINE SOCIETY.
CHARTER OF THE MARINE SOCIETY OF THE CITY OF NEW-YORK.
New-York: 1796.

30883　NEW YORK. CITY. MISSIONARY SOCIETY.
THE ADDRESS AND CONSTITUTION OF THE NEW-YORK MISSIONARY SOCIETY.
[Vignette.]
New-York: Printed by T. and J. Swords, No. 99 Pearl-street.—1796.—pp.
(19). 8vo.　　　　　　　　AAS. BM. JCB. MHS. NYHS. NYPL. UTS.

30884　NEW YORK. CITY. NEW YORK INSURANCE COMPANY.
ARTICLES OF ASSOCIATION OF THE NEW-YORK INSURANCE COMPANY.
New-York: Printed by John Childs, No. 7, Garden-Street. 1796. pp. [20.]
8vo.　　　　　　　　　　　　　　　　　　　　　　　　　　NYPL.

30885　NEW YORK. CITY. SOCIETY FOR PROMOTING THE MANUMISSION OF SLAVES.
THE CONSTITUTION OF THE NEW-YORK SOCIETY FOR PROMOTING THE MANUMISSION
OF SLAVES, AND PROTECTING SUCH OF THEM AS HAVE BEEN, OR MAY BE, LIB-
ERATED.
New-York: 1796. pp. 19. 8vo.

30886　NEW YORK. CITY. TONTINE ASSOCIATION.
THE CONSTITUTION AND NOMINATIONS OF THE SUBSCRIBERS TO THE TONTINE
COFFEE-HOUSE. [Ornaments.]
New-York: Printed in the year 1796. pp. (2), [47.] 4to.
AAS. JCB. NL. NYHS. NYPL.

Under the terms of the Agreement, the property was divided, in 1876,
when the original nominees were reduced by death to seven. The
original cost of each share was $200, and the amount received, when
the property was sold at auction, in 1881, was $138,550.

30887   NEW YORK. CITY. WASHINGTON MILITARY SOCIETY.
THE CONSTITUTION AND BYE-LAWS OF THE NEW YORK MILITARY SOCIETY. PUB-
LISHED BY ORDER OF THE SOCIETY, 27TH. OCT. 1796.
New-York: Printed by William A. Davis, No. 438 Pearl Street. 1796. pp.
[12.] 12mo.   MHS. NYPL.

30888   THE NEW-YORK GAZETTE AND GENERAL ADVERTISER. NUMB. 2192. FRIDAY,
JANUARY 1, [—NUMB. 2505. SATURDAY, DECEMBER 31, 1796.]
*Published (daily) by A. M'Lean, Franklin's Head, No. 116, Pearl-Street.
late 41, Hanover-Square, nearly opposite the New-York Bank.* 1796. fol.

30889   THE NEW-YORK MAGAZINE; OR, LITERARY REPOSITORY. [JANUARY-DECEMBER]
1796. NEW SERIES —· VOL. I. [Ornament.]
New-York: Printed and sold by T. and J. Swords, No. 99 Pearl-street. 1796.
pp. vii, ii, 672, 12 plates. 8vo. AAS. BPL. HC. HSP. JCB. LCP. LOC. NYHS. NYPL. YC.

30890   THE NEW-YORK PRICES CURRENT. VOL. I. NO. 1. JANUARY, [—VOL. II. No.
53, MONDAY, DECEMBER 26, 1796.]
New-York: Published weekly by James Oram, 1796. 4to.

Established, as a weekly, by James Oram. With the issue for June 3,
1797, the title was changed to *Oram's New-York Price-Current, and
Marine Register.* With the issue for May 25, 1799, this was changed
to *New-York Price-Current;* and, with the issue for June 26, 1802, to
Oram's New-York Price-Current. In September, 1804, Oram disposed
of his interests to Alexander Ming and William Young; and, with the
issue for September 8, 1804, the title was changed to *Ming & Young's
New-York Price-Current.* Young died September 15, 1805; and, with
the issue for September 21, 1805, the title was changed to *Ming's New-
York Price-Current.* With the issue for January 30, 1813, Samuel Dickinson became the publisher, and the title was changed to *Dickinson's
(formerly) Ming's New-York Price-Current;* but, with the issue for
March, 20, 1813, the title reverted to *Ming's New-York Price-Current,*
Dickinson continuing as publisher up to the issue for November 19,
1814, when Alexander Ming resumed publication. With the issue for
May 4, 1816, the number of pages was increased to eight, changing
back to four pages, with the issue for May 24, 1817, when publication
was made semi-weekly; and, with the issue for December 6, 1817, it
was decreased to two pages. Publication was, apparently, discontinued
at the end of the year 1817.

30891   THE NEW-YORK WEEKLY MAGAZINE; OR, MISCELLANEOUS REPOSITORY: FORMING
AN INTERESTING COLLECTION OF ORIGINAL AND SELECT LITERARY PRODUCTIONS
IN PROSE AND VERSE: CALCULATED FOR INSTRUCTION AND RATIONAL ENTERTAIN-
MENT—THE PROMOTION OF MORAL AND USEFUL KNOWLEDGE—AND TO ENLARGE
AND CORRECT THE UNDERSTANDINGS OF YOUTH. VOLUME I. [WEDNESDAY, JULY
1, 1795.—WEDNESDAY, JUNE 29, 1796.] [Four lines of verse.] [Ornament.]
New-York: Printed and published by John Bull, No. 115, Cherry-street
M,DCC,XCVI. pp. viii, 416, frontispiece. 4to.   LOC.

30892   —— THE NEW-YORK WEEKLY MAGAZINE; OR, MISCELLANEOUS REPOSITORY. VOL.
II. No. 53. WEDNESDAY. JULY 6, 1796. [—No. 78. WEDNESDAY, DECEMBER
28, 1796.]
*New-York: Printed by John Bull, No. 115, Cherry-Street, where every kind
of printing work is executed with the utmost accuracy, elegance and dispatch.—
Subscriptions for this Magazine (at 2s per month) are taken in at the Printing-
Office, and by E. Mitchell, Bookseller, No. 9, Maiden-Lane.* 1796. pp. 208. 4to.
     AAS. BA. HSP. LOC. NYHS. NYSL. WHS. YC.
In January, 1797, John Bull disposed of his interests in the Magazine
to Thomas Burling, junior.

30893   THE NEWBURGH PACKET. VOL. III. No. 110. TUESDAY, JANUARY 5, [—VOL. IV. No. 161, TUESDAY, DECEMBER 27, 1796.]

Newburgh, [N. Y.] Published by Lucius Cary. 1796. fol.

In the fall of this year, Cary removed his Press to Geneva and, in December, established there the *Ontario Gazette and Western Chronicle.* There appears to be good evidence that David Denniston continued publication of the Packet certainly into June of the following year.

30894   NEWMAN, JOHN

THE COLUMBIAN CALENDAR, OR NEW-ENGLAND ALMANACK FOR THE YEAR OF OUR LORD 1797: BEING THE FIRST AFTER BISSEXTILE, OR LEAP YEAR, AND THE TWENTY-FIRST OF AMERICAN INDEPENDENCE, WHICH COMMENCED JULY 4, 1776. CONTAINING A VARIETY OF MATTER CURIOUS, USEFUL AND ENTERTAINING. THE ASTRONOMICAL CALCULATIONS BY JOHN NEWMAN, PHILOM.

Printed at the Minerva Press in Dedham, and sold by the groce, dozen, or single, by David Heaton, in Wrentham. [1796.] 12mo.   AAS. NYPL.

30895   NEWPORT. RHODE ISLAND. BANK OF RHODE ISLAND.

RESOLVED, THAT THE FOLLOWING ACTS AND RESOLUTIONS BE PUBLISHED FOR THE INFORMATION OF THE STOCKHOLDERS OF THE BANK OF RHODE-ISLAND, AND SUCH PERSONS AS MAY HAVE TO TRANSACT BUSINESS WITH THE BANK. [Twenty-nine lines.] BY ORDER OF THE PRESIDENT AND DIRECTORS, MOSES SEIXAS, CASHIER.

Newport, [Printed by Henry Barber] January 5, 1796. Broadside. fol. JCB.

30896   NEWPORT. RHODE ISLAND. STAR FIRE SOCIETY.

ARTICLES OF THE STAR FIRE SOCIETY.

Newport: Printed by Henry Barber, 1796.   NHS.

30897   THE NEWPORT MERCURY. No. 1759. TUESDAY, JANUARY 5, [—No. 1810. TUESDAY, DECEMBER 27, 1796.]

Newport (Rhode Island) Published by Henry Barber, near the State-House. 1795. fol.   AAS. LOC. NHS. RIHS. RL.

30898   NEWTON, JOHN   1725–1807

AN AUTHENTIC NARRATIVE OF SOME REMARKABLE AND INTERESTING PARTICULARS IN THE LIFE OF JOHN NEWTON. COMMUNICATED IN A SERIES OF LETTERS TO THE REV. MR. HAWEIS, RECTOR OF ALDWINCKLE, NORTHAMTONSHIRE; [Six lines of Scripture texts.]

New-York: Printed by W. A. Davis, for C. Davis, No. 212, Water-Street. 1796. pp. (2), (2), 248, portrait. 12mo.   AAS. NYPL.

30899   —— *General title:* LETTERS AND SERMONS, WITH A REVIEW OF ECCLESIASTICAL HISTORY, AND HYMNS. BY JOHN NEWTON, RECTOR OF ST. MARY, WOOLNOTH, LONDON. IN SIX VOLUMES. VOL. IV. [—V.]

Philadelphia: Printed by William Young, Bookseller, No. 52, Second-Street, the corner of Chesnut-Street. M,DCC,XCVI. 2 vols. pp. (2), viii, 340; xviii, 320. 12mo.   AAS.

Second title: SIX DISCOURSES, OR SERMONS, AS INTENDED FOR THE PULPIT. ALSO, TWENTY SERMONS PREACHED IN THE PARISH-CHURCH OF OLNEY. BY JOHN NEWTON, RECTOR OF ST. MARY, WOOLNOTH, LONDON.

Philadelphia: Printed by William Young, Bookseller, No. 52, Second-Street, corner of Chesnut-Street. M,DCC,XCVI. pp. (2), viii, 340.

NEWTON, John, continued.

Third title: LETTERS AND SERMONS, WITH A REVIEW OF ECCLESIASTICAL HISTORY, AND HYMNS. BY JOHN NEWTON, RECTOR OF ST. MARY, WOOLNOTH, LONDON. IN SIX VOLUMES. VOL. V.

Philadelphia: Printed by William Young, Bookseller, No. 52, Second-Street, the corner of Chesnut-Street. M,DCC,XCVI. pp. xviii, 320.

This volume contains besides A Review of Ecclesiastical history, in two books, The Guilt and danger of such a Nation as this! A sermon preached in the Parish Church of St. Mary, Woolnoth, on Wednesday, February 21, 1781. The day appointed for a general fast. pp. 293-320.

30900 —— A MONUMENT TO THE PRAISE OF THE LORD'S GOODNESS, AND TO THE MEMORY OF DEAR ELIZA CUNNINGHAM, [PUBLISHED FOR THE BENEFIT OF A CHARITABLE INSTITUTION.] [Three lines of Scripture texts.] THE FIRST AMERICAN EDITION.

Philadelphia: Printed for Willam Rogers, by Lang & Ustick. 1796. pp. 30. 8vo. AAS. JCB.

30901 —— VERSES . . . ON HIS MARRIAGE, AND THE DEATH OF HIS WIFE IN 1790. BY JOHN NEWTON.

New-York: Printed by William A. Davis, 1796. pp. 12. 24mo.

30902 NEWTON, THOMAS 1704-1782
DISSERTATIONS ON THE PROPHECIES, WHICH HAVE REMARKABLY BEEN FULFILLED, AND AT THIS TIME ARE FULFILLING IN THE WORLD. BY THOMAS NEWTON, D. D. LATE LORD BISHOP OF BRISTOL.

Printed at Northampton, (Massachusetts) [For Isaiah Thomas, Worcester, and Thomas and Andrews, Boston] by William Butler, M,DCC,XCVI. pp. (2), (5), 591. 8vo. AAS. BA.

30903 NEWTOWN. NEW HAMPSHIRE. BAPTIST CHURCH.
A CONFESSION OF FAITH AND CHURCH ORDER: ADOPTED BY THE BAPTIST CHURCH OF CHRIST IN NEWTOWN, NEW-HAMPSHIRE. CONSTITUTED, FEBRUARY 17TH, 1796. [Two lines from] PAUL.

Printed at Exeter, by Henry Ranlet, for Rev. John Peak, pastor of said Church. M,DCC,XCVI. pp. 16. 8vo. AAS.

30904 NICCOLAI or NICOLAI, VALENTIN –1799
A FAVORITE SONATA [I.] BY NICCOLAI.

[Philadelphia:] Published by G. Willig, No. 165 *Mt. St.* [1796.] pp. 7. 4to. NYPL.

30905 NICHOLS, THOMAS
POVERTY AND RICHES. A SERMON PREACHED BEFORE THE MASONIC LODGE AT MANCHESTER, VERMONT. BY THE REV. THOMAS NICHOLS, MINISTER OF ST. JAMES CHURCH, ARLINGTON, VERMONT.

Bennington: Printed by Anthony Haswell. 1796.

30906 THE NIGHTINGALE, OR, A MELANGE DE LITTERATURE; A PERIODICAL PUBLICATION. [Three lines from] MILTON. EDITED BY JOHN LATHROP, JUN. VOL. I. FROM MAY TO AUGUST, 1796.

Boston: Printed [by John Russell & Co.] for the Proprietors, at their Office, Quaker-Lane. MDCCXCVI. pp. (12), 432. 12mo. AAS. BPL. LOC. NYPL. YC.

All that was published. Issued three times a week, each number containing twelve pages, with title and index. The second volume was announced as a weekly continuation, but no copies are known.

30907   THE NIGHTINGALE, continued.
—— PROSPECTUS OF THE NIGHTINGALE. A NEW EVENING PAPER.
[Boston: Printed by John Russell & Co. January 13th, 1796.] pp. 12.
12mo.   AAS.

30908   NORFOLK HERALD. VOL. 2. No. 56. SATURDAY, JANUARY 2, [—VOL. 3. No. 209.
SATURDAY, DECEMBER 31, 1796.]
Norfolk: Published on Mondays, Thursdays and Saturdays, by Willett &
O'Connor, near the Market. 1796. fol.   LOC.
Beginning with the issue for November 3d, the title was altered to
The Norfolk Herald & public advertiser, and so continued.

30909   NORTH CAROLINA. STATE.
A COLLECTION OF THE STATUTES OF THE PARLIAMENT OF ENGLAND IN FORCE IN
THE STATE OF NORTH CAROLINA, PUBLISHED ACCORDING TO A RESOLVE OF
THE GENERAL ASSEMBLY.
Newbern: Printed by Francois –X. Martin. 1796. 4to.

30910   —— JOURNAL OF THE HOUSE OF COMMONS OF THE GENERAL ASSEMBLY OF NORTH-
CAROLINA, NOVEMBER AND DECEMBER SESSION, 1795.
[Halifax: Printed by Hodge & Wills, 1796.] pp. 57. fol.   NCSL.

30911   —— JOURNAL OF THE SENATE OF THE GENERAL ASSEMBLY OF NORTH-CAROLINA,
NOVEMBER AND DECEMBER SESSION, 1795.
[Halifax: Printed by Hodge & Wills, 1796.] pp. 46. fol.   NCSL.

30912   —— LAWS OF NORTH-CAROLINA. AT A GENERAL ASSEMBLY BEGUN AND HELD AT
THE CITY OF RALEIGH, ON THE SECOND DAY OF NOVEMBER, IN THE YEAR OF OUR
LORD ONE THOUSAND SEVEN HUNDRED AND NINETY-FIVE, AND IN THE TWENTIETH
YEAR OF AMERICAN INDEPENDENCE: BEING THE FIRST SESSION OF THE SAID AS-
SEMBLY. [—9 DECEMBER, 1795.] [Colophon:]
Edenton: Printed by Hodge & Wills, Printers to the State. [1796.] pp. 31,
(1). fol.   LOC. NCSL. NCU. NYPL.

30913   NORTH-CAROLINA GAZETTE. VOL. XI. No. 521. SATURDAY, JANUARY 2, [—No.
572. SATURDAY, DECEMBER 31, 1796.]
Newbern: Printed by Francois –X. Martin. 1796. fol.

30914   THE NORTH-CAROLINA JOURNAL. No. 181. MONDAY, JANUARY 4, [—No. 232.
MONDAY. DECEMBER, 26, 1796.]
Halifax: Printed by Abraham Hodge, joint printer to the State with H.
Wills. 1796. fol.   AAS. HSP. LOC.

30915   THE NORTH-CAROLINA MINERVA, AND FAYETTEVILLE ADVERTISER. VOL. 1.
NUMB. 1. THURSDAY, MARCH 24, [—NUMB. 42. SATURDAY, DECEMBER 31, 1796.]
Fayetteville: Published by Hodge & Boylan. 1796. fol.
Established, as a weekly, by Abraham Hodge, and William Boylan,
and continued by them at Fayetteville into March, 1799, when they
removed their Press to Raleigh, and continued its publication there,
without change in numbering, in May, 1799, as *The North-Carolina*
Minerva, and Raleigh Advertiser. Late in 1800, the sub-title was
dropped from the heading; and in May, 1803, the title was changed to
Minerva; or, Anti-Jacobin, when Hodge retired from the firm. Early
in 1805, this title was shortened to *The Minerva.* And in November,
1809, altered to *The Raleigh Minerva.* In May, 1810, Alexander Lucas
became associated with William Boylan, as editor; and, in November,
1810, Boylan withdrew, and the paper was published by Alexander
Lucas and Abraham H. Boylan, the latter withdrawing some time
after 1812, when Lucas became sole publisher into 1819, when——
Harvey was admitted to partnership as Lucas and Harvey, under whose
direction it was continued beyond the period of this work.

30916 NORTHWEST TERRITORY.
LAWS OF THE TERRITORY OF THE UNITED STATES NORTH - - WEST OF THE OHIO:
ADOPTED AND MADE BY THE GOVERNOUR AND JUDGES, IN THEIR LEGISLATIVE
CAPACITY, AT A SESSION BEGUN ON FRIDAY, THE XXIX DAY OF MAY, ONE THOUSAND
SEVEN HUNDRED AND NINETY-FIVE, AND ENDING ON TUESDAY THE TWENTY-FIFTH
DAY OF AUGUST FOLLOWING: WITH AN APPENDIX OF RESOLUTIONS AND THE OR-
DINANCE FOR THE GOVERNMENT OF THE TERRITORY. BY AUTHORITY.
Cincinnati: Printed by W. Maxwell. M,DCC,XCVI. pp. [225.] 4to.
JCB. LOC. NYPL.

Known as Maxwell's Code. The first book printed in the Territory.
A facsimile reprint has been made.

30917 —— A TABLE OF THE VARIATIONS IN THE LAWS OF THE TERRITORY, AS PRINTED
BY W. MAXWELL, AND THE BOOKS OF LAWS IN THE SECRETARY'S OFFICE. COM-
PILED BY THOMAS GOUDY.
Cincinnati: Printed by Samuel Freeman and Son. July 1796.

"The copy of the Laws of the Territory printed by Mr. Maxwell, has
been compared by the Secretary with the books in his office. and very
material errors discovered therein. A Table of the variations has
been published, and will be furnished by Mr. Goudy to those persons
who receive the Laws from the Secretary's office. A few additional
copies thereof have been struck off, by the Printer for the information
of those who may procure the Laws by purchase, and are to be had at
his office in Front Street. Sign of the three Tons. Price six cents."

30918 —— PLAT OF THE SEVEN RANGES OF TOWNSHIPS, BEING PART OF THE TERRITORY
OF THE UNITED STATES N. W. OF THE RIVER OHIO, WHICH BY A LATE ACT OF
CONGRESS ARE DIRECTED TO BE SOLD.
[*Philadelphia: Printed for Mathew Carey,* 1796.]

157th Pennsylvania District Copyright, issued to Mathew Carey, as
Proprietor, 30 September, 1796.

30919 THE NORWICH [Cut of] PACKET. VOL. XXII. No. 1138. THURSDAY, JANUARY 7,
[—VOL. XXIII. No. 1189. THURSDAY, DECEMBER 29, 1796.]
*Norwich, (Connecticut)—Published by John Trumbull, a few rods west of the
Meeting-House.* 1796. fol.
AAS.

30920 NOTH UND HÜLFSBÜCHLEIN FÜR BAUERSLEUTE.
Philadelphia: Gedruckt bey Neal und Kammerer. 1796.

30921 NOYES, JAMES
AN ASTRONOMICAL DIARY OR ALMANACK, FOR THE YEAR OF CHRISTIAN ÆRA, 1797.
BEING FIRST AFTER BISSEXTILE OR LEAP YEAR. CALCULATED FOR THE MERIDIAN
OF PORTSMOUTH, LAT. 43 DEG. 5 MIN. NORTH. BUT WILL SERVE FOR ANY OF THE
ADJACENT STATES. BY JAMES NOYES. [Eight lines of verse.]
Printed at Dover, and for sale by the gross, dozen or single, at the Sun office.
[1796] pp. (24). 12mo.
LOC.

30922 OBSERVATIONS ON DR. MACKRILL'S HISTORY OF THE YELLOW FEVER. BY A GEN-
TLEMAN OF THE FACULTY.
Baltimore: Printed by John Hayes. 1796. pp. 60. 12mo.
SGO.

30923 OBSERVATOR, pseudonym.
THOUGHTS ON CHRISTIAN BAPTISM, DEDUCED FROM SCRIPTURE. BY OBSERVATOR.
OCCASIONED BY CERTAIN EXPRESSIONS USED AND DIRECTIONS GIVEN IN A SERMON
DELIVERED BEFORE THE PRESBYTERIAN CHURCH IN THE CITY OF NEW-YORK,
MARCH 13, 1796. BY A LEARNED AND PIOUS DIVINE.
*New-York Printed and sold by W. Durell, at his Printing Office, No. 208,
Pearl Street. 1796. pp. 27. 8vo.* AAS. JCB. NYPL.

30924 ODE ON THE BIRTH-DAY OF THE PRESIDENT OF THE UNITED STATES. 1796. HENCE!
PALE ENVY'S STEP PROFANE! [Two columns of verse, with chorus.]
[Philadelphia: 1796.] Broadside. fol. LCP.

30925 ODES FOR THE FOURTH OF JULY. 1796.
[Providence: 1796.] Broadside. 4to.

30926 ONTARIO GAZETTE AND WESTERN CHRONICLE. VOL. I. NUMB. 1. FRIDAY, DECEM-
BER 16, [—NUMB. 3. FRIDAY, DECEMBER 30, 1796.]
*Published every Friday, by Lucius Cary, in Geneva, County of Ontario—
State of New-York. 1796. fol.*

Established, as a weekly, by Lucius Cary, and continued by him probably to the end of the first volume in December, 1797,—the sub-title in
the meantime having been dropped from the heading. It is probable
that Cary removed his printing office early in the following year to
Canandaigua, and in April, 1798, established there, with the same volume numbering, his *Ontario Gazette.*

30927 THE ORACLE OF DAUPHIN. AND HARRISBURGH ADVERTISER. VOL. IV. No. 12.
MONDAY, JANUARY 4, [—VOL. V. No. 11. WEDNESDAY, DECEMBER 28, 1796.]
*Printed by John Wyeth, at his Office in Mulberry-Street, Harrisburgh
1796. fol.*

30928 THE ORACLE OF THE DAY. [Motto.] No. 10 OF VOL. VI. SATURDAY, JANUARY 2,
[—No. 10 OF VOL. VII. WEDNESDAY, DECEMBER 28, 1796.]
*Published every Saturday morning, by Charles Peirce, in Court-Street, Ports-
mouth, New-Hampshire. 1796. fol.* AAS.

Beginning in January, the size of the paper was enlarged to royal folio;
and publication was made weekly on Saturdays, which, before June,
was changed to Thursdays, and in November to Wednesdays. With the
change, "Open to all, and influenced by none" was added, after the
motto, in the heading.

30929 THE ORANGE NIGHTINGALE, AND NEWBURY MORNING STAR. VOL. I. No. 1.
THURSDAY, MAY 12, [—No. 33. MONDAY, DECEMBER 26, 1796.]
Newbury, (Vermont): Printed by Nathaniel Coverly, jun'r. 1796. fol.

Established, as a weekly, by Nathaniel Coverly, junior, and continued
by him into September, 1797. Before May, 1797, the title was changed
to *Orange Nightingale, and New-Hampshire Advertiser.*

30930 ORIENTAL [cut] TRUMPET. VOL. I. No. 1. THURSDAY, DECEMBER 15, [—No. 3.
THURSDAY, DECEMBER 29, 1796.]
*Portland—(Dist. of Maine)—Published by John Rand, at his Office in Mid-
dle-Street, near the head of Fish-Street. 1796. fol.* AAS.

Established, as a weekly, by John Rand. With the issue for April 25,
1798, William Burdick was admitted to partnership, as Rand and Burdick. And the title was enlarged to, *Oriental Trumpet: or, town and
country gazette.* With the issue for November 5th, Burdick withdrew,
and John Rand continued publication, probably, to the end of the
fourth volume, in December, 1800, when it was discontinued.

30981   OSWALD, JAMES
ONE KIND KISS, BEFORE WE PART. A FAVORITE SONG COMPOSED BY DR. JACKSON
AND SUNG BY MRS. HODGKINSON. PRICE 20 CENTS.
[*Philadelphia:*] *Printed at Carr's Musical Repositories.* [1796.] pp. (2).
4to.   HSP.

30982   OTSEGO COUNTY. NEW YORK. BAPTIST ASSOCIATION.
MINUTES OF THE OTSEGO BAPTIST ASSOCIATION.
Cooperstown: Printed by Elihu Phinney. 1796. 8vo.

30983   OTSEGO HERALD: OR, WESTERN ADVERTISER. [MOTTO.] VOL. I. NUMB. 40. FRI-
DAY, JANUARY 1, [—VOL. II. NUMB. 92. THURSDAY, DECEMBER 29, 1796.]
☞ *Cooperstown: Printed and published (every Thursday, at two dollars per
annum) by Elihu Phinney, at his Printing-Office, first door east of the Court-
House; . . .* 1796. fol.

30984   OTTO, JOHN C.   1775 – 1845
AN INAUGURAL ESSAY ON EPILEPSY, SUBMITTED TO THE EXAMINATION OF THE REV.
JOHN EWING, S. T. P. PROVOST; THE TRUSTEES AND MEDICAL FACULTY OF THE
UNIVERSITY OF PENNSYLVANIA, ON THE 17TH DAY OF MAY, 1796. FOR THE DE-
GREE OF DOCTOR OF MEDICINE. BY JOHN C. OTTO, A.M. MEMBER OF THE MEDI-
CAL AND CHEMICAL SOCIETIES OF PHILADELPHIA.
Philadelphia: Printed by Lang & Ustick, M,DCC,XCVI. pp. (55). 8vo.
AAS. PU. SGO.

30985   PACKARD, ASA   – 1843
A SERMON, PREACHED AT SURRY, AT THE ORDINATION OF THE REV. PERLEY
HOWE, SEPTEMBER 16, 1795. BY ASA PACKARD, A.M. PASTOR OF THE CHURCH
IN MARLBOROUGH, (MASSACHUSETTS).
Walpole, New Hampshire. By David Carlisle, jun. 1796. pp. 30. 8vo.
AAS. JCB.

30986   PACKARD, HEZEKIAH   1761 – 1849
A CATECHISM, CONTAINING THE FIRST PRINCIPLES OF RELIGIOUS AND SOCIAL DUTIES.
ADAPTED TO THE CAPACITIES OF CHILDREN AND YOUTH, AND BENEFICIAL TO
HEADS OF FAMILIES. BY HEZEKIAH PACKARD, MINISTER OF CHELMSFORD.
[Four lines from] MOSES.
Printed by Samuel Hall, No. 53 Cornhill, Boston. 1796. pp. (84). 12mo.
AAS. JCB. NYPL.

97th Massachusetts District Copyright, issued to Hezekiah Packard,
as Author, 26 April, 1796.

30987   PADDY'S RESOURCE: BEING A SELECT COLLECTION OF ORIGINAL AND MODERN PATRI-
OTIC SONGS, TOASTS AND SENTIMENTS, COMPILED FOR THE USE OF ALL FIRM PA-
TRIOTS. FIRST AMERICAN EDITION.
Philadelphia: Printed for, and sold by T. Stephens. M,DCC,XCVI. pp. [72],
frontispiece. 12mo.   LOC.

30988   PAGE, JOHN   1744 – 1808
AN ADDRESS TO THE CITIZENS OF THE DISTRICT OF YORK, IN VIRGINIA. BY THEIR
REPRESENTATIVE, JOHN PAGE, OF ROSEWELL.
[*Philadelphia:* 1796.] pp. (32). 8vo.   BA. HC. HSP.
Dated, Rosewell, (Gloucester County), Aug. 5th, 1796.

30939   PAGE, REED
A SERMON, DELIVERED AT THE ORDINATION OF THE REV. JABEZ P. FISHER, A. B. TO THE PASTORAL CARE OF THE CHURCH IN NOTTINGHAM WEST, FEBRUARY 24, 1796. BY REED PAGE, A. M. PASTOR OF THE CHURCH IN HANCOCK.
Printed at Amherst, by Samuel Cushing. MDCCXCVI. pp. 48. 8vo. AAS. JCB.

30940   PAIN, WILLIAM   1730–1790
THE PRACTICAL HOUSE CARPENTER; OR, YOUTH'S INSTRUCTOR: CONTAINING A GREAT VARIETY OF USEFUL DESIGNS IN CARPENTRY AND ARCHITECTURE; AS CENTERING FOR GROINS, NICHES, &C. EXAMPLES FOR ROOFS, SKY LIGHTS, &C. THE FIVE ORDERS LAID DOWN BY A NEW SCALE. MOULDINGS, &C. AT LARGE, WITH THEIR ENRICHMENTS. PLANS, ELEVATIONS AND SECTIONS OF HOUSES FOR TOWN AND COUNTRY, LODGES, HOT-HOUSES, GREEN-HOUSES, STABLES, &C. DESIGN FOR A CHURCH, WITH PLAN, ELEVATION, AND TWO SECTIONS; AN ALTAR-PIECE, AND PULPIT. DESIGNS FOR CHIMNEY-PIECES, SHOP-FRONTS, DOOR-CASES. SECTION OF A DINING-ROOM AND LIBRARY. VARIETY OF STAIR-CASES, WITH MANY OTHER IMPORTANT ARTICLES, AND USEFUL EMBELLISHMENTS. TO WHICH IS ADDED, A LIST OF THE PRICE OF CARPENTERS' WORK. THE WHOLE ILLUSTRATED, AND MADE PERFECTLY EASY, BY 148 COPPER PLATES, WITH EXPLANATIONS TO EACH, BY WILLIAM PAIN, AUTHOR OF THE PRACTICAL BUILDER, AND BRITISH PALLADIO. THE FIRST AMERICAN FROM THE FIFTH LONDON EDITION, WITH ADDITIONS.
Boston: Printed and sold by William Norman, Bookseller and Stationer, No. 75, Newbury-Street. 1796. pp. 16, 146 plates, (7), (1). 4to.   AAS.

30941   PAINE, THOMAS   1737–1809
THE AGE OF REASON; BEING AN INVESTIGATION OF TRUE AND OF FABULOUS THEOLOGY. PART THE SECOND. BY THOMAS PAINE, AUTHOR OF THE WORKS ENTITLED — COMMON SENSE — RIGHTS OF MAN, PART FIRST AND SECOND — AND DISSERTATIONS ON FIRST PRINCIPLES OF GOVERNMENT.
London, Printed. New-York, Re-printed by Mott & Lyon, for Fellows & Adam and J. Reid. 1796. pp. 199, (1), (1). 12mo.   LOC.

30942   —— — THE AGE OF REASON. PART THE SECOND. BEING AN INVESTIGATION OF TRUE AND FABULOUS THEOLOGY. BY THOMAS PAINE, AUTHOR OF THE WORKS ENTITLED COMMON SENSE, — RIGHTS OF MAN, PART FIRST AND SECOND, — THE FIRST PART OF THE AGE OF REASON, — AND DISSERTATIONS ON FIRST PRINCIPLES OF GOVERNMENT.
[Philadelphia:] Printed [by Benjamin Franklin Bache] for the Booksellers. MDCCXCVI. pp. vii, (100). 8vo.   AAS. JCB.

131st Pennsylvania District Copyright, issued to Benjamin Franklin Bache, as Proprietor, 6 April, 1796. Editions of this Part were advertised by George Keatinge, No. 149 Market Street, Baltimore; and by John West, No. 75 Cornhill, Boston, perhaps with their imprints. "The following latest works of Thomas Paine, are published at the Office of the Aurora, No. 112 Market-Street. The editions are published under the eye of the author, and are therefore correct." Age of Reason. 1st Part. Age of Reason, 2d Part. Dissertations on the First Principles of Government. Decline and fall of the English System of Finance.

30943   —— *Half-title:* DOWNFALL OF THE FUNDING SYSTEM.
Title: THE DECLINE AND FALL OF THE ENGLISH SYSTEM OF FINANCE. BY THOMAS PAINE, AUTHOR OF COMMON SENSE, AMERICAN CRISIS, AGE OF REASON, &C. "ON THE VERGE, NAY EVEN IN THE GULPH OF BANKRUPTCY." DEBATES IN PARLIAMENT.
New-York, Printed by Mott & Lyon, for J. Fellows, from a London copy, taken from a French edition. 1796. pp. (56). 8vo.   AAS. BA. LOC.

PAINE, THOMAS, continued.

30944 —— —— *Half-title:* THOMAS PAINE ON THE FUNDING SYSTEM.

Title: THE DECLINE & FALL OF THE ENGLISH SYSTEM OF FINANCE. BY THOMAS PAINE, AUTHOR OF COMMON SENSE, AMERICAN CRISIS, AGE OF REASON, &C. [One line from] DEBATES IN PARLIAMENT. SECOND AMERICAN EDITION.

New-York: Printed by William A. Davis, for J. Fellows, from a London copy of the Paris edition. 1796. pp. (58), (1). 12mo. AAS. BM.

30945 —— —— THE DECLINE AND FALL OF THE ENGLISH SYSTEM OF FINANCE. BY THOMAS PAINE, AUTHOR OF COMMON SENSE, RIGHTS OF MAN, AGE OF REASON, &C.

Philadelphia: Printed by John Page, No. 67, Mulberry Street, for Benj. Franklin Bache, No. 112 High Street. 1796. pp. (2), (33). 8vo. AAS. BA. BM. JCB. NYPL.

30946 —— —— *Half-title:* THE DECLINE AND FALL OF THE ENGLISH SYSTEM OF FINANCE.

Heading: THE DECLINE AND FALL OF THE ENGLISH SYSTEM OF FINANCE. BY THOMAS PAINE, AUTHOR OF COMMON SENSE, RIGHTS OF MAN, AGE OF REASON, &C.

Philadelphia: Printed by John Page, No. 67 Mulberry Street, for Benj. Franklin Bache, No. 112 High Street. 1796. pp. (2), (33), [33]–(40). 8vo. AAS,

Second heading: SPEECH OF THOMAS PAINE, AS DELIVERED IN THE CONVENTION JULY 7, 1795. WHEREIN HE ALLUDES TO THE PRECEDING WORK. pp. [33] — (40).

30947 —— —— THE DECLINE AND FALL OF THE ENGLISH SYSTEM OF FINANCE. BY THOMAS PAINE, AUTHOR OF COMMON SENSE, AMERICAN CRISIS, RIGHTS OF MAN, AGE OF REASON, &C. [One line from] DEBATES IN PARLIAMENT.

Philadelphia: Printed [by Henry Sweitzer] for Robert Campbell & Co. No. 40, South Second-Street. 1796. pp. (27), (1). 8vo. AAS. LOC.

30948 —— —— THE DECLINE AND FALL OF THE ENGLISH SYSTEM OF FINANCE BY THOMAS PAINE, AUTHOR OF COMMON SENSE, AMERICAN CRISIS, RIGHTS OF MAN, AGE OF REASON, &C. [One line from] DEBATES IN PARLIAMENT.

Philadelphia: Printed [by Henry Sweitzer] for Robert Campbell & Co. No. 40, South Second-Street. 1796. pp. (58), (1). 8vo. LOC.

30949 —— DISSERTATION ON FIRST PRINCIPLES OF GOVERNMENT, BY THOMAS PAINE, AUTHOR OF COMMON SENSE; RIGHTS OF MAN; AGE OF REASON, &C. [Ornament.]

Paris: Printed at the English Press. Carlisle: Re-printed by James Steel, 1796. pp. 36. 12mo. JCB.

30950 —— —— THE FIRST PRINCIPLES OF GOVERNMENT. BY THOMAS PAINE: TO WHICH IS ADDED, HIS SPEECH, DELIVERED IN THE CONVENTION, JULY 7, 1795, ON THE DECLARATION OF RIGHTS AND THE CONSTITUTION.

New-York: Printed for John Fellows, No. 60, Wall-Street. 1796.

30951 —— LETTER TO GEORGE WASHINGTON, PRESIDENT OF THE UNITED STATES OF AMERICA. ON AFFAIRS PUBLIC AND PRIVATE. BY THOMAS PAINE, AUTHOR OF THE WORKS ENTITLED, COMMON SENSE, RIGHTS OF MAN, AGE OF REASON, &C.

Philadelphia: Printed by Benj. Franklin Bache, No. 112 Market street. 1796. [Entered according to law.] pp. (2), (76), (1). 8vo. AAS. BA. BM. JCB. LOC. MHS. NYHS. NYPL. VSL.

Reprinted in Baltimore, and in London, in 1797; and, New York, in 1802. 160th Pennsylvania District Copyright, issued to Benjamin Franklin Bache, as Proprietor, 18 November, 1796. Contains a List of his books.

30952 PAINE, Tom, pseudonym.
TOM PAINE'S JESTS; BEING AN ENTIRELY NEW AND SELECT COLLECTION OF PATRI-
OTIC BON MOTS, REPARTEES, ANECDOTES, EPIGRAMS, OBSERVATIONS, &C. ON PO-
LITICAL SUBJECTS. BY THOMAS PAINE, AND OTHER SUPPORTERS OF THE RIGHTS
OF MAN. TO WHICH IS ADDED, A TRIBUTE TO THE SWINISH MULTITUDE: BEING
A CHOICE COLLECTION OF PATRIOTIC SONGS. SPEAK TRUTH AND SHAME THE DEVIL.
SERIA MIXTA JOCIS.
Philadelphia: Printed for Mathew Carey, No. 118, Market-Street. M.DCC.-
XCVI. pp. (72). 12mo.   AAS. BU. JCB. LOC. NYPL.
Second title: A TRIBUTE TO THE SWINISH MULTITUDE: BEING A CHOICE COLLEC-
TION OF PATRIOTIC SONGS. COLLECTED BY THE CELEBRATED R. THOMSON. pp.
(31)—[72].

The Dedication is dated by the Editor, London, September 2d, 1793.
This edition differs very materially from the edition issued by Mathew
Carey in 1794.

30953 PALMER, JOHN, JUNIOR
THE HAUNTED CAVERN. A NOVEL.
*Baltimore: Printed by Christopher Jackson. Sold by George Keatinge, No.
149, Market-Street.* 1796.

30954 —— — THE HAUNTED CAVERN: A CALEDONIAN TALE. [Eight lines of verse.]
BY JOHN PALMER, JUNIOR.
Bennington: Re-printed by Anthony Haswell, for the Booksellers, New York.
1796. pp. 197, frontispiece. 12mo.   VtU.

30955 PALMER, ROBERT F.
THE PRODIGAL REFORMED. BY A VIRGINIA FARMER. CONTENTS. THE AUTHOR'S
BIRTH, AND ORIGIN, HIS EDUCATION, AND PROFESSION, HIS TRAVELS THROUGH
ENGLAND, IRELAND, FRANCE, ALGIERS, AND AMERICA.
Richmond? 1796.

7th Virginia District Copyright, issued to Robert F. Palmer, as Author,
23 September, 1796.

30956 PANTHER, ABRAHAM
A VERY SURPRISING NARRATIVE OF A YOUNG WOMAN, WHO WAS DISCOVERED IN A
ROCKY CAVE; AFTER HAVING BEEN TAKEN BY THE SAVAGE INDIANS OF THE WIL-
DERNESS, IN THE YEAR 1777, AND SEEING NO HUMAN BEING FOR THE SPACE OF
NINE YEARS.
Greenfield: Printed by Thomas Dickman, 1796.

30957 —— — A VERY SURPRISING NARRATIVE OF A YOUNG WOMAN, WHO WAS DISCOV-
ERED IN GLOOMY MANSION OF A ROCKY CAVE! AFTER HAVING BEEN TAKEN FROM
HER COMPANIONS BY THE SAVAGE INDIANS. THIRD WINDSOR EDITION.
[Windsor:] Printed by Alden Spooner. 1796. 12mo.

30958 PAPERS RESPECTING INTRUSIONS BY CONNECTICUT CLAIMANTS. [Colophon:]
[Philadelphia:] Printed by Hall & Sellers, 1796. pp. [24]. 8vo. JCB. NYPL.

30959 PARKER, ISAAC   1768 – 1830
AN ORATION, DELIVERED AT CASTINE, JULY 4, 1796, AT THE CELEBRATION OF THE
TWENTIETH ANNIVERSARY OF AMERICAN INDEPENDENCE. BY ISAAC PARKER,
ESQ. [Ornament.]
Printed by Samuel Hall, No. 53, Cornhill, Boston. 1796. pp. [15.] 8vo.
BM. LOC.

30960   PASCALIS-OUVIERE, FELIX   1750 – 1833
MEDICO-CHEMICAL DISSERTATIONS ON THE CAUSES OF THE EPIDEMIC, CALLED YEL-
LOW FEVER; AND ON THE BEST ANTIMONIAL PREPARATIONS FOR THE USE OF
MEDICINE. BY A PHYSICIAN, PRACTITIONER IN PHILADELPHIA.

*Philadelphia: From the Press of Snowden & M'Corkle, No. 47, North Fourth-
Street. 1796.* pp. [41], (1), (1). 8vo.   LOC. SGO.

30961   A PASTORAL VISIT TO THE AFFLICTED.
Printed at Keene, Newhampshire; by Cornelius Sturtevant, junior, & Co.
M,DCCXCVI. pp. (12). 12mo.   AAS.

Reprinted from the 1737 edition.

30962   PATERSON, WILLIAM   1745 – 1806
THE CHARGE OF JUDGE PATTERSON TO THE JURY, . . . IN THE CASE OF VAN-
HORNE'S LESSEE AGAINST DORRANCE: TRIED AT A CIRCUIT COURT FOR THE UNITED
STATES, HELD AT PHILADELPHIA, APRIL TERM 1795: WHEREIN THE CONTROVER-
TED TITLE TO THE WYOMING LANDS, BETWEEN THE CLAIMANTS UNDER PENNSYL-
VANIA AND CONNECTICUT, RECEIVED A DECISION.

Philadelphia: Printed by Samuel H. Smith, No. 118, Chesnut-Street. 1796.
pp. [41], (1). 8vo.   AAS. CLS. LOC.

"This Charge highly concerns every one interested in such disputes."
Reprinted in Philadelphia in 1801.

30963   PATTILLO, HENRY
A GEOGRAPHICAL CATECHISM, TO ASSIST THOSE WHO HAVE NEITHER MAPS NOR
GAZETTEERS, TO READ NEWS-PAPERS, HISTORY, OR TRAVELS; WITH AS MUCH OF
THE SCIENCE OF ASTRONOMY, AND THE DOCTRINE OF THE AIR, AS IS JUDGED
SUFFICIENT FOR THE FARMER, WHO WISHES TO UNDERSTAND SOMETHING OF THE
WORKS OF GOD AROUND HIM; AND FOR THE STUDIOUS YOUTH, WHO HAVE OR HAVE
NOT A PROSPECT OF FURTHER PROSECUTING THOSE SUBLIME SCIENCES. BY HENRY
PATTILLO, A. M. GRANVILLE.

Halifax: Printed by Abraham Hodge. M,DCC,XCVI. pp. 62. 8vo. NCU.

30964   PAULUS EMILIUS, pseudonym.
A LETTER ADDRESSED TO [WILLIAM CLIFFTON] THE AUTHOR OF THE GROUP OR
ELEGANT REPRESENTATION ILLUSTRATED. BY PAULUS EMILIUS. [Eight lines of
quotations.]

Philadelphia: Printed for the Author, M,DCC,XCVI. pp. (2), (9). 8vo. LOC.

Advertised, by William Cobbett, as: A Letter addressed to the Author
of the Group: in which is contained; the substance of things unexpected, and the evidence of things not seen. Being a mirror, in which
the painted will peradventure discern appropriate light and shade.
Also a word in season to Mr. Stephens, &c. &c. [Five lines from
Shakespear.]

30965   PAYSON, SETH   1758–1820
A SERMON, DELIVERED AT THE ORDINATION OF THE REV. JOSEPH BROWN, TO THE
PASTORAL CARE OF THE CHURCH IN SHAPLEIGH, PROVINCE OF MAINE, OCTOBER
14TH, MDCCXCV. BY SETH PAYSON. PUBLISHED BY DESIRE OF THE HEARERS.

Printed at Dover, by Samuel Bragg, for the Subscribers. 1796. pp. 24. 8vo.
AAS. JCB.

30966   PEACOCK, LUCY   1786–1816
VISIT FOR A WEEK, OR HINTS ON THE IMPROVEMENT OF TIME. CONTAINING, ORIGINAL TALES, ENTERTAINING STORIES, INTERESTING ANECDOTES, AND SKETCHES FROM NATURAL AND MORAL HISTORY. TO WHICH IS ADDED, A POETICAL APPENDIX. DESIGNED FOR THE AMUSEMENT OF YOUTH. [Four lines from] VOLTAIRE. EMBELLISHED WITH AN ELEGANT FRONTISPIECE.
     Philadelphia: Printed by Ormrod and Conrad, No. 41, Chesnut-Street. 1796. pp. (2), (2), 275, (1), frontispiece. 12mo.   AAS. LOC.

30967   PEALE, CHARLES WILLSON   1741–1827
A SCIENTIFIC AND DESCRIPTIVE CATALOGUE OF PEALE'S MUSEUM, BY C. W. PEALE, MEMBER OF THE AMERICAN PHILOSOPHICAL SOCIETY, AND A. M. F. J. BEAUVOIS, MEMBER OF THE SOCIETY OF ARTS AND SCIENCES OF ST. DOMINGO; OF THE AMERICAN PHILOSOPHICAL SOCIETY; AND CORRESPONDENT TO THE MUSEUM OF NATURAL HISTORY AT PARIS. [Cut of open book.] NATURE. [Five lines of verse.]
     Philadelphia: Printed by Samuel H. Smith, No. 118, Chesnut-Street. M.DCC.XCVI. pp. (xii), 44. 8vo.   JCB. LCP. LOC. NYPL.
     Ends with the catch-word, The. 135th Pennsylvania District Copyright, issued to Charles Wilson Peale, as Author and Proprietor, 13 May, 1796. No. 1 of Description of Peale's Museum, in English, and in French, was received in Charleston, for the Subscribers, by Freneau & Paine, July 13, 1796.

30968   PECK, JEDIDIAH
THE POLITICAL WARS OF OTSEGO: OR DOWNFALL OF JACOBINISM AND DESPOTISM: BEING A COLLECTION OF PIECES, LATELY PUBLISHED IN THE OTSEGO HERALD. TO WHICH IS ADDED, AN ADDRESS TO THE CITIZENS OF THE UNITED STATES; AND EXTRACTS FROM JACK TAR'S JOURNALS, KEPT ON BOARD THE SHIP LIBERTY. CONTAINING A SUMMARY ACCOUNT OF HER ORIGIN, BUILDERS, MATERIALS, USE — AND HER DANGEROUS VOYAGE, FROM THE LOW LANDS OF CAPE MONARCHY, TO THE PORT OF FREE REPRESENTATIVE GOVERNMENT. BY THE AUTHOR OF THE PLOUGH-JOGGER.
     Cooperstown: Printed for the Author, by E. Phinney. M,DCC,XCVI. pp. 122, (1), (3). 8vo.   BA. LOC.
     Contains a three-page List of subscribers' names.

30969   PEARCE, WILLIAM
AMIDST THE ILLUSIONS. FROM HARTFORD BRIDGE OR THE SKIRTS OF A CAMP. AS SUNG BY MISS BROADHURST.
     Sold at Carr's Musical Repository's Philadelphia & N. York, & by J. Carr, Baltimore. Price 25 cents. [1796.] 4to.   YC.

30970   PEIRCE, JOHN, JUNIOR
THE NEW AMERICAN SPELLING-BOOK: IN THREE PARTS. CONTAINING, I. TABLES OF COMMON WORDS, FROM ONE TO FIVE SYLLABLES; TOGETHER WITH SEVERAL TABLES CONTAINING A LARGE NUMBER OF NAMES OF PERSONS, PLACES, TOWNS, COUNTIES, TOWNSHIPS, RIVERS, CREEKS, &C. &C. ON THIS CONTINENT: WITH NATURAL AND EASY LESSONS DISPOSED THROUGH THE WHOLE, WHICH ARE ADAPTED TO THE CAPACITIES OF SMALL CHILDREN; AND YET SO AS THOSE OF RIPER YEARS MAY RECEIVE SENSIBLE INSTRUCTIONS THERE FROM. II. A COLLECTION OF WORDS OF TWO, THREE AND FOUR SYLLABLES, DIVIDED INTO THREE TABLES: BEING ACCENTED AND EXPLAINED FOR THE BETTER INSTRUCTION OF YOUTH IN THE KNOWLEDGE OF WORDS, AS WELL AS SPELLING; TOGETHER WITH A LARGE TABLE OF WORDS NEARLY THE SAME IN SOUND, BUT DIFFERENT IN SPELLING AND SIGNIFICATION; WITH READING LESSONS AT THE END OF EACH TABLE. III. A VERY PLAIN AND EASY INTRODUCTION TO ENGLISH GRAMMAR, PARTICULARLY ADAPTED TO THE CAPACITIES OF YOUTH, AND INTENDED FOR THE USE OF SCHOOLS. COMPILED BY JOHN PEIRCE, JUN. THE SECOND EDITION.
     Philadelphia: Printed by Joseph Crukshank. 1796.

30971   PELHAM, WILLIAM
AT PELHAM'S BOOK STORE AND CIRCULATING LIBRARY, No. 59 CORNHILL, BOSTON,
A GENERAL ASSORTMENT OF BOOKS AND STATIONARY.
[Boston: 1796.] Broadside.   MHS.

30972   PENN, WILLIAM   1644 – 1718
NO CROSS, NO CROWN: A DISCOURSE SHEWING THE NATURE AND DISCIPLINE OF THE
HOLY CROSS OF CHRIST; AND THAT THE DENIAL OF SELF, AND DAILY BEARING OF
CHRIST'S CROSS, IS THE ALONE WAY TO THE REST AND KINGDOM OF GOD. TO
WHICH ARE ADDED, THE LIVING AND DYING TESTIMONIES OF MANY PERSONS OF
FAME AND LEARNING, BOTH OF ANCIENT AND MODERN TIMES, IN FAVOUR OF THIS
TREATISE. IN TWO PARTS. BY WILLIAM PENN. [Four lines of Scripture texts.]
Philadelphia: Printed by Jacob Johnson & Co. No. 147, High-Street. M.-
DCC.XCVI. pp. 358. 8vo.   AAS. NYPL.

30973   PENNSYLVANIA. STATE.
ACCOUNTS OF THE TREASURY OF PENNSYLVANIA, FROM THE FIRST OF JANUARY TO
THE THIRTY-FIRST OF DECEMBER [1795]. INCLUSIVE.
Philadelphia: Printed by Francis & Robert Bailey, at Yorick's Head, No.
116, High-Street. [1796.] pp. (12). fol.   LOC.

30974   —— — ACCOUNTS OF THE TREASURY OF PENNSYLVANIA, FROM THE FIRST OF JAN-
UARY TO THE THIRTY-FIRST OF DECEMBER [1795], INCLUSIVE. [Ornament.]
Philadelphia: Printed by Zachariah Poulson, junior, number eighty, Chesnut-
Street. [1796.] pp. (12). fol.   LOC.

30975   —— ACT OF THE LEGISLATURE OF PENNSYLVANIA OF THIRD APRIL 1792 [FOR THE
SALE OF THE VACANT LAND WITHIN THIS COMMONWEALTH] AND OPINIONS THERE-
ON, TO THE PERSONS EMIGRATING TO LANDS IN PENNSYLVANIA NORTH AND WEST
OF THE OHIO AND ALLEGHANY RIVERS AND CONEWANGO CREEK . . . [Signed,
Jared Ingersoll, and seven others.]
[Philadelphia: Printed by Hall & Sellers.] May 13th, 1796. pp. (10).
8vo.   AAS.

30976   —— ACTS OF THE GENERAL ASSEMBLY OF THE COMMONWEALTH OF PENNSYLVANIA.
PASSED AT A SESSION, WHICH WAS BEGUN AND HELD AT THE CITY OF PHILADEL-
PHIA ON TUESDAY, THE FIRST DAY OF DECEMBER, IN THE YEAR ONE THOUSAND
SEVEN HUNDRED AND NINETY-FIVE, AND OF THE INDEPENDENCE OF THE UNITED
STATES OF AMERICA, THE TWENTIETH. [—23 DECEMBER, 1795.] PUBLISHED BY
AUTHORITY.
Philadelphia: Printed by Hall and Sellers, No. 51, Market-Street. D.-
MCC.XCVI [sic 1796.] pp. (2). [89.] fol.   LOC.

30977   —— A COMPILATION OF THE LAWS OF THE STATE OF PENNSYLVANIA, RELATIVE TO
THE POOR, FROM THE YEAR 1700, TO 1795, INCLUSIVE. PUBLISHED FOR THE
GUARDIANS OF THE POOR. [Edited by W. Franklin.]
Philadelphia: Printed by Zachariah Poulson, junior. 1796. pp. (2), 112;
10. 8vo.   AAS. BM. HC. LCP. MHS.
Second title: ORDINANCES, RULES AND BYE-LAWS FOR THE ALMS-HOUSE, AND
HOUSE OF EMPLOYMENT. pp. 10.

30978   —— JOURNAL OF THE FIRST SESSION OF THE SIXTH HOUSE OF REPRESENTATIVES OF
THE COMMONWEALTH OF PENNSYLVANIA, WHICH COMMENCED AT PHILADELPHIA,
ON TUESDAY, THE FIRST DAY OF DECEMBER, IN THE YEAR OF OUR LORD ONE
THOUSAND SEVEN HUNDRED AND NINETY-FIVE, AND OF THE COMMONWEALTH THE
TWENTIETH. [— 4 APRIL, 1796.] [Arms.]
Philadelphia: Printed by Francis & Robert Bailey, at Yorick's Head, No.
116, High-Street. M,DDC,XCV [sic 1795.] pp. [487.] fol.   LOC.

PENNSYLVANIA. STATE, continued.

30979 — TAGEBUCH DES SECHSTEN HAUSES DER REPRÄSENTANTEN DER REPUBLIK PENN-SYLVANIEN: 1795-1796.

Philadelphia: Gedruckt bey Steiner u Kammerer. 1796.

30980 — JOURNAL OF THE SENATE OF THE COMMONWEALTH OF PENNSYLVANIA. COMMENCING ON TUESDAY THE FIRST DAY OF DECEMBER, IN THE YEAR OF OUR LORD ONE THOUSAND AND SEVEN HUNDRED AND NINETY-FIVE, AND OF THE INDEPENDENCE OF THE UNITED STATES OF AMERICA THE TWENTIETH. [— 4 APRIL, 1796.] VOLUME VI.

Philadelphia: Printed by Zachariah Poulson, junior, number eighty, Chesnut-Street. [1796.] pp. (249). fol.   LOC.

30981 — REPORT OF THE REGISTER-GENERAL OF THE STATE OF THE FINANCES OF PENNSYLVANIA, FOR THE YEAR M,DCC,XCV.

Philadelphia: Printed by Francis & Robert Bailey, at Yorick's Head, No. 116, High-Street. [1796.] pp. (19). fol.   LOC.

30982 — — REPORT OF THE REGISTER-GENERAL OF THE STATE OF THE FINANCES OF PENNSYLVANIA, FOR THE YEAR 1795. [Ornament.]

Philadelphia: Printed by Zachariah Poulson, junior, number eighty, Chesnut-Street. [1796.] pp. (19). fol.   LOC.

30983 — PUBLIC NOTICE. FRIDAY THE FOURTH DAY OF NOVEMBER NEXT, IS THE DAY APPOINTED BY LAW, FOR THE PEOPLE TO MEET AT THEIR RESPECTIVE PLACES OF ELECTION TO CHOOSE BY WRITTEN TICKETS FIFTEEN ELECTORS ON BEHALF OF THIS STATE, OF A PRESIDENT AND VICE-PRESIDENT OF THE UNITED STATES. . . . ELECTORS. THOMAS M'KEAN, [and fourteen others.]. EXTRACT OF A LETTER FROM THOMAS PAINE, DATED PARIS, JULY 30TH, 1796. [Thirty lines.]

[Philadelphia: Printed by Benjamin Franklin Bache, 1796.] Broadside. 8vo.   HSP.

30984 — — PUBLIC NOTICE. FRIDAY THE FOURTH DAY OF NOVEMBER NEXT, IS THE DAY APPOINTED BY LAW, FOR THE PEOPLE TO MEET AT THEIR RESPECTIVE PLACES OF ELECTION, TO CHOOSE BY WRITTEN TICKETS, FIFTEEN ELECTORS ON BEHALF OF THIS STATE, OF A PRESIDENT AND VICE-PRESIDENT OF THE UNITED STATES. [Fourteen lines.] CITIZENS OF PENNSYLVANIA! THE FOLLOWING MAXIMS AND OPINIONS ARE TAKEN FROM MR. ADAMS'S DEFENCE OF THE AMERICAN CONSTITUTIONS, AND BY THEM YOU WILL BE ABLE TO JUDGE FOR YOURSELF WHETHER THE MAN THAT HOLDS SUCH DOCTRINES IS A FIT PERSON TO BE ELECTED PRESIDENT OF THE UNITED STATES. [Two columns.] A REPUBLICAN.

[Philadelphia: 1796.] Broadside. fol.   HSP.

30985 — (CIRCULAR.) PHILADELPHIA, SEPT. 25, 1796. SIR, THE REPUBLICAN MEMBERS OF THE STATE LEGISLATURE AND OF CONGRESS FROM THIS STATE, BEFORE THEIR LATE ADJOURNMENT HAD A MEETING TO FRAME A TICKET FOR ELECTORS OF THE PRESIDENT AND VICE-PRESIDENT. [Thirty-two lines.] M. LEIB, CHAIRMAN. REPUBLICAN TICKET. THOMAS M'KEAN, [and fourteen others.] ACTION OF CITIZENS OF THE COUNTY OF CUMBERLAND. [Six lines.] WILLIAM BROWN, CHAIRMAN. OCTOBER 15TH, 1796.

[Carlisle: Printed by George Kline, 1796.] Broadside. fol.   HSP.

30986 THE PENNSYLVANIA GAZETTE. NUMBER 3416. WEDNESDAY, JANUARY 6, [— NUMBER 3467. WEDNESDAY, DECEMBER 28, 1796.]

Philadelphia: Printed by Hall and Sellers, at the New Printing-Office near the Market. 1796. fol.   AAS. HC. HSP. LCP. PSL.

30987   THE PENNSYLVANIA HERALD, AND YORK GENERAL ADVERTISER. VOL. VII.
No. 48. TOTAL NO. 360. WEDNESDAY, JANUARY 6, [— VOL. VIII. No. 47. TOTAL
NO. 411. WEDNESDAY, DECEMBER 28, 1796.]
York: Printed every Wednesday, by John Edie. 1796. fol.   YHS.

30988   PENNSYLVANIA LAND COMPANY.
THE SUBSCRIBERS, PROPRIETORS OF LANDS IN THE STATE OF PENNSYLVANIA, FIND-
ING IT NECESSARY TO PROTECT THEIR PROPERTY FROM UNLAWFUL INTRUSIONS,
HAVE AGREED TO FORM THEMSELVES INTO AN ASSOCIATION ON THE FOLLOWING
TERMS AND PRINCIPLES.
[Philadelphia:] June 7, 1796. Broadside.

30989   PENNSYLVANISCHER CALENDER. AUF DAS 1797 STE JAHR CHRISTI.
Ephrata: Gedruckt bey Benjamin Mayer. [1796.]

30990   THE PENNYWORTH OF WIT. [Colophon:]
*[Boston: Printed by Thomas Fleet, jun.?] Sold at the Bible & Heart, in
Cornhill.* [1796.] Broadside. fol.   AAS. BPL.

30991   —— A PENNY WORTH OF WIT. [Cut of ship.] [A poem.]
Hudson: Printed and sold at Stoddard's Printing-Office. [1796.] pp. (8).
16mo.   AAS.

30992   PERRY, DAVID   1746–1817
A SHORT VIEW AND DEFENCE OF THE ECCLESIASTICAL RIGHTS OF MAN, IN A SERMON
DELIVERED ON CHRISTMAS DAY, A. D. 1795. BY DAVID PERRY, MINISTER OF THE
GOSPEL IN RIDGWAY [*sic* RICHMOND, MASSACHUSETTS.] [Two lines from] ST.
PAUL.
Danbury: Printed by Ely & Nichols. M,DCC,XCVI. pp. 20. 12mo. BA. UTS.

30993   PERRY, WILLIAM
THE ROYAL STANDARD ENGLISH DICTIONARY. IN WHICH THE WORDS ARE NOT ONLY
RATIONALLY DIVIDED INTO SYLLABLES, ACCURATELY ACCENTED, THEIR PART OF
SPEECH PROPERLY DISTINGUISHED, AND THEIR VARIOUS SIGNIFICATIONS ARRANGED
IN ONE LINE; BUT, LIKEWISE, BY A KEY TO THIS WORK, COMPRISING THE VARIOUS
SOUNDS OF THE VOWELS AND CONSONANTS, DENOTED BY TYPOGRAPHICAL CHARAC-
TERS, AND ILLUSTRATED BY EXAMPLES, WHICH RENDER IT INTELLIGIBLE TO THE
WEAKEST CAPACITY. IT EXHIBITS THEIR TRUE PRONUNCIATION, ACCORDING TO THE
PRESENT PRACTICE OF MEN OF LETTERS, EMINENT ORATORS AND POLITE SPEAK-
ERS, IN LONDON. UPON A PLAN PERFECTLY PLAIN, AND ENTIRELY NEW. TO WHICH
IS PREFIXED, A COMPREHENSIVE GRAMMAR OF THE ENGLISH LANGUAGE. TO THE
WHOLE ARE ADDED, THE SCRIPTURE PROPER NAMES IN THE OLD AND NEW TESTA-
MENTS, NAMES OF THE PRINCIPAL CITIES, RIVERS, MOUNTAINS, &C. IN THE KNOWN
WORLD: ALSO, THE ANCIENT AND MODERN POETS, PHILOSOPHERS, AND STATESMEN.
&C. WITH THEIR PROPER PRONUNCIATION POINTED OUT. THE FOURTH AMERICAN
WORCESTER EDITION, CAREFULLY REVISED AND CORRECTED. BY WILLIAM PERRY,
LECTURER IN THE ACADEMY AT EDINBURGH, AUTHOR OF THE ONLY SURE GUIDE
TO THE ENGLISH TONGUE, THE MAN OF BUSINESS, THE ORATOR, &C. &C.
*Printed at Worcester, Massachusetts, at the Press of Isaiah Thomas, by L.
Worcester, for said Thomas. Sold in Worcester, by Thomas, Son & Thomas—In
Boston, by Thomas & Andrews, D. West, E. Larkin, S. Hall, J. West and other
Booksellers.—In Baltimore, by Thomas, Andrews & Butler.—In Albany, by Thomas,
Andrews & Penniman.* 1796. pp. (2), (2), 594+. Square 12mo.   AAS. BA.

30994   THE [cut] PHENIX; OR WINDHAM HERALD. VOL. V. NUMB. 252. SATURDAY, JANU-
ARY 2, [— VOL. VI. NUMB. 304. SATURDAY, DECEMBER 31, 1796.]
Windham: Printed by John Byrne, in the lower room of the Court-House.
1796. fol.   AAS. CHS. NYHS.

30995   PHILADELPHIA. PENNSYLVANIA.
BY THE MAYOR, ALDERMEN AND CITIZENS OF PHILADELPHIA. AN ORDINANCE TO PREVENT THE ERECTION OF WOODEN BUILDINGS WITHIN CERTAIN LIMITS IN THE CITY OF PHILADELPHIA. [Forty-six lines.] MATTHEW CLARKSON, MAYOR. EN- ACTED INTO AN ORDINANCE, AT PHILADELPHIA, THE SIXTH DAY OF JUNE, ANNO DOMINI, ONE THOUSAND SEVEN HUNDRED AND NINETY-SIX. WILLIAM H. TOD, CLERK TO THE CORPORATION.

[Philadelphia: 1796.] Broadside. fol.   HSP.

30996   —— REPORT OF A COMMITTEE OF THE SELECT COUNCIL OF PHILADELPHIA. READ NOVEMBER 10TH, 1796.

Philadelphia: Printed by Zachariah Poulson, junior. 1796. pp. 24. 8vo. JCB.

30997   PHILADELPHIA. PENNSYLVANIA. BAPTIST ASSOCIATION.
MINUTES OF THE PHILADELPHIA BAPTIST ASSOCIATION, HELD AT PHILADELPHIA, OCTOBER 4TH, 5TH, & 6TH, 1796.

[Philadelphia: 1796.] pp. 8. 4to.   BU.

30998   PHILADELPHIA. PENNSYLVANIA. CHURCHES.
AN ACCOUNT OF THE BAPTISMS AND BURIALS IN THE UNITED CHURCHES OF CHRIST CHURCH AND ST. PETER'S . . .

Philadelphia: 1796. Broadside. fol.   LCP.

30999   PHILADELPHIA. PENNSYLVANIA. CABINET AND CHAIR-MAKERS.
THE PHILADELPHIA CABINET & CHAIR-MAKERS' BOOK OF PRICES. INSTITUTED MARCH 4, 1796.

Philadelphia:—Printed by Richard Folwell, No. 33 Mulberry St. MDCC- XCVI. pp. 28. 8vo.   HSP.

31000   PHILADELPHIA. PENNSYLVANIA. FRIENDSHIP FIRE COMPANY.
ARTICLES OF THE FRIENDSHIP FIRE COMPANY OF THE NORTHERN LIBERTIES, IN- STITUTED IN THE YEAR, 1796. [Four columns.] [Colophon:]

[Philadelphia:] Printed by Jane Aitken, No. 20, North Third Street. [1796.] Broadside. fol.   HSP.

31001   PHILADELPHIA. PENNSYLVANIA. LIBRARY COMPANY.
THIRD SUPPLEMENT TO THE CATALOGUE OF BOOKS, BELONGING TO THE LIBRARY COMPANY OF PHILADELPHIA. TO WHICH IS PREFIXED, A CONTINUATION OF THE BYE-LAWS AND REGULATIONS OF THE COMPANY. COMMUNITER BONA PROFUND- ERE DEORUM EST.

Philadelphia: Printed by Zachariah Poulson, junior, Librarian, Number eighty, Chesnut-Street. June 30, 1796. pp. 38. 8vo.   AAS. LOC. NYPL.

31002   PHILADELPHIA. PENNSYLVANIA. NEW THEATRE.
PLAYBILL OF RICHARD III. GIVEN AT THE NEW THEATRE, AUGUST 31, 1796.

[Philadelphia: 1796.] Broadside. 4to.

31003   PHILADELPHIA. PENNSYLVANIA. SOCIETY OF UNITARIAN CHRISTIANS.
CONSTITUTIONAL RULES OF THE SOCIETY OF UNITARIAN CHRISTIANS, AT PHILADEL- PHIA, AGREED UPON, (HAVING BEEN PREVIOUSLY READ AND PROPOSED FOR CON- SIDERATION) AT A MEETING OF THE SOCIETY, HELD AT THE UNIVERSITY OF PENN- SYLVANIA, ON SUNDAY THE 28TH OF AUGUST, 1796.

Philadelphia: Printed by Joseph Gales, No. 145, North Second-Street. 1796. pp. (7). 8vo.   BM. LOC.

31004   THE PHILADELPHIA GAZETTE & UNIVERSAL DAILY ADVERTISER. [Motto.] VOL. XIII. No. 2244. FRIDAY, JANUARY 1, [—No. 2555. SATURDAY, DECEMBER 31, 1796.]
> *Printed and published by Andrew Brown, at Washington's Head, in Chesnut-Street,—No. 29—between Front and Second Streets.* 1796. fol.
>
> AAS. BA. BM. HSP. LCP. PSL. WHS.

31005   THE PHILADELPHIA MINERVA. VOL. I. No. 48. SATURDAY, JANUARY 2, [—VOL. II. No. 48. WHOLE NO. 100. SATURDAY, DECEMBER 31, 1796.]
> *[Philadelphia:] Printed by Woodruff & Pechin, No. 224, Market-Street, near Seventh-Street.* 1796. 4to.   AAS. HC. HSP. LCP. LOC. NYHS. WHS.

In May, the Printers dissolved partnership; and, from that date, publication was carried on by John Turner, at the same Printing-office, until July 23d, when it was moved to, "between 72 & 74 Chesnut-Street." In August, "Utile dulci," was added to the heading.

31006   PHILADELPHISCHE [cut] CORRESPONDENZ. [Motto.] NUM. 470. FREYTAG, DEN 1 JANUARY, [—NUM. 574. FREYTAG, DEN 30 DECEMBER, 1796.]
> *Diese Zeitung wird alle Dienstag und Freytag heraus gegeben von Steiner und Kammerer, in der Rees-Strasse, zwischen der Zweyten-und Dritten-Strasse. No.* 85. . . . 1796. fol.   HSP. PSL.

31007   PHILLIPS, JOHN
A NARRATIVE SHEWING WHY THE REV. J. PHILLIPS IS NOT IN CONNECTION WITH THE EPISCOPALIAN METHODISTS. WITH A DEFENCE OF THE DOCTRINES HELD AND TAUGHT BY THE AUTHOR. MOST HUMBLY ADDRESSED TO THE MINISTERS AND MEMBERS OF THAT SOCIETY IN PARTICULAR, AND TO THE PUBLIC IN GENERAL. TOGETHER WITH A SUMMARY ACCOUNT OF HIS CONNEXION WITH, &C. THE REV. W. HAMMET. [Four lines of quotations.]
> *Charleston: Printed for the Author, by J. M'Iver, No. 47, Bay.* MDCC-XCVI. pp. 36. 8vo.   NYHS.

31008   PHILLIPS, NATHANIEL
PHILLIPS's UNITED STATES DIARY; OR AN ALMANACK, FOR THE YEAR OF OUR LORD, 1797: BEING THE FIRST AFTER LEAP YEAR, AND TWENTY-FIRST OF AMERICAN INDEPENDENCE. [Eight lines. U. S. and R. I. Arms. Four lines of verse.]
> *Printed at Warren (R. I.) by Nathaniel Phillips. Great encouragement given to wholesale purchasers.* [1796.] pp. (24). 12mo.   AAS. LOC. RIHS.

31009   PICCINI, NICOLO   1728 – 1800
OVERTURE LA BUONA FIGLIUOLA. ARRANGED FOR THE PIANOFORTE.
> *Philadelphia: Published by G. Willig, 165 Market Street.* [1796.]   NYPL.

31010   PIGOTT, CHARLES   – 1794
POLITICAL CURIOSITIES, INCLUDING AN ACCOUNT OF THE STATE OF POLITICAL AFFAIRS IN EUROPE. BY A SOCIETY OF PATRIOTS. [Vignette.]
> *Printed for Richard Lee, No. 84, Mulberry-Street, near the corner of Third-Street, Philadelphia.* [1796.] pp. (2), (23), (1); (19), (1); [8]; [8]; [16]; (16); (16); (12), (4); [8]; [8]; (16); (4); (8). 8vo.   AAS. LOC. NYPL.

A general title-page, and Dedication to Peter Porcupine, printed in Philadelphia, for a collection of the original issues of nineteen political tracts, printed and "published by Citizen Richard Lee, at the British Tree of Liberty," London, 1794-1795. Charles Pigott, author of "The Jockey Club," was the author of some ten of the tracts.

31011 PIGOTT, CHARLES, continued.
—— A POLITICAL DICTIONARY: EXPLAINING THE TRUE MEANING OF WORDS. ILLUS-TRATED AND EXEMPLIFIED IN THE LIVES, MORALS, CHARACTER AND CONDUCT OF THE FOLLOWING MOST ILLUSTRIOUS PERSONAGES, AMONG MANY OTHERS. THE KING, QUEEN, PRINCE OF WALES, DUKE OF YORK, POPE PIUS VI, EMPEROR, KING OF PRUSSIA, THE TIGRESS OF RUSSIA, DUKES OF BRUNSWICK, PORTLAND, RICHMOND, NEWCASTLE, LEEDS. EARLS CHATHAM, FITZWILLIAM, DARLINGTON, SPENCER, HOWE, CHESTERFIELD. LORDS GRENVILLE, MORNINGTON, MOIRA, MOUNTMORRIS, MULGRAVE, FITZGERALD, HARVEY. JUDGES KENYON AND LOUGH-BOROUGH. HON. FRANK NORTH. SIRS GEORGE SAVILLE, GILBERT ELLIOT, FRANCIS MOLYNEUX, WATKIN LEWES, ROGER CURTIS, SIDNEY SMYTHE, FRANCIS SYKES, RICHARD HILL, LANDGRAVE OF HESSE CASSEL. MADAME SCHWELLEN-BERGEN. MESSRS. PITT, FOX, BURKE, DUMOURIER, WARREN HASTINGS, WYND-HAM, POWIS, DUNDAS, THORNTON, WILBERFORCE, REEVES, ARTHUR YOUNG, GEORGE HANGER, CHARLES JENKINSON, COL. TARLETON, BROOK WATSON, ALDER-MAN CURTIS, ANDERSON, LE MESURIER, SANDERSON, BISHOPS AND CLERGY, CHARLES I. AND LOUIS XVI. BY THE LATE CHARLES PIGOTT, ESQ. AUTHOR OF THE JOCKEY CLUBS, &C. &C.

New-York—Printed for Thomas Greenleaf, No. 54, Wall-Street. M,DCC,-XCVI. pp. 198. 12mo.
AAS. BM. JCB. LOC. NYPL.

31012 PIKE, SAMUEL 1717–1777
A PLAIN AND FULL ACCOUNT OF THE CHRISTIAN PRACTICES OBSERVED BY THE CHURCH IN ST. MARTINS-LE-GRAND IN LONDON, AND OTHER CHURCHES (COMMONLY CALLED SANDEMANIAN) IN FELLOWSHIP WITH THEM. TO WHICH IS ADDED, AN ADDRESS FROM SAMUEL PIKE, TO A CHRISTIAN CHURCH IN LONDON.
Danbury, (Connecticut): Printed by Ely & Nichols. 1796.

31013 PINCHARD, Mrs. ——
THE BLIND CHILD, OR ANECDOTES OF THE WYNDHAM FAMILY. WRITTEN FOR THE USE OF YOUNG PEOPLE. BY A LADY.
Worcester: Printed by Isaiah Thomas, jun. Sold wholesale and retail at his Bookstore, at the Sign of Johnson's Head.—1796. pp. 190, frontispiece. 32mo.
AAS.

31014 —— THE TWO COUSINS, A MORAL STORY, FOR THE USE OF YOUNG PERSONS. IN WHICH IS EXEMPLIFIED THE NECESSITY OF MODERATION AND JUSTICE TO THE ATTAINMENT OF HAPPINESS. BY THE AUTHOR OF THE "BLIND CHILD," AND "DRAMATIC DIA-LOGUES." [Ten lines from] BEAUMONT AND FLETCHER.
From the Press of Samuel Etheridge, sold by him, and by the Booksellers. Boston, 1796. pp. 142, frontispiece. 24mo.
AAS. NYPL.

31015 THE PITTSBURGH GAZETTE. VOLUME IX. NUMBER 487. SATURDAY, JANUARY 2, [— VOLUME X. NUMBER 539. SATURDAY, DECEMBER 31, 1796.]
Pittsburgh: Printed by John Scull, in Front Street, next door to the corner of Market Street. . . . 1796. fol.

31016 PLAYFAIR, WILLIAM 1759–1823
THE HISTORY OF JACOBINISM, ITS CRIMES, CRUELTIES AND PERFIDIES: COMPRISING AN INQUIRY INTO THE MANNER OF DISSEMINATING, UNDER THE APPEARANCE OF PHILOSOPHY AND VIRTUE, PRINCIPLES WHICH ARE EQUALLY SUBVERSIVE OF OR-DER, VIRTUE, RELIGION, LIBERTY AND HAPPINESS. BY WILLIAM PLAYFAIR. WITH AN APPENDIX, BY PETER PORCUPINE, CONTAINING A HISTORY OF THE AMERICAN JACOBINS, COMMONLY DENOMINATED DEMOCRATS. VOL. I. [—II.] [Three lines from] BURKE.
Philadelphia: Printed for William Cobbett, north Second Street, opposite Christ Church. 1796. 2 vols. pp. 30, (35)–385; 301; (48). 8vo.
AAS. HSP. JCB. LOC. NYPL.

PLAYFAIR, WILLIAM, continued.
Second title: HISTORY OF THE AMERICAN JACOBINS, COMMONLY DENOMINATED DEMOCRATS. BY PETER PORCUPINE. [Three lines from] BURKE.
Philadelphia: Printed for William Cobbett, north Second Street, opposite Christ Church. Nov. 1796. pp. (48.)

31017 PLEYEL, IGNAZ JOSEPH   1757 – 1831
HENRY'S COTTAGE MAID—A FAVORITE SONG—COMPOSED BY PLEYEL. [Two eight-line verses, with music.]
New York Printed for G. Gilfert & Co. at their Musical Magazine No. 177 Broadway. [1796.] pp. (2). fol.   JCB.

31018 PLUMMER, JONATHAN, JUNIOR
THE AWFUL MALIGNANT FEVER AT NEWBURYPORT IN THE YEAR 1796. [Cuts of forty-four coffins.] AN ELEGIAC EPISTLE TO THE MOURNERS, ON THE DEATH OF FORTY-FOUR PERSONS WHO DIED OF A MALIGNANT FEVER IN NEWBURYPORT AND THE ADJACENT TOWNS, IN THE SUMMER AND AUTUMN OF THE YEAR 1796—TO-GETHER WITH A SHORT ACCOUNT OF THAT ALARMING DISORDER.—BY JONATHAN PLUMMER, JUN. [Colophon:]
[Newburyport:] Printed for and sold by the Author—Price 4½d. [1796.] Broadside. fol.   EI. NYHS.

31019 POLAR STAR. [AND] BOSTON DAILY [cut] ADVERTISER. VOL. I. No. 1. THURSDAY, OCTOBER 6, [— No. 74. SATURDAY, DECEMBER 31, 1796.]
[Boston:]   Printed by Alexander Martin, No. 71, State-Street, opposite the Custom-House, for the Proprietors. 1796. fol.   AAS. BA.

Edited by John Daly Burk. The first daily newspaper established in Boston. It was enlarged soon after publication was begun. With the issue for November 14th, the cut of a star was placed over the sub-title, and the word "and" added, as given above. Publication was discontinued, probably, with the issue for February 2, 1797, — the last number located.

31020 POLITICAL GAZETTE. VOL. I. No. 37. TUESDAY, JANUARY 5, [— VOL. II. No. 36. TOTAL NO. 88. FRIDAY, DECEMBER 30, 1796.]
Newburyport, (Massachusetts)—Published on Tuesday [Friday], by William Barrett, west corner of Market-Square . . . 1796. fol.

31021 POOR WILL'S ALMANACK, FOR THE YEAR OF OUR LORD, 1797; BEING THE FIRST AF-TER BISSEXTILE OR LEAP-YEAR. [Eighteen lines.]
Philadelphia: Printed for and sold by Joseph Crukshank, No. 87, High-Street. [1796.] pp. (36). 12mo.   AAS. HSP. LOC. RIHS.

Contains, Address to the free Africans and other people of colour in the United States.

31022 POOR WILL'S POCKET ALMANACK, FOR THE YEAR 1797; BEING THE FIRST AFTER BISSEXTILE OR LEAP-YEAR. [Eighteen lines.]
Philadelphia: Printed for and sold by Joseph Crukshank, No. 87, High-Street. [1796.] pp. (38). 32mo.   AAS. HSP.

31023 POPE, ALEXANDER   1688–1744
AN ESSAY ON MAN: IN FOUR EPISTLES. TO HENRY ST. JOHN, LORD BOLINGBROKE.
Litchfield, (Connecticut): Printed by Collier and Buel. 1796.

31024 —— —— AN ESSAY ON MAN: IN FOUR EPISTLES. TO HENRY ST. JOHN, LORD BOLING-BROKE.
New-York: Printed by John Tiebout. 1796. 24mo.

31025 POPE, ALEXANDER, continued.

—— — AN ESSAY ON MAN: IN FOUR EPISTLES. TO HENRY ST. JOHN, LORD BOLING-BROKE. WRITTEN IN THE YEAR M,DCC,XXXII. BY ALEXANDER POPE, ESQ.

Providence (Rhode Island): Printed by and for Carter and Wilkinson, and sold at their Book and Stationary Store, opposite the Market. 1796. pp.[72]. *12mo.*

AAS. RIHS.

Contains, The Universal prayer, Deo opt. max.; and The Dying christian to his soul, Ode.

31026 —— — AN ESSAY ON MAN: IN FOUR EPISTLES TO H. ST. JOHN, LORD BOLINGBROKE: TO WHICH IS ADDED, THE UNIVERSAL PRAYER. BY ALEXANDER POPE, ESQ. [Ornament.]

Printed at Worcester: by Isaiah Thomas, jun. Sold wholesale and retail at his Bookstore. February—1796. *pp.* 44. *24mo.* AAS. HC.

31027 —— A SELECT COLLECTION OF POEMS, VIZ. AN ESSAY ON MAN, AN ESSAY ON CRITICISM, THE MESSIAH, &C. BY ALEXANDER POPE, ESQ. TOGETHER WITH AN ACCOUNT OF THE LIFE OF THE AUTHOR.

New-London: From Springer's Press. For J. Springer & S. Green. 1796. pp. 132. 18mo. AAS. NYPL.

31028 POPE, AMOS   1771 – 1837

POPE'S MASSACHUSETTS, RHODE-ISLAND, CONNECTICUT, NEW-HAMPSHIRE AND VERMONT ALMANAC FOR THE YEAR OF OUR LORD 1797. . . . BY AMOS POPE.

Printed at Boston by John W. Folsom, No. 30 Union-Street. [1796.] *pp.* (32). *16mo.*

31029 PORT-ROYAL, Messieurs DE

THE ROYAL CONVERT: OR, THE FORCE OF TRUTH. BEING A WONDERFUL AND STRANGE RELATION OF THE CONVERSION OF VARANES, PRINCE OF PERSIA, AND TWO YOUNG LADIES, TO THE CHRISTIAN FAITH: THEIR TRIALS AND SUFFERINGS ON THAT ACCOUNT; OF THE STRANGE DEATH OF ONE OF THE LADIES, AND OF THE PRINCE'S SUCCESS OVER HIS ENEMIES, AND CONVERTING AT LAST HIS CRUEL FATHER, & HIS WHOLE KINGDOM. WRITTEN IN FRENCH BY THE MESSIEURS OF PORT ROYAL, AND NOW NEWLY TRANSLATED INTO ENGLISH. THE FIRST EXETER EDITION.

Printed and sold by H. Ranlet, Main-Street, Exeter. 1796. pp. 96. *12mo.*

AAS.

31030 THE POTOWMAC GUARDIAN, AND BERKELEY ADVERTISER. VOL. 6. NUMBER 268. MONDAY, JANUARY 4, [—VOL. VII. NUMBER 318. THURSDAY, DECEMBER 29, 1796.]

Martinsburg, Virginia: Printed and published, every Monday, by N. Willis, Burke-Street. 1796. fol.

From January 14th, Thursday was made the day of publication. In February, the spelling of Potowmac in the title was changed to Potomak; and, in June, was changed to &.

31031 POTTER, NATHANIEL   1770 – 1843

AN ESSAY ON THE MEDICINAL PROPERTIES AND DELETERIOUS QUALITIES OF ARSENIC. SUBMITTED TO THE EXAMINATION OF THE TRUSTEES AND MEDICAL FACULTY OF THE UNIVERSITY OF PENNSYLVANIA FOR THE DEGREE OF DOCTOR OF MEDICINE.

Philadelphia: Printed by W. W. Woodward. 1796. pp. (2), 64. 8vo.

BM. SGO.

Reprinted in Caldwell's Medical Theses. Vol. I. Philadelphia, 1805.

31032 THE POUGHKEEPSIE JOURNAL. TOTAL NUM. 546. WEDNESDAY, JANUARY 6, [—
TOTAL NUM. 596. WEDNESDAY, DECEMBER 28, 1796.]
Poughkeepsie, Dutchess County—Printed and published by Nicholas Power,
at the Post-Office. 1796. fol. AAS.

In April, Richard Vanderburgh was admitted to partnership, at first
as, Nicholas Power & Company, and afterwards as, Nicholas Power and
Richard Vanderburgh, until November, when the partnership was dissolved.

31033 POWERS, PETER   1729 – 1800
AN HUMBLE INQUIRY INTO THE NATURE OF COVENANTING WITH GOD. BY THE REV.
PETER POWERS, PASTOR OF THE CHURCH AT DEER ISLE.
Printed at Newburyport, by Blunt & March. 1796. pp. 44. 8vo.
AAS. BA. JCB.

31034 POWERS, THOMAS   1776 – 1796
THE DYING SPEECH OF THOMAS POWERS, (WRITTEN BY HIS OWN HAND) TO WHICH
IS ADDED, A LETTER FROM A BLACK WOMAN, SENT TO HIM WHILE UNDER SENTENCE
OF DEATH: ALSO, AN AFFECTING LETTER DELIVERED TO HIM ON TUESDAY MORN-
ING, PREVIOUS TO HIS EXECUTION.
Haverhill (New-Hampshire): Printed and sold by Nathaniel Coverly. 1796.

31035 —— — THE LAST WORDS, AND DYING SPEECH OF THOMAS POWERS, WHO WAS EX-
ECUTED AT HAVERHILL, THE 28TH JULY [1796.]
Windsor: Printed by Alden Spooner. 1796.

31036 —— — THE NARRATIVE AND CONFESSION OF THOMAS POWERS, WHO IS TO BE
HUNG AT HAVERHILL, THE TWENTY-EIGHTH OF JULY, FOR A RAPE.
Hanover: Printed by Dunham and True. 1796.

31037 —— — THE NARRATIVE AND CONFESSION OF THOMAS POWERS, A NEGRO, FOR-
MERLY OF NORWICH IN CONNECTICUT, WHO WAS IN THE 20TH YEAR OF HIS AGE.
HE WAS EXECUTED AT HAVERHILL, IN THE STATE OF NEW-HAMPSHIRE, ON THE
28TH JULY, 1796, FOR COMMITTING A RAPE. [Cut.] PRICE, SINGLE, 4½.
Norwich, Printed [by John Trumbull] August 19th, 1796. pp. — 12 —
12mo. LOC.

31038 PRAYERS, THANKSGIVINGS, AND MEDITATIONS TO ASSIST THE DEVOUT CHRISTIAN IN
HIS PREPARATION FOR AND ATTENDANCE ON THE LORD'S SUPPER.
Haverhill: Printed by Peter Edes. 1795.

31039 PRESBYTERIAN CHURCH IN KENTUCKY.
EXTRACTS FROM THE MINUTES AND PAPERS OF THE TRANSYLVANIA PRESBYTERY;
AND OTHER DOCUMENTS RELATIVE TO JAMES MOORE'S TRIALS FOR THE GOSPEL
MINISTRY IN THE PRESBYTERIAN CHURCH.
Lexington: Printed by J. H. Stewart. 1796.

31040 PRESBYTERIAN CHURCH IN NEW JERSEY AND NEW YORK.
A BRIEF ACCOUNT OF THE ASSOCIATED PRESBYTERIES; AND A GENERAL VIEW OF
THEIR SENTIMENTS CONCERNING RELIGION AND ECCLESIASTICAL ORDER. BY A
CONVENTION OF SAID PRESBYTERIES. [Eight lines of Scripture texts.]
Printed in Catskill, by M. Croswell — 1796. pp. iv, 102, (6). 12mo.
AAS. BM. JCB. NYHS. NYPL.

Second title: AN ACT, TO INCORPORATE SUNDRY PERSONS AS TRUSTEES OF THE
SOCIETY, INSTITUTED IN MORRIS-COUNTY, FOR THE PROMOTION OF LEARNING AND
RELIGION. PASSED AT BURLINGTON, MAY 30TH, 1787. pp. (6).

31041   PRESBYTERIAN CHURCH IN THE UNITED STATES OF AMERICA.
ACTS AND PROCEEDINGS OF THE GENERAL ASSEMBLY OF THE PRESBYTERIAN CHURCH; IN THE UNITED STATES OF AMERICA, A. D. 1795 & 1796.
Philadelphia: Printed by Samuel H. Smith No. 118 Chesnut Street. M.-DCC.XCVI. pp. [17.] 8vo.   AAS. MHS. NYPL. PHS. PTS.

31042   PRESIDENT II. BEING OBSERVATIONS ON THE LATE OFFICIAL ADDRESS OF GEORGE WASHINGTON: DESIGNED TO PROMOTE THE INTEREST OF A CERTAIN CANDIDATE FOR THE EXECUTIVE, AND TO EXPLODE THE PRETENSIONS OF OTHERS. ADDRESSED TO THE PEOPLE OF THE UNITED STATES.
[Philadelphia:] Printed for the Author 1796. pp. (16). 8vo.   LOC.

31043   —— PRESIDENT II. BEING OBSERVATIONS ON THE LATE OFFICIAL ADDRESS OF GEORGE WASHINGTON: DESIGNED TO PROMOTE THE INTEREST OF A CERTAIN CANDIDATE FOR THE EXECUTIVE, AND TO EXPLODE THE PRETENTIONS OF OTHERS. ADDRESSED TO THE PEOPLE OF THE UNITED STATES.
Newark, New-Jersey. Printed by Daniel Dodge, and Co. 1796. pp. (16). 8vo.   BA. HSP. NYHS. NYPL.

31044   PRESIDENTS MARCH. [FOR PIANO, GERMAN FLUTE OR VIOLIN.]
New York: Printed and sold by G. Gilfert. No. 177 Broadway. [1796.] pp. (2). fol.   JCB.

31045   PRESTON, FRANCIS
ADDRESS TO THE PEOPLE OF THE CONGRESSIONAL DISTRICT COMPOSED OF THE COUNTIES OF WYTHE, WASHINGTON, MONTGOMERY, GREEN BRIAR, KANHAWA, GRAYSON, RUSSELL AND LEE. . . .
Philadelphia: M.DCC.XCVI. pp. [29.] 8vo.   JCB. LOC.

31046   PRICE, JONATHAN
A CHART OF THE SEA COASTS, FROM CAPE HENRY TO CAPE ROMAN, AND OF THE INLETS, SOUNDS AND RIVERS OF NORTH-CAROLINA, TO THE TOWNS OF EDENTON, WASHINGTON, NEWBERN AND WILMINGTON. BY JONATHAN PRICE, AND JOHN STROTHER.
Newbern: Printed by Francois-X. Martin. 1796,

North Carolina District Copyright, issued to Jonathan Price and John Strother, as Authors, 7 March, 1796.

31047   —— A MAP OF THE STATE OF NORTH-CAROLINA, AGREEABLE TO ITS PRESENT BOUNDARIES. BY JONATHAN PRICE, AND JOHN STROTHER.
Newbern: Printed by Francois-X. Martin. 1796.

North Carolina District Copyright, issued to Jonathan Price and John Strother. as Authors, 9 March, 1796.

31048   PRIDEAUX, HUMPHREY   1648 – 1724
THE HISTORY OF THE LIFE OF THE GREAT IMPOSTOR MAHOMET: CONTAINING, I. HIS BIRTH AND PARENTAGE. II. OF HIS WIVES. III. HIS JOURNEY INTO HEAVEN, AND THE EXTRAORDINARY THINGS WHICH HE SAW. IV. OF HIS PUBLISHING THE ALCORAN. V. HIS WARS, WITH MANY OTHER EXTRAORDINARY PARTICULARS. VI. HIS DEATH AND BURIAL AT MEDINA, &C. BY HUMPHREY PRIDEAUX, D. D. DEAN OF NORWICH. [Double lines.]
Philadelphia: Printed and sold by Stewart & Cochran, No. 34, South Second-street. M,DCC,XCVI. pp. (126). 24mo.   AAS.

To the reader, dated, Norwich, March 15, 1697.

31049   PRIESTLEY, JOSEPH   1733 – 1804
CONSIDERATIONS ON THE DOCTRINE OF PHLOGISTON AND THE DECOMPOSITION OF
WATER. BY JOSEPH PRIESTLEY, L. L. D. F. R. S. &C. &C. [One line of Latin from]
HORACE.
> *Philadelphia: Printed by Thomas Dobson, at the Stone-House, No. 41, South
> Second Street. 1796.*

> 142d Pennsylvania District Copyright, issued to Thomas Dobson, as
> Proprietor, 19 July, 1796.

31050   —— DISCOURSES RELATING TO THE EVIDENCES OF REVEALED RELIGION, DELIVERED
IN THE CHURCH OF THE UNIVERSALISTS AT PHILADELPHIA 1796. AND PUBLISHED
AT THE REQUEST OF MANY OF THE HEARERS. BY JOSEPH PRIESTLEY, L. L. D.
F. R. S. &C. &C. [Four lines from] I. PETER III. 15. VOL. I.
> *Philadelphia: Printed by Thomas Dobson, at the Stone-House, No. 41, South
> Second Street. 1796.*   AAS. BA. BM. HC. LCP.

> 141st Pennsylvania District Copyright, issued to Thomas Dobson, as
> Proprietor, 19 July, 1796.

31051   —— —— DISCOURSES RELATING TO THE EVIDENCES OF REVEALED RELIGION, DE-
LIVERED IN THE CHURCH OF THE UNIVERSALISTS, AT PHILADELPHIA, 1796. AND
PUBLISHED AT THE REQUEST OF MANY OF THE HEARERS. BY JOSEPH PRIESTLEY,
L. L. D. F. R. S. &C. &C. [Two lines from] I PET. iii. 15. [VOL. I.]
> *Philadelphia: Printed by John Thompson.* MDCCXCVI. pp. xx. (1), (1),
> 426. 8vo.   AAS.

31052   —— EXTRACTS FROM DOCTOR PRIESTLEY'S CATECHISM FOR CHILDREN AND YOUNG
PERSONS. THE FOURTH EDITION.
> *Salem: Printed by William Carlton.* 1796. pp. 12, 12mo.
>   BA. BM. EI. HC. NYPL.

31053   —— A GENERAL VIEW OF THE ARGUMENTS FOR THE UNITY OF GOD, AND AGAINST
THE DIVINITY AND PRE-EXISTENCE OF CHRIST; FROM REASON, FROM THE SCRIP-
TURES, AND FROM HISTORY. BY JOSEPH PRIESTLEY.
> *New-York: Printed for John Fellows, No. 60, Wall-Street.* 1796.

31054   —— MISCELLANEOUS OBSERVATIONS RELATING TO EDUCATION. MORE ESPECIALLY
AS IT RESPECTS THE CONDUCT OF THE MIND. THE FIRST AMERICAN EDITION. BY
JOSEPH PRIESTLEY, LL. D. F. R. S. [One line of Latin from] HORACE.
> *New-London: Printed by J. Springer, for T. C. Green, and S. Green; and
> J. Trumbull, Norwich.* 1796. pp. x, 102, (2). 12mo.   AAS. BA. LOC. NYPL.

31055   —— UNITARIANISM EXPLAINED AND DEFENDED IN A DISCOURSE DELIVERED IN THE
CHURCH OF THE UNIVERSALISTS, AT PHILADELPHIA, 1796. BY JOSEPH PRIESTLEY,
LL. D. F. R. S. &C. &C. [Six lines of Scripture texts.]
> *Philadelphia: Printed by John Thompson.* 1796. Copyright secured ac-
> cording to law. pp. viii, 32. 8vo.   AAS. BA. BM. CLS. MHS.

> 140th Pennsylvania District Copyright, issued to Thomas Dobson, as
> Proprietor, 19 July, 1796. Reprinted in London, in 1833.

31056   PRINCE GEORGE COUNTY, MARYLAND.
TO THE GENERAL ASSEMBLY OF MARYLAND: PERMIT A PLAIN PLANTER TO SUG-
GEST TO YOUR CONSIDERATION THE FOLLOWING MODE OF DIVIDING PRINCE GEORGE
AND ANNE-ARUNDEL COUNTIES . . . THE VOTES FOR PRINCE GEORGE COUNTY
TO BE TAKEN AT THE CITY OF WASHINGTON, . . . [Signed by forty-two plant-
ers.] PRINCE GEORGE'S COUNTY, 8TH DECEMBER, 1796.
> *[Annapolis: Printed by Frederick Green.* 1796.] Broadside. 4to.

AUCTION
VALUES

31057   PROTESTANT EPISCOPAL CHURCH IN NEW JERSEY.
PROCEEDINGS OF A CONVENTION OF THE PROTESTANT EPISCOPAL CHURCH IN THE
STATE OF NEW-JERSEY, HELD AT ELIZABETH-TOWN, ON WEDNESDAY AND THURS-
DAY, THE 1ST. AND 2D. OF JUNE, 1796.
Elizabeth-Town: Printed by Shepard Kollock. M.DCC.XCVI. pp. (2),
(64)–[81.] 8vo.   AAS.
Reprinted.

31058   PROTESTANT EPISCOPAL CHURCH IN NEW YORK.
JOURNAL OF THE PROCEEDINGS OF THE PROTESTANT EPISCOPAL CHURCH IN THE
STATE OF NEW-YORK, HELD IN TRINITY CHURCH, IN THE CITY OF NEW-YORK.
New-York: Printed by Hugh Gaine. 1796.

31059   PROVIDENCE. RHODE ISLAND.
PROVIDENCE, JUNE 29TH, 1796. (CIRCULAR.) GENTLEMEN, THE FREE MEN OF
THE TOWN OF PROVIDENCE, DEEPLY IMPRESSED WITH THE INEQUALITY AND IN-
JUSTICE OF THE ESTIMATE OF THE RATEABLE PROPERTY OF THE STATE, AS RE-
PORTED BY SEVEN OF THE STATE'S COMMITTEE, AND ADOPTED BY THE GENERAL
ASSEMBLY, AT THEIR LAST SESSION, HAVE TAKEN THE SUBJECT INTO CONSIDERA-
TION AT A TOWN-MEETING HOLDEN THIS DAY, AND HAVE UNANIMOUSLY PASSED THE
RESOLUTIONS, COPIES OF WHICH WE HAVE THE HONOUR HEREWITH TO TRANSMIT
YOU. [Two columns.] WITH PROPER SENTIMENTS OF CONSIDERATION AND RE-
SPECT, YOUR VERY HUMBLE SERVANTS, IN BEHALF OF THE TOWN: MOD-
ERATOR.   CLERK.
[Providence: Printed by Bennett Wheeler, 1796.] Broadside. fol.
BU. JCB. RIHS.

31060   —— PROVIDENCE, JULY 27, 1796. GENTLEMEN, AT A MEETING OF THE COMMITTEES
APPOINTED BY EIGHT TOWNS IN THE COUNTIES OF PROVIDENCE AND BRISTOL, AT
THE TOWN-HOUSE IN PROVIDENCE, TO CONSULT ON THE PRESENT SITUATION OF
THEIR RESPECTIVE TOWNS, AND OF THE STATE AT LARGE, IT WAS VOTED TO AD-
JOURN THE MEETING TO THE FIFTEENTH DAY OF AUGUST NEXT, . . . THE OB-
JECT OF THIS MEETING IS . . . PARTICULARLY THE UNEQUAL OPERATION OF THE
NEW ESTIMATE, THE IMPERFECTIONS OF OUR JUDICIARY SYSTEM, AND THE WANT
OF A CONSTITUTION OF STATE GOVERNMENT . . . [Nine lines]. BY ORDER AND
IN BEHALF OF THE MEETING AFORESAID, DANIEL MOWRY, MODERATOR. JAMES
BURRILL, JUN. SEC'RY. A TRUE COPY: TO THE TOWN-CLERK AND MEMBERS OF
THE TOWN-COUNCIL OF THE TOWN OF
[Providence: Printed by Bennett Wheeler? 1796.] Broadside. fol.   RIHS.
Printed entirely in script letters.

31061   —— AT A CONVENTION OF DELEGATES FROM EIGHT TOWNS IN THE COUNTIES OF
PROVIDENCE AND BRISTOL, HOLDEN BY ADJOURNMENT AT THE TOWN-HOUSE IN
PROVIDENCE, ON THE FIFTEENTH DAY OF AUGUST, 1796, – – – THE FOLLOWING
LETTERS WERE DIRECTED TO BE PRINTED, AND SENT TO THE MEMBERS OF THE
GENERAL ASSEMBLY, AND THE TOWN-COUNCILS AND TOWN-CLERKS OF THE SEV-
ERAL TOWNS, WITH A REQUEST THAT THEY MAY BE READ IN OPEN TOWN-MEETING.
TO THE FREEMEN OF THE STATE OF RHODE-ISLAND AND PROVIDENCE PLANTA-
TIONS. . . . AN ACT FOR TAKING A GENERAL ESTIMATE OF THE RATEABLE
PROPERTY WITHIN THE STATE, AND OF THAT BELONGING TO THE INHABITANTS
BEING WITHOUT THE STATE. . . . IN THE HOUSE OF REPRESENTATIVES, JUNE
18, 1796. . . . TO THE FREEMEN OF THE STATE OF RHODE-ISLAND AND PROVI-
DENCE PLANTATIONS. . . . IN BEHALF OF THE CONVENTION OF DELEGATES,
ASSEMBLED AT PROVIDENCE ON THE 15TH DAY OF AUGUST, 1796 — WITH PROPER
SENTIMENTS OF CONSIDERATION AND RESPECT, WE ARE YOUR VERY HUMBLE
SERVANTS, DANIEL MOWRY, MODERATOR, JAMES BURRILL, JUN. SEC'RY. A TRUE
COPY:
[Providence: Printed by Bennett Wheeler, 1796.] pp. (2). fol.   RIHS.

31062   PROVIDENCE. RHODE ISLAND. CARPENTERS.
RULES FOR HOUSE-CARPENTERS WORK IN THE TOWN OF PROVIDENCE.
Printed at Providence by Carter and Wilkinson, M,DCC,XCVI. 12mo.
BU. RIHS.

31063   PROVIDENCE. RHODE ISLAND. ST. JOHN'S LODGE
PROVIDENCE, NOVEMBER [5] 1796. BROTHER, YOU ARE REQUESTED TO ATTEND
THE FUNERAL OF OUR DECEASED BROTHER JOHN FRANCIS, THIS AFTERNOON, AT
[THREE] O'CLOCK.——THE LODGE WILL CONVENE AT THE [COUNCIL CHAMBER]
AT [TWO] O'CLOCK; PROPERLY CLOTHED. BY ORDER, B. WHEELER, SECRETARY.
[Providence: Printed by Bennett Wheeler, 1796.] Broadside. 16mo.
BU. JCB.

31064   THE PROVIDENCE GAZETTE. VOL. XXXIII. No. 1670. SATURDAY, JANUARY 2,
[—No. 1722. SATURDAY, DECEMBER 31, 1796.]
*Printed and published by Carter and Wilkinson, at the Post-Office, opposite
the Market; . . . 1796. fol.* AAS. BU. LOC. RIHS. RL.

31065   PUGLIA, SANTIAGO FELIPE
THE BLUE SHOP; OR, IMPARTIAL AND HUMOROUS OBSERVATIONS ON THE LIFE AND
ADVENTURES OF PETER PORCUPINE, WITH THE REAL MOTIVES WHICH GAVE RISE
TO HIS ABUSE OF OUR DISTINGUISHED PATRIOTIC CHARACTERS; TOGETHER WITH A
FULL AND FAIR REVIEW OF HIS LATE SCARE-CROW. BY JAMES QUICKSILVER.
*Philadelphia: Printed by Moreau de St. Méry, No. 84, corner of Front and
Walnut Streets. August 1796. pp. (52). 8vo.* CLS. LOC. NYPL.

Also attributed to Joseph Scott on the authority of Mathew Carey.
145th Pennsylvania District Copyright, issued to Moreau de St. Méry,
as Proprietor, 22 August, 1796.

31066   —— THE POLITICAL MASSACRE, OR UNEXPECTED OBSERVATIONS ON THE WRITINGS
OF OUR PRESENT SCRIBBLERS. BY JAMES QUICKSILVER, AUTHOR OF THE BLUE
SHOP. [Vignette.]
*Philadelphia: Printed by Moreau de St. Méry, No. 84, corner of Front and
Walnut Streets. September 1796. pp. (29), (2). 8vo.* LOC.

151st Pennsylvania District Copyright, issued to M. L. E. Moreau de
St. Méry, as Proprietor, 17 September, 1796.

31067   RADCLIFFE, ANN WARD   1764 – 1822
THE CASTLES OF ATHLIN AND DUNBAYNE. A HIGHLAND STORY. [Two lines from]
CAWTH. BY ANNE RATTCLIFFE [*sic*], AUTHORESS OF A SICILIAN ROMANCE, RO-
MANCE OF THE FOREST, MYSTERIES OF EUDOLPHO, ETC.
*Philadelphia: Published by Thomas Bradford, Printer, Bookseller and Sta-
tioner, No. 8, South Front Street. 1796. pp. (260), (2). 12mo.* NYPL.

31068   RAINBOW, THOMAS, AND HANNAH, ROBERT
CATALOGUE OF THE BOOKS IN THE NORFOLK CIRCULATING LIBRARY.
*Norfolk: Printed by Willett & O'Connor, for Rainbow & Hannah, at the Nor-
folk Circulating Library. 1796.*

James Hunter disposed of the Norfolk Circulating Library to Rainbow
and Hannah, September 21, 1795.

31069   RALLING, JOHN
MISCELLANEOUS SKETCHES IN PROSE AND VERSE, WRITTEN FOR THE SPIRITUAL IM-
PROVEMENT OF MANKIND. . . . BY JOHN RALLING, AUTHOR OF THE PLAN ON
FREEDOM AND LIBERTY, AND VARIOUS OTHER LITTLE TRACTS.
Newburyport: Printed by William Barrett, 1796. pp. 24. 12mo. BU.

31070   RAMSAY, ANDREW MICHAEL   1686 – 1743
LES VOYAGES DE CYRUS; AVEC UN DISCOURS SUR LA THÉOLOGIE ET LA MYTHOLOGIE
DES PAIËNS. PAR M. DE RAMSAY. TRADUIT, ET MIS DANS L'ORDRE LE PLUS
CONVENABLE, POUR HÂTER LES PROGRÈS DE CEUX QUI S'APPLIQUENT AUX LANGUES
FRANÇAISE ET ANGLAISE, PAR J. E. G. M. DE LA GRANGE, AVOCAT AU CONCEIL
SUPÉRIEUR DU CAP-FRANÇOIS; TRADUCTEUR DU JOURNAL EN FRANCE, PAR J.
MOORE. TOME PREMIER [—SECOND.] ENRÉGISTRE SUIVANT LA LOI.

Philadelphie: Imprimé pour James Rivington, chez, Ornrod et Conrad.
M.DCC.XCVI. 2 tomes. pp. (2), (2), (4), 141, 141 ; (2), (2), 96, 97, 73, 73, frontispiece. 12mo.   AAS. JCB. NYPL.

Second title: THE TRAVELS OF CYRUS; TO WHICH IS ANNEXED, A DISCOURSE UP-
ON THE THEOLOGY AND MYTHOLOGY OF THE PAGANS. BY M. DE RAMSAY. TRANS-
LATED, AND DISPOSED IN THE MOST CONVENIENT ORDER, FOR THE GREATER IM-
PROVEMENT OF THOSE WHO APPLY THEMSELVES TO THE FRENCH AND ENGLISH
LANGUAGES. BY J. E. G. M. DE LA GRANGE. LL. L. COUNSELLOR AT LAW IN THE
SUPREME COURT OF CAPE-FRANÇOIS, AND TRANSLATOR OF J. MOORE'S JOURNAL
IN FRANCE. VOLUME I. [—II.] ENTERED ACCORDING TO LAW.

Philadelphia: Printed for James Rivington, by Ormrod and Conrad, M.-
DCC.XCVI. 2 vols. pp. 141; 97, 73.

The French and English versions are on opposite pages—each with
separate pagination. In addition to the Discourse, there is a Letter
from M. Freret, member of the Academy of Inscriptions at Paris, to
the Author, concerning the chronology of his work. pp. 64-73.

31071   RAMSAY, DAVID   1749 – 1815
A SKETCH OF THE SOIL, CLIMATE, WEATHER, AND DISEASES OF SOUTH-CAROLINA.
READ BEFORE THE MEDICAL SOCIETY OF THAT STATE. BY DAVID RAMSAY, M. D.
VICE-PRESIDENT OF THE SOCIETY. [Printer's mark.]

Charleston: Printed by W. P. Young, Franklin's Head, No. 43, Broad-street.
MDCCXCVI. pp. (2), (2), 30, 3 tables. 8vo.

                 AAS. BM. BPL. HC. JCB. LOC. MHS. NYPL. SCHS.

Copy-right secured according to Law.

31072   RANDOLPH, EDMUND JENNINGS   1753 – 1813
POLITICAL TRUTH: OR ANIMADVERSIONS ON THE PAST AND PRESENT STATE OF PUBLIC
AFFAIRS; WITH AN INQUIRY INTO THE TRUTH OF THE CHARGES PREFERRED
AGAINST MR. RANDOLPH.

Philadelphia: Printed by Samuel Harrison Smith, No. 118. Chesnut-street.
M.DCC.XCVI. pp. 44. 8vo.   AAS. BA. BPL. JCB. LOC. MHS. NYPL.

"Of the numerous pamphlets which have appeared lately under a political name, this certainly ranks foremost for elegant language, and
sound reasoning."

31073   RANLET, HENRY
THE COMPLETE NEW-HAMPSHIRE REGISTER; CONTAINING A LIST OF THE OFFICERS,
EXECUTIVE, LEGISLATIVE AND JUDICIARY IN THE SERVICE OF THE UNITED STATES,
WITH MANY OTHER COMMUNICATIONS, IN THIS STATE, NOT HITHERTO PUBLISHED
IN A WORK OF THIS KIND. TO WHICH IS ADDED, AN ALMANACK FOR THE YEAR
1797. THE WHOLE COMPRISING A VALUABLE COLLECTION OF INTERESTING AND
USEFUL MATTER, SUITABLE FOR SUCH A WORK. [Four lines of verse.]

*Printed at Exeter by H. Ranlet, and sold at his Book-Store by the hundred,
dozen or single.* 1796. pp. (52); (40). 12mo.   AAS. NL.

RANLET, HENRY, continued.
Second title: THE NEW-HAMPSHIRE DIARY; OR ALMANACK: FOR THE YEAR OF OUR LORD 1797. BEING THE FIRST AFTER BISSEXTILE OR LEAP-YEAR, AND THE TWENTY-FIRST OF THE AMERICAN INDEPENDENCE. CALCULATED FOR THE MERIDIAN OF BOSTON, LAT. 42 DEG. 25 M. N. BUT WILL SERVE FOR THE ADJACENT STATES WITH LITTLE VARIATION. CONTAINING A VARIETY OF USEFUL AND ENTERTAINING MATTER, SUITABLE FOR SUCH A WORK. [Vignette.]
Printed at Exeter, by H. Ranlet, and sold at his Book-Store by the groce, dozen, or single. [1796.] pp. (40).

31074 THE RECORDER. VOL. VII. No. 228. TUESDAY, JANUARY 5, [—VOL. – No. –
— — 1796.]
Troy: Printed by George Gardner, a few rods west of the Meeting-House. 1796. fol.

How long continued is not known.

31075 RED AND BLACK; OR THE FATES AT FARO, A SERIOUS DRAMA; BEING A PICTURE OF THE SECRET INTRIGUES AND DELUSIONS RECENTLY PRACTISED, BY THE MANAGERS OF THE FRENCH BANK, IN PHILADELPHIA; WITH A DELINKATION OF THE AFFECTING INCIDENTS RESULTING THEREFROM. ALSO, CHARACTERS SUPPORTING THE BANKS, &C. DESIGNED AS A MORROR [*sic*] FOR GAMESTERS, AND OTHERS WHO FEEL A PROPENSITY TO HAZARD THEIR FORTUNES AND REPUTATION AT THE TABLE. [Two lines from] POPE.
Philadelphia: Printed for the Author by W. W. Woodward, No. 17, Chesnut-Street. 1796. 8vo.

31076 REDFIELD, NATHAN
A TREATISE OF SURVEYING, CONTAINING BOTH THE THEORY AND PRACTICE OF THAT ART. IN TWO PARTS. PART 1. CONTAINING ARITHMETIC AND GEOMETRY, SO FAR AS IS NECESSARY FOR THE MEASURING OF LANDS IN THE COMMON METHOD BY PROTRACTION. PART 2. CONTAINING PLANE TRIGONOMETRY, PERFORMED BY THE USE OF TABLES OF NATURAL SINES AND TANGENTS; TOGETHER WITH ITS APPLICATION TO THE MEASUREMENT OF HEIGHTS AND DISTANCES, AND PARTICULARLY TO THE SURVEYING OF LANDS IN A MODE PECULIARLY FITTED FOR THE USE OF SURVEYORS IN AMERICA. BY NATHAN REDFIELD.
Hartford? 1796.

Connecticut District Copyright, issued to Nathan Redfield, as Author, 12 February, 1796.

31077 REFLECTIONS ON THE INCONSISTENCY OF MAN, PARTICULARLY EXEMPLIFIED IN THE PRACTICE OF SLAVERY IN THE UNITED STATES.
New York: Printed and sold by John Buel, corner of Water Street and Fly Market. 1796. pp. 27. 8vo.   NYHS.

31078 REID, JOHN, publisher.
THE AMERICAN ATLAS: CONTAINING THE FOLLOWING MAPS, VIZ. 1. NORTH-AMERICA 2. SOUTH AMERICA 3. UNITED STATES 4. NEW-HAMPSHIRE 5. PROVINCE OF MAINE 6. MASSACHUSETTS 7. VERMONT 8. RHODE-ISLAND 9. CONNECTICUT 10. NEW-YORK 11. NEW-JERSEY 12. PENNSYLVANIA 13. DELAWARE AND MARYLAND 14. VIRGINIA 15. KENTUCKY, WITH THE ADJOINING TERRITORIES 16. NORTH-CAROLINA 17. SOUTH-CAROLINA 18. GEORGIA 19. TENNESSEE 20. WEST INDIES
New-York: Published by John Reid, Bookseller and Stationer, No. 106 *Water-Street.* 1796. pp. (2), 20 maps. fol.   AAS. BA. BPL. HC. JCB. NYPL.

A separate issue of the Atlas originally designed to accompany Winterbotham's Historical view of the United States.

31079   THE RELIGIOUS INQUIRER. No. 1, JUNE 24, 1796.
Norwich: Printed by John Trumbull, 1796.

Proposals for a monthly paper of eight pages, octavo,—ninety-six pages a year—with the above title, were made, by John Trumbull, May 19, 1796.

31080   THE REMARKABLE HISTORY OF AUGI: OR: A PICTURE OF TRUE HAPPINESS. TO-GETHER WITH THE STORY OF THE DREAMER. FIRST AMERICAN EDITION.
Worcester: Printed by Isaiah Thomas, jun. . . . —1796. pp. 31. 32mo. AAS.

31081   THE REPUBLICAN CITIZEN, AND FARMER AND PLANTER'S CHRONICLE. AGRI-CULTURE IS ABOVE ALL!! VOL. I. NUMB. I. WEDNESDAY, JUNE 1, [— NUMB. XXXI. WEDNESDAY, DECEMBER 28, 1796.]
Fredericksburg (Va.): Published (every Wednesday) by Lancelot A. Mullin, [Market-Street, west corner of the upper Tobacco Inspection.] 1796. fol.

Established, as a weekly, by Lancelot A. Mullin, and continued by him certainly to June 14, 1797—the last number located.

31082   REPUBLICAN GAZETTEER. [Motto.] VOL. 1. NUMB. 1. TUESDAY, NOVEMBER 22, [— NUMB. 6. TUESDAY, DECEMBER 27, 1796.]
Printed by Moses Davis. Concord, Newhampshire. 1796. fol.

Established, as a weekly, by Moses Davis, in continuation, and con-tinuing the advertisements of *The Federal Mirror*, with the motto: "Here you may range the world from pole to pole; increase your knowledge, and delight your soul"—at small expense. And continued to April 4, 1797, when the title was changed to *The New Star*.

31083   REPUBLICAN JOURNAL. [Motto.] VOL. I. No. 15. WEDNESDAY, JANUARY 6, [— VOL. I. No. 41. WEDNESDAY, JULY 6, 1796.]
Poughkeepsie, Printed and published by Nathan Douglas, near the Episcopal Church. 1796. fol.

With the issue of June 29th, Douglas sold his interests to Richard Van-derburgh & Company, and, in partnership with Stiles Nichols, estab-lished in October at Danbury, Connecticut, a newspaper with the same title. The above is the last number located.

31084   REPUBLICAN JOURNAL. [Motto.] VOL. I. No. 1. MONDAY, OCTOBER 3, [— No. 13. MONDAY, DECEMBER 26, 1796.]
Printed & published by Douglas & Nichols, near the Court-House, in Dan-bury. 1796. fol.

Established, as a weekly, by Nathan Douglas and Stiles Nichols, and continued by them certainly to the issue of January 6, 1800—the last number located. The motto reads: "A people ignorant, can never enjoy freedom; a people immoral are unworthy of the blessing."—Muir.

31085   REPUBLICAN JOURNAL; AND DUMFRIES WEEKLY ADVERTISER. VOL. I. No. XXXIV. THURSDAY, JANUARY 7, [—VOL. II. No. XXI. THURSDAY, NOVEMBER 3, 1796.]
Dumfries, (Virginia): Printed by J. Kempe & T. Thornton. 1796. fol.   HC.

With the issue for April 7th, James Kempe withdrew, and publication was continued by Thomas Thornton, up to November 3d,—the last number located. There appears to be some doubt that the title in April was not American Journal.

31086   A REVIEW OF THE QUESTION, IN WHOM HAS THE CONSTITUTION VESTED THE TREATY
POWER? WITH INCIDENTAL ILLUSTRATIONS; AND A SHORT DISCUSSION OF THE RIGHT
OF THE HOUSE TO CALL ON THE PRESIDENT, IN A LATE INSTANCE, FOR CERTAIN
PAPERS. BY A SENATOR OF THE UNITED STATES.
   Philadelphia: Printed by Samuel Harrison Smith, No. 118, *Chesnut-Street.*
1796. pp. [35], (1). 8vo.   BA. JCB. LOC. NYPL.

31087   RHEES, MORGAN JOHN   1760 – 1804
THE GOOD SAMARITAN. AN ORATION DELIVERED ON SUNDAY EVENING, MAY 22,
1796, IN BEHALF OF THE PHILADELPHIA SOCIETY FOR THE INFORMATION AND
ASSISTANCE OF PERSONS EMIGRATING FROM FOREIGN COUNTRIES. BY MORGAN J.
RHEES. PUBLISHED BY REQUEST; — FOR THE BENEFIT OF THE SOCIETY. [Three
lines of Scripture texts.]
   Philadelphia: Printed by Lang & Ustick, 1796. *Price* 25 *cents.* pp. 20.
8vo.   AAS. BA. HC. JCB. LOC. NYPL.

31088   RHODE ISLAND. STATE.
OCTOBER, 1795. AT THE GENERAL ASSEMBLY OF THE GOVERNOR AND COMPANY
OF THE STATE OF RHODE-ISLAND AND PROVIDENCE – PLANTATIONS. BEGUN AND
HOLDEN AT SOUTH-KINGSTOWN, WITHIN AND FOR THE STATE AFORESAID, ON THE
LAST MONDAY IN OCTOBER, IN THE YEAR OF OUR LORD ONE THOUSAND SEVEN
HUNDRED AND NINETY-FIVE, AND IN THE TWENTIETH YEAR OF INDEPENDENCE.
[Colophon:]
   Warren (Rhode-Island): Printed by Nathaniel Phillips, Printer to the State.
M,DCC,XCVI. pp. 32. fol.   JCB. RIHS.

31089   —— FEBRUARY, 1796. AT THE GENERAL ASSEMBLY OF THE GOVERNOR AND COM-
PANY OF THE STATE OF RHODE-ISLAND. AND PROVIDENCE – PLANTATIONS, BEGUN
AND HOLDEN BY ADJOURNMENT, AT PROVIDENCE, WITHIN AND FOR THE STATE
AFORESAID, ON THE FIRST MONDAY IN FEBRUARY, IN THE YEAR OF OUR LORD
ONE THOUSAND SEVEN HUNDRED AND NINETY-SIX, AND IN THE TWENTIETH YEAR
OF INDEPENDENCE. [Colophon:]
   Warren (Rhode Island): Printed by Nathaniel Phillips, Printer to the State.
M,DCC,XCVI. pp. 37. fol.   JCB. LOC. RIHS.

31090   —— MAY, 1796. AT THE GENERAL ASSEMBLY OF THE GOVERNOR AND COMPANY
OF THE STATE OF RHODE-ISLAND AND PROVIDENCE – PLANTATIONS. BEGUN AND
HOLDEN AT NEWPORT, WITHIN AND FOR THE STATE AFORESAID. ON THE FIRST
WEDNESDAY IN MAY, IN THE YEAR OF OUR LORD ONE THOUSAND SEVEN HUNDRED
AND NINETY-SIX, AND IN THE TWENTIETH YEAR OF INDEPENDENCE.
   [*Warren: Printed by Nathaniel Phillips,* 1796.] pp. 24. fol. JCB. LOC. RIHS.

31091   —— JUNE, 1796. AT THE GENERAL ASSEMBLY OF THE GOVERNOR AND COMPANY
OF THE STATE OF RHODE-ISLAND, AND PROVIDENCE – PLANTATIONS, IN NEW-
ENGLAND, IN AMERICA; BEGUN AND HOLDEN BY ADJOURNMENT. AT NEWPORT,
WITHIN AND FOR THE STATE AFORESAID, ON THE SECOND MONDAY IN JUNE, IN
THE YEAR OF OUR LORD ONE THOUSAND SEVEN HUNDRED AND NINETY-SIX, AND
IN THE TWENTIETH YEAR OF INDEPENDENCE. [Colophon:]
   Warren (Rhode-Island): Printed by Nathaniel Phillips, Printer to the State.
M,DCC,XCVI. pp. 29. fol.   HSP. JCB. LOC. RIHS.

31092   —— OCTOBER, 196 [*sic* 1796.] AT THE GENERAL ASSEMBLY OF THE GOVERNOR
AND COMPANY OF THE STATE OF RHODE-ISLAND. AND PROVIDENCE – PLANTA-
TIONS, BEGUN AND HOLDEN AT PROVIDENCE, WITHIN AND FOR THE STATE. AFORE-
SAID, ON THE LAST MONDAY IN OCTOBER, IN THE YEAR OF OUR LORD ONE THOU-
SAND SEVEN HUNDRED AND NINETY-SIX, AND IN THE TWENTY-FIRST YEAR OF
INDEPENDENCE. [Colophon:]
   Warren (Rhode-Island): Printed by Nathaniel Phillips, Printer to the State.
[1796.] pp. 23. fol.   HSP. JCB. LOC. RIHS.

31093   RHODE ISLAND. State, continued.
—— State of Rhode Island and Providence Plantations. June session A. D. 1796. [An Act directing the mode of choosing Representatives to Congress.]
[Warren: Printed by Nathaniel Phillips. 1796.] Broadside.   RISL.

31094   —— State of Rhode-Island, &c. In General Assembly. June session, A.D. 1796. An Act for granting and apportioning a Tax of twenty thousand dollars, upon the inhabitants of this State. [Colophon:]
Warren (Rhode-Island): Printed by Nathaniel Phillips, Printer to the State. M,DCC,XCVI. pp. 4. fol.   RIHS.

31095   —— At a General Assembly of the State of Rhode-Island and Providence Plantations. In the House of Representatives, June 18, A.D. 1796. The underwritten Representatives dissent from the Bill for establishing an estimate of the value of rateable property in the several towns in this State, [Three columns. Signed, Welcome Arnold, and fourteen others.]

Followed by: At a town-meeting of the freemen of the town of Providence, legally warned and assembled at the Town House in said town on the 23d day of June, A. D. 1796. Resolved, as the sense of this meeting. That no assessment of this town's apportionment of the State tax, as ordered by the General Assembly, at their June session, shall be made by the assessors of this town; such apportionment being manifestly unconstitutional. [Three lines.]

Followed by: At a town-meeting of the freemen of the town of Providence, legally warned and assembled at the Town-House in said town, on the twenty-ninth day of June, A. D. 1796. Whereas, the committee at the last meeting to write circular letters to certain towns on the subject of the estimate lately adopted by the General Assembly, have made a report of a draught of a letter to this meeting; — It is voted and resolved that the said draught be approved of. [Nine lines.] A true copy, witness, Geo. Tillinghast. town-clerk. [Colophon:]
[Providence:] Printed by B. Wheeler. [1796.] Broadside. fol. BU. LOC. RIHS.

31096   —— By his excellency Arthur Fenner, esquire, governor, captain-general and commander in chief of the State of Rhode-Island, and Providence-Plantations. To the town-clerk of the town of   Greeting. Benjamin Bourn, esquire, the first Representative of this State in the Congress of the United States, having been appointed, under the authority of Congress, District Judge of the State aforesaid, and accepted his said appointment, whereby his seat in Congress is become vacant: [Ordering town-meetings on the fifteenth day of November, to elect a successor for the period of the fourth Congress.] Given under my hand and the seal of the said State, this fourth day of November, A. D. 1796, and in the twenty-first year of independence. By his excellency's command.
[Warren: Printed by Nathaniel Phillips, 1796.] Broadside. fol.   RIHS.

31097   RHODE ISLAND. College of, now Brown University.
[Ornament.] Commencement of Rhode-Island College, September 7, 1796. Order of the day. [Twenty-nine lines. Ornament. Colophon:]
[Providence:] Printed by Carter and Wilkinson. [1796.] Broadside. fol.   BU. JCB.

31098   RHODE ISLAND COLLEGE, continued.
       —— VIRO AMPLISSIMO, JABEZ BOWEN, ARMIGERO, COLLEGII RHOD. INSULÆ QUOD PROVIDENTIÆ EST. CANCELLARIO; REVERENDO JONATHANI MAXCY, PRÆSIDI; SOCIIS AC CURATORIBUS HUICCE COLLEGIO INVIGILANTIBUS; ERUDITIS PROFESSORIBUS AC TUTORIBUS SPECTATIS; REVERENDIS ECCLESIARUM CHRISTI PASTORIBUS; OMNIBUS UBIQUE GENTIUM MÆCENATIBUS: HASCE THESES JUVENES IN ARTIBUS INITIATI, [Seventeen names.] HUMILLIMÈ DEDICANT. [Three columns.] [Colophon:]
         Habita in solennibus Academicis Providentiæ Rep. Ins. Rhod. et Prov. Plant. die septimo Septembris, A. D. M,DCC,XCVI. Rerumque publicarum Fœderatarum Americæ summæ potestatis XXI. *Providentiæ: Typis Carter et Wilkinson.* Broadside. fol.   BU.

31099   RICHARD, OLD FATHER, pseudonym.
       POOR RICHARD REVIVED: BEING THE FARMER'S DIARY: OR BARBER & SOUTHWICK'S ALBANY ALMANACK; FOR 1797. BY OLD FATHER RICHARD, MATHEMAT.
         Albany: Printed and sold by Barber and Southwick, two doors below the Dutch Church, State-Street. [1796.] pp. (36). 12mo.

31100   RICHARDSON, SAMUEL   1689–1761
       THE HISTORY OF CLARISSA HARLOWE.
         Cooperstown: Printed by Elihu Phinney. 1796

31101   —— THE HISTORY OF PAMELA; OR, VIRTUE REWARDED. ABRIDGED FROM THE WORKS OF SAMUEL RICHARDSON, ESQ. [And, Edwin and Adela: a tale.]
         New-York: Printed by Mott & Lyon, for Evert Duyckinck, & Co. No. 110 *Pearl-street.* pp. 144. 12mo.   AAS.

31102   THE RICHMOND AND [cut] MANCHESTER ADVERTISER. [Motto.] VOL. III. NO. 73. WHOLE NO. 282. SATURDAY, JANUARY 2, [— VOL. IV. NO. 62. WHOLE NO. 371. FRIDAY, NOVEMBER 18, 1796.]
         Richmond—Printed (on Wednesdays and Saturdays) by Samuel Pleasants, jun. Opposite Bowler's and next door below the Columbia Tavern. 1796. fol.   LOC.
       In April, the printing-office was "near the Vendue-Office," and so continued. Beginning November 22d, the title was changed to *Virginia Argus.*

31103   RICHMOND [cut] CHRONICLE. [Motto.] NUMB. 300. FRIDAY, JANUARY 1, [— NUMB. 363. TUESDAY, AUGUST 9, 1796.]
         Richmond: Printed [Tuesdays and Fridays] by John Dixon, near the Market. 1796. fol.
       In April, Saturday was substituted for Friday as one of the days of publication. The above is the last number located. In July, 1797, Dixon established *The Observatory; or, a view of the times.*

31104   RIGHTS OF MAN:—BY JOHN WINTER. VOL. II. NO. 103. WEDNESDAY, JANUARY 6, [— VOL. III. NO. 154. WEDNESDAY, DECEMBER 28, 1796.]
         Frederick-Town (Maryland): Printed by John Winter, at his Office, in Patrick-Street. . . . . 1796. fol.

31105   RILEY, GEORGE
       THE BEAUTIES OF THE CREATION; OR, A NEW MORAL SYSTEM OF NATURAL HISTORY; DISPLAYED IN THE MOST SINGULAR, CURIOUS, AND BEAUTIFUL QUADRUPEDS, BIRDS, INSECTS, TREES, AND FLOWERS: DESIGNED TO INSPIRE YOUTH WITH HUMANITY TOWARDS THE BRUTE CREATION, AND BRING THEM EARLY ACQUAINTED WITH THE WONDERFUL WORKS OF THE DIVINE CREATOR. SECOND AMERICAN EDITION. [Three lines from] BLACKMORE ON THE CREATION.
         Philadelphia: Printed by William Young, Bookseller, No. 52, *Second, corner of Chesnut-Street.* 1796. pp. 343, (5). 12mo.   AAS. JCB. LOC.
       Pages (344)–(348) contains Books, etc. published, and to be sold by William Young.

31106   RIOFFE, Honoré, baron   1764–1813
REVOLUTIONARY JUSTICE DISPLAYED; OR, AN INSIDE VIEW OF THE VARIOUS PRISONS
OF PARIS, UNDER THE GOVERNMENT OF ROBESPIERRE AND THE JACOBINS. TAKEN
PRINCIPALLY FROM THE JOURNALS OF THE PRISONERS THEMSELVES. "AH LIBERTY
HOW HAST THOU BEEN SPORTED WITH." MAD ROLAND. TRANSLATED FROM THE
FRENCH. WITH AN APPENDIX — CONTAINING — AN ACCOUNT OF THE PROMULGA-
TION OF THE NEW RELIGION OF FRANCE, THE IMPIOUS ATTACK ON THE ANCIENT,
AND THE VIOLATION AND PLUNDER OF THE SACRED RECEPTACLES OF THE DEAD.

*Philadelphia: Printed for Benjamin Davies, No. 68, High-street, by Richard
Folwell, No. 33, Mulberry-street.* [1796.] pp. (180). 12mo.   AAS.

Contains, A list of books, &c. for sale at Benjamin Davies' Bookstore,
No. 68, High-street. pp. 177–180. "Entered agreeable to law." 126th
Pennsylvania District Copyright, issued to Benjamin Davies, as Pro-
prietor, 5 February, 1796. And the seventeenth work deposited in the
Office of the Secretary of State, under the copyright law, July, 1796.

31107   RIPPON, John   1751–1826
AN ACCOUNT OF THE LONDON MISSIONARY SOCIETY EXTRACTED FROM DR. RIPPON'S
BAPTIST ANNUAL REGISTER. TO WHICH IS ADDED, THE STATE OF RELIGION AT
SIERRA LEONE, IN AFRICA. FROM NUMBERS 10 AND 11 OF THE REGISTER. WITH
[a translation of] AN EVANGELICAL HYMN, COMPOSED IN THE BENGAL LANGUAGE,
1788. BY RAM RAM BOSHOO, A HINDOO MUNSHEE.

Philadelphia: Printed by Lang & Ustick, 1796. pp. (2), [16], (2). 8vo.
       AAS. NYPL.

To the American reader, signed, W. Rogers. T. Ustick. Philadelphia,
February 18th, 1796. With printed wrappers.

31108   RISING SUN. VOL. III. No. 119. FRIDAY, JANUARY 1, [— VOL. IV. No. 171. FRI-
DAY, DECEMBER 30, 1796.]

Kingston, (Ulster County). Printed by William Copp, and Samuel Freer.
1796. fol.

31109   THE RISING SUN. [Motto.] VOL. I. No. 22. TUESDAY, JANUARY 5, [—VOL. II. No.
21. WHOLE NO. 73. TUESDAY, DECEMBER 27, 1796.]

*[Printed and published] By Cornelius Sturtevant, jun. & Co. Keene,
(Newhampshire).* 1796. fol.   AAS.

31110   ROBBINS, Chandler   1738–1799
A DISCOURSE DELIVERED BEFORE THE HUMANE SOCIETY OF THE COMMONWEALTH
OF MASSACHUSETTS, AT THEIR SEMIANNUAL MEETING, JUNE 14TH, 1796. BY
CHANDLER ROBBINS, D. D. MINISTER OF THE FIRST CHURCH IN·PLYMOUTH. [One
line from] LUKE XV. 24. [Printer's mark.]

Boston: Printed by Thomas Fleet, jun. at the Bible & Heart Cornhill. MDCC-
XCVI. pp, (36). 4to. AAS. BA. BM. BPL. HC. JCB. LOC. MHS. NYHS. NYPL. SGO. YC.

31111   —— A SERMON PREACHED AT PLYMOUTH, DECEMBER 22, 1793: BEING THE ANNI-
VERSARY OF THE LANDING OF OUR ANCESTORS IN THAT PLACE, IN 1620. PUB-
LISHED AT THE REQUEST OF THOSE WHO HEARD IT, AND OTHERS; WITH SOME EN-
LARGEMENTS, AND PARTICULAR ANECDOTES RELATING TO THEIR SUFFERINGS
BEFORE THEY LEFT ENGLAND; NEVER BEFORE PUBLISHED. BY CHANDLER ROB-
BINS, D. D. [Six lines from] ISA. LXXVIII. 5, 6, 7.

— Printed at Boston — Stockbridge: Re-printed by Loring Andrews. 1796.
pp. [46.] 16mo.   AAS. CHS. JCB. LOC. UTS.

31112   ROBBINS, Ephraim
A Friendly letter to the rev. mr. [Henry] Cumings, containing several queries upon certain observations in his sermon on Natural religion. [Three lines from] Paul.
Newburyport: Printed by William Barrett, Market-Square, for the Author. 1796. pp. [19.] 8vo.   AAS. BA. NYHS.
To the Christian reader, is signed, E. R. Carlisle, December 1, 1796.

31113   ROBERTSON, Joseph   1726 – 1802
A Clear and practical system of punctuation: abridged from Robertson's Essay on punctuation. [By Thaddeus Mason Harris.] For the use of schools. [Second ? edition.]
Printed at Boston, by I. Thomas and E. T. Andrews, Faust's Statue, No, 45 Newbury Street. 1796.

31114   ROGERS, James
The Authority and duty of Christ's ministers. A sermon, preached at Long Cane, July 29th, 1794. at the ordination of the rev. William Blackstock. By the rev. James Rogers, member of the Associate Reformed Presbytery of the Carolinas and Georgia. Published at the request of the Presbytery. [Ornament.]
Charleston: Printed by J. MacIver, No. 47, Bay. MDCCXCVI. pp. (27). 8vo.   LOC.

31115   ROGERS, William   1751 – 1824
A Sermon. occasioned by the death of the rev. Oliver Hart. a. m. who departed this life, Dec. 31, 1795, in the 73d year of his age. Preached at Hopewell, New-Jersey, April. 24. 1796. By William Rogers. d. d. professor of English and belles lettres in the University of Pennsylvania. [Published by particular request.] [Three lines of quotations.]
Philadelphia, Printed by Lang & Ustick, M,DCC.XCVI. pp. (39). 8vo.
     AAS. BM. JCB. NYHS. NYPL.

31116   ROLLIN, Charles   1661 – 1741
The Life of Alexander the great, king of Macedon. Compiled from ancient history. By mr. Rollin, late principal of the University of Paris, professor of eloquence in the Royal College, and member of the Royal Academy of Inscriptions and belles-lettres. Translated from the French.
Providence: Printed by B. Wheeler, for Joseph J. Todd, at the Bible and Anchor. MDCCXCVI. pp. 257, (1). 12mo.   AAS. BU. JCB. LOC. NYPL. RIHS.
The last page consists of an advertisement of Todd's Bookstore and Circulating Library, for town and country.

31117   ROMAN CATHOLIC CHURCH.
Catéchisme, ou abrégé de la foi Catholique. Publie par ordre de mgr. l'Archevêque de Paris, pour les fidèles de son Diocèse, et enseigné dans les missions de rr. pp. Capucins aux isles sous le vent de l' Amérique.
Baltimore: de l' Imprimerie de S. Sorer. 1796. pp. 113. 24mo.   AAS.

31118   —— La Journée du chretien, sanctifiée par la priere et la meditation. Nouvelle edition.
Baltimore: De l' Imprimerie de William Pechin. MDCCXCVI. pp. (2). [284 *sic* 311.] 24mo.   AAS.

31119   ROOT, Erastus   1773–1846
An Introduction to arithmetic for the use of common schools. By Erastus Root, a. b. The second edition.
> *Norwich: Printed and sold by Thomas Hubbard.* M.DCC.XCVI. *(With the privilege of copy-right.)* pp. 105. 12mo.   AAS. BA. MHS. NYPL.

31120   ROULSTONE'S Knoxville Gazette, and weekly advertiser. No. 3. Monday, November 14, [— No. 9. Monday, December 26, 1796.]
> *Knoxville, [State of Tennessee.] Published by George Roulstone.* 1796. fol.

In continuation of *Knoxville Gazette, and weekly advertiser.*

31121   ROUSSEAU, Jean Jacques   1712–1778
The Confessions of J. J. Rousseau, citizen of Geneva. Part I.; to which is added, the Reveries of a solitary walker; Part II.; to which is added, a new collection of letters from the Author; translated from the French.
> *New-York:* 1796. 2 vols. 12mo.

31122   —— Eloisa: or, a series of original letters. collected and published by J. J. Rousseau, citizen of Geneva. Translated from the French Together with, the sequel of Julia: or, the new Eloisa. (Found amongst the Author's papers after his decease.) First American edition. Vol. I. [— III.]
> *Philadelphia: Printed for Samuel Longcope.* M.DCC.XCVI. 3 vols. pp. 274; 267; — . 12mo,   AAS. NYPL.

31123   —— Letters of an Italian nun and an English gentleman. Translated from the French of J. J. Rousseau. [Two lines of Italian quotation.] Fifth edition.
> *Philadelphia: Printed for Mathew Carey, No. 118, Market-Street.* 1796. pp. (130). 12mo.   AAS.

31124   —— Letters of an Italian nun and an English gentleman. Translated from the French of J. J. Rousseau. [Two lines of Italian quotation.] First Worcester edition.
> *Worcester, Massachusetts, From the Press of Thomas, Son and Thomas. No-vember—1796.* pp. 196, portrait. 12mo.   AAS.

The portrait, engraved by Doolittle, is "Published by Thomas, Son & Thomas, Jan'y 1797."

31125   ROWE, Elizabeth Singer   1674–1737
Devout exercises of the heart, in meditation and soliloquy. prayer and praise. By the late pious and ingenious mrs. Elizabeth Rowe. Revised and published at her request, by Isaac Watts, d. d.
> *Dedham: Printed and sold by Nathaniel and Benjamin Heaton, at their Office near the Court-House.* M,DCC,XCVI. pp. 142. (2). 12mo.   AAS. HC. JCB.

31126   ROWLAND, William Frederick   1763–1843
A Sermon, delivered in presence of his excellency John Taylor Gilman, esquire, governor, the honorable the Council, Senate, and House of Representatives, of the State of New-Hampshire, convened at Exeter on the day of the anniversary election, June 2. 1796. By William F. Rowland. a. m. pastor of the first church in Exeter.
> *Printed at Exeter, by Henry Ranlet, for the General Court.* M,DCC.XCVI. pp. 32. 8vo.   AAS. BA. BM. LOC. NYHS. NYPL.

31127 ROWLANDSON, MARY WHITE
A NARRATIVE OF THE CAPTIVITY SUFFERINGS AND REMOVES OF MRS. MARY ROW-
LANDSON, WHO WAS TAKEN PRISONER BY THE INDIANS, WITH SEVERAL OTHERS;
AND TREATED IN THE MOST BARBAROUS AND CRUEL MANNER BY THOSE VILE SAV-
AGES: WITH MANY OTHER REMARKABLE EVENTS DURING HER TRAVELS. WRITTEN
BY HER OWN HAND. FOR HER PRIVATE USE, AND NOW MADE PUBLIC AT THE EARN-
EST DESIRE OF SOME FRIENDS AND FOR THE BENEFIT OF THE AFFLICTED.
*Haverhill, New Hampshire: Printed and sold by Nathaniel Coverly and Son,
near the Court-House.* [1796.] pp. 64. 16mo.

31128 ROWSON, SUSANNA HASWELL   1761–1824
AMERICANS IN ENGLAND, OR, LESSONS FOR DAUGHTERS. A COMEDY. BY THE AUTHOR
OF CHARLOTTE TEMPLE, ETC. ETC.
Boston: 1796. 12mo.

31129 —— IN VAIN THE VERDURE OF SPRING. THE MUSIC COMPOSED BY BENJAMIN CARR.
Philadelphia: Printed by G. Willig. [1796.]

31130 —— SLAVES IN ALGIERS; OR, A STRUGGLE FOR FREEDOM: A PLAY, INTERSPERSED
WITH SONGS, IN THREE ACTS. AS PERFORMED WITH GREAT APPLAUSE AT THE
THEATRES, IN PHILADELPHIA AND BALTIMORE.—WRITTEN BY MRS. ROWSON, LATE
OF THE PHILADELPHIA. NOW OF THE BOSTON THEATRE.
Boston: 1796. 12mo.

31131 [U. S. arms.] THE ROYAL PRIMER; OR, AN EASY AND PLEASANT GUIDE TO THE ART
OF READING. EMBELLISHED WITH CUTS.
Printed and sold by Samuel Hall, No. 53, Cornhill, Boston.—1796. pp. (72).
48mo.   AAS. MHS.

31132 RUDDOCK, SAMUEL A.
A GEOGRAPHICAL VIEW OF ALL THE POST TOWNS IN THE UNITED STATES OF AMER-
ICA, AND THEIR DISTANCES FROM EACH OTHER, ACCORDING TO THE ESTABLISHMENT
OF THE POST MASTER GENERAL. BY SAMUEL A. RUDDOCK, ACCOMPTANT, BOSTON.
[Boston: 1796.] Broadside. 4to.   HC. MHS.
An engraved plate. 99th Massachusetts District Copyright, issued to
Samuel A. Ruddock, as Author, 12 May, 1796.

31133 —— —— A GEOGRAPHICAL VIEW OF ALL THE POST TOWNS IN THE UNITED STATES
OF AMERICA, AND THEIR DISTANCES FROM EACH OTHER ACCORDING TO THE ESTAB-
LISHMENT OF THE POST MASTER GENERAL. ALSO, THE LATITUDE AND LONGITUDE
OF ALL PRINCIPAL TOWNS FROM THE MOST ACCURATE AND AUTHENTIC CALCULA-
TIONS. TO WHICH IS ADDED, A VIEW OF THE LENGTH AND BREADTH OF THE SEV-
ERAL UNITED STATES, INCLUDING THE NUMBER OF COUNTIES. SQUARE MILES, AND
NUMBER OF ACRES THEY SEPARATELY CONTAIN, TOGETHER WITH THE LATITUDES
AND LONGITUDES THEY ARE DIVIDEDLY BETWEEN. LIKEWISE THE NUMBER OF IN-
HABITANTS THEY DISJOINTLY CONTAINED AT THE LAST CENSUS. IN LIKE MANNER
THE TIME WHEN THEY SINGLY RATIFIED THE FEDERAL CONSTITUTION. WITH THE
RATES OF POSTAGE OF LETTERS FROM ONE PLACE TO ANOTHER, &C.
*Boston: Sold by Samuel Hall, James White, David West, and at the Boston
Book-Store.* 1796. 2' x 2'.

** · As there were a few copies delivered to some of the Subscribers (more than 800) before the Press was thoroughly corrected, those
who may have such will please exchange them at the Boston Book-
Store,—there is only a few literal errors."

31134 —— VALUABLE TABLES, FOR RENDERING THE VALUE OF FEDERAL MONEY EASY AND
INTELLIGIBLE; AND LIKEWISE FOR COMPUTING INTEREST IN DOLLARS, DIMES,
CENTS AND MILLS.
Litchfield: Printed by Thomas Collier. 1796.

31135   RUDDOCK, SAMUEL A., continued.
—— — VALUABLE TABLES. NO. 1. A TABLE SHEWING THE VALUE OF ANY NUM-
BER OF CENTS FROM ONE TO ONE HUNDRED, IN SHILLINGS, PENCE AND FARTHINGS,
RENDERING THE VALUE OF THE FEDERAL CURRENCY EASY AND INTELLIGIBLE.
NO. 2. VALUE OF ENGLISH AND PORTUGUESE GOLD, IN DOLLARS, CENTS AND MILLS.
NO. 3. VALUE OF FRENCH AND SPANISH GOLD, IN DOLLARS, CENTS AND MILLS.
NO. 4. A TABLE OF SIMPLE INTEREST AT 6 PER CENT, IN DOLLARS, CENTS, DIMES
AND MILLS.
    Newfield: Printed by Beach & Jones, near the Bridge. 1796.

31136   —— — I. A TABLE SHEWING THE VALUE OF ANY NUMBER OF CENTS FROM 1 TO
100, IN THE STATES WHERE DOLLARS PASS FOR 6s. II. A TABLE FOR REDUCING
SHILLINGS, PENCE, AND FARTHINGS INTO DOLLARS, CENTS AND MILLS. ALSO, A
METHOD OF REDUCING POUNDS, SHILLINGS, PENCE, AND FARTHINGS INTO DOLLARS,
CENTS AND MILLS.
    Norwich: Printed by John Trumbull. 1796. Broadside. fol.

31137   —— — VALUABLE TABLES, FOR REDUCING LAWFUL TO FEDERAL MONEY.
    Rutland: Printed by James Kirkaldie, for S. Williams & Co. 1796.

31138   —— — VALUABLE TABLES. NO. I. A TABLE SHOWING THE VALUE OF ANY NUM-
BER OF CENTS, FROM ONE TO ONE HUNDRED, IN SHILLINGS, PENCE, AND FARTHINGS.
NO. II. VALUE OF ENGLISH AND PORTUGUESE GOLD, IN DOLLARS, CENTS, AND MILLS.
NO. III. VALUE OF FRENCH AND SPANISH GOLD, IN DOLLARS. CENTS AND MILLS.
NO. IV. A TABLE OF SIMPLE INTEREST, AT 6 PER CENT. PER ANNUM, IN DOLLARS,
DIMES, CENTS. AND MILLS.
    Windsor: Printed by Alden Spooner. 1796.

31139   RULES OF ARITHMETIC: CONTAINING ALL THE USEFUL TABLES IN MONEY, WEIGHTS
AND MEASURES.
    Philadelphia: 1796. 12mo.

31140   RUM, Sir RICHARD, pseudonym.
THE INDICTMENT AND TRIAL OF SIR RICHARD RUM, AND CAPTAIN WHISKEY; WITH
ADDITIONS AND IMPROVEMENTS. [Cut.]
    Philadelphia: Printed for Robert Stewart, travelling Bookseller. Price 8d.
—1796. pp. 24. 12mo.   JCB.

31141   THE RURAL MAGAZINE: OR VERMONT REPOSITORY. DEVOTED TO LITERARY, MORAL,
HISTORICAL, AND POLITICAL IMPROVEMENT. VOL. II. [JANUARY – DECEMBER,
1796.] [Edited by Rev. Samuel Williams, LL. D.]
    *Rutland: Printed by James Kirkaldie, for S. Williams & Co. a few rods
north of the State House.* [1796.] pp. 620, (4). 8vo.
         AAS. BA. BM. BPL. LOC. MHS. NYHS. NYPL. YC.

31142   THE RURAL REPOSITORY. [Motto.] VOL. I. NO. 12. THURSDAY, JANUARY 7, [—
VOL. II. NO. 63. THURSDAY, DECEMBER 29, 1796.]
    *Published every Thursday by Charles Prentiss, south of the Meeting house, in
Leominster, (Massachusetts.)* 1796. fol.   AAS.

31143   RUSH, BENJAMIN   1745–1813
AN EULOGIUM, INTENDED TO PERPETUATE THE MEMORY OF DAVID RITTENHOUSE,
LATE PRESIDENT OF THE AMERICAN PHILOSOPHICAL SOCIETY, DELIVERED BEFORE
THE SOCIETY IN THE FIRST PRESBYTERIAN CHURCH, IN HIGH-STREET, PHILADEL-
PHIA, ON THE 17TH DEC. 1796. AGREEABLY TO APPOINTMENT. BY BENJAMIN
RUSH, A MEMBER OF THE SOCIETY.
    *Philadelphia: Printed for J. Ormrod, No. 41, Chesnut Street, by Ormrod &
Conrad. Copy-right secured.* [1796.] pp. (46). 8vo.
         AAS. BA. BM. BPL. HC. JCB. MHS. NYPL. RIHS. SGO.

81144 RUSH, BENJAMIN, continued.

—— MEDICAL INQUIRIES AND OBSERVATIONS: CONTAINING AN ACCOUNT OF THE BILIOUS REMITTING AND INTERMITTING YELLOW FEVER, AS IT APPEARED IN PHILADELPHIA IN THE YEAR 1794. TOGETHER WITH AN INQUIRY INTO THE PROXIMATE CAUSE OF FEVER; AND A DEFENCE OF BLOOD-LETTING AS A REMEDY FOR CERTAIN DISEASES. BY BENJAMIN RUSH, M. D. PROFESSOR OF THE INSTITUTES, AND OF CLINICAL MEDICINE, IN THE UNIVERSITY OF PENNSYLVANIA. VOLUME IV.

Philadelphia; Printed by Thomas Dobson, at the Stone-House, No. 41, South Second-Street. 1796. pp. vii, (1), (vii)—ix, 258. 8vo. BPL. NYPL. SGO.

Forming Volume IV of his Works.

81145 THE RUTLAND HERALD: A REGISTER OF THE TIMES. [Motto.] VOL. II. No. 5. MONDAY, JANUARY 4, [—— VOL. III. No. 4. MONDAY, DECEMBER 26, 1796.]

Rutland, State of Vermont:—Printed by J. Kirkaldie, for S. Williams, & Co., in the Main-Street, a few rods south of the State-House, . . . 1796. fol. AAS.

James Kirkaldie, the printer, died August 9th, aged 26 years, and was succeeded by John S. Hutchins, on October 3, 1796.

81146 S., G.

A NEW INTRODUCTION TO READING: OR A COLLECTION OF EASY LESSONS, ARRANGED ON AN IMPROVED PLAN: CALCULATED TO ACQUIRE WITH EASE A THEORY OF SPEECH, AND TO FACILITATE THE IMPROVEMENT OF YOUTH. DESIGNED AS AN INTRODUCTION TO THE SPEAKER. TO WHICH IS ADDED A CHRONOLOGICAL TABLE. AND EMBELLISHED WITH A FINE ENGRAVING. THE FIFTH EDITION, CORRECTED. COMPILED BY THE PUBLISHER. [Three lines from] DYER.

Philadelphia: Printed by Henry and Patrick Rice. 1796. pp. viii, (7), 328, frontispiece. 12mo. NYPL.

Who the Publisher, G. S., is is not shown in the book. "The third and fourth editions were published within a year of each other, and the fourth contained two plates."

81147 S., R.

JACHIN AND BOAZ; OR, AN AUTHENTIC KEY TO THE DOOR OF FREEMASONRY, BOTH ANCIENT AND MODERN. CALCULATED NOT ONLY FOR THE INSTRUCTION OF EVERY NEW MADE MASON; BUT ALSO FOR THE INFORMATION OF ALL WHO INTEND TO BECOME BRETHREN. CONTAINING, I. A CIRCUMSTANTIAL ACCOUNT OF ALL THE PROCEEDINGS IN MAKING A MASON, WITH THE SEVERAL OBLIGATIONS OF AN ENTERED APPRENTICE, FELLOW-CRAFT, AND MASTER; THE PRAYERS, AND ALSO THE SIGN, GRIP, AND PASS-WORD OF EACH DEGREE, WITH THE CEREMONY OF THE MOP AND PAIL. II. THE MANNER OF OPENING A LODGE, AND SETTING THE CRAFT TO WORK. III. THE ENTERED APPRENTICE, FELLOW-CRAFT, AND MASTER'S LECTURES, VERBATIM, AS DELIVERED IN ALL LODGES; WITH THE SONG AT THE CONCLUSION OF EACH PART. IV. THE ORIGIN OF MASONRY; DESCRIPTION OF SOLOMON'S TEMPLE; HISTORY OF THE MURDER OF THE GRAND MASTER HIRAM BY THE THREE FELLOW-CRAFTS; THEIR DISCOVERY AND PUNISHMENT; THE BURIAL OF HIRAM BY KING SOLOMON'S ORDER; WITH THE FIVE POINTS OF FELLOWSHIP, &C. V. THE CEREMONY OF THE INSTALMENT OF THE MASTERS OF DIFFERENT LODGES ON ST. JOHN'S DAY—DESCRIPTION OF THE REGALIA, &C. VI. CEREMONIES USED AT THE FUNERAL OF A MASON. VII. A SAFE AND EASY METHOD PROPOSED, BY WHICH A MAN MAY OBTAIN ADMITTANCE INTO ANY LODGE, WITHOUT PASSING THROUGH THE FORM REQUIRED, AND THEREBY SAVE A GUINEA OR TWO IN HIS POCKET. VIII. ANTHEMS, ODES, SONGS, TOASTS, &C. ILLUSTRATED WITH A BEAUTIFUL FRONTISPIECE OF THE REGALIA, JEWELS, AND EMBLEMATICAL ORNAMENTS BELONGING TO MASONRY. AND AN ACCURATE PLAN OF THE DRAWING ON THE FLOOR OF A LODGE, INTERSPERSED WITH A VARIETY OF NOTES AND REMARKS, NECESSARY TO EXPLAIN AND RENDER THE WHOLE CLEAR TO THE MEANEST CAPACITY. BY A GENTLEMAN BELONGING TO

S., R., continued.

THE JERUSALEM LODGE; A FREQUENT VISITOR AT THE QUEEN'S ARMS, ST. PAUL'S CHURCH-YARD; THE HORN, IN FLEET-STREET; CROWN AND ANCHOR, STRAND; AND THE SALUTATION, NEWGATE STREET. TRY ME—PROVE ME. A NEW EDITION, GREATLY ENLARGED AND IMPROVED.

New-York: Printed by Tiebout & O'Brien, for Evert Duyckinck & Co. Book-sellers and Stationers, No. 110, Pearl-Street. M,DCC,XCVI. pp. (iv), (2), (58), frontispiece. 8vo.   AAS. LOC.

31148   SAINT PIERRE, JACQUES HENRI BERNARDIN DE   1737–1814
PAUL ET VIRGINIE, HISTOIRE INDIENNE. PAR JACQUES-HENRI-BERNARDIN DE SAINT PIERRE. AVEC FIGURES. . . . MISERIS SUCCURRERE DISCO. ÆNEID LIB. I.

à Boston: Imprimé pour Guillaume Spotswood et Joseph Nancrede. 1796. 2 tomes. pp. 291; — ; 3 plates. 32mo.   AAS.

Second title: PAUL AND VIRGINIA, AN INDIAN STORY. TRANSLATED FROM THE FRENCH OF J. H. B. DE SAINT PIERRE. AUTHOR OF THE STUDIES OF NATURE, BY H. HUNTER, D.D. EMBELLISHED WITH ENGRAVINGS. . . . MISERIS SUCCURRERE DISCO. ÆNEID, LIB. I. I HAVE LEARNED TO SUCCOUR THE DISTRESSED.

Boston: Printed for W. Spotswood & J. Nancrede. 1796. pp. 291; — ; 3 plates.

The French and English texts are on opposite pages.

31149   —— PAUL ET VIRGINIE, HISTOIRE INDIENNE. PAR JACQUES-HENRI-BERNARDIN DE SAINT PIERRE. AVEC FIGURES. [One line of Latin from] ÆNEID LIB. I.

à Boston: Imprimé pour Guillaume Spotswood et Joseph Nancrede. 1796. pp. 264, 3 plates. 32mo.

31150   —— PAUL AND VIRGINIA, AN INDIAN STORY. TRANSLATED FROM THE FRENCH OF J. H. B. DE SAINT PIERRE. AUTHOR OF THE STUDIES OF NATURE. BY H. HUNTER, D. D. EMBELLISHED WITH ENGRAVINGS. [Two lines of quotations.]

Boston: Printed for W. Spotswood & J. Nancrede. 1796. pp. 264, 3 plates. 32mo.   AAS.

31151   SALEM. MASSACHUSETTS.
MEMORIAL TO UNITED STATES HOUSE OF REPRESENTATIVES, RELATING TO THE TREATY WITH GREAT BRITAIN.

Salem: Printed by William Carlton. April 22, 1796. Broadside.   EI.

31152   SALEM. MASSACHUSETTS. AMITY FIRE CLUB.
ARTICLES OF THE AMITY FIRE CLUB ASSOCIATED IN SALEM, FEBRUARY 10, 1796. [With list of members.]

Salem: Printed by William Carlton. 1796. pp. 12. 12mo.   EI.

31153   THE SALEM GAZETTE. VOLUME X. NUMBER 482. TUESDAY, JANUARY 5, [—NUMBER 564. FRIDAY, DECEMBER 30, 1796.]

Printed and Published by William Carlton, Essex-Street, between Washington and Market-Streets, Salem, Massachusetts. 1796. fol.   AAS. EI. HC. LOC.

Beginning in June, the Gazette was published as a semi-weekly on Tuesdays and Fridays.

31154   SALIMENT, GEORGE EDWARD
MINUETTO WITH EIGHT VARIATIONS FOR THE FLUTE AND VIOLONCELLO COMPOSED BY GEO. ED. SALIMENT.

Printed by B. Carr & sold at his Musical Repositories New York & Philadelphia. [1796.] 4to.

31155   SALTONSTALL, WINTHROP   1775–1802
AN INAUGURAL DISSERTATION ON THE CHEMICAL AND MEDICAL HISTORY OF SEPTON, AZOTE, OR NITROGENE; AND ITS COMBINATIONS WITH THE MATTER OF HEAT AND THE PRINCIPLE OF ACIDITY. SUBMITTED TO THE PUBLIC EXAMINATION OF THE FACULTY OF PHYSIC UNDER THE AUTHORITY OF THE TRUSTEES OF COLUMBIA COLLEGE IN THE STATE OF NEW-YORK: WILLIAM SAMUEL JOHNSON, LL. D. PRESIDENT: FOR THE DEGREE OF DOCTOR OF PHYSIC, ON THE THIRD DAY OF MAY, 1796. BY WINTHROP SALTONSTALL . . .

      New-York: Printed by T. and J. Swords. 1796. pp. 68. 8vo.

                                               HC. RIMS. SGO.

31156   SALZMANN, CHRISTIAN GOTTHILF   1744–1811
ELEMENTS OF MORALITY, FOR THE USE OF CHILDREN: WITH AN INTRODUCTORY ADDRESS TO PARENTS. TRANSLATED FROM THE GERMAN OF THE REV C. G. SALZMANN. [By Mary Wollstonecraft.] ILLUSTRATED WITH TWENTY COPPER PLATES. [By —— Weston.] IN TWO VOLUMES. VOL. I. [— II.]

      Philadelphia: Printed by J. Hoff & H. Kammerer, jun. M,DCC,XCVI. 2 vols. pp. 248, 10 plates; 259. (1), (2), 10 plates. 12mo.   AAS. HC.

31157   —— — ELEMENTS OF MORALITY, FOR THE USE OF CHILDREN; WITH AN INTRODUCTORY ADRESS [*sic*] TO PARENTS. TRANSLATED FROM THE GERMAN OF THE REV. C. G. SALZMANN. [By Mary Wollstonecraft.] THE THIRD AMERICAN EDITION.

      Wilmington: Printed by Joseph Johnson Market-Street opposite the Bank. 1796. pp. 232. 12mo.   AAS.

31158   SAMOUAL, JEAN BAPTISTE, and LOUIS
DESCRIPTION OF A PLANTATION. SITUATED AT PETIT ST. LOUIS. NEAR PORT-DE-PAIX, IN THE NORTHERN PART OF HISPANIOLA; WITH ALL THE BUILDINGS. BELONGING TO THE SAME AND NECESSARY TO CARRY ON THE CULTIVATION OF SUCH PLANTATION; NOW OFFERED TO BE EXCHANGED. BY J. B. & L. SAMOUAL, PROPRIETORS, FOR GOODS. PRINCIPALLY EAST-INDIA, AND PARTLY PUBLIC PAPERS ON ST. DOMINGO, PROPERLY CERTIFIED AND SIGNED BY THE PUBLIC FUNCTIONARIES, AND APPROVED BY THE GENERAL IN CHIEF. TOUSSAINT. THIS BEAUTIFUL PLANTATION, A PLAN OF WHICH IS ANNEXED, WAS SURVEYED IN 1785. BY THE KING'S SURVEYOR: AND THE FOLLOWING EXPLANATORY OBSERVATIONS ARE THE SUBSTANCE OF A *Proces-verbal* , SIGNED BY A NUMBER OF RESPECTABLE PLANTERS, WHOSE PROPERTY LIES CONTIGUOUS TO IT. THE CERTIFICATE OF IT. TRANSLATED IN THE ENGLISH LANGUAGE, TOGETHER WITH THE FRENCH ORIGINAL OF IT, SHALL BE EXHIBITED TO ANY GENTLEMAN WHO MAY PROPOSE BECOMING A PURCHASER.

      [Boston? 1796.] pp. [12,] map. 12mo.   AAS. BA. MHS.

      Title of Map: PLAN OF THE PLANTATION OF M. SAMOUAL SITUATED IN THE DISTRICT OF THE RIVER BARE AT PORT ST. LOUIS OF THE NORTH. SURVEYED BY US THE 17TH OCTR 1785. NAZE KINGS SURVEYOR. $7\frac{1}{2}$ x 10.

31159   SAVAGE, EDWARD   1761–1817
LIBERTY IN THE FORM OF THE GODDESS OF YOUTH, GIVING SUPPORT TO THE BALD-EAGLE. PAINTED AND ENGRAVED BY E. SAVAGE.

      Philadelphia: 1796. Broadside. fol.

31160   —— — LIBERTY GIVING SUPPORT TO THE BALD-EAGLE. A PRINT.

      Baltimore: Published by James Smith & Co. 1796.

31161　SAY, BENJAMIN
A SHORT COMPILATION OF THE EXTRAORDINARY LIFE AND WRITINGS OF THOMAS SAY;
IN WHICH IS FAITHFULLY COPIED, FROM THE ORIGINAL MANUSCRIPT, THE UNCOM-
MON VISION WHICH HE HAD WHEN A YOUNG MAN. BY HIS SON.

*Philadelphia: Printed and sold by Budd and Bartram, No. 58, North Sec-
ond street.* 1796. pp. (32.) 151, (1). 12mo.　AAS. BA. BM. JCB. NYPL. WiPL.

159th Pennsylvania District Copyright, issued to Stacy Budd and
Archibald Bartram, as Proprietors, 17 November, 1796. Reprinted in
New York in 1805.

31162　SCHENCK, WILLIAM
AN ATTEMPT TO DELINEATE THE CHARACTER AND REWARD OF THE FAITHFUL SER-
VANTS OF CHRIST, IN A SERMON, PREACHED AT THE FUNERAL OF THE REV. NOAH
WETMORE, A. M. LATE MINISTER AT BROOKHAVEN, LONG ISLAND, MARCH 10, 1796.
BY WILLIAM SCHENCK, A. B. & M. V. D. AT HUNTINGTON, LONG-ISLAND. [Three
lines from] PAUL. PUBLISHED AT THE REQUEST; AND BY THE WIDOW AND CHIL-
DREN OF THE DECEASED.

Sag-Harbor: Printed by David Frothingham. [1796.] pp. (–27–) 8vo.
LOC. NYPL.

31163　SCHILLER, JOHANN CHRISTOPH FRIEDRICH VON　　　1759–1805
THE GHOST-SEER; OR, APPARITIONIST. FROM THE GERMAN OF SCHILLER.

New-York: Printed by T. & J. Swords. 1796. pp. 120. 12mo.

31164　——— — THE GHOST-SEER, OR THE APPARITIONIST.
Charleston: Printed by W. P. Young. 1796.

31165　SCHNEIDER, PETER
MERKWÜRDIGE PROPHEZEYUNG EINES EINSIEDLERS, WELCHER 15 JAHRE ALLEIN
IN DER WÜSKEN GEWOHNET. ENTDECKT VON DR. PETER SCHNEIDER. VIERTE
AUFLAGE.

Ephrata: Gedruckt bey Benjamin Mäyer. 1796.

31166　SCHUYLER, PHILIP JOHN　　　　　　　　　　　1733–1804
REMARKS ON THE REVENUE, OF THE STATE OF NEW-YORK. BY PHILIP SCHUYLER,
A MEMBER OF THE SENATE OF THAT STATE.

*Albany: Printed by Charles R. and George Webster, at their Bookstore, in the
White House, corner of State and Pearl-Streets, opposite the City-Tavern.* MDCC-
XCVI. pp. [24.] 4to.　　　　　　AAS. BA. BPL. LOC. NYHS. NYPL.

31167　SCHUYLKILL AND SUSQUEHANNA NAVIGATION.
CANAL LOTTERY, NO. TWO. SCHEME OF A LOTTERY AUTHORIZED BY AN ACT EN-
TITLED "AN ACT TO ENABLE THE PRESIDENT AND MANAGERS OF THE SCHUYLKILL
AND SUSQUEHANNA NAVIGATION, AND THE PRESIDENT AND MANAGERS OF THE
DELAWARE AND SCHUYLKILL CANAL NAVIGATION, TO RAISE BY WAY OF LOTTERY,
THE SUM OF FOUR HUNDRED THOUSAND DOLLARS, FOR THE PURPOSE OF COMPLET-
ING THE WORKS IN THEIR ACTS OF INCORPORATION MENTIONED." [Forty lines.]

[Philadelphia: Printed by Zachariah Poulson, junior. April 20th, 1796.]
Broadside. fol.　　　　　　　　　　　　　　　　HSP.

31168　SCOTT, JOSEPH, JUNIOR
JOSEPH SCOTT, JUN. AT HIS SHOP, NO. 6, DOCK-SQUARE, BOSTON (NEAR THE MAR-
KET) IMPORTS FROM THE MANUFACTORIES . . . .

[Boston: 1796.] Broadside.　　　　　　　　　　　EI.

31169   SEAMAN, VALENTINE   1770–1817
AN ACCOUNT OF THE EPIDEMIC YELLOW FEVER, AS IT APPEARED IN THE CITY OF
NEW-YORK IN THE YEAR 1795. CONTAINING BESIDES ITS HISTORY, &C. THE MOST
PROBABLE MEANS OF PREVENTING ITS RETURN AND OF AVOIDING IT IN CASE IT
SHOULD AGAIN BECOME EPIDEMIC. BY VALENTINE SEAMAN, M. D. ONE OF THE
PHYSICIANS OF THE HEALTH COMMITTEE OF NEW-YORK IN 1795. [Eight lines of
verse.]

> *New-York: Printed by Hopkins, Webb & Co. No. 40, Pine-Street.* –1796.–
> pp. ix, 150. 8vo.   BPL. JCB. 8GO.

> 39th New York District Copyright, issued to Valentine Seaman, as
> Author, 23 April. 1796.

31170   SEARSON, JOHN   1750–
THE ART OF CONTENTMENT: WITH SEVERAL ENTERTAINING PIECES OF POETRY
DESCRIPTIVE OF THE PRESENT TIME IN THE U. STATES OF AMERICA. BY JOHN
SEARSON, FORMERLY A MERCHANT OF PHILADELPHIA.

> *Baltimore: Printed for the Author, by W. Pechin.* [1796.] pp, 226. 12mo.
>   BM.

> Dedicated to George Washington.

31171   SEDAINE, MICHEL JEAN   1719–1797
THE DESERTER: A COMIC OPERA. IN TWO ACTS. BY C. DIBDIN. AS PERFORMED
AT THE BOSTON THEATRE. SECOND BOSTON EDITION.

> *Boston: Printed for Lemuel Blake.* 1796. pp. 32. 12mo.   AAS.

31172   SELECT PAMPHLETS: VIZ. 1. LESSONS TO A YOUNG PRINCE, BY AN OLD STATESMAN,
ON THE PRESENT DISPOSITION IN EUROPE TO A GENERAL REVOLUTION. 2. APPEAL
FROM THE NEW TO THE OLD WHIGS, IN CONSEQUENCE OF SOME LATE DISCUSSIONS
IN PARLIAMENT. 3. ADDRESS TO THE HOUSE OF REPRESENTATIVES OF THE UNITED
STATES. 4. FEATURES OF MR. JAY'S TREATY. 5. SHORT ACCOUNT OF THE MALIG-
NANT FEVER, PREVALENT IN PHILADELPHIA, IN THE FALL OF 1793.—BY MATHEW
CAREY. 6. DR. NASSY'S ACCOUNT OF THE SAME FEVER. 7. OBSERVATIONS ON DR.
RUSH'S ENQUIRY INTO THE ORIGIN OF THE LATE EPIDEMIC FEVER—BY MATHEW
CAREY. 8. REVOLUTION OF AMERICA—BY THE ABBE RAYNAL.

> *Philadelphia: Published by Mathew Carey, No. 118 Market-Street.* 1796.
> *(Price two dollars.)* pp. (2), (4), (9)-68, 5 plates; (93), (2); [48]; 51; 103, (9);
> (26); (23); 72. 8vo.   AAS. LOC. NL.

> *Second title:* LESSONS TO A YOUNG PRINCE, BY AN OLD STATESMAN, ON THE PRES-
> ENT DISPOSITION IN EUROPE TO A GENERAL REVOLUTION. THE SIXTH EDITION.
> WITH THE ADDITION OF A LESSON ON THE MODE OF STUDYING AND PROFITING BY
> THE REFLECTIONS ON THE FRENCH REVOLUTION: BY THE RIGHT HONORABLE ED-
> MUND BURKE. EMBELLISHED BY FIVE COPPERPLATES, DELINEATING FIVE POLIT-
> ICAL CONSTITUTIONS IN A MODE ENTIRELY NEW. [Three lines of Latin from] CIC.
> DE DIV. LIB. ii. VER. 4. [By David Williams.]

> *London—Printed: New-York, Re-printed by Childs and Swaine. Sold by
> Berry and Rogers, No. 35, Hanover-Square.*—1791.— pp. (4), (9)-68, 5 plates.

> *Third title:* AN APPEAL FROM THE NEW TO THE OLD WHIGS, IN CONSEQUENCE OF
> SOME LATE DISCUSSIONS IN PARLIAMENT. RELATING TO THE REFLECTIONS ON THE
> FRENCH REVOLUTION. BY THE RIGHT HONOURABLE EDMUND BURKE.

> *London:—Printed. New-York: Re-printed by Childs and Swaine. Sold by
> Berry and Rogers, New-York; the principal booksellers in Philadelphia; Thomas
> and Andrews, Boston; and W. P. Young, Charleston, South Carolina.*—1791.—
> pp. (93), (2).

SELECT PAMPHLETS, continued.
Fourth title: ADDRESS TO THE HOUSE OF REPRESENTATIVES OF THE UNITED STATES, ON LORD GRENVILLE'S TREATY. [Two lines of quotations.] [By Mathew Carey.]
Philadelphia: Printed by Samuel Harrison Smith, for Mathew Carey. 1796. pp. [48.]

Fifth title: FEATURES OF MR. JAY'S TREATY. TO WHICH IS ANNEXED A VIEW OF THE COMMERCE OF THE UNITED STATES, AS IT STANDS AT PRESENT, AND AS IT IS FIXED BY MR. JAY'S TREATY. [By Alexander James Dallas.]
Philadelphia: Printed for Mathew Carey, by Lang & Ustick. 1795. pp. 51.

Sixth title: A SHORT ACCOUNT OF THE MALIGNANT FEVER, LATELY PREVALENT IN PHILADELPHIA: WITH A STATEMENT OF THE PROCEEDINGS THAT TOOK PLACE ON THE SUBJECT IN DIFFERENT PARTS OF THE UNITED STATES. BY MATHEW CAREY. SECOND EDITION.
Philadelphia: Printed by the Author, November 23, 1793. pp. (103), (9).

Seventh title: OBSERVATIONS ON THE CAUSE, NATURE, AND TREATMENT OF THE EPIDEMIC DISORDER, PREVALENT IN PHILADELPHIA. BY D. NASSY, M.D. MEMBER OF THE AMERICAN PHILOSOPHICAL SOCIETY, &c. [Translated from the French.]
Philadelphia: Printed by Parker & Co. for M. Carey. Nov. 26,—1793. pp. 26.

Eighth title: OBSERVATIONS ON DR. RUSH'S ENQUIRY INTO THE ORIGIN OF THE LATE EPIDEMIC FEVER IN PHILADELPHIA: BY MATHEW CAREY.
Philadelphia: From the Press of the Author. December 14, 1793. pp. 23.

Ninth title. THE REVOLUTION OF AMERICA. BY THE ABBE RAYNAL, AUTHOR OF THE PHILOSOPHICAL AND POLITICAL HISTORY OF THE ESTABLISHMENTS AND COMMERCE OF THE EUROPEANS IN BOTH THE INDIES. THE SECOND EDITION. PRICE ONE DOLLAR.
Philadelphia: Printed for Robert Bell, in Third Street. M,DCC,LXXXII. pp. 72.

31173 —— SELECT PAMPHLETS: VIZ. 1. POLITICAL PROGRESS OF BRITAIN—OR AN IMPARTIAL HISTORY OF THE ABUSES IN THE GOVERNMENT OF THE BRITISH EMPIRE, FROM THE REVOLUTION IN 1688, TO THE PRESENT TIME. 2. POLITICAL PROGRESS OF BRITAIN—PART II. 3. A BONE TO GNAW FOR THE DEMOCRATS—OR OBSERVATIONS ON A PAMPHLET, ENTITLED, THE POLITICAL PROGRESS OF BRITAIN. 4. GUILLOTINA. 5. DEMOCRATIAD. 6. TRIAL OF MAURICE MARGAROT, BEFORE THE HIGH COURT OF JUSTICIARY, AT EDINBURGH, FOR SEDITIOUS PRACTICES. 7. INDUSTRY, A POEM, BY COL. HUMPHREYS. 8. OBSERVATIONS ON A PAMPHLET, ENTILED [*sic*], "CONSIDERATIONS ON THE ORDER OF CINCINNATI."
Philadelphia: Published by Mathew Carey, No. 118, Market-Street. 1796. (*Price two dollars.*) pp. (2), (120); [96]; v, [66]; (14); (22); (166), portrait; [22], (2); 28, (4). 8vo. AAS.

Second title: THE POLITICAL PROGRESS OF BRITAIN; OR, AN IMPARTIAL HISTORY OF ABUSES IN THE GOVERNMENT OF THE BRITISH EMPIRE, IN EUROPE, ASIA, AND AMERICA. FROM THE REVOLUTION, IN 1688, TO THE PRESENT TIME: THE WHOLE TENDING TO PROVE THE RUINOUS CONSEQUENCES OF THE POPULAR SYSTEM OF TAXATION, WAR, AND CONQUEST. "THE WORLD'S MAD BUSINESS." PART FIRST. THIRD EDITION.
Philadelphia: Printed by and for Richard Folwell, No. 33, Mulberry-street. 1795. [*Price half a dollar.*] pp. (120).

SELECT PAMPHLETS, continued.

Third title: THE POLITICAL PROGRESS OF BRITAIN: OR, AN IMPARTIAL HISTORY OF ABUSES IN THE GOVERNMENT OF THE BRITISH EMPIRE, IN EUROPE, ASIA, AND AMERICA. FROM THE REVOLUTION, IN 1688, TO THE PRESENT TIME: THE WHOLE TENDING TO PROVE THE RUINOUS CONSEQUENCES OF THE POPULAR SYSTEM OF TAXATION, WAR, AND CONQUEST. NOW BARRABAS WAS A ROBBER. PART SECOND.

Philadelphia: Printed for Richard Folwell, No. 33, Mulberry-street. And sold in New-York by James Rivington. 1795. *[Price three shillings.]* pp. 96.

Fourth title: A BONE TO GNAW, FOR THE DEMOCRATS; OR, OBSERVATIONS ON A PAMPHLET, ENTITLED, "THE POLITICAL PROGRESS OF BRITAIN." [Two lines of French from] LA POMPADOUR.

Philadelphia: Printed by Thomas Bradford, No. 8, South Front Street. 1795. pp. v, [66.]

Fifth title: THE GUILLOTINA, OR A DEMOCRATIC DIRGE, A POEM. BY THE AUTHOR OF THE "DEMOCRATIAD." [Twelve lines of verse.]

Philadelphia: Sold at the Political Book-Store, South Front-Street, No. 8. [1796.] pp. (14).

Sixth title: THIRD EDITION. THE DEMOCRATIAD, A POEM, IN RETALIATION, FOR THE "PHILADELPHIA JOCKEY CLUB." [Two lines of verse.] BY A GENTLEMAN OF CONNECTICUT.

Philadelphia: Published by Thomas Bradford, Printer, Book-seller & Stationer, No. 8, South Front Street. 1796. pp. [22.]

Seventh title: THE TRIAL OF MAURICE MARGAROT, BEFORE THE HIGH COURT OF JUSTICIARY, AT EDINBURGH, ON THE 13TH AND 14TH OF JANUARY, 1794, ON AN INDICTMENT FOR SEDITIOUS PRACTICES. TAKEN IN SHORTHAND BY MR. RAMSEY.

London: Printed.—New-York: Re-printed, by James Carey, No. 91, Broad-street. [1794.] pp. (166), portrait.

Eighth title: A POEM ON INDUSTRY. ADDRESSED TO THE CITIZENS OF THE UNITED STATES OF AMERICA. BY COLONEL DAVID HUMPHREYS, MINISTER RESIDENT AT THE COURT OF LISBON.

Philadelphia: Printed for Mathew Carey, No. 118, Market-street. October 14, 1794. pp. [22], (2).

Ninth title: OBSERVATIONS ON A LATE PAMPHLET, ENTITLED, "CONSIDERATIONS UPON THE SOCIETY OR ORDER OF THE CINCINNATI," CLEARLY EVINCING THE INNOCENCE AND PROPRIETY OF THAT HONOURABLE AND RESPECTABLE INSTITUTION. IN ANSWER TO VAGUE CONJECTURES, FALSE INSINUATIONS, AND ILL-FOUNDED OBJECTIONS. BY AN OBSCURE INDIVIDUAL. [Six lines of quotations.]

Philadelphia: Printed and sold by Robert Bell, in Third-Street. Price one-fourth of a dollar. M,DCC,LXXXIII. pp. 28, (4).

31174 —— SELECT PAMPHLETS: VIZ. 1. RIGHTS OF MAN—PART THE FIRST—BEING AN ANSWER TO MR. BURKE'S ATTACK ON THE FRENCH REVOLUTION—BY THOMAS PAINE. 2. RIGHTS OF MAN — PART THE SECOND — COMBINING PRINCIPLE AND PRACTICE. 3. VINDICATION OF MR. RANDOLPH'S RESIGNATION. 4. NEW-YEAR'S GIFT FOR THE DEMOCRATS. 5. POLITICAL TRUTH. 6. CAUTIONARY HINTS TO CONGRESS, RESPECTING THE DISPOSAL OF THE WESTERN LANDS. 7. SHORT HISTORY OF THE NATURE AND CONSEQUENCES OF EXCISE LAWS—INCLUDING SOME ACCOUNT OF THE RECENT INTERRUPTION TO THE MANUFACTORIES OF SNUFF AND REFINED SUGARS. 8. PLATTE'S DISCOVERY OF SUBTERRANEAN TREASURES — CONTAINING USEFUL EXPLANATIONS CONCERNING ALL MANNER OF MINES AND MINERALS.

Philadelphia: Published by Mathew Carey, No. 118, Market-Street. 1796. *(Price two dollars.)* pp. (2), 76; 87, (1); [103]; [71]; 44; 13, (2); [116]; (24). 8vo.

AAS.

SELECT PAMPHLETS, continued.

Second title: RIGHTS OF MAN: PART THE FIRST. BEING AN ANSWER TO MR. BURKE'S ATTACK ON THE FRENCH REVOLUTION. BY THOMAS PAINE, SECRETARY FOR FOREIGN AFFAIRS TO CONGRESS IN THE AMERICAN WAR, AND AUTHOR OF THE WORK INTITLED COMMON SENSE.

> *London: Printed; New-York: Re-printed by Berry, Rogers, and Berry, No. 35, Hanover-square.* M.DCC.XIII. [sic 1792.] pp. 76.

Third title: RIGHTS OF MAN: PART THE SECOND. COMBINING PRINCIPLE AND PRACTICE. BY THOMAS PAINE, SECRETARY FOR FOREIGN AFFAIRS TO CONGRESS IN THE AMERICAN WAR, AND AUTHOR OF THE WORK INTITLED COMMON SENSE.

> *London: Printed: New-York: Reprinted by Berry, Rogers, and Berry, No. 35, Hanover-square.* M.DCC.XCIII. pp. 87,(1).

Fourth title: A VINDICATION OF MR. RANDOLPH'S RESIGNATION.

> *Philadelphia: Printed by Samuel H. Smith, No. 118, Chesnut street.* M,DCC,-XCV. pp. [103.]

Fifth title: SECOND EDITION. A NEW YEAR'S GIFT TO THE DEMOCRATS, OR, OBSERVATIONS ON A PAMPHLET, ENTITLED, "A VINDICATION OF MR. RANDOLPH'S RESIGNATION." BY PETER PORCUPINE. [Six lines of verse from] SWIFT.

> *Philadelphia: Published by Thomas Bradford, Printer, Book-seller & Stationer, No. 8, South Front-Street.* 1796. pp. (71).

Sixth title: POLITICAL TRUTH: OR ANIMADVERSIONS ON THE PAST AND PRESENT STATE OF PUBLIC AFFAIRS; WITH AN INQUIRY INTO THE TRUTH OF THE CHARGES PREFERRED AGAINST MR. RANDOLPH.

> *Philadelphia: Printed by Samuel Harrison Smith, No. 118, Chesnut-street.* M.DCC.XCVI. pp. 44.

Seventh title: CAUTIONARY HINTS TO CONGRESS RESPECTING THE SALE OF THE WESTERN LANDS, BELONGING TO THE UNITED STATES. SECOND EDITION.

> *Philadelphia: Printed for Mathew Carey, by Lang & Ustick, Feb 24, 1796.* pp. [13], (2).

Eighth title: A SHORT HISTORY OF THE NATURE AND CONSEQUENCES OF EXCISE LAWS; INCLUDING SOME ACCOUNT OF THE RECENT INTERRUPTION TO THE MANUFACTORIES OF SNUFF AND REFINED SUGAR. NEMO ME IMPUNE LACESSIT. THE HORROR OF ALL FREE STATES.

> *Philadelphia: Printed for the Booksellers. December 7, 1795.* pp. [116.]

Ninth title: A DISCOVERY OF SUBTERRANEAN TREASURE, VIZ. ALL MANNER OF MINES & MINERALS, FROM THE GOLD TO THE COAL, WITH PLAIN DIRECTIONS AND RULES FOR FINDING THEM IN ALL KINGDOMS AND COUNTRIES. ALSO THE ART OF MELTING, REFINING AND ASSAYING THEM MADE PLAIN AND EASY TO EVERY ORDINARY CAPACITY, SO THAT THEY MAY WITH SMALL CHARGE TRY THE VALUE OF SUCH ORES AS SHALL BE FOUND EITHER BY RULE OR ACCIDENT. TO WHICH IS ADDED, A REAL EXPERIMENT, TO TRY WHETHER A PIECE OF GOLD BE TRUE OR COUNTERFEIT, WITHOUT DEFACING OR ALTERING THE FORM THEREOF, WITH MORE CERTAINTY THAN ANY GOLDSMITH OR REFINER COULD FORMERLY DO. ALSO A SURE WAY TO TRY WHAT COLOUR ANY BERRY, LEAF, FLOWER, STALK, ROOT, FRUIT, SEED, BARK OR WOOD WILL GIVE: TOGETHER WITH DIRECTIONS FOR MAKING COLOURS THAT SHALL NOT STAIN NOR FADE. VERY NECESSARY FOR EVERY ONE TO KNOW, WHETHER HE BE A TRAVELLER BY LAND OR SEA, OR IN WHAT COUNTRY, DOMINION, OR PLANTATION SOEVER HE MAY INHABIT. BY MR. GABRIEL PLATTES.

> *Philadelphia: Printed* M,DCC,XCII. pp. (24).

31175 SELECT PLAYS: CONTAINING, 1. WILD OATS. BY MR. O'KEEFE. 2. LIONEL AND
CLARISSA. BY MR. BICKERSTAFF. 3. LOVE IN A VILLAGE. BY THE SAME. 4. THE
SUSPICIOUS HUSBAND. BY DR. HOADLEY. [Ornament.]
> *Philadelphia: Published by Mathew Carey*, M,DCC,XCVI. pp. (2), [72];
> 72; 58, (2): (2), (2), 68, 12mo. AAS.

Second title: WILD OATS: OR, THE STROLLING GENTLEMAN. A COMEDY IN FIVE
ACTS, AS PERFORMED AT THE THEATRE-ROYAL, COVENT GARDEN. BY JOHN
O'KEEFE, ESQ.
> *Dublin: Printed for the Booksellers.* M.DCC.LXCIII [sic 1793.] pp. [72.]

Third title: LIONEL AND CLARISSA: OR, THE SCHOOL FOR FATHERS. A COMIC
OPERA: WRITTEN BY MR. BICKERSTAFF. MARKED WITH THE VARIATIONS ON THE
MANAGER'S BOOK, AT THE THEATRE ROYAL, IN DRURY-LANE.
> *Philadelphia: Printed by W. W. Woodward, for Mathew Carey, No.* 118,
> *Market-street.* 1794. pp. 72.

Fourth title: LOVE IN A VILLAGE. A COMIC OPERA. WRITTEN BY MR. BICKER-
STAFF. AS PERFORMED AT THE NEW THEATRE, IN PHILADELPHIA. [Ornament.]
> *From the Press of M. Carey, March* 1, M,DCC,XCIV. pp. 58, (2).

Fifth title: THE SUSPICIOUS HUSBAND, A COMEDY. BY THE RIGHT REVEREND
DR. BENJAMIN HOADLEY. [Vignette.]
> *Philadelphia: Printed by William Spotswood.* MDCCXCI. pp. (2), (2), 68.

31176 SEVEN WISE MISTRESSES.
ROMAN STORIES: OR, THE HISTORY OF THE SEVEN WISE MISTRESSES OF ROME.
CONTAINING, SEVEN DAYS ENTERTAINMENT, IN MANY PLEASANT AND WITTY TALES
OR STORIES. WHEREIN THE TREACHERY OF EVIL COUNSELLORS IS DISCOVERED;
INNOCENCY CLEARED; AND THE WISDOM OF SEVEN WISE MISTRESSES DISPLAYED.
> *Concord: Printed by Russell and Davis.* 1796.

31177 SEWALL, DANIEL   1755–1842
AN ASTRONOMICAL DIARY, OR ALMANAC, FOR THE YEAR OF CHRISTIAN ÆRA, 1797:
BEING FIRST AFTER BISSEXTILE OR LEAP YEAR. CALCULATED FOR THE MERIDIAN
OF PORTSMOUTH, NEW-HAMPSHIRE, LAT. 43 DEG. 5 MIN. NORTH. AND DESIGNED
CHIEFLY FOR THE STATE OF NEW-HAMPSHIRE, AND DISTRICT OF MAINE. CON-
TAINING EVERY THING NECESSARY FOR AN ALMANAC, WITH A VARIETY OF ENTER-
TAINING AND USEFUL MATTERS. BY DANIEL SEWALL. [Eleven lines of verse.]
> *Portsmouth, New-Hampshire: Printed by Charles Peirce, in Court-street,
> sold by him wholesale and retail; also, by the Author, at his Office in York, and by
> most of the Shop-keepers in town and country.* [1796.] pp. (24). 12mo.
> AAS. LOC. NHHS.

31178 SEWALL, STEPHEN   1734–1804
THE SCRIPTURE HISTORY, RELATING TO THE OVERTHROW OF SODOM AND GOMORRAH,
AND TO THE ORIGIN OF THE SALT SEA, OR LAKE OF SODOM. BY STEPHEN SEWALL,
A. M. AND A. A. S. LATE PROFESSOR IN THE UNIVERSITY OF CAMBRIDGE.
> *Boston: Printed for William P. & Lemuel Blake, at the Boston Bookstore
> No.* 1, *Cornhill.* 1796. pp. 30. 8vo. AAS. BA. HC. JCB.

31179 SHAFTSBURY. VERMONT. BAPTIST ASSOCIATION.
MINUTES OF THE SHAFTSBURY ASSOCIATION, AT THEIR ANNUAL CONVENTION, HELD
IN WEST STOCKBRIDGE, 1796.
> [*Without Place or Printer.* 1796.]

31180   SHAKESPEARE, William   1564–1616
THE PLAYS AND POEMS OF WILLIAM SHAKESPEARE. CORRECTED FROM THE LAT-
EST AND BEST LONDON EDITIONS, WITH NOTES, BY SAMUEL JOHNSON, L. L. D. TO
WHICH ARE ADDED, A GLOSSARY AND THE LIFE OF THE AUTHOR. EMBELLISHED
WITH A STRIKING LIKENESS FROM THE COLLECTION OF HIS GRACE THE DUKE OF
CHANDOS. FIRST AMERICAN EDITION. VOL. IV. [— VIII.]

     Philadelphia : Printed and sold by Bioren & Madan. MDCCXCVI. 5 vols.
pp. 447: 392; 388; 452; 304; 128. 12mo.   AAS. BPL. LOC. NYPL.

31181   SHAW, Robert
THE GENTLEMAN'S AMUSEMENT, OR COMPANION FOR THE GERMAN FLUTE. ARRANGED
AND ADAPTED BY R. SHAW. No. 6 [— 7.]

     Philadelphia : Printed at Carr & Co's Musical Repository. [1796.] pp. 44–76.
4to.   LOC.

31182   —— — THE GENTLEMAN'S AMUSEMENT. A SELECTION OF SOLOS, DUETTS, OVER-
TURES, ARRANGED AS DUETTS, RONDOS & ROMANCES FROM THE WORKS OF PLEYEL,
HAYDN, MOZART, HOFFMEISTER, FISCHER, SHIELD, DR. ARNOLD, SALIMENT, ETC.
SEVERAL AIRS, DANCES, MARCHES, MINUETTS & SCOTCH REELS. SIXTY FOUR SELECT
SONGS FROM THE FAVORITE OPERAS & DIBDINS LATEST PUBLICATIONS WITH SOME
GENERAL REMARKS FOR PLAYING THE FLUTE WITH TASTE AND EXPRESSION AND A
DICTIONARY OF MUSICAL TERMS. THE WHOLE SELECTED, ARRANGED & ADAPTED
FOR ONE, TWO, & THREE GERMAN FLUTES OR VIOLINS BY R. SHAW OF THE THEATRE
CHARLESTOWN & B. CARR. FORMING THE CHEAPEST, AND MOST COMPLETE COLLEC-
TION EVER OFFERED TO THE PUBLIC; THE CONTENTS BEING SELECTED FROM THE
BEST AUTHORS, AND WHAT, PURCHASED IN ANY OTHER MANNER WOULD AMOUNT TO
MORE THAN THREE TIMES THE PRICE. PRICE BOUND SIX DOLLARS. UNBOUND FIVE
DOLLARS OR IN 12 SINGLE NUMBERS AT 50 CENTS EACH.

     *[Philadelphia :] Printed for the Editors and sold at B. Carr's Musical Re-
positories Philadelphia and New-York and J. Carr's Baltimore.* [1796.] pp. 77.
4to.   LOC.

31183   SHE LEFT ME AH! FOR GOLD—A FAVORITE SONG. [Two eight-line verses, with music.]

     *New-York : Printed for G. Gilfert & Co. at their Musical Magazine, No.
177 Broadway.* [1796.] pp. (2). fol.   JCB.

31184   SHERIDAN, Thomas   1719–1788
A COMPLETE DICTIONARY OF THE ENGLISH LANGUAGE, BOTH WITH REGARD TO
SOUND AND MEANING: ONE MAIN OBJECT OF WHICH IS, TO ESTABLISH A PLAIN AND
PERMANENT STANDARD OF PRONUNCIATION. TO WHICH IS PREFIXED, A PROSODIAL
GRAMMAR. BY THOMAS SHERIDAN, A. M. [Five lines of Latin from] QUINCT.
L. I. C. 4. THE SIXTH EDITION, CAREFULLY REVISED AND CORRECTED BY THE REV.
JOHN ANDREWS, D. D. RECTOR OF ST. JAMES, BRISTOL, AND PROFESSOR OF RHET-
ORICK AND BELLES LETTRES IN THE COLLEGE AND ACADEMY OF PHILADELPHIA.

     *Philadelphia : Printed for W. Young, Mills and Son, Booksellers and Sta-
tioners, No. 52 Second-Street corner of Chesnut-Street.* M.DCC.XCVI. Unpaged.
8vo.   BA.

     This edition is printed one column to the page.

31185   SHERIDAN, Thomas, continued.
—— — A Complete Dictionary of the English language, both with regard to sound and meaning: one main object of which is, to establish a plain and permanent standard of pronunciation. To which is prefixed, a Prosodial grammar. By Thomas Sheridan, a.m. [Five lines of Latin from] Quinct. L. i. c. 4. The sixth edition.

> *Philadelphia: Printed for W. Young, Mills & Son, Booksellers and Stationers, No. 52, Second-Street, corner of Chesnut-Street.* M,DCC,XCVI. Unpaged; pp. (2), 8, (2), 60. 8vo.
>   AAS. NYPL.

> This edition is printed two columns to the page. Philadelphia, October 6, 1796. ☞The Editors of this impression have been guided by the first and last editions published under the Author's inspection: and by the corrections and abridgements of the Rev. Dr. John Andrews, of the University of Pennsylvania.

31186   —— A Course of lectures on elocution. A new edition. By Thomas Sheridan, a.m.

> *Printed at Providence (Rhode-Island) by Carter & Wilkinson, and sold at the Providence Book-Store, opposite the Market.* M.DCC.XCVI. pp. 256. 12mo.
>   AAS. JCB. LOC. RIHS.

31187   SHIPPEN, John
The Story of Palemon and Eliza. Founded on fact. By a Student of Dickinson College. [Seven lines of verse.]

> *Harrisburgh: Printed by John Wyeth, May* 30, 1796. pp. 13, (1). 16mo. AAS.

31188   SHIPPING Articles.
Articles of agreement between the master and mariners of the —— whereof —— is master, now bound from the port of —— [Eight lines, with ruled table for names, wages, etc. With] An Act for the government and regulation of seamen in the merchant's service. [Colophon:]

> *Philadelphia: Printed by Samuel Harrison Smith, Cherry-Alley, between Fourth and Fifth Streets.* [1796.] pp. (2). fol.   JCB.

31189   SHOEMAKER, Abraham
Poulson's Town and country Almanac, for the year of our Lord, 1797; . . . [Cut.]

> *Philadelphia: Printed and sold by Zachariah Poulson, junior, No. 80, Chesnut-Street, eight doors below Third-Street.* [1796.] pp. (48). 12mo. AAS. LOC.

31190   SHRUBSOLE, William   1729–1797
Christian memoirs, or a review of the present state of religion in England, in the form of a new pilgrimage to the Heavenly Jerusalem; containing, by way of allegorical narrative, a great variety of dialogues on the most interesting subjects, and adventures of religious persons. By W. Shrubsole.

> *Philadelphia: Printed by Isaac Neale and Heinrich Kammerer, jun. No. 24, North Third Street.* 1796. pp. 400. 8vo.

31191   SIBBES, Richard   1577–1635
Divine meditations and holy contemplations.

> *Philadelphia: Printed by Stephen C. Ustick, No.79, North Third-Street.* 1796.

AUCTION
VALUES

31192   SIBLEY, SOLOMON   1769–1846
AN ORATION, DELIVERED AT MENDON, JULY 4, 1796, AT THE CELEBRATION OF THE
TWENTIETH ANNIVERSARY OF AMERICAN INDEPENDENCE. BY SOLOMON SIBLEY,
A. B. STUDENT AT LAW. [Ornament.]
> *Printed by Samuel Hall, No. 53, Cornhill, Boston.* 1796. pp. 16. 8vo.
>   BA. BM. JCB.

31193   SIMMONS, AMELIA
AMERICAN COOKERY, OR THE ART OF DRESSING VIANDS, FISH, POULTRY AND VEGE-
TABLES, AND THE BEST MODES OF MAKING PASTES, PUFFS, PIES, TARTS, PUDDINGS,
CUSTARDS AND PRESERVES, AND ALL KINDS OF CAKES, FROM THE IMPERIAL PLUMB
TO PLAIN CAKE. ADAPTED TO THIS COUNTRY, AND ALL GRADES OF LIFE. BY AMELIA
SIMMONS, AN AMERICAN ORPHAN. PUBLISHED ACCORDING TO ACT OF CONGRESS.
> *Hartford: Printed by Hudson & Goodwin, for the Author.* 1796. pp. 46, (1).
> 8vo.   CHS. NYPL.

Connecticut District Copyright, issued to Amelia Simmons, as Author,
28 April, 1796. And the thirteenth work deposited in the Office of the
Secretary of State, under the Copyright Law, 26 May, 1796.

31194   SIMS, JAMES   1741–1820
OBSERVATIONS ON THE SCARLATINA ANGINOSA, COMMONLY CALLED *The* ULCERATED
SORE THROAT. BY JAMES SIMS, M. D. PRESIDENT OF THE MEDICAL SOCIETY IN
LONDON. WITH SOME REMARKS BY THOMAS BULFINCH, M. D, [Vignette.]
> *Printed and sold by Samuel Hall, No. 53, Cornhill, Boston.* 1796. pp. [16.]
> 8vo.   AAS. BA. BM. NYPL. SGO.

A second edition was printed in Boston in 1803.

31195   SKINNER, ICHABOD LORD   1767–1852
A DISCOURSE ON MUSIC; DELIVERED FEBRUARY 1796, AT A SINGING LECTURE, IN
NORTH BOLTON.
> *Hartford: Printed by Hudson & Goodwin.* 1796. pp. 18. 8vo.   CHS. WL. YC.

31196   SMITH, ADAM   1723–1790
AN INQUIRY INTO THE NATURE AND CAUSES OF THE WEALTH OF NATIONS. BY ADAM
SMITH, LL. D. AND F. R. S. OF LONDON AND EDINBURGH: ONE OF THE COMMISSION-
ERS OF HIS MAJESTY'S CUSTOMS IN SCOTLAND; AND FORMERLY PROFESSOR OF MORAL
PHILOSOPHY IN THE UNIVERSITY OF GLASGOW. IN THREE VOLUMES. VOL. I [—
III.] A NEW EDITION.
> *Philadelphia: Printed by Thomas Dobson, at the Stone House, No. 41, S.
> Second Street.* 1796. 3 vols. pp. 412; 430; 387, (53). 12mo.   AAS. BPL. NYPL.

31197   SMITH, CHARLES   1768–1808
THE GENTLEMAN'S POLITICAL POCKET ALMANAC, FOR THE YEAR 1797. BY CHARLES
SMITH. COPY-RIGHT SECURED.
> *New-York: Printed by J. Buel, for C. Smith, No. 51, Maiden-Lane.* [1796.]
> pp. (59), (1). 2 portraits. 24mo.   AAS. JCB. NYHS. NYPL.

The portraits are of Thomas Jefferson, and James Madison.

31198   SMITH, CHARLOTTE TURNER   1749–1806
D'ARCY. A NOVEL. BY CHARLOTTE SMITH.
> *Philadelphia: Printed by James Carey, No. 83, North Second-Street.*
> 1796. 12mo.

31199 SMITH, DANIEL   1740–1818
A SHORT DESCRIPTION OF THE STATE OF TENNASSE, LATELY CALLED THE TERRI-
TORY OF THE UNITED STATES, SOUTH OF THE RIVER OHIO; TO ACCOMPANY AND
EXPLAIN A MAP OF THAT COUNTRY.
  *Philadelphia: Printed for Mathew Carey. No. 118, Market-Street By Lang
and Ustick, March 9.* 1796. pp. 36. 12mo.   MHS.

31200 —— — A SHORT DESCRIPTION OF THE STATE OF TENNESSEE, LATELY CALLED THE
TERRITORY OF THE UNITED STATES, SOUTH OF THE RIVER OHIO. TO WHICH IS
PREFIXED, THE CONSTITUTION OF THAT STATE.
  *Philadelphia: Printed for Mathew Carey, No. 118, Market-Street, by Lang
and Ustick, Sept. 20.* 1796. pp. 44. 12mo. BA. LOC. NYHS.

31201 SMITH, ELIAS   1769–1846
AN ESSAY ON THE FALL OF ANGELS AND MEN; WITH REMARKS ON DR. EDWARDS'S
NOTION OF FREEDOM OF THE WILL: ALSO A BLOW AT THE ROOT OF UNIVERALIAN-
ISM.
  Boston: Re-printed by Benjamin Edes, in Kilby-Street, 1796. pp. 53, (1).
8vo.   NYHS.

31202 —— — AN ESSAY ON THE FALL OF ANGELS AND MEN; WITH REMARKS ON DR. ED-
WARDS'S NOTION OF THE FREEDOM OF THE WILL, AND THE SYSTEM OF UNIVERSAL-
ITY. [Signed E. S.]
  *Wilmington (Delaware) Printed Middletown (Connecticut) Reprinted by
Moses H. Woodward,* 1796. pp. (50). 8vo.   AAS. BA.

31203 SMITH, EUNICE
PRACTICAL LANGUAGE INTERPRETED: IN A DIALOGUE BETWEEN A BELIEVER AND
AN UNBELIEVER. IN TWO PARTS. REPRESENTING A BELIEVER UNDER THE IN-
FLUENCE OF GRACE, SPEAKING CANAAN'S LANGUAGE. PART I. REPRESENTS AN
UNBELIEVER UNDER THE INFLUENCE OF A CARNAL MIND, REFUSING TO ACCEPT OF
THE INVITATIONS OF THE GOSPEL; WHOSE PRACTICE OFTEN SPEAKS PLAINER AND
LOUDER THAN WORDS, SAYING OF CHRIST THE KING, WE WILL NOT HAVE THIS
MAN TO REIGN OVER US. PART II. SHEWS SOME OF THE LANGUAGE OF A SOUL
UNDER CONVICTION; AND HOW THE UNBELIEVER BECOMES A BELIEVER.
  Dover: Printed by Samuel Bragg, jr. 1796. pp. 23. 12mo.

31204 SMITH, HUGH   1730–1790
LETTERS TO MARRIED WOMEN, ON NURSING AND THE MANAGEMENT OF CHILDREN.
BY THE LATE HUGH SMITH, M. D. SECOND AMERICAN EDITION.
  Philadelphia: Printed for Mathew Carey, by Lang and Ustick. M.DCC.-
XCVI. pp. 153. 12mo.   AAS. 3GO.

31205 SMITH, JOHN BLAIR   1756–1799
ORATIO INAUGURALIS, DE INSTITUTIONE JUVENTUTIS, HABITA APUD SCHENECTADIAM,
IN BELGARUM TEMPLO, KALENDIS MAIAE, ANNO MDCCXCVI. A JOANNE BLAIR
SMITH, D. D. PRAES: COLL: CONCORDIAE.
  Schenectadiæ: Apud Cornelium P, Wyckoff. 1796. pp. 16. 8vo.

31206 SMITH, JOSHUA   –1795
DIVINE HYMNS, OR SPIRITUAL SONGS, FOR THE USE OF RELIGIOUS ASSEMBLIES, AND
PRIVATE CHRISTIANS: BEING A COLLECTION BY JOSHUA SMITH, AND OTHERS. THE
SIXTH EDITION, REVISED BY SEVERAL GENTLEMEN WITH SOME ALTERATIONS BY
ONE OF THE ELDERS OF THE BAPTIST CHURCH.
  Poughkeepsie: Printed and sold by Nathan Douglas. 1796.
  "The very rapid sale of Smith's Hymns has induced the Editor to pub-
  lish this his third edition." This edition was also advertised, as above,
  in Danbury, Connecticut by Douglas and Nichols, in October, 1796,
  upon the removal of Nathan Douglas to that place.

31207   SMITH, PRESERVED   1759–1834
A DISCOURSE, DELIVERED IN CHESTER ON TUESDAY THE 15TH OF MARCH, 1796, BE-
FORE AN ASSEMBLY OF ANTIENT, FREE, AND ACCEPTED MASONS, CONVENED FOR
THE PURPOSE OF INSTALLING A LODGE IN THAT TOWN. BY PRESERVED SMITH,
A. M. PUBLISHED AT THE REQUEST OF THE BRETHREN.
Printed at West-Springfield by Edward Gray. M,DCC,XCVI. pp. [22.] 12mo.
AAS.

31208   SMITH, SAMUEL HARRISON   1772–1845
(CIRCULAR.) PHILADELPHIA, FEBRUARY 20, 1796. SIR, IN COMPLIANCE WITH THE
RECOMMENDATION OF A NUMBER OF GENTLEMEN, I HAVE DETERMINED TO SUBMIT
TO PUBLIC PATRONAGE THE PUBLICATION OF A NEWSPAPER, THE PLAN OF WHICH
IS ANNEXED. [Fourteen lines.] SAMUEL H. SMITH. PROPOSALS BY SAMUEL H.
SMITH, No. 118, CHESNUT STREET, FOR PRINTING BY SUBSCRIPTION, A NEWSPAPER,
TO APPEAR TWICE A DAY, CALLED THE NEW WORLD, OR THE MORNING AND EVEN-
ING GAZETTE. . . .
[Philadelphia: Printed by Samuel Harrison Smith, 1796.] pp. (3). 4to.
HSP.

31209   SMITH, WILLIAM LOUGHTON   1758–1812
A COMPARATIVE VIEW OF THE CONSTITUTIONS OF THE SEVERAL STATES WITH EACH
OTHER, AND WITH THAT OF THE UNITED STATES: EXHIBITING IN TABLES THE
PROMINENT FEATURES OF EACH CONSTITUTION, AND CLASSING TOGETHER THEIR
MOST IMPORTANT PROVISIONS UNDER THE SEVERAL HEADS OF ADMINISTRATION;
WITH NOTES AND OBSERVATIONS. BY WILLIAM SMITH, OF SOUTH CAROLINA, L. L. D.
AND MEMBER OF THE CONGRESS OF THE UNITED STATES. DEDICATED TO THE
PEOPLE OF THE UNITED STATES.
*Philadelphia: Printed by John Thompson, and sold by all the Booksellers in
the United States.* 1796. pp. (2), (2), (2), [4], 6 folded tables, [9]–[34]. 4to.
AAS. BA. BM. BPL. HC. .JCB. LOC. MHS. NYHS. NYPL. SCHS.

170th Pennsylvania District Copyright, issued to John Thompson, as
Proprietor, 24 January, 1797. Published in two states. Priced; fine
paper, hot-pressed, 1.25, and common paper, 1.00. Some slight variations in tables v. and vi. — numbered and not numbered — and in the
quality of paper used, differentiate copies seen. Used as a text-book
in the College of New Jersey.

31210   —— AN ORATION, DELIVERED IN ST. PHILIP'S CHURCH, BEFORE THE INHABITANTS
OF CHARLESTON, SOUTH-CAROLINA, ON THE FOURTH OF JULY, 1796, IN COMMEM-
ORATION OF AMERICAN INDEPENDENCE. BY APPOINTMENT OF THE AMERICAN
REVOLUTION SOCIETY, AND PUBLISHED AT THE REQUEST OF THAT SOCIETY, AND
ALSO OF THE SOUTH-CAROLINA STATE SOCIETY OF CINCINNATI. BY WILLIAM
SMITH, A MEMBER OF THE REVOLUTION SOCIETY, AND REPRESENTATIVE IN THE
CONGRESS OF THE UNITED STATES.
Printed by W. P. Young, No. 43, Broad-Street, Charleston. [1796.] pp. (2).
(2), 40. 8vo.   AAS. BA. BPL. HC. LOC. MHS. NYPL.
(Entered according to Law.)

31211   —— — AN ORATION, DELIVERED IN ST. PHILIP'S CHURCH, BEFORE THE INHABI-
TANTS OF CHARLESTON, SOUTH-CAROLINA, ON THE FOURTH OF JULY, 1796, IN
COMMEMORATION OF AMERICAN INDEPENDENCE. BY APPOINTMENT OF THE
AMERICAN REVOLUTION SOCIETY, AND PUBLISHED BY REQUEST OF THAT SOCIETY,
AND ALSO OF THE SOUTH-CAROLINA STATE SOCIETY OF CINCINNATI. BY WILLIAM
SMITH, A MEMBER OF THE REVOLUTION SOCIETY, AND REPRESENTATIVE IN THE
CONGRESS OF THE UNITED STATES. SECOND EDITION.
Printed by W. P. Young, No. 43, Broad-Street, Charleston. [1796.] pp. (2).
(2), 40. 8vo.   BA. BPL. HC. JCB. MHS.

SMITH, WILLIAM LOUGHTON, continued.

31212 —— THE PRETENSIONS OF THOMAS JEFFERSON TO THE PRESIDENCY EXAMINED; AND THE CHARGES AGAINST JOHN ADAMS REFUTED. ADDRESSED TO THE CITIZENS OF AMERICA IN GENERAL; AND PARTICULARLY TO THE ELECTORS OF THE PRESIDENT. [First part.]

[Philadelphia: Printed by John Fenno.] United States, October, 1796. pp. (64). 8vo.   AAS. BA. CLS. HC. HSP. JCB. LOC. MHS. NYHS. NYPL. YC.

31213 —— —— *Half-title:* THE PRETENSIONS OF JEFFERSON AND THE CHARGES AGAINST ADAMS EXAMINED. PART THE SECOND.

Title: THE PRETENSIONS OF THOMAS JEFFERSON TO THE PRESIDENCY EXAMINED; AND THE CHARGES AGAINST JOHN ADAMS REFUTED. ADDRESSED TO THE CITIZENS OF AMERICA IN GENERAL, AND PARTICULARLY TO THE ELECTORS OF THE PRESIDENT. PART THE SECOND.

[Philadelphia: Printed by John Fenno.] United States, November, 1796. pp. (2), (42). 8vo.   AAS. BA. CLS. JCB. LOC. NYHS. NYPL.

These essays were first published in the "Gazette of the United States" from October 14 — November 24, 1796, under the signature of Phocion. In their preparation, Mr. Smith is said to have been assisted by Oliver Wolcott. Pages 39-42 contain an "Appendix: Vindication of Mr. Adams's Defence of the American Constitutions." Signed, Union. Eastern Shore, Maryland. 26th Oct. 1796. Which was written by William Vans Murray.

31214 SMOLLETT. TOBIAS GEORGE   1721–1771
THE HISTORY OF ENGLAND, FROM THE REVOLUTION TO THE END OF THE AMERICAN WAR, AND PEACE OF VERSAILLES IN 1783. IN SIX VOLUMES. DESIGNED AS A CONTINUATION OF MR. HUME'S HISTORY. BY T. SMOLLETT, M. D. AND OTHERS. VOL. I. [— II.] A NEW EDITION, WITH CORRECTIONS AND IMPROVEMENTS.

Philadelphia: Printed for Robert Campbell & Co. by Henry Sweitzer. M.DCC.XCVI. 2 vols. pp. 576, portrait of Smollett; 568, portrait of George I. 8vo.   AAS. LCP. NYPL.

31215 SMYTH, ALEXANDER   1765–1830
THE THIRD AND LAST LETTER FROM ALEXANDER SMYTH TO FRANCIS PRESTON. 1796.

[Richmond: Printed by Samuel Pleasants, jun. 1796.] pp. [46]. 16mo. NYPL.

Dated, Wythe County, 20th November, 1796.

31216 SNOWDEN, RICHARD
THE AMERICAN REVOLUTION: WRITTEN IN SCRIPTURAL, OR, ANCIENT HISTORICAL STYLE. "HONI SOIT QUI MAL Y'PENSE." BY RICHARD SNOWDEN.

Baltimore: Printed by W. Pechin, No. 10, *Second-street.* [1796.] pp. 360. 12mo.   AAS. BA. BM. JCB. LCP. LOC. NL.

31217 —— THE COLUMBIAD; OR A POEM ON THE AMERICAN WAR, IN THIRTEEN CANTOES. BY RICHARD SNOWDEN.

Baltimore: Printed by W. Pechin, No. 10, *Second-street.* pp. 44. 12mo.
AAS. BA. BM. JCB. LCP. LOC. NL.

The Preface is signed, A New-Jersey Farmer.

31218 SOBERSIDES, SOLOMON, pseudonym.
A PRETTY NEW YEAR'S GIFT; OR, ENTERTAINING HISTORIES, FOR THE AMUSEMENT AND INSTRUCTION OF YOUNG LADIES AND GENTLEMEN, IN WINTER EVENINGS. THE SECOND WORCESTER EDITION.

Worcester, (Massachusetts). Printed by Thomas, Son & Thomas. 1796. pp. 135, (1). 32mo.   AAS.

31219　SOUTH CAROLINA. State.
Acts and Resolutions of the General Assembly of South Carolina. Passed
in Nov. and Dec, 1795. [Arms.]
Charleston: Printed by W. P. Young and D. Faust, State Printers. Feb.
1796. pp. 59, (2); 88, (2). fol. LOC. MHS.

31220　SOUTH CAROLINA. State. Courts.
The Rules and orders of the Courts of Sessions and Common Pleas, of the
Court of Equity, and the Federal Court, in South-Carolina.
New-York: Printed by T. and J. Swords, No. 99 Pearl-street. —1796.—
pp. 48. 8vo. BA. NYHS.

31221　THE SOUTH-CAROLINA and Georgia Almanac, for the year of our Lord,
1797: being the first after leap year, and (till the 4th of July) the
twenty-first of American independence. [Nine lines.]
Charleston: Printed by J. M'Iver . . . [1796.] pp, (36). 12mo. SCHS.

31222　THE SOUTH-CAROLINA State Gazette and General Advertiser. Friday,
January 1, [— Friday, December 30, 1796.]
Columbia, South-Carolina: Published by Young & Faust. 1796. fol.

31223　THE SOUTH-CAROLINA State Gazette and Timothy's & Mason's [cuts] Daily
Advertiser. [Motto.] Vol. lvii. No. 4951. Friday, January 1, [— No. 5252.
Saturday, December 31, 1796.]
Charleston: Published by Timothy & Mason. 1796. fol.

Without imprint, and numbering irregular. The heading is elaborate,
with a figure of Liberty on the left. Continental soldier on the right,
Fame, with trumpet, over. With two oval cuts. On the left, the State
seal: Palmetto tree. South Carolina. Animis opibusque parati. On
the right, a female figure, and Dum spiro spero spes. And the two fold
motto.

31224　SOUTHERN Centinel, and Gazette of the State. Vol. iii. Numb. cxxxv.
Thursday, January 7, [— Vol. iv. Numb. 186. Thursday, December 29, 1796.]
Augusta: Printed by Alexander M'Millan, Printer to the State. 1796. fol.

31225　SPALDING or Spaulding, Joshua　　　　　　　　　　1760–1825
Sentiments, concerning the coming and kingdom of Christ; collected from
the Bible, and from the writings of many antient, and some modern, believers: in nine lectures; with an appendix. By Joshua Spalding, minister of the Gospel, at the Tabernacle in Salem. [Two lines from] Jesus
Christ.
Salem: Printed by Thomas C. Cushing, MDCCXCVI. [Published according
to Act of Congress.] pp. (2),(2),(2),(2), 273. 12mo. AAS. BM. EI. NYHS. NYPL.

95th Massachusetts District Copyright, issued to Joshua Spalding, as
Author, 16 February, 1796. And the tenth work deposited in the Office
of the Secretary of State, under the Copyright law, 14 April, 1796.

31226　SPOONER'S Vermont Journal. Vol. xiii. Number 649. Monday, January 4, [—
Vol. xiv. Number 701. Friday, December 30, 1796.]
Vermont:—Printed and published by Alden Spooner, on the west side of the
Main Street, in Windsor. 1796. fol. AAS. NYPL.

The imprint was shortened in June by omitting "Vermont," and "in
Windsor."

31227   SPRINGFIELD. Massachusetts. Library Company.
     Catalogue of books in the Springfield Library Company. [320 titles.]
       Springfield: Printed by Francis Stebbins. 1796.

31228   STANFORD, John   1754–1834
     The Christian's pocket library. Edited by John Stanford, a. m. Vol. i.
     No. 1. [— 6.]
       New-York: 1796. portrait. 16mo.   BM.

       Engraved title-page, and portrait, woodcuts. A second volume was
       published in New York, in 1800.

31229   STANHOPE, Philip Dormer, 4th earl of Chesterfield   1694–1773
     Principles of politeness, and of knowing the world: by the late Lord
     Chesterfield. With additions, by the rev. dr. John Trusler. Contain-
     ing every instruction necessary to complete the gentleman and man of
     fashion, to teach him a knowledge of life, and make him well received
     in all companies. For the improvement of youth: yet not beneath the
     attention of any.
       *Greenfield, (Massachusetts:) Printed by Thomas Dickman, and sold at his
     Bookstore in Greenfield.* MDCCXCVI. pp. 178. 24mo.   AAS. JCB. LOC.

31230   THE STATE Gazette & New-Jersey Advertiser. Independence, 21st year.
     Federal government, 8th year. No. 45 of Vol. iv. Whole no. 201. Tues-
     day July 12, [— No. 17 of Vol. v. Whole no. 225. Tuesday, December 27,
     1796.]
       Printed by Matthias Day, Trenton. 1796. fol.   AAS.

       In continuation of the *New-Jersey State Gazette.*

31231   STATE [R. I. Arms] Gazette, and town and country advertiser. Vol. i, No. 1.
     Monday, January 4, [— No. 52, Saturday, (evening) July 2, 1796.]
       *Providence (Rhode-Island) Published on Mondays and Thursdays, by Joseph
     Fry, directly opposite the Market.* . . . 1796. 4to.   AAS. NYPL. RIHS.

       In May the days of publication were changed to Wednesdays and Sat-
       urdays. Established, as a semi-weekly, by Joseph Fry, and continued
       by him to the end of the first volume, in July, when it was probably
       discontinued.

31232   STATE Gazette of North-Carolina. Vol. xi. Numb. 521. Thursday, January
     7, [— Numb. 564. Thursday, December 28, 1796.]
       Edenton: Printed by Henry Wills, joint printer to the State with A. Hodge.
     1796. fol.   AAS.

31233   STAUNTON Gazette. Vol. i. No. 46. Wednesday, December 7, [—No. 49.
     Wednesday, December 28, 1796.]
       Staunton: Printed by Wise and Adams.

       In continuation of *The Virginia Gazette.*

31234   STEBBINS, Josiah   1766–1829
     An Address to the senior class in Yale-College: delivered in the chapel,
     as a response to the valedictory oration, which closed the public per-
     formances exhibited by the class after their examination, July 20, 1796.
     By Josiah Stebbins, esquire, a tutor of the college. Printed at the
     desire of the students. [Two lines of verse.]
       New-Haven: Printed by T. & S. Green. [1796.] pp. 23. 8vo.
                                     AAS. JCB. MHS. NYPL.

31235   STEPHENS, THOMAS
     STEPHENS'S PHILADELPHIA DIRECTORY, FOR 1796; OR, ALPHABETICAL ARRANGE-
MENT: CONTAINING THE NAMES, OCCUPATIONS, AND PLACES OF ABODE OF THE
CITIZENS: WITH A REGISTER OF THE EXECUTIVE, LEGISLATIVE, AND JUDICIAL
MAGISTRATES OF THE UNITED STATES, AND THE STATE OF PENNSYLVANIA, WITH
THEIR SALARIES; THE GOVERNORS OF THE DIFFERENT STATES; AND THE MAGIS-
TRATES OF THE CITY: ALSO, AN ACCOUNT OF THE DIFFERENT SOCIETIES, CHARI-
TABLE AND LITERARY INSTITUTIONS, WITH THE NAMES OF THEIR PRESENT OFFI-
CERS; AND AN ACCURATE TABLE OF THE DUTIES ON GOODS, WARES, AND MERCHAN-
DIZE, TOGETHER WITH A GENERAL ABSTRACT FROM THE REVENUE LAWS—RELA-
TIVE TO THE DUTY OF MASTERS OF VESSELS—OF THE OWNERS OR CONSIGNEES OF
GOODS—OF OFFICERS OF THE CUSTOMS—OF THE PAYMENT OF DUTIES, &C. AND OF
THE MANNER IN WHICH GOODS MUST BE IMPORTED. TO ALL WHICH ARE ADDED, A
COMPLETE ACCOUNT OF THE POST OFFICE ESTABLISHMENT—THE BANKS, AND DIF-
FERENT MONIES, &C. WITH AN ALPHABETICAL LIST OF THE STREETS, LANES, AND
ALLEYS.

       *Philadelphia: Printed for Thomas Stephens, No. 60 South Second Street; by
W. [W.] Woodward. Entered according to Act of Congress.* [1796.] pp. 19, (1),
286, 69, (2), plan. 12mo.   BPL. HC. LCP. LOC.

       Second heading: A SHORT ACCOUNT OF PHILADELPHIA. pp. 69.

       Title of plan: STEPHENS PLAN OF THE CITY OF PHILADELPHIA.

       125th Pennsylvania District Copyright, issued to Thomas Stephens, as
Proprietor, 7 January, 1796.

31236   STERLING, WILLIAM A.
     THE CHILD'S INSTRUCTOR: BEING AN EARLY INTRODUCTION TO THE ORTHOGRAPHY
OF THE COLUMBIAN LANGUAGE. CONTAINING A CHOICE SELECTION OF EARLY
SPELLING AND READING LESSONS, PROPERLY ARRANGED TO LEAD THE LEARNER BY
DEGREES TO A COMPETENT KNOWLEDGE OF THE RUDIMENTS OF READING. SUITED
TO THE CAPACITY OF YOUTH. BY WILLIAM A. STERLING, SCHOOLMASTER.

       Fairhaven: Printed and sold by Judah P. Spooner. MDCCXCVI. pp. 48.
12mo.

31237   STEWART, JOHN, "Walking"   1749–1822
     PROSPECTUS OF A SERIES OF LECTURES, OR A NEW PRACTICAL SYSTEM OF HUMAN
REASON, CALCULATED TO DISCHARGE THE MIND FROM A GREAT MASS OF ERROR,
AND TO FACILITATE ITS LABOUR IN THE APPROXIMATION OF MORAL TRUTH, DI-
VESTED OF ALL METAPHYSICAL PERPLEXITIES AND NULLITIES; ACCOMODATED TO
THE MOST ORDINARY CAPACITIES, IN A SIMPLE METHOD. WHICH DISPENSES EQUALLY
WITH THE STUDY OF THE COLLEGE, OR THE LECTURE OF MUSTY LIBRARIES. BY
JOHN STEWART, THE TRAVELLER.

       *Philadelphia: Printed by Thomas Dobson, at the Stone House, No. 41, South
Second Street.* M,DCC,XCVI. pp. [16.] 8vo.   AAS. LOC.

31238   ——— THE REVELATION OF NATURE, WITH THE PROPHESY OF REASON. [Two lines
of verse.]

       *New-York: Printed by Mott & Lyon, for the Author. In the fifth year of
intellectual existence, or the publication of the Apocalypse of Nature, 3000 years
from the Grecian Olympiads, and 4800 from recorded knowledge in the Chinese
tables of eclipses, beyond which chronology is lost in fable.* [1796.] pp. xxxix,
104. 12mo.   AAS. BU. LOC. NYPL.

31239   STEWART'S KENTUCKY HERALD. VOL. I. NUMB. 47. TUESDAY, JANUARY 5, [— VOL.
II. NUMB. 98. DECEMBER 27, 1796.]

       Lexington: Printed by James H. Stewart; . . . 1796. fol.

     Supplements were added to the issues of October 18th, and 25th.

31240 STONE, NATHANIEL   –1848
Half-title: MR. STONE'S AND MR. UNDERWOOD'S SERMONS, AT THE OPENING OF A
NEW MEETING-HOUSE IN DENNIS.

First title: THE DUTY OF WORSHIPPING GOD IN HIS HOUSE, CONSIDERED IN A
SERMON, DELIVERED DECEMBER 17TH, 1795, ON OCCASION OF OPENING A NEW
MEETING-HOUSE IN THE SOUTH PART OF DENNIS. BY NATHANIEL STONE, A. M. PAS-
TOR OF THE CHURCH IN THAT TOWN. PUBLISHED BY DESIRE OF THE HEARERS.
Printed at Boston, by Manning & Loring, Spring-Lane. Feb. 1796. pp. 17;
14. 8vo.   AAS. JCB. MHS. NYHS.

Second title: PUBLIC WORSHIP CONSIDERED AND RECOMMENDED. A SERMON DE-
LIVERED AT DENNIS, DECEMBER 17, 1795, AT THE OPENING OF A NEW MEETING-
HOUSE. BY NATHAN UNDERWOOD, A. M. PASTOR OF THE SOUTH CHURCH IN HAR-
WICH. PUBLISHED BY DESIRE OF THE HEARERS.
Printed at Boston, by Manning & Loring, Spring-Lane. Feb. 1796. pp. 14.

31241 STONINGTON. CONNECTICUT. BAPTIST ASSOCIATION.
MINUTES OF THE STONINGTON ASSOCIATION, HELD AT GROTON, OCTOBER 18TH
AND 19TH, 1796.
New-London: Printed by James Springer? 1796.   BM.

31242 STORY, ISAAC, JUNIOR   1774-1803
ALL THE WORLD'S A STAGE. A POEM, IN THREE PARTS. [Five lines from] POPE'S
ESSAY ON MAN. THE STRANGER.
Newburyport: Printed by William Barrett. 1796. pp. [15.] 8vo. HC. NYPL.

31243 STREBECK, GEORGE
A SERMON. PREACHED (BY COURTSEY) [*sic*] IN THE GERMAN REFORMED CHURCH,
AT NEW-YORK, BY REV. GEORGE STREBECK.
New-York: Printed by Tiebout & O'Brien, 1796. pp. 16. 8vo.   NYHS.

31244 STRONG, CYPRIAN   1743–1811
A SECOND INQUIRY, INTO THE NATURE AND DESIGN OF CHRISTIAN BAPTISM. INTENDED
AS A VINDICATION AND FURTHER ILLUSTRATION, OF THE SENTIMENTS ADVANCED IN
A FORMER INQUIRY, ON THE SAME SUBJECT. BY CYPRIAN STRONG, A. M. PASTOR
OF THE FIRST CHURCH IN CHATHAM. [Printers mark.]
Hartford: Printed by Hudson & Goodwin. 1796. pp. 117, (1). 8vo.
                          AAS. BA. BM. CHS. HC. JCB. LOC. NYPL. UTS. YC.

31245 STRONG, JOSEPH   1753–1834
A SERMON, DELIVERED AT THE FUNERAL OF HIS EXCELLENCY SAMUEL HUNTINGTON,
GOVERNOR OF THE STATE OF CONNECTICUT; WHO DIED JANUARY 5TH, 1796. BY
JOSEPH STRONG, PASTOR OF THE FIRST CHURCH IN NORWICH. [Printer's mark.
Ornament.]
Hartford: Printed by Hudson and Goodwin. M,DCC,XCVI. pp. 19. 8vo.
                           AAS. JCB. LOC. MHS. NYHS. NYPL. UTS. YC.

31246 STRONG, NATHAN   1748–1816
THE DOCTRINE OF ETERNAL MISERY RECONCILEABLE WITH THE INFINITE BENEV-
OLENCE OF GOD, AND A TRUTH PLAINLY ASSERTED IN THE CHRISTIAN SCRIPTURES.
BY NATHAN STRONG, PASTOR OF THE NORTH PRESBYTERIAN CHURCH IN HART-
FORD. [Printers mark.]
Hartford: Printed by Hudson and Goodwin. 1796. pp. 408. 8vo.
                        AAS. BA. BM. BPL. BU. JCB. LOC. NYPL. UTS. YC.
Published according to Act of Congress.

31247　STRONG, NEHEMIAH　　　　　　　　　　　　　　　1729–1807
AN ASTRONOMICAL DIARY, CALENDAR, OR ALMANACK, FOR THE YEAR OF OUR LORD,
1797: AND FROM THE CREATION OF THE WORLD, 5746, AND TILL JULY 4TH, THE
21ST OF AMERICAN INDEPENDENCE. BEING THE FIRST AFTER BISSEXTILE, OR
LEAP YEAR. CONTAINING, ALL THINGS NECESSARY FOR SUCH A COMPOSITION.
ADAPTED TO THE HORIZON AND MERIDIAN OF HARTFORD, LAT. 41 DEG. 56 MIN.
NORTH: LONG. 72 DEG. 56 MIN. WEST, OF THE ROYAL OBSERVATORY (OR FLAM-
STEEDIAN HOUSE) IN GREENWICH, ACCORDING TO THE LATEST OBSERVATIONS;
BUT MAY SERVE INDIFFERENTLY FOR ALL THE TOWNS IN CONNECTICUT, AND THE
ADJACENT STATES. BY NEHEMIAH STRONG, LATE PROFESSOR OF MATHEMATICS,
AND NATURAL PHILOSOPHY OF YALE COLLEGE. [Eight lines of verse.]
　　Hartford: Printed by Elisha Babcock. [1796.] pp. (24). 12mo. AAS. CHS. YC.

31248　——　STRONG'S ASTRONOMICAL DIARY, CALENDAR, OR ALMANACK, FOR THE YEAR OF
OUR LORD, 1797: AND FROM THE CREATION OF THE WORLD, 5746: AND THE
TWENTY-FIRST OF AMERICAN INDEPENDENCE. BEING THE FIRST AFTER BISSEX-
TILE OR LEAP YEAR. [Eight lines.]
　　West-Springfield: Printed by Edward Gray. [1796.] pp. (24). 12mo.
　　　　　　　　　　　　　　　　　　　　　　　　　　AAS. LOC.

　　Spurious. "There is none of Strong's genuine Almanacks for sale but
　　those printed by Elisha Babcock—those printed by Ned Gray, and sell-
　　ing by Mr. Patten were not calculated by Nehemiah Strong, esq. nor
　　by any other person by the name of Strong. (So says Nehemiah Strong,
　　esq.)" January 2, 1797.

　　"Nehemiah Strong says that he has never known or heard of any per-
　　son but himself, by the name of Strong, who has ever calculated or
　　published any Almanack, either in this or in any other State." Feb. 8,
　　1798. New Milford.

31249　——　SHEET ALMANAC FOR THE YEAR 1797.
　　Hartford: Printed by Elisha Babcock, 1796. Broadside.

31250　——　STAFFORD'S ALMANACK, FOR THE YEAR OF OUR LORD, 1797. AND FROM THE
CREATION OF THE WORLD 5746. AND THE 21ST OF AMERICAN INDEPENDENCE.
BEING THE FIRST AFTER BISSEXTILE OR LEAP-YEAR. WHEREIN ARE CONTAINED,
ALL THINGS NECESSARY TO SUCH A COMPOSITION. ADAPTED TO THE HORIZON AND
MERIDIAN OF NEW-HAVEN. [Fourteen lines.]
　　Printed and sold by T. & S. Green, New-Haven. [1796.] pp. (24). 12mo.
　　　　　　　　　　　　　　　　　　　　　AAS. CHS. LOC. NYPL. YC.

　　In his address to the reader, dated, New-Milford, June 24, 1796, the
　　Author states "This is the 22d astronomical performance of this kind,
　　which the Author has, under the same signature, offered the public,
　　since he first undertook the business."

31251　STROTHER, JOHN
A TREATISE ON THE DISTILLATION OF ARDENT SPIRITS FROM MATERIALS OF THE
GROWTH OF THE UNITED STATES. BY JOHN STROTHER.
　　Richmond? 1796.
　　8th Virginia District Copyright, issued to John Strother, as Author,
　　23 September, 1796.

31252　THE (cut) SUN. DOVER GAZETTE, AND COUNTY ADVERTISER. [Motto.] NUMBER 18,
OF VOL. I. WHOLE NUMBER 18. WEDNESDAY, JANUARY 6, [—NUMBER 17, OF
VOL. II. WHOLE NUMBER 69. WEDNESDAY, DECEMBER 28, 1796.]
　　Published on Wednesdays—By Samuel Bragg, jun. at his Printing-Office,
　　near the Court-House, Dover. . . . 1796. fol.　　　　AAS.

31253   THE SUNBURY AND NORTHUMBERLAND GAZETTE. VOL. IV. NO. 27. SATURDAY, JANUARY 2, [—VOL. V. NO. 27. SATURDAY, DECEMBER 31, 1796.]
Northumberland—Printed by George Schusler. 1796. fol.

31254   SUNDAY MONITOR. "HOW SWEET THE TOIL, WHEN PHILANTHROPY'S THE CAUSE." VOL. I. NO, 1. SUNDAY, DECEMBER 18, 1796.
Baltimore: Printed by Philip Edwards. 1796. pp. (4). fol.   MdHS.

The first issue of a Sunday newspaper in the United States, and, apparently, the only issue made. It is a noticeable fact, that both this attempt, and that of *The Weekly Museum*, in January, 1797, to establish Sunday journalism, should have been made under the Charter of Maryland.

31255   SWANWICK, JOHN   1760-1798
BRITISH HONOUR AND HUMANITY; OR, THE WONDERS OF AMERICAN PATIENCE, AS EXEMPLIFIED IN THE MODEST PUBLICATIONS, AND UNIVERSAL APPLAUSE OF MR. WILLIAM COBBET [*sic*]; INCLUDING A VARIETY OF ANECDOTES AND REMARKS, PERSONAL AND POLITICAL, AND A SURVEY OF THE MODERN STATE OF AMERICAN NEWSPAPERS: BY A FRIEND TO REGULAR GOVERNMENT.
Philadelphia: Printed for and sold by Robert Campbell, No. 40, South Second Street. 1796. pp. (58). 8vo.   AAS. BA. BPL. HC. JCB. LCP. LOC. NL. NYPL.

Preface dated, Philadelphia, Octob. 8, 1796. This is sometimes erroneously attributed to Mathew Carey; but it is more probably written by John Swanwick, of whom, in a large measure, it is a defence.

31256   —— A ROASTER; OR, A CHECK TO THE PROGRESS OF POLITICAL BLASPHEMY: INTENDED AS A BRIEF REPLY TO PETER PORCUPINE, ALIAS BILLY COBLER. BY SIM SANSCULOTTE.
Philadelphia: Printed by J. Johnson. M,DCC,XCVI. pp. [21.] 8vo.
                                        AAS. JCB. LOC. NYHS.

"What," says William Cobbett, "can I say worse of the blundering performance, than that it bears all the internal evidence of being written by the blunderbus author who disgusted the city with Rub from Snub."
See my X:30727, to which this is a "brief reply."

31257   SWEDENBORG or SWEDBERG, EMANUEL   1688-1772
THE DELIGHTS OF WISDOM CONCERNING CONJUGIAL LOVE: AFTER WHICH FOLLOW THE PLEASURES OF INSANITY CONCERNING SCORTATORY LOVE. TRANSLATED FROM THE LATIN OF THE HON. EMANUEL SWEDENBORG, A NATIVE OF SWEDEN. ORIGINALLY PUBLISHED AT AMSTERDAM IN THE YEAR 1768.
Philadelphia: Printed by Francis & Robert Bailey, at Yorick's-Head, No. 116, High-Street. 1796. pp. viii, vi, (521), (2). 8vo.   AAS. JCB. LOC. NYPL.

31258   —— THE WISDOM OF ANGELS CONCERNING THE DIVINE PROVIDENCE. TRANSLATED FROM THE LATIN OF THE HON. EMANUEL SWEDENBORG. ORIGINALLY PUBLISHED AT AMSTERDAM, ANNO 1764.
Printed at Boston by Isaiah Thomas and Ebenezer T. Andrews, Faust's Statue, No. 45. Newbury Street. July, 1796. pp. 543. 8vo.   AAS. HC. JCB. NYPL.

31259   SWIFT, ZEPHANIAH   1759-1823
A SECOND ADDRESS, TO THE REVEREND MOSES C. WELCH, CONTAINING AN ANSWER TO HIS LETTER TO THE CORRESPONDENT. [Eighteen lines of quotations.]
Windham: Printed by John Byrne. 1796. pp. 43. 8vo.
                                     AAS. CLA. JCB. LOC. UTS.

31260   SWIFT, ZEPHANIAH, continued.
—— A SYSTEM OF THE LAWS OF THE STATE OF CONNECTICUT. IN SIX BOOKS. BY ZEPHANIAH SWIFT. VOLUME II. [Ornament.]

> *Windham: Printed by John Byrne, for the Author.* 1796. pp. v, 479, (6), 6, plate. 8vo.   AAS. BM. BPL. HC. LOC. LIHS. NYHS. YC.

> Contains an interesting six page List of Subscribers. Connecticut District Copyright issued to Zephaniah Swift, as Author, 26 February, 1796.

31261   SYMMES, JOHN CLEVES   1742–1814
ON THE FIRST SETTLEMENT OF THE NORTH WEST TERRITORY.

> *Cincinnati: Printed by William Maxwell.* 1796.

> "Judge Symmes' pamphlet On the first settlement of this country."
> See United States. Letter of the Attorney General. March 11, 1796.

31262   SYMMES, WILLIAM   1762–1807
AN ORATION, DELIVERED IN THE MEETING HOUSE OF THE FIRST PARISH IN PORTLAND, JUNE 24TH, 5796. AT THE REQUEST AND IN THE PRESENCE OF THE LODGE OF FREE AND ACCEPTED MASONS, CONGREGATED THERE, IT BEING THE ANNIVERSARY FESTIVAL OF ST. JOHN, THE BAPTIST. BY WILLIAM SYMMES, J. W. OF THE LODGE.

> *Printed at Portland, by brother John K. Baker.* 5796. [1796.] pp. 16. 4to.
>   AAS. BA. JCB.

31263   A TABLE FOR RECEIVING AND PAYING GOLD AT THE PRESENT STANDARD, ACCORDING TO THE ACT OF CONGRESS REGULATING FOREIGN COINS. PASSED THE 9TH OF FEBRUARY, 1793. CALCULATED FOR THE USE OF THE BANK OF THE UNITED STATES.
> *Newbern: Printed by Francis –X. Martin.* 1796.

31264   TABLES AND INSTRUCTIONS TO REDUCE LAWFUL MONEY TO FEDERAL, AND SHOW THE INTEREST OF DOLLARS IN DECIMALS, &C.
> *Hallowell: Printed and sold by Peter Edes.* 1796.

> "By dozen or single."

31265   TABLES, SHEWING IN THREE DIFFERENT VIEWS, THE COMPARATIVE VALUE OF THE CURRENCY OF THE STATE OF NEW-YORK, WITH DOLLARS, CENTS AND MILLS, AND STERLING MONEY; ALSO, OF FRENCH CROWNS, WITH DOLLARS, CENTS AND MILLS, AND WITH CURRENCY, AND OF FOREIGN COINED GOLD, WITH DOLLARS, CENTS AND MILLS.
> *New-York: Printed by Francis Childs & Co.* 1795. pp. 33. 12mo.

31266   —— TABLES, SHEWING IN THREE DIFFERENT VIEWS, THE COMPARATIVE VALUE OF THE CURRENCY, OF THE STATES OF NEW-HAMPSHIRE, MASSACHUSETTS, RHODE-ISLAND, CONNECTICUT, VIRGINIA, VERMONT AND KENTUCKY, WITH DOLLARS, CENTS AND MILLS, AND STERLING MONEY; ALSO, OF FRENCH CROWNS, WITH DOLLARS, CENTS AND MILLS, AND WITH CURRENCY, AND OF FOREIGN COINED GOLD, WITH DOLLARS, CENTS & MILLS.
> *Portsmouth, New-Hampshire: Printed and sold by Charles Peirce.* 1796.

> 14th New Hampshire District Copyright, issued to Charles Peirce, as Proprietor, 2 March, 1796.

31267   TAPPAN, DAVID   1752–1803
A DISCOURSE DELIVERED TO THE STUDENTS OF HARVARD COLLEGE, SEPTEMBER 6, 1796. DESIGNED FOR THE SPECIAL BENEFIT OF THE NEW CLASS, WHICH LATELY JOINED THE SOCIETY; BY DAVID TAPPAN, HOLLISIAN PROFESSOR OF DIVINITY IN SAID UNIVERSITY.

> *Boston: Printed by Manning & Loring.* 1796. pp. [20.] 8vo.
>   AAS. BA. HC. JCB. LOC. NYHS. NYPL. UTS.

31268
    TAYLOR, Amos
      The Genuine experience, and dying address, of mrs. Dolly Taylor, of Reading, (Vermont) who departed this life, May 19th, 1794. Actually dictated by herself, and taken from her lips, but a little before her death. Now published, with her husband's testimony concerning her, for whom he mourns, but not without hope. The third edition: — carefully revised by the Author.

        Windsor: Printed by Alden Spooner, for the Author. M,DCC,XCV. pp. (8)+ 8vo.   AAS.

31269
    —— — The Genuine experience, and dying address, of mrs. Dolly Taylor, of Reading, (Vermont,) who departed this life, May 19th, 1794. Actually dictated by herself, and taken from her lips. but a little before her death. Now published, with her husband's testimony concerning her, for whom he mourns, but not without hope. The fourth edition:—carefully revised by the Author.

        Bennington: Printed [by Anthony Haswell] for Amos Taylor, and sold by him at his book store in Whitingham. 1796. pp. 12. 12mo.   AAS. JCB.

31270
    —— The Scholar's primer, or child's best helpmate to Columbian literature. Published for the use of small children in families and schools. Containing a larger collection of spelling, and easy familiar lessons for the youth of America, than the genius of man has hitherto compiled. By Amos Taylor, tutor.

        Bennington: Printed by Anthony Haswell. 1796.

31271
    TAYLOR, George Keith
      Substance of a Speech delivered in the House of Delegates of Virginia, on the Bill to amend the penal laws of this Commonwealth. By George Keith Taylor.

        Richmond: Printed by Samuel Pleasants, jun. M,DCC,XCVI. pp. 36. 4to.   BA. HC. VSL.

31272
    TAYLOR, Jeremy   1613–1667
      The Life of our blessed Saviour Jesus Christ: with considerations and discourses upon the conception, nativity, circumcision, baptism. temptation, preaching, miracles, passion, resurrection, and His ascension into Heaven. Including several unanswerable arguments obvious to the meanest capacity, in defence of the divinity of our holy Redeemer, and the truth of the christian religion. Likewise, the Lives, acts and deaths of the holy Evangelists and Apostles, as recorded by the primitive fathers, and ancient writers of unquestionable veracity. By J. Taylor, b. d.

        Greenfield, (Massachusetts:) Printed by Thomas Dickman, and sold at his Bookstore. 1796. pp. 152. 12mo.   AAS. BM. JCB. NYPL.

      Second title: The Lives of the holy Evangelists and Apostles; with their martyrdoms, for preaching the Gospel of our Lord Jesus Christ. pp. (2), (105)—152.

      An abridgment from William Cave.

31273   TAYLOR, JEREMY, continued.

—— — THE LIFE OF OUR BLESSED SAVIOUR JESUS CHRIST, WITH CONSIDERATIONS AND DISCOURSES UPON THE CONCEPTION, NATIVITY, CIRCUMCISION BAPTISM, TEMPTATION, PREACHING, MIRACLES, PASSION, RESURRECTION, AND HIS ASCENSION INTO HEAVEN. INCLUDING SEVERAL UNANSWERABLE ARGUMENTS, OBVIOUS TO THE MEANEST CAPACITY, IN DEFENCE OF THE DIVINITY OF OUR HOLY REDEEMER, AND THE TRUTH OF THE CHRISTIAN RELIGION. — LIKEWISE, THE LIVES, ACTS, AND DEATHS OF THE HOLY EVANGELISTS AND APOSTLES, AS RECORDED BY THE PRIMITIVE FATHERS, AND ANCIENT WRITERS OF UNQUESTIONABLE VERACITY. BY J. TAYLOR, B. D.

Printed at Newburyport, by Blunt and March for Samuel Larkin, Bookseller and Stationer, Portsmouth. MDCCXCVI. pp. 248, (1). 12mo.

AAS. BA. BM. JCB. NYPL.

"It is sufficient recommendation, that it has in the course of the last year, run through an edition of one thousand copies."

31274   TAYLOR, JOHN   1762–1840

AN ORATION, DELIVERED ON THE ANNIVERSARY OF INDEPENDENCE, AT DEERFIELD, ON THE FOURTH OF JULY, 1796. BY JOHN TAYLOR, A. M. [Printer's mark.]

Printed and sold at Greenfield, Massachusetts, by Thomas Dickman. MDCC-XCVI. pp. 20. 4to.   CHS. HC. MHS. NYHS. NYPL. YC.

31275   THE TELEGRAPHE. [Motto.] VOL. I. No. 48. TUESDAY (EVENING) JANUARY 5, [—VOL. II. No. 65. TUESDAY (EVENING), MAY 3, 1796.]

Carlisle: Printed by Steel & M'Clean, at the Sign of the Printing-Press in York-Street.—1796. fol.

At the close of the first volume, February 9th, John S. McClean withdrew, and publication was continued in the name of James Steel to May 3d—the last number located.

31276   TEMPLE, SAMUEL

A CONCISE INTRODUCTION TO PRACTICAL ARITHMETIC; IN WHICH, ALL THE RULES, THAT OCCUR IN COMMON BUSINESS, ARE APPLIED TO THE FEDERAL CURRENCY. DESIGNED FOR THE USE OF SCHOOLS IN THE UNITED STATES. BY SAMUEL TEMPLE, A. M. [Cut of two crowns.]

Boston: Printed and sold by Samuel Hall, No. 53, Cornhill. 1796. *[With the privilege of copy right.]* pp. 116. 12mo.   AAS.

31277   TENNESSEE. STATE.

ACTS PASSED AT THE FIRST GENERAL ASSEMBLY OF THE STATE OF TENNESSEE: BEGUN AND HELD AT KNOXVILLE, ON MONDAY, THE TWENTY-EIGHTH OF MARCH, ONE THOUSAND SEVEN HUNDRED AND NINETY-SIX. [—23 April, 1796.]

Knoxville: Printed by George Roulstone, Printer to the State. M,DCC,-XCVI. pp. [78.] 8vo.   LOC.

31278   —— THE CONSTITUTION OF THE STATE OF TENNESSEE.

Knoxville, Printed by George Roulstone, Printer to the State. 1796. pp. 16. 8vo.   NYPL.

31279   —— — CONSTITUTION OF THE STATE OF TENNESSEE. UNANIMOUSLY ESTABLISHED IN CONVENTION AT KNOXVILLE, ON THE SIXTH DAY OF FEBRUARY, ONE THOUSAND SEVEN HUNDRED AND NINETY SIX. [Ornament.]

Philadelphia: Printed for Thomas Condie, No. 20, Carters Alley. M,DCC,-XCVI. pp. [33.] 12mo.   HC. LOC. NYHS. NYPL.

31280   TENNESSEE. State, continued.
—— *Heading:* Journal of the proceedings of a Convention, begun and held at Knoxville, on the eleventh day of January, 1796, for the purpose of framing a Constitution or form of government of the people.
Knoxville: Printed by George Roulstone. 1796.   LOC.
Reprinted in Nashville, in 1852.

31281   —— Journal of the House of Representatives of the State of Tennessee: begun and held at Knoxville, on Monday, the twenty-eighth of March, one thousand seven hundred and ninety-six. [Heavy lines.]
Knoxville: Printed by George Roulstone, Printer to the State. M,DCC,-XCVI. pp. 80. 8vo.   JCB.

31282   —— State of Tenesse. [*sic*] John Sevier, Esq. Governor and commander in chief in and over the same. A Proclamation. [Convening the General Assembly, Saturday, July 30th, 1796, on an Act of the Government annulling several Acts of the Legislature.] Given under my hand and seal, at Knoxville, this 11th day of July, one thousand seven hundred and ninety-six, and in the twenty-first year of American independence. John Sevier. By the Governor. Wm. Maclin, sec'ry.
Knoxville: Printed by George Roulstone. 1796. Broadside.

31283   THACHER, Peter   1752–1802
Half-title: Doctor Thacher's Sermon on the death, and doctor Welsh's Eulogy to the memory, of the honourable Nathaniel Gorham, Esq. MDCCXCVI.
Title: A Sermon, preached at Charlestown, June 19, 1796, and occasioned by the sudden death of the honourable Nathaniel Gorham, Esquire, æt. 59. By Peter Thacher, D. D. minister of a church in Boston. [Ornament.]
Printed by Samuel Hall, in Cornhill, Boston. MDCCXCVI. pp. [25]; [15], (1). 4to.   AAS. BA. HC. JCB. MHS.
Second title: An Eulogy, delivered June 29, 1796, at the meeting-house in Charlestown, in the Commonwealth of Massachusetts, in memory of the honourable Nathaniel Gorham, esquire, who died June 11, 1796. By doctor Thomas Welsh, member of the American Academy of Arts and Sciences, and fellow of the Massachusetts Medical Society. [One line from] Tristram Shandy. [Ornament.]
Printed by Samuel Hall, in Cornhill, Boston. MDCCXCVI. pp. [15], (1).
The last page contains A Dirge. By the Rev. Thaddeus Mason Harris.
Set to music by Mr. Oliver Holden.

31284   —— A Sermon preached to the Society in Brattle-street, Boston, April 17, 1796; and occasioned by the death of the Hon. Thomas Russell, Esq. By Peter Thacher, D. D. pastor of the church in Brattle-street.
Boston: Printed by Benjamin Sweetser, corner of Wing's-Lane. M.DCC.-XCVI. pp. [32.] 8vo.   AAS. BA. BM. BPL. HC. JCB. MHS. NYPL.

31285   THACHER, Samuel
An Oration, pronounced July 4, 1796, at the request of the inhabitants of the town of Concord, in commemoration of the twentieth anniversary of American independence. By Samuel Thacher. [One line of Latin quotation.] [Ornaments.]
Printed by Samuel Hall, No. 53, Cornhill, Boston. 1796. pp. 24. 8vo.   AAS. BA. JCB.

31286   **THACHER, Thomas**   1756–1812
A SERMON PREACHED AT MILTON, THE LORD'S DAY AFTER THE INTERMENT OF THE REVEREND NATHANIEL ROBBINS, A. M. PASTOR OF SAID CHURCH. WHO EXPIRED THE 19TH DAY OF MAY, A. D. 1795. ÆT. 69. BY THOMAS THACHER, A. M. MINISTER OF A CHURCH IN DEDHAM.
> *Boston: Printed by Thomas Fleet, jun. Cornhill.* MDCCXCVI. pp. (26); (2), 28. 8vo.   AAS. BA. BPL. JCB. MHS. NYHS. NYPL.

Second title: THE COMFORTABLE CHAMBERS, OPENED AND VISITED, UPON THE DEPARTURE OF THAT AGED AND FAITHFUL SERVANT OF GOD, MR. PETER THATCHER, THE NEVER TO BE FORGOTTEN PASTOR OF MILTON, WHO MADE HIS FLIGHT THITHER, ON DECEMBER 17, 1727. BY COTTON MATHER, D. D. & F. R. S. [THE LAST SERMON THE AUTHOR EVER DELIVERED.]
> *Boston: Re-printed by Thomas Fleet, jun. Cornhill.* MDCCXCVI. pp. (2), 28.

With "A Short account of the town of Milton." pp. (2).

31287   **THAYER, Nathaniel**   1769–1840
A SERMON, PREACHED DECEMBER 23, AT THE FUNERAL OF THE REV. TIMOTHY HARRINGTON; LATE SENIOR MINISTER OF THE CHURCH IN LANCASTER; WHO DIED DECEMBER 18, 1795, IN THE EIGHTIETH YEAR OF HIS AGE. BY NATHANIEL THAYER, A. M. SURVIVING MINISTER OF SAID CHURCH.
> *Amherst, Newhampshire, From the Press of Biglow and Cushing.* MDCCXCVI. pp. 19. 8vo.   AAS. BA. BM. JCB. LOC. MHS. NYPL.

Printed by request of the Selectmen of Lancaster.

31288   THE THEOLOGICAL MAGAZINE, OR SYNOPSIS OF MODERN RELIGIOUS SENTIMENT. ON A NEW PLAN. [Seven lines of quotations.] VOL. I. [JULY, 1795,—JUNE, 1796.]
> *New-York: Printed by T. and J. Swords, for Cornelius Davis.* 1796. pp. viii, 480. 8vo.   AAS. BA. BM. BPL. JCB. LOC. MHS. NYHS. NYPL. PTS. YC.

A bi-monthly publication continued to February, 1799.

31289   —— THE THEOLOGICAL MAGAZINE, OR SYNOPSIS OF MODERN RELIGIOUS SENTIMENT. ON A NEW PLAN. [VOL. II. No. 1. SEPTEMBER AND OCTOBER, No. 2. NOVEMBER AND DECEMBER, 1796.]
> *New-York: Printed by T. and J. Swords, for Cornelius Davis.* 1796. pp. 160. 8vo.   AAS.

31290   **THOMAS, Isaiah**   1749–1831
CATALOGUE OF BOOKS TO BE SOLD BY THOMAS, SON & THOMAS, AT THEIR BOOKSTORE, IN WORCESTER, MASSACHUSETTS: CONSISTING OF HISTORY, VOYAGES, TRAVELS, GEOGRAPHY, ANTIQUITIES, PHILOSOPHY, NOVELS, MISCELLANIES, DIVINITY, PHYSIC, SURGERY, ANATOMY, ARTS, SCIENCES, HUSBANDRY, ARCHITECTURE, NAVIGATION, MATHEMATICKS, LAW, PERIODICAL PUBLICATIONS, POETRY, PLAYS, MUSIC. &C. &C. &C. OCTOBER, MDCCXCVI.
> *Printed at Worcester, Massachusetts, by Thomas, Son & Thomas.* [1796.] pp. 47. 12mo.   AAS. MHS.

31291   THOMAS'S MASSACHUSETTS, CONNECTICUT, RHODEISLAND, NEWHAMPSHIRE, & VERMONT ALMANACK, WITH AN EPHEMERIS, FOR THE YEAR OF OUR LORD, 1797: BEING THE FIRST AFTER BISSEXTILE, OR LEAP YEAR, AND TWENTY-FIRST OF THE INDEPENDENCE OF UNITED COLUMBIA. FROM CREATION, ACCORDING TO THE SCRIPTURES, 5789. [Five lines.] WITH THE PRESIDENT'S ADDRESS, AND THE FEE BILL. [Cut. Four lines from] THOMSON.
> *Printed at Worcester, Massachusetts, for Isaiah Thomas. Sold by Thomas, Son & Thomas, in Worcester; by Thomas & Andrews, S. Hall, B. Larkin, D. West, E. Larkin, J. Boyle, W. Spotswood, J. West, J. Nancrede, and at the Boston Bookstore, in Boston; and by the other Booksellers, in town and country. Price 7 dols. per gross—75 cents dozen—10 cents single.* [1796.] pp. (48). 12mo.   AAS. LOC. NYPL. YC.

31292   THOMAS'S MASSACHUSETTS SPY: OR, THE WORCESTER GAZETTE. [Mottoes.] VOL.
XXIV. No. 1183. WEDNESDAY, JANUARY 6, [— VOL. XXV. No. 1237. WEDNESDAY,
DECEMBER 28, 1796.]

> *Printed at Worcester, (Massachusetts) by Leonard Worcester, at his Office, near*
> *the South Meeting House, for Isaiah Thomas. . . . 1796. fol.*   AAS.

> Beginning May 25th, the imprint reads: "Leonard Worcester at the
> Old Printing Office, near the Court House, for Isaiah Thomas.". July
> 27th, Isaiah Thomas entered into partnership with his son, Isaiah
> Thomas, junior, and Alexander Thomas, junior, under the firm name
> of Thomas, Son, and Thomas.

31293   THOMAS, ANDREWS, AND PENNIMAN.
AMERICAN PUBLICATIONS CATALOGUE OF BOOKS FOR SALE, WHOLESALE OR RETAIL,
AT THE BOOK STORE OF THOMAS, ANDREWS & PENNIMAN, ALBANY.

> *[Albany: Printed by Barber and Southwick. 1796.] Broadside. fol.*

31294   THOMAS, ROBERT BAILEY   1766–1846
No. V. THE FARMER'S ALMANACK, CALCULATED ON A NEW AND IMPROVED PLAN,
FOR THE YEAR OF OUR LORD, 1797. BEING THE FIRST AFTER BISSEXTILE, OR
LEAP-YEAR, AND TWENTY-FIRST OF THE INDEPENDENCE OF AMERICA. [Six lines.]
BY ROBERT B. THOMAS. [Cut. Four lines of verse.]

> *Boston: Printed by Manning & Loring, for John West, Proprietor of the*
> *copy-right, and for sale at his Book-store, No. 75, Cornhill, and sold by the other*
> *Booksellers in Boston. Sold also by Cushing & Carlton, and J. Dabney, Salem;*
> *by Edmund M. Blunt, Newburyport; by the Author, and M. Smith, Sterling; and*
> *at various other places. [Price seven dollars per groce, 75 cents per dozen, and 10*
> *cents single.] [1796.] pp. (48). 12mo.*   AAS. LOC. MHS.

31295   —— ROBERT B. THOMAS, HAS FOR SALE AT HIS BOOK & STATIONARY STORE, IN
STERLING, THE FOLLOWING BOOKS & STATIONARY, TO WHICH ADDITIONS ARE CON-
STANTLY MAKING. —— [Colophon:]

> *Leominster: Printed by Charles Prentiss—1796. pp. (4). 8vo.*   AAS. LOC.

31296   THOMAS, WILLIAM
HODGE'S NORTH-CAROLINA ALMANACK, FOR THE YEAR OF OUR LORD, 1797; BEING
THE FIRST AFTER BISSEXTILE OR LEAP-YEAR, AND THE 21ST-22D OF AMERICAN
INDEPENDENCE. CALCULATED FOR THE STATE OF NORTH-CAROLINA, BEING PRE-
CISELY ADAPTED TO THE MERIDIAN AND LATITUDE OF THE CITY OF RALEIGH; BUT
WILL SERVE WITHOUT SENSIBLE ERROR FOR ANY OF THE STATES ADJACENT. CON-
TAINING THE LUNATIONS, RISING AND SETTING OF THE SUN, MOON AND SEVEN STARS,
SOLAR AND LUNAR ECLIPSES, REMARKABLE DAYS, FESTIVALS, &C. ALSO, A VARIETY
OF USEFUL AND AMUSING ARTICLES.

> *Halifax: Printed and sold by Abraham Hodge, [1796.]*

31297   THOMPSON, WILLIAM
THE BALTIMORE TOWN AND FELL'S POINT DIRECTORY, CONTAINING THE NAMES,
OCCUPATIONS AND PLACES OF ABODE OF THE INHABITANTS; ARRANGED IN ALPHA-
BETICAL ORDER: — ALSO — A REGISTER OF THE EXECUTIVE, LEGISLATIVE, AND
JUDICIAL MAGISTRATES OF THE UNITED STATES AND OF THE STATE OF MARYLAND,
WITH THEIR SALARIES; TOGETHER WITH A LIST OF THE DUTIES PAYABLE AT THE
PORT OF BALTIMORE —— AND AN ABRIDGED ALMANAC, SHEWING THE DAYS OF
THE WEEK AND MONTH FOR THE YEAR, &C. &C. THE FIRST EDITION. BY [William]
THOMPSON AND [James] WALKER.

> *Baltimore: Printed for the Proprietors, by Pechin & Co. No. 27, Gay-street.*
> *[1796.] pp. 99, (1). 12mo.*   AAS. MDHS.

31298   THORNTON, ELISHA
THE NEW-ENGLAND ALMANACK, OR LADY'S AND GENTLEMAN'S DIARY, FOR THE YEAR
OF OUR LORD CHRIST 1797: BEING THE FIRST AFTER BISSEXTILE, OR LEAP-YEAR,
AND THE TWENTY-FIRST OF AMERICAN INDEPENDENCE, WHICH COMMENCED JULY
4, 1776. [Seventeen lines.] THE ASTRONOMICAL CALCULATIONS BY ELISHA
THORNTON, AND ELIAB WILKINSON, PHILOM.
> *Printed at Providence (R. I.) by Carter and Wilkinson, and sold wholesale
> and retail, at their Book and Stationary Store, opposite the Market. [Great al-
> lowance made to those who purchase quantities.]* [1796.] pp. (24). 12mo.
>   AAS. HSP. LOC. RIHS.

31299   THOUGHTS ON THE LAWFULNESS OF WAR; HUMBLY SUBMITTED TO THE SERIOUS CON-
SIDERATION OF THE TEACHERS OF EVERY CHURCH OR SECT AMONG CHRISTIANS. BY
A CLERGYMAN OF THE CHURCH OF ENGLAND. "I AM FOR PEACE." PS. CXX. 17.
> *London printed: 1796. Philadelphia Re-printed by D. Humphreys, No. 48,
> Spruce-Street.* M.DCC.XCVI. pp. 20. 8vo.   LOC.

31300   THUMB, TOM. pseudonym.
TOM THUMB'S FOLIO; OR, A NEW PENNY PLAYTHING FOR LITTLE GIANTS.
> *New-York:* 1796. 32mo.

31301   TILLOTSON, DANIEL
SONG ON VACATION. SET TO MUSIC BY DAVID B. WILCOXSON. YALE COLLEGE.
JANUARY 1, 1796.
> *[New-Haven: Printed by Thomas and Samuel Green.* 1796.] Broadside.

31302   TO THE FREE AND INDEPENDENT CITIZENS OF   FRIENDS AND COUNTRYMEN,
WE ARE NOW AT A CRISIS IN OUR NATIONAL AFFAIRS, AWFULLY IMPORTANT AND
ALARMING. [In opposition to the Treaty with Great Britain.]
> *[Boston?* 1796.] Broadside.   MHS.

31303   TO THE FREEMEN OF THE TOWN OF PROVIDENCE. . . . [Colophon:]
> *Providence: Printed by B. Wheeler.* [1796.] Broadside. fol.

31304   TO THE HONORABLE THE HOUSE OF REPRESENTATIVES OF THE UNITED STATES. THE
MEMORIAL OF THE SUBSCRIBERS, MERCHANTS AND TRADERS OF   RESPECT-
FULLY REPRESENTS . . . [On Treaty with Great Britain.]
> *[Boston:* 1796.] Broadside.   MHS.

31305   TO THE HONOURABLE THE HOUSE OF REPRESENTATIVES OF THE UNITED STATES. THE
MEMORIAL OF THE SUBSCRIBERS, CITIZENS OF   IN MASSACHUSETTS. . . .
[On carrying into operation the Treaty with Great Britain.]
> *[Boston: April 28.* 1796.] Broadside.   MHS.

31306   TO THE SELECTMEN OF THE TOWN OF LYNNFIELD, REQUESTING CO-OPERATION IN SUCH
MEASURES AS SHALL BE THOUGHT BEST ADAPTED TO INDUCE THE HOUSE OF REP-
RESENTATIVES TO VOTE THE SUPPLIES NECESSARY FOR THE COMPLETION OF THE
TREATY WITH GREAT BRITAIN.
> *[Salem: Printed by William Carlton.* 1796.] Broadside.   EI.

31307   THE TOCSIN. FRIDAY, JANUARY 1, [—SATURDAY, DECEMBER 31, 1796.]
> *Published by Wait, Robinson & Baker, at the Hook, Hallowell, [District of
> Maine] [Massachusetts.]* 1796. fol.

> Howard S. Robinson withdrew January 15th, and Wait & Baker dis-
> posed of their interests in September, to Benjamin Poor, who continued
> publication with the issue for September 30th.

31308   TORREY, JOHN
SCRIPTURAL AND ALLEGORICAL POEMS ON THE DOWNFALL OF SUPERSTITION. BY JOHN
TORREY. [Two lines of verse.]
New-York: 1796.

43d New York District Copyright, issued to John Torrey, as Author,
7 July, 1796.

31309   TOWN & COUNTRY ALMANAC; FOR VIRGINIA, PENNSYLVANIA, DELAWARE, MARY-
LAND AND KENTUCKY—FOR THE YEAR OF OUR LORD—1797; —BEING THE FIRST
AFTER BISSEXTILE OR LEAP-YEAR: —THE TWENTY-FIRST YEAR OF AMERICAN IN-
DEPENDENCE, AND THE NINTH OF THE FEDERAL GOVERNMENT. CONTAINING (BE-
SIDES EVERY THING NECESSARY IN AN ALMANAC) A VARIETY OF PIECES IN PROSE
& VERSE.
*Baltimore: Printed by W. Pechin, No. 15, Market-st.—for J. Hagerty, and
Thomas, Andrews and Butler.* [1796.] pp. (36). 12mo.   LOC.

31310   TRAIL, ROBERT   1642–1716
THIRTEEN SERMONS ON THE THRONE OF GRACE, FROM HEB. IV.16.—FIRST PRINTED
IN 1696. LIKEWISE, A SERMON ON THE FOLLOWING QUESTION, BY WHAT MEANS
MAY MINISTERS BEST WIN SOULS? FROM I TIM. IV. 16.—FIRST PRINTED IN 1683.
AND A VINDICATION OF THE PROTESTANT DOCTRINE CONCERNING JUSTIFICATION,
AND OF ITS PREACHERS AND PROFESSORS, FROM THE UNJUST CHARGE OF ANTI-
NOMIANISM. FIRST PRINTED IN 1699. BY THE LATE REVEREND MR. ROBERT
TRAILL, A. M. MINISTER OF THE GOSPEL IN LONDON.
Philadelphia: Printed and sold by John M'Culloch, 1796. pp. viii, 13–292,
(4). 8vo.   AAS. NYPL.

31311   THE TRAITOR DETECTED, OR, AN EXAMINATION OF MR. RANDOLPH'S VINDICATION.
[Seven lines of verse.]
Baltimore: 1796.

31312   THE TREATY—ITS MERITS AND DEMERITS FAIRLY DISCUSSED AND DISPLAYED.
[Boston: 1796.] pp. [141.] 8vo.   AAS. BA. HC. HSP. JCB. LOC. MHS. NYHS.

Contains: The Treaty.—Objections to the Treaty.—Objections refuted.
—The Federalist. Nos. 1-4.—The Constitutionalist. Nos. 1-4.—The
Federalist. Nos. 5-8.—A Letter from the President of the United States
to the Selectmen of Boston.—Action of the Boston Chamber of Commerce.

31313   TRENCK, FRIEDRICH, freiherr VON DER   1726-1794
THE LIFE OF BARON FREDERICK TRENCK. CONTAINING HIS ADVENTURES HIS CRUEL
AND EXCESSIVE SUFFERINGS, DURING TEN YEARS IMPRISONMENT, AT THE FORTRESS
OF MAGDEBURG, BY COMMAND OF THE LATE KING OF PRUSSIA. [WITH ANECDOTES
OF THE LIFE OF ALEXANDER SCHELL, AN OFFICER OF THE GUARD, IN GLATZ, WHO
DELIVERED ME FROM PRISON, ON THE 26TH OF DECEMBER, 1746, AND DESERTED
IN MY COMPANY.—WRITTEN AS A SUPPLEMENT TO MY OWN HISTORY.] TRANSLA-
TED FROM THE GERMAN, BY THOMAS HOLCROFT. [Ornament.]
New-York: Printed and sold by William Durell, No. 208, Pearl-street.
M,DCC,XCVI. pp. 187, plate. 24mo.   AAS.

31314   TREZIULNEY, ——
A LETTER TO WASHINGTON BY JASPER DWIGHT, OF VERMONT.
*Printed at Philadelphia, for the Author, [by Benjamin Franklin Bache],
and sold by the Booksellers.* Dec. 1796. pp. (48). 8vo.   HSP.

TREZIULNEY,—— continued.

31315　—— — A LETTER TO GEORGE WASHINGTON, PRESIDENT OF THE UNITED STATES : CONTAINING STRICTURES ON HIS ADDRESS OF THE SEVENTEENTH OF SEPTEMBER, 1796, NOTIFYING HIS RELINQUISHMENT OF THE PRESIDENTIAL OFFICE. BY JASPER DWIGHT, OF VERMONT.

Printed at Philadelphia, for the Author, [by Benjamin Franklin Bache], and sold by the Booksellers. Dec. 1796. pp. (48). 8vo.

AAS. BA. CLS. HSP. JCB. LOC. MHS. NYHS. NYPL.

This unjust and abusive invective against George Washington— more so, even, than the Letter of Thomas Paine, or the hostile criticism of the *Aurora*—is usually attributed to his political enemy, William Duane, whose subsequent marriage to the widow of Benjamin Franklin Bache, gave his embittered soul complete control of that paper's opinions. In the "Autobiography of Mathew Carey," as given in the "New-England Magazine," VI: 105, he states: "A Pole by the name of Treziulney, who acted as bookkeeper for Mr. Duane, wrote a pamphlet the object of which was to prove the utter incapacity of General Washington as displayed during the Revolution." This purpose has been, apparently, edited out of this pamphlet; but the evidence of foreign thought in the body of the work is strong; and the intense hatred edited in, to the opening and closing pages, could only be that of a man who was without citizenship in any country, or political principle which was not opposed to the public opinion of every country wherever he had lived.

31316　TRIMMER, SARAH KIRBY　　　　　　　　　　1741–1810
AN EASY INTRODUCTION TO THE KNOWLEDGE OF NATURE. ADAPTED TO THE CAPACITIES OF CHILDREN. BY MRS. TRIMMER. REVISED, CORRECTED, AND GREATLY AUGMENTED; AND ADAPTED TO THE UNITED STATES OF AMERICA. [And, A Winter evening's conversation.]

Boston: Printed by Manning and Loring, for David West. 1796. pp. 147, 8. 24mo.　　　　　　　　　　　　　　　AAS.

31317　TRUELOVE, NURSE, pseudonym.
NURSE TRUELOVE'S CHRISTMAS BOX. THE THIRD WORCESTER EDITION.

Printed at Worcester, Massachusetts, by Thomas, Son & Thomas. MDCCXCVI. pp. (2), (2), 4–29, (1), frontispiece. 32mo.　　　AAS.

31318　TRUMBULL, BENJAMIN　　　　　　　　　　1735–1820
PROPOSALS FOR PUBLISHING BY SUBSCRIPTION. A COMPLETE HISTORY OF CONNECTICUT. FROM THE TIME OF THE EMIGRATION OF ITS FIRST PLANTERS FROM ENGLAND, IN 1630 TO 1712. BY BENJAMIN TRUMBULL, A. M.

Hartford : Printed by Hudson & Goodwin. April, 1796. Broadside. nar. fol.

31319　TUCKER, ST. GEORGE　　　　　　　　　　1752–1827
A DISSERTATION ON SLAVERY: WITH A PROPOSAL FOR THE GRADUAL ABOLITION OF IT, IN THE STATE OF VIRGINIA. BY ST. GEORGE TUCKER, PROFESSOR OF LAW IN THE UNIVERSITY OF WILLIAM AND MARY, AND ONE OF THE JUDGES OF THE GENERAL COURT, IN VIRGINIA. [Four lines from] MONTESQUIEU.

Philadelphia: Printed for Mathew Carey, No. 118, Market-street, 1796. pp. (2), (2), (2), (9)–106. 8vo.　　AAS. BA. BM. HC. JCB. LOC. MHS. NYPL.

156th Pennsylvania District Copyright, issued to Mathew Carey, as Proprietor, 30 September, 1796. Reprinted, in an edition of one hundred copies, by John Carter Brown, for private circulation, in New York in 1861.

31320

TUCKER, St. George, continued.
—— The Probationary Odes of Jonathan Pindar, esq. a cousin of Peter's, and candidate for the post of poet laureate to the C. U. S. In two parts. [Two lines of Latin from] Hor.

Philadelphia: Printed for Benj. Franklin Bache. M,DCC,XCVI. *[Copyright secured.]* pp. 103. 12mo.　　　AAS. BU. HC. LCP. LOC. MHS. NYPL.

Second title: The Probationary Odes of Jonathan Pindar, esq. a cousin of Peter's, and late poet laureat elect to the C. U. S. Part second. With notes, critical and explanatory, by Christopher Clearsight, esq. [One line of Latin from] Hor. pp. (2), (49)–103.

The address to the author of the Notes, in part second, is signed Timothy Touchpenny. The first part was printed in Freneau's "National Gazette", in June, July and August, 1793, and has sometimes been attributed to Philip Freneau. 148th Pennsylvania District Copyright issued to Benjamin Franklin Bache. as Proprietor, 1 September, 1796.

31321

TURNBULL, Robert James　　　　　　　　　1775–1833
A Visit to the Philadelphia Prison; being an accurate and particular account of the wise and humane administration adopted in every part of that building; containing also an account of the gradual reformation, and present improved state, of the penal laws of Pennsylvania: with observations on the impolicy and injustice of capital punishments. In a letter to a friend. By Robert J. Turnbull. [Three lines from] Rights of Man.

Philadelphia: Printed by Budd & Bartram, No. 58, North Second Street. M,DCC,XCVI. pp. (iv), 108, folded table. 8vo.
　　　　　　　　　　　　BA. BM. LCP. LOC. NYHS. NYPL. RIHS.

Reprinted from the Charleston Daily Gazette, February, 1796. Reprinted in London, in 1797. 147th Pennsylvania District Copyright, issued to Robert J. Turnbull, as Author, 31 August, 1796.

31322

TURNER, Richard junior　　　　　　　　　1753–1788
An Abridgment of the Arts and Sciences: being a short, but comprehensive system, of useful and polite learning. Divided into lessons. Adapted to the use of schools and academies. By R. Turner, jun. of Magdalen-Hall, Oxford.

New-London: Printed and sold by James Springer [Beach Street.] 1796. pp. 167, (1). 24mo.　　　　　　　　AAS. CHS.

31323

TURNER, Robert
Botanoaotia, the British and American physician; or, the nature and virtues of English and American plants. By Robert Turner, botanolog. stud.
Hartford: Printed? for Nathaniel Patten. 1796.

Proposals for printing by subscription, as soon as five hundred subscribers are obtained, in a volume of near 400 pages, were made by Nathaniel Patten, July 19, 1796.

31324

TWAMLEY, Josiah
Dairying exemplified or the business of cheese-making: laid down from approved rules, collected from the most experienced dairy-women of several counties. Digested under various heads; from a series of observations during thirty years practice in the cheese trade. By J. Twamley. The first American edition, from the second British, corrected and improved.

Providence (Rhode Island). Printed by and for Carter and Wilkinson, and sold at their Book and Stationary Store, opposite the Market. 1796. pp. 78, (5). 12mo.　　　　　　　AAS. LOC. RIHS.

31325   TWILIGHT, pseudonym.
TWILIGHT'S ORATIONS, OR REVELATIONS OF POLITICS, IN XVII CHAPTERS. THEY ARE SEVERALLY INTRODUCED AND CONCLUDED BY PRAYER. CHAP. I. JESUS CHRIST IS THE POLITICAL KING, AND ONLY LAWFUL HEAD OF GOVERNMENTS IN CHRISTENDOM. PRICE TWELVE AND A HALF CENTS.

Second title: THE REVELATION OF POLITICS, AND NEW MORAL LIBERTY; OR TEMPLE OF JESUS CHRIST, IN THE HISTORIC PAGE OF JEWS AND CHRISTIANS. BY TWILIGHT.
Norfolk: Printed by Willett and O'Connor. [1796.] pp. (2), (35). 12mo.

31326   THE TWO BABES IN THE WOOD: TOGETHER WITH DIVINE SONGS FOR CHILDREN. BY ISAAC WATTS, D. D.
Poughkeepsie: Printed by Nathan Douglas. 1796. 12mo.

31327   TYLER, JOHN   1742–1823
SERMON TO MASONS, NORWICH, JUNE 24, 1796.
Norwich: Printed by John Sterry & Co. 1796. pp. 28. 8vo.

31328   TYTLER, JAMES   1747–1805
PAINE'S SECOND PART OF THE AGE OF REASON ANSWERED. BY JAMES TYTLER, AUTHOR OF THE REMARKS ON PAINE'S FIRST PART OF THE AGE OF REASON. BY A CITIZEN OF THE WORLD, PUBLISHED AT BELFAST IN IRELAND, 1794. [Five lines of Scripture texts.]
Salem: Printed by Thomas C. Cushing, 1796. pp. [107.] 12mo.
                                        AAS. BA. EI. LOC. MHS. NYPL.

31329   UNITED BAPTIST ASSOCIATION.
MINUTES OF THE UNITED BAPTIST ASSOCIATION, FORMERLY CALLED THE KEHUKEE ASSOCIATION, HELD AT PARKER'S MEETING-HOUSE ON MEHERRIN, HERTFORD COUNTY, NORTH CAROLINA, SEPTEMBER 1796. [Colophon:]
Halifax: Printed by Abraham Hodge. [1796.] 4to.   JCB.

31330   UNITED BRETHREN, OR MORAVIANS.
TÄGLICHEN LOOSUNGEN, UND LEHRTEXTE DER BRÜDERGEMEINDE FÜR DAS JAHR 1797.
Lancaster: Gedruckt bey Johann Albrecht & Comp. 1796. 8vo.

31331   UNITED STATES OF AMERICA.
ACTS PASSED AT THE FIRST SESSION OF THE FOURTH CONGRESS OF THE UNITED STATES OF AMERICA: BEGUN AND HELD AT THE CITY OF PHILADELPHIA, IN THE STATE OF PENNSYLVANIA, ON MONDAY, THE SEVENTH OF DECEMBER, ONE THOUSAND SEVEN HUNDRED AND NINETY-FIVE, AND OF THE INDEPENDENCE OF THE UNITED STATES, THE TWENTIETH. PUBLISHED BY AUTHORITY.
Philadelphia: Printed by Francis Childs. MDCCXCVI, pp. 137, (46), (iv).
8vo.   AAS. JCB. MHS.

31332   —— — ACTS PASSED AT THE FIRST SESSION OF THE FOURTH CONGRESS OF THE UNITED STATES OF AMERICA: BEGUN AND HELD AT THE CITY OF PHILADELPHIA, IN THE STATE OF PENNSYLVANIA, ON MONDAY THE SEVENTH OF DECEMBER, ONE THOUSAND SEVEN HUNDRED AND NINETY-FIVE [— 1 JUNE, 1796], AND OF THE INDEPENDENCE OF THE UNITED STATES, THE TWENTIETH.
Richmond: Printed by Augustine Davis, Printer for the Public. M,DCC,-XCVI. pp. [55], [13], (1). fol.   NYPL. VSL.

The Appendix contains, Treaties with Great Britain, Algiers, and certain Indian tribes.

UNITED STATES, continued.

31333 —— AN ACT DIRECTING CERTAIN EXPERIMENTS TO BE MADE TO ASCERTAIN CERTAIN UNIFORM STANDARDS OF WEIGHTS AND MEASURES IN THE UNITED STATES. MAY 19TH, 1796. [Colophon:]
[Philadelphia:] Printed by John Fenno. [1796.] Broadside. fol.

31334 —— — AN ACT DIRECTING CERTAIN EXPERIMENTS TO BE MADE TO ASCERTAIN UNIFORM STANDARDS OF WEIGHTS AND MEASURES FOR THE UNITED STATES.
[Philadelphia:] Printed by John Fenno. [1796.] pp. (8). 8vo. AAS.

31335 —— FOURTH CONGRESS OF THE UNITED STATES: AT THE FIRST SESSION, BEGUN AND HELD AT THE CITY OF PHILADELPHIA, IN THE STATE OF PENNSYLVANIA, ON WEDNESDAY, THE SEVENTH OF DECEMBER, ONE THOUSAND SEVEN HUNDRED, AND NINETY-FIVE. AN ACT FOR LAYING DUTIES ON CARRIAGES FOR THE CONVEYANCE OF PERSONS. APPROVED—MAY THE TWENTY-EIGHTH, 1796. GO. WASHINGTON, PRESIDENT OF THE UNITED STATES.
[Philadelphia: Printed by Francis Childs. 1796.] pp. 8. 4to. JCB.

31336 —— FOURTH CONGRESS OF THE UNITED STATES: AT THE FIRST SESSION, BEGUN AND HELD AT THE CITY OF PHILADELPHIA, IN THE STATE OF PENNSYLVANIA, ON MONDAY, THE SEVENTH OF DECEMBER, ONE THOUSAND SEVEN HUNDRED AND NINETY-FIVE. AN ACT FOR THE RELIEF AND PROTECTION OF AMERICAN SEAMEN. APPROVED, MAY TWENTY-EIGHTH, 1796. GO: WASHINGTON, PRESIDENT OF THE UNITED STATES.
[Philadelphia: Printed by Francis Childs. 1796.] pp. (2). fol.

31337 —— — EXTRACT FROM THE ACT OF CONGRESS, PASSED THE 28TH DAY OF MAY, 1796, ENTITLED "AN ACT FOR THE RELIEF AND PROTECTION OF AMERICAN SEAMEN." SECTION 5-6. [Thirty-five lines.]
[Philadelphia: Printed by Francis Childs. 1796.] Broadside. fol. JCB.

31338 —— — EXTRACT FROM THE ACT OF CONGRESS, PASSED THE 28TH DAY OF MAY, 1796, ENTITLED "AN ACT FOR THE RELIEF AND PROTECTION OF AMERICAN SEAMEN." [Ornament.] SECTION 5-6. [Twenty-nine lines.] A TRUE EXTRACT. [Signed, Jeremiah Olney, collector.]
[Providence: Reprinted by Carter and Wilkinson. 1796.] Broadside. fol. JCB.

31339 —— — DISTRICT OF SALEM AND BEVERLY. EXTRACT FROM AN ACT OF THE CONGRESS OF THE UNITED STATES OF AMERICA, ENTITLED "AN ACT FOR THE RELIEF AND PROTECTION OF AMERICAN SEAMEN."
[Salem: Printed by William Carlton. 1796.] Broadside. EI.

31340 —— EXTRACT FROM THE ACT OF CONGRESS, PASSED THE 28TH DAY OF MAY, 1796, ENTITLED "AN ACT FOR THE RELIEF AND PROTECTION OF AMERICAN SEAMEN."
Baltimore: 1796.

31341 —— FOURTH CONGRESS OF THE UNITED STATES: AT THE FIRST SESSION, BEGUN AND HELD AT THE CITY OF PHILADELPHIA, IN THE STATE OF PENNSYLVANIA, ON MONDAY, THE SEVENTH OF DECEMBER, ONE THOUSAND SEVEN HUNDRED AND NINETY-FIVE. AN ACT IN ADDITION TO AN ACT, INTITULED "AN ACT SUPPLEMENTARY TO THE ACT, INTITULED "AN ACT TO PROVIDE MORE EFFECTUALLY FOR THE COLLECTION OF THE DUTIES ON GOODS, WARES AND MERCHANDIZE IMPORTED INTO THE UNITED STATES, AND ON THE TONNAGE OF SHIPS OR VESSELS." [And another Act.]
[Philadelphia: Printed by Francis Childs. 1796.] pp. (4). fol. JCB.

UNITED STATES, continued.

31342 —— FOURTH CONGRESS OF THE UNITED STATES: AT THE FIRST SESSION, BEGUN AND HELD AT THE CITY OF PHILADELPHIA, IN THE STATE OF PENNSYLVANIA, ON MONDAY, THE SEVENTH OF DECEMBER. ONE THOUSAND SEVEN HUNDRED AND NINETY-FIVE. AN ACT MAKING FURTHER APPROPRIATIONS FOR THE YEAR ONE THOUSAND SEVEN HUNDRED AND NINETY-SIX. [Forty-one lines.] APPROVED —— JUNE THE FIRST 1796. GO. WASHINGTON, PRESIDENT OF THE UNITED STATES. [And four other Acts.]
[Philadelphia: Printed by Francis Childs. 1796.] pp. (4). fol. JCB.

31343 —— FOURTH CONGRESS OF THE UNITED STATES: AT THE FIRST SESSION BEGUN AND HELD AT THE CITY OF PHILADELPHIA IN THE STATE OF PENNSYLVANIA, ON WEDNESDAY THE SEVENTH OF DECEMBER, ONE THOUSAND SEVEN HUNDRED AND NINETY-FIVE. AN ACT MAKING FURTHER PROVISION . . . REVENUE CUTTERS . . . APPROVED—MAY THE TWENTY-SEVENTH, 1796.
[Philadelphia: Printed by Francis Childs. 1796.] pp. (2). fol.

31344 —— AN ACT MAKING A PARTIAL APPROPRIATION FOR THE SUPPORT OF THE MILITARY ESTABLISHMENT FOR THE YEAR 1796. [Colophon:]
[Philadelphia:] Printed by Francis Childs. [1796.] Broadside. fol.

31345 —— AN ACT PROVIDING PASSPORTS FOR THE SHIPS AND VESSELS OF THE UNITED STATES. APPROVED JUNE 1ST, 1796. GO. WASHINGTON.
[Philadelphia: Printed by Francis Childs. 1796.] pp. (2). 4to. JCB.

31346 —— FOURTH CONGRESS OF THE UNITED STATES: AT THE FIRST SESSION, BEGUN AND HELD AT THE CITY OF PHILADELPHIA IN THE STATE OF PENNSYLVANIA, ON WEDNESDAY THE SEVENTH OF DECEMBER, ONE THOUSAND SEVEN HUNDRED, AND NINETY-FIVE. AN ACT RELATIVE TO QUARANTINE.
[Philadelphia: Printed by Francis Childs. 1796.] pp. (3). fol.

31347 —— FOURTH CONGRESS OF THE UNITED STATES: AT THE FIRST SESSION, BEGUN AND HELD AT THE CITY OF PHILADELPHIA IN THE STATE OF PENNSYLVANIA, ON WEDNESDAY THE SEVENTH OF DECEMBER, ONE THOUSAND SEVEN HUNDRED AND NINETY-FIVE. AN ACT TO REGULATE THE TRADE AND INTERCOURSE WITH THE INDIAN TRIBES AND TO PRESERVE PEACE ON THE FRONTIERS. APPROVED—MAY THE NINETEENTH, 1796. GO. WASHINGTON. PRESIDENT OF THE UNITED STATES.
[Philadelphia: Printed by Francis Childs. 1796.] pp. (4). fol.

31348 —— FOURTH CONGRESS OF THE UNITED STATES: AT THE FIRST SESSION, BEGUN AND HELD AT THE CITY OF PHILADELPHIA IN THE STATE OF PENNSYLVANIA, ON WEDNESDAY THE SEVENTH OF DECEMBER, ONE THOUSAND SEVEN HUNDRED AND NINETY-FIVE. AN ACT TO SUSPEND IN PART THE ACT ENTITLED "AN ACT TO ALTER THE ACT ENTITLED "AN ACT FOR LAYING CERTAIN DUTIES ON SNUFF AND REFINED SUGAR. APPROVED MAY THIRTIETH, 1796. GO. WASHINGTON, PRESIDENT OF THE UNITED STATES.
[Philadelphia: Printed by Francis Childs. 1796.] pp. (2). fol.

31349 —— 11TH MARCH, 1796. COMMITTED TO A COMMITTEE OF THE WHOLE HOUSE REPORT . . . A BILL AUTHORIZING A LOAN FOR THE CITY OF WASHINGTON.
[Philadelphia: Printed by Francis Childs. 1796.] pp. (3). fol.

31350 —— 14TH MARCH, 1796. A BILL FOR THE RELIEF AND PROTECTION OF AMERICAN SEAMEN.
[Philadelphia: Printed by Francis Childs. 1796.] pp. (4). fol.

UNITED STATES, continued.

31351 —— DEBATES IN THE HOUSE OF REPRESENTATIVES OF THE UNITED STATES, DURING THE FIRST SESSION OF THE FOURTH CONGRESS. PART I. UPON THE CONSTITUTIONAL POWERS OF THE HOUSE, WITH RESPECT TO TREATIES.
Philadelphia: Printed for Benj. Franklin Bache, by Bioren & Madan. Sold at No. 112, Market-street. 1796. pp. (386). 8vo. AAS. BA. HC. JCB. LOC. NYHS.

31352 —— —— DEBATES IN THE HOUSE OF REPRESENTATIVES OF THE UNITED STATES, DURING THE FIRST SESSION OF THE FOURTH CONGRESS. PART II. UPON THE SUBJECT OF THE BRITISH TREATY.
Philadelphia: Printed for Benj. Franklin Bache, by Bioren & Madan. Sold at No. 112, Market-Street. 1796. pp. (362). 8vo. AAS. BA. HC. LOC. NYHS.
Reprinted in a second edition in Philadelphia, in 1808.

31353 —— DEBATES IN THE HOUSE OF REPRESENTATIVES OF THE UNITED STATES DURING THE FIRST SESSION OF THE FOURTH CONGRESS, UPON THE CONSTITUTIONAL POWERS OF THE HOUSE, WITH RESPECT TO TREATIES, AND UPON THE SUBJECT OF THE BRITISH TREATY.
Philadelphia: Printed for Benj. Franklin Bache, by Bioren & Madan. Sold at No. 112, Market-Street. 1796. pp. (8). 8vo. BA. BPL. BU. JCB. LOC.

31354 —— JOURNAL OF THE HOUSE OF REPRESENTATIVES OF THE UNITED STATES. AT THE FIRST SESSION OF THE FOURTH CONGRESS. ANNO M.DCC.XCV. AND OF THE INDEPENDENCE OF THE UNITED STATES THE TWENTIETH. [7 December, 1795—1 June, 1796.]
Philadelphia: Printed by Francis Childs. M.DCC.XCV. [1796.] pp. 537, (1), (34). 8vo. AAS. BA. BPL. BU. HC. NYPL.

31355 —— JOURNAL OF THE SENATE OF THE UNITED STATES OF AMERICA, BEING THE FIRST SESSION OF THE FOURTH CONGRESS, BEGUN AND HELD AT THE CITY OF PHILADELPHIA, DECEMBER 7TH, 1795, [—1 JUNE, 1796.] AND IN THE TWENTIETH YEAR OF THE SOVEREIGNTY OF THE SAID UNITED STATES.
Philadelphia: Printed by John Fenno. M.DCC.XCV. [1796.] pp. 346, vi, xxi. 8vo. AAS. BA. BPL. BU. HC.

31356 —— THE LAWS OF THE UNITED STATES OF AMERICA. IN THREE VOLUMES. VOL. I. [—II.] PUBLISHED BY AUTHORITY.
Philadelphia: Printed by Richard Folwell, No. 33, Mulberry-Street. 1796. 2 vols. pp. 495; 576. 8vo. JCB. MHS.
The third volume though dated 1796 was not printed before 1797. Contains the Acts passed by the first, second, third, and fourth Congress. Complete sets are frequently found with Childs and Swaine's New York, 1795 edition erroneously substituted for Volume one of Folwell's edition. "This edition published under an order of the Congress of the United States, has many peculiar advantages. . . . There is one copious, luminous Index (in Volume three), compiled by Zephaniah Swift, esq. referring to all the volumes, and comprising in itself a complete Digest of all the Laws of the United States."

31357 —— A LIST OF THE NAMES, AND PLACES OF ABODE, OF THE MEMBERS OF THE SENATE, AND HOUSE OF REPRESENTATIVES, OF THE UNITED STATES; AND THEIR OFFICERS. [Three columns.]
[Philadelphia: Printed by John Fenno. 1796.] Broadside. fol. AAS. BA.

31358 —— MR. BLOUNT'S MOTION 6 APRIL 1796. IN THE COMMITTEE OF THE WHOLE HOUSE ON THE MESSAGE FROM THE PRESIDENT OF THE UNITED STATES OF THE 30TH ULT.
[Philadelphia: Printed by Francis Childs. 1796.] 8vo. BA.

UNITED STATES, continued.

31359   —— Mr. Harper's Motion. 31st December 1795. Committed to a committee of the whole House, on Monday next. Resolved, That the Secretary of the Treasury do lay before this House, as speedily as possible, a tariff of duties payable in the ports of the United States, . . .

[Philadelphia: Printed by Francis Childs—1796.] pp. (2). 8vo. AAS. BA.

31360   —— Mr. Kitchell's Motion. [On Treaties in the House of Representatives.] 1st April 1796, Referred to the committee of the whole House, on Wednesday next, to whom is committed the Message from the President of the United States of the 30th ultimo. Published by order of the House of Representatives.

[Philadelphia: Printed by Francis Childs. 1796.] pp. (4). 8vo. AAS. BA.

31361   —— Mr. Maclay's Motion. [Not "to concur in passing the laws necessary for carrying the said Treaty into effect."] 14th April 1796, Referred to a committee of the whole House, on the state of the Union.

| Philadelphia: Printed by Francis Childs. 1796.] pp. (2). 8vo. AAS. BA.

31362   —— Mr. Samuel Smith's Motion. 4th January, 1796. Resolved, That from and after the   day of   next, it shall not be lawful for any foreign ship or other vessel, to land within the territory of the United States, any goods, wares or merchandize, except such as shall be the produce, growth or manufucture *[sic]* of the nation to which such ship or other vessel may belong.

[Philadelphia: Printed by Francis Childs. 1796.] pp. (2). 8vo. AAS. BA.

31363   —— Mr. Samuel Smith's Motion. 7th May, 1796. Committed to a committee of the whole House, on Monday next. Resolved, That it shall not be lawful to sell within the United States, any vessel or goods captured from a Prince or State, or from the subjects or citizens of a Prince or State with which the United States are at peace . . . Published by order of the House of Representatives.

[Philadelphia: Printed by Francis Childs. 1796.] pp. (2). 8vo.
AAS. BA. NYPL.

31364   —— Proceedings of the House of Representatives of the United States, in the case of Robert Randall and Charles Whitney. 13 January, 1796. Published by order of the House of Representatives.

[Philadelphia: Printed by Francis Childs. 1796.] pp. (32). 8vo.
AAS. BA. JCB.

31365   —— In the House of Representatives of the United States, Monday, the 4th of January, 1796. A Message, in writing, was received from the President of the United States, by mr. Dandridge, his secretary, as followeth: "Gentlemen of the Senate and House of Representatives, A letter from the minister plenipotentiary of the French Republic, received on the 22d of last month, covered an address, dated the 21st of October, 1794, from the Committee of public safety to the Representatives of the United States in Congress; and also informed me, that he was instructed by the Committee, to present to the United States, the colours of France. . . . Go. Washington." United States, January 4th, 1796.

[Philadelphia: Printed by Francis Childs. 1796.] pp. (7). 8vo. AAS. LOC.

UNITED STATES, continued.

31366 —— [MADE THE 11TH DECEMBER, 1795.] THE COMMITTEE APPOINTED ON THE 7TH INSTANT, TO PREPARE AND REPORT SUCH STANDING RULES AND ORDERS OF PROCEEDINGS, AS ARE PROPER TO BE OBSERVED IN THIS HOUSE, REPORT, THAT THE FOLLOWING BE ESTABLISHED AS THE STANDING RULES AND ORDERS OF THE HOUSE OF REPRESENTATIVES OF THE UNITED STATES: . . .
[Philadelphia: Printed by Francis Childs. 1796.] pp. (11). 8vo. AAS.

31367 —— —— [Ornamental line.] STANDING RULES AND ORDERS, OF THE HOUSE OF REPRESENTATIVES OF THE UNITED STATES. [Ornament.] [Colophon:]
[Philadelphia:] Printed by Francis Childs. [1796.] pp. (11). 8vo.

31368 —— [MADE THE 14TH OF DECEMBER, 1795:] REPORT FROM THE COMMITTEE APPOINTED TO PREPARE AND REPORT AN ADDRESS TO THE PRESIDENT OF THE UNITED STATES, IN ANSWER TO HIS SPEECH TO BOTH HOUSES OF CONGRESS.
[Philadelphia:] Printed by F. Childs. [1796.] pp. (4). 8vo. AAS. BA.

31369 —— REPORT OF THE COMMITTEE OF CLAIMS, ON THE PETITION OF BENJAMIN TITCOMB. 22D DECEMBER, 1795, READ, AND CONSIDERATION POSTPONED UNTIL MONDAY NEXT. 29TH DECEMBER, 1795, COMMITTED TO A COMMITTEE OF THE WHOLE HOUSE, ON MONDAY NEXT. PUBLISHED BY ORDER OF THE HOUSE OF REPRESENTATIVES.
[Philadelphia, Printed by Francis Childs. 1796.] pp. (4). 8vo. AAS.

31370 —— [MADE THE 29TH OF DECEMBER, 1795.] REPORT OF THE COMMITTEE, TO WHOM WERE REFERRED THE REPORTS ON THE MEMORIAL OF PARKER, HOPKINS AND MEERS [of Savannah in Georgia.] PUBLISHED BY ORDER OF THE HOUSE OF REPRESENTATIVES.
[Philadelphia: Printed by Francis Childs. 1796.] pp. (4). 8vo. AAS.

31371 —— [MADE THE 4TH OF JANUARY, 1796, AND COMMITTED TO A COMMITTEE OF THE WHOLE HOUSE, TO-MORROW.] REPORT OF THE COMMITTEE OF CLAIMS ON THE PETITION OF JOHN BAPTIST DUMON. PUBLISHED BY ORDER OF THE HOUSE OF REPRESENTATIVES.
[Philadelphia: Printed by Francis Childs. 1796.] pp. (4). 8vo. AAS. BA.

31372 —— [MADE THE 11TH OF JANUARY, 1796, AND COMMITTED TO A COMMITTEE OF THE WHOLE HOUSE, ON WEDNESDAY NEXT.] REPORT OF THE COMMITTEE OF COMMERCE AND MANUFACTURES, ON THE PETITIONS OF JOHN DEVEREUX, WILLIAM AND ARCHIBALD M'NEAL, MOSES MYERS, WILLIAM SMITH AND JOSHUA CARTER, AND WRIGHT WHITE. PUBLISHED BY ORDER OF THE HOUSE OF REPRESENTATIVES.
[Philadelphia: Printed by Francis Childs. 1796.] pp. (6). 8vo. AAS. BA.

31373 —— [MADE THE 13TH OF JANUARY, 1796.] REPORT OF THE COMMITTEE OF ELECTIONS TO WHOM WAS RECOMMITTED THEIR REPORT, ON THE MEMORIAL OF JOHN RICHARDS.
[Philadelphia: Printed by Francis Childs. 1796.] pp. (6). 8vo. AAS.

31374 —— [MADE THE 26TH OF JANUARY, 1796, AND COMMITTED TO A COMMITTEE OF THE WHOLE HOUSE, ON MONDAY NEXT.] REPORT OF THE COMMITTEE OF CLAIMS, ON THE PETITION OF SILAS CLARK. PUBLISHED BY THE HOUSE OF REPRESENTATIVES.
[Philadelphia: Printed by Francis Childs. 1796.] pp. (4). 8vo. AAS. BA.

31375 —— [MADE THE 26TH OF JANUARY, 1796.] REPORT OF THE COMMITTEE OF CLAIMS ON THE PETITION OF JOHN GRIFFIN. PUBLISHED BY ORDER OF THE HOUSE OF REPRESENTATIVES.
[Philadelphia: Printed by Francis Childs. 1796.] pp. (4). 8vo. AAS. BA.

UNITED STATES, continued.

31376 —— [MADE THE 26TH OF JANUARY, 1796, AND COMMITTED TO A COMMITTEE OF THE WHOLE HOUSE ON MONDAY NEXT.] REPORT OF THE COMMITTEE OF CLAIMS, ON A MOTION OF THE 11TH INSTANT, RESPECTING OFFICERS AND SOLDIERS OF THE LATE ARMY AND NAVY OF THE UNITED STATES, ENTITLED TO ARREARAGES OF PAY, OR OTHER EMOLUMENTS. PUBLISHED BY ORDER OF THE HOUSE OF REPRESENTATIVES.

[Philadelphia: Printed by Francis Childs. 1796.] pp. (6). 8vo.   AAS.

31377 —— REPORT OF THE COMMITTEE OF ELECTIONS, TO WHOM WAS REFERRED THE PETITION OF MATTHEW LYON, OF THE STATE OF VERMONT, COMPLAINING OF AN UNDUE ELECTION AND RETURN OF ISRAEL SMITH, TO SERVE AS A MEMBER·OF THE HOUSE OF REPRESENTATIVES, FOR THE SAID STATE, IN THE FOURTH CONGRESS OF THE UNITED STATES, 27TH JANUARY 1796, READ, AND WEDNESDAY NEXT ASSIGNED FOR CONSIDERATION. 4TH FEBRUARY 1796, FARTHER CONSIDERATION POSTPONED UNTIL MONDAY NEXT. PUBLISHED BY ORDER OF THE HOUSE OF REPRESENTATIVES.

[Philadelphia: Printed by Francis Childs. 1796.] pp. (4). 8vo.   AAS. BA.

31378 —— [MADE THE 29TH OF JANUARY, 1796, AND COMMITTED TO A COMMITTEE OF THE WHOLE HOUSE, ON WEDNESDAY NEXT.] REPORT OF THE COMMITTEE, APPOINTED TO ENQUIRE INTO THE ACTUAL STATE OF THE NAVAL EQUIPMENT ORDERED BY A FORMER LAW OF THE UNITED STATES, AND TO REPORT WHETHER ANY AND WHAT FURTHER PROVISION IS NECESSARY TO BE MADE ON THIS SUBJECT. PUBLISHED BY ORDER OF THE HOUSE OF REPRESENTATIVES.

[Philadelphia: Printed by Francis Childs. 1796.] pp. (5). 8vo.   AAS. BA.

31379 —— [MADE THE 4TH OF FEBRUARY, 1796, AND COMMITTED TO A COMMITTEE OF THE WHOLE HOUSE, ON MONDAY NEXT.] REPORT OF THE COMMITTEE OF WAYS AND MEANS, TO WHOM IT WAS REFERRED TO REPORT, WHETHER FURTHER MEASURES ARE NECESSARY TO REINFORCE THE EXISTING PROVISIONS FOR THE PUBLIC DEBT. PUBLISHED BY ORDER OF THE HOUSE OF REPRESENTATIVES.

[Philadelphia: Printed by Francis Childs. 1796.] pp. (4). 8vo.   AAS. BA.

31380 —— [MADE THE 8TH OF FEBRUARY, 1796, AND COMMITTED TO A COMMITTEE OF THE WHOLE HOUSE, TO-MORROW.] REPORT OF THE COMMITTEE OF COMMERCE AND MANUFACTURES, ON THE PETITIONS OF ISRAEL LORING, — SUNDRY MERCHANTS OF PHILADELPHIA AND NEW YORK, — JOSE ROIZ SILVA, — NEHEMIAH SOMES AND JAMES STRANGE. PUBLISHED BY ORDER OF THE HOUSE OF REPRESENTATIVES.

[Philadelphia: Printed by Francis Childs. 1796.] pp. (6). 8vo.   AAS. BA.

31381 —— 23D FEBRUARY, 1796. READ AND COMMITTED TO A COMMITTEE OF THE WHOLE HOUSE, ON THURSDAY NEXT. REPORT OF THE COMMITTEE OF WAYS AND MEANS, ON THE PROVISIONS REQUISITE FOR IMPROVING THE INTERNAL REVENUES OF THE UNITED STATES; AND FOR MORE EFFECTUALLY SECURING THE COLLECTION OF THE SAME. PUBLISHED BY ORDER OF THE HOUSE OF REPRESENTATIVES.

[Philadelphia: Printed by Francis Childs. 1796.] pp. (4). 8vo.   AAS. BA.

31382 —— 25TH FEBRUARY, 1796. REFERRED TO A COMMITTEE OF THE WHOLE HOUSE, ON MONDAY NEXT. REPORT ON THE LEGISLATIVE PROVISION NECESSARY FOR THE RELIEF OF AMERICAN SEAMEN IMPRESSED INTO THE SERVICE OF FOREIGN POWERS; AND ON A MODE OF FURNISHING AMERICAN SEAMEN WITH EVIDENCE OF THEIR CITIZENSHIP. PUBLISHED BY ORDER OF THE HOUSE OF REPRESENTATIVES.

[Philadelphia: Printed by Francis Childs. 1796.] pp. (4). 8vo.   AAS. BA.

UNITED STATES, continued.

31383 —— REPORT OF THE COMMITTEE TO WHOM WAS REFERRED THE MESSAGE FROM THE PRESIDENT OF THE UNITED STATES, OF THE SECOND ULTIMO, ACCOMPANYING THE COPY OF A LETTER FROM THE GOVERNOR OF THE TERRITORY SOUTH OF THE RIVER OHIO, TO THE SECRETARY AT WAR, DATED THE NINETEENTH OF DECEMBER LAST. 10TH MARCH, 1796, COMMITTED TO A COMMITTEE OF THE WHOLE HOUSE, ON MONDAY NEXT. PUBLISHED BY ORDER OF THE HOUSE OF REPRESENTATIVES.
[Philadelphia: Printed by Francis Childs. 1796.] pp. (6). 8vo.
AAS. BA. JCB.

31384 —— REPORT OF THE COMMITTEE OF ELECTIONS, TO WHOM WERE REFERRED THE MEMORIALS AND PETITIONS OF SUNDRY CITIZENS AND ELECTORS OF THE SECOND MIDDLE DISTRICT OF THE STATE OF MASSACHUSETTS, COMPLAINING OF AN UNDUE ELECTION AND RETURN OF JOSEPH BRADLEY VARNUM, TO SERVE AS A MEMBER OF THIS HOUSE, FOR THE SAID STATE. 15TH MARCH, 1796, COMMITTED TO A COMMITTEE OF THE WHOLE HOUSE, TO-MORROW. PUBLISHED BY ORDER OF THE HOUSE OF REPRESENTATIVES.
[Philadelphia: Printed by Francis Childs. 1796.] pp.(4). 8vo.   AAS. BA.

31385 —— REPORT OF THE COMMITTEE OF WAYS AND MEANS, ON THE STATE OF THE RECEIPTS AND EXPENDITURES OF THE UNITED STATES, AND THE EXISTING AND APPROACHING EXIGENCIES FOR WHICH PROVISION WILL BE REQUISITE. 17TH MARCH, 1796. COMMITTED TO A COMMITTEE OF THE WHOLE HOUSE, ON MONDAY SE'NNIGHT. PUBLISHED BY ORDER OF THE HOUSE OF REPRESENTATIVES.
[Philadelphia: Printed by Francis Childs. 1796.] pp. (11). 8vo.   AAS. BA.

31386 —— REPORT OF THE COMMITTEE APPOINTED TO ENQUIRE WHETHER ANY, AND WHAT ALTERATIONS OUGHT TO BE MADE IN THE PRESENT MILITARY ESTABLISHMENT OF THE UNITED STATES. 25TH MARCH 1796, COMMITTED TO A COMMITTEE OF THE WHOLE HOUSE, ON MONDAY NEXT. PUBLISHED BY ORDER OF THE HOUSE OF REPRESENTATIVES.
[Philadelphia: Printed by Francis Childs. 1796.] pp. (4). 8vo.   AAS. BA.

31387 —— REPORT OF THE COMMITTEE APPOINTED TO ENQUIRE IF ANY, AND WHAT ALTERATIONS ARE NECESSARY TO BE MADE IN THE ACT TO ESTABLISH THE POST-OFFICE AND POST-ROADS WITHIN THE UNITED STATES. 4TH APRIL, 1796, COMMITTED TO A COMMITTEE OF THE WHOLE HOUSE, ON MONDAY NEXT. PUBLISHED BY ORDER OF THE HOUSE OF REPRESENTATIVES.
[Philadelphia: Printed by Francis Childs. 1796.] pp.(4). 8vo.   AAS. BA.

31388 —— *Heading:* REPORT OF THE COMMITTEE TO WHOM WAS REFERRED THE MESSAGE OF THE PRESIDENT OF THE UNITED STATES OF THE 8TH OF APRIL, 1796, RELATIVE TO THE TERRITORY OF THE UNITED STATES, SOUTH WEST OF THE RIVER OHIO.
[Philadelphia: Printed by Francis Childs. 1796.] pp.(5). 8vo.   AAS. JCB.

31389 —— *Heading:* 12TH APRIL 1796, COMMITTED TO A COMMITTEE OF THE WHOLE HOUSE, ON TUESDAY NEXT. REPORT FROM THE COMMITTEE, TO WHOM WAS REFERRED THE MESSAGE FROM THE PRESIDENT OF THE UNITED STATES, OF THE 8TH INSTANT, RELATIVE TO THE TERRITORY OF THE UNITED STATES SOUTH OF THE RIVER OHIO; TOGETHER WITH SUNDRY DOCUMENTS ACCOMPANYING THE SAME. . . . RESOLVED, THAT . . . THE STATE OF TENNESSEE IS HEREBY DECLARED TO BE ONE OF THE SIXTEEN UNITED STATES OF AMERICA.
[Philadelphia: Printed by Francis Childs. 1796.] pp. (2). 8vo.   AAS. BA.

31390 —— REPORT OF THE COMMITTEE TO WHOM WERE REFERRED SO MUCH OF THE REPORT OF THE SECRETARY OF STATE, MADE THE 13TH OF JULY, 1790; AND THE MESSAGE OF THE PRESIDENT OF THE UNITED STATES, OF THE 8TH OF JANUARY, 1795, AS RELATES TO WEIGHTS AND MEASURES. 12TH APRIL, 1796. COMMITTED TO A COMMITTEE OF THE WHOLE HOUSE, ON MONDAY NEXT. PUBLISHED BY ORDER OF THE HOUSE OF REPRESENTATIVES.
[Philadelphia: Printed by Francis Childs. 1796.] pp.(7). 8vo.   AAS. BA.

UNITED STATES, continued.

31391   —— REPORT OF THE COMMITTEE APPOINTED TO ENQUIRE INTO THE TRUTH OF THE INFORMATION, THAT A SON OF GENERAL LA FAYETTE, IS NOW WITHIN THE UNITED STATES, AND ALSO, WHAT MEASURES IT WILL BE PROPER TO TAKE, IF THE SAME BE TRUE, TO EVINCE THE GRATEFUL SENSE ENTERTAINED BY THIS COUNTRY, FOR THE SERVICES OF HIS FATHER. 26TH APRIL, 1796. ORDERED TO LIE ON THE TABLE. PUBLISHED BY ORDER OF THE HOUSE OF REPRESENTATIVES.

[Philadelphia : Printed by Francis Childs. 1796.] pp. (4). 8vo.   AAS. BA.

31392   —— REPORT OF THE COMMITTEE OF WAYS AND MEANS, TO WHOM IT WAS REFERRED TO ENQUIRE WHETHER THE BANK OF THE UNITED STATES ARE WILLING TO CONTINUE THE LOANS MADE BY THEM TO GOVERNMENT, IN ANTICIPATION OF THE PUBLIC REVENUE, OR ANY PART THEREOF, BY NEW LOANS, ON TERMS SIMILAR TO THOSE ON WHICH THE SAID ANTICIPATIONS ARE OBTAINED. 3D MAY, 1796. REFERRED TO THE COMMITTEE OF THE WHOLE HOUSE, ON THE BILL MAKING PROVISION FOR THE PAYMENT OF CERTAIN DEBTS OF THE UNITED STATES. PUBLISHED BY ORDER OF THE HOUSE OF REPRESENTATIVES.

[Philadelphia : Printed by Francis Childs. 1796.] pp. (4). 8vo.   AAS. BA.

31393   —— REPORT OF THE COMMITTEE OF CLAIMS, ON THE MEMORIAL OF SAMUEL G. FOWLER AND CHRISTOPHER FOWLER, ADMINISTRATORS OF SAMUEL FOWLER, DECEASED. 7TH MAY, 1796. COMMITTED TO A COMMITTEE OF THE WHOLE HOUSE, ON MONDAY NEXT. PUBLISHED BY ORDER OF THE HOUSE OF REPRESENTATIVES.

[Philadelphia : Printed by Francis Childs. 1796.] pp. (4). 8vo.   AAS. BA.

31394   —— REPORT OF THE COMMITTEE APPOINTED TO TAKE INTO CONSIDERATION THE STATE OF THE FORTIFICATION OF OUR HARBOURS; THE MEASURES WHICH HAVE BEEN PURSED [*sic*] FOR OBTAINING PROPER SITES FOR ARSENALS, AND FOR REPLENISHING OUR MAGAZINES WITH MILITARY STORES; AND TO REPORT WHAT FURTHER MEASURES ARE NECESSARY RESPECTING THE SAME. 9TH MAY, 1796. COMMITTED TO THE COMMITTEE OF THE WHOLE HOUSE, TO-MORROW. PUBLISHED BY ORDER OF THE HOUSE OF REPRESENTATIVES.

[Philadelphia : Printed by Francis Childs. 1796.] pp. (4). 8vo.   AAS. BA.

31395   —— REPORT OF THE COMMITTEE ON THE PETITION OF SUNDRY INHABITANTS OF THE COUNTIES OF ST. CLAIR & RANDOLPH, IN THE TERRITORY NORTH-WEST OF THE RIVER OHIO. 12TH MAY 1796, ORDERED TO LIE ON THE TABLE. 13TH MAY 1796, COMMITTED TO A COMMITTEE OF THE WHOLE HOUSE, ON MONDAY NEXT.

[Philadelphia : Printed by Francis Childs. 1796.] pp. [11.] 8vo.

                     AAS. BA. JCB.

Petition for repeal of the anti-slavery clause in the Ordinance of 1787.

31396   —— REPORT OF THE COMMITTEE OF CLAIMS, ON THE PETITION OF CATHERINE GREENE, WIDOW OF THE LATE MAJOR-GENERAL GREENE, DECEASED, 13TH MAY, 1796. COMMITTED TO A COMMITTEE OF THE WHOLE HOUSE ON MONDAY NEXT. PUBLISHED BY ORDER OF THE HOUSE OF REPRESENTATIVES.

[Philadelphia : Printed by Francis Childs. 1796.] pp. (6). 8vo.   AAS. BA.

31397   —— REPORT OF THE COMMITTEE OF ELECTIONS, TO WHOM WAS RECOMMITTED THE PETITION OF MATHEW [*sic*] LYON, OF THE STATE OF VERMONT, COMPLAINING OF AN UNDUE ELECTION AND RETURN OF ISRAEL SMITH, TO SERVE AS A MEMBER OF THE HOUSE OF REPRESENTATIVES FOR THE SAID STATE, IN THE FOURTH CONGRESS OF THE UNITED STATES. 13TH MAY, 1796. ORDERED TO LIE ON THE TABLE.

[Philadelphia : Printed by Francis Childs. 1796.] pp. (4). 8vo.   AAS.

UNITED STATES, continued.

31398 —— REPORT OF THE COMMITTEE OF CLAIMS, TO WHOM WAS COMMITTED THE BILL SENT FROM THE SENATE, INTITULED, "AN ACT, MAKING AN EXTRA ALLOWANCE TO CERTAIN CLERKS IN THE PUBLIC OFFICES, AND TO THE WIDOWS OF CERTAIN DECEASED CLERKS." 17TH MAY, 1796. COMMITTED TO A COMMITTEE OF THE WHOLE HOUSE, TO-MORROW.

[Philadelphia: Printed by Francis Childs. 1796.] pp. [4.] 8vo. AAS. BA.

31399 —— REPORT OF THE COMMITTEE OF CLAIMS, ON THE PETITION OF ALEXANDER FOWLER. 17TH MAY, 1796. COMMITTED TO A COMMITTEE OF THE WHOLE HOUSE, TO-MORROW.

[Philadelphia: Printed by Francis Childs. 1796.] pp. [5.] 8vo. AAS.

31400 —— REPORT OF THE COMMITTEE OF WAYS AND MEANS, RELATIVE TO APPROPRIATIONS FOR THE MILITARY AND NAVAL ESTABLISHMENTS, AND FOR THE PAYMENT OF MILITARY PENSIONS. 18TH MAY, 1796. COMMITTED TO A COMMITTEE OF THE WHOLE HOUSE, ON FRIDAY NEXT. PUBLISHED BY ORDER OF THE HOUSE OF REPRESENTATIVES.

[Philadelphia: Printed by Francis Childs. 1796.] pp. (12). 8vo. AAS. BA.

31401 —— REPORT OF THE COMMITTEE OF CLAIMS, ON THE PETITION OF OLIVER POLLOCK, 26TH MAY, 1796. COMMITTED TO A COMMITTEE OF THE WHOLE HOUSE, TO-MORROW. PUBLISHED BY ORDER OF THE HOUSE OF REPRESENTATIVES.

[Philadelphia: Printed by Francis Childs. 1796.] pp. (4). 8vo. AAS.

31402 —— A COLLECTION OF THE SPEECHES OF THE PRESIDENT OF THE UNITED STATES TO BOTH HOUSES OF CONGRESS, AT THE OPENING OF EVERY SESSION, WITH THEIR ANSWERS. ALSO THE ADDRESSES TO THE PRESIDENT, WITH HIS ANSWERS, FROM THE TIME OF HIS ELECTION: WITH AN APPENDIX, CONTAINING THE CIRCULAR LETTER OF GENERAL WASHINGTON TO THE GOVERNORS OF THE SEVERAL STATES, AND HIS FAREWELL ORDERS TO THE ARMIES OF AMERICA, AND THE ANSWER. DEDICATED TO THE CITIZENS OF THE UNITED STATES OF AMERICA. [By Solomon Cotton, junior.] PUBLISHED ACCORDING TO ACT OF CONGRESS.

Printed at Boston, by Manning and Loring, for Solomon Cotton, jun. Bookseller and Stationer, sold by him, at his Bookstore, No. 51, *Marlborough-Street. July,* 1796. pp. 282, (1). 12mo. AAS. BA. HC. LOC. MHS. NYPL.

Contains a three-page list of Subscribers' names. 102d Massachusetts District Copyright, issued to Solomon Cotton, junior, as Proprietor, 11 July, 1796. The Boston Athenæum also has a variant edition of this year, "with a correction."

31403 —— THE CONSTITUTIONS OF THE UNITED STATES, ACCORDING TO THE LATEST AMENDMENTS: TO WHICH ARE ANNEXED, THE DECLARATION OF INDEPENDENCE; AND THE FEDERAL CONSTITUTION; WITH THE AMENDMENTS THERETO. THIS EDITION CONTAINS THE LATE CONSTITUTIONS OF NEW-HAMPSHIRE, KENTUCKY AND TENNESSEE, NOT IN ANY FORMER ONE.

Philadelphia: Printed by E. Oswald, for W. Woodhouse, Bookseller, No. 6, *South Front-Street.* M,DCC,XCVI. pp. 250. 12mo.

AAS. BM. HC. JCB. LOC. MdHS. NYPL.

31404 —— —— THE DECLARATION OF INDEPENDENCE AND CONSTITUTION OF THE UNITED STATES; TO WHICH IS PREFIXED THE CONSTITUTION OF THE STATE OF NEW-YORK.

New-York: Printed by John Bull, Editor of the Weekly Magazine, and sold by the Booksellers in general. 1796. pp. 37. 8vo. AAS.

UNITED STATES, continued.

31405 —— —— FEDERAL CONSTITUTION; WITH THE AMENDMENTS (WITH CONSTITUTIONS OF VERMONT, GEORGIA AND KENTUCKY: WITH THE REGULATIONS FOR THE GOVERNMENT OF THE TERRITORY NORTH-WEST OF THE RIVER OHIO: ALSO THE AMENDMENTS TO THE CONSTITUTION OF MARYLAND NOT IN ANY FORMER EDITION. *Philadelphia:* 1796.

31406 —— MESSAGE FROM THE PRESIDENT OF THE UNITED STATES, ACCOMPANYING A MEMORIAL OF THE COMMISSIONERS APPOINTED BY VIRTUE OF THE ACT FOR ESTABLISHING THE TEMPORARY AND PERMANENT SEAT OF THE GOVERNMENT OF THE UNITED STATES. 8TH JANUARY, 1796, REFERRED TO—MR. JEREMIAH SMITH, MR. THATCHER, MR. FINDLEY, MR. BRENT, AND MR. TATOM. 25TH JANUARY, 1796, REPORT MADE, AND COMMITTED TO A COMMITTEE OF THE WHOLE HOUSE, ON MONDAY NEXT. PUBLISHED BY ORDER OF THE HOUSE OF REPRESENTATIVES.
[Philadelphia: Printed by Francis Childs. 1796.] pp. (13). 8vo.   AAS. BA.

31407 —— [RECEIVED THE 13TH OF JANUARY, 1796.] MESSAGE FROM THE PRESIDENT OF THE UNITED STATES, ACCOMPANYING AN OFFICIAL STATEMENT OF THE EXPENDITURE TO THE END OF THE YEAR 1795, FROM THE SUMS HERETOFORE GRANTED TO DEFRAY THE CONTINGENT CHARGES OF THE GOVERNMENT. PUBLISHED BY ORDER OF THE HOUSE OF REPRESENTATIVES.
[Philadelphia: Printed by Francis Childs. 1796.] p. (11). 8vo.   AAS. BA.

31408 —— MESSAGE FROM THE PRESIDENT OF THE UNITED STATES, ACCOMPANYING A COPY OF THE TREATY CONCLUDED BETWEEN THE UNITED STATES AND THE DEY AND REGENCY OF ALGIERS. 8TH MARCH, 1796, READ AND ORDERED TO LIE ON THE TABLE. 9TH MARCH, 1796, COMMITTED TO THE COMMITTEE OF THE WHOLE HOUSE, ON THE STATE OF THE UNION. PUBLISHED BY ORDER OF THE HOUSE OF REPRESENTATIVES.
[Philadelphia: Printed by Francis Childs. 1796.] pp. (11). 8vo.   AAS.

31409 —— *Heading:* GEORGE WASHINGTON, PRESIDENT OF THE UNITED STATES OF AMERICA. TO ALL TO WHOM THESE PRESENTS SHALL COME, —— GREETING: WHEREAS A TREATY OF PEACE AND AMITY HAS BEEN CONCLUDED IN THE MANNER HEREINAFTER-MENTIONED BY THE PLENIPOTENTIARY OF THE UNITED STATES OF AMERICA, AND THE DEY AND REGENCY OF ALGIERS; WHICH TREATY, WRITTEN IN THE ARABIC LANGUAGE, BEING TRANSLATED INTO THE LANGUAGE OF THE UNITED STATES IS IN THE WORDS FOLLOWING, TO WIT: A TREATY OF PEACE AND AMITY CONCLUDED THIS PRESENT DAY I —— IMA ARTASI, THE TWENTY-FIRST OF THE LUNA SAFER, YEAR OF THE HEGIRA 1210, CORRESPONDING WITH SATURDAY THE FIFTH OF SEPTEMBER, ONE THOUSAND SEVEN HUNDRED AND NINETY-FIVE, BETWEEN HASSAN BASHAW, DEY OF ALGIERS, HIS DIVAN AND SUBJECTS, AND GEORGE WASHINGTON, PRESIDENT OF THE UNITED STATES OF NORTH AMERICA, AND THE CITIZENS OF THE SAID UNITED STATES, . . . [Text of Treaty.] IN TESTIMONY WHEREOF, I HAVE CAUSED THE SEAL OF THE UNITED STATES OF AMERICA TO BE AFFIXED TO THESE PRESENTS, AND SIGNED THE SAME WITH MY HAND. DONE AT THE CITY OF PHILADELPHIA, THE SEVENTH DAY OF MARCH, ONE THOUSAND SEVEN HUNDRED AND NINETY-SIX, AND OF THE INDEPENDENCE OF THE UNITED STATES OF AMERICA, THE TWENTIETH. GO: WASHINGTON. BY THE PRESIDENT, TIMOTHY PICKERING, SECRETARY OF STATE.
[Philadelphia: Printed by Francis Childs. 1796.] pp. (8). 8vo.   AAS.

31410 —— —— TREATY OF PEACE AND AMITY, CONCLUDED SEPTEMBER 5, 1795, BETWEEN HASSAN BASHAW, DEY OF ALGIERS, HIS DIVAN AND SUBJECTS; AND GEORGE WASHINGTON, PRESIDENT OF THE UNITED STATES OF NORTH AMERICA, AND THE CITIZENS OF THE SAID UNITED STATES. WITH THE PRESIDENT'S PROCLAMATION, ANNOUNCING ITS RATIFICATION, AS PUBLISHED IN THE PHILADELPHIA GAZETTE, MARCH 9, 1796.
[Philadelphia:] *Printed by Ormrod & Conrad, No. 41, Chesnut-street.* 1796. pp. (12). 12mo.   LOC.

UNITED STATES, continued.

31411 —— MESSAGE FROM THE PRESIDENT OF THE UNITED STATES, ACCOMPANYING A COPY OF THE TREATY OF AMITY, COMMERCE AND NAVIGATION, BETWEEN THE UNITED STATES OF AMERICA AND GREAT-BRITAIN. 1ST MARCH, 1796. READ, AND ORDERED TO BE COMMITTED TO THE COMMITTEE OF THE WHOLE HOUSE ON THE STATE OF THE UNION.
[Philadelphia: Printed by Francis Childs. 1796.] pp. (32). 8vo.
AAS. JCB. LOC.

31412 —— — *Heading:* BY GEORGE WASHINGTON, PRESIDENT OF THE UNITED STATES OF AMERICA; A PROCLAMATION. WHEREAS A· TREATY OF AMITY, COMMERCE AND NAVIGATION, BETWEEN THE UNITED STATES OF AMERICA AND HIS BRITANNIC MAJESTY, WAS CONCLUDED AND SIGNED AT LONDON, ON THE NINETEENTH DAY OF NOVEMBER, ONE THOUSAND· SEVEN HUNDRED AND NINETY-FOUR, BY THE PLENI- POTENTIARIES OF THE UNITED STATES AND OF HIS BRITANNIC MAJESTY, DULY AND RESPECTIVELY AUTHORIZED FOR THAT PURPOSE. . . . [Text of Treaty with additional article.] IN TESTIMONY WHEREOF, I HAVE CAUSED THE SEAL OF THE UNITED STATES OF AMERICA, TO BE AFFIXED TO THESE PRESENTS, AND SIGNED THE SAME WITH MY HAND. DONE AT THE CITY OF PHILADELPHIA THE 29TH DAY OF FEBRUARY ONE THOUSAND SEVEN HUNDRED AND NINETY-SIX, AND OF THE IN- DEPENDENCE OF THE UNITED STATES OF AMERICA, THE TWENTIETH. GO: WASH- INGTON. BY THE PRESIDENT TIMOTHY PICKERING, SECRETARY OF STATE.
[Philadelphia: Printed by Francis Childs. 1796.] pp. (30). 8vo.
AAS. BA. MHS.

31413 —— — THE TREATY OF COMMERCE AND NAVIGATION BETWEEN AMERICA AND GREAT BRITAIN. WITH THE OBSERVATIONS OF TWO RESPECTABLE WRITERS, FOR AND AGAINST THE INSTRUMENT.
Boston: Printed by John Russell, Quaker Lane. 1796.

31414 —— — TREATY OF AMITY, COMMERCE & NAVIGATION, BETWEEN HIS BRITANNIC MAJESTY AND THE UNITED STATES OF AMERICA, WITH THE PRESIDENT'S PROCLA- MATION, ANNOUNCING ITS RATIFICATION, AS PUBLISHED IN THE PHILADELPHIA GAZETTE, ON TUESDAY THE 1ST OF MARCH, 1796.
Philadelphia: Printed by Ormrod & Conrad, No. 41, Chesnut-street. 1796. pp. (45). 12mo.
LOC.

31415 —— — THE PRESIDENT'S MESSAGE. ON THE TREATY PAPERS. [Two columns.] GEO. WASHINGTON. UNITED STATES, MARCH 30, 1796. [Colophon:]
[Boston:] Done by A. Martin, Orrery Press. [1796.] Broadside, fol.
Printed on silk.
AAS. MHS.

31416 —— — THE PRESIDENT'S MESSAGE. ON THE TREATY PAPERS. CENTINEL-OFFICE, APRIL 7, 1796. A GENTLEMAN THIS INSTANT ARRIVED FROM NEW-YORK, HAS FAVORED US WITH THE FOLLOWING HIGHLY INTERESTING AND MAGNANIMOUS COMMUNICATION OF THE PRESIDENT OF THE UNITED STATES, TO THE HOUSE OF REPRESENTATIVES, ON WEDNESDAY THE 30TH ULT. [Two columns.] GEO. WASH- INGTON. UNITED STATES, MARCH 30, 1796. ☞ THIS MESSAGE HAS BEEN COM- MITTED TO A COMMITTEE OF THE WHOLE; FOR YESTERDAY.
[Boston: Printed by Benjamin Russell. 1796.] Broadside. fol. AAS. MHS.

31417 —— — MESSAGE FROM THE PRESIDENT OF THE UNITED STATES, ASSIGNING THE REASONS WHICH FORBID HIS COMPLIANCE WITH THE RESOLUTION OF THE TWENTY- FOURTH INSTANT, REQUESTING "A COPY OF THE INSTRUCTIONS, CORRESPONDENCE AND OTHER DOCUMENTS, RELATIVE TO THE TREATY LATELY CONCLUDED BETWEEN THE UNITED STATES AND GREAT-BRITAIN." 30TH MARCH 1796, ORDERED TO LIE ON THE TABLE. PUBLISHED BY ORDER OF THE HOUSE OF REPRESENTATIVES.
[Philadelphia: Printed by Francis Childs. 1796.] pp. (6). 8vo. AAS. BA.

UNITED STATES, continued.

31418 —— MESSAGE FROM THE PRESIDENT OF THE UNITED STATES, ACCOMPANYING A COPY OF THE TREATY OF FRIENDSHIP, LIMITS AND NAVIGATION, BETWEEN THE UNITED STATES AND THE KING OF SPAIN. 29TH MARCH 1796, REFERRED TO THE COMMITTEE OF THE WHOLE HOUSE, ON THE STATE OF THE UNION. PUBLISHED BY ORDER OF THE HOUSE OF REPRESENTATIVES.

[Philadelphia: Printed by Francis Childs. 1796.] pp. (19). 8vo. AAS. BA.

31419 —— —— A TREATY BETWEEN THE UNITED STATES AND HIS CATHOLIC MAJESTY, 27TH, OCTOBER, 1795.

[Philadelphia:] Printed by John Fenno, Printer to the Senate of the United States. 1796. pp. 19. 8vo. HC. NYHS.

31420 —— PRESIDENT'S MESSAGE. PHILADELPHIA, MARCH 31. THE FOLLOWING IS A COPY OF THE MESSAGE FROM THE PRESIDENT, WHICH WAS YESTERDAY READ IN THE HOUSE OF REPRESENTATIVES OF THE UNITED STATES. [Two columns.] GEO. WASHINGTON, UNITED STATES, MARCH 30.

[Philadelphia: 1796.] Broadside. fol. AAS.

31421 —— MESSAGE FROM THE PRESIDENT OF THE UNITED STATES, ACCOMPANYING THE TRANSLATION OF A LETTER FROM THE MINISTER OF THE FRENCH REPUBLIC, TO THE SECRETARY OF STATE, 25TH MARCH 1796, ORDERED TO LIE ON THE TABLE. PUBLISHED BY ORDER OF THE HOUSE OF REPRESENTATIVES.

[Philadelphia: Printed by Francis Childs. 1796.] pp. (2). 8vo. AAS. BA.

31422 —— OFFICIAL LETTERS TO THE HONORABLE AMERICAN CONGRESS, WRITTEN DURING THE WAR BETWEEN THE UNITED COLONIES AND GREAT BRITAIN, BY HIS EXCELLENCY GEORGE WASHINGTON, COMMANDER IN CHIEF OF THE CONTINENTAL FORCES, NOW PRESIDENT OF THE UNITED STATES. COPIED, BY SPECIAL PERMISSION, FROM THE ORIGINAL PAPERS PRESERVED IN THE OFFICE OF THE SECRETARY OF STATE, PHILADELPHIA. VOL. I. [-II.] SECOND BOSTON EDITION.

Boston: Printed by Manning & Loring for S. Hall, W. Spotswood, J. White, Thomas & Andrews, D. West, E. Larkin, W. P. Blake, and J. West. 1796. 2 vols. pp. 340, portrait; 356. 12mo. AAS. BA. BM. JCB. LOC. NYPL.

Edited by John Carey, of Philadelphia. Issued with and without the portrait.

31423 —— —— OFFICIAL LETTERS TO THE HONORABLE AMERICAN CONGRESS, WRITTEN DURING THE WAR BETWEEN THE UNITED COLONIES AND GREAT-BRITAIN, BY HIS EXCELLENCY GEORGE WASHINGTON, COMMANDER IN CHIEF OF THE CONTINENTAL FORCES: NOW PRESIDENT OF THE UNITED STATES. COPIED, BY SPECIAL PERMISSION, FROM THE ORIGINAL PAPERS PRESERVED IN THE OFFICE OF THE SECRETARY OF STATE, PHILADELPHIA. VOL. I. [-II.]

New-York: Printed and sold by Samuel Campbell, No. 124, Pearl-Street. M,DCC,XCVI. 2 vols. pp. 296; (2), 311. 8vo. AAS. BA. BM. LOC. NYHS. NYPL.

There are two impressions of Volume I. differing, typographically, throughout. Copies of both varieties are in the New York Public Library.

31424 —— SPEECH OF THE PRESIDENT OF THE UNITED STATES, TO BOTH HOUSES OF CONGRESS, ON WEDNESDAY, DECEMBER 7, 1796.

[Philadelphia: Printed by Francis Childs. 1796.] pp. 9. 8vo. AAS.

31425 —— —— SPEECH OF THE PRESIDENT OF THE UNITED STATES, TO BOTH HOUSES OF CONGRESS, DECEMBER 7, 1796. [Vignette.]

Philadelphia: Printed for J. Ormrod, No. 41, Chesnut Street, by Ormrod & Conrad. 1796. pp. (12). 8vo. LOC.

UNITED STATES, continued.

31426 —— — SPEECH OF THE PRESIDENT OF THE UNITED STATES, TO BOTH HOUSES OF CONGRESS, DECEMBER 7, 1796. [Two columns.] GO: WASHINGTON. UNITED STATES, 7TH DECEMBER, 1796.
[Philadelphia? 1796.] Broadside. fol.   AAS.

31427 —— — PRESIDENT'S SPEECH. AMERICAN CONGRESS HOUSE OF REPRESENTATIVES WEDNESDAY, DECEMBER 7. THE HOUSE BEING ASSEMBLED, A MESSAGE WAS SENT TO THE SENATE, TO INFORM THEM THAT THEY WERE READY AGREEABLY TO APPOINTMENT TO RECEIVE ANY COMMUNICATION WHICH THE PRESIDENT OF THE UNITED STATES MIGHT THINK PROPER TO MAKE TO THEM. THE SENATE ACCORDINGLY ATTENDED, AND PRECISELY AT TWELVE O'CLOCK, THE PRESIDENT ENTERED, AND AFTER HAVING TAKEN HIS SEAT, DELIVERED THE FOLLOWING ADDRESS:
[Newport: Printed by Henry Barber, 1796.] Broadside. fol.   LOC.

31428 —— [MADE THE 26TH JANUARY, 1796.] LETTER AND REPORT OF THE ATTORNEY GENERAL, TO WHOM WAS REFERRED THE PETITION OF JAMES MACKEY. PUBLISHED BY ORDER OF THE HOUSE OF REPRESENTATIVES.
[Philadelphia: Printed by Francis Childs. 1796.] pp. (8). 8vo.   AAS. BA.

31429 —— LETTER FROM THE ATTORNEY GENERAL, ACCOMPANYING HIS REPORT ON THE PETITION OF SUNDRY INHABITANTS OF THE COUNTY OF ST. CLAIR, IN THE TERRITORY NORTH-WEST OF THE RIVER OHIO. [Against George Turner, one of the judges of that Territory.] 10TH MAY, 1796. REFERRED TO MR. BRADBURY, MR. GILMAN, MR. HARTLEY MR. HEATH AND MR. ORR. PUBLISHED BY ORDER OF THE HOUSE OF REPRESENTATIVES.
[Philadelphia: Printed by Francis Childs. 1796.] pp. (8). 8vo.   AAS. BA.

31430 —— LETTER FROM THE ATTORNEY-GENERAL, ACCOMPANYING HIS REPORT ON THE RESOLUTION OF THE EIGHTH ULTIMO, RELATIVE TO THE CONTRACT ENTERED INTO BETWEEN THE UNITED STATES AND JOHN CLEVES SYMMES. 5TH MAY, 1796, COMMITTED TO A COMMITTEE OF THE WHOLE HOUSE, TO-MORROW. 22D DECEMBER 1796, COMMITTED TO A COMMITTEE OF THE WHOLE HOUSE, ON TUESDAY NEXT. PUBLISHED BY ORDER OF THE HOUSE OF REPRESENTATIVES.
[Philadelphia: Printed by Francis Childs. 1796.] pp. (6). 8vo. AAS. BA.

31431 —— A REPORT OF THE ATTORNEY GENERAL TO TO *[sic]* CONGRESS; CONTAINING, A COLLECTION OF CHARTERS, TREATIES, AND OTHER DOCUMENTS, RELATIVE TO AND EXPLANATORY OF THE TITLE TO THE LAND SITUATE IN THE SOUTH WESTERN PARTS OF THE UNITED STATES; AND CLAIMED BY CERTAIN COMPANIES UNDER A LAW OF THE STATE OF GEORGIA, PASSED JANUARY 7, 1795. PRINTED BY ORDER OF THE SENATE OF THE UNITED STATES.
Philadelphia: Printed by John Fenno, Printer to the Senate of the United States. 1796. pp.[171.] 8vo.   AAS. BA. BPL. CLS. DERGL. HC. JCB.

31432 —— LETTER FROM THE SECRETARY OF STATE. INCLOSING THE ESTIMATES REFERRED TO IN THE PRESIDENT'S MESSAGE OF THE 29TH ULTIMO, RELATIVE TO THE TREATY WITH SPAIN, AND OTHER FOREIGN NATIONS, AND WITH THE INDIAN TRIBES. 7TH APRIL, 1796. COMMITTED TO A COMMITTEE OF THE WHOLE HOUSE, ON THE STATE OF THE UNION. PUBLISHED BY ORDER OF THE HOUSE OF REPRESENTATIVES.
[Philadelphia: Printed by Francis Childs. 1796.] pp. (11). 8vo. AAS. BA.

31433 —— LETTER FROM THE SECRETARY OF STATE, ENCLOSING THE REPORTS OF THE LATE AND PRESENT DIRECTOR OF THE MINT EXHIBITING THE STATE OF THAT ESTABLISHMENT, AND SHEWING THE NECESSITY OF SOME FURTHER LEGISLATIVE PROVISIONS TO RENDER IT MORE EFFICIENT AND SECURE. 14TH DECEMBER 1795, COMMITTED TO A COMMITTEE OF THE WHOLE HOUSE, ON THE STATE OF THE UNION.
Philadelphia: Printed by Francis and Robert Bailey, at Yorick's Head, No. 116, High-Street. M,DCC.XCV. pp. [14.] 8vo.   AAS. BA.

UNITED STATES, continued.

31434   —— An Account of the receipts and expenditures of the United States, for the year 1795. Stated in pursuance of the standing order of the House of Representatives of the United States, passed on the thirtieth day of December, one thousand seven hundred and ninety-one. Published by order of the House of Representatives.

Philadelphia: Printed by John Fenno, No. 119, Chesnut-Street. MDCCXCVI. pp. [83], (18). fol.   AAS. BA. JCB. MHS.

Second title: Appendix, containing statements shewing the operation of the funds for reducing the domestic debt, to the close of the year 1795. Also, statements of the foreign and domestic debts of the United States, and of the expenditure of the proceeds of foreign loans to the same period. pp. (18).

31435   —— Accounts of the Treasurer of the United States, of payments and receipts of public monies, commencing the first of January, aud [*sic*] ending the thirty-first of December, 1795. Also his account of receipts and expenditures for the War Department, from the first of January, to the thirty-first of December 1795. Published by order of the House of Representatives.

[*Philadelphia: Printed by John Fenno.* 1796.] pp. 148. 8vo.   AAS. BA. BU.

31436   —— Circular relative to vessels and property captured by privateers. June 30, 1796.

[*Philadelphia: Printed by William Ross.* 1796.] Broadside.

31437   —— Circular of instructions relative to the shipment of American seamen. July 19, 1796.

[*Philadelphia: Printed by William Ross.* 1796.] pp. (2).

31438   —— Circular relating to relief and protection of American seamen and proof of citizenship. July 19, 1796.

[*Philadelphia: Printed by William Ross.* 1796.] pp. (2).

31439   —— Circular directing returns of exports to be made to the register of the Treasury. July 22, 1796.

[*Philadelphia: Printed by William Ross.* 1796.] Broadside.

31440   —— Circular of instructions relative to passports for ships and vessels of the United States. August 15, 1796.

[*Philadelphia: Printed by William Ross.* 1796.] Broadside.

31441   —— Circular of instruction to collectors relative to return of exports. September 8, 1796.

[*Philadelphia: Printed by William Ross.* 1796.] pp. (2).

31442   —— Circular of instructions relative to bonds to secure payment of duties. November 17, 1796.

[*Philadelphia: Printed by William Ross.* 1796.] Broadside.

31443   —— Circular relating to the cargoes of prize-vessels. November 26, 1796.

[*Philadelphia: Printed by William Ross.* 1796.] pp. (2).

31444   —— An Estimate for an appropriation of monies, for the services of the year 1796. Accompanying a Letter and Report from the Secretary of the Treasury, received 14th December, 1795. Published by order of the House of Representatives.

[*Philadelphia: Printed by John Fenno.* 1796.] pp. [29.] 8vo.   AAS. BA. JCB.

UNITED STATES, continued.

31445 —— INSTRUCTIONS RELATIVE TO FORMS TO BE USED BY RECEIVERS OF PUBLIC MON-
EYS, AND METHOD OF CONDUCTING THE SALES OF CERTAIN LANDS SURVEYED IN
PURSUANCE OF AN ORDINANCE OF CONGRESS PASSED MAY 20, 1785.
[Philadelphia: 1796.]

31446 —— LETTER FROM THE SECRETARY OF THE TREASURY, ACCOMPANYING A REPORT AND
ESTIMATES OF THE SUMS NECESSARY TO BE APPROPRIATED FOR THE SERVICE FOR
THE YEAR 1797; ALSO, A STATEMENT OF THE RECEIPTS AND EXPENDITURES AT
THE TREASURY OF THE UNITED STATES, FOR ONE YEAR, PRECEDING THE FIRST OF
OCTOBER, 1796. 16TH DECEMBER 1796, ORDERED TO LIE ON THE TABLE.
[Philadelphia: Printed by W. Ross. 1796.] pp. 33 8vo.   AAS. BA. JCB.

31447 —— [PRESENTED TO THE HOUSE THE 4TH OF JANUARY, 1796.] LETTER OF THE
SECRETARY OF THE TREASURY, TO THE CHAIRMAN OF THE COMMITTEE OF WAYS
AND MEANS; ACCOMPANYING A STATEMENT OF THE DEBTS OF THE UNITED STATES,
WITH A VIEW OF THE SUMS WHICH WILL BE ANNUALLY REQUISITE FOR DISCHARG-
ING THEM.
[Philadelphia: Printed by Francis Childs. 1796.] pp. 16. fol.   BA. JCB.

31448 —— LETTER FROM THE SECRETARY OF THE TREASURY, ACCOMPANYING A REPORT
AND STATEMENTS MADE IN PURSUANCE OF TWO RESOLUTIONS OF THE HOUSE OF
REPRESENTATIVES, TAKEN JANUARY 18, 1796.
[Philadelphia: Printed by Francis Childs. 1796.] fol.   BA. BPL.

31449 —— LETTER FROM THE SECRETARY OF THE TREASURY ACCOMPANYING A RETURN OF
THE EXPORTS OF THE UNITED STATES, OCTOBER 1790—30 SEPTEMBER 1795.
ALSO, LETTER FROM THE COMMISSIONER OF REVENUE. [25 JANUARY 1796.]
[Philadelphia: Printed by Francis Childs. 1796.] fol.   BA.

31450 —— LETTER FROM THE SECRETARY OF THE TREASURY, RELATIVE TO ADDITIONAL
PROVISIONS FOR THE EXECUTION OF THE ACT MAKING FURTHER PROVISIONS FOR
THE SUPPORT OF PUBLIC CREDIT AND REDEMPTION OF THE PUBLIC DEBT. 3 FEB-
RUARY, 1796.
[Philadelphia: Printed by Francis Childs. 1796.] fol.   BA.

31451 —— LETTER FROM THE SECRETARY OF THE TREASURY ACCOMPANYING SUNDRY
STATEMENTS, MADE IN PURSUANCE OF THE RESOLUTIONS OF THE 2D OF MARCH,
1795, AND THE 26TH OF FEBRUARY, 1796; AS ALSO, AN EXPLANATORY REPORT
THEREON BY THE COMMISSIONER OF THE REVENUE, RESPECTING THE INTERNAL
REVENUE OF THE UNITED STATES.—7TH MARCH, 1796—READ AND ORDERED TO
LIE ON THE TABLE. [PUBLISHED BY ORDER OF THE HOUSE OF REPRESENTATIVES.]
[Philadelphia: Printed by Francis Childs. 1796.] pp. 40, 2 folded sheets.
fol.   BA. JCB.

31452 —— LETTER FROM THE SECRETARY OF THE TREASURY, TO THE CHAIRMAN OF THE
COMMITTEE OF WAYS AND MEANS. PUBLISHED BY ORDER OF THE HOUSE OF REPRE-
SENTATIVES, THE 12TH OF MARCH, 1796.
[Philadelphia: Printed by Francis Childs. 1796.] pp. 4. fol.   JCB.

31453 —— LETTER AND REPORT OF THE SECRETARY OF THE TREASURY, ON THE PETI-
TIONS OF HOPLEY YEATON, AND OF GEORGE HOUSE, JEREMIAH GREENMAN AND
EBENEZER PERKINS. 15TH MARCH, 1796, ORDERED TO LIE ON THE TABLE. 16TH
MARCH, 1796. COMMITTED TO A COMMITTEE OF THE WHOLE HOUSE, ON TUES-
DAY NEXT. PUBLISHED BY ORDER OF THE HOUSE OF REPRESENTATIVES.
[Philadelphia: Printed by Francis Childs. 1796.] pp. (7). 8vo.   AAS. BA.

UNITED STATES, continued.

31454 —— LETTER AND REPORT OF THE SECRETARY OF THE TREASURY, ON THE MEMORIAL OF SUNDRY MERCHANTS OF THE CITY OF PHILADELPHIA. 16TH MARCH, 1796, COMMITTED TO A COMMITTEE OF THE WHOLE HOUSE, ON MONDAY NEXT. PUBLISHED BY ORDER OF THE HOUSE OF REPRESENTATIVES.
[Philadelphia: Printed by Francis Childs. 1796.] pp. (4). 8vo.   AAS.   BA.

31455 —— LETTER FROM THE SECRETARY OF THE TREASURY, ACCOMPANYING AN ABSTRACT OF THE OFFICIAL EMOLUMENTS AND EXPENDITURES OF THE OFFICERS OF THE CUSTOMS, FOR THE YEAR 1795. AS ALSO, AN EXPLANATORY LETTER THEREON, FROM THE COMPTROLLER OF THE TREASURY.—4TH APRIL, 1796.—REFERRED TO THE COMMITTEE OF COMMERCE AND MANUFACTURES.
[Philadelphia: Printed by Francis Childs. 1796.] pp. 12. fol.   BA.   JCB.

31456 —— LETTER FROM THE SECRETARY OF THE TREASURY TO THE CHAIRMAN OF THE COMMITTEE OF WAYS AND MEANS, RELATIVE TO AN INACCURACY WHICH HAS BEEN DISCOVERED IN THE PRINTED STATEMENT OF RECEIPTS AND EXPENDITURES FOR THE YEAR 1794. PUBLISHED BY ORDER OF THE HOUSE OF REPRESENTATIVES, 18TH APRIL, 1796.
[Philadelphia: Printed by Francis Childs. 1796.] pp. (6). fol.   AAS.   BA.

31457 —— LETTER FROM THE SECRETARY OF THE TREASURY, ACCOMPANYING A STATEMENT OF GOODS, WARES AND MERCHANDIZE, EXPORTED FROM THE UNITED STATES, FROM THE FIRST OF OCTOBER 1794, TO THE THIRTIETH OF SEPTEMBER 1795, INCLUSIVE. 12TH MAY, 1796. ORDERED TO LIE ON THE TABLE. PUBLISHED BY ORDER OF THE HOUSE OF REPRESENTATIVES.
[Philadelphia: Printed by Francis Childs. 1796.] pp. (11). 8vo.   AAS.   BA.

31458 —— LETTER FROM THE SECRETARY OF THE TREASURY, ACCOMPANYING AN ESTIMATE OF THE RECEIPTS AND EXPENDITURES FOR 1796. 18 MAY, 1796.
[Philadelphia: Printed by Francis Childs. 1796.] fol.   BA.

31459 —— [PRESENTED TO THE HOUSE, THE 19TH OF JANUARY, 1796.] STATEMENT SHEWING THE FINAL LIQUIDATION OF THE FRENCH LOANS, AND THEIR FULL REIMBURSEMENT AT THE TREASURY, UPON THE PRINCIPLES OF THE LOAN OPENED FOR THE FOREIGN DEBT UNDER THE ACT MAKING FURTHER REVISION FOR THE SUPPORT OF PUBLIC CREDIT AND FOR THE REDEMPTION OF THE PUBLIC DEBT.
[Philadelphia: Printed by Francis Childs. 1796.] pp. (2). fol.   BA.

31460 —— [RECEIVED THE 14TH DECEMBER, 1795.] SUNDRY ESTIMATES AND STATEMENTS RELATIVE TO APPROPRIATIONS FOR THE SERVICE OF THE YEAR 1796, AND TO THE EXPENDITURES OF CERTAIN SUMS HERETOFORE APPROPRIATED. PUBLISHED BY ORDER OF THE HOUSE OF REPRESENTATIVES.
[Philadelphia: Printed by Francis Childs. 1796.] ⁺pp. 28: 8vo.
AAS.   BA.   JCB.

31461 —— TREASURY DEPARTMENT, COMPTROLLER'S OFFICE, SEPTEMBER 26, 1796. (CIRCULAR TO MARSHALS.) SIR, THE DIFFICULTIES WHICH ARE EXPERIENCED IN ADJUSTING THE ACCOMPTS OF SOME OF THE MARSHALS, RENDER IT INDISPENSABLY NECESSARY THAT A UNIFORM MODE OF EXHIBITING THEM SHOULD BE PRESCRIBED AND ESTABLISHED. . . .
[Philadelphia: Printed by William Ross. 1796.] pp. (2). 4to.   NYPL.

31462 —— [RECEIVED THE 18TH DECEMBER, 1795.] REPORT OF THE COMMISSIONERS OF THE SINKING FUND, STATING THE AMOUNT OF THEIR PURCHASES, AND OTHER PROCEEDINGS, SINCE THEIR REPORT OF THE 18TH OF NOVEMBER, 1794. PUBLISHED BY ORDER OF THE HOUSE OF REPRESENTATIVES.
[Philadelphia:] Printed by Francis Childs. [1796.] pp. (14). 8vo. AAS. BA. JCB.

UNITED STATES, continued.

31463 —— REPORT OF THE COMMISSIONERS OF THE SINKING FUND, STATING THE AMOUNT OF THEIR PURCHASES, AND OTHER PROCEEDINGS, SINCE THEIR REPORT OF THE 18TH OF DECEMBER 1795. 16TH DECEMBER 1796, ORDERED TO LIE ON THE TABLE. PUBLISHED BY ORDER OF THE HOUSE OF REPRESENTATIVES.

[Philadelphia: Printed by Francis Childs. 1796.] pp. 6. 8vo. AAS. BA.

31464 —— — A COMPLETE AND ACCURATE DESCRIPTION OF THE SINKING FUND; SHEWING THE QUARTERLY DIMINUTION OF THE PRESENT 6 PER CENT STOCK OF THE UNITED STATES, AND THEIR REAL VALUE, ON THE FIRST DAYS OF EACH QUARTER.

Boston: Printed by John Russell, Quaker-Lane. 1796.

31465 —— ORDERS AND DIRECTIONS FOR CONDUCTING THE MINT OF THE UNITED STATES, ESTABLISHED BY ELIAS BOUDINOT, DIRECTOR OF SAID MINT. NOVEMBER 2, 1795.

Philadelphia: Printed by John Fenno, No. 119, *Chesnut-Street.* 1796. pp, [36.] 8vo. LOC.

31466 —— [RECEIVED THE 14TH DECEMBER, 1795.] LETTER FROM THE SECRETARY OF WAR, ACCOMPANYING SUNDRY STATEMENTS & REPORTS, RELATIVE TO, I. THE PRESENT MILITARY FORCE OF THE UNITED STATES, II. MEASURES WHICH HAVE BEEN PURSUED TO OBTAIN PROPER SITES FOR ARSENALS, III. MEASURES WHICH HAVE BEEN TAKEN TO REPLENISH THE MAGAZINES WITH MILITARY STORES. IV. MEASURES WHICH HAVE BEEN TAKEN TO OPEN A TRADE WITH THE INDIANS, V. PROGRESS MADE IN PROVIDING MATERIALS FOR THE FRIGATES, AND IN BUILDING THEM. PUBLISHED BY ORDER OF THE HOUSE OF REPRESENTATIVES.

[Philadelphia: Printed by Francis Childs. 1796.] pp. [22.] 8vo.
AAS. BA. JCB. LOC.

31467 —— LETTER AND REPORTS OF THE SECRETARY AT WAR, TO THE COMMITTEE APPOINTED TO ENQUIRE INTO THE NAVAL EQUIPMENT OF THE UNITED STATES. PUBLISHED BY THE ORDER OF THE HOUSE OF REPRESENTATIVES, THE 2D MARCH, 1796.

[Philadelphia: Printed by Francis Childs. 1796.] pp. 11 fol. BA. JCB.

31468 —— [RECEIVED THE 20TH OF JANUARY 1796.] REPORT FROM THE DEPARTMENT OF WAR, RELATIVE TO THE FORTIFICATIONS OF THE PORTS AND HARBOURS OF THE UNITED STATES. PUBLISHED BY ORDER OF THE HOUSE OF REPRESENTATIVES.

[Philadelphia: Printed by Francis Childs. 1796.] pp. [9]. 8vo.
AAS. BA. JCB.

31469 —— REGULATIONS FOR THE ORDER AND DISCIPLINE OF THE TROOPS OF THE UNITED STATES. BY BARON STEUBEN. TO WHICH ARE ADDED, THE MANUAL EXERCISE AND EVOLUTIONS OF THE CAVALRY.

New-London: Printed by Samuel Green, 1796.

31470 —— — REGULATIONS FOR THE ORDER AND DISCIPLINE OF THE TROOPS OF THE UNITED STATES. BY BARON DE STEUBEN. TO WHICH ARE ADDED, THE MANUAL AND EVOLUTIONS OF THE CAVALRY. THE WHOLE EXEMPLIFIED BY NINE HANDSOME COPPERPLATES, AND FULL BOUND, WHICH RENDER IT FAR PREFERABLE TO ANY OTHER EDITION NOW IN USE.

Providence: Printed by Carter and Wilkinson, and sold at the Providence Book-Store, opposite the Market. 1796.

UNITED STATES, continued.
31471 —— — STEUBEN'S MILITARY DISCIPLINE FOR THE REGULATION OF THE TROOPS OF
THE UNITED STATES.
Baltimore: Printed by P. Edwards & J. W. Allen. 1796.

31472 —— — STEUBEN'S MILITARY DISCIPLINE, FOR THE REGULATION OF THE TROOPS OF
THE UNITED STATES. ORNAMENTED WITH CUTS, &C. WITH THE ARTICLES OF
WAR ANNEXED.
Edenton: Printed by Henry Wills. 1796.

31473 —— PAPERS, RELATIVE TO AN APPLICATION TO CONGRESS, FOR AN EXCLUSIVE RIGHT
OF SEARCHING FOR AND WORKING MINES, IN THE NORTH-WEST AND SOUTH-WEST
TERRITORY. BY N [icholas] I. ROOSEVELT & J [acob] MARK, AND THEIR ASSOCI-
ATES. FEBRUARY 10. 1796.
[Philadelphia:] Printed by Samuel Harrison Smith. [1796.] pp. [28.]
8vo.   AAS. BA. LOC. NYPL.

31474 THE UNITED STATES AND NEW-HAMPSHIRE REGISTER, FOR THE YEAR 1797.
BEING THE 21ST—22D, OF NATIONAL INDEPENDENCE. CONTAINING A GREAT
VARIETY OF USEFUL & ENTERTAINING MATTER.
Printed at Dover, for the citizens of the United States. By Samuel Bragg, jr.
[1796.] pp. (90). 18mo.   LOC. NL.

31475 THE UNITED STATES CHRISTIAN MAGAZINE. VOL. I. NO. 2 SEPTEMBER, [—
No. 3 —— 1796.]
New-York: Printed by T. & J. Swords, No. 99 Pearl-Street. 1796. pp. 77–
236. 8vo.   BA. HSP. LOC. MHS. PTS. YC.

Owing to the withdrawal of the publication fund, this Magazine was
not continued beyond the third number.

31476 [U S arms.] UNITED STATES CHRONICLE. [R I arms.] VOL. XIII. NUMBER 625.
THURSDAY, JANUARY 7, [—NUMBER 676. THURSDAY, DECEMBER 29, 1796.]
Published by Bennett Wheeler, in the Market-House Chambers, Providence,
1796. fol.   AAS. HC. LOC. NYHS. RIHS.

In September, the Printing Office was moved to his new "Office in
Westminster Street, a few rods westward of the Great Bridge," and
directly opposite the Turk's Head.

31477 THE UNMASKED NABOB OF HANCOCK COUNTY: OR, THE SCALES DROPT FROM THE
EYES OF THE PEOPLE.
Portsmouth, N. H. Printed by Charles Peirce, Proprietor of the work. 1796.
pp. 24. 12mo.   AAS. LOC. MHS.

Second title: THE APPEAL OF THE TWO COUNTIES OF LINCOLN AND HANCOCK,
FROM THE FORLORN HOPE OR, MOUNT OF DISTRESS; TO THE GENERAL COURT, OR,
TO ALL THE WORLD. [Ornament.]
Portsmouth, N. H. Printed by Charles Peirce, Proprietor of the work. 1796.
pp. (12)–24.

A vigorous attack upon General Henry Knox's claim to the Waldo
Patent of land in the District of Maine.

31478   DER UNPARTHEYISCHE READING ADLER. [Cut of eagle and scroll with] "WIR SUCHEN KEIN LOB AUS DEN GRUNDSÄTZEN EINIGER PARTHEY, HOFFEN ES ABER DURCH UNSER EINLIEGEN FÜR DAS GEMEINE BESTE, ZU VERDIENEN." NO. 1. DIENSTAG DEN 29 NOVEMBER, 1796.

> *[Gedruckt und] Herausgegeben von Jacob Schneider und Georg Gerrish in der Deutsch-und Englischen Buchdruckerey in Reading in der Pennstrasse.* 1796. fol.   AAS.

>> Established, as a weekly, by Jacob Schneider and Georg Gerrish. The above issue was a preliminary number, regular publication beginning with the issue for January 3, 1797, after which Gerrish withdrew and publication was made in the name of Schneider and Comp. up to July, 1802, when Johann Ritter was admitted to partnership as Schneider & Ritter. In March, 1804, Schneider withdrew, and Charles A. Kessler was admitted to partnership as Ritter and Comp. who continued publication beyond the period of this work — Kessler dying in 1823; and Ritter in 1851. In 1797, the title was changed to *Der Unpartheyische Readinger Adler;* and this was shortened to *Der Readinger Adler,* in 1801; and to *Readinger Adler,* in 1810.

31479   DIE UNPARTHEYISCHE YORK GAZETTE. NO. 1. FREITAG, FEBRUAR 19, [— No. 45. DIENSTAG, DEZEMBER 27, 1796.]

> *York: Gedruckt und Herausgegeben von Salomon Mayer.* 1796. fol.   YHS.

>> Established, as a weekly, by Saloman Mayer, and continued by him to July 18, 1797, — the last number located.

31480   USSHER, GEORGE NEVILLE
THE ELEMENTS OF ENGLISH GRAMMAR, METHODICALLY ARRANGED FOR THE ASSISTANCE OF YOUNG PERSONS, WHO STUDY THE ENGLISH LANGUAGE GRAMMATICALLY: TO WHICH IS ADDED A CONCISE TREATISE OF RHETORIC. DESIGNED PARTICULARLY FOR THE USE OF LADIES' BOARDING SCHOOLS. BY G. NEVILLE USSHER. THE SECOND AMERICAN EDITION, TO WHICH IS NOW ADDED A SHORT TREATISE ON PUNCTUATION.

> *Printed at Exeter, by Henry Ranlet, and sold at his Book-Store, Main-Street, by the dozen or single.* M,DCC,XCVI. pp. 110. 8vo.   AAS. BA. LOC. NYPL.

31481   VAILL, JOSEPH   1751–1838
NOAH'S FLOOD: A POEM. IN TWO PARTS. PART I. CONTAINS AN HISTORICAL ACCOUNT OF THE DELUGE, TAKEN FROM THE BIBLE; INTERSPERSED WITH CONJECTURAL OBSERVATIONS. PART II. IS DESIGNED AS A MORAL IMPROVEMENT OF THE SUBJECT. TO WHICH ARE ADDED, THE FOLLOWING PIECES IN POETRY, VIZ. YOUTH CAUTIONED AGAINST VICE. ON HAPPINESS. A NEW-YEAR'S HYMN. [Two lines from] PSALMIST. BY JOSEPH VAIL, A. M. PASTOR OF THE THIRD CHURCH IN EAST-HADDAM.

> *New-London:—Printed by Samuel Green.* 1796. pp. [28]. 8vo.
>   AAS. BU. NYHS. UTS.

31482   A VALUABLE COLLECTION OF BOOKS IN DIFFERENT DEPARTMENTS OF LITERATURE AND SCIENCE. [2100 lots.]

> *Philadelphia:* 1796. 8vo.

31483   VATTEL, EMERICH DE   1714–1767
THE LAW OF NATIONS: OR, PRINCIPLES OF THE LAW OF NATURE; APPLIED TO THE CONDUCT AND AFFAIRS OF NATIONS AND SOVEREIGNS. A WORK TENDING TO DISPLAY THE TRUE INTEREST OF POWER. BY M. DE VATTEL. FIRST AMERICAN EDITION, CORRECTED AND REVISED FROM THE LATEST LONDON EDITION. [Three lines of Latin from] CICER. SOMN. SCIPION. TRANSLATED FROM THE FRENCH.

> *New-York: Printed and sold by Samuel Campbell,* 124 *Pearl-Street,* 1796. pp. 563. 8vo.   AAS. BM. HC. NYPL.

>> Page xlvi of the contents is misnumbered xxxvi.

31484   THE VENDUE, ON SIX MONTH'S CREDIT. A NEW SONG. BY THE AUTHOR OF SIMON SAD.
Poughkeepsie: Printed by Nicholas Power. 1796.

31485   DER VERBESSERTE HOCH DEUTSCHE AMERICANISCHE LAND UND STAATS CALEN-
DER. AUF DAS JAHR. . . . 1797. DER DREIZEHNTEN MAL HERAUSGEGEBEN.
Friedrich Stadt, Maryland: Gedruckt bey Matthias Bartgiss. [1796.]

31486   VERMONT. STATE.
ACTS AND LAWS, PASSED BY THE LEGISLATURE OF THE STATE OF VERMONT, AT THEIR
SESSION HOLDEN AT RUTLAND, ON THE SECOND THURSDAY OF OCTOBER, ONE THOU-
SAND SEVEN HUNDRED AND NINETY-SIX. [— 8 NOVEMBER, 1796.]
Bennington: Printed by Anthony Haswell. 1796. pp. [185.] 8vo.
AAS. LOC. NYPL.

31487   —— BY HIS EXCELLENCY THOMAS CHITTENDEN, ESQ. CAPTAIN GENERAL GOVERNOR,
COMMANDER IN CHIEF, IN AND OVER THE STATE OF VERMONT. A PROCLAMATION.
. . . APPOINT THURSDAY, THE FIRST DAY OF DECEMBER NEXT TO BE OBSERVED
AS A DAY OF PUBLICK THANKSGIVING, PRAYER, AND PRAISE, THROUGHOUT THIS
STATE. . . . GIVEN UNDER MY HAND IN THE COUNCIL CHAMBER, AT RUTLAND
THIS TWENTY-SEVENTH DAY OF OCTOBER, IN THE YEAR OF OUR LORD, ONE THOU-
SAND SEVEN HUNDRED AND NINETY-SIX; AND IN THE TWENTIETH YEAR OF OUR IN-
DEPENDENCE. THOMAS CHITTENDEN. BY HIS EXCELLENCY'S COMMAND TRUMAN
SQUIER, SEC'RY. GOD SAVE THE PEOPLE.
[Rutland: 1796.] Broadside.

31488   —— A JOURNAL OF THE PROCEEDINGS OF THE GENERAL ASSEMBLY OF THE STATE
OF VERMONT, AT THEIR SESSION HELD AT WINDSOR, OCTOBER 8, 1795.
Rutland: Printed by order of the Legislature. [1796.] pp. 170. 4to.   AAS.

31489   —— A LIST OF ARREARAGES OF TAXES DUE FROM THE SEVERAL TOWNS IN THE STATE
OF VERMONT ON THE 21ST DAY OF OCTOBER A. D. 1796.
*Rutland, Vermont: Printed at the Herald Office by order of the Legislature
for the use of members.* [1796.] pp. 11. 4to.   AAS.

31490   —— THE STATE OF VERMONT, IN ACCOUNT CURRENT WITH THE HON. SAMUEL MAT-
TOCKS AS TREASURER, FROM SEPTEMBER 15, 1795, TO SEPTEMBER 15TH, 1796.
[Rutland: 1796.] Broadside. fol.

31491   THE VERMONT CHRONICLE AND [U. S. arms] THE WINDHAM ADVERTISER. PLIANT
AS READS [*sic*] WHERE STREAMS OF FREEDOM GLIDE; — FIRM AS THE HILLS, TO
STEM OPPRESSION'S TIDE. VOL. I. NO. 1. MONDAY, JULY 4, [— NO. 16. MONDAY,
OCTOBER 17, 1796.]
*Printed by John Goold, jun. a few rods south of the Meetinghouse, in West-
minster. 1796.* fol.   AAS. HC.
Established, as a weekly, by John Goold, junior, and continued by him
to October 17th, — the last number located.

31492   VERMONT GAZETTE. [Motto.] NUMB. 32 OF VOL. XIII. WHOLE NUMBER 656. FRI-
DAY, 1ST JANUARY, [— NUMB. 32 OF VOL. XIV. WHOLE NUMBER 708. FRIDAY,
DECEMBER 30, 1796.]
Bennington: Printed and published by Anthony Haswell. 1796. fol.
The motto was changed to: Let truth and candor grace the varying page,
—The palm of youth,—the dignity of age. Beginning with the issue
for August 19th, the imprint was changed to: Printed at Bennington,
by O. C. Merrill, for Anthony Haswell, and so continued to the end of
the year. In January, 1797, Haswell sold the Gazette, and one-half interest in the Printing Office, to Orsamus C. Merrill, and Reuben Langdon, who began with a new numbering, the *Tablet of the Times.*

31493   A VIEW OF THE QUARTERLY DIMUNITION OF THE FUNDED SIX PER CENT STOCKS OF THE UNITED STATES OF AMERICA. BY WHICH MAY BE SEEN THE REAL VALUE OF ANY SUM OF THE PRESENT SIX PER CENT STOCK (TOGETHER WITH THE REAL VALUE OF THE DEFERRED SIX PER CENT STOCK) ON THE FIRST DAYS OF JANUARY, APRIL, JULY AND OCTOBER IN EACH YEAR FROM THE YEAR 1796 TO THE YEAR 1825, IN-CLUSIVELY; TO WHICH IS ADDED THE LAW MAKING PROVISIONS FOR THE REDEMP-TION OF THE PUBLIC DEBT, &c. VALUABLE TO STOCKHOLDERS AND NEGOTIATORS; BUT USELESS TO ALL OTHERS, AS THEY CANNOT UNDERSTAND ITS CONTENTS.

Boston: Printed by John Russell, Quaker-Lane. 1796.   JCB.

31494   THE VILLAGE HARMONY, OR YOUTH'S ASSISTANT TO SACRED MUSICK. CONTAINING A CONCISE INTRODUCTION TO THE GROUNDS OF MUSICK, WITH SUCH A COLLECTION OF THE MOST APPROVED PSALM TUNES, ANTHEMS, AND OTHER PIECES, IN THREE AND FOUR PARTS, AS ARE MOST SUITABLE FOR DIVINE WORSHIP. DESIGNED FOR THE USE OF SCHOOLS AND SINGING SOCIETIES. THE SECOND EDITION.

Printed at Exeter, by H. Ranlet, and sold at his Book-store. 1796. pp. 190.

"To which is added eighty pages of the best musick current."

31495   VILLAGE MESSENGER. [Motto.] No .1, OF VOL. I. SATURDAY, JANUARY 9, [—No.52. TUESDAY, DECEMBER 27, 1796.]

[Printed and published] By Biglow and Cushing, Amherst, Newhampshire, 1796. fol.   AAS.

Established, as a weekly, by William Biglow, and Samuel Cushing, with the motto, "Whatsoever things are true—Whatsoever things are pure." In July, 1796, Biglow withdrew, and Samuel Cushing contin-ued its publication alone to April 18, 1797, when he disposed of his interests to Samuel Preston, who changed the motto to, "Old things shall pass away—and all things become new," enclosing the title, etc. in an oval ornamental border, and by whom publication was continued until 5 December, 1801, when it was discontinued.

31496   VIRGILIUS MARO, PUBLIUS   BC 70–19
THE WORKS OF VIRGIL: TRANSLATED INTO LITERAL ENGLISH PROSE; WITH SOME EXPLANATORY NOTES. BY CALEB ALEXANDER, A. M.

Printed at Worcester, Massachusetts, by Leonard Worcester, for David West, of Boston. MDCCXCVI. pp. 673, (1). 12mo.   AAS. BM. NYPL.

The Latin text, with a literal prose translation, on opposite pages. 100th Massachusetts District Copyright, issued to David West, as Pro-prietor, 26 May, 1796. And the fourteenth work deposited in the Office of the Secretary of State, under the Copyright law, 24 June, 1796.

31497   VIRGINIA. STATE.
ABRIDGMENT OF THE PUBLIC PERMANENT LAWS OF VIRGINIA. THE REPEALING CLAUSES IN THE SEVERAL LAWS WHICH HAVE THEM, ARE REDUCIBLE TO A FEW FORMS, AND ARE ALIKE IN GENERAL. TO PREVENT THE SWELLING OF THE BOOK UNNECESSARILY, AND YET TO GIVE AT THE SAME TIME THE OPERATIVE WORDS OF EVERY LAW, REFERENCE IS MADE AT THE CLOSE OF EVERY LAW TO THE FORM OF REPEAL AS IT IS SET FORTH VERBATIM IN THE APPENDIX. EVERY ACT PASSED ON OR AFTER OCTOBER 19, 1792, IS TO BE UNDERSTOOD TO CONTAIN THE FOLLOWING CLAUSE OF COMMENCEMENT: "THIS ACT SHALL COMMENCE IN FORCE FROM AND AFTER THE PASSING THEREOF;" UNLESS ITS COMMENCEMENT SHALL BE PARTICU-LARLY EXPRESSED TO BE ON A DIFFERENT DAY, OR IN A DIFFERENT FORM. THOSE ACTS WHICH PASSED BEFORE THE 19TH OF OCTOBER, 1792, AND COMMENCE THEIR OPERATION ON A DIFFERENT DAY FROM THE DAY OF THEIR PASSING, WILL BE SPECIFIED. THE DATE PREFIXED TO EACH LAW IS THE DAY ON WHICH IT PASSED.

Richmond: Printed by Augustine Davis, M,DCC,XCVI. pp. (2), 385 [386]. 4to.   VSL.

VIRGINIA, continued.

31498   —— ACT OF THE COMMONWEALTH OF VIRGINIA, FOR REGULATING THE MILITIA; TO-
GETHER WITH THE ACTS OF THE CONGRESS OF THE UNITED STATES, MORE EFFEC-
TUALLY TO PROVIDE FOR THE NATIONAL DEFENCE, BY ESTABLISHING AN UNIFORM
MILITIA THROUGHOUT THE UNITED STATES—AND, FOR CALLING FORTH THE MILITIA
TO EXECUTE THE LAWS OF THE UNION, SUPPRESS INSURRECTIONS, AND REPEL IN-
VASIONS.

Richmond: Printed by Augustine Davis, Printer for the Public. M.DCC.-
XCVI. pp. [86]; [26.] 4to.   JCB. LOC.

Second title: RULES AND ARTICLES FOR THE BETTER GOVERNMENT OF THE TROOPS
RAISED, OR TO BE RAISED AND KEPT IN PAY BY AND AT THE EXPENCE OF THE
UNITED STATES OF AMERICA.

Richmond: Printed by Aug: Davis, Printer for the Public. M,DCC,XCVI.
pp. [26.]

31499   —— ACTS PASSED AT A GENERAL ASSEMBLY OF THE COMMONWEALTH OF VIRGINIA.
BEGUN AND HELD AT THE CAPITOL, IN THE CITY OF RICHMOND, ON TUESDAY, THE
TENTH DAY OF NOVEMBER, ONE THOUSAND SEVEN HUNDRED AND NINETY-FIVE.
[—28 DECEMBER, 1795.] [Ornament.]

Richmond: Printed by Augustine Davis, Printer for the Public. M,DCC,-
XCVI. pp. [59.] fol.   HSP. LOC. NYPL. VSL.

31500   —— ACTS OF THE GENERAL ASSEMBLY OF VIRGINIA FOR REGULATING PILOTS, AND
ASCERTAINING THEIR FEES, WITH THE RATES OF PILOTAGE.

Norfolk: Printed by Willett & O'Connor. 1796.

31501   —— VIRGINIA. IN THE HOUSE OF DELEGATES, TUESDAY, DECEMBER THE 13TH, 1796.
ORDERED THAT THE PUBLIC PRINTER BE DIRECTED TO STRIKE OFF TWO THOU-
SAND COPIES OF THE FOLLOWING RESOLUTION, TO BE DISTRIBUTED AMONG THE
SEVERAL COUNTIES OF THIS COMMONWEALTH, FOR THE CONSIDERATION OF THE
GOOD PEOPLE THEREOF, ATTEST, JOHN STEWART, C. H. D. [Regarding petitions
for a revision of the Constitution.]

[Richmond: Printed by Augustine Davis, 1796.] Broadside. fol.   LOC.

31502   —— JOURNAL OF THE HOUSE OF DELEGATES OF THE COMMONWEALTH OF VIRGINIA,
BEGUN AND HELD AT THE CAPITOL, IN THE CITY OF RICHMOND, ON TUESDAY, THE
TENTH DAY OF NOVEMBER, ONE THOUSAND SEVEN HUNDRED AND NINETY-FIVE.
[—29 DECEMBER, 1795.]

Richmond: Printed by Augustine Davis, Printer for the public. M,DCC,-
XCV. [1796.] pp. 138. fol.   BU. JCB. VSL.

31503   —— JOURNAL OF THE SENATE OF THE COMMONWEALTH OF VIRGINIA, BEGUN AND
HELD AT THE CAPITOL, IN THE CITY OF RICHMOND, ON TUESDAY THE TENTH DAY
OF NOVEMBER, ONE THOUSAND SEVEN HUNDRED AND NINETY-FIVE. [—29 DE-
CEMBER, 1795.]

Richmond: Printed by Thomas Nicolson. 1796.

No copy in manuscript, or in print, is known.

31504   —— LIST OF PENSIONERS CONTINUED BY THE HONORABLE THE EXECUTIVE, FOR THE
YEAR 1795, TO BE PAID OUT OF THE REVENUE TO BE COLLECTED FOR THAT
YEAR. . . .

[Richmond: Printed by Augustine Davis, 1796.] Broadside. fol.   LOC.

VIRGINIA, continued.

31505 —— To the worshipful the County Court of .... GENTLEMEN, THE LAST GENERAL ASSEMBLY HAVING AUTHORISED ME, WITH THE ADVICE OF COUNCIL, TO RAISE AS MANY ADDITIONAL COMPANIES OF ARTILLERY AND TROOPS OF CAVALRY AS WILL CONSTITUTE A REGIMENT OF EACH, IN THE FOUR RESPECTIVE DIVISIONS OF THE MILITIA IN THE STATE, AND TO APPOINT THE NECESSARY OFFICERS TO COMMAND THEM. [Seventeen lines. Signed, R. F. Brooke] RICHMOND, FEBRUARY 12TH, 1796.

[Richmond: Printed by Augustine Davis, 1796.] Broadside. fol. LOC.

31506 THE VIRGINIA ALMANAC FOR THE YEAR OF OUR LORD 1797. BY THE NORTH MOUNTAIN PHILOSOPHER.

Winchester: Printed and sold by Richard Bowen. [1796.]

31507 THE VIRGINIA AND N. CAROLINA ALMANACK FOR 1797; CONTAINING IN ADDITION TO WHAT IS GENERALLY GIVEN, A NUMBER OF USEFUL RECEIPTS, CURIOUS BON MOTS, AND LAUGHABLE ANECDOTES. NOT BEFORE PUBLISHED IN AN ALMANACK. TO IT IS LIKEWISE ADDED, WHAT MUST BE HIGHLY INTERESTING TO EVERY MAN IN THIS COUNTRY, THE PRESIDENT'S ADDRESS, DECLINING TO BE CONSIDERED A CANDIDATE FOR THE IMPORTANT OFFICE OF FIRST MAGISTRATE OF THE UNITED STATES. . . .

Norfolk: Printed and sold by Willett & O'Connor. [1796.]

31508 VIRGINIA [cut] ARGUS. VOL. IV. No. 63. WHOLE NO. 372. TUESDAY, NOVEMBER 22, [—VOL. IV. No. 74. WHOLE NO. 383. FRIDAY, DECEMBER, 30, 1796.]

Richmond, (Virg)—Printed (on Tuesdays and Fridays) by Samuel Pleasants, jun., near the Vendue-Office. 1796. fol.

In continuation of *The Richmond and Manchester Advertiser.*

31509 THE VIRGINIA GAZETTE. VOL. I. No. 1. FRIDAY, JANUARY 22, [—No. 45. FRIDAY, NOVEMBER 25, 1796.]

Staunton: Printed by John Wise for Robert Douthat. 1796. fol.

Established, as a weekly, from and in continuation of Throckmorton's The Virginia Gazette, and continued by them into September, 1796, when Douthat disposed of his interests to John Wise and —— Adams, who continued publication to December, 1796, when they changed the title to *Staunton Gazette.*

31510 THE VIRGINIA GAZETTE, AND GENERAL ADVERTISER. VOL. X. NUMB. 496. WEDNESDAY, JANUARY 6, [—VOL. XI. NUMB. 547. WEDNESDAY, DECEMBER 28, 1796.]

[Richmond:] Printed by Aug. Davis, Printer for the public. 1796. fol.

31511 VIRGINIA GAZETTE & PETERSBURG INTELLIGENCER. NUMBER 651. FRIDAY, JANUARY 1, [—NUMBER 755, FRIDAY, DECEMBER 30, 1796.]

Published every Tuesday and Friday by William Prentis. 1796. fol.

31512 VIRGINIA GAZETTE AND WEEKLY ADVERTISER. NUMBER 671. MONDAY, JANUARY 4, [—NUMBER 723. MONDAY, DECEMBER 26, 1796.]

Richmond: Published by Thomas Nicolson, two doors above the Eagle-Tavern. 1796. fol.

31513 THE VIRGINIA HERALD, AND FREDERICKSBURG & FALMOUTH ADVERTISER. VOL. VIII. NUMB. 482. FRIDAY, JANUARY 1, [—VOL. IX. NUMB. 586. FRIDAY, DECEMBER 29, 1796.]

Fredericksburg (Va): Published on Tuesdays and Fridays, by T. Green. 1796. fol.

31514 VIRTUE AND VICE: OR THE HISTORY OF CHARLES CAREFUL, AND HARRY HEEDLESS. SHEWING THE GOOD EFFECTS OF CAUTION AND PRUDENCE, AND THE MANY INCONVENIENCES THAT HARRY HEEDLESS EXPERIENCED FROM HIS RASHNESS AND DISOBEDIENCE, WHILE MASTER CAREFUL BECAME A GREAT MAN, ONLY BY HIS MERIT. THE SECOND WORCESTER EDITION.
Printed at Worcester, Massachusetts. By Thomas, Son & Thomas. And sold wholesale and retail, at their Bookstore. MDCCXCVI. pp. 61, (2). 32mo.   AAS.

31515 THE VOCAL COMPANION. BEING A CHOICE COLLECTION OF THE MOST APPROVED SONGS, CATCHES, DUETS, &C.
Philadelphia: Printed for Mathew Carey, No. 118, Market-street. 1796. pp. (196), frontispiece. 12mo.   AAS. LOC.

31516 VOLNEY, CONSTANTIN FRANÇOIS DE CHASSEBŒUF, comte DE   1757–1820
THE LAW OF NATURE, OR PRINCIPLES OF MORALITY, DEDUCED FROM THE PHYSICAL CONSTITUTION OF MANKIND AND THE UNIVERSE. BY C.–F. VOLNEY. [Two lines from] POPE.
Philadelphia: Printed for T. Stephens, by F. & R. Bailey. 1796. pp. viii, (2), 161, portrait. 18mo.   BM. LOC. NYPL.
This translation was reprinted in London this year. 128th Pennsylvania District Copyright, issued to Thomas Stephens, as Proprietor,—March, 1796.

31517 —— THE RUINS: OR A SURVEY OF THE REVOLUTIONS OF EMPIRES. BY M. VOLNEY. ONE OF THE DEPUTIES OF THE NATIONAL ASSEMBLY OF 1789, AND AUTHOR OF TRAVELS INTO SYRIA AND EGYPT. TRANSLATED FROM THE FRENCH. [Six lines from] CH. IV, PAGE 24.
New-York: Printed by William A. Davis, for E. Duyckinck & Co. T. & J. Swords, N. Judah, Rogers & Berry, Fellows & Adam, J. Reid, J. Harrisson, D. Dunham, T. Allen, P. A. Mesier, and B. Gomez, Bookseller.—1796.—pp. 305, 3 plates, map. 12mo.   AAS. BA. JCB. NYPL.
Concludes: End of the first part.

31518 VOLTAIRE, FRANÇOIS MARIE AROUET DE.   1694–1778
THE PHILOSOPHICAL DICTIONARY, FOR THE POCKET TRANSLATED FROM THE FRENCH EDITION CORRECTED BY THE AUTHOR. [Vignette portrait of Voltaire.]
Catskill, Printed by T: & M. Croswel [sic] *for selves and J. Fellows & E. Duyckinck, New York.* 1796. pp. (2), (2), (4), 336. 16mo.   AAS. LOC. NYPL.
With engraved title-page by T. R. Maverick.

31519 WADSWORTH, BENJAMIN   1750–1826
SOCIAL THANKSGIVING A PLEASANT DUTY. A SERMON, PREACHED ON THE DAY OF ANNUAL THANKSGIVING THROUGH THE COMMONWEALTH OF MASSACHUSETTS, DECEMBER 15, 1796. BY BENJAMIN WADSWORTH, A. M. PASTOR OF THE FIRST CHURCH IN DANVERS.
Printed at Salem, by Thomas C. Cushing. [1796.] pp. [38,] errata. 8vo.
AAS. BA. EI. HC. JCB. NHHS. NYPL.

31520 WALKER, ROBERT   1716–1783
SERMONS ON PRACTICAL SUBJECTS. BY ROBERT WALKER, LATE ONE OF THE MINISTERS OF THE HIGH CHURCH OF EDINBURGH. TO WHICH IS PREFIXED, AN ACCOUNT OF THE AUTHOR'S LIFE, AND A CHARACTER OF HIM: BY HUGH BLAIR, D. D. THE FIRST AMERICAN EDITION. IN TWO VOLUMES. VOL. I.
Albany: Printed and sold by John M' Donald, Bookseller, No. 18, State-Street. M,DCC,XCVI. pp. (2), [iv], (4), 285. 8vo.   AAS. HC.
The second volume was published in 1797. Part of the edition of the first volume was destroyed by fire.

31521   WARNER, Effingham
SELECT PIECES OF RELIGIOUS SUBJECTS, WRITTEN BY EFFINGHAM WARNER: TO WHICH ARE PREFIXED, A SHORT SKETCH OF HIS LIFE AND CHARACTER. [Four lines of quotations.]
Printed at New-York, by James Oram, No. 33 Liberty-Street. 1796. pp. (2), 104. 12mo.   AAS. BM. NYPL.

31522   WARREN, John   1753–1815
AN EULOGY ON THE HONOURABLE THOMAS RUSSELL, ESQ. LATE PRESIDENT OF THE SOCIETY FOR PROPAGATING THE GOSPEL AMONG THE INDIANS AND OTHERS, IN NORTH AMERICA; THE HUMANE SOCIETY OF THE COMMONWEALTH OF MASSACHUSETTS; THE AGRICULTURAL SOCIETY; THE SOCIETY FOR THE ADVICE OF IMMIGRANTS; THE BOSTON CHAMBER OF COMMERCE; AND THE NATIONAL BANK IN BOSTON. WHO DIED AT BOSTON, APRIL 8, 1796. DELIVERED, MAY 4, 1796, BEFORE THE SEVERAL SOCIETIES TO WHICH HE BELONGED. BY JOHN WARREN.
Boston: Printed by Benjamin Sweetser, corner of Wing's-Lane. M,DCC,XCVI. pp. [31], [3.] 4to.   AAS. BA. BM. BPL. BU. JCB. LOC. MHS. NYHS. NYPL. SGO. UTS.

The appended pages contain: A Monody on the death of the honourable Thomas Russell, esq; sung at the Eulogy of Doctor John Warren; in the church in Brattle-street, on Wednesday, May 4, 1796. Written at the request of the several Societies, of which he was a member. Set to music by Mr. Hans Gram. pp. (3).

31523   WARREN, RHODE ISLAND. BAPTIST ASSOCIATION.
MINUTES OF THE WARREN ASSOCIATION, HELD AT THE BAPTIST MEETING-HOUSE IN CHARLTON, SEPTEMBER 13 AND 14, 1796.
Boston: Printed by Manning & Loring. M,DCC,XCVI. pp. 10. 12mo.   AAS. JCB. NYPL.

31524   WARWICK. NEW YORK. BAPTIST ASSOCIATION.
MINUTES OF THE WARWICK BAPTIST ASSOCIATION, HELD AT PLEASANT VALLEY, ULSTER COUNTY, MAY 31, 1796.
New-York: Printed by T. & J. Swords. 1796. 4to.

31525   WASHINGTON, George   1732–1799
THE ADDRESS OF HIS EXCELLENCY GEORGE WASHINGTON, PRESIDENT OF THE UNITED STATES OF AMERICA: TO THE PEOPLE OF THE SAID STATES: ON HIS DECLINING TO BE A CANDIDATE FOR THE OFFICE OF PRESIDENT AT THE ENSUING ELECTION.
Albany: Printed and sold by Barber & Southwick, Faust's Statue, below the Dutch Church, State-Street. 1796. pp. 22. 8vo.   NYHS.

31526   —— — THE PRESIDENT'S ADDRESS TO THE PEOPLE OF THE UNITED STATES, ON HIS DECLINING ANOTHER ELECTION.
Amherst, Newhampshire: Printed by Samuel Cushing. [1796.] pp. 35. 12mo.   JCB.

31527   —— — ADDRESS OF GEORGE WASHINGTON, TO THE PEOPLE OF THE UNITED STATES PREPARATORY TO HIS DECLINATION.
Printed for George Keatinge . . . Baltimore. 1796. pp. 23. 12mo.   BM. BPL.

31528   —— — ADDRESS OF GEORGE WASHINGTON, PRESIDENT OF THE UNITED STATES, TO THE PEOPLE OF AMERICA, PRESENTED 17TH SEPTEMBER, 1796, ON APPRISING THEM THAT HE DECLINED BEING CONSIDERED AMONG THE NUMBER OF THOSE OUT OF WHOM A CHOICE IS TO BE MADE OF ONE, TO ADMINISTER THE EXECUTIVE GOVERNMENT OF THE UNITED STATES. "BEGIN WITH THE INFANT IN HIS CRADLE, LET THE FIRST WORD HE LISPS BE WASHINGTON."
Bennington: From the Press of A. Haswell, Annoque Domini. 1796. pp. 45. 24mo.   BA.

WASHINGTON, GEORGE, continued.

31529   —— — ADDRESS OF GEORGE WASHINGTON, ON DECLINING BEING CONSIDERED A CANDIDATE FOR THE PRESIDENCY OF THE UNITED STATES.
[Without place or Printer.] 1796. pp. 22. 8vo.   MHS.

31530   —— — THE LEGACY OF THE FATHER OF HIS COUNTRY. ADDRESS OF GEORGE WASHINGTON, PRESIDENT OF THE UNITED STATES, TO HIS FELLOW CITIZENS, ON DECLINING BEING CONSIDERED A CANDIDATE FOR THEIR FUTURE SUFFRAGES. "IT IS A LEGACY WORTHY SUCH A FATHER."—SHAKSPEARE.
Printed at Boston, by John Russell—and sold at his Office, Quaker-Lane; and by David West, No. 36, Marlborough-Street. 1796. pp. 43. 16mo.
       AAS. BA. JCB. LOC. MHS.
"Elegantly printed, from new type, on vellum paper."

31531   —— — THE PRESIDENT'S ADDRESS TO THE PEOPLE OF THE UNITED STATES.
Boston: Printed by Benjamin Sweetser. 1796.
"Worthy a page of marble—and a cover of gold!"

31532   —— — AN ADDRESS TO THE PEOPLE OF THE UNITED STATES, BY GEORGE WASHINGTON, ESQUIRE.
Chambersburg: Printed by Dover & Harper. DCCXCVI [sic 1796.] pp. [19.] 8vo.   NYPL.

31533   —— — AN ADDRESS OF THE PRESIDENT TO THE PEOPLE OF THE UNITED STATES ON HIS DECLINING BEING CONSIDERED A CANDIDATE FOR THE PRESIDENCY AT THE ENSUING ELECTION.
Charleston: Printed by Timothy & Mason. 1796.

31534   —— — THE ADDRESS TO THE PEOPLE OF THE UNITED STATES. FROM GEORGE WASHINGTON, PRESIDENT.
New-Castle: Printed by Samuel and John Adams. 1796. pp. (21). 8vo.
       LOC. NYPL.
The copy in the Library of Congress is in large paper format, in folio, —the best example of the Press of the Printers.

31535   —— — THE RESIGNATION OF HIS EXCELLENCY GEORGE WASHINGTON, PRESIDENT OF THE UNITED STATES; AND HIS ADDRESS TO THE CITIZENS OF THE UNITED STATES, SEPTEMBER 17TH, 1796. [U. S. arms.]
Printed at New-York, by James Oram, No. 33, Liberty-Street. [1796.] pp. 26. 8vo.   JCB.

31536   —— — ADDRESS OF THE PRESIDENT, TO THE PEOPLE OF THE UNITED STATES.
New-York: Printed by John Tiebout, No. 358, Pearl-Street. 1796. pp. 36. 18mo.   LOC. NYPL.

31537   —— — PRESIDENT WASHINGTON'S RESIGNATION, AND ADDRESS TO THE CITIZENS OF THE UNITED STATES, SEPTEMBER 17, 1796. AN INVALUABLE LEGACY TO AMERICANS. [Vignette.]
Newburyport: Printed by William Barrett. 1796. pp. (19). 8vo.
       AAS. LOC. NYPL.

31538   —— — *Heading:* COLUMBIA'S LEGACY; OR, WASHINGTON'S FAREWELL ADDRESS. TO THE PEOPLE OF THE UNITED STATES.
[Newburyport: Printed by Angier March. Sold at Barrett's Book-store, Market-Square. 1796.] pp. (3)–[50], (1). 24mo.   NYPL.
"This "Code of political morality" is published in a pamphlet, and put a low price, that no citizen may be deprived of so valuable a production."

WASHINGTON, GEORGE, continued.

31539 —— — TO THE PEOPLE OF THE UNITED STATES. FRIENDS AND FELLOW CITIZENS, THE PERIOD FOR A NEW ELECTION OF A CITIZEN TO ADMINISTER THE EXECUTIVE GOVERNMENT OF THE UNITED STATES BEING NOT FAR DISTANT, . . . I SHOULD NOW APPRISE YOU OF THE RESOLUTION I HAVE FORMED, TO DECLINE BEING CONSIDERED AMONG THE NUMBER OF THOSE OUT OF WHOM A CHOICE IS TO BE MADE. [Six columns.] G. WASHINGTON. UNITED STATES, 17TH SEPTEMBER, 1796. [Colophon:]
> *Newport, (R. I.) Printed by Henry Barber.* [1796.] pp. (2). fol.   AAS.

31540 —— — THE ADDRESS OF GEORGE WASHINGTON, PRESIDENT OF THE UNITED STATES TO HIS FELLOW-CITIZENS, ON DECLINING BEING CONSIDERED AS A CANDIDATE FOR THEIR FUTURE SUFFRAGES.
> *Norwich: Printed by Thomas Hubbard.* 1796. pp. 34. 12mo.

31541 —— — THE ADDRESS OF GEORGE WASHINGTON, PRESIDENT OF THE UNITED STATES, TO HIS FELLOW-CITIZENS, ON DECLINING BEING CONSIDERED A CANDIDATE FOR THEIR SUFFRAGES.
> *Norwich: Printed by John Trumbull,* 1796.

31542 —— — *Heading:* THE PRESIDENT'S ADDRESS TO THE PEOPLE OF THE UNITED STATES. . . . GEO: WASHINGTON. UNITED STATES, 17TH SEPTEMBER, 1796.
> *[Philadelphia:* 1796.] pp. [16.] 8vo.   BA. JCB. NYPL.

This is the first edition of the Address.

31543 —— — THE PRESIDENT'S ADDRESS TO THE PEOPLE OF THE UNITED STATES, ANNOUNCING HIS INTENTION OF RETIRING FROM PUBLIC LIFE AT THE EXPIRATION OF THE PRESENT CONSTITUTIONAL TERM OF PRESIDENCY. [Signed, G. WASHINGTON. UNITED STATES, 17TH SEPTEMBER, 1796.]
> *Philadelphia: Printed for J. Ormrod, No. 41, Chesnut-Street, By Ormrod & Conrad.* 1796. pp. (23). 8vo.   HC. HSP. LCP. LOC. NYPL.

31544 —— — THE PRESIDENT'S ADDRESS TO THE PEOPLE OF THE UNITED STATES. ANNOUNCING HIS INTENTION OF RETIRING FROM PUBLIC LIFE AT THE EXPIRATION OF THE PRESENT CONSTITUTIONAL TERM OF PRESIDENCY. [Vignette.] ORMROD'S SECOND EDITION.
> *Philadelphia: Printed for J. Ormrod, No. 41, Chesnut-Street, by Ormrod & Conrad.* 1796. pp. (23). 8vo.   CLS. JCB. LOC. NYPL.

31545 —— — COLUMBIA'S LEGACY; OR, WASHINGTON'S VALUABLE ADVICE TO HIS FELLOW CITIZENS, PUBLISHED BY HIM AT THE PERIOD OF ANNOUNCING HIS INTENTION OF RETIRING FROM PUBLIC LIFE AT THE EXPIRATION OF THE PRESENT CONSTITUTIONAL TERM OF THE PRESIDENCY OF THE UNITED STATES. TO WHICH IS ADDED, HIS SPEECH TO CONGRESS, AT THEIR PRESENT SESSION, WHICH TERMINATES HIS POLITICAL CAREER.
> *Philadelphia: Printed by H. Sweitzer & J. Ormrod, December 10th,* 1796. pp. 89. 32mo.   LOC. NYPL.

Second title: THE PRESIDENT'S SPEECH, TO THE CONGRESS OF THE UNITED STATES, AT THEIR SESSION BEGUN AND HELD ON MONDAY DEC. 5, 1796.
> *Philadelphia: Printed by H. Sweitzer & J. Ormrod, December 10th,* 1796. pp. (2), (2), (65)–89.

31546 —— — THE PRESIDENT'S ADDRESS TO THE PEOPLE OF THE UNITED STATES, ANNOUNCING HIS DESIGN OF RETIRING FROM PUBLIC LIFE, AT THE EXPIRATION OF THE PRESENT CONSTITUTIONAL TERM OF THE PRESIDENTSHIP.
> *Philadelphia: Printed for the Proprietors, at No. 118, Chesnut-Street, September 20,* 1796. pp. [16.] 8vo.   LOC.

WASHINGTON, George, continued.

31547   —— — The President's Address to the people of the United States, September 17, 1796, intimating his resolution of retiring from public service, when the present term of presidency expires. [U. S. arms.]

> *Philadelphia: Printed for W. Young, Mills & Son, No. 52, Second-street, corner of Chesnut-street.* M,DCC,XCVI. pp. (28). 8vo.   BM. NYPL.

31548   —— — *Heading:* The President's Address to the people [*sic*] of the United States.

> [*Without place or Printer.* 1796.] pp. 24. 8vo.   LOC.

31549   —— — The Address of resignation of our worthy President George Washington.

> *Poughkeepsie: Printed by Nicholas Power.* 1796.

31550   —— — Address of George Washington, to the people of the United States, announcing his resolution to retire from public life. Containing an invaluable legacy of good advice, worthy to be had in perpetual remembrance.

> *Printed at Providence, by Carter and Wilkinson, and sold at their Book-Store, opposite the Market.* 1796. pp. (22). 8vo.   JCB. LOC. NYPL. RIHS.

31551   —— — The Legacy of the Father of his Country. Address of George Washington, President of the United States, to his fellow citizens, on declining being considered a candidate for their future suffrages. "It is a Legacy worthy such a Father." Shakespeare.

> *Printed at Stockbridge, by Loring Andrews.* 1796. pp. 26. 8vo.   BA. LOC.

"The important truths which the Address contains are at this time particularly interesting to all who love their country."

31552   —— — George Washington's Resignation of the presidency of the United States of America: September 17th, 1796.

> *Windsor: Printed by Alden Spooner.* M,DCC,XCVI.. pp. 23. 12mo.   AAS.

31553 **WASHINGTON'S** march [and, The President's march.]

> *New York: Printed and sold by B. Carr.* 1796.

31554 —— The President's march. [and Washington's march.]

> *Philadelphia: Printed and sold by Benjamin Carr.* 1796.

The music of both is the same.

31555 —— Washington's march. [and, Washington's march at the battle of Trenton.]

> *Philadelphia. Published & sold at G. Willig's Musical Magazine.* [1796.]

31556 **WASHINGTON** Advertiser. Number 1. Wednesday, March 9, [— Number 19, Wednesday, May 11, 1796.]

> *Greenleaf's Point, City of Washington. Published by John Crocker & Co.* 1796. 4to.   HC.

Established, as a semi-weekly, by John Crocker, in succession to the *Impartial Observer, and Washington Advertiser,* and continued to the issue for May 11th—the last number located. And succeeded by the following:

31557   THE WASHINGTON [cut] Gazette. Number 1 of Volume i. From Saturday,
         June 11, to Wednesday, June 15, [— Number 54. From Wednesday, Decem-
         ber 28, to Saturday, December 31, 1796.]
             City of Washington: Published by Benjamin More, every Wednesday and
             Saturday, price 4 dollars per ann. (one dollar to be paid at the end of every quar-
             ter) at the house next west of the Hotel, where subscriptions will be thankfully re-
             ceived,—handbills, &c. printed at the shortest notice. 1796. fol.   AAS. HC. LOC.
             The cut is a representation of Liberty and Justice, with an all-seeing
             eye between the figures, with the motto, Nunquam dormio. Established,
             as a semi-weekly, by Benjamin More, and continued by him into March,
             1798. The venture appears as an unprofitable one. With the issue for
             July 26, 1797, publication was temporarily suspended "until the pub-
             lication is attended with some profit to the Publisher;" and when re-
             sumed with the issue for September 16, 1797, it was as a weekly on
             Saturdays, and the cut dropped from the heading. The issue for De-
             cember 23, 1797, announced that the next number "would not appear
             until the week after Christmas." The final issue, for March 17-24, 1798,
             editorially states: "I shall not be able to continue the publication of
             the Washington Gazette, except some friend should lend a helping hand.
             HOPE has led me into a thicket of difficulties—and appears to be de-
             parting from me."

31558   WASHINGTON [cut] Patrol. [Mottoes.] Vol. i. No. 33. Wednesday, January
         6, [—   — 1796.]
             Salem. (Washington County) State of New-York:—Printed by W. W. Wands
             & S. J. Honeywood, . . . 1796. fol.
             Discontinued within its first year. And succeeded, in 1798, by the
             Northern Centinel,

31559   THE WASHINGTON Spy. Vol. vi. Num. 283. Wednesday, January 6, [—No.
         334. Wednesday, December 28, 1796.]
             Elizabeth (Hager's) Town, (Maryland) Printed by Phebe Herbert, at her
             Printing-Office in the Main Street leading to the Western country. . . . 1796. fol.
             The partnership of Phebe Herbert and John D. Carey, was dissolved
             by mutual consent, June 1, 1796, Phebe Herbert continuing the publi-
             cation of The Spy.

31560   WATSON, Elkanah   1758–1842
         Land for sale. The following lots and parts of lots in the County of
             Onondago, Viz . . . Elkanah Watson, Albany, March 15, 1796. [Colo-
             phon:]
             Printed by Barber & Southwick, Albany. [1796.] Broadside. fol.

31561   WATSON, Richard   1737-1816
         An Apology for christianity, in a series of letters addressed to Edward
             Gibbon, Esq. author of the History of the decline and fall of the Roman
             Empire. Being a necessary and instructive appendix thereto. By R. Wat-
             son, d. d. f. r. s. lord bishop of Landaff, and regius professor of divinity
             in the University of Cambridge.
             New-Brunswick Printed by Abraham Blauvelt. 1796.

31562   —— — An Apology for christianity, in a series of letters, addressed to
             Edward Gibbon, esq. author of the History of the decline and fall of
             the Roman Empire. Being a necessary and instructive appendix thereto.
             By R. Watson, d. d. f. r. s. lord bishop of Landaff, and regius professor
             of divinity in the University of Cambridge.
             Philadelphia: Printed by James Carey, No. 83, North Second-Street. 1796.
             [Price twenty-five cents.] pp. (56). 8vo.   AAS. BA. CLS. JCB. LOC. MHS. NYPL.

WATSON, RICHARD, continued.

31563   —— —— AN APOLOGY FOR CHRISTIANITY. IN A SERIES OF LETTERS, ADDRESSED TO EDWARD GIBBON, ESQ. AUTHOR OF THE HISTORY OF THE DECLINE AND FALL OF THE ROMAN EMPIRE. BEING A NECESSARY AND INSTRUCTIVE APPENDIX THERETO. BY R. WATSON, D. D. F. R. S. LORD BISHOP OF LANDAFF, AND REGIUS PROFESSOR OF DIVINITY IN THE UNIVERSITY OF CAMBRIDGE, THIRD AMERICAN EDITION.
    Schenectady: Printed by Cornelius P. Wyckoff. 1796. pp. 144. 24mo.   AAS.

31564   —— —— AN APOLOGY FOR THE BIBLE, IN A SERIES OF LETTERS, ADDRESSED TO THOMAS PAINE, AUTHOR OF A BOOK ENTITLED, THE AGE OF REASON, PART THE SECOND, BEING AN INVESTIGATION OF TRUE AND OF FABULOUS THEOLOGY. BY R. WATSON, D. D. F. R. S. LORD BISHOP OF LANDAFF, AND REGIUS PROFESSOR OF DIVINITY IN THE UNIVERSITY OF CAMBRIDGE.
    Albany: Printed and sold by Barber & Southwick, Faust's Statue, below the Dutch Church, State Street. 1796. pp. (192). 12mo.   AAS. JCB. NYPL.

31565   —— —— AN APOLOGY FOR THE BIBLE, IN A SERIES OF LETTERS, ADDRESSED TO THOMAS PAINE, AUTHOR OF A BOOK, ENTITLED THE AGE OF REASON, PART THE SECOND, BEING AN INVESTIGATION OF TRUE AND OF FABULOUS THEOLOGY. BY R. WATSON, D. D. F. R. S. LORD BISHOP OF LANDAFF, AND REGIUS PROFESSOR OF DIVINITY IN THE UNIVERSITY OF CAMBRIDGE.
    Boston: Printed by Manning & Loring, for James White, at Franklin's Head, Court-Street, 1796. pp. 168. 8vo.   AAS. BA. BM. JCB. LOC. NYPL.

31566   —— —— AN APOLOGY FOR THE BIBLE; IN A SERIES OF LETTERS, ADDRESSED TO THOMAS PAINE, AUTHOR OF A BOOK, ENTITLED, THE AGE OF REASON, PART THE SECOND; BEING AN INVESTIGATION OF TRUE AND OF FABULOUS THEOLOGY. BY R. WATSON, D. D. F. R. S. LORD BISHOP OF LANDAFF, AND REGIUS PROFESSOR OF DIVINITY IN THE UNIVERSITY OF CAMBRIDGE.
    Lancaster, Printed and sold by W. Hamilton, and W. & R. Dickson, Kingstreet, 1796. pp. (118). 8vo.   JCB. LOC. NYPL.

31567   —— —— AN APOLOGY FOR THE BIBLE, IN A SERIES OF LETTERS, ADDRESSED TO THOMAS PAINE, AUTHOR OF A BOOK ENTITLED, THE AGE OF REASON, PART THE SECOND, BEING AN INVESTIGATION OF TRUE AND OF FABULOUS THEOLOGY. BY R. WATSON, D. D. F. R. S. LORD BISHOP OF LANDAFF, AND REGIUS PROFESSOR OF DIVINITY IN THE UNIVERSITY OF CAMBRIDGE.
    New-Brunswick: Printed by Abraham Blauvelt. 1796. pp. (2), (201). 24mo.   AAS. JCB. LOC. NYPL.

31568   —— —— AN APOLOGY FOR THE BIBLE. IN A SERIES OF LETTERS, ADDRESSED TO THOMAS PAINE, AUTHOR OF A BOOK ENTITLED, THE AGE OF REASON, PART THE SECOND. BEING AN INVESTIGATION OF TRUE AND OF FABULOUS THEOLOGY. BY R. WATSON, D. D. F. R. S. LORD BISHOP OF LANDAFF, AND REGIUS PROFESSOR OF DIVINITY IN THE UNIVERSITY OF CAMBRIDGE.
    New-York: Printed by John Bull, No. 115, Cherry-Street, 1796. pp. (iv), (242), (10). 8vo.   AAS. JCB. LOC. NYPL.

31569   —— —— AN APOLOGY FOR THE BIBLE, IN A SERIES OF LETTERS, ADDRESSED TO THOMAS PAINE, AUTHOR OF A BOOK ENTITLED, THE AGE OF REASON, PART THE SECOND, BEING AN INVESTIGATION OF TRUE AND OF FABULOUS THEOLOGY. BY R. WATSON, D. D. F. R. S. LORD BISHOP OF LANDAFF, AND REGIUS PROFESSOR OF DIVINITY IN THE UNIVERSITY OF CAMBRIDGE.
    New-York: Printed by T. and J. Swords, No. 99 Pearl-street. —1796.— pp. (178), (1). 12mo.   AAS. JCB. LOC. NYPL.

    In two states—a few copies printed on fine paper, and neatly bound and lettered.

WATSON, Richard, continued.

31570 —— — An Apology for the Bible, in a series of letters, addressed to Thomas Paine, author of a book entitled, The Age of Reason, part the second, being an investigation of true and of fabulous theology. By R. Watson, d. d. f. r. s. lord bishop of Landaff, and regius professor of divinity in the University at Cambridge.

Newburgh: Printed by David Denniston.—1796.—pp. (228). 12mo. AAS.

An interesting list of Subscribers' names stops at the letter P at the ending of signature T.

31571 —— — An Apology for the Bible, in a series of letters, addressed to Thomas Paine, author of a book entitled, The Age of Reason, part the second, being an investigation of true and of fabulous theology. By R. Watson, d. d. f. r. s. lord bishop of Landaff, and regius professor of divinity in the University of Cambridge.

Philadelphia: Printed by James Carey, No. 83, North Second-Street. 1796. *[Price three-eighths of a dollar.]* pp. (2), (80). 8vo. AAS. JCB. LOC. NYHS. NYPL.

31572 —— — An Apology for the Bible, in a series of letters, addressed to Thomas Paine, author of a book entitled, The Age of Reason, part the second, being an investigation of true and of fabulous theology. By R. Watson, d. d. f. r. s. lord bishop of Landaff, and regius professor of divinity in the University of Cambridge. Second Philadelphia edition.

Philadelphia: Printed by James Carey, No. 83, North Second-Street. 1796. *[Price three-eighths of a dollar.]* pp. (2), (80). 8vo. AAS. BA. JCB. LOC.

31573 —— — An Apology for the Bible, in a series of letters, addressed to Thomas Paine, author of a book entitled The Age of Reason, part the second, being an investigation of true and of fabulous theology. By R. Watson, d. d. f. r. s. lord bishop of Landaff, and regius professor of divinity in the University of Cambridge.

Philadelphia: Printed for W. Young, Mills & Son, No. 52, corner of Second and Chesnut Streets, by W. Woodward. 1796. pp. 206. 8vo. AAS. JCB. LOC.

31574 WATTS, Isaac 1674–1748
The Beauties of the late rev. dr. Isaac Watts; containing the most striking and admired passages in the works of that justly celebrated divine, philosopher, moralist, and poet: equally calculated for the communication of polite and useful knowledge, and the increase of wisdom and happiness. To which is added, the Life of the Author. [Edited by Mason Locke Weems.]

Elizabeth-Town: Printed by Shepard Kollock. M,DCC,XCVI. pp. (2), 229, (5). 18mo. AAS BA. JCB. NYPL.

31575 —— Dr. Watts's Catechism for little children.
Windham: Printed by John Byrne. 1796.

31576 —— Dr. Watts' Catechisms and Prayers, for children and youth. To which are added, his Preservative from the sins and follies of childhood and youth; and a large catalogue of remarkable Scripture names, collected for the use of children, and explained for their better acquaintance with the Holy Scriptures.

Charleston: Printed by W. P. Young, No. 43, Broad-Street. 1796.

31577 —— Divine and moral songs, attempted in easy language for the use of children. Revised and corrected. By Isaac Watts, d. d.

Boston: Printed and sold by Samuel Hall, in Cornhill. 1796. pp. 70. 24mo. AAS.

WATTS, Isaac, continued.

31578   —— Divine and moral songs for children; revised and altered so as to render them of general use. [with, A Catechism. and Prayers.] By Isaac Watts, d. d.

> *Leominster: Printed by Charles Prentiss. Sold wholesale & retail at his Bookstore.* 1796. pp. 72. 24mo.   AAS.

An edition was printed for Robert B. Thomas, Sterling, this year.

31579   —— Logic: or, the right use of reason, in the inquiry after truth. With a variety of rules to guard against error in the affairs of religion and human life, as well as in the sciences. By Isaac Watts, d. d. Second American edition.

> *Printed at Newburyport, by W. Barrett, for Thomas and Andrews, Faust's Statue, No. 45, Newbury-Street, Boston, July,* 1796. pp. 285. 12mo.
>   AAS. JCB. NYPL.

31580   —— Miscellaneous thoughts, in prose and verse, on natural, moral and divine subjects: written chiefly in younger years. By I. Watts, d. d. [One line of Latin from] Hor. The first American edition.

> *Elizabeth-Town: Printed and sold by Shepard Kollock.* M,DCC,XCVI. pp. 240, (3). 12mo.   AAS. NYPL.

31581   —— Reliquiæ juveniles. Miscellaneous thoughts, in prose and verse, on natural, moral, and divine subjects; written chiefly in younger years. To which is added, remnants of time, employed in prose and verse. By I. Watts, d. d. [One line of Latin from] Hor. First American edition, with large additions.

> *Printed for William P. Blake, No. 59, Cornhill, Boston; by Charles Peirce, Portsmouth.* 1796. pp. xii, 304. 12mo.   AAS. JCB. NYPL.

31582   THE WAY to be happy in a miserable world. The sixth edition.
> *Norwich: Printed by John Trumbull.* 1796. pp. 23. 12mo.

31583   WEATHERWISE, Abraham, pseudonym.
Weatherwise's Almanack, for the year of our Lord 1797. Being the first after bissextile, or leap-year; [Twenty lines.]

> *Printed at Boston and sold by J. Boyle, C. Bingham, B. Larkin, Wm. Pelham, E. Larkin, J. Nancrede, J. West, J. Bumstead,* . . . [1796.] pp. (24) 12mo.   AAS. BM.

31584   WEBSTER, Noah, junior   1758–1843
An American selection of lessons, in reading and speaking. Calculated to improve the minds and refine the taste of youth. And also, to instruct them in the geography, history and politics of the United States. To which is prefixed, Rules in elocution, and directions for expressing the principal passions of the mind. Being the third part of a Grammatical institute of the English language. By Noah Webster, jun esquire [Two lines from] Mirabeau. The second Albany edition.

> *Printed by Charles R. & George Webster, [with privilege of copy-right]. At their Bookstore, in the White House, corner of State and Pearl-Streets, opposite the City-Tavern, Albany;* 1796. ☞ *Sold at said Bookstore, by wholesale and retail.* pp. 289, (1). 12mo.   AAS.

WEBSTER, NOAH, JUNIOR, continued.

31585 —— — AN AMERICAN SELECTION OF LESSONS IN READING AND SPEAKING. CALCU-
LATED TO IMPROVE THE MINDS AND REFINE THE TASTE OF YOUTH. AND ALSO TO
INSTRUCT THEM IN THE GEOGRAPHY, HISTORY, AND POLITICS OF THE UNITED STATES.
TO WHICH ARE PREFIXED, RULES IN ELOCUTION, AND DIRECTIONS FOR EXPRESSING
THE PRINCIPAL PASSIONS OF THE MIND. BEING THE THIRD PART OF A GRAMMATICAL
INSTITUTE OF THE ENGLISH LANGUAGE. TO WHICH IS ADDED, AN APPENDIX, CON-
TAINING SEVERAL NEW DIALOGUES. BY NOAH WEBSTER, JUN. ESQUIRE. AUTHOR
OF "DISSERTATIONS ON THE ENGLISH LANGUAGE," "COLLECTION OF ESSAYS AND
FUGITIVE WRITINGS," &C. THOMAS AND ANDREWS' SIXTH EDITION. WITH MANY
CORRECTIONS AND IMPROVEMENTS, BY THE AUTHOR. [Two lines from] MIRABEAU.

*Printed at Boston, by Isaiah Thomas and Ebenezer T. Andrews. At Faust's
Statue, No. 45, Newbury Street. Sold, wholesale and retail, at their Bookstore; by
said Thomas, at his Bookstore in Worcester; and by Thomas, Andrews and Butler,
Booksellers, Baltimore. Jan. 1796.* pp. 239, (1), (2), portrait. 12mo. AAS. NYPL.

Frontispiece portrait headed: Part III.—Sixth edition.—1796.

31586 —— — AN AMERICAN SELECTION OF LESSONS IN READING AND SPEAKING. CALCU-
LATED TO IMPROVE THE MINDS AND REFINE THE TASTE OF YOUTH. AND ALSO TO
INSTRUCT THEM IN THE GEOGRAPHY, HISTORY, AND POLITICS OF THE UNITED STATES.
TO WHICH ARE PREFIXED, RULES IN ELOCUTION, AND DIRECTIONS FOR EXPRESSING
THE PRINCIPAL PASSIONS OF THE MIND. BEING THE THIRD PART OF A GRAMMATICAL
INSTITUTE OF THE ENGLISH LANGUAGE. TO WHICH IS ADDED, AN APPENDIX, CON-
TAINING SEVERAL NEW DIALOGUES. BY NOAH WEBSTER, JUN. ESQUIRE. AUTHOR
OF "DISSERTATIONS ON THE ENGLISH LANGUAGE," "COLLECTION OF ESSAYS AND
FUGITIVE WRITINGS," &C. THOMAS AND ANDREWS' SEVENTH EDITION. WITH MANY
CORRECTIONS AND IMPROVEMENTS, BY THE AUTHOR. [Two lines from] MIRABEAU.

*Printed at Boston, by Isaiah Thomas and Ebenezer T. Andrews, at Faust's
Statue, No. 45, Newbury Street. Sold, wholesale and retail, at their Bookstore; by
said Thomas, at his Bookstore in Worcester; and by Thomas, Andrews and Butler,
Booksellers, Baltimore. June, 1796.* pp. [240], portrait. 12mo. AAS.

Frontispiece portrait headed: Part III.—seventh edition.—1796.

31587 —— — AN AMERICAN SELECTION OF LESSONS IN READING AND SPEAKING. CALCU-
LATED TO IMPROVE THE MINDS AND REFINE THE TASTE OF YOUTH. AND ALSO TO
INSTRUCT THEM IN THE GEOGRAPHY, HISTORY, AND POLITICS OF THE UNITED
STATES. TO WHICH ARE PREFIXED, RULES IN ELOCUTION, AND DIRECTIONS FOR EX-
PRESSING THE PRINCIPAL PASSIONS OF THE MIND. BEING THE THIRD PART OF A
GRAMMATICAL INSTITUTE OF THE ENGLISH LANGUAGE. TO WHICH IS ADDED, AN
APPENDIX, CONTAINING SEVERAL NEW DIALOGUES. BY NOAH WEBSTER, JUN. ES-
QUIRE, AUTHOR OF "DISSERTATIONS ON THE ENGLISH LANGUAGE," "COLLECTION OF
ESSAYS AND FUGITIVE WRITINGS," &C. THOMAS AND ANDREWS' EIGHTH EDITION.
WITH MANY CORRECTIONS AND IMPROVEMENTS, BY THE AUTHOR. [Two lines from]
MIRABEAU.

*Printed at Boston, by Isaiah Thomas and Ebenezer T. Andrews, at Faust's
Statue, No. 45, Newbury Street. Sold, wholesale and retail, at their Bookstore; by
said Thomas, at his Bookstore in Worcester; and by Thomas, Andrews and Butler. Booksellers, Baltimore.—June, 1796.* pp. [240], (2), portrait. 12mo.

AAS. BA. YC.

Frontispiece portrait headed: Part III.—Eighth edition.—1796.

WEBSTER, Noah, junior, continued.

31588   — — An American selection of lessons in reading and speaking. Calculated to improve the minds and refine the taste of youth. And also, to instruct them in the geography, history, and politics of the United States. To which are prefixed, Rules in elocution, and directions for expressing the principal passions of the mind. Being the third part of a Grammatical institute of the English language. To which is added, an appendix, containing several new dialogues. By Noah Webster, jun. esquire. Author of "Dissertations on the English language," "Collection of essays and fugitive writings," &c. Thomas and Andrews' ninth edition. With many corrections and improvements, by the Author. [Two lines from] Mirabeau.

Printed at Boston, by Isaiah Thomas and Ebenezer T. Andrews, at Faust's Statue, No. 45, Newbury Street. Sold, wholesale and retail, at their Bookstore; by Thomas, Son & Thomas, in Worcester; by Thomas, Andrews & Butler, in Baltimore; and by Thomas, Andrews & Penniman, in Albany—Dec. 1796. pp. [240,] frontispiece. 12mo.   JCB. LOC.

Frontispiece portrait of Noah Webster, jun. esq. headed: Part III.—
Ninth edition.—1796. Another "Ninth edition" bears the date of 1797.

31589   — — An American selection of lessons in reading and speaking. Calculated to improve the minds and refine the taste of youth. To which are prefixed Rules in elocution, and directions for expressing the principal passions of the mind. Being the third part of a Grammatical institute of the English language. By Noah Webster, jun. 'Author of 'Dissertations on the English language,' 'Collection of essays and fugitive writings,' 'The Prompter,' &c. The eleventh edition.

Hartford: Printed by Hudson & Goodwin. [With the privilege of copy right.] [1796.] pp. [261], (2). 12mo.   HC. NYPL.

31590   — The American spelling book: containing an easy standard of pronunciation. Being the first part of a Grammatical institute of the English language. To which is now first added, an appendix, containing a Moral catechism and a Federal catechism. By Noah Webster, jun. esquire, Author of "Dissertations on the English language," "Collection of essays and fugitive writings, &c. Thomas & Andrews' thirteenth edition. With many corrections and improvements by the Author.

Printed at Boston, by Isaiah Thomas and Ebenezer T. Andrews, Faust's Statue, No. 45, Newbury Street. Sold wholesale and retail, at their Bookstore; by said Thomas at his Bookstore in Worcester; and by the Booksellers in town and country. MDCCXCVI. pp. 156, portrait. 12mo.

31591   — — The American spelling book: containing an easy standard of pronunciation. Being the first part of a Grammatical institute of the English language. To which is now first added, an appendix, containing a Moral catechism and a Federal catechism. By Noah Webster, jun. esquire. Author of "Dissertations on the English language," "Collection of essays and fugitive writings," &c. Thomas & Andrews' fourteenth edition. With many corrections and improvements by the Author.

Printed at Boston, by Isaiah Thomas and Ebenezer T. Andrews, Faust's Statue, No. 45, Newbury Street. Sold wholesale and retail, at their Bookstore; by said Thomas at his Bookstore in Worcester; and by the Booksellers in town and country. MDCCXCVI. pp. 156, portrait. 12mo.

WEBSTER, NOAH, JUNIOR, continued.

31592 —— — THE AMERICAN SPELLING BOOK: CONTAINING AN EASY STANDARD OF PRO-
NUNCIATION. BEING THE FIRST PART OF A GRAMMATICAL INSTITUTE OF THE EN-
GLISH LANGUAGE. IN THREE PARTS. BY NOAH WEBSTER, JUNR. ESQUIRE. THE
EIGHTEENTH CONNECTICUT EDITION.

*Hartford: Printed by Hudson and Goodwin. [With the privilege of copy-
right.]* [1796.] pp. 165, (1). 12mo. NYPL.

The year of publication is taken from the Table of numbers on page
119.

31593 —— A COLLECTION OF PAPERS ON THE SUBJECT OF BILIOUS FEVERS, PREVALENT IN
THE UNITED STATES FOR A FEW YEARS PAST. COMPILED BY NOAH WEBSTER,
JUN. MEMBER OF THE SOCIETY FOR PROMOTING AGRICULTURE, ARTS AND MANU-
FACTURES IN THE STATE OF NEW-YORK, AND HONORARY MEMBER OF THE HIS-
TORICAL SOCIETY IN BOSTON.

*New-York: Printed by Hopkins, Webb and Co. No. 40, Pine-street. 1796.
[Published according to Act of Congress.]* pp. (x), [ix], 52, (2), (53)–60, (61)–144,
(145)–156, (157)–170, (171)–199, (201)–246.. 8vo.

AAS. BM. BPL. HC. HSP. LCP. LIHS. LOC. MHS. NYHS. NYPL. SGO. WL. YC.

Second title: AN ACCOUNT OF THE EPIDEMIC YELLOW FEVER, AS IT APPEARED IN
THE CITY OF NEW-YORK IN THE YEAR 1795. CONTAINING, BESIDES ITS HISTORY,
&C. THE MOST PROBABLE MEANS OF PREVENTING ITS RETURN, AND OF AVOIDING
IT, IN CASE IT SHOULD AGAIN BECOME EPIDEMIC. BY VALENTINE SEAMAN, M. D.
ONE OF THE PHYSICIANS OF THE HEALTH COMMITTEE OF NEW-YORK IN 1795.
[Eight lines from] ARMSTRONG.

*New-York: Printed by Hopkins, Webb & Co. No. 40, Pine-street.—1796.—
[Entered according to law.]* pp. [ix], 52.

Third title: LETTERS TO WILLIAM BUEL. PHYSICIAN, ON THE FEVER WHICH PRE-
VAILED IN NEW-YORK, IN 1795. BY E. H. SMITH. TO WHICH IS PREFIXED, AN
ACCOUNT OF THE FEBRILE DISEASES OF SHEFFIELD, (Massachusetts) IN THE YEARS
1793, 1794 AND 1795. BY W. BUEL. pp. (2), (53)—144.

Fourth title: LETTERS FROM DOCTORS TAYLOR AND HANSFORD, TO THE PUBLISH-
ER. pp. (2), (147)—153.

The copy in the New York Public Library contains mss. notes and corrections by the Author. 44th New York District Copyright, issued to
Noah Webster, junior, as Author, 8 July, 1796.

31594 —— A GRAMMATICAL INSTITUTE OF THE ENGLISH LANGUAGE, COMPRISING AN EASY,
CONCISE AND SYSTEMATIC METHOD OF EDUCATION. DESIGNED FOR THE USE OF
ENGLISH SCHOOLS IN AMERICA. IN THREE PARTS. PART SECOND: CONTAINING A
PLAIN AND COMPREHENSIVE GRAMMAR, GROUNDED ON THE TRUE PRINCIPLES AND
IDIOMS OF THE LANGUAGE. BY NOAH WEBSTER, JUN. ESQUIRE, AUTHOR OF "DIS-
SERTATIONS ON THE ENGLISH LANGUAGE," "COLLECTION OF ESSAYS AND FUGITIVE
WRITINGS," &C.

*Albany: Printed by Charles R. & George Webster, and sold at their Book-
store, in the White-House, corner of State and Pearl-streets. 1796. (With the
privilege of copy-right for the first, second and third parts of Websters Grammatical Institute.)* pp. 115, (1). 12mo. LOC. NYHS. NYPL.

WEBSTER, NOAH, JUNIOR, continued.

31595 —— — A GRAMMATICAL INSTITUTE OF THE ENGLISH LANGUAGE; COMPRISING AN EASY, CONCISE AND SYSTEMATIC METHOD OF EDUCATION. DESIGNED FOR THE USE OF ENGLISH SCHOOLS IN AMERICA. IN THREE PARTS. PART SECOND. CONTAINING A PLAIN AND COMPREHENSIVE GRAMMAR, GROUNDED ON THE TRUE PRINCIPLES AND IDIOMS OF THE LANGUAGE. BY NOAH WEBSTER, JUN. ESQUIRE. AUTHOR OF "DISSERTATIONS ON THE ENGLISH LANGUAGE," "COLLECTION OF ESSAYS AND FUGITIVE WRITINGS," &C. THOMAS AND ANDREWS' FOURTH EDITION. WITH MANY CORRECTIONS AND IMPROVEMENTS, BY THE AUTHOR.

> *Printed at Boston, by Isaiah Thomas and Ebenezer T. Andrews, at Faust's Statue, No. 45, Newbury Street. Sold, wholesale and retail, at their Bookstore; by said Thomas, at his Bookstore in Worcester; by Thomas, Andrews & Butler, in Baltimore; and by Thomas, Andrews & Penniman, in Albany.—Nov.* 1796. pp. 116, portrait. 12mo.   HC. NYPL.

Portrait headed: Part II. Thomas & Andrews' fourth edition.

31596 —— — A GRAMMATICAL INSTITUTE OF THE ENGLISH LANGUAGE; COMPRISING AN EASY, CONCISE AND SYSTEMATIC METHOD OF EDUCATION. DESIGNED FOR THE USE OF ENGLISH SCHOOLS IN AMERICA. IN THREE PARTS. PART SECOND. CONTAINING A PLAIN AND COMPREHENSIVE GRAMMAR, GROUNDED ON THE TRUE PRINCIPLES AND IDIOMS OF THE LANGUAGE. BY NOAH WEBSTER, JUN. ESQUIRE. AUTHOR OF "DISSERTATIONS ON THE ENGLISH LANGUAGE," "COLLECTION OF ESSAYS AND FUGITIVE WRITINGS," &C. THE FIFTH CONNECTICUT EDITION.

> *Hartford: Printed by Hudson & Goodwin.* 1796. pp. 136, (2). 12mo.
>   AAS. CHS. LOC. NL. NYPL. WL. YC.

31597 —— THE PROMPTER: OR, A COMMENTARY ON COMMON SAYINGS AND SUBJECTS; WHICH ARE FULL OF COMMON SENSE, THE BEST SENSE IN THE WORLD. "TO SEE ALL OTHERS' FAULTS AND FEEL OUR OWN."

> *Leominster: Printed by Charles Prentiss.* MDCCXCVI. pp. 44. 16mo. LEPL.

31598 —— — THE PROMPTER: OR, A COMMENTARY ON COMMON SAYINGS AND SUBJECTS; WHICH ARE FULL OF COMMON SENSE, THE BEST SENSE IN THE WORLD. "TO SEE ALL OTHERS FAULTS AND FEEL OUR OWN."

> *New-York: Printed by George Bunce & Co.* 1796.

31599 —— — THE PROMPTER: OR, A COMMENTARY ON COMMON SAYINGS AND SUBJECTS; WHICH ARE FULL OF COMMON SENSE, THE BEST SENSE IN THE WORLD. TO *see* ALL OTHERS' FAULTS AND *feel* OUR *own*."

> *Philadelphia: Printed for Mathew Carey, No.* 118, *Market-Street.* 1796. pp. (95). 12mo.   BM. EI. LOC. NJHS. NYPL.

31600 *Heading:* THE WEDDING: AN EPIC POEM,

> [*Without place or Printer.* 1796.] pp. (8). 8vo.   AAS.

This poem, without a title page, may be the same, advertised in Rutland, Vermont, in 1797, as: "The Marriage: an epic poem. Written by an Eminent American poet." *q. v.*

31601   THE WEEKLY ADVERTISER, OF READING, IN THE COUNTY OF BERKS. NO. 1. SATUR-
DAY, MAY 7, [— NO. 35. SATURDAY, DECEMBER 31, 1796.]
*This paper is published every Saturday by Jungmann and Company, in the
Printing-Office of Reading, at the rate of one dollar per annum, one half dollar to
be paid at subscribing, and half a dollar at the expiration of every six months.*
1796. 4to.

Established, as a weekly, by Gottlob Jungmann and Company, and
continued by them to February, 1800, when Carl A. Bruckmann was
admitted to partnership as Jungmann & Bruckmann. With the issue
for August 23, 1806, Bruckmann withdrew, and publication was continued by Gottlob Jungmann alone to August 1811, when a new series,
with new serial numbering, was begun, published by Gottlob Jungmann
and Company. In June, 1814, the title was changed to *The Weekly Advertiser of Reading, for Berks and Schuylkill County*, and in January
1815, publication was made in the names of Gottlob & John E. Jungmann. In September, 1815, the title was again changed to *The Reading
Weekly Advertiser for the Counties of Berks & Schuylkill*, which continued
until publication was discontinued in April, 1816.

31602   WEEKLY [U. S. arms] MONITOR. VOL. 12. NUMB. 563. WEDNESDAY, MAY 18, [—
VOL. XII. No. 594. WEDNESDAY, DECEMBER 28, 1796.]
Litchfield, (Connecticut): Printed by Thomas Collier. 1796. fol.   AAS.
In continuation of the *Litchfield Monitor, and agricultural register*. Va-
riously Lichfield and Litchfield; and T., Tho., and Thomas Collier.

31603   THE WEEKLY MUSEUM. VOL. VIII. NUMBER 399. SATURDAY, JANUARY 2, [—VOL.
IX. NUMBER 451. SATURDAY, DECEMBER 31, 1796.]
*New-York: Printed and published by John Harrisson, at his Printing-Office
(Yorick's Head) No. 3 Peck-Slip.* 1796. 4to.   AAS. HSP. LOC. NYHS. WHS.

31604   ——— ADDRESS OF THE CARRIER OF THE WEEKLY MUSEUM TO HIS PATRONS, WITH THE
COMPLIMENTS OF THE SEASON. [Two columns of verse.]
[New-York: Printed by John Harrisson, 1796.] Broadside. fol.

31605   WEEKLY [seal] ORACLE. VOL. I. No. 1. SATURDAY, OCTOBER 22, [— No. 11. SAT-
URDAY, DECEMBER 31, 1796.]
*New-London: Printed and published by James Springer, at his Printing-
Office, Beach-Street.* 1796. 4to.

Established, as a weekly, by James Springer, and continued by him to
October 27, 1801—the last number located. In October, 1797, the paper
was enlarged to folio, and the title altered to *Springer's Weekly Oracle*,
until its publication ceased.

31606   THE WEEKLY REGISTER. VOL. V. No. 7. WEDNESDAY, JANUARY 6, [— OCTOBER ?,
1796.]
Norwich: Printed by Thomas Hubbard, 24 rods west of the Meeting-House.
1796. fol.

In November, Thomas Hubbard removed his press to Chelsea Landing,
now a part of Norwich, and there established, with a new numbering,
The Chelsea Courier.

31607   WELCH, MOSES COOK   1754–1824
THE ADDRESSER ADDRESSED; OR A LETTER TO THE CORRESPONDENT; CONTAINING
SOME FREE REMARKS ON HIS "ADDRESS TO THE REV. MOSES C. WELCH." HUM-
BLY DEDICATED TO THE HONORABLE ZEPHANIAH SWIFT, ESQ. BY MOSES C. WELCH,
A. M. PASTOR OF A CHURCH IN MANSFIELD. [Two lines from] KING SOLOMON.
Norwich: Printed by Thomas Hubbard. M,DCC,XCVI. pp. 36. 8vo.
                                          AAS. CHS. JCB. NYPL. UTS.

31608   WELCH, Moses Cook, continued.
—— An Eulogy, pronounced at the funeral of dea. Benjamin Chaplin, late of Mansfield in Connecticut, March 27th, 1795. By Moses C. Welch, a. m. pastor of a church in Mansfield.
Norwich: Printed by Thomas Hubbard. 1796. pp. 10. 8vo.
           AAS. CHS. JCB. LOC. YC.
This is usually found stitched with David Avery's Two sermons, *q. v.*

31609   WELLES, Noah   1718–1776
A Vindication of the validity and divine right of Presbyterian ordination, as set forth in dr. Chauncy's Sermon at the Dudleian lecture, and mr. Welle's [*sic*] Discourse upon the same subject. In answer to the exceptions of mr. Jeremiah Leamimg [*sic*], contained in his late Defence of the episcopal government of the church. By Noah Welles, a. m. pastor of the first church in Stanford. [Four lines of Scripture texts.]
Re-printed at Litchfield, by T. Collier. [1796.] pp. 189. 8vo.   AAS.
The first edition was printed in New Haven, in 1767.

31610   WERDEN, Peter   1728–1808
Letters to a friend; containing remarks on a pamphlet written by Job Scott entitled "The Baptism of Christ, a Gospel ordinance, being altogether inward, spiritual, &c. By Peter Werden.
Printed at Lansingburgh, by Wm. W. Wands, for the Author. MDCCXCVI, pp. 64. 8vo.   AAS.

31611   WESLEY, John   1703–1791
A Dialogue between a predestinarian, and his friend.
Printed at Boston. MDVIIXCVI. [sic 1796.] pp. 11. 12mo.

31612   WEST, Benjamin   1730–1813
An Astronomical diary or Almanack, for the year of christian æra, 1797. Being first after bissextile or leap year. Calculated for the meridian of Portsmouth, lat. 43 deg. 5 min. north. But will serve for any of the adjacent states. By Isaac Bickerstaff. [Eight lines of verse.]
Printed at Dover, and for sale by the gross dozen or single, at the Sun Office. [1796.] pp. (24). 12mo.   AAS. NHHS.
Contains, A humorous tale. The negro. By Mr. Bowles. Method of making butter in winter. Roads. Anecdotes.

31613   —— An Astronomical diary: or Almanack, for the year of our Lord 1797: being the first after bissextile, or leap-year; and the twenty-first of the independence of the United States of America. [Fourteen lines.] By Isaac Bickerstaff, esq. [Four lines of verse.]
Printed at Boston, and sold by J. Boyle, C. Bingham, B. Larkin, Wm. Pelham, E. Larkin, J. Nancrede, J. West, J. Bumstead, and other Booksellers in town and country. [1796.] pp. (24). 12mo.   AAS. LOC. NYHS.

31614   —— — The Federal Almanack, for the year of our Lord 1797: being the first after bissextile, or leap-year; and the twenty-first of the independence of the United States of America. [Eleven lines.] Calculated for the meridian and latitude of Boston, but will serve without sensible variation for the adjacent states. [Four lines of verse.]
Printed at Boston, and sold by J. Boyle, C. Bingham, B. Larkin, Wm. Pelham, E. Larkin, J. Nancrede, J. West, J. Bumstead, and other Booksellers in town and country. [1796.] pp. (24). 12mo.   AAS. LOC. NYHS.
From the same forms, and essentially the same as the preceding, with change of title only.

WEST, BENJAMIN, continued.

31615 —— BICKERSTAFFS GENUINE ALMANACK, FOR THE YEAR OF OUR LORD, 1797. [Cut of astronomer taking an observation.] BEING FIRST AFTER BISSEXTILE, OR LEAP-YEAR; AND THE 21ST OF THE INDEPENDENCE OF AMERICA.

Boston: Printed and sold by J. White, near Charles-river Bridge, and by most of the Booksellers. [1796.] pp. (24). 12mo.

31616 —— THE TOWN AND COUNTRY ALMANACK, FOR THE YEAR OF OUR LORD, 1797. BE-ING THE FIRST AFTER BISSEXTILE, OR LEAP YEAR, AND TWENTY FIRST OF THE INDEPENDENCE OF AMERICA. FITTED TO THE TOWN OF NORWICH, BUT WILL SERVE FOR THE STATE OF CONNECTICUT, RHODE ISLAND, NEW-HAMPSHIRE, MASSACHU-SETTS, NEW YORK, AND VERMONT. [Eleven lines.] BY ISAAC BICKERSTAFF, AS-TRONOMER.

Printed in Norwich, (Connecticut), by John Trumbull, and sold at his Print-ing-Office, a few rods west from the Meeting House, in large or small quantities. [1796.] pp. (48). 12mo.   AAS. CHS. HSP. NYPL. YC.

Contains, the Affecting history of the dreadful distresses of Frederick Manheim and family. And the Morgan Indian Narrative.

31617 —— WEBSTER'S CALENDAR; OR THE ALBANY ALMANACK, FOR THE YEAR OF OUR LORD 1797: BEING THE 1ST AFTER BISSEXTILE OR LEAP YEAR; OF AMERICAN IN-DEPENDENCE (WHICH WAS DECLARED THE 4TH OF JULY, 1776) PART OF THE 21ST AND 22D YEARS. FROM THE CREATION OF THE WORLD 5746. CALCULATED FOR THE MERIDIAN OF ALBANY; NORTH LATITUDE 42 DEGREES 45 MINUTES—FROM THE EN-GLISH OBSERVATORY 73 DEGREES AND 8 MINUTES WEST. BY ISAAC BICKERSTAFF, ESQ. CONTAINING, AS USUAL, A GREAT VARIETY OF NEW USEFUL AND ENTERTAIN-ING PIECES.

Albany: Printed by Charles R. and George Webster, in the White House, cor-ner of State and Pearl-Streets. Sold at their Bookstore, Albany; by William W. Wands, at his Printing-Office, Lansingburgh; by Jacob Dockstader, at his Print-ing Office, Johnstown; by Samuel Colt, Canandargua—and, by all the Post-riders from said Offices. ☞ *Great allowance to those who buy large quantities.* [1796.] pp. (36). 12mo.   AAS. BPL. HC.

Contains, On reading the President's Address. A poem. America's legacy; being the Address of George Washington, on his declining a re-election to the Presidency.

31618 —— WHEELER'S NORTH-AMERICAN CALENDAR, OR AN ALMANACK, FOR THE YEAR OF OUR LORD 1797; BEING THE FIRST AFTER BISSEXTILE, OR LEAP YEAR, AND THE TWENTY FIRST OF AMERICAN INDEPENDENCE. [U. S. arms.]

Printed at Providence, and sold by B. Wheeler, by the groce, dozen, or single, cheap for cash. [1796.] pp. (24). 12mo.   AAS. JCB. RIHS.

31619 WEST, JOHN
THE BOSTON DIRECTORY, CONTAINING THE NAMES OF THE INHABITANTS, THEIR OCCU-PATIONS, PLACES OF BUSINESS, AND DWELLING-HOUSES; ALSO A LIST OF THE TOWN OFFICERS, PUBLIC OFFICES, WHERE AND BY WHOM KEPT; BANKS, &C. &C. TO WHICH IS PREFIXED, A GENERAL DESCRIPTION OF BOSTON. ORNAMENTED WITH A PLAN OF THE TOWN, TAKEN FROM ACTUAL SURVEY. [BY OSGOOD CARLETON.]

Boston: Printed by Manning & Loring, for John West, No. 75 Cornhill. June, 1796. pp. 117, plan. 12mo.   AAS. BA. BPL. HC.

The second Directory of Boston, none having been printed between the years 1789 and 1796. The Plan was also issued separately, "on fine paper, handsomely coloured."

31620 WESTERN Centinel. Vol. III. No. 1. Wednesday, January 6, [-- No. 52. Wednes-
day, December 28, 1796.]
*Printed by O. P. Easton, near the Post-Office, in Whitestown, Herkimer
County, State of New-York.* 1796. fol.

31621 WESTERN Inland Lock Navigation Company.
Western Inland Lock Navigation. The Directors of the Western Inland
Lock Navigation Company, have determined to construct a canal, to con-
nect the waters of the Mohawk River, with those of Wood'Creek, and
to clear the banks of that Creek, of the timber growing and laying
thereon. . . . Ph. Schuyler, president. New-York, January 18th, 1796.
[New-York: 1796.] Broadside. fol.   NYPL.

31622 WESTERN and Northern Inland Lock Navigation Companies.
New-York. In Senate, February 10, 1796. Resolved, That the Report of
the Western Inland Lock Navigation Companies, be forthwith printed in
the news-paper published by the Printer to this State. By order, Abraham B. Bancker, clerk. To the honourable the Legislature of the State
of New-York, In Senate and Assembly convened. The Directors of the
Western and Northern Lock Navigation Companies, Respectfully report,
That in the summer and fall, ensuing the incorporation of the subscribers to the said Companies, surveys were made . . . Ph. Schuyler, president. [Colophon:]
[New-York:] Printed by William Robins, for the Printer to the State.
[1796.] Broadside. fol.   NYPL.

31623 —— Report of the directors of the Western and Northern Inland Lock
Navigation Companies, in the State of New-York, to the Legislature:
together with the Report of mr. William Weston, engineer.
New-York: Printed by George Forman, No. 156, Front-street.—1796.—pp.
(20). 4to.   BM. NYHS. NYPL.

31624 THE WESTERN Telegraphe, and Washington Advertiser. Free, but not
licentious. Vol. I. No. 21. Tuesday, January 5, [— Vol. II. No. 72. Tues-
day, December 27, 1796.]
*Washington (Pennsylvania): Printed by Colerick, Hunter & Beaumont.—
Subscriptions and advertisements taken in at Washington, by the Editors; Union-
Town, by Samuel King; Brownsville by Jacob Bowman; Pittsburgh, by Jeremiah
Barker; McKee's Point, by John Speir; Charlestown, (Mouth of Buffaloe), by
Richard Spier; West Liberty, by William M'Kinley [and Wm. Skinner]; in Mor-
gan-Town, by Hugh M'Neely; in Frederick-Town, by Isaac Jenkinson; in Mid-
dletown, by Samuel Urie; in Marietta, by Joseph Lincoln, and in Greensburgh, by
John Badollet.* 1796. fol.

31625 WHARTON, Charles Henry   1748–1833
A Short and candid enquiry into the proofs of Christ's divinity; in which
doctor Priestley's opinion concerning Christ, is occasionally considered.
In a letter to a friend. By Charles H. Wharton, d. d. and member of
the Philosophical Society of Philadelphia. [Five lines from] St. John 1st.
Epist, c. II, v. 23-24.
Philadelphia: Printed by Ormrod & Conrad, No. 41, Chesnut street. 1796.
pp. (59), (1). 8vo.   AAS. JCB. LOC.

Dated, Prospect Hill, March 31st, 1791. 138th Pennsylvania District
Copyright, issued to John Ormrod, as Proprietor, 24 June, 1796.

AUCTION
VALUES

31626 WHITELAW, JAMES
A CORRECT MAP OF THE STATE OF VERMONT FROM ACTUAL SURVEY: EXHIBITING
THE COUNTY AND TOWN LINES, RIVERS, LAKES, PONDS, MOUNTAINS, MEETING
HOUSES, MILLS, PUBLIC ROADS. ETC., ANNO DOMINI 1795. BY JAMES WHITELAW,
ESQ., SURVEYOR-GENERAL OF THE STATE OF VERMONT.
[*Rutland: Published by S. Williams & Co.* 1796.]
Twice copyrighted. First when Proposals were issued in October, 1795.
Second: 6th Vermont District Copyright, issued to James Whitelaw, as
Author, 20 June, 1796. And published October 31, 1796.

31627 WHITESTOWN GAZETTE. VOL. I. No. 1. TUESDAY, JUNE 7, [— No. 30. TUESDAY,
DECEMBER 27, 1796.]
*Published by Samuel Wells,— Whitestown, (Herkimer County). Opposite the
Meeting-House.* 1796. fol.   AAS.
Established, as a weekly, by Samuel Wells. With the issue for July
12, 1796, William M'Lean was admitted to partnership, as Wells and
M'Lean. In September, 1796, Wells withdrew, and publication was
continued in the name of William M'Lean, into August, 1798, when he
removed his Press to Utica, and publication was resumed, in Septem-
ber, 1798, without change of numbering, as the *Whitestown Gazette.*
And Cato's Patrol.

31628 WHITING, SAMUEL   1744–1819
AN ORATION, DELIVERED AT THE CELEBRATION OF AMERICAN INDEPENDENCE, AT
SHEFFIELD, JULY 4TH, 1796. BY SAMUEL WHITING, ESQUIRE. PUBLISHED AT
THE REQUEST OF THE COMMITTEE.
Printed at Stockbridge, by Loring Andrews. 1796. pp. 17. 8vo.   LOC. UTS.

31629 WHITMAN, KILBORN   1764–1835
A SERMON, DELIVERED JUNE 10TH, 1795, AT THE ORDINATION OF JOSHUA CUSHMAN,
TO THE PASTORAL CARE OF THE CHRISTIAN SOCIETY IN WINSLOW. BY KILBORN
WHITMAN, OF PEMBROKE. [One line from] PAUL,
Printed at Hallowell, Hook, by Wait & Baker. 1796. pp. 36. 12mo. AAS. JCB.

31630 WHITNEY, JOSIAH   1731–1824
A SERMON, OCCASIONED BY THE DEATH OF THE REV. NOADIAH RUSSEL, A. M. OF
THOMPSON; WHO DEPARTED THIS LIFE ON TUESDAY THE 27TH DAY OF OCTOBER,
1795, AND DELIVERED AT HIS FUNERAL, ON THE FRIDAY FOLLOWING. BY JOSIAH
WHITNEY, A. M. PASTOR OF THE FIRST CHURCH IN BROOKLYN. [Seven lines from]
DR. YOUNG.
Providence: Printed by Carter & Wilkinson, opposite the Market. MDCC-
XCVI. pp. (27). 8vo.   AAS. BM. CHS. HC. JCB. LOC. NYPL. RIHS. UTS. YC.

31631 WHITNEY, PETER   1744–1816
THE DUTY OF PRAISING THE WORKS OF GOD, TO SUCCEEDING GENERATIONS, CONSID-
ERED AND APPLIED, IN A DISCOURSE, DELIVERED AT NORTHBOROUGH ON WEDNES-
DAY, JUNE 1ST, 1796. BY PETER WHITNEY, A. M. PASTOR OF THE CHRISTIAN
CHURCH AND SOCIETY IN NORTHBOROUGH.
*Printed at Worcester, by Thomas, Son & Thomas. Sold by them at their
Worcester Bookstore* 1796. pp. 23. 8vo.   AAS. BA. JCB. LOC. MHS. NYPL. UTS.
"Rev.Mr.Whitney's Half Century Sermon in Northborough,June,1796."

31632 WHITTEMORE, JOSEPH
JOSEPH WHITTEMORE, PRESENTS THE FOLLOWING ADDRESS TO HIS FRIENDS,PATRONS,
AND CUSTOMERS, WISHING THEM, MOST SINCERELY, A HAPPY NEW YEAR. [Forty
lines.]
Boston: January 1, 1796. Broadside. fol.   HSP.

31633   WHITTINGTON, Sir RICHARD   –1423
THE FAMOUS HISTORY OF SIR RICHARD WHITTINGTON, THREE TIMES LORD MAYOR
OF LONDON.
Dover: Printed by Samuel Bragg, jun. 1796.

31634   WILLIAMS, HELEN MARIA   1762–1827
LETTERS CONTAINING A SKETCH OF THE POLITICS OF FRANCE, FROM THE THIRTY-FIRST
OF MAY, 1793, TILL THE TWENTY-EIGHTH OF JULY, 1794, AND OF THE SCENES
WHICH HAVE PASSED IN THE PRISONS OF PARIS. BY HELEN MARIA WILLIAMS.
*Philadelphia: Printed for Mathew Carey, William Young, Thomas Dobson,
H. & P. Rice, and John Ormrod.* M,DCC,XCVI. pp. (283). 12mo.   AAS. JCB.

31635   —— LETTERS CONTAINING A SKETCH OF THE SCENES WHICH PASSED IN VARIOUS DE-
PARTMENTS OF FRANCE DURING THE TYRANNY OF ROBESPIERRE; AND OF THE
EVENTS WHICH TOOK PLACE IN PARIS ON THE 28TH OF JULY, 1794. BY HELEN
MARIA WILLIAMS. [Ornament.]
*Philadelphia: From the Press of Snowden & M'Corkle, No. 47, N. Fourth-
street.* 1796. pp. (160). 12mo.   AAS. NYPL.

31636   WILLIAMS, NATHAN   1735–1829
THE BLESSEDNESS OF THE DEAD WHO DIE IN THE LORD, ILLUSTRATED IN A SERMON
PREACHED AT THE FUNERAL OF THE REV. NATHAN STRONG, SENIOR PASTOR OF THE
CHURCH OF CHRIST IN COVENTRY, WHO DIED NOVEMBER 7TH, 1795, IN THE 79TH
YEAR OF HIS AGE. BY NATHAN WILLIAMS, D. D. PASTOR OF THE CHURCH IN TOL-
LAND.
Hartford: Printed by Hudson & Goodwin. 1796. pp. 28. 8vo.
      AAS. BM. CHS. JCB. LOC. NYPL. UTS. YC.

31637   WILLIAMS, SAMUEL   1743–1817
THE VERMONT ALMANAC AND REGISTER FOR THE YEAR OF OUR LORD 1797: BEING
THE FIRST AFTER LEAP-YEAR, AND UNTIL JULY FOURTH, THE TWENTY-FIRST OF THE
INDEPENDENCE OF AMERICA. FITTED TO THE LATITUDE AND LONGITUDE OF RUT-
LAND: LATITUDE 43° 21′ NORTH, LONGITUDE 2.9 EAST OF PHILADELPHIA.
*Printed at Rutland, (Vermont.) [By James Kirkaldie.] And sold wholesale
and retail at the Printing-Office.* [1796.] pp. (60). 12mo.   AAS. BM. NYHS.
Contains, A chronological history of 1794 and 1795.

31638   WILLIAMS, SIMON FINLEY
AN ORATION, DELIVERED ON THE FOURTH OF JULY, 1796. BEING THE ANNIVERSARY
OF THE AMERICAN INDEPENDENCE, AT MEREDITH BRIDGE. BY THE REV. SIMON
FINLEY WILLIAMS, A. B. [Three lines of Latin from] VIRGIL. PUBLISHED BY THE
DESIRE OF A NUMBER OF THE GENTLEMEN PRESENT.
Printed at Dover: by Samuel Bragg, jun. for the Subscribers. MDCCXCVI.
pp† [24.] 8vo.   AAS.

31639   WILLIAMS, THOMAS
THE AGE OF CREDULITY: A LETTER TO NATHANIEL BRASSEY HALHED, ESQ. M. P. IN
ANSWER TO HIS TESTIMONY IN FAVOUR OF RICHARD BROTHERS. WITH AN APPEN-
DIX, IN VINDICATION OF THE SCRIPTURE PROPHECIES. BY THE AUTHOR OF "THE
AGE OF INFIDELITY" — AND OTHER TRACTS. MENE, MENE, TEKEL, UPHARSIN.
DANIEL.
*Philadelphia: Printed by Lang & Ustick, for Thomas Ustick, No. 79, North
Third Street.* May, 1796. pp. [45], (2). 8vo.   AAS. BM. JCB. LOC. NYPL.

31640   —— THE AGE OF INFIDELITY.—PART II.—IN ANSWER TO THE SECOND PART OF THE
AGE OF REASON. WITH SOME ADDITIONAL REMARKS UPON THE FORMER. BY A
LAYMAN. [Four lines of verse from] YOUNG.
*Philadelphia: Printed by Lang & Ustick, and sold at No, 79, North Third
Street, and by the Booksellers.* 1796. pp. iv, (1), (5)–(67). 8vo.   AAS. HC.

31641　WILLISON, JOHN　　　　　　　　　　　　　　　　1680–1750
THE AFFLICTED MAN'S COMPANION: OR A DIRECTORY FOR PERSONS AND FAMILIES,
AFFLICTED WITH SICKNESS OR ANY OTHER DISTRESS. WITH DIRECTIONS TO THE
SICK, BOTH UNDER AND AFTER AFFLICTION. ALSO, DIRECTIONS TO THE FRIENDS OF
THE SICK AND OTHERS WHO VISIT THEM. AND LIKEWISE TO ALL, HOW TO PREPARE
BOTH FOR SICKNESS AND DEATH; AND HOW TO BE EXERCISED AT THE TIME OF DY-
ING. TO WHICH IS ADDED, A COLLECTION OF COMFORTABLE TEXTS OF SCRIPTURE,
VERY SUITABLE FOR DYING BELIEVERS.—THE CHOICE SAYINGS OF EMINENT DYING
SAINTS.—THE AUTHOR'S LAST ADVICE TO HIS WIFE AND CHILDREN: AND HIS DYING
WORDS, WRITTEN BY HIMSELF, AND FOUND AMONG HIS PAPERS AFTER HIS DEATH.
BY THE REVEREND MR. JOHN WILLISON, LATE MINISTER OF THE GOSPEL IN DUN-
DEE. [Line of twelve stars.] VERY NECESSARY FOR ALL FAMILIES.
　　Wilmington, Printed by Joseph Johnson. 1796. pp. 272. 12mo. AAS. JCB. WIPL.

31642　WILMER, JAMES JONES　　　　　　　　　　　　　　1749–
AN ADDRESS TO THE CITIZENS OF THE UNITED STATES, ON NATIONAL REPRESENTA-
TION; WITH A SKETCH OF THE ORIGIN OF GOVERNMENT, AND THE STATE OF PUBLIC
AFFAIRS. BY JAMES JONES WILMER.
　　　Baltimore: Printed by William Pechin. [1796.] pp. 16. 8vo.　　　BA.

31643　THE WILMINGTON CHRONICLE, AND NORTH-CAROLINA WEEKLY ADVERTISER.
[Motto.] VOL. II. NO. 1. THURSDAY, JANUARY 14, [—VOL. III. NO. 4. THURSDAY,
AUGUST 4, 1796.]
　　　*Wilmington: Printed by John Bellew, at his Office, corner of Market and Sec-
ond Streets.* 1796. fol.

　　The above is the last number located.

31644　WILSON, JOHN
AN INAUGURAL EXPERIMENTAL DISSERTATION ON DIGESTION, SUBMITTED TO THE EX-
AMINATION OF THE REV. JOHN EWING, S. T. P. PROVOST; THE TRUSTEES AND MEDI-
CAL FACULTY OF THE UNIVERSITY OF PENNSYLVANIA, ON THE 17TH DAY OF MAY,
1796. FOR THE DEGREE OF DOCTOR OF MEDICINE. BY JOHN WILSON, A. M. OF
PENNSYLVANIA, MEMBER OF THE PHILADEDHHIA [*sic*] MEDICAL SOSIETY [*sic.*]
[One line of Latin from] CIC. ORAT. AD BRUT.
　　　Philadelphia: Printed by Lang & Ustick. M.DCC.XCVI. pp. (25), 8vo.
　　　　　　　　　　　　　　　　　　　　　　　　AAS. LOC. SGO.

31645　WINCHESTER, ELHANAN　　　　　　　　　　　　　1751–1797
A PLAIN POLITICAL CATECHISM. INTENDED FOR THE USE OF SCHOOLS, IN THE
UNITED STATES OF AMERICA: WHEREIN THE GREAT PRINCIPLES OF LIBERTY, AND
OF THE FEDERAL GOVERNMENT, ARE LAID DOWN AND EXPLAINED, BY WAY OF QUES-
TION AND ANSWER. MADE LEVEL TO THE LOWEST CAPACITIES. BY ELHANAN WIN-
CHESTER.
　　　Greenfield, (Mass.) From the Press of T. Dickman: Sold at his Book Store.
MDCCXCVI. pp. [107.] 18mo.　　　　　　　　　　　　　BM. LOC.

31646　—— — A PLAIN POLITICAL CATECHISM. INTENDED FOR THE USE OF SCHOOLS, IN
THE UNITED STATES OF AMERICA: WHEREIN THE GREAT PRINCIPLES OF LIBERTY,
AND OF THE FEDERAL GOVERNMENT, ARE LAID DOWN AND EXPLAINED, IN THE WAY
OF QUESTION AND ANSWER. MADE LEVEL TO THE LOWEST CAPACITIES. BY ELHA-
NAN WINCHESTER.
　　　Philadelphia: Printed by R. Folwell. 1796. pp. 96. 12mo.

　　119th Pennsylvania District Copyright, issued to Elhanan Winchester,
as Author, 24 December, 1795. The second work deposited in the Office
of the Secretary of State, under the Copyright law, 5 February, 1796.

31647   WINTERBOTHAM, William   1763–1829
AN HISTORICAL, GEOGRAPHICAL, COMMERCIAL, AND PHILOSOPHICAL VIEW OF THE UNITED STATES OF AMERICA, AND OF THE EUROPEAN SETTLEMENTS IN AMERICA AND THE WEST-INDIES. BY W. WINTERBOTHAM. THE FIRST AMERICAN EDITION, WITH ADDITIONS AND CORRECTIONS. IN FOUR VOLUMES. VOL. I. [—IV.]

New-York: Printed by Tiebout and O'Brien, for John Reid, Bookseller and Stationer, No. 106, Water-Street. 1796. 4 vols. pp. vi, (1), 590, portrait of Washington, plate; (2), (2), 493, portrait of Penn, plate; (2), (2), 519, portrait of Franklin, 2 plates, 3 plans; (2), (2), 516, (8), (9), (1), portrait of Author, 15 plates. 8vo.   AAS. BA. BPL. BU. HC. JCB. LOC. NYHS. NYPL.

Contains a list of about eight hundred subscribers. An Atlas of twenty folio maps accompanies the work with a cover title: The Atlas for Winterbotham's History of America,—which was also issued separately by the publisher, as "The American Atlas." A second edition was printed in Boston, in 1828.

31648   —— — AN HISTORICAL, GEOGRAPHICAL AND PHILOSOPHICAL VIEW OF THE CHINESE EMPIRE; COMPREHENDING A DESCRIPTION OF THE FIFTEEN PROVINCES OF CHINA, CHINESE TARTARY; TRIBUTARY STATES; NATURAL HISTORY OF CHINA; GOVERNMENT, RELIGION, LAWS, MANNERS AND CUSTOMS, LITERATURE, ARTS, SCIENCES, MANUFACTURES, &C. BY W. WINTERBOTHAM. TO WHICH IS ADDED, A COPIOUS ACCOUNT OF LORD MACARTNEY'S EMBASSY, COMPILED FROM ORIGINAL COMMUNICATIONS. IN TWO VOLUMES. VOL. I. [— II.]

London printed: Philadelphia, Re-printed for Richard Lee, Dunning, Hyer, and Palmer—Printers. 1796. 2 vols. pp. (2), (2), 303, (2), (2); 322, (3), (3). 8vo.   AAS. JCB. LOC.

31649   THE WISCASSET TELEGRAPH. "THE WILDERNESS SHALL BUD AND BLOSSOM LIKE THE ROSE. VOL. I. NO. 1. SATURDAY, DECEMBER 3, [— VOL I. NO. V. SATURDAY, DECEMBER 31, 1796.]

Printed and published by J. N. Russell and H. Hoskins, corner of Main and Fore-Streets, Wiscasset. 1796. fol.

Established, as a weekly, by Joseph N. Russell, and Henry Hoskins. Under date of April 1, 1797, Russell withdrew, and publication was continued in the name of Henry Hoskins. In November, 1797, John W. Scott was admitted to partnership, and publication was discontinued by them probably in November, 1798.

31650   WISDOM IN MINIATURE: OR THE YOUNG GENTLEMAN AND LADY'S MAGAZINE — [NO. I.] BEING A COLLECTION OF SENTENCES, DIVINE AND MORAL. TRAIN UP A CHILD IN THE WAY HE SHOULD GO, AND WHEN HE IS OLD HE WILL NOT DEPART FROM IT.

Hartford: Printed by J. Babcock. 1796. pp. 30. 32mo.   AAS. NYPL.

31651   —— WISDOM IN MINIATURE: OR THE YOUNG GENTLEMAN AND LADY'S PLEASING INSTRUCTOR, BEING A COLLECTION OF SENTENCES, DIVINE, MORAL AND HISTORICAL. SELECTED FROM THE WRITINGS OF MANY INGENIOUS AND LEARNED AUTHORS, BOTH ANCIENT AND MODERN. INTENDED NOT ONLY FOR THE USE OF SCHOOLS, BUT AS A POCKET COMPANION FOR THE YOUTH OF BOTH SEXES IN AMERICA. SECOND WORCESTER EDITION.

Printed at Worcester, (Massachusetts), by Thomas, Son & Thomas: sold wholesale and retail, at their Bookstore.—October, 1796. pp. 192, frontispiece. 32mo.   AAS. BM. JCB. NYPL.

31652 EIN WOHL EINGERICHTETES DEUTSCHES A. B. C—BUCHSTABIR-UND LESEBUCH ZUM
GEBRAUCH DEUTSCHER SCHULEN. ENTHALTEND: DAS A B C, NEBST VIELEN ARTEN
BUCHSTABIR-UND LESEÜBUNGEN. EINE ANWEISUNG DAS DEUTSCHE RECHT ZU LER-
NEN, MIT EINEM KURZEN UNTERRICHT VOM SCHREYBEN UND RECHNEN. ETLICHE
ANGENEHME UND LEHRREICHE ERZÄHLUNGEN, FABELN MIT KUPFERN, UND POETIS-
CHE STÜCKE. EINE KURZE ERDBESCHREIBUNG UND EIN SINNRECHES BILD VOR DEM
BUCHE. [Printer's mark.]
> *Germantaun: Gedruckt bey Michael Billmeyer,* 1796. pp. xiv, 120, frontis-
> piece and 7 cuts. 12mo.   AAS. LOC. NYPL.

31653 WOLLSTONECRAFT afterwards GODWIN, MARY   1759–1797
LETTERS WRITTEN DURING A SHORT RESIDENCE IN SWEDEN, NORWAY, AND DENMARK.
BY MARY WOLLSTONECRAFT. FIRST AMERICAN EDITION.
> *Printed for & sold by J. Wilson & J. Johnson, Booksellers, Wilmington,*
> (*Del.*) 1796. pp. (218), (2), (2), (1), (12). 12mo.   AAS. BM. DHS. JCB. WIPL.
> The appended twelve pages contain Books sold at J. Wilson's Store in
> Wilmington—name and place added with ink.

31654 WOODS, LEONARD   1774–1854
ENVY WISHES, THEN BELIEVES. AN ORATION, DELIVERED AT COMMENCEMENT, HAR-
VARD UNIVERSITY, CAMBRIDGE, JULY 20TH, 1796. BY LEONARD WOODS. [Orna-
ment.]
> *Leominster,* (*Massachusetts*) *Printed by Charles Prentiss.* 1796. pp. 16. 8vo.
>   AAS. BM. HC. JCB. LOC. MHS. NYPL.

31655 WOODS'S NEWARK GAZETTE AND NEW-JERSEY ADVERTISER. No. 35. VOL. V. NUMB.
243. WEDNESDAY, JANUARY 6, [—NO. 34. VOL. VI. NUMB. 294. WEDNESDAY, DE-
CEMBER, 28, 1796.]
> *Newark, New-Jersey. Printed by John Woods, near the Episcopal Church.*
> . . . 1796. fol.
> Beginning May 11th, the Gazette was reduced in size to three columns,
> enclosed in heavy borders.

31656 WOODSTOCK. VERMONT. BAPTIST ASSOCIATION.
MINUTES OF THE WOODSTOCK ASSOCIATION, HELD AT WOODSTOCK, IN THE STATE OF
VERMONT, SEPTEMBER 28TH AND 29TH, 1796.
> [*Norwich: Printed by John Trumbull,* 1796.] pp. [8.] 8vo.   AAS.

31657 WORCESTER, NOAH   1758–1837
A SERMON DELIVERED AT HAVERHILL, NEW HAMPSHIRE, JULY 28, 1796, AT THE
EXECUTION OF THOMAS POWERS, WHO WAS EXECUTED FOR A RAPE, COMMITTED AT
LEBANON, ON THE 7TH OF DECEMBER, 1795. BY NOAH WORCESTER, A. M. PASTOR
OF A CHURCH IN THORNTON.
> *Haverhill, New-Hampshire: Printed and sold by N. Coverly.* MDCCXCVI.
> pp. 33. 8vo.   JCB.

31658 WORCESTER, SAMUEL   1770–1821
AN ORATION, PRONOUNCED AT NEWIPSWICH, ON THE ANNIVERSARY OF AMERICAN IN-
DEPENDENCE, JULY 4, 1796. BY SAMUEL WORCESTER, A. B.
> *Amherst, Newhampshire, Printed by Samuel Cushing.* MDCCXCVI. pp. 24.
> 8vo.   BA. JCB. NYPL.

31659 WORCESTER, THOMAS   1768–1831
A THANKSGIVING SERMON. DELIVERED NOVEMBER 12, 1795. BY THOMAS WOR-
CESTER, V. D. M. PASTOR OF THE CONGREGATIONAL CHURCH IN SALISBURY. [Orna-
ment.]
> *Newburyport: Printed by John Mycall,* M,DCC,XCVI. pp. (31). 8vo.
>   AAS. JCB.

31660   WORKMAN, Benjamin
THE AMERICAN ACCOUNTANT; OR, SCHOOLMASTERS' NEW ASSISTANT: COMPRISED IN FOUR BOOKS. BOOK I. CONTAINING ARITHMETIC OF WHOLE NUMBERS,—DIVERS DENOMINATIONS, AND THE COMMON RULES, TO THE END OF THE DOUBLE RULE OF THREE. BOOK II. FRACTIONS, VULGAR AND DECIMAL. BOOK III. MERCANTILE ARITHMETIC; OR ALL THE RULES NECESSARY FOR FORMING A COMPLETE ACCOUNTANT; METHODICALLY ARRANGED AND LARGELY EXEMPLIFIED. BOOK IV. EXTRACTIONS, PROGRESSIONS, &C. BEING THE HIGHER RULES OF ARITHMETIC. AND INCLUDING ALL THE QUESTIONS IN THE PHILADELPHIA EDITION OF GOUGH, WITH MANY OTHERS. THE RULES ARE EITHER NEW, OR THOSE OF THAT TREATISE SO COMPENDIZED, AS TO BE BOTH BRIEF AND PERFECTLY APPLICABLE. THE WHOLE ADAPTED TO THE COMMERCE OF THE UNITED STATES; AND COMPREHENDING EVERYTHING NECESSARY TO A COMPLETE PRACTICAL KNOWLEDGE OF THE SCIENCE OF ARITHMETIC. BY BENJAMIN WORKMAN. THE THIRD EDITION. REVISED AND CORRECTED BY R. PATTERSON, A. M. PROFESSOR OF MATHEMATICS IN THE UNIVERSITY OF PENNSYLVANIA.
Philadelphia: Printed for William Young, No. 52, the corner of Second and Chesnut-Streets. M,DCC,XCVI. pp. (2), (2), (13)–220, (4). 12mo.   AAS.

31661   —— ELEMENTS OF GEOGRAPHY, DESIGNED FOR YOUNG STUDENTS IN THAT SCIENCE. IN SEVEN SECTIONS. SECT. I. OF THE SOLAR SYSTEM. SECT. II. OF THE EARTH IN PARTICULAR. SECT. III. OF MAPS AND GLOBES. THE THREE FOREGOING SECTIONS CONTAIN THE SCIENTIFIC OR ASTRONOMICAL PART OF GEOGRAPHY, DIGESTED IN A CLEAR AND COMPREHENSIVE MANNER. SECT. IV. OF THE DIFFERENT RELIGIONS, GOVERNMENTS, AND LANGUAGES OF NATIONS. SECT. V. OF THE POLITICAL DIVISIONS OF THE EARTH, INTO EMPIRES, KINGDOMS, &C. OR THE HISTORICAL PART OF GEOGRAPHY. SECT. VI. OF NATURAL PHILOSOPHY; OR THE PROPERTIES OF MATTER, &C. SECT. VII. OF CHRONOLOGY. BY BENJAMIN WORKMAN, A. M. THE SIXTH EDITION. ILLUSTRATED WITH, 1. A MAP OF THE WORLD. 2. A PLATE OF THE SOLAR SYSTEM. 3. A MAP OF NORTH AMERICA. 4. A MAP OF THE UNITED STATES. 5. A MAP OF SOUTH AMERICA. 6. A MAP OF EUROPE. 7. A MAP OF ASIA. 8. A MAP OF AFRICA.
Philadelphia: Printed and sold by John M'Culloch, No. 1, North Third-Street.—1796. *[Entered according to Act of Congress.]* pp. 180, 7 maps, 1 plate. 24mo.   AAS. JCB.

31662   —— FATHER TAMMANY'S ALMANAC, FOR THE YEAR 1797.
Philadelphia: Printed and sold by John M'Culloch? [1796.]

31663   —— A TREATISE OF ARITHMETIC, IN THEORY AND PRACTICE; CONTAINING EVERY THING IMPORTANT IN THE STUDY OF ABSTRACT AND APPLICATE NUMBERS. ADAPTED TO THE COMMERCE OF GREAT-BRITAIN AND IRELAND. BY JOHN GOUGH. TOGETHER WITH MANY VALUABLE ADDITIONS AND AMENDMENTS, MORE PARTICULARLY FITTING THE WORK FOR THE IMPROVEMENT OF THE AMERICAN YOUTH. BY BENJAMIN WORKMAN, A. M. THE SECOND EDITION. REVISED AND ENLARGED BY R. PATTERSON, A. M. PROFESSOR OF MATHEMATICS IN THE UNIVERSITY OF PENNSYLVANIA.
Philadelphia: Printed for William Young, No. 52, the corner of Second and Chesnut-streets. M,DCC,XCVI. pp. vi, (2), (13)–(376). 12mo.   AAS.

31664   THE WORLD DISPLAYED; OR, A CURIOUS COLLECTION OF VOYAGES AND TRAVELS. SELECTED AND COMPILED FROM THE WRITERS OF ALL NATIONS; BY SMART, GOLDSMITH, & JOHNSON. FIRST AMERICAN EDITION, CORRECTED & ENLARGED. IN EIGHT VOLUMES. VOL. VI. [— VIII.]
Philadelphia: [Printed by John Thompson.] Published by Dobelbower, Key, and Simpson. 1796. 3 vols. pp. (2), (2), 464, (2), 6 plates; (2), 510, (2), 6 plates; (2). 464, (26), (2), portrait of James Cook, map, 5 plates. 8vo.
    AAS. NYPL.
Engraved title-pages. Contains a twenty-six page List of subscribers.

31665   WORTMAN, TUNIS   –1822
AN ORATION ON THE INFLUENCE OF SOCIAL INSTITUTION UPON HUMAN MORALS AND
HAPPINESS, DELIVERED BEFORE THE TAMMANY SOCIETY, AT THEIR ANNIVERSARY
ON THE TWELFTH OF MAY, 1796. BY T. WORTMAN. [Five lines from] EDMUND
BURKE'S VINDICATION OF NATURAL SOCIETY.

New-York: Printed by C. C. Van Alen, & Co. No. 60, *Wall Street.* 1796.
pp. [31.] 8vo.   AAS. BA. LOC. NYHS. NYPL.

31666   WIJNPERSSE, DIONIJSIUS VAN DE   1724–1808
A PROOF OF THE TRUE AND ETERNAL GODHEAD OF OUR LORD JESUS CHRIST; AGAINST
MODERN ATTACKS. BY DIONYSIUS VAN DE WYNPERSSE, D. D. PROFESSOR OF PHI-
LOSOPHY, MATHEMATICS, AND ASTRONOMY, AT LEYDEN. WHICH GAINED THE HIGH-
EST PRIZE OF THE HAGUE SOCIETY, FOR THE DEFENCE OF CHRISTIANITY, 1792.
TRANSLATED FROM THE DUTCH, BY THOMAS BELL, MINISTER, GLASGOW.

Philadelphia: Printed by William Young, Bookseller, No. 52, *Second-Street,
corner of Chesnut-Street.* M,DCC,XCVI. pp. (v),(1),(13)–198. 12mo AAS. NYPL.

31667   WYTHE, GEORGE   1726-1806
Caption-title: A REPORT OF THE CASE BETWEEN FIELD AND HARRISON, DETER-
MINED BY THE HIGH COURT OF CHANCERY, IN WHICH THE DECREE WAS REVERSED
BY THE COURT OF APPEALS.

Richmond: Printed and sold by Thomas Nicolson. M,DCC,XCVI. pp. [32.]
8vo.   BA. VSL.

31668   ——   *Caption-title:* [REPORT OF THE CASE] BETWEEN WILLIAM FOWLER AND SU-
SANNA HIS WIFE, PLAINTIFFS AND TRACY SAUNDERS, AN INFANT, BY JAMES PAT-
TERSON, HIS GUARDIAN, DEFENDANT. [Also, THE CASE OF GOODELL AND CLOUGH
VS. JOHN BULLOCK.]

[Richmond: Printed by Thomas Nicolson. 1796.] pp. [28.] 8vo.   LOC.

31669   ——   *Caption-title:* [REPORT OF THE CASE OF] LOVE AGAINST DONELSON AND HODG-
SON.

[Richmond: Printed by Thomas Nicolson. 1796.] pp. [34.] 8vo.   LOC.

31670   ——   *Caption-title:* [REPORT OF THE CASE] BETWEEN JOSEPH WILKINS AND JOHN
TAYLOR.

[Richmond. Printed by Thomas Nicolson. 1796.] pp. [30],(1). 8vo. LOC.

31671   ——   *Caption-title:* [REPORT OF THE CASE] BETWEEN WILLIAM YATES AND SARAH
HIS WIFE . . . AND ABRAHAM SALLE, BERNARD MARKHAM, EDWARD MOSELEY,
BENJAMIN HARRIS AND WILLIAM WAGER HARRIS . . .

[Richmond: Printed by Thomas Nicolson. 1796.] pp. [30](1). 8vo. LOC.

31672   ——   *Caption-title:* [REPORT OF THE] CASE UPON STATUTE FOR DISTRIBUTION [OF
THE GOODS OF AN INTESTATE. Signed, THE EDITOR.]

Richmond: Printed by Thomas Nicolson, 1796. pp.[38.] 8vo. AAS. LOC. VSL.

31673   YALE COLLEGE.
Catalogue of the members of Yale-College. 1796. [Two columns.]

     [New-Haven: Printed by Thomas and Samuel Green. 1796.] Broadside.
fol.
                        NL.

31674   —— Catalogus senatus academici et eorum qui munera et officia academica
gesserunt, quique aliquovis fuerunt in Collegio Yalensi, quod est in Novo-
Portu Reipublicæ Connecticuttensis in Nov-Anglia. [Heavy line.]

     Novi-Portus: Excudebant Thomas et Samuel Green, Universitatis Typographi.
[1796.] pp. 36. 8vo.
                      BM. JCB. NYPL, YC.

31675   —— Illustrissimo Olivero Wolcott, arm. ll. d. Reipublicæ Connecticuttensis
gubernatori: honoratissimo Jonathani Trumbull, arm. vice-gubernatori;
clarissimisque proceribus politiæ nostræ civilis: reverendo pariter ac
honorando Timotheo Dwight, s.t. d. Collegii Yalensis præsidi, . . . Hasce
Theses, in comitiis publicis Collegii Yalensis . . . Anno Domini m,dcc,-
xcvi, publicé exhibendas candidatis Baccalaureales . . . Humillimè
dedicant. . . . [Colophon:]

     Habita in Comitiis Academicis Novo Portu Connecticutensium, M,DCC,XCVI.
E. Typis Thomæ et Samuelis Green, Universitatis Typographorum. Broadside. fol.

31676   YANKEE Doodle, an original American air, arranged with variations for
the pianoforte.

     Baltimore: Printed by J. Carr, Music Store, No. 6 *Gay Street, Baltimore, and
B. Carr's Musical Repositories, Market Street, Philadelphia and William Street,
New York,* 1796.

31677   YOUNG, Edward   1683–1765
The Complaint: or, night-thoughts on life, death, and immortality. To
which is prefixed, the life of the author. [One line of Latin from] Virg.

     New-York: Printed by John Tiebout, No. 358, *Pearl-Street, for N. Bell, Book-
seller and Stationer.* M,DCC,XCVI. pp. xii, 266, frontispiece. 12mo. AAS. LOC.

31678   —— —— The Complaint: or, night-thoughts on life, death, and immortality.
To which is prefixed, the life of the author. [One line of Latin from] Virg.

     New-York: Printed by John Tiebout, No. 358, *Pearl-Street, for J. Reid, J.
Harrisson, C. Davis, E. Mitchell, P. A. Mesier, C. Smith, J. S. Mott, J. Lyon, and
N. Bell.* M,DCC,XCVI. pp. 266, frontispiece. 12mo.   AAS. NYPL.

     The frontispiece, of a night scene in a churchyard, is engraved by Scoles
from the engraving in the former impression, and is headed "First New-
York edition." The text of both impressions is from the same plates,

31679   YOUNG, John
A Free and natural inquiry into the propriety of the christian faith. By
John Young, esq. of New-Hampshire, in North America.

     Portsmouth? 1796.

     15th New Hampshire District Copyright, issued to John Young, as
Author, 20 June, 1796.

31680 YOUNG, JOHN, continued.
—— THE POOR MAN'S COMPANION; OR MISCELLANEOUS OBSERVATIONS, CONCERNING PENAL AND SANGUINARY LAWS, THE MODE AND NATURE OF EVIDENCE, AND, AN INQUIRY INTO THE PROPRIETY AND POLICY OF PUNISHMENT. BY JOHN YOUNG, ESQ. OF NEWHAMPSHIRE, IN NEW ENGLAND.

 Newbury, (Vermont) Printed by Nathaniel Coverly, and sold at his Book-store, near the Court-House. [1796.] pp. 100. 12mo.   AAS.

 The copyright of this publication is secured to the Author, agreeably to the Act of Congress. 18th New Hampshire District Copyright, issued to John Young, as Author, 20 October, 1796.

31681 YOUNG, WILLIAM P.
CATALOGUE OF BOOKS, CONTAINING BESIDES HIS FORMER COLLECTION, A CONSIDERABLE IMPORTATION, PER THE CAROLINA, FROM LONDON, JUST OPENED, THE BEST EDITIONS. IN SUPERB BINDINGS, INCLUDING, ALSO, HIS ASSORTMENT OF STATIONARY.

 Charleston: Printed by W. P. Young, at Franklin's Head, No. 43, Broad-Street. 1796.

31682 —— PALLADIUM OF KNOWLEDGE: OR, THE CAROLINA AND GEORGIA ALMANAC, FOR THE YEAR OF OUR LORD 1797, AND 21–22 OF AMERICAN INDEPENDENCE. [Ten lines.]

 Charleston: Printed by W. P. Young, sold at his Book-Store, No. 43, Broad-Street. [1796.] pp. (50). 12mo.   AAS. LOC. NYHS.

31683 DIE ZIERDE DE JUGEND.
 Lancaster: Gedruckt bey Joh. Albrecht & Comp. 1796. pp. 58. 12mo.

31684 ZIMMERMANN, JOHANN GEORG, ritter von.   1788–1795
SOLITUDE CONSIDERED WITH RESPECT TO ITS INFLUENCE UPON THE MIND AND THE HEART. WRITTEN ORIGINALLY IN GERMAN BY M. ZIMMERMANN, AULIC COUNSELLOR AND PHYSICIAN TO HIS BRITANNIC MAJESTY AT HANOVER. TRANSLATED FROM THE FRENCH OF J. B. MERCIER. [Six lines of French from] LA FONTAINE, LE SONGE D'UN HABITANT DU MOGOL. L. XI, FABLE IV.

 Albany: Printed by Barber & Southwick, Faust's Statue, State-Street—1796. pp. 280. 8vo.   AAS. BA. JCB. LOC. NYPL.

31685 —— —— SOLITUDE CONSIDERED WITH RESPECT TO ITS INFLUENCE UPON THE MIND AND HEART. TRANSLATED FROM THE FRENCH OF J. B. MERCIER.
 New-York: Printed by Mott & Lyon, for Thomas Dunn. [1796.] 12mo.

1797

31686 ABOLITION SOCIETIES in the United States.
MINUTES OF THE PROCEEDINGS OF THE FOURTH CONVENTION OF DELEGATES FROM THE
ABOLITION SOCIETIES ESTABLISHED IN DIFFERENT PARTS OF THE UNITED STATES,
ASSEMBLED AT PHILADELPHIA, ON THE THIRD DAY OF MAY, ONE THOUSAND SEVEN
HUNDRED AND NINETY-SEVEN, AND CONTINUED, BY AJOURNMENTS, UNTIL THE NINTH
DAY OF THE SAME MONTH, INCLUSIVE. [Ornament.]
*Philadelphia: Printed by Zachariah Poulson, junior, number eighty, Ches-
nut-Street.* 1797. pp. (59). 8vo.   AAS. BM. HSP. JCB. LOC. NYHS. NYPL.

31687 —— TO THE SOCIETY FOR PROMOTING THE ABOLITION OF SLAVERY. TO INFORM YOU
OF OUR PROCEEDINGS—TO SOLICIT YOUR FURTHER ADVICE AND ASSISTANCE — AND
TO REQUEST YOUR SPECIAL ATTENTION TO THE ORIGINAL OBJECT OF OUR MEET-
INGS—WE NOW ADDRESS YOU, . . . [Signed, JOSEPH BLOOMFIELD, PRESIDENT
THOS. P. COPE SECRETARY.]
Philadelphia: [Printed by Zachariah Poulson, junior.] May 9th, 1797. pp.
(2). fol.   HSP.

31688 ADAMS, ——
SKETCHES OF THE HISTORY, GENIUS, DISPOSITION, ACCOMPLISHMENTS, EMPLOYMENTS,
CUSTOMS AND IMPORTANCE OF THE FAIR SEX, IN ALL PARTS OF THE WORLD. INTER-
SPERSED WITH MANY SINGULAR AND ENTERTAINING ANECDOTES. BY A FRIEND TO
THE SEX. "NATURE MADE YOU TO TEMPER MAN." OTWAY.
Philadelphia: Printed by Samuel Sansom, jun. No. 27, Mulberry-Street.
[1796.] pp. viii, 292. 12mo.   AAS. BM.

31689 ADAMS, JOHN   1735–1826
A DEFENCE OF THE CONSTITUTIONS OF GOVERNMENT OF THE UNITED STATES OF
AMERICA, AGAINST THE ATTACK OF M. TURGOT IN HIS LETTER TO DR. PRICE DATED
THE TWENTY-SECOND DAY OF MARCH, 1778. BY JOHN ADAMS, LL. D. PRESIDENT
OF THE UNITED STATES. [One line from] POPE. IN THREE VOLUMES. VOL. I.
THE THIRD EDITION.
*Philadelphia: Printed by Budd and Bartram, for William Cobbett, opposite
Christ Church.* 1797. pp. 6, xxxiii, 392, portrait. 8vo.   AAS. BM. JCB. NYPL.

Contains an interesting List of Subscribers. The portrait, by Copley,
is engraved by J. Smithers.

31690 —— — A DEFENCE OF THE CONSTITUTIONS OF GOVERNMENT OF THE UNITED
STATES OF AMERICA, AGAINST THE ATTACK OF M. TURGOT IN HIS LETTER TO DR.
PRICE DATED THE TWENTY-SECOND DAY OF MARCH, 1778. BY JOHN ADAMS, LL. D.
PRESIDENT OF THE UNITED STATES. [Twelve lines of quotations.] IN THREE
VOLUMES. VOL. II. THE THIRD EDITION.
*Philadelphia: Printed by H. Sweitzer, for William Cobbett, opposite Christ
Church.* 1797. pp. (2), (2), (2), 451. 8vo.   AAS. BM. JCB. NYPL.

31691 —— — A DEFENCE OF THE CONSTITUTIONS OF GOVERNMENT OF THE UNITED
STATES OF AMERICA, AGAINST THE ATTACK OF M. TURGOT IN HIS LETTER TO DR.
PRICE DATED THE TWENTY-SECOND DAY OF MARCH, 1778. BY JOHN ADAMS, LL. D.
PRESIDENT OF THE UNITED STATES. [Six lines from] JOHNSON'S ADVENTURER.
NO. 45. IN THREE VOLUMES. VOL. III. THE THIRD EDITION.
*Philadelphia: Printed by William Young, for William Cobbett, opposite
Christ Church.* 1797. pp. (2), 528, (36). 8vo.   AAS. BM. JCB. NYPL.

31692   ADAMS, John   1750–1814
THE FLOWERS OF MODERN TRAVELS; BEING ELEGANT, ENTERTAINING AND INSTRUC-
TIVE EXTRACTS, SELECTED FROM THE WORKS OF THE MOST CELEBRATED TRAVEL-
LERS; SUCH AS LORD LYTTLETON, SIR W. HAMILTON, BARON DE TOTT, DR. JOHNSON,
DR. MOORE, DR. TROIL, ADDISON, BRYDONE, COX, WRAXALL, SAVARY, TOPHAM,
SHERLOCK, DOUGLAS, SWINBURNE, LADY M. W. MONTAGUE, &C, &C. INTENDED
CHIEFLY FOR YOUNG PEOPLE OF BOTH SEXES. BY THE REV. JOHN ADAMS, A. M.
[Six lines of quotations.] VOL. I. [—II.]
> *Boston: Printed for John West, No. 75, Cornhill. 1797. 2 vols. pp. (324);*
> 312. 12mo.   AAS. BM. LOC. NYPL.

31693   ADAMS, Samuel
FOR SALE, BY SAMUEL ADAMS, TRUCKMAN, AT HIS HOUSE IN ELLIOT STREET, AND AT
HIS WHARF AT THE BOTTOM OF CROSS-STREET, BOSTON. . . .
> *[Boston: 1797.]* Broadside.   MHS.

31694   ADDISON, Alexander   1759–1807
CAUSES AND ERROR OF COMPLAINTS AND JEALOUSY OF THE ADMINISTRATION OF THE
GOVERNMENT. BEING A CHARGE TO THE GRAND JURIES OF THE COUNTIES OF THE
FIFTH CIRCUIT, OF THE STATE OF PENNSYLVANIA, AT MARCH SESSIONS, 1797. BY
ALEXANDER ADDISON, PRESIDENT OF THE COURTS OF COMMON PLEAS OF THE CIR-
CUIT.
> *Philadelphia: Printed by T, Dobson, No. 41, South Second Street. 1797. pp.*
> 24. 8vo.   NYPL.

31695   ADDRESS TO THE INHABITANTS OF THE CITY AND LIBERTIES OF PHILADELPHIA.
> *Philadelphia: 1797.* Broadside. fol.   SGO.

31696   AN AFFECTIONATE LETTER FROM A SOLICITOUS MOTHER TO HER ONLY SON, BOTH
LIVING IN NEW ENGLAND.
> *Amherst, Newhampshire. Printed by Samuel Preston. 1797.*

31697   THE AGE OF ERROR; OR, A POETICAL ESSAY ON THE COURSE OF HUMAN ACTION. BY
A PHILADELPHIAN. [One line of Latin from] PER. SAT. I. 1.
> *Philadelphia: Printed for the Author. 1797. pp. 16. 8vo.*   AAS. BU. JCB.

> 193d Pennsylvania District Copyright, issued to Mathew Carey, as Pro-
> prietor, 13 November, 1797. By "a youth of nineteen."

31698   AIKIN, John   1747–1822
EVENINGS AT HOME; OR, THE JUVENILE BUDGET OPENED. CONSISTING OF A VARIETY
OF MISCELLANEOUS PIECES, FOR THE INSTRUCTION AND AMUSEMENT OF YOUNG PER-
SONS. VOL. I. [— VI.] SECOND EDITION.
> *Philadelphia: Printed by T. Dobson, at the Stone House, No. 41, S. Second-*
> *Street. 1797. 6 vols. in two. pp. iv, 330, (2); iv, 314, (2). 12mo.* AAS. NYPL.

31699   —— — EVENINGS AT HOME, OR THE JUVENILE BUDGET OPENED. CONSISTING OF A
VARIETY OF MISCELLANEOUS PIECES, FOR THE INSTRUCTION AND AMUSEMENT OF
YOUNG PERSONS.
> *Salem: Printed by Thomas C. Cushing. 1797. 2 vols. 12mo.*

31700   —— JUVENILE TRIALS FOR ROBBING ORCHARDS, TELLING FIBS, AND OTHER HEINOUS
OFFENCES. BY MASTER TOMMY LITTLETON, SECRETARY TO THE COURT; WITH A
SEQUEL BY DR. AIKIN. [Two lines of verse.]
> *Boston: Printed for F. Nichols. 1797. [Price twenty cents.] pp. (2), 118.*
> 24mo.   AAS. NYPL.

31701   AITKEN, JOHN, editor.
THE SCOTS MUSICAL MUSEUM. BEING A COLLECTION OF THE MOST FAVORITE SCOTS
TUNES, ADAPTED TO THE VOICE, HARPSICHORD, AND PIANOFORTE.
*Philadelphia: Printed, and sold at the Bookstores, and by John Aitken, the
Editor, No. 193, South Second Street.* 1797.

31702   THE ALBANY CENTINEL. NO. 1. OF VOL. I. TUESDAY, JULY 4, [— NO. 52. FRI-
DAY, DECEMBER 29, 1797.]
*Published every Tuesday and Friday, by Loring Andrews & Co. at the Print-
ing-Office in Maiden-Lane, west of Masters' Lodge; where subscriptions advertisements, &c. for this paper will be received. Communications for the Albany Centinel
will also be received by the copartners, Thomas, Andrews & Penniman, at the Albany
Bookstore, sign of Franklin's Head, State-Street.* 1797. fol.   AAS.

Established, as a semi-weekly, by Loring Andrews, formerly of Boston,
and Stockbridge; his co-partners being Isaiah Thomas, Ebenezer Turell Andrews, and Obadiah Penniman, who operated the Albany Bookstore. On October 2, 1798, the co-partnership was dissolved by mutual
consent—Loring Andrews continuing publication, as sole proprietor to
July, 1801, when, by purchase, Daniel Whiting, and David Leavenworth
became Proprietors and Publishers. In April, 1802, Samuel Whiting
was admitted to partnership, as Whiting, Leavenworth and Whiting.
And in April, 1803, David Leavenworth withdrew, the paper being
printed from that date by Asa H. Center, for Daniel & Samuel Whiting.
In September, 1803, Eleazer F. Backus was admitted to partnership, as
Whiting, Backus & Whiting. In October, 1804, Center ceased to be
printer, his place in the imprint being taken, in May, 1805, by William
Tucker. In March, 1806, Daniel Whiting withdrew, the firm name becoming Backus & Whiting, this arrangement continuing to November
10, 1806, its last number, when they sold their interests to Isaac Mitchell, who established, in continuation, the *Republican Crisis.*

31703   THE ALBANY CHRONICLE. VOL. I. NO. 9. MONDAY, JANUARY 2, [— VOL. II, NO.
60. MONDAY, DECEMBER 25, 1797.]
*[Albany:] Published every Monday, by John M'Donald & Co. on the east side
of Middle-Alley, three doors from the corner or State-Street.* 1797. fol.

With the issue for August 28th, the title was changed to, *Albany Chronicle: or, journal of the times.* Edited by John M'Donald, and printed
by Joseph Fry and Henry C. Southwick, corner of Dock Street and
Mark Lane.

31704   THE ALBANY GAZETTE. VOL. XIII. NUMB. 1055. MONDAY, JANUARY 2, [— VOL.
XIV. NUMB. 1158. FRIDAY, DECEMBER 29, 1797.]
*Printed every Monday and Friday by Charles R. and George Webster, at their
Bookstore, in the White House. corner of State and Pearl-Streets, opposite the City
Tavern. . . .* 1797. fol.

31705   THE ALBANY [N. Y. arms] REGISTER, VOL. IX. NUMBER 521. MONDAY, JANUARY
2, [— VOL. X. NUMBER 624. FRIDAY, DECEMBER 29, 1797.]
*Published on Mondays and Fridays, by Barber & Southwick, at Faust's
Statue, below the Dutch Church, State-Street.* 1797. fol.

In August, there was added to the imprint: "Or at their Book-Store,
two doors north of the City-Hall, in Court-Street."

31706   ALDEN, ABNER   1758–1820
AN INTRODUCTION TO READING AND SPELLING. BEING THE FIRST PART OF A COLUM-
BIAN EXERCISE. CONTAINING SELECTION OF WORDS IN COMMON USE, ARRANGED AND
DIVIDED IN SUCH A MANNER AS WILL LEAD THE LEARNER TO A RIGHT PRONUNCIA-
TION. TOGETHER WITH A VARIETY OF LESSONS FOR READING. BY ABNER ALDEN, A.M.

    *Printed at Boston, by Isaiah Thomas and Ebenezer T. Andrews, Faust's
Statue, No. 45 Newbury-Street.* 1797.

    112th Massachusetts District Copyright, issued to Isaiah Thomas and
Ebenezer T. Andrews, as Proprietors, 11 February, 1797.

31707   —— AN INTRODUCTION TO SPELLING AND READING, IN TWO VOLUMES. BEING THE
FIRST AND SECOND PARTS OF A COLUMBIAN EXERCISE. THE WHOLE COMPRISING
AN EASY AND SYSTEMATICAL METHOD OF TEACHING AND OF LEARNING THE ENGLISH
LANGUAGE. BY ABNER ALDEN, A.M. VOL. II. CONTAINING I. LANGUAGE—SIMPLE
SOUNDS—DIPHTHONGS—SYLLABLES—ACCENT AND EMPHASIS—LETTERS—OTHER
CHARACTERS, &C. II. WORDS IN WHICH THE SAME CONSONANT IS SILENT, PLACED
IN THE SAME TABLE. III. DIAGRAPHS—WORDS IN WHICH DIFFERENT VOWELS HAVE
THE SAME SOUND, PLACED UNDER THE SAME NUMBER. IV. DERIVATIVE WORDS—
THOSE WHICH END ALIKE, PLACED IN THE SAME TABLE. V. A VARIETY OF LESSONS
FOR READING, &C. PUBLISHED ACCORDING TO ACT OF CONGRESS.

    *Printed at Boston, by I. Thomas and E. T. Andrews. Sold by them, at their
Bookstore, Faust's Statue, No. 45, Newbury Street; by said Thomas, at Worcester;
by Thomas, Andrews & Penniman, at Albany; and by Thomas, Andrews & Butler,
at Baltimore.*—Nov. 1797. pp. 192. 12mo.   AAS.

    136th Massachusetts District Copyright, issued to Isaiah Thomas and
Ebenezer T. Andrews, as Proprietors, 2 January, 1798.

31708   ALEXANDER, CALEB   1755–1828
THE YOUNG GENTLEMEN AND LADIES' INSTRUCTOR: BEING A SELECTION OF NEW PIECES;
DESIGNED AS A READING BOOK FOR THE USE OF SCHOOLS AND ACADEMIES; CON-
TAINING SUBJECTS HISTORICAL, GEOGRAPHICAL, MORAL, BIOGRAPHICAL, ANECDOTAL,
INSTRUCTIVE AND ENTERTAINING; ALSO, DIALOGUES AND ORATIONS, WITH CRITICAL
REMARKS ON READING, ACCENTUATION, EMPHASIS, ELEMENTS OF GESTURES AND
ORATORY. BY CALEB ALEXANDER, A.M. AUTHOR OF "A GRAMMATICAL SYSTEM OF
THE ENGLISH LANGUAGE." THE YOUNG GENTLEMEN AND LADIES SPELLING BOOK,
AND "THE WORKS OF VIRGIL TRANSLATED INTO LITERAL ENGLISH PROSE."

    *Boston: Printed for E. Larkin, and W. P. & L. Blake, (Proprietors of the
work.) Sold, wholesale and retail, at their respective Bookstores..* 1797. pp. 228.
12mo.   AAS. HC.

    129th Massachusetts District Copyright, issued to William P. and
Lemuel Blake, as Proprietors, 19 September, 1797. Preface dated,
Mendon. July, 1797.

31709   —— —— THE YOUNG LADIES AND GENTLEMEN'S SPELLING-BOOK: CONTAINING A
CRITERION OF RIGHTLY SPELLING AND PRONOUNCING THE ENGLISH LANGUAGE: IN-
TERSPERSED WITH MANY EASY LESSONS IN READING, ENTERTAINING FABLES AND
COLLECTIONS OF MORAL SENTENCES. INTENDED FOR THE USE OF COMMON SCHOOLS.
BY CALEB ALEXANDER, A.M. AUTHOR OF "THE WORKS OF VIRGIL, TRANSLATED
INTO LITERAL ENGLISH PROSE." "A GRAMMATICAL INSTITUTE OF THE LATIN LAN-
GUAGE. "A GRAMMATICAL SYSTEM OF THE ENGLISH LANGUAGE." "AND A GRAM-
MATICAL SYSTEM OF THE GRECIAN LANGUAGE," &C. &C.

    *Providence: Printed and sold by Carter & Wilkinson, opposite the Market-
House.* 1797.

    "The Publishers having purchased for fourteen years the copy-right of
this work, and propose keeping a constant supply on hand."

31710   ALLDRIDGE, W. J.
THE UNIVERSAL MERCHANT, IN THEORY AND PRACTICE: IMPROVED AND ENLARGED BY W. J. ALLDRIDGE, ASSAYER OF METALS, AND AUTHOR OF THE GOLDSMITH'S REPOSITORY. FIRST AMERICAN EDITION.
Philadelphia: Printed by F. & R. Baily [sic] *at Yorick's Head, No. 116 High-Street.* M,DCC,XCVII. pp. (2), xxxi, 338, [68], 14. 8vo. AAS. JCB. MHS.

31711   —— — THE UNIVERSAL MERCHANT, IN THEORY AND PRACTICE: IMPROVED AND ENLARGED. BY W. J. ALLDRIDGE, ASSAYER OF METALS, AND AUTHOR OF THE GOLDSMITH'S REPOSITORY, FIRST AMERICAN EDITION.
Philadelphia: Printed by Francis and Robert Bailey, at Yorick's-Head, No. 116. High-Street, M,DCC,XCVII. pp. v,xxxi, 338, [68], 14, (6). 8vo. AAS. JCB.

A corrected edition. Contains a six-page list of Subscribers' names.

31712   ALLEN, BENJAMIN   1771–1836
AN ORATION, IN DEFENCE OF DIVINE REVELATION; TOGETHER WITH THE VALEDICTORY ADDRESSES; DELIVERED IN THE BAPTIST MEETING-HOUSE, IN PROVIDENCE, AT THE COMMENCEMENT OF RHODE-ISLAND COLLEGE, SEPTEMBER 6, A. D. 1797. BY BENJAMIN ALLEN, A. B. PUBLISHED BY REQUEST.
Providence: Printed by Carter and Wilkinson, and sold at their Book-Store, opposite the Market. M,DCC,XCVII. pp. (16). 8vo. AAS. BM. JCB. NYPL. RIHS.

31713   ALLEN, PAUL, JUNIOR   1775–1826
AN ORATION, ON THE NECESSITY OF POLITICAL UNION AT THE PRESENT DAY: DELIVERED AT THE BAPTIST MEETING-HOUSE, IN PROVIDENCE, AT THE COMMENCEMENT OF RHODE-ISLAND COLLEGE, A. D. 1797. BY PAUL ALLEN, JUN. A. B. CANDIDATE FOR THE DEGREE OF MASTER IN THE ARTS.
Providence: Printed by Carter and Wilkinson, and sold at their Book-Store, opposite the Market. M,DCC,XCVII. pp. (8) 8vo. AAS. BM. JCB. NYPL. RIHS.

31714   ALLINE, HENRY   1748–1784
HYMNS, AND SPIRITUAL SONGS. BY HENRY ALLINE, LATE MINISTER OF THE GOSPEL, AT FALMOUTH, IN NOVA-SCOTIA. THE THIRD EDITION. WITH SOME ENLARGEMENTS.
Printed at Dover, by Samuel Bragg, jun. and for sale at his Office, and in Boston, by John West.—1797. pp. vi, 388, (18). 24mo. AAS. HC.

31715   —— A SERMON, PREACHED AT FORT-MIDWAY: ON THE 19TH OF FEBRUARY, 1783. BY HENRY ALLINE, MINISTER OF THE GOSPEL AT FALMOUTH, NOVA-SCOTIA. [Vignette.]
Re-printed at Dover: by Samuel Bragg, jr. M,DCC,XCVII. pp. 39. 8vo. AAS.

31716   ALLSTON, WILLIAM
AN INAUGURAL ESSAY ON DROPSY, OR THE HYDROPIC STATE OF FEVER. SUBMITTED TO THE EXAMINATION OF THE REV. JOHN EWING, S. T. P. PROVOST, THE TRUSTEES AND MEDICAL FACULTY OF THE UNIVERSITY OF PENNSYLVANIA, ON THE TWELFTH DAY OF MAY, 1797. FOR THE DEGREE OF DOCTOR OF MEDICINE. BY WILLIAM ALLSTON, OF GEORGE-TOWN, SOUTH-CAROLINA, MEMBER OF THE PHILADELPHIA MEDICAL AND CHEMICAL SOCIETIES.
Philadelphia: Printed by William W. Woodward, No. 17, Chesnut-Street. 1797. pp. 60. 8vo. AAS. SGO.

31717   AMERICAN ACADEMY OF COMPLIMENTS: OR, THE COMPLETE AMERICAN SECRETARY. WITH A COLLECTION OF THE NEWEST SONGS.
Wilmington: Printed by Peter Brynberg. 1797.

31718   THE AMERICAN FARMER'S GUIDE: OR A NEW AND EXCELLENT TREATISE ON AGRI-CULTURE. WHEREIN THE PLANTER AND FARMER WILL SEE SUCH A JUDICIOUS METHOD FOR THE MANAGEMENT OF STOCK-RASIING [*sic*] MANURE-ENRICHING AND IMPROVING HIS LANDS THAT THEY SHALL PRODUCE THE MOST PLENTIFUL CROPS, AND IN A FEW YEARS BECOME AS VALUABLE AS THOSE OF ENGLAND OR FRANCE.

       Philadelphia: Reprinted for the Rev. Mason L. Weems, by Jacob Johnson & Co. (Price one quarter of a dollar.) [1795.] pp. 83. 12mo.   APS. HSP. LOC.

       See, also, No. 234 of the excellent "Weems Bibliography," by Emily Ellsworth Ford Skeel.

31719   AMERICAN GAZETTE & GENERAL ADVERTISER. VOL. III. No. 281. TUESDAY, JANU-ARY 3, [— VOL. IV. No. 367. TUESDAY, NOVEMBER 7, 1797.]

       Norfolk: Printed every Tuesday and Friday, by William Davis. 1797. fol.

       The above is the last number located.

31720   THE AMERICAN IN ALGIERS, OR THE PATRIOT OF SEVENTY-SIX IN CAPTIVITY. A POEM, IN TWO CANTOS. [Two lines from] FRENEAU.

       New-York: Printed and sold by J. Buel, No. 153, Water-Street, corner of Fly-Market. M.DCC.XCVII. pp. 36. 12mo.   BA. BU. LOC. NYHS.

31721   AMERICAN INTELLIGENCER. VOL. II. No. 73. TUESDAY, JANUARY 3, [— VOLUME III. NUMBER 120. TUESDAY, NOVEMBER 28, 1797.]

       West-Springfield, (Massachusetts:) Published by Edward Gray, a few rods west of the Meeting-House. 1797. fol.   AAS.

       The above is the last number located.

31722   THE AMERICAN LADIES POCKET BOOK, WITH AN ALMANAC, FOR THE YEAR 1798.

       Philadelphia: Published by William Y. Birch, No. 17, South Second Street. [1797.]

       Title-page and frontispiece engraved.

31723   AMERICAN [U. S. arms] MERCURY. VOL. XIII. No. 652. MONDAY, JANUARY 2, [— VOL. XIV. No. 703. MONDAY, DECEMBER 25, 1797.]

       Published by Elisha Babcock—Hartford. 1797. fol.   AAS. CHS. YC.

31724   THE AMERICAN MORAL & SENTIMENTAL MAGAZINE, CONSISTING OF A COLLECTION OF SELECT PIECES, IN PROSE AND VERSE, FROM THE BEST AUTHORS, ON RELIGIOUS, MORAL, AND SENTIMENTAL SUBJECTS, CALCULATED TO FORM THE UNDERSTANDING, AND IMPROVE THE HEART. [Seven lines from] THOMSON. VOL. I. [MONDAY, JULY 3, — MONDAY, DECEMBER 4, 1797.]

       New-York: Printed by the Editor, [Thomas Kirk] 112, Chatham-Street, next door to the Tea-Water Pump. 1797. pp. 370 [sic 384], (iv). 8vo.

                          BA. HSP. LOC. NYHS. NYPL. WHS. YC.

31725   THE AMERICAN SPECTATOR, OR MATRIMONIAL PRECEPTOR. A COLLECTION (WITH ADDITIONS AND VARIATIONS) OF ESSAYS, EPISTLES, PRECEPTS AND EXAMPLES, RE-LATING TO THE MARRIED STATE, FROM THE MOST CELEBRATED WRITERS, ANCIENT AND MODERN. ADAPTED TO THE STATE OF SOCIETY IN THE AMERICAN REPUBLIC. PUBLISHED ACCORDING TO ACT OF CONGRESS.

       Boston: Printed by Manning & Loring, for David West, Proprietor of the Copy-Right. 1797. pp. 286, frontispiece. 12mo.   AAS. BM. JCB. LOC. NYPL.

       107th Massachusetts District Copyright, issued to David West, as Proprietor, 30 December, 1796.

31726   AMERICAN SPY. VOL. VI. NUMBER 301. TUESDAY, JANUARY 3, [— VOL. VII. NUM-
BER 342. TUESDAY, DECEMBER 26, 1797.]

> *Lansingburgh: Printed every Tuesday, in the Post-Office, by William W.*
> *Wands.* 1797. fol.

> In June, William W. Wands withdrew, and the Press was sold to Rob-
> ert Moffitt & Co. who established *The Northern Budget*, continuing the
> advertisements of the Spy. After an interval of ten weeks, Charles R.
> Webster resumed publication of the *American Spy*, with continuous
> numbering, and continued it to 28 August, 1798.

31727   AMERICAN TELEGRAPHE. & FAIRFIELD COUNTY GAZETTE. VOL. II. NO. 40. WHOLE
NO. 92. WEDNESDAY, JANUARY 4, [—VOL. III. NO. 38. WHOLE NO. 142. WEDNES-
DAY, DECEMBER 27, 1797.]

> *Newfield, near Fairfield, [Connecticut]: Printed and published by Lazarus*
> *Beach, Printer, Bookseller and Stationer, opposite Mr. Hinman's Inn.* 1797.
> fol.   AAS.

> With the issue for April 5th, the name was shortened to *American*
> *Telegraphe*, with this motto: Receive instruction and not silver, and
> knowledge rather than choice gold.

31728   THE AMERICAN UNIVERSAL MAGAZINE. VOL. I. [NO. V. MONDAY, JANUARY 2, —
NO. VIII. MONDAY, MARCH 20, 1797.]

> *Philadelphia: Printed for Richard Lee.* [1797.] pp. (2), 448, (8), 10 plates.
> 8vo.   AAS. BM. BPL. BU. HSP. LCP. LOC. NYHS. NYPL. RIHS. WHS. YC.

> Established as a weekly, and bi-weekly, by Richard Lee. And con-
> tinued to March, 1798. The general title page is engraved. Numbers
> I-IV were Printed in 1796, by Samuel H. Smith, for Richard Lee, No.
> 131 Chesnut-Street. V-VI. Printed by Budd & Bartram, for Richard
> Lee. VII. Printed by Snowden & M'Corkle, for Richard Lee. VIII.
> Printed for Richard Lee, No. 4, Chesnut-Street, near the wharf.

31729   —— THE AMERICAN UNIVERSAL MAGAZINE. VOL. II. [NO. IX. MONDAY, APRIL 3,
— MONDAY, JUNE 13, 1797.] [Cut.]

> *Philadelphia: Printed [by Samuel H. Smith] for Richard Lee.* [1797.] pp.
> (2), 404, (6), 6 plates. 8vo.

31730   —— THE AMERICAN UNIVERSAL MAGAZINE. VOL. III. [MONDAY, JULY 10, — MON-
DAY, NOVEMBER 15, 1797.] [Cut.]

> *Philadelphia: Printed by Saml. H. Smith and Thos. Smith.* [1797.] pp. (2),
> 464, 8, 7 plates. 8vo.

31731   THE AMERICAN TUTOR'S ASSISTANT; OR, A COMPENDIOUS SYSTEM OF PRACTICAL
ARITHMETIC; CONTAINING THE SEVERAL RULES OF THAT USEFUL SCIENCE, CONCISELY
DEFINED, METHODICALLY ARRANGED, AND FULLY EXEMPLIFIED. THE WHOLE PAR-
TICULARLY ADAPTED TO THE EASY AND REGULAR INSTRUCTION OF YOUTH IN OUR
AMERICAN SCHOOLS: BY SUNDRY TEACHERS IN AND NEAR PHILADELPHIA. THE
SECOND EDITION.

> *Philadelphia: Printed and sold by Zachariah Poulson, junior, No. 80, Ches-*
> *nut-Street.* 1796.

31732   THE AMERICAN TUTOR'S ASSISTANT, continued.
—— THE AMERICAN TUTOR'S ASSISTANT; OR, A COMPENDIOUS SYSTEM OF PRACTICAL ARITHMETIC; CONTAINING, THE SEVERAL RULES OF THAT USEFUL SCIENCE CONCISELY DEFINED, METHODICALLY ARRANGED, AND FULLY EXEMPLIFIED. THE WHOLE PARTICULARLY ADAPTED TO THE EASY AND REGULAR INSTRUCTION OF YOUTH IN OUR AMERICAN SCHOOLS: BY SUNDRY TEACHERS IN AND NEAR PHILADELPHIA. THE THIRD EDITION.

> *Philadelphia: Printed and sold by Zachariah Poulson, junior, No. 80, Chesnut-Street.* 1797. pp. (2), (2), 200. 12mo.   AAS. LCP.

The Preface is signed by John Todd, Zachariah Jess, William Waring, Jeremiah Paul. "Entered according to law."

31733   AMERICANISCHER STADT UND LAND KALENDER AUF DAS 1798STE JAHR CHRISTI, WELCHES EIN GEMEINES JAHR IST VON 365 TAGEN.

> *Philadelphia: Gedruckt und zu haben bey Carl Cist, in der Zweyten-strasse, No. 104, nah am Eck der Rehs-strasse.* [1797.] pp. (46). 4to.   LOC.

31734   AMES, FISHER   1758–1808
Half-title: THE SECOND EDITION OF MR. AMES'S SPEECH, IN CONGRESS, THURSDAY, APRIL, 1796.

Title: THE SPEECH OF MR. AMES, IN THE HOUSE OF REPRESENTATIVES OF THE UNITED STATES, WHEN IN COMMITTEE OF THE WHOLE, ON THURSDAY, APRIL 28, 1796, IN SUPPORT OF THE FOLLOWING MOTION: RESOLVED, THAT IT IS EXPEDIENT TO PASS THE LAWS NECESSARY TO CARRY INTO EFFECT THE TREATY LATELY CONCLUDED BETWEEN THE UNITED STATES AND THE KING OF GREAT-BRITAIN.

> *Boston: Printed by Jno & J. N. Russell, Quaker-Lane, sold by them; and by William P. Blake, No. 1, Cornhill. [Price 25 cents.]* [1797.] pp. 52. 8vo.

This edition is "printed on fine paper."   HSP. JCB. NYPL.

31735   THE AMUSING COMPANION: OR, INTERESTING STORY TELLER. BEING A COLLECTION OF MORAL, SENTIMENTAL AND MISCELLANEOUS TALES. [Four lines of verse.]

> *Charlestown: Printed by John Lamson, for John W. Folsom, No. 30, Union-Street, Boston.* MDCCXCVII. pp. 284, (3). 16mo.   JCB.

31736   ANDREWS, JOHN   1746–1813
AN ADDRESS TO THE GRADUATES IN MEDICINE: DELIVERED AT A MEDICAL COMMENCEMENT IN THE UNIVERSITY OF PENNSYLVANIA, HELD MAY 12, 1797. TO WHICH IS PREFIXED, THE PRAYER, MADE USE OF ON THAT OCCASION. BY JOHN ANDREWS . . . PUBLISHED BY REQUEST.

> *Philadelphia: Printed by Ormrod & Conrad.* 1797. pp. 19. 8vo. NYPL. SGO.

31737   ANDREWS, ROBERT
THE VIRGINIA ALMANACK, FOR THE YEAR OF OUR LORD, 1798. BEING THE SECOND AFTER LEAP-YEAR; AND THE TWENTY-SECOND OF AMERICAN INDEPENDENCE. [Thirteen lines.]

> *Richmond: Printed by T. Nicolson, just above the Eagle-Tavern.* [1797.] pp. (38). 16mo.   VSL.

31738   ANDREWS'S WESTERN [cut] STAR. NO. 7. OF VOL. VIII. WHOLE NO. 371. MONDAY, JANUARY 2, [— NO. 15 OF VOL. VIII. WHOLE NO. 379. MONDAY, FEBRUARY 27, 1797.]

> *Printed at Stockbridge, Massachusetts, by Loring Andrews, . . .* 1797. fol. AAS.

With the above issue, Andrews disposed of his interests to Benjamin Rosseter, and Herman Willard, who continued publication as *The Western Star.*

31739 AN APPEAL TO THE CANDID, UPON THE PRESENT STATE OF RELIGION AND POLITICS
       IN CONNECTICUT.
          [New-Haven: Printed by T. & S. Green, 1797.] pp. 23 [24.] 12mo. BA. BM.
       An extra page numbered 61, is inserted between pages 15 and 16.

31740 APPLETON, JESSE   1772–1819
          THE IMMENSITY OF GOD. A SERMON, DELIVERED TO THE CONGREGATIONAL SOCIETY
       IN HAMPTON, NOVEMBER 14, 1797; AT THE DEDICATION OF THEIR NEW HOUSE, FOR
       PUBLIC WORSHIP. BY JESSE APPLETON, A. M. MINISTER OF THE CONGREGATIONAL
       CHURCH IN HAMPTON. [Two lines from] EXOD. III. 5.
          Newburyport:—Printed by Edmund M. Blunt—1797. pp. 32. 8vo.
                                                 BA. HC. JCB. NYHS.

31741 THE ARABIAN NIGHTS ENTERTAINMENTS. CONSISTING OF ONE THOUSAND AND ONE
       STORIES, TOLD BY THE SULTANESS OF THE INDIES, TO DIVERT THE SULTAN FROM A
       CRUEL VOW HE HAD MADE, TO MARRY A LADY EVERY DAY, AND HAVE HER PUT TO
       DEATH NEXT MORNING, TO AVENGE HIMSELF FOR THE DISLOYALTY OF HIS FIRST
       SULTANESS. CONTAINING A FAMILIAR ACCOUNT OF THE CUSTOMS, MANNERS, AND
       RELIGION OF THE EASTERN NATIONS, THE TARTARS, PERSIANS, AND INDIANS, &c.
       THE SECOND AMERICAN EDITION, FREELY TRANSCRIBED FROM THE ORIGINAL TRANS-
       LATION. VOL. I. [— II.]
          *Printed at Exeter, by H. Ranlet, for Thomas and Andrews. Faust's Statue, No.
       45 Newbury-street, Boston. 1797.* 2 vols. pp. 272; 280. 16mo.   AAS.

31742 —— THE ARABIAN NIGHTS ENTERTAINMENTS. CONSISTING OF ONE THOUSAND AND
       ONE STORIES, TOLD BY THE SULTANESS OF THE INDIES, TO DIVERT THE SULTAN
       FROM A CRUEL VOW HE HAD MADE, TO MARRY A LADY EVERY DAY, AND HAVE HER
       PUT TO DEATH NEXT MORNING, TO AVENGE HIMSELF FOR THE DISLOYALTY OF HIS
       FIRST SULTANESS. CONTAINING A FAMILIAR ACCOUNT OF THE CUSTOMS, MANNERS,
       AND RELIGION OF THE EASTERN NATIONS, THE TARTARS, PERSIANS, AND INDIANS, &c.
          Wilmington: Printed by Peter Brynberg. 1797.

31743 —— THE ORIENTAL MORALIST, OR THE BEAUTIES OF THE ARABIAN NIGHTS ENTER-
       TAINMENTS. TRANSLATED FROM THE ORIGINAL, AND ACCOMPANIED WITH SUITABLE
       REFLECTIONS ADAPTED TO EACH STORY. BY THE REVEREND MR. J. COOPER. AU-
       THOR OF THE HISTORY OF ENGLAND, &C. &C. &C. THE FIRST AMERICAN EDITION.
          Dover: Printed by Samuel Bragg, jr. for Wm. T. Clap, Boston. 1797. pp.
       (2), (2), (2), (8), 232, (1). 12mo.   AAS.

31744 ARBLAY, FRANCES BURNEY D'   1752–1840
          CAMILLA: OR, A PICTURE OF YOUTH. BY THE AUTHOR OF EVELINA AND CECILIA.
       IN THREE VOLUMES. VOL. I. [— III.] FIRST BOSTON EDITION.
          *Boston: Printed by Manning & Loring, for S. Hall, W. Spotswood, J. White,
       Thomas & Andrews, D. West, E. Larkin, W. P. & Lemuel Blake, and J. West. 1797.*
       pp. (2), (2), 328; (2), (2), 353; (2), (2), 342, (3). 12mo. AAS. BA. HC. JCB. LOC.

31745 —— —— CAMILLA: OR, A PICTURE OF YOUTH. BY THE AUTHOR OF EVELINA AND
       CECILIA.
          New-York: Printed by John Bull, for Samuel Campbell. 1797. 5 vols. 12mo.
                                                              LOC. NYPL.

31746 —— —— CAMILLA: OR, A PICTURE OF YOUTH. BY THE AUTHORESS OF EVELINA AND
       CECILIA. FIVE VOLUMES IN THREE. VOL. I. [— III.] [Vignette.]
          Philadelphia: Printed by Ormrod & Conrad, Chesnut-street. 1797. 3 vols.
       pp. (2), 326; (2), 335; (2), (2), 352. 12mo.   AAS.

31747 —— EVELINA: OR, A YOUNG LADY'S ENTRANCE INTO THE WORLD. IN TWO VOLUMES.
          New-York: Printed by Jacob S. Mott, for E. Duyckinck, 1797. 2 vols. 12mo.
                                                              NYPL.

31748   ARGENSON, RENE LOUIS DE VOYER, marquis D'   1694-1757
ESSAYS, CIVIL, MORAL, LITERARY, & POLITICAL. WRITTEN AFTER THE MANNER OF
M. DE MONTAGNE: INTERSPERSED WITH CHARACTERS, PORTRAITS & ANECDOTES.
BY THE CELEBRATED MARQUIS D'ARGENSON, MANY YEARS PRIME MINISTER OF
FRANCE; — AND WHO WAS HONOURED WITH THE PARTICULAR INTIMACY OF THE
LATE KING OF PRUSSIA. TRANSLATED FROM HIS VALUABLE MANUSCRIPTS. FIRST
AMERICAN EDITION.
> *Printed at Worcester, Massachusetts, by Thomas, Son & Thomas: sold by them
> at the Worcester Bookstore.—March—1797.—pp.228. 12mo.* AAS. HC. JCB. NYPL.

31749   THE ARGUS. "PRESS TO ONE CENTRE STILL, THE GEN'RAL GOOD." VOL. I. No. 1.
THURSDAY, JANUARY 12, [— No. 50. MONDAY, DECEMBER 25, 1797.]
> *Printed and published by Cornelius Sturtevant jun. & Co. at Putney, Vermont.*
> 1797. fol.
                                                                              AAS.
The change in day of publication was made in August. Established,
as a weekly, by Cornelius Sturtevant, junior, Abijah Wilder, and Elias
Sturtevant, and continued by them to June 4, 1798, when the partnership was dissolved—and publication continued by Cornelius Sturtevant
alone. In November, 1798, the title was changed to *Putney Argus*,
under which it was continued to February 26, 1799—the last number
located.

31750   THE ARGUS; AND NEW-JERSEY CENTINEL. VOL. II. No. 65. THURSDAY, JANUARY
5, [— OCTOBER ? 1797.]
> *Published (weekly) by Alexander M'Kenzie, Bridge Town.* 1797. fol.
No copies are known after November 10. 1796, but publication was
probably continued to the close of the second volume in October, 1797.

31751   ARGUS. GREENLEAF'S NEW [cut] DAILY ADVERTISER. [Motto.] NUMBER 517. MON-
DAY, JANUARY 2, [— NUMBER 825. SATURDAY, DECEMBER 30, 1797.]
> ☞ *New-York—Edited, printed, and published (every morning) by Thomas
> Greenleaf, No. 54, Wall-Street—six doors from the Tontine Coffee-house.* 1797. fol.
                                                                    LOC. NYHS. NYPL.

31752   ARNAUD, FRANÇOIS THOMAS MARIE DE BACULARD D'   1718-1805
FANNY: OR THE HAPPY REPENTANCE. FROM THE FRENCH OF M. D'ARNAUD.
> *Printed and sold by H. Ranlet, Exeter.* 1796. pp. 38, (2). 16mo.   JCB.

31753   ARNOLD, JOSIAH LYNDON   1768-1796
POEMS. BY THE LATE IOSIAS LYNDON ARNOLD, ESQR, OF ST. JOHNSBURY, (VERMONT),
FORMERLY OF PROVIDENCE, AND A TUTOR IN RHODE-ISLAND COLLEGE, [Edited by
James Burrill, junior.]
> *Printed at Providence, by Carter & Wilkinson, and sold at their Bookstore,
> opposite the Market.* M.DCC.XCVII. pp. 141.   AAS. BM. BU. JCB. MHS. NYPL.

31754   ARNOLD, SAMUEL JAMES   1774-1852
LITTLE SALLY. A FAVORITE SONG SUNG IN THE SHIPWRECK. COMPOSED BY DR.
[Samuel] ARNOLD. PRICE 25 CENTS.
> *New-York: Printed and sold at J. Hewitt's Musical Repository, No. 131,
> William Street. Sold also by B. Carr, Philadelphia & J. Carr Baltimore.* [1797.]
> pp. (2). 4to.
                                                                              LOC.

31755   ASSOCIATE REFORMED CHURCH IN NORTH AMERICA.
EXTRACT FROM THE MINUTES OF THE ACTS AND PROCEEDINGS OF THE ASSOCIATE
REFORMED SYNOD, MET AT PHILADELPHIA, MAY 29, 1797, AND CONTINUED BY AD-
JOURNMENTS. PUBLISHED BY ORDER OF SYNOD.
> *New-York: Printed by T. & J. Swords, No. 99 Pearl-street.—1797.—pp.*
> (10). 8vo.
                                                                    AAS. NYHS. NYPL.

31756 AURORA [cut] GENERAL ADVERTISER. SURGO UT PROSIM. NUM. 1880. MONDAY,
       JANUARY 2, [— NUM. 2173. SATURDAY, DECEMBER 30, 1797.]
           *Published (daily) by Benj. Franklin Bache, No. 112, Market Street, between
       Third and Fourth Streets, Philadelphia. 1797. fol.*
                                 AAS. BM. HSP. LCP. MdHS. NYPL. PSL.

31757 AUSTIN, SAMUEL   1760–1830
       A SERMON, DELIVERED AT WORCESTER, ON THE DAY OF PUBLIC THANKSGIVING, OB-
       SERVED THROUGHOUT THE COMMONWEALTH OF MASSACHUSETTS, DECEMBER 15TH,
       MDCCXCVI. BY SAMUEL AUSTIN, A. M.
           Printed at Worcester, by Leonard Worcester. MDCCXCVII. pp. 24. 8vo.
                            AAS. BA. BM. CLS. HC. JCB. LOC. MHS. NYPL. UTS. YC.
       Contains two pages of verse from Thomson's Seasons.

31758 B., J.
       FOUR SERMONS, ON THE SECOND COMING OF CHRIST, AND THE FUTURE MISERY OF
       THE WICKED. BY J. B.
           Philadelphia: Printed by Ormrod & Conrad, No. 41, Chesnut-street. 1797.
       pp. 84. 12mo.   JCB.

31759 BACHE, BENJAMIN FRANKLIN   1769–1798
       REMARKS OCCASIONED BY THE LATE CONDUCT OF MR. WASHINGTON, AS PRESIDENT OF
       THE UNITED STATES. M.DCC.XCVI.
           *Philadelphia: Printed for Benjamin Franklin Bache, No. 112, Market-
       Street.* 1797. *[Copy-right secured according to law.]* pp. [iv], [84]. 8vo.
                            AAS. BA. HC. HSP. LOC. MHS. NYHS. VSL.

       185th Pennsylvania District Copyright, issued to Benjamin Franklin
       Bache, as Proprietor, 23 June, 1797.

31760 BACHE'S PHILADELPHIA AURORA. NO. I. MONDAY, APRIL 3, AND TUESDAY, APRIL
       4, [— NO. 117. FRIDAY, DECEMBER 29, AND SATURDAY, DECEMBER 30, 1797.]
           Published (tri-weekly) by Benj. Franklin Bache, No. 112 Market Street.
       1797. fol.

       Established, as a tri-weekly edition of the *Aurora,* by Benjamin Frank-
       lin Bache, and continued under this title, without numbering, to March
       10, 1800, when the title was changed, by Bache's successor, William
       Duane, to *The Philadelphia Aurora,* and this page heading changed to
       Aurora, for the Country, as a column heading, in November, 1800.
       From June, 1817, the column heading was *Aurora* only, beyond the
       period of this work. The editorial changes were the same as in the
       daily paper.

31761 BACKUS, AZEL   1765–1817
       A SERMON, DELIVERED AT THE FUNERAL OF HIS EXCELLENCY OLIVER WOLCOTT,
       GOVERNOR OF THE STATE OF CONNECTICUT; WHO DIED 1ST DECEMBER, 1797. BY
       AZEL BACKUS, A. M. PASTOR OF THE CHURCH IN BETHLEM.
           Printed at Litchfield, by T. Collier. [1797.] pp. 23. 8vo.
                            AAS. BA. BM. JCB. MHS. NYHS. NYPL. RIHS.
       In two states—some copies on thick paper with variations.

31762 BACKUS, CHARLES   1749–1803
       FIVE DISCOURSES, ON THE TRUTH AND INSPIRATION OF THE BIBLE. PARTICULARLY
       DESIGNED FOR THE BENEFIT OF YOUTH. BY CHARLES BACKUS, A. M, PASTOR OF A
       CHURCH IN SOMERS. PUBLISHED ACCORDING TO ACT OF CONGRESS.
           Hartford: Printed by Hudson & Goodwin, 1797. pp. 173. 12mo.
                            AAS. BA. BM. JCB. LOC. NYPL. UTS. YC.

31763 BAILEY, EBENEZER
A FUNERAL ELEGY; OR, AN ELEGIAC ESSAY ON THE DEATH OF MISS RHODA BAILEY
. . . [of Westmoreland, New Hampshire.]
[Printed by Cornelius Sturtevant, jun. & Co. Putney, Vermont. 1797.]
8vo.   BM.

31764 BAILEY, FRANCIS   1735–1815
BAILEY'S POCKET ALMANAC, FOR THE YEAR OF OUR LORD, MDCCXCVIII; AND OF THE
EMPIRE THE TWENTY-SECOND. THE SECOND AFTER BISSEXTILE, OR LEAP-YEAR.
[Six lines of verse. U. S. arms.]
*Philadelphia: Printed by Francis Bailey, at Yorick's Head, No. 116, High-
street.* [1797.] pp. (32). 32mo.   HSP. LOC.

31765 BALL, HEMAN   1764–1821
A SERMON DELIVERED BEFORE THE WORSHIPFUL MASTER, THE WARDENS AND
BRETHREN OF UNION LODGE, AT MIDDLEBURY, JUNE 27TH, 1797: BEING THE
FESTIVAL OF ST. JOHN, THE BAPTIST. BY HEMAN BALL, A. M. PASTOR OF A CHURCH
IN RUTLAND, VERMONT. PUBLISHED AT THE REQUEST OF THE LODGE.
Printed at Rutland, Vermont, by Josiah Fay, for S. Williams & Co. MDCC-
XCVII. pp. 23. 12mo.

31766 BALLOU, SILAS   1753–1837
NEW HYMNS, ON VARIOUS SUBJECTS, VIZ. ON THE CREATION OF THE WORLD . . .
ON THE EARLY AND EXTENSIVE PROMISES OF GOD . . . ON THE APPLICATION
OF THE BLESSED COMFORTER . . . BY SILAS BALLOU . . .
Newbury, Vermont: Printed by Nathaniel Coverly, jun'r, 1797. pp. 184+
12mo.   HC. NYPL.

31767 BALTIMORE. MARYLAND.
AN ACT TO ERECT BALTIMORE-TOWN, IN BALTIMORE-COUNTY, INTO A CITY, AND TO
INCORPORATE THE INHABITANTS THEREOF.
Baltimore: Printed by John Hayes, March 13, 1797. pp. 15, (1). 8vo. NYPL.

31768 —— ORDINANCES OF THE CORPORATION OF THE CITY OF BALTIMORE, PASSED AT
THEIR FIRST SESSION, HELD APRIL 1797. WITH THE ACT OF INCORPORATION PRE-
FIXED.
Baltimore: Printed by John Hayes. 1797. 8vo.

31769 BALTIMORE. MARYLAND. LIBRARY COMPANY.
CATALOGUE OF THE BOOKS, &C. BELONGING TO THE LIBRARY COMPANY OF BALTIMORE;
WITH THE BY-LAWS OF THE COMPANY, AND LIST OF MEMBERS.
Baltimore: Printed by John Hayes. 1797. 12mo.

31770 BARBAULD, ANNA LÆTITIA AIKIN   1743–1825
HYMNS IN PROSE FOR CHILDREN. BY MRS. BARBAULD.
Boston: Printed and sold by W. Spotswood. 1797. pp. iv, 29, (3). 18mo.
                                                             JCB.

31771 BARLOW, JOEL   1754–1812
THE HASTY-PUDDING: A POEM, IN THREE CANTOS; IN RECOMMENDATION OF SIMPLICITY
OF DIET. BY JOEL BARLOW, ESQ. AUTHOR OF THE VISION OF COLUMBUS, CONSPIR-
ACY OF KINGS, REVISION OF DR. WATTS' PSALMS, ADVICE TO PRIVILEGED ORDERS,
&C. &C. AND NOW CONSUL FOR THE UNITED STATES AT ALGIERS. [Three lines of
quotations.]
New-London: Printed and sold by Charles Holt. 1797.

BARLOW, JOEL, continued.

31772 —— — THE HASTY-PUDDING; A POEM, IN THREE CANTOS. WRITTEN AT CHAMBERY, IN SAVOY, JAN. 1793. BY JOEL BARLOW, ESQ.
Printed and sold at the Printing-Office in Fairhaven. [1797.] pp. 16. 16mo.
           LOC.

31773 —— — THE HASTY-PUDDING: A POEM, IN THREE CANTOS. WRITTEN AT CHAMBERY, IN SAVOY, JAN. 1793. BY JOEL BARLOW, ESQ. OMNE TULIT PUNCTUM QUI MISCUIT UTILE DULCI. HE MAKES A GOOD BREAKFAST WHO MIXES PUDDING WITH MOLASSES.
Printed by Rosseter & Willard, Stockbridge.—1797. pp. 16. 16mo.   BU.

31774 **BARNARD, THOMAS**   1748–1814
A SERMON, DELIVERED ON THE DAY OF ANNUAL THANKSGIVING, DECEMBER 15, 1796. BY THOMAS BARNARD, D. D. PASTOR OF THE NORTH CHURCH IN SALEM. PUBLISHED AT THE REQUEST OF THE HEARERS AND OTHERS.
Printed by Thomas C. Cushing, Essex-Street, Salem. [1797.] pp. [22.]
8vo.   AAS. BM. CHS. CLA. HC. NYPL. YC.

31775 **BARTGIS'S FEDERAL GAZETTE, OR THE FREDERICK-TOWN AND COUNTY WEEKLY ADVERTISER.** VOL. IV. No. 243. THURSDAY, JANUARY 5, [— VOL. V, No. 294. WEDNESDAY, DECEMBER 27, 1797.]
Printed every Thursday, by Matthias Bartgis, at his English & German Printing-Office, the upper end of Market-Street, Frederick-Town; . . . 1797. fol.   MDHS.

In May, the day of publication was changed to Wednesday. And, beginning August 30th, a cut of the United States Arms divided the heading. With the issue for August 30, 1797, the title was changed to *Bartgis's Federal Gazette, or the Frederick County Weekly Advertiser.*

31776 **BARTLETT, JOSIAH**   1759–1820
AN ADDRESS: DELIVERED AT WARREN HALL, IN CHARLESTOWN, AT THE REQUEST OF KING SOLOMON'S LODGE, FEBRUARY 22, 1797. BY JOSIAH BARTLETT . . .
Charlestown: Printed by John Lamson. [1797.] pp. 16. 8vo.   BA. HC. MHS.

With Prayer by Rev. Jedidiah Morse.

31777 **BARTON, BENJAMIN SMITH**   1766–1816
NEW VIEWS OF THE ORIGIN OF THE TRIBES AND NATIONS OF AMERICA. BY BENJAMIN SMITH BARTON, M. D. CORRESPONDENT-MEMBER OF THE SOCIETY OF THE ANTIQUARIES OF SCOTLAND; MEMBER OF THE AMERICAN PHILOSOPHICAL SOCIETY; FELLOW OF THE AMERICAN ACADEMY OF ARTS AND SCIENCES OF BOSTON; CORRESPONDING MEMBER OF THE MASSACHUSETTS HISTORICAL SOCIETY, AND PROFESSOR OF MATERIA MEDICA, NATURAL HISTORY AND BOTANY, IN THE UNIVERSITY OF PENNSYLVANIA,
Philadelphia: Printed, for the Author, by John Bioren. 1797. pp. xii, cix, 83. 8vo.   AAS. BA. BM. HC. JCB. MHS. NYHS. NYPL.

184th Pennsylvania District Copyright, issued to Benjamin Smith Barton, as Author, 16 June, 1797.

31778 **THE BATH GAZETTE, AND GENERAL ADVERTISER.** [Motto.] VOL. I. No. 3. THURSDAY, JANUARY 5, [— VOL. II. No. 2. THURSDAY, DECEMBER 28, 1797.]
Bath, County of Steuben, State of New-York: Published weekly by William Kersey and James Edie, . . . 1797. fol.

31779   BAXTER, Richard   1615–1691
A Call to the Unconverted, to turn and live; and accept of Mercy, while it may be had; as ever they will find mercy, in the day of their extremity from the living God.—To which is added—Converse with God in solitude, together with the dying thoughts, of the Author. By the late revered and pious mr. Richard Baxter.

       New-Brunswick: Printed by Abraham Blauvelt. 1797. pp. 307, (5). 12mo.
                                                            AAS.
       Contains five pages of Subscribers' names.

31780   BAY, William   1773–1865
An Inaugural dissertation on the operation of pestilential fluids upon the large intestines, termed by nosologists dysentery. Submitted to the public examination of the faculty of physic, under the authority of the trustees of Columbia College in the State of New-York, William Samuel Johnson, LL. D. president, for the degree of doctor of physic, on the 3d of May, 1797. By William Bay, citizen of the State of New-York. [Eight lines of Latin verse.]

       New-York: Printed by T. and J. Swords, Printers to the Faculty of Physic of Columbia College, No. 99 Pearl-street.—1797.—pp. 109. 8vo.
                                       AAS. BA. HC. MHS. RIMS. SGO.

31781   BAZIN, John
John Bazin, at his store, No. 32, Cornhill, near the market, Boston . . .

       [Boston:] From the Press of S. Etheridge, No. 9, Newbury-Street. [1797.] Broadside.
                                                              EI.

31782   BEDDOES, Thomas   1760–1808
Observations on the nature and cure of calculus, sea scurvey, consumption, catarrh, and fever: together with conjectures upon several other subjects of physiology and pathology. By Thomas Beddoes, m. d.

       Philadelphia: Printed by T. Dobson, at the Stone House. No. 41, South Second Street. 1797. pp. xvi, 278, (1). 8vo.
                                                     AAS. NYPL.

31783   THE [cut] BEE. Volume I. Number 1. Wednesday, June 14, [— Number 29. Wednesday, December 27, 1797.]

       New-London: Printed and published by Charles Holt. 1797. fol.
                                                     LOC. NYHS. YC.

       Established, as a weekly, by Charles Holt, and continued by him to June 23, 1802, when its publication ceased. In the issue for February 19, 1800, the Publisher announced that, "on the 2d of April next, with No. 137, the publication of *The Bee* must be suspended — for a length of time not to be determined by the Editor;" and the issue for that date, was edited from the New London Gaol, where Holt had been confined for an article in *The Bee*, opposing the enlistment of recruits for the army. From the same editorial sanctum he announced his intention to publish *The Bee*, as a political and mercantile newspaper on an enlarged and improved plan; and, after his sentence was concluded, he revived his paper with the issue for August 27, 1800. After discontinuing *The Bee* at New London, Holt removed his Press to Hudson, New York, and established a paper with the same name there on August 17, 1802.

AUCTION VALUES

31784   BEERS, ANDREW   1749–1824
BEERS'S ALMANAC FOR THE YEAR OF OUR LORD 1798: BEING THE SECOND AFTER BISSEXTILE, OR LEAP-YEAR, AND 22D YEAR OF AMERICAN INDEPENDENCE, 'TILL 4TH OF JULY. CALCULATED FOR THE MERIDIAN OF HARTFORD, LATITUDE 42 DEGREES, 56 MIN. NORTH—LONGITUDE 72 DEG. 50 MIN. WEST, AND WILL SERVE FOR ANY OF THE ADJACENT STATES, WITHOUT ANY ESSENTIAL DIFFERENCE. CONTAINING ALSO, THE LUNATIONS, CONJUNCTIONS, ECLIPSES, JUDGMENT OF WEATHER, RISING AND SETTING OF THE PLANETS, LENGTH OF DAYS AND NIGHTS, COURTS, &C. TOGETHER WITH USEFUL TABLES, PIECES OF INSTRUCTION AND ENTERTAINMENT, &C. &C. BY ANDREW BEERS, PHILOM.

> *Hartford: Printed by Hudson & Goodwin.* [1797.] pp. (36). 12mo.
>   AAS. NYPL. YC.

The American Antiquarian Society has a variant with no other difference than the imprint is in two lines, the other having three lines.

31785   —— — BEERS'S ALMANAC FOR THE YEAR OF OUR LORD 1798: [Thirteen lines.] BY ANDREW BEERS, PHILOM.

> *Troy: Printed and sold by Luther Pratt.* [1797.] pp. (36). 12mo.   AAS.

There is no difference, except the imprint, in this and the preceding entry, printed at Hartford.

31786   —— THE FARMER'S AMERICAN ALMANAC FOR THE YEAR OF OUR LORD CHRIST, — 1798 — AND FROM CREATION, 5747, BEING THE SECOND AFTER BISSEXTILE, OR LEAP YEAR, AND 22D OF AMERICAN INDEPENDENCE, TILL THE 4TH OF JULY. CALCULATED FOR THE MERIDIAN OF DANBURY, IN THE STATE OF CONNECTICUT; LATITUDE 41° 50''N. —LONG. 73° 37'' W. BUT MAY SERVE FOR THE ADJACENT STATES. CONTAINING, A VERY GREAT VARIETY OF USEFUL AND ENTERTAINING MATTER. BY ANDREW BEERS, PHILOM.

> *Danbury: Printed and sold by the gross, dozen or single, by Douglas & Nichols.* [1797.] pp. [34], (2). 12mo.   AAS. HSP. YC.

31787   —— GLORIA GREENLEAF'S NEW-YORK, CONNECTICUT, & NEW-JERSEY ALMANACK, OR DIARY, FOR THE YEAR OF OUR LORD, 1798; [Eighteen lines, with cut.]

> *Printed at New-York—By Thomas Greenleaf. Mundi.* [1797.] pp. [36.] 12mo.   LIHS. NJHS. NYHS. NYPL. YC.

31788   —— STODDARD'S DIARY: OR, THE COLUMBIA ALMANACK, FOR THE YEAR OF OUR LORD 1798: BEING THE SECOND AFTER BISSEXTILE OR LEAP YEAR, AND OF AMERICAN INDEPENDENCE (WHICH WAS DECLARED THE 4TH OF JULY, 1776) PART OF THE 22D AND 23D YEARS: CALCULATED FOR LATITUDE 42 DEGREES NORTH, AND FOR A MERIDIAN 3 DEGREES EAST OF GEORGETOWN, THE INTENDED PERMANENT RESIDENCE OF CONGRESS. CONTAINING, BESIDES WHAT IS USUAL AND NECESSARY IN COMPOSITIONS OF THIS NATURE, MANY THINGS, NEW, USEFUL AND ENTERTAINING. BY ANDREW BEERS, PHILOM.

> *Hudson: Printed and sold by Ashbel Stoddard.* 🖝 *Great allowance to those who purchase quantities.* [1797.] pp. (36). 12mo.   AAS. NYPL.

Contains, Courts in New York, Western Massachusetts, Connecticut, and places and times for holding Federal Courts in every State. Interest. Interesting prophecy. New method of courtship. Roads. The Upas, or poison tree. Singular advantages of ugliness.

31789 BEERS, ANDREW, continued.

—— WEBSTER'S CALENDAR: OR, THE ALBANY ALMANACK, FOR THE YEAR OF OUR LORD, 1798: BEING THE 2D AFTER BISSEXTILE OR LEAP YEAR; OF AMERICAN INDEPENDENCE (WHICH WAS DECLARED THE 4TH OF JULY, 1776) PART OF THE 22D AND 23D YEARS; FROM THE CREATION OF THE WORLD 5747. CALCULATED FOR THE MERIDIAN OF ALBANY; NORTH LATITUDE 42 DEGREES 45 MINUTES; FROM THE ENGLISH OBSERVATORY, 73 DEGREES AND 8 MINUTES WEST. BY ANDREW BEERS, PHILOM. CONTAINING, AS USUAL, A GREAT VARIETY OF NEW, USEFUL AND ENTERTAINING PIECES.

Albany: Printed by Charles R. and George Webster, in the White House, corner of State & Pearl-Streets: sold at their Bookstore, Albany; at Webster's Printing-Office, Lansingburgh; by Jacob Dockstader, at his Printing-Office, Johnstown; and by all the Post-Riders from said Offices. ☞ *Great allowance to those who buy by wholesale.* [1797.] pp. (36). 12mo. AAS. EI. LOC. NYSL.

Contains, Witchcraft: a Virginia anecdote. Mode of constructing terrace roofs, &c. True happiness at home, Officers of government of the United States. Of New-York. Of Albany. Different forms of government. Civil liberty. Divine rights of Kings. Art of war. Religion of the Persians. William Rufus. Drunkenness. Pleasure. Description of a blazing star. Description of Hell-Gate. Dates of false silver coins. Dull times. The Bridge of Schaffhausen. And of Wettingen, Switzerland. Heights of different giants. Maxims. Courts. Roads. Interest.

31790 BEETE, ——

THE MAN OF THE TIMES; OR, A SCARCITY OF CASH. A FARCE. AS PERFORMED, WITH UNIVERSAL APPLAUSE, AT THE CHURCH-STREET THEATRE, CHARLESTON. WRITTEN BY MR. BEETE, COMEDIAN. [Printer's mark.]

Charleston: Printed by W. P. Young, State-printer, 43, Broad-Street. [Copy-right secured according to law.] [1797.] pp. (2), (2), 38. 16mo.
BPL. CLS. NYPL.

31791 BELCHER, SUPPLY 1751–1836

MR. BELCHER'S CELEBRATED ORDINATION ANTHEM, WHICH WAS PERFORMED IN HALLOWELL AND AUGUSTA. TOGETHER WITH A NUMBER OF OTHER FUGUING PIECES NEVER BEFORE PUBLISHED.

Printed typographically at Boston. By Isaiah Thomas and Ebenezer T. Andrews. [1797.] *For sale by Peter Edes, Augusta. Price 20 cents.*

31792 BELKNAP, DANIEL 1771–1815

THE HARMONIST'S-COMPANION. CONTAINING A NUMBER OF AIRS SUITABLE FOR DIVINE WORSHIP: TOGETHER WITH AN ANTHEM FOR EASTER, AND A MASONIC ODE, NEVER BEFORE PUBLISHED. COMPOSED BY DANIEL BELKNAP, TEACHER OF MUSIC, IN FRAMINGHAM. [One line from] PSAL. CXLIX. 1. PUBLISHED ACCORDING TO ACT OF CONGRESS.

Printed, typographically, at Boston, by Isaiah Thomas and Ebenezer T. Andrews, Faust's Statue No. 45, Newbury-Street.—Oct. 1797. pp. 31,(1). obl. 16mo.
AAS. NYPL.

131st Massachusetts District Copyright, issued to Daniel Belknap, as Author, 14 October, 1797.

31793 BELKNAP, JEREMY 1744–1798

SACRED POETRY. CONSISTING OF PSALMS AND HYMNS, ADAPTED TO CHRISTIAN DEVOTION, IN PUBLIC AND PRIVATE. SELECTED FROM THE BEST AUTHORS, WITH VARIATIONS AND ADDITIONS. BY JEREMY BELKNAP, D. D. THE SECOND EDITION, WITH IMPROVEMENTS.

Boston: Printed for Thomas & Andrews and D. West. November, 1797. pp. 263. 18mo. AAS. BM. NYPL.

31794   BELL, Benjamin   1749–1806
A TREATISE ON THE THEORY AND MANAGEMENT OF ULCERS: WITH A DISSERTATION ON WHITE SWELLINGS OF THE JOINTS. TO WHICH IS PREFIXED, AN ESSAY ON THE CHIRURGICAL TREATMENT OF INFLAMMATION AND ITS CONSEQUENCES. BY BENJAMIN BELL, MEMBER OF THE ROYAL COLLEGE OF SURGEONS, ONE OF THE SURGEONS TO THE ROYAL INFIRMARY, AND FELLOW OF THE ROYAL SOCIETY OF EDINBURGH. [One line of Latin from] TACIT.

> *Printed at Boston, by I. Thomas and E. T. Andrews, Faust's Statue, No. 45, Newbury Street. Sold, wholesale and retail, at their Bookstore: by said Thomas, Andrews & Penniman, in Albany; and by Thomas, Andrews & Butler, in Baltimore. June,* 1797. pp. 264, plate. 8vo.   AAS. SGO.

31795   BELL, Benjamin   1752–1836
AN IMPARTIAL HISTORY OF THE TRIAL OF BENJAMIN BELL, A. M. FOR THE PRETENDED CRIME OF EXTORTION: EXEMPLIFIED IN A SERIES OF LETTERS. [Seven lines of quotations.] BY BENJAMIN BELL, LATE PASTOR OF A CHURCH IN WINDSOR AND CORNISH.

> *Printed at Windsor, by Oliver Farnsworth, at the Press of Alden Spooner.* M,DCC,XCVII. pp. 155. 8vo.   AAS. BA. BPL. NYHS. YC.

31796   BELLAMY, Joseph   1719–1790
AN ESSAY ON THE NATURE AND GLORY OF THE GOSPEL OF JESUS CHRIST: ON THE NATURE AND CONSEQUENCES OF SPIRITUAL BLINDNESS; AND ON THE NATURE AND CONSEQUENCES OF DIVINE ILLUMINATION. DESIGNED AS A SUPPLEMENT TO THE AUTHOR'S LETTERS AND DIALOGUES, ON THE NATURE OF LOVE TO GOD, FAITH IN CHRIST, AND ASSURANCE OF A TITLE TO ETERNAL LIFE. BY JOSEPH BELLAMY, D. D. MINISTER OF THE GOSPEL AT BETHLEM. . . .

> *Printed at Worcester, for Isaiah Thomas,* 1797. pp. 307. 12mo.
>   AAS. LCP. NYHS. NYPL. RIHS. YC.

31797   BENJAMIN, Asher   1773–1845
THE COUNTRY BUILDER'S ASSISTANT: CONTAINING A COLLECTION OF NEW DESIGNS OF CARPENTRY AND ARCHITECTURE; WHICH WILL BE PARTICULARLY USEFUL, TO COUNTRY WORKMEN IN GENERAL. ILLUSTRATED WITH NEW AND USEFUL DESIGNS OF FRONTISPIECES, CHIMNEY PIECES, &c. TUSCAN, DORIC, IONIC, AND CORINTHIAN ORDERS, WITH THEIR BASES, CAPITALS, AND ENTABLATURES: ARCHITRAVES FOR DOORS, WINDOWS AND CHIMNEYS: CORNICES, BASE, AND SURBASE MOULDINGS FOR ROOMS: DOORS, AND SASHES, WITH THEIR MOULDINGS: THE CONSTRUCTION OF STAIRS, WITH THEIR RAMP AND TWIST RAILS: PLAN, ELEVATION, AND ONE SECTION OF A MEETINGHOUSE, WITH THE PULPIT AT LARGE: PLANS AND ELEVATIONS OF HOUSES: THE BEST METHOD OF FINDING THE LENGTH, AND BACKING OF HIP RAFTERS: ALSO, THE TRACING OF GROINS, ANGLE BRACKETS, CIRCULAR SOFFITS IN CIRCULAR WALLS, &c. CORRECTLY ENGRAVED ON THIRTY COPPER PLATES; WITH A PRINTED EXPLANATION TO EACH. BY ASHER BENJAMIN.

> *Printed at Greenfield (Massachusetts) by Thomas Dickman.* M,DCC,XCVII. pp. (2), (30), 30 plates. 4to.   AAS

31798   BENTLEY, William   1759–1819
Half-title: THE REV. BROTHER BENTLEY'S DISCOURSE, AND BROTHER DANA'S ADDRESS; AT THE CONSECRATION OF THE BENEVOLENT LODGE IN AMHERST.

> *First title:* A DISCOURSE, DELIVERED AT AMHERST, AUGUST 10, 1797; BEFORE THE MOST WORSHIPFUL NATHANIEL ADAMS, OF THE GRAND LODGE OF NEWHAMPSHIRE, AND THE OFFICERS OF THE GRAND LODGE OF MASSACHUSETTS; AT THE INSTALLATION OF THE BENEVOLENT LODGE, UNDER THE RIGHT WORSHIPFUL SAMUEL DANA, ESQ. [Four lines of Latin quotations.] BY THE REV. BROTHER WILLIAM BENTLEY, A. M. F. H. S.

> *[Amherst:] Samuel Preston, Printer.* 1797. pp. 24; 12. 8vo.   AAS. BA. HC.

BENTLEY, WILLIAM, continued.
Second title: AN ADDRESS, DELIVERED IN AMHERST, AUGUST 10, 1797; BEFORE
THE OFFICERS OF THE GRAND LODGES OF NEWHAMPSHIRE AND MASSACHUSETTS;
AT THE CONSECRATION OF THE BENEVOLENT LODGE. BY THE HON. BROTHER SAMUEL
DANA, ESQ. MASTER OF THE BENEVOLENT LODGE. [One line of Latin from
Horace.] PUBLISHED AT THE REQUEST OF THE LODGE.
[Amherst:] Samuel Preston, Printer. 1797. pp. 12.

31799 —— *Half-title:* THE REV. BROTHER BENTLEY'S DISCOURSE, AND BROTHER DIX'S AD-
DRESS; AT THE CONSECRATION OF WASHINGTON LODGE IN ROXBURY.

First title: A DISCOURSE, DELIVERED IN ROXBURY, OCTOBER 12, 5796; BEFORE
THE GRAND LODGE OF FREE AND ACCEPTED MASONS IN THE COMMONWEALTH OF
MASSACHUSETTS; (THE MOST WORSHIPFUL PAUL REVERE, ESQ. MASTER,) AT THE
REQUEST OF THE MEMBERS OF WASHINGTON LODGE, ON OCCASION OF THE CONSECRA-
TION OF THE LODGE AND THE INSTALLATION OF OFFICERS. BY THE REV. BROTHER
WILLIAM BENTLEY, A. M. F. H. S. [Three lines of Latin from] LUCRETIUS.
Boston: William Spotswood. 1797. pp. [21]: [10]. 8vo.

AAS. BM. HC. MHS. NYPL.

Second title: A SALUTATORY ADDRESS, ON THE SOCIAL INFLUENCE AND MERIT OF
FREE MASONRY: DELIVERED IN PUBLIC ASSEMBLY AT THE REQUEST OF THE OFFI-
CERS AND MEMBERS OF WASHINGTON LODGE IN ROXBURY, AT THEIR CONSECRATION,
OCTOBER 12, A. L. 5796. BY BROTHER WILLIAM DIX, A. M.
Boston: William Spotswood. 1797. pp. [10.]

31800 —— A FUNERAL DISCOURSE, DELIVERED IN THE EAST MEETING HOUSE, SALEM, ON
THE SUNDAY AFTER THE DEATH OF MAJOR-GENERAL JOHN FISKE, WHO DIED SEP-
TEMBER 28, 1797, ÆT. 53. BY WILLIAM BENTLEY, A. M. PASTOR OF THE SECOND
CONGREGATIONAL CHURCH IN SALEM.
Salem: Printed by Thomas C. Cushing. 1797. pp. 37. 8vo.

AAS. BA. BM. BPL. EI. HC. JCB. MHS. NYHS. NYPL.

31801 BERESFORD, RICHARD   1755–1803
ARISTOCRACY THE BANE OF LIBERTY; LEARNING THE ANTIDOTE. DESIGNED TO
RECOMMEND THE GENERAL ESTABLISHMENT OF FREE SCHOOLS AND COLLEGES IN
REPUBLICKS. BY RICHARD BERESFORD, A MEMBER FROM SOUTH-CAROLINA IN THE
REVOLUTION CONGRESS. [Four lines of verse from] CATO.
Charleston: Printed by W. P. Young, Printer to the State. Dec. 1797. pp.
(2), 37. 8vo.   AAS. CLS.

31802 —— NUGÆ CANORÆ; CONSISTING OF A FEW MINOR POEMS. BY THE AUTHOR OF A
PLEA FOR LITERATURE. [Printer's mark.]
Charleston: Printed by W. P. Young, Franklin's Head, No. 43 Broad-Street.
M.DCC.XCVII. pp. 28. 8vo.   BU. LOC.

31803 —— SKETCHES OF FRENCH AND ENGLISH POLITICKS IN AMERICA, IN MAY, 1797. BY
A MEMBER OF THE OLD CONGRESS.
*Charleston: Printed for the Author, by W. P. Young, Franklin's Head, No.
43, Broad-Street.* M.DCC.XCVII. pp. (2), 65. 8vo.   AAS. CLS. HC. HSP. LOC. NYPL.

31804 BERQUIN, ARNAUD   1750–1791
SELECT STORIES. FROM THE FRENCH OF M. BERQUIN.
Philadelphia: Printed by ·H. Kammerer jun. 1797. 12mo.

31805 BERTODY, FRANCIS
THE ART OF CURING ONE'S SELF OF THE VENEREAL DISEASE. BY DR. BERTODY. [In
French and English.]
*Boston: Printed for and sold by the Author, Leverett Street, West-Boston
third house from the Brewery.* 1797.

31806   BIBLIA.
THE HOLY BIBLE, CONTAINING THE OLD AND NEW TESTAMENTS: TRANSLATED OUT OF
THE ORIGINAL TONGUES, AND WITH THE FORMER TRANSLATIONS DILIGENTLY COM-
PARED AND REVISED, BY THE SPECIAL COMMAND OF KING JAMES I, OF ENGLAND.
[One line of Hebrew text, from Genesis II, 17, in an ornamental border.]

*United States of Columbia. Printed at Worcester, Massachusetts, by Isaiah
Thomas. Sold by him in Worcester, by wholesale, bound or in sheets. Sold also by
said Thomas and Andrews, in Boston, and by the Booksellers in the United States
of Columbia.* 1797. pp. (2), (2), (674); (2), (288), [unpaged.] 12mo. AAS. NYPL.

Second title: THE NEW TESTAMENT OF OUR LORD AND SAVIOUR JESUS CHRIST.
TRANSLATED OUT OF THE ORIGINAL GREEK, AND WITH THE FORMER TRANSLATIONS
DILIGENTLY COMPARED AND REVISED, BY THE SPECIAL COMMAND OF HIS MAJESTY
KING JAMES I, OF ENGLAND. [Two lines of Greek text, in an ornamental border.]

*United States of Columbia. Printed at Worcester, Massachusetts, by Isaiah
Thomas. Sold by him in Worcester, by wholesale, bound or in sheets. Sold also by
said Thomas and Andrews, in Boston, and by the Booksellers in the United States
of Columbia.* 1797. pp. (2), (288). [unpaged.]

The first issue of Thomas' standing duodecimo edition. An error in
Acts VI, 3, "Whom *ye* may appoint over this business" has been noted.
"Four different sizes of the Bible have now passed through the Presses
of the Proprietor, viz. Folio, with fifty copperplate representations of
Scripture history.—Royal quarto, with and without Concordance.—
Large demy octavo with and without Apocrypha.—And demy 12mo.
This last is just issued from the press, the types for which were procured at a very great expence, are exceedingly well-executed, and employed a number of workmen 4 years to complete them. They are now
all standing, and are to be kept ready at all times for the press, in the
same manner as they are at the Royal Printing Offices in London and
Edinburgh, and the University Printing Houses of Oxford and Cambridge, in England:—a constant supply (of coarse and fine copies) bound
or in sheets, and in any quantity will be kept by the Editor at the Worcester Bookstore. As the execution of the plan on which this small
Bible is printed, in order to make the price proportionately low to those
imported from Scotland and England has been attended with a very
heavy expence to the undertaker, and employed a larger capital than
any work issued from an American press, he hopes suitable encouragement will be given to the undertaking."

31807   —— THE HOLY BIBLE, CONTAINING THE OLD AND NEW TESTAMENTS: TRANSLATED
OUT OF THE ORIGINAL TONGUES; AND WITH THE FORMER TRANSLATIONS DILIGENTLY
COMPARED AND REVISED. [Printer's mark.]

*New-York: Printed and sold by Hugh Gaine, at his Book-Store and Print-
ing-Office, at the Bible, in Hanover-Square.* M,DCC,XCVII. pp. 408. 12mo. NYPL.

Second title: THE NEW TESTAMENT OF OUR LORD AND SAVIOUR JESUS CHRIST,
NEWLY TRANSLATED OUT OF THE ORIGINAL GREEK; AND WITH THE FORMER TRANS-
LATIONS DILIGENTLY COMPARED AND REVISED. [Printer's mark.]

*New-York: Printed and sold by Hugh Gaine, at his Book-Store and Print-
ing-Office, at the Bible, in Hanover-Square.* M,DCC,XCII.

A second impression of Gaine's 1792 edition of the Bible, in which the
general title-page has been reset, and a few typographical changes made
in the text of the Old Testament. The New Testament is without any
change from the edition printed in 1792.

BIBLIA, continued.

31808 —— THE HOLY BIBLE, CONTAINING THE OLD AND NEW TESTAMENTS: TOGETHER WITH THE APOCRYPHA; TRANSLATED OUT OF THE ORIGINAL TONGUES: AND WITH THE FORMER TRANSLATIONS, DILIGENTLY COMPARED AND REVISED. NUMBER XVII–XXX.

Philadelphia: Printed for John Thompson and Abraham Small, [from the Hot-press of John Thompson.] fol.

31809 —— THE HOLY BIBLE, ABRIDGED: OR, THE HISTORY OF THE OLD AND NEW TESTAMENTS. ILLUSTRATED WITH NOTES, AND ADORNED WITH CUTS FOR THE USE OF CHILDREN.

Wilmington: Printed and sold by Peter Brynberg. 1797. pp. 136. 24mo. AAS.

31810 BIBLIA. OLD TESTAMENT. PSALMS.
AN IMITATION OF THE PSALMS OF DAVID; CAREFULLY SUITED TO THE CHRISTIAN WORSHIP: BEING AN IMPROVEMENT OF THE FORMER VERSIONS OF THE PSALMS. ALLOWED BY THE GENERAL ASSEMBLY, OF THE PRESBYTERIAN CHURCH, IN THE UNITED STATES, TO BE USED IN CHURCHES AND PRIVATE FAMILIES, ALL THINGS WRITTEN IN THE LAW OF MOSES, AND THE PROPHETS, AND THE PSALMS CONCERNING ME, MUST BE FULFILLED. [Barlow's version.]

Albany: Printed by Charles R. and George Webster, in the White House, corner of State and Pearl-streets. Sold by Webster and Steel, T. Spencer, and J. Chestney, Albany—A. Stoddard, Hudson. [June 12th, 1795.] pp. (2), 306: 338, (1). 24mo. AAS.

Second title: THE PSALMS OF DAVID IN METRE. TRANSLATED, AND DILIGENTLY COMPARED WITH THE ORIGINAL TEXT, AND FORMER TRANSLATIONS. MORE PLAIN, SMOOTH AND AGREEABLE TO THE TEXT, THAN ANY HERETOFORE. ALLOWED BY THE AUTHORITY OF THE GENERAL ASSEMBLY OF THE KIRK OF SCOTLAND, AND APPOINTED TO BE SUNG IN CONGREGATIONS AND FAMILIES. WITH AN EXPOSITION, OR, A BRIEF VIEW OF THE CONTENTS OF EACH PSALM. BY MR. MATTHEW HENRY, AUTHOR OF THE COMMENTARY ON THE BIBLE.

Albany: Printed by Charles R. and George Webster, in the White House, corner of State and Pearl-streets. Sold by Webster and Steel, T. Spencer and A. Ellison, Albany—W. W. Wands, Lansingburgh—A. Stoddard, Hudson—J. Shurtleff, Schenectady—D. Rogers, Ballston—R. Dodge, Johnstown—and O. P. Easton, Whitestown. [1795.] pp. 338.

A correction of my IX:26652, and 26659.

31811 —— PSALMS CAREFULLY SUITED TO THE CHRISTIAN WORSHIP IN THE UNITED STATES OF AMERICA. BEING AN IMPROVEMENT OF THE OLD VERSIONS OF THE PSALMS OF DAVID. ALLOWED BY THE REVEREND SYNOD OF NEW-YORK AND PHILADELPHIA, TO BE USED IN CHURCHES AND PRIVATE FAMILIES. [Three lines of Scripture text.]

Elizabeth-Town: Printed by Shepard Kollock, for T. Allen, Bookseller and Stationer, No. 186, Pearl-Street, New-York. M,DCC,XCVII.. pp. 314, (10); (2), 286. 18mo. AAS. JCB.

Second title: HYMNS AND SPIRITUAL SONGS. IN THREE BOOKS. I. COLLECTED FROM THE SCRIPTURES. II. COMPOSED ON DIVINE SUBJECTS. III. PREPARED FOR THE LORD'S SUPPER, BY I. WATTS, D. D. [Four lines of quotations.]

Elizabeth-Town: Printed by Shepard Kollock for T. Allen, Bookseller and Stationer, No. 186, Pearl Street, New-York. M,DCC,XCVII. pp. (2), 286.

BIBLIA, continued.

31812 —— — PSALMS, CAREFULLY SUITED TO THE CHRISTIAN WORSHIP IN THE UNITED STATES OF AMERICA. BEING AN IMPROVEMENT OF THE OLD VERSIONS OF THE PSALMS OF DAVID. ALLOWED BY THE REVEREND SYNOD OF NEW-YORK AND PHILADELPHIA, TO BE USED IN CHURCHES AND PRIVATE FAMILIES.
Wilmington: Printed by Peter Brynberg. 1797. pp. 287, (20). 24mo.

31813 —— THE PSALMS OF DAVID IN METRE: TRANSLATED AND DILIGENTLY COMPARED WITH THE ORIGINAL TEXT AND FORMER TRANSLATIONS: MORE PLAIN, SMOOTH, AND AGREEABLE TO THE TEXT, THAN ANY HERETOFORE: ALLOWED BY THE AUTHORITY OF THE GENERAL ASSEMBLY OF THE KIRK OF SCOTLAND, AND APPOINTED TO BE SUNG IN CONGREGATIONS AND FAMILIES. WITH NOTES, EXHIBITING THE CONNEXION, EXPLAINING THE SENSE; AND FOR DIRECTING AND ANIMATING THE DEVOTION. BY JOHN BROWN, MINISTER OF THE GOSPEL IN HADDINGTON. [Two lines from] I COR. XIV. 15.
Carlisle: Printed for Archibald Loudon. By George Kline. MDCCXCVII. pp. 336. 12mo.   AAS.

31814 —— DER PSALTER DES KÖNIGS UND PROPHETEN DAVIDS, VERDEUTSCHET VON D. MARTIN LUTHER.
Ephrata: Gedruckt bey Benjamin Meyer, 1797. 16mo.

31815 —— DAS KLEINE DAVIDISCHE PSALTERSPIEL DER KINDER ZIONS, VON ALTEN UND NEUEN AUSERLESENEN GEISTES GESÄNGEN, ALLEN WAHREN HEILS—,BEGIERIGEN SÄULINGEN DER WEISHEIT, INSONDERHEIT ABER DENEN GEMEINDEN DES HERRN, ZUM DIENST UND GEBRAUCH MIT FLEISS ZUSAMMEN GETRAGEN IN GEGENWÄRTIG-BELIEBIGER FORM UND ORDNUNG. NEBST EINEM DREYSACHEN, DARZU NÜTZLICHEN UND DER MATERIEN HALBEN NÖTHIGEN REGISTER. ZWEYTE VERBESSERTE AUFLAGE.
Baltimore: Gedruckt bey Samuel Saur, 1797. pp. 572; 55. 12mo.   AAS.

Second title: DIE KLEINE HARFE, GESTIMMET VON UNTERSCHIEDLICHEN LIEBLICHEN LIEDERN ODER LOB-GESÄNGEN, WELCHE GEHÖRET WERDEN VON DEN ENDEN DER ERDEN, ZU EHREN DEM GERECHTEN . . . ZWEYTE AUFLAGE.
Baltimore: Gedruckt bey Samuel Saur. 1797. pp. 55.
Some copies have the first edition of Die Kleine Harfe, with the Chesnuthill, 1792, imprint, appended.

31816 —— — DAS KLEINE DAVIDISCHE PSALTERSPEIL DER KINDER ZIONS, VON ALTEN UND NEUEN AUSERLESENEN GEISTES GESÄNGEN, ALLEN WAHREN HEILSBEGIERIGEN SÄUGLINGEN DER WEISHEIT, INSONDERHEIT ABER DENEN GEMEINDEN DES HERRN, ZUM DIENST UND GEBRAUCH, MIT FLEISS ZUSAMMEN GETRAGEN IN GEGENWÄRTIG-BELIEBIGER FORM UND ORDUNG. NEBST EINEM DREYSACHEN, DARZU NÜTZLICHEN UND DER MATERIEN HALBEN NÖTHIGEN REGISTER.
Germantaun: Gedruckt bey Michael Billmeyer, 1797. pp. (2), (4), 572, (22), 21, (1). 8vo.   AAS. BU.

31817 BIBLIA. NEW TESTAMENT.
THE NEW TESTAMENT OF OUR LORD AND SAVIOUR JESUS CHRIST, NEWLY TRANSLATED OUT OF THE ORIGINAL GREEK: AND WITH THE FORMER TRANSLATIONS DILIGENTLY COMPARED AND REVISED.
Lancaster: Printed by J. Bailey and W. & R. Dickson, in Kingstreet. 1797. Unpaged. 12mo.

31818 —— — THE NEW TESTAMENT OF OUR LORD AND SAVIOUR JESUS CHRIST, NEWLY TRANSLATED OUT OF THE ORIGINAL GREEK: AND WITH THE FORMER TRANSLATIONS DILIGENTLY COMPARED AND REVISED.
New-Haven: Published by Edward O'Brien; also sold wholesale and retail by John Turner, Philadelphia. 1797. 12mo.   AAS. BM.

31819　BIBLIA, continued.
—— A CATHOLIC LITURGY, OR FORM OF PRAYER. CHRISTIANS OF ALL DENOMINATIONS MAY UNITE IN THESE PRAYERS, AS THEY ALLUDE TO NO DOCTRINES, BUT SUCH AS ARE UNIVERSALLY PROFESSED BY ALL WHO CALL THEMSELVES CHRISTIANS.
　　Printed by Samuel Hall, No. 53, Cornhill, Boston, 1797. pp. 44, (1). 8vo.
JCB. LOC. NYHS.
　　Contains: Matthew, v: 1-20; vi:19-34; vii: 1-12. Romans, xii. Colossians, iii. James, i. The selections were made by Nathan Davies.

31820　BICHENO, JAMES　　　　　　　　　　　　　　　　　　　–1831
THE SIGNS OF THE TIMES: OR, THE OVERTHROW OF THE PAPAL TYRANNY IN FRANCE, THE PRELUDE OF DESTRUCTION TO POPERY AND DESPOTISM, BUT OF PEACE TO MANKIND. BY J. BICHENO. [One line from] MATT. XXIV. 44.
　　London — Printed. Philadelphia — Re-printed by Joseph Gales, No. 145, North Second Street. 1797. pp. (2), (2), 40. 8vo.　　　　AAS.

31821　—— THE SIGNS OF THE TIMES: OR, THE DARK PROPHECIES OF SCRIPTURE ILLUSTRATED BY THE APPLICATION OF PRESENT IMPORTANT EVENTS. PART II. WRITTEN IN GREAT-BRITAIN. BY J. BICHENO.
　　Philadelphia: Printed by Joseph Gales, No. 126, N. Second-street, for Richard Davison. 1797. pp. (2), (40). 8vo.　　　　AAS. LOC.
　　Page 6 omitted in numbering.

31822　BICKNELL, ALEXANDER　　　　　　　　　　　　　　　　–1796
THE ENGLISH HERMIT, OR HISTORY AND ADVENTURES OF PHILIP QUARLL, WHO HAS LIVED THIRTY YEARS UPON AN UNINHABITED ISLAND WITHOUT ANY HUMAN ASSISTANCE, STILL CONTINUES TO RESIDE, AND WILL NOT COME AWAY. EMBELLISHED WITH A NUMBER OF ENGRAVINGS, AND A FRONTISPIECE.
　　Boston: Printed and sold by William Spotswood, No. 55. Marlborough-Street. 1795.

31823　—— —— THE HERMIT; OR THE UNPARALLELLED SUFFERINGS AND SURPRISING ADVENTURES OF PHILIP QUARLL, AN ENGLISHMAN: WHO WAS LATELY DISCOVERED UPON AN UNINHABITED ISLAND IN THE SOUTH SEA, WHERE HE LIVED ABOVE FIFTY YEARS, WITH OUT ANY HUMAN ASSISTANCE.
　　Brattleborough, (Vt.): Printed by Benjamin Smead. 1797.

31824　BIGELOW, TIMOTHY　　　　　　　　　　　　　　　　1767–1821
AN ORATION, PRONOUNCED AT CAMBRIDGE, BEFORE THE P B K, AT THEIR ANNUAL MEETING ON THURSDAY, JULY 21, 1796. IT BEING THE DAY FOLLOWING THE PUBLIC COMMENCEMENT. BY TIMOTHY BIGELOW.
　　Boston: Printed by Manning & Loring. 1797. pp. 15. 8vo.
AAS. BA. BM. HC. JCB. NYPL.

31825　BINGHAM, CALEB　　　　　　　　　　　　　　　　　1757–1817
THE AMERICAN PRECEPTOR; BEING A NEW SELECTION OF LESSONS FOR READING AND SPEAKING. DESIGNED FOR THE USE OF SCHOOLS. BY CALEB BINGHAM, A. M. AUTHOR OF THE COLUMBIAN ORATOR, CHILD'S COMPANION, &C. "TRAIN UP A CHILD IN THE WAY HE SHOULD GO,—" THE FOURTH EDITION. PUBLISHED ACCORDING TO ACT OF CONGRESS.
　　Boston: Printed by Manning and Loring, for the Author; and sold at his Book-Store, No. 44, Cornhill; sold also by Thomas & Andrews, D. West, J. West, J. White, E. Larkin, W. P. & L. Blake, &c. &c. 1797. pp. 228. 12mo.
AAS. BM. NYPL.

31826　—— AN ASTRONOMICAL AND GEOGRAPHICAL CATECHISM, FOR THE USE OF CHILDREN.
　　Albany: Printed by Loring Andrews & Co. for Thomas, Andrews & Penniman, at the Albany Bookstore, Sign of Franklin's Head, No. 45, State Street. 1797.
　　"First published in Boston where it had a very extensive circulation."

BINGHAM, Caleb, continued.

31827 —— The Columbian Orator: containing a variety of original and selected pieces; together with rules; calculated to improve youth and others in the ornamental and useful art of eloquence. By Caleb Bingham, a. m. author of the American preceptor, Young ladies accidence, &c. [Three lines from] Rollin. Published according to Act of Congress.

Boston: Printed by Manning & Loring, for the Author, No. 44, for David West, No. 56, and for John West, No. 75, Cornhill. May, 1797. pp. 288. 12mo.
BM. JCB.

144th Massachusetts District Copyright, issued to Caleb Bingham, as Author, 17 May, 1798.

31828 —— The Young lady's accidence: or, a short and easy introduction to English grammar. Designed, principally, for the use of young learners, more especially those of the fair sex, though proper for either. By Caleb Bingham, a. m. Author of the Child's companion, American preceptor, and Columbian orator. [Two lines of verse.] The tenth edition. Published according to Act of Congress.

Printed at Boston by I. Thomas and E. T. Andrews, at Faust's Statue, No. 45, Newbury-Street, for the Author; and sold by him, No. 44, Cornhill—1797. pp. 60. 24mo.
AAS. JCB.

31829 **BIRD, John**
To the honorable the General Assembly of Connecticut . . . The Remonstrance of John Bird . . . Dated at Troy, this 23d day of August, 1797. [Colophon:]

Printed by Luther Pratt, Troy. [1797.] Broadside.
JCB.

31830 **BISHOP, Abraham**   1763–1844
Georgia speculation unveiled; in two numbers. [Entitled, Northern raps for Georgia knuckles.] By Abraham Bishop. [Signed, A. B. New-Haven. Oct. 14, 1797.]

Hartford: Printed by Elisha Babcock. [Copy-right secured.] 1797. pp. [39.] 8vo.   AAS. BA. BM. DERGL. HC. JCB. LOC. MHS. NYHS. NYPL. RIHS. YC.

"Designed as a counter-part to "State of facts" published by the Georgia Company." A second part,—different from the second number—was printed in 1798.

31831 **BISSE, Thomas**   167– –1731
The Beauty of holiness in the common prayer: as set forth in four sermons preached at the Rolls Chapel, in 1716. By Thomas Bisse, d. d. The first American, from the seventh London, edition.

Boston: Printed by Manning & Loring. 1797. pp. 94. 12mo.   AAS. JCB.

31832 **BLACK, Robert**
An Inaugural dissertation on fractures. Submitted to the examination of the rev. John Ewing, s. t. p. provost, the trustees and medical faculty of the University of Pennsylvania. On the 12th day of May, 1797. For the degree of doctor of medicine. By Robert Black, of Pennsylvania, member of the Philadelphia Medical and Chemical Societies. Puta, lege, et observa studiose.

Philadelphia. Printed by Ormrod & Conrad, 41, Chesnut-Street. [1797.] pp. (6). (5)–(46). 8vo.   AAS. BM.

31833   BLAIR, HUGH   1718–1800
ESSAYS ON RHETORIC. ABRIDGED CHIEFLY FROM DOCTOR BLAIR'S LECTURES ON THAT SCIENCE. THIRD AMERICAN EDITION, WITH ADDITIONS AND IMPROVEMENTS.

Printed at Boston, by Samuel Etheridge, for Thomas and Andrews: sold at their Bookstore; by Thomas, Andrews and Penniman, Albany; and by Thomas, Andrews and Butler, Baltimore. May, 1797. pp. 249. 12mo.   AAS. NYPL.

31834   BLAIR, ROBERT   1699–1746
THE GRAVE. A POEM. THE HOUSE APPOINTED FOR ALL LIVING. JOB. BY ROBERT BLAIR. [Ornament.]

Elizabeth-Town: Printed by Shepard Kollock, for Cornelius Davis, No. 94, Water-Street. New-York. M,DCC,XCVII. pp. 26. 12mo.   AAS.

Has the same collation as in "A Collection of poems" this year.

31835   BLAKE, WILLIAM P.
CATALOGUE OF AMERICAN EDITIONS OF BOOKS FOR SALE BY WILLIAM P. AND LEMUEL BLAKE. NO. 1, CORNHILL, BOSTON.

Boston: Printed for William P. and Lemuel Blake. 1797. Broadside. fol.

31836   BLAUVELT, ABRAHAM
BLAUVELT'S AMERICAN ALMANAC FOR THE YEAR 1798.

New-Brunswick, N. J. Printed by Abraham Blauvelt. [1797.]

31837   BLEECKER, ANN ELIZA SCHUYLER   1752–1783
THE HISTORY OF MARIA KITTLE. BY ANN ELIZA BLEECKER. IN A LETTER TO MISS TEN EYCK.

Hartford: Printed by Elisha Babcock. 1797. pp. 70. 12mo.   LOC.

"A pathetic story, founded on facts."

31838   BLOUNT, CHARLES   1654–1693
GREAT IS DIANA OF THE EPHESIANS; OR, THE ORIGINAL OF IDOLATRY.

New-London: Printed by Charles Holt. 1797. 12mo.

31839   BOADEN, JAMES   1762–1839
THE SECRET TRIBUNAL: A PLAY, IN FIVE ACTS. BY JAMES BOADEN, AUTHOR OF FONTAINVILLE FOREST. AS PERFORMED AT THE THEATRE-ROYAL, COVENT-GARDEN. [Two lines from] MILTON.

London: Printed. Philadelphia: Re-printed and sold by James Humphreys, No. 74, North Third-street. 1797. pp. 45, (1). 12mo.   AAS. LOC. NYPL.

31840   BODDILY, JOHN
THE SUBSTANCE OF A DISCOURSE, DELIVERED AT THE DEDICATION OF THE SECOND PRESBYTERIAN MEETING-HOUSE IN NEWBURYPORT, DEC. 22, 1796. BY JOHN BODDILY, MINISTER OF THE GOSPEL. PUBLISHED BY DESIRE.

Newburyport—From the Press of William Barrett, Market-Square. Jan. 1797. pp. [18.] 8vo.   AAS. JCB.

31841   —— THE SUBSTANCE OF A SERMON, PREACHED BEFORE THE SECOND PRESBYTERIAN SOCIETY IN NEWBURYPORT, JAN. 8, 1797. ENTITLED, THE DIFFERENCE BETWEEN THE MERE FORM AND THE POWER OF GODLINESS, BY JOHN BODDILY, MINISTER OF THE GOSPEL. I. PETER III. 15. [Two lines.]

Newburyport—From the Press of William Barrett, Market-Square. Jan. 1797. pp. [19.] 8vo.   AAS. BA. BM. JCB.

31842 BOGARDUS, JACOB
To be sold, at private sale, the messuage and farm, now occupied by the sub-
scriber, Jacob Bogardus. [About 228 acres beginning near the main street in
Catskill. Colophon:]
Catskill (New York): Printed by M. Croswell. 1797. Broadside. fol.

31843 BOGATZKY, KARL HEINRICH VON   1690–1754
A Golden Treasury, for the children of God, whose treasure is in Heaven;
consisting of select texts of the Bible, with practical observations in
prose and verse, for every day in the year. By C. H. V. Bogatzky. With
some alterations and improvements by various hands. Also, a preface for
the right use of this book. Together with a few forms of prayer for
private use. [One line from] MATT. VI, 21.
New-York: Printed by Wilson & Kirk, 299, *Broad-Way.* 1797. pp. xvi, 376.
obl. 32mo.   AAS. JCB. NYPL.

31844 BOOTH, ABRAHAM   1734–1806
Glad tidings to perishing sinners; or, the genuine gospel a complete war-
rant for the ungodly to believe in Jesus. By Abraham Booth. [Five lines
of quotations.]
Philadelphia: Printed by Stephen C. Ustick; sold at No. 79. *North Third
Street.* 1797. pp. 237, 2. 12mo.   AAS. NYPL.

The two appended pages contain: Books, for sale by S. C. Ustick.

31845 BORDLEY, JOHN BEALE   1727–1804
Queries selected from a paper of the Board of Agriculture in London, on
the nature and principles of vegetation: with answers and observations.
By J. B. B.
/ *Philadelphia: Printed by Charles Cist,* 1797.] pp. [16.] 8vo.   BA. LOC.

31846 —— Sketches on rotations of crops, and other rural matters. To which are
annexed intimation on manufactures; on the fruits of agriculture; and
on new sources of trade, interfering with products of the United States
of America, in foreign markets. [Signed, B. JANUARY, 1794.]
Philadelphia: Printed by Charles Cist, No. 104, *North Second Street.*
M,DCC,XCVII. pp. (2), [76], [11.] 8vo.   AAS. BA. CLB. LOC.

Contains, a printed slip on Ice houses. Dated, January 23d, 1797.
168th Pennsylvania District Copyright, issued to Charles Cist, as Proprietor, 20 January, 1797.

31847 BOSTON. MASSACHUSETTS.
By order of the selectmen of Boston. The Legislature of this Commonwealth having at their last session among other Acts, passed and enacted
two, which intimately concern the inhabitants of this town the one entitled, "An Act to secure the town of Boston against damage from fires;"
—and the other entitled "An Act for the extinguishment of fire, and to
direct the proceedings thereat;"—the selectmen to give the most timely
notice thereof to the inhabitants in general, and to call their attention
to the same more immediately than may be effected by the common and
usual method of promulgating the laws, have procured such extracts from
the said Acts as are most necessary to be generally known, to be published and ordered the same to be publickly posted up in different parts
of the town, that no inhabitant may unwarily infringe the same. [Two
columns.]
[Boston: Printed by Benjamin Edes, 1797.] Broadside. fol.

31848   BOSTON. MASSACHUSETTS, continued.
—— NOTIFICATION. THE FREEHOLDERS AND OTHER INHABITANTS OF THE TOWN OF BOSTON, QUALIFIED AS THE LAW DIRECTS, ARE HEREBY NOTIFIED TO MEET AT FAN-EUIL-HALL ON THURSDAY THE 11TH DAY OF MAY . . .
      [Boston: 1797.] Broadside.   LOC.

31849   —— REPORT PRINTED BY ORDER OF THE TOWN, FOR THE INFORMATION OF THE IN-HABITANTS, TO BE CONSIDERED AT THE ADJOURNMENT, ON THURSDAY, 21ST INSTANT. [Upon vagrant strangers.]
      [Boston: 1797.] Broadside.   BPL.

31850   BOSTON. MASSACHUSETTS. BOSTON CAVALRY.
BOSTON, NOV. 30, 1797. SIR, THE FOLLOWING IS A STATEMENT OF THE ACCOUNTS OF THE BOSTON CAVALRY, FROM THE ORIGIN OF THE CORPS TO THE PRESENT PERIOD . . .
      [Boston: 1797.] pp. 8, table. 8vo.   BPL.

31851   BOSTON. MASSACHUSETTS. DISPENSARY.
Heading: INSTITUTION OF THE BOSTON DISPENSARY FOR THE MEDICAL RELIEF OF THE POOR.
      [Boston: 1797.] pp. 14. 16mo.   JCB.

31852   BOSTON. MASSACHUSETTS. FEDERAL STREET SCHOOL.
REGULATIONS FOR THE GOVERNMENT OF THE SCHOOL IN FEDERAL STREET. ADOPTED BY THE PROPRIETORS. "ORDER IS HEAVEN'S FIRST LAW."
      Printed at Boston. 1797. pp. 16, (8). 16mo.   BA.
The text is followed by four blank leaves.

31853   BOSTON. MASSACHUSETTS. HAYMARKET THEATRE.
HAYMARKET THEATRE. MONDAY EVENING, JANUARY 9, 1797. [Play bill of The Jew, and Rosina, with Barrett, Powell, Williamson, Dickinson, and others in the cast.]
      [Boston: 1797.] Broadside. fol.

31854   BOSTON. MASSACHUSETTS. MUTUAL FIRE INSURANCE COMPANY.
Heading: REPORT OF A COMMITTEE, CHOSEN TO DIGEST A PLAN, AND FORM RULES AND REGULATIONS FOR A MUTUAL FIRE INSURANCE COMPANY. . . . NATHAN BOND. ELISHA TICKNOR. BOSTON, FEBRUARY 21, 1797.
      [Boston: Printed by Thomas Fleet. 1797.] pp. (12). 12mo.   AAS.

31855   THE BOSTON [cut] GAZETTE, AND REPUBLICAN JOURNAL. [Motto.] No. 2203. MONDAY, JANUARY 2, [— No. 2254. MONDAY, DECEMBER 25, 1797.]
      Printed by Benjamin Edes, in Kilby-Street, Boston. 1797. fol.   AAS. LOC. MHS.

31856   THE BOSTON PRICE-CURRENT [cut] AND MARINE INTELLIGENCER. COMMERCIAL AND MERCANTILE. VOL. II. No. 86. MONDAY, JANUARY 2, [— VOL. III. No. 33. THURSDAY, DEC. 28, 1797.]
      Printed at Boston, [by John Russell,] on Mondays and Thursdays, in Quaker-Lane, near State-Street. 1797. fol.   AAS. BA. MHS.
The words "Commercial Gazette," changed to "Russell's Commercial Gazette," September 7th, in the heading, were not intended to be a part of the title. The words "Commercial and mercantile" were dropped in March.

31857   BOWDOIN, James   1752–1811
OPINIONS RESPECTING THE COMMERCIAL INTERCOURSE BETWEEN THE UNITED STATES
OF AMERICA, AND THE DOMINIONS OF GREAT-BRITAIN, INCLUDING OBSERVATIONS
UPON THE NECESSITY AND IMPORTANCE OF AN AMERICAN NAVIGATION ACT. BY A
CITIZEN OF MASSACHUSETTS. "FAS EST ET AB HOSTE DOCERI." [Ornament.]
   Boston: Printed and sold by Samuel Hall, No. 53, Cornhill. 1797. pp. [16],
   (1). 8vo.   AAS. BA. BM. HC. JCB. LOC. MHS. NYPL..

31858   BOWDOINHAM. MAINE. BAPTIST ASSOCIATION.
MINUTES OF THE BOWDOINHAM ASSOCIATION, HELD AT THE BAPTIST MEETING-HOUSE
IN THOMASTON, AUGUST 23 AND 24, 1797. [Ornament.]
   Boston: Printed by Manning and Loring. M,DCC,XCVII. pp. [8]. 8vo.
                                                      AAS. JCB.

31859   BOWEN'S VIRGINIA GAZETTE: AND THE WINCHESTER CENTINEL. VOL. IX. No. 457.
FRIDAY, JANUARY 6, [— VOL. X. No. 508. FRIDAY, DECEMBER 27, 1797.]
   Winchester: Printed by R. Bowen. 1797. fol.

31860   BRAAM HOUCKGEEST, ANDREAS EVERARD VAN   1739–1796
VOYAGE DE L'AMBASSADE DE LA COMPAGNIE DES INDES ORIENTALES HOLLANDAISES,
VERS L'EMPEREUR DE LA CHINE, DANS LES ANNÉES 1794 & 1795: OÙ SE TROUVE
LA DESCRIPTION DE PLUSIEURS PARTIES DE LA CHINE INCONNUES AUX EUROPÉENS,
& QUE CETTE AMBASSADE À DONNÉ L'OCCASION DE TRAVERSER: LE TOUT TIRÉ DU
JOURNAL D'ANDRÉ EVERARD VAN BRAAM HOUCKGEEST. CHEF DE LA DIRECTION
DE LA COMPAGNIE DES INDES ORIENTALES HOLLANDAISE À LA CHINE, & SECOND
DANS CETTE AMBASSADE; ANCIEN DIRECTEUR DE LA SOCIÉTÉ DES SCIENCES & ARTS
DE HARLEM EN HOLLANDE; DE LA SOCIÉTÉ PHILOSOPHIQUE DE PHILADELPHIE,
&C. &C. ET ORNÉ DE [DIX-HUIT] CARTES & DE GRAVURES. PUBLIÉ EN FRANÇAIS
PAR M. L. E. MOREAU DE SAINT-MÉRY. TOME PREMIER.
   *A Philadelphie: Et se trouve chez L'Editeur, Imprimeur-Libraire au coin de
la Premiere rue Sud & de Walnut, No. 84. Les principaux Libraires des Etats-
Unis d'Amerique. Les Libraires des principales Villes d'Europe.* 1797. pp. lxxx,
487, 7 plates, 2 maps. 4to.   BM. NYPL.

   Dedicated to George Washington. The second volume was published
   in 1798. 182d Pennsylvania District Copyright, issued to André Everard Van Braam Houckgeest, as Proprietor, 13 June, 1797.

31861   BRACKEN, HENRY   1697–1764
THE GENTLEMAN'S POCKET FARRIER: SHOWING HOW TO USE YOUR HORSE ON A JOUR-
NEY; AND WHAT TREATMENTS ARE PROPER FOR COMMON ACCIDENTS THAT MAY
BEFAL HIM ON THE ROAD. TO WHICH IS ADDED, TEN MINUTES ADVICE TO EVERY
PURCHASER OF A HORSE.
   Washington, (Pennsylvania): Printed by John Colerick.. 1797. 16mo.

31862   BRACKENRIDGE, HUGH HENRY, formerly HUGH MONTGOMERY   1748–1816
MODERN CHIVALRY: CONTAINING THE ADVENTURES OF CAPTAIN JOHN FARRAGO, AND
TEAGUE O'REGAN, HIS SERVANT. VOLUME IV. BY H. H. BRACKENRIDGE. [One
line of Latin from] JUVENAL.
   Philadelphia: Printed and sold by John M'Culloch, No. 1, North Third-Street.
M,DCC,XCVII. [*Entered according to Act of Congress.*] pp.160. 12mo. JCB. NYPL.

   The first and second volumes were printed in Philadelphia in 1792, and
   the third volume in Pittsburgh, in 1793.

31863   BRADLEY, Daniel
An Oration, delivered at Lavana, at request of the Scipio Lodge, before a
large and respectable audience, on the anniversary of St. John, June 24,
1797: By Dan Bradley, esq.

Printed by William M'Lean,—Whitestown, (Herkimer County.) 1797.

31864   BRADMAN, Arthur
A Narrative of the extraordinary sufferings of mr. Robert Forbes, his wife
and five children; during an unfortunate journey through the wilderness
from Canada to Kennebeck River, in which three of their children were
starved to death. To which is added, a Narrative of the captivity and
escape of mrs. Frances Scott, an inhabitant of Washington County, Virginia.

*Elizabeth (Hager's) Town: Printed by Thomas Grieves, near the Court-House.
1797.*

31865   BRIDGHAM, Samuel Willard   1774–1840
An Oration, on the propriety of introducing the science of Jurisprudence
into a course, of classical education. Pronounced in the Baptist meeting-
house, in Providence, at the anniversary commencement of Rhode-Island
College, September 6th, A. D. 1797. By Samuel W. Bridgham, a candidate
for the degree of master in the arts. Published at the request of the
students.

Providence: Printed by Carter and Wilkinson. M,DCC,XCVII. pp. (7).
8vo.   AAS. JCB. NYPL. RIHS.

31866   BRIGGS, Ephraim   –1799
A Sermon, delivered at the ordination of the Reverend Ephraim Briggs, to
the pastoral charge of the church of Christ in Chatham, July 20, 1796.
By Ephraim Briggs, a. m. pastor of the church in Halifax. To which is ad-
ded, the Charge, by the reverend Oakes Shaw, of Barnstable; and the
Right hand of fellowship, by the reverend Nathan Stone of Dennis.

Printed by S. Hall, No. 53, Cornhill, Boston. 1797. pp. 27. 8vo.   JCB.

31867   BRIGGS, Isaac
Briggs's Maryland, Pennsylvania and Virginia Almanac; or Baltimore
ephemeris, for the year of our Lord, 1798; likewise a variety of pieces
in prose and verse.

Baltimore: Printed by W. Pechin, No. 15, Baltimore-Street. [1797.] pp.
(36). 12mo.   AAS.

Dated, Sharon, Montgomery county, (Maryland) 7th of second month,
1797.

31868   —— The Maryland & Virginia Almanac; or Washington ephemeris: for the
year of our Lord, 1798; being the second after leap-year. Adapted to
the latitude and meridian of Washington; and consequently to the States
above mentioned. [Seventeen lines.] Likewise, the Way to wealth, Advice
to young tradesmen, and several useful tables.

George-Town: Printed by Green, English & Co. [1797.] pp. (32). 12mo.   VBL.

The Author's Preface is signed, Isaac Briggs. Sharon, Montgomery
County (Maryland) 7th of second month, 1797.

AUCTION
VALUES

31869   BRIGGS, Isaac, continued.
—— — The Maryland & Virginia Almanac; or Washington ephemeris; for the year of our Lord 1798; being the second after leap-year. Adapted to the latitude and meridian of Washington; and consequently to the States above mentioned. [Seventeen lines.] Likewise, The Way to wealth, Advice to young tradesmen, and several useful tables.
> *George-Town: Printed by Green, English & Co. for the Rev. Mason L. Weems.* [1797.] pp. (32). 12mo.   LOC.

> See, also, No. 236 of the excellent "Weems Bibliography," by Emily Ellsworth Ford Skeel.

31870   —— The Virginia Almanack, or Ephemeris: for the year of our Eord [*sic*], 1798: being the second after leap-year. [Eighteen lines.]
> *Richmond: Printed and sold by Samuel Pleasants, jun. near the Vendue Office.* [1797.] pp. [38.] 12mo.   VSL.

> The Preface is signed, Isaac Briggs, Sharon, Montgomery County (Mar.) 7th of second month, '97.

31871   BRISSOT de WARVILLE, Jacques Pierre   1754–1793
New travels in the United States of America. Performed in 1788, by J. P. Brissot de Warville, Translated from the French. [Five lines of quotations.]
> *From the Press of Joseph Bumstead, Union-Street—Boston.* 1797. pp. 276, (3), folded table. 12mo.   AAS. BPL. HC. JCB. LCP. MHS. NYPL.

> "This volume comprises his two first volumes. His third, on the Commerce of America has been before published in English."

31872   BROCKWAY, Thomas   1745–1807
A sermon, delivered at the ordination of the Rev. Bezaleel Pinneo, to the pastoral charge of the first church and society in Milford, October 26th, 1796. By Thomas Brockway, A. M. pastor of the church in the second society of Lebanon.
> *New-Haven—Printed by T. & S. Green.* M,DCC,XCVII. pp. (30). 8vo.   AAS. CLA. HC. JCB. UTS.

> The Charge, by B. Trumbull, D. D. The Right hand of fellowship, by Rev. D. Tullar.

31873   BROOKE. Frances Moore   1724–1789
When William at eve. Song from "Rosina."
> *New-York: Printed and sold by G. Gilfert, No. 177, Broadway.* [1797.] Broadside. 4to.   LOC.

31874   BROOKE, Henry   1706–1783
The History of a reprobate; being the life and adventures of David Doubtful. By Henry Brooke esq. author of the Fool of quality, Juliet Grenville, Gustavus Vasa, &c. &c.
> *Boston: Printed and sold by William Spotswood, No. 55. Marlborough-Street.* 1795.

31875   BROOM, Jacob
By Legislative authority: A Lottery! For raising four thousand dollars, clear of all expenses, for the purpose of aiding the subscriber in the re-establishment of his cotton manufactory. . . . Jacob Broom. Wilmington, Delaware, July 24th, 1797.
> [*Wilmington: Printed by Samuel & John Adams.* 1797.] Broadside. fol.

31876   BROOME, Ralph
    STRICTURES ON MR. BURKE'S TWO LETTERS, ADDRESSED TO A MEMBER OF THE PRESENT PARLIAMENT: ON THE PROPOSALS FOR PEACE WITH THE "REGICIDE DIRECTORY OF FRANCE." PART THE FIRST.

    Philadelphia: Printed by John Thompson, and sold by the Booksellers of Philadelphia, New-York, and Baltimore. 1797. pp. iv, [50.] 8vo.   LOC.

31877   BROTHERS, Richard   1757–1824
    A REVEALED KNOWLEDGE OF THE PROPHECIES AND TIMES. BOOK THE FIRST. WROTE UNDER THE DIRECTION OF THE LORD GOD, AND PUBLISHED BY HIS SACRED COMMAND: IT BEING THE FIRST SIGN OF WARNING FOR THE BENEFIT OF ALL NATIONS. CONTAINING, WITH OTHER GREAT AND REMARKABLE THINGS NOT REVEALED TO ANY OTHER PERSON ON EARTH, THE RESTORATION OF THE HEBREWS TO JERUSALEM, IN THE YEAR 1798; UNDER THEIR REVEALED PRINCE AND PROPHET RICHARD BROTHERS.

    West-Springfield: Printed by Edward Gray. For Asaph Chilson of Buckland, and to be sold by said Chilson by the dozen or single. M,DCC,XCVII. pp. [72]; [111]; [37]; [19.] 12mo.   AAS. JCB. NYPL.

    Second title: A REVEALED KNOWLEDGE OF THE PROPHECIES AND TIMES, PARTICULARLY OF THE PRESENT TIME, THE PRESENT WAR, AND THE PROPHECY NOW FULFILLING. THE YEAR OF THE WORLD 5913. BOOK THE SECOND. CONTAINING, WITH OTHER GREAT AND REMARKABLE THINGS, NOT REVEALED TO ANY OTHER PERSON ON EARTH, THE SUDDEN AND PERPETUAL FALL OF THE TURKISH, GERMAN, AND RUSSIAN EMPIRES. WROTE UNDER THE DIRECTION OF THE LORD GOD, AND PUBLISHED BY HIS SACRED COMMAND; IT BEING A SECOND SIGN OF WARNING FOR THE BENEFIT OF ALL NATIONS. BY THE MAN THAT WILL BE REVEALED TO THE HEBREWS AS THEIR PRINCE AND PROPHET.

    West-Springfield: Printed by Edward Gray, for Asaph Chilson, of Buckland, and to be sold by said Chilson, by the dozen or single. M,DCC,XCVII. pp. [111].

    Third title: TESTIMONY OF THE AUTHENTICITY OF THE PROPHECIES OF RICHARD BROTHERS, AND OF HIS MISSION TO RECALL THE JEWS. BY NATHANIEL BRASSEY HALHED, M. P. AND GOD SAID, "LET THERE BE LIGHT."

    West-Springfield: Printed by Edward Gray, for Asaph Chilson, of Buckland, and to be sold by said Chilson, by the dozen or single. M,DCC,XCVII. pp. [37.]

    Fourth title: A CALCULATION ON THE COMMENCEMENT OF THE MILLENNIUM, AND A SHORT REPLY TO DR HORNE'S PAMPHLET ENTITLED "SOUND ARGUMENT, DICTATED BY COMMON SENSE." TOGETHER WITH CURSORY OBSERVATIONS ON THE "AGE OF CREDULITY." BY NATHANIEL BRASSEY HALHED, M. P. TO WHICH IS ADDED AN ORIGINAL LETTER FROM MR. BROTHERS, TO PHILIP STEPHENS, ESQ. WITH HIS ANSWER. A PAPER IS SUBJOINED, POINTING OUT THOSE PARTS OF MR. BROTHER'S PROPHECIES THAT HAVE BEEN ALREADY FULFILLED. "EYES YE HAVE AND SEE NOT."

    West-Springfield: Printed by Edward Gray, for Asaph Chilson, of Buckland, and to be sold by said Chilson, by the dozen or single. M,DCC,XCVII. pp. [19.]

31878   BROWN, Clark   1772–1817
    A CATECHISM, IN THREE PARTS: DESIGNED FOR THE USE OF CHILDREN. PART I—CONTAINING GENERAL INSTRUCTIONS IN RELIGIOUS KNOWLEDGE. PART II.—CONTAINING EXPLANATORY DIRECTIONS, RESPECTING THE GENERAL DESIGN & USE OF THE BIBLE. PART III.—CONTAINING A KNOWLEDGE OF THE CHRISTIAN RELIGION IN PARTICULAR. BY CLARK BROWN, B. D. M.

    Newbedford:—Printed by John Spooner. 1797. pp. 31. 16mo.   AAS. BA.

31879   BROWN, John   1722–1787
An Essay towards an easy, plain, practical, and extensive explication of the Assembly's Shorter Catechism. By mr. John Brown, minister at Haddington. [Ten lines of quotations.] [Publisher's monogram.]
> *Carlisle: Printed for Archibald Loudon, by George Kline.* MDCCXCVII.
pp. xvi, 354. 12mo.   AAS. LOC. NYPL.

31880   BROWN or Bruno, John   1735–1788
The Elements of medicine; or, a translation of the Elementa Medicinæ Brunonis. With large notes, illustrations, and comments. By the Author of the original work. The sixth edition.
> *Fairhaven: Printed by James Lyon, at Voltaire's Head.* M,DCC,XCVII.
pp. xiv, 404, (11). 12mo.   AAS. JCB.

31881   BROWN, Samuel   1769–1830
An Inaugural dissertation on the bilious malignant fever. Read at a public examination, held by the medical professors, before the Rev. Joseph Willard, s. t. d. president, and the governors in the University at Cambridge. For the degree of Bachelor in medicine, July 10, 1797. By Samuel Brown, a. m. [Four lines of verse.]
> *Printed at Boston, by Manning & Loring,* 1797. pp. [54.] 8vo.
>   AAS. BA. BM. LOC. MHS. NYPL. SGO.

31882   BROWN, William Hill   1766–1793
West Point preserved or the treason of Arnold. An historical tragedy in five acts. By William Hill Brown, late of Boston.
> *Boston:* 1797.

114th Massachusetts District Copyright, issued to Margaret Brown, as Proprietor, 11 March, 1797.

31883   BROWNE, Joseph
Treatise on the yellow fever; shewing its origin, cure and prevention. By Joseph Browne.
> *New-York: Printed [by Thomas Greenleaf] at the Argus Office.* [1797.] pp.
31. 8vo.   NYHS.

31884   BROWNSON, Oliver
A New collection of sacred harmony. Containing a set of psalm tunes, hymns and anthems, likewise the necessary rules of psalmody. By Oliver Brownson.
> *Simsbury, (Conn.): Printed [by Thomas and Samuel Green, New-Haven] and sold by the Author.* 1797. pp. 56. obl. 8vo.

Title-page, and music engraved by Z. Howe.

31885   BRUNT, Jonathan, junior
A Few particulars of the life of Jonathan Brunt, junior, printer & bookseller. [Third edition, corrected.] Also, The Excellency of pure or incorrupted liberty, when compared with the present prevailing licentious liberty.
> *Written, Printed and sold by himself only.* October, 1797. pp. [8.] 8vo. LOC.

The first two editions were, also, probably printed at this date: and another edition printed in Frankfort, Kentucky, in 1804.

31886   BUCHAN, WILLIAM   1729–1805
DOMESTIC MEDICINE: OR, A TREATISE ON THE PREVENTION AND CURE OF DISEASES,
BY REGIMEN AND SIMPLE MEDICINES. WITH AN APPENDIX, CONTAINING A DISPENSA-
TORY FOR THE USE OF PRIVATE PRACTITIONERS. BY WILLIAM BUCHAN, M. D. FEL-
LOW OF THE ROYAL COLLEGE OF PHYSICIANS, EDINBURGH: REVISED AND ADAPTED
TO THE DISEASES AND CLIMATE OF THE UNITED STATES OF AMERICA, BY SAMUEL
POWEL GRIFFITTS, M. D. LATE PROFESSOR OF MATERIA MEDICA IN THE UNIVER-
SITY OF PENNSYLVANIA, SECOND EDITION.
> *Philadelphia: Printed by Thomas Dobson, at the Stone-House, No. 41, South
> Second Street.* 1797. pp. xxxi, 757, (2). 8vo.   AAS. SGO.

> Contains, a two-page list of Books published by Thomas Dobson.

31887   —— — DOMESTIC MEDICINE, OR A TREATISE ON THE PREVENTION AND CURE OF
DISEASES BY REGIMEN AND SIMPLE MEDICINES. WITH AN APPENDIX, CONTAINING
A DISPENSATORY FOR THE USE OF PRIVATE PRACTITIONERS. BY WILLIAM BUCHAN,
M. D. FELLOW OF THE ROYAL COLLEGE OF PHYSICIANS, EDINBURGH. ADAPTED TO
THE CLIMATE AND DISEASES OF AMERICA. BY ISAAC CATHRALL.
> *Philadelphia: Printed by Richard Folwell.* 1797. pp. 512, 8vo. NYPL. SGO.

> 191st Pennsylvania District Copyright, issued to Richard Folwell, as
> Proprietor, 30 August, 1797.

31888   —— — DOMESTIC MEDICINE: OR, A TREATISE ON THE PREVENTION AND CURE OF
DISEASES, BY REGIMEN AND SIMPLE MEDICINES. WITH AN APPENDIX, CONTAINING
A DISPENSATORY FOR THE USE OF PRIVATE PRACTITIONERS. BY WILLIAM BUCHAN,
M. D. FELLOW OF THE ROYAL COLLEGE OF PHYSICIANS, EDINBURGH. THE TWEN-
TIETH EDITION CONTAINING ALL THE IMPROVEMENTS.
> *Waterford: Printed by and for James Lyon & Co.* 1797. pp. xxiv, (476),
> 17. 8vo.   AAS.

31889   BUELL, SAMUEL   1716–1798
SINCERE REIGNING LOVE TO CHRIST, CONSIDERED IN ITS NATURE, INFLUENCE AND USE-
FULNESS, BOTH WITH RESPECT TO THE PRIVATE CHRISTIAN, AND A MINISTER OF THE
GOSPEL. A SERMON DELIVERED AT THE ORDINATION OF THE REVEREND JOSEPH
HAZARD, TO THE PASTORAL CHARGE OF THE CHURCH IN SOUTHOLD, FIRST SOCIETY,
JUNE 7, 1797. BY SAMUEL BUELL, D. D. PASTOR OF THE CHURCH IN EAST-HAMP-
TON. [Six lines of Scripture texts.]
> *New-London: Printed by Samuel Green.* 1797. pp. 30. 8vo.
>   AAS. CHS. LOC. MHS. NYPL..

31890   BUNN, MATTHEW
A SHORT NARRATIVE OF THE LIFE AND SUFFERINGS OF MATTHEW BUNN, AFTER HIS
ARRIVAL AT THE BRITISH GARRISON AT DETROIT, AT WHICH PLACE HE ARRIVED
THE 30TH OF APRIL, 1792. FROM HIS INDIAN CAPTIVITY; AN ACCOUNT WHEREOF
WAS LATELY PUBLISHED, ENTITLED, "A JOURNAL OF THE ADVENTURES OF MAT-
THEW BUNN A NATIVE OF BROOKFIELD, MASSACHUSETTS," &C.
> *[Without Place or Printer.] Printed in the year* 1797. pp. (36). 12mo.
>   AAS. HEH.

31891   BUNYAN, JOHN   1628–1688
GRACE ABOUNDING TO THE CHIEF OF SINNERS: OR, A BRIEF AND FAITHFUL RELATION
OF THE EXCEEDING MERCY OF GOD IN CHRIST TO HIS POOR SERVANT JOHN BUNYAN
. . . ALL WHICH WAS WRITTEN BY HIS OWN HAND . . . SECOND NEW-YORK
EDITION.
> *New-York: Printed by J. Tiebout, for Evert Duyckinck.* 1797. pp. 108.
> 24mo.   NYPL.

31892   BURGES, TRISTAM   1770–1853
SOLITUDE AND SOCIETY CONTRASTED. AN ORATION, PRONOUNCED AT THE ANNUAL MEETING OF THE PHILOLOGICAL SOCIETY, IN MIDDLEBOROUGH, ON WEDNESDAY, THE 7TH OF JUNE, 1797. BY TRISTAM BURGES, A. B. [Two lines of Latin from] Q. H. FLACCIUS.

     Providence: Printed by Carter and Wilkinson. M,DCC,XCVII. pp. (24). 8vo.
                              AAS. BM. JCB. NYPL. RIHS.

     Contains, two Odes, sung on the anniversary of the Philological Society, June 7, A. D. 1797. pp. 22-24.

31893   BURK, JOHN DALY   1775–1808
BUNKER-HILL; OR THE DEATH OF GENERAL WARREN: AN HISTORIC TRAGEDY. IN FIVE ACTS. BY JOHN BURK, LATE OF TRINITY COLLEGE, DUBLIN. AS PLAYED AT THE THEATRES IN AMERICA, FOR FOURTEEN NIGHTS, WITH UNBOUNDED APPLAUSE. COPYRIGHT SECURED ACCORDING TO LAW.

     New-York: Printed by T. Greenleaf. M,DCC,XCVII. pp. 55. 12mo.
                              AAS. BM.

     Dedicated to Aaron Burr, esq.

31894   BURKE, EDMUND   1729–1797
A LETTER FROM THE RT. HONOURABLE EDMUND BURKE TO HIS GRACE THE DUKE OF PORTLAND. ON THE CONDUCT OF THE MINORITY IN PARLIAMENT. CONTAINING FIFTY-FOUR ARTICLES OF IMPEACHMENT AGAINST THE RT. HON. C. J. FOX. FROM THE ORIGINAL COPY, IN THE POSSESSION OF THE NOBLE DUKE.

     London: Printed. Philadelphia: Re-printed for James Humphreys, No. 74, North Third-Street, the corner of Cherry Alley. 1797. pp. [56.] 8vo.
                              AAS. LCP. LOC. NYPL.

     Editor's Advertisement, dated, Philadelphia, June 5, 1797, states: that the English edition was suppressed immediately after it was printed and only seventy or eighty copies of it got abroad.

31895   —— TWO LETTERS ADDRESSED TO A MEMBER OF THE PRESENT PARLIAMENT, ON THE PROPOSALS FOR PEACE WITH THE REGICIDE DIRECTORY OF FRANCE. BY THE RIGHT HON. EDMUND BURKE.

     Philadelphia: Printed for William Cobbett, in Second Street, opposite Christ-Church, and J. Ormrod No. 41, Chesnut Street. By Bioren and Madan. 1797. pp. (64); (22). 8vo.   AAS. BA. JCB. LOC. MHS. NYHS. NYPL.

31896   BURLINGTON. NEW JERSEY. LIBRARY.
ADDITIONAL CATALOGUE OF BOOKS IN THE BURLINGTON LIBRARY.
     Burlington: Printed by Isaac Neale. 1797.

31897   BURLINGTON MERCURY. [Motto.] NUMBER 45. FRIDAY, JANUARY 6, [—— NUMBER 56. FRIDAY, MARCH 24, 1797.]
     Burlington—(State of Vermont)—Printed every Friday, by Donnelly and Hill, directly opposite the Court-House. 1797. fol.

     The above is the last number located.

31898   BURNET, GILBERT   1643–1715
SOME ACCOUNT OF THE LIFE AND DEATH OF JOHN WILMOT, EARL OF ROCHESTER. WHO DIED JULY 26, 1680. WRITTEN BY HIS OWN DIRECTION ON HIS DEATH-BED. BY GILBERT BURNET, LORD BISHOP OF SARUM. TO WHICH IS PREFIXED AN ACCOUNT OF THE AUTHOR'S LIFE.

     Albany: Printed by J. M'Donald. MDCCXCVII. pp. xx, (139). 12mo.
                              AAS. WIPL.

31899   BURNHAM, RICHARD   1749–1810
HYMNS, PARTICULARLY DESIGNED FOR THE USE OF THE CONGREGATION MEETING TO-
GETHER IN EDWARD STREET, SOHO, IN LONDON. BY RICHARD BURNHAM, MINISTER
OF THE GOSPEL. SING YE PRAISES WITH UNDERSTANDING. PSALM XLVII. 7.
            Boston: Printed by Thomas Hall, for J. Asplund. 1796. pp. 20, 320 [268.]
24mo.   AAS.

         We have before, IX: 26579, had occasion to refer to the peculiar ideas of
         printing and publishing of John Asplund, the editor of this work. In
         the above. without so much, apparently, as saying "by your leave" he
         has taken the work of a Baptist minister of a poor parish in London,
         and deliberately changed the Author's arrangement of the text first, by
         an arbitrary division of his own into classes of no known system, and
         second, by an attempted arrangement by which the number of the hymn
         and the number of the page would correspond. So long as the Hymnal
         Pegasus observes the regulation trot of four, or five, four-line octosyl-
         labic verses, the system works like a charm; but when, probably from a
         shortage of oats, the hymn consists of less than the regular number of
         verses. the system fails and we have, as in this case, 320 hymns and
         only 268 pages—a deception for which the editor, not the reverend
         Author, is to blame.

31900   BURR, JONATHAN   –1842
A COMPENDIUM OF ENGLISH GRAMMAR, FOR THE USE OF SCHOOLS AND PRIVATE IN-
STRUCTORS. TO WHICH ARE ANNEX'D EXERCISES CORRESPONDING TO THE GRAMMAR.
BY JONATHAN BURR, A. M.
            Boston: 1797. 12mo.   BM.

         120th Massachusetts District Copyright, issued to Jonathan Burr, as
         Author, 31 July, 1797.

31901   BURRILL, GEORGE RAWSON   1770–1818
AN ORATION, DELIVERED IN THE BENEVOLENT CONGREGATIONAL MEETING-HOUSE,
ON THE FOURTH OF JULY, A. D. 1797, IN COMMEMORATION OF AMERICAN INDEPEN-
DENCE, BY GEORGE R. BURRILL, ESQ. ECCE SPECTACULUM DIGNUM! PUBLISHED
BY REQUEST.
            Providence: Printed by Carter and Wilkinson, and sold at their Book-Store.
1797. pp. (2), (18). 8vo.   AAS. BA. JCB. NYPL. RIHS.

31902   BUTLER, JAMES
FORTUNE'S FOOT-BALL; OR, THE ADVENTURES OF MERCUTIO. FOUNDED ON MATTERS
OF FACT. A NOVEL, IN TWO VOLUMES. BY JAMES BUTLER. VOL. I.
            Harrisburgh, Pennsylvania: Printed by John Wyeth. 1797. *[Entered ac-
cording to law.]* pp. 192. 12mo.   AAS. BM. LOC. NYPL.

         The second volume was printed in 1798.

31903   CADET DE GASSICOURT, CHARLES LOUIS   1769–1821
THE TOMB OF JAMES MOLAI; OR, THE SECRET OF THE CONSPIRATORS. TRANSLATED
[from the French,] BY A GENTLEMAN OF BOSTON. ADDRESSED TO THOSE WHO
WISH TO KNOW EVERYTHING.
            Boston: Printed by Benjamin Edes, Kilby-Street — 1797. pp. (22). 8vo.
                                                    AAS. BA. LOC. MHS. NYHS.

31904   CALENDRIER REPUBLICAIN POUR L'AN VI [1798] DE LA REPUBLIQUE FRANCAISE,
ET LE XXIIME DE L'INDEPENDENCE AMERICAINE. EMBELLI D'UN PORTRAIT DE
BUONAPARTE. [Twenty-four lines. Cut.]
            Philadelphie: De l'imprimerie de Benj. Franklin Bache, No. 112 *rue de
Marche.* [1797.] pp. (48) portrait. 48mo.   LOC.

31905   CALLENDER, James Thomson   1758–1803
The American annual register, or, historical memoirs of the United States, for the year 1796.

> *Philadelphia: Printed and sold by Bioren & Madan, No. 77, Dock-street. January 19th, 1797.* pp. vii, (288) 8vo.
>   AAS. BA. BPL. HC. JCB. LOC. MHS. NYHS. NYPL.

> Entered according to law. 167th Pennsylvania District Copyright, issued to Bioren and Madan, as Proprietors, 19 January, 1797. This edition was soon disposed of, and a new edition was issued later in the year under the following title:

31906   —— —— The History of the United States for 1796; including a variety of interesting particulars relative to the federal government previous to that period.

> *Philadelphia: From the Press of Snowden & M'Corkle, No. 47, North Fourth-Street.* 1797. pp. viii, 312. 8vo.   AAS. BA. HC. JCB. LCP. NL. NYHS. NYPL. VSL.

> 186th Pennsylvania District Copyright, issued to Snowden and Mc-Corkle, as Proprietors, 24 June, 1797. First published in eight weekly numbers, at eight pence each. Chapters v and vi contain the unfounded charges of peculating against Alexander Hamilton which brought out his famous Reynold's pamphlet. The copy in the New York Public Library contains mss. annotations by George Bancroft.

31907   CALLENDER, John   1772–1833
An Oration, pronounced July 4, 1797, at the request of the inhabitants of the town of Boston, in commemoration of the anniversary of American independence. By John Callender. [Six lines of verse from] Cowper.

> *Boston: Printed and sold by Benjamin Edes, Kilby Street.—1797.* pp. 19. 8vo.   AAS. BA. BM. HC. JCB. MHS. NYPL.

31908   CAMBRIDGE. Massachusetts. Friendly Fire Society.
The Rules and regulations of the Friendly Fire Society, instituted at Cambridge. March 17th, 1797.

> *Printed at Boston, for the Society, by Seth H. Moore. March,* 1797. pp. 8. 16mo.   JCB.

31909   CAMILLUS, pseudonym.
The Political reformer: or a proposed plan of reformations in the laws and governments of the United States of America: calculated to promote human happiness. To which are added, Strictures on John Adams's Defence of the Constitutions of government of the United States of America. [Signed, Camillus.]

> *Philadelphia: Printed for the Author, by W. W. Woodward, No. 17, Chesnut Street.* 1797. pp. 73. 8vo.   BA. BPL. JCB. LOC. MHS. NYPL.

> "Camillus" was also used as a pseudonym by Alexander Hamilton.

31910   CAMP, John   1753–1821
A Sermon, delivered at the Academy in Cooperstown, on the 27 of December 1796, before the members of Otsego Lodge, it being the festival of St. John the Evangelist; by the Reverend John Camp, a. m. pastor of the church of Christ, in New-Canaan. To which is added, the Speech of count T ——, at the initiation of his son; and the Address of the Grand Lodge of Pennsylvania, to the President of the United States, with his Answer.

> *Cooperstown: Printed by Elihu Phinney.* 1797.

31911   CAMPBELL, DONALD   1751–1804
A JOURNEY OVER LAND TO INDIA, PARTLY BY A ROUTE NEVER GONE BEFORE BY ANY EUROPEAN, BY DONALD CAMPBELL, OF BARBRECK, ESQ. WHO FORMERLY COMMANDED A REGIMENT OF CAVALRY IN THE SERVICE OF HIS HIGHNESS THE NABOB OF THE CARNATIC. IN A SERIES OF LETTERS TO HIS SON. COMPREHENDING HIS SHIPWRECK AND IMPRISONMENT WITH HYDER ALI AND HIS SUBSEQUENT NEGOCIATIONS AND TRANSACTIONS IN THE EAST. [Two lines of Latin quotation.]
> *Philadelphia: Printed by T. Dobson, at the Stone House, No. 41, South Second-Street. 1797. pp. 424, 6. 8vo.*   AAS.

31912   CAMPBELL. JOHN POAGE   1767–1814
A SERMON ON SACRED MUSIC: PREACHED BEFORE A PUBLIC CONCERT IN WASHINGTON. BY REV. JOHN P. CAMPBELL. PUBLISHED BY REQUEST.
> *Washington, (K.) Printed by Hunter and Beaumont. 1797.*

31913   CAMPBELL, ROBERT
ROBERT CAMPBELL AND CO'S. CATALOGUE FOR 1797: CONTAINING A VERY EXTENSIVE AND VALUABLE COLLECTION OF BOOKS [2605 titles] IN THE DIFFERENT DEPATMENTS [*sic*] OF LITERATURE AND SCIENCE; NOW SELLING AT VERY REDUCED PRICES, AT No. 40, SOUTH SECOND-STREET: WHERE COUNTRY STORE-KEEPERS, PUBLIC AND PRIVATE LIBRARIES, ARE SUPPLIED ON VERY LOW TERMS. N. B. A LIBERAL PRICE WILL BE GIVEN FOR LIBRARIES OR PARCELS OF BOOKS.
> *Philadelphia: [January 1st.] 1797. pp. (2), 90, (2). 8vo.*   AAS.

31914   CAREY, JAMES
ANTICIPATION! PORCUPINE'S DESCENT INTO HELL: OR, AN ELEGY ON HIS DEATH. A MOCK-HEROIC POEM. BY HENRY HEDGEHOG. THE SECOND EDITION, CORRECTED.
> *Philadelphia: Printed by James Carey, No. 83, North Second-street. September 25, 1797. pp. [8.] 8vo.*   LOC.

31915   CAREY'S DAILY ADVERTISER, A LITERARY, POLITICAL, & COMMERCIAL EVENING GAZETTE. "NOTHING EXTENUATE — NOR SET DOWN AUGHT IN MALICE." — SHAKESPEARE. VOL. I. NO. 1. THURSDAY EVENING, FEBRUARY 9, [— No. 185. TUESDAY EVENING, SEPTEMBER 12, 1797.]
> *Philadelphia: Printed by James Carey, No. 83, North Second-Street. 1797. fol.*

> Established, as a daily, by James Carey, in continuation of *The Daily Advertiser*, and succeeded in January, 1798, by *Carey's United States Recorder*, a tri-weekly publication. The above is the last number located.

31916   CARITAT, HOCQUET
CATALOGUE OF THE CIRCULATING LIBRARY OF H. CARITAT.
> *New-York: Printed for H. Caritat, Pearl-Street, No. 3. 1797.*

31917   CARLISLE. PENNSYLVANIA. LIBRARY COMPANY.
THE RULES OF THE CARLISLE LIBRARY COMPANY; WITH A CATALOGUE OF BOOKS BELONGING THERETO.
> *Carlisle: Printed by George Kline. [1797.] pp. 15. 8vo.*   LOC.

31918   CARPENTER, THOMAS
THE AMERICAN SENATOR. OR A COPIOUS AND IMPARTIAL REPORT OF THE DEBATES IN THE CONGRESS OF THE UNITED STATES: INCLUDING ALL TREATIES, ADDRESSES, PROCLAMATIONS, &C. WHICH OCCUR DURING THE PRESENT SESSION, BEING THE SECOND OF THE FOURTH CONGRESS. BY THOMAS CARPENTER. VOL. II.
> *Philadelphia: Printed for the Author. 1797. pp. (368), (4). 8vo.*
>   AAS. BM. LOC.

CARPENTER, THOMAS, continued.

31919　　——　—　THE AMERICAN SENATOR. OR A COPIOUS AND IMPARTIAL REPORT OF THE DEBATES IN THE CONGRESS OF THE UNITED STATES: INCLUDING ALL TREATIES, ADDRESSES, PROCLAMATIONS, &C. WHICH OCCUR DURING THE PRESENT SESSION, BEING THE SECOND OF THE FOURTH CONGRESS. VOL. III.

Philadelphia: Printed for the Editor, by William W. Woodward, No. 17, Chesnut Street. 1797. pp. (2),(2), (369)–(787), (4), (8). 8vo.　　AAS. BM. LOC.

Contains an eight page list of Subscribers' names.

31920　　CARVER, JONATHAN　　　　　　　　　　　　　1710–1780
THREE YEARS TRAVELS THROUGHOUT THE INTERIOR PARTS OF NORTH-AMERICA, FOR MORE THEN [*sic*] FIVE THOUSAND MILES, CONTAINING AN ACCOUNT OF THE GREAT LAKES, AND ALL THE LAKES, ISLANDS AND RIVERS, CATARACTS, MOUNTAINS, MINERALS, SOIL AND VEGETABLE PRODUCTIONS OF THE NORTH-WEST REGIONS OF THAT VAST CONTINENT; WITH A DESCRIPTION OF THE BIRDS, BEASTS, REPTILES, INSECTS, AND FISHES PECULIAR TO THE COUNTRY. TOGETHER WITH A CONCISE HISTORY OF THE GENIUS, MANNERS, AND CUSTOMS OF THE INDIANS INHABITING THE LANDS THAT LIE ADJACENT TO THE HEADS AND TO THE WESTWARD OF THE GREAT RIVER MISSISSIPPI; AND AN APPENDIX, DESCRIBING THE UNCULTIVATED PARTS OF AMERICA, THAT ARE THE MOST PROPER FOR FORMING SETTLEMENTS. BY CAPTAIN JONATHAN CARVER, OF THE PROVINCIAL TROOPS IN AMERICA.

Printed by John Russell, for David West, No. 56, Cornhill, Boston. 1797. pp. xvi, (5)–312. 12mo.　　AAS. BA. HC. JCB. LOC. NYPL.

Contains Vocabularies of the Chippewa and Naudowessie languages, pp. 341-253.

31921　　CARY, THOMAS, JUNIOR　　　　　　　　　　　　　–1820
A SERMON, DELIVERED AT CHARLESTOWN, JULY 23, 1797. BY THOMAS CARY, A. M. PASTOR OF THE FIRST CHURCH IN NEWBURY-PORT. PUBLISHED AT THE REQUEST OF THE HEARERS; TO WHOM IT IS RESPECTFULLY INSCRIBED.

Charlestown: Printed by John Lamson, at his Office near the Bridge. [1797.] pp. 24. 8vo.　　AAS. BA. BM. JCB. MHS. UTS.

31922　　CATLIN, JACOB　　　　　　　　　　　　　　　1758–1826
THE MORAL CHARACTER OF CHRIST THE STANDARD OF SOCIAL VIRTUE. A SERMON DELIVERED IN NEW-MARLBOROUGH; ON THE FIRST DAY OF THE YEAR OF OUR LORD, 1796; BEFORE THE FREE AND ACCEPTED MASONS OF THE CINCINNATUS LODGE; IT BEING THE DAY OF THEIR INSTALMENT. PUBLISHED AT THE REQUEST OF THE LODGE. BY JACOB CATLIN, A. M. PASTOR OF THE FIRST CHURCH OF CHRIST IN NEW-MARLBOROUGH.

Stockbridge: Printed by Loring Andrews. 1797. pp. 22. 12mo.　　AAS. BPL.

31923　　THE CATSKILL PACKET. VOL. V. NUMBER 1. SATURDAY, JANUARY 7, [— No. 52. SATURDAY, DECEMBER 30, 1797.]

Catskill, (State of New-York): Printed by Mackay Croswell. [1797.] fol.

31924　　CECIL, RICHARD　　　　　　　　　　　　　　　1748–1810
A FRIENDLY VISIT TO THE HOUSE OF MOURNING. [Eleven lines of quotations.]

Hartford: Printed for Nathaniel Patten, 1797.

31925　　——　A FRIENDLY VISIT TO THE HOUSE OF MOURNING. IN THE DAY OF ADVERSITY CONSIDER.

Wiscasset, District of Maine. Printed by J. N. Russell and H. Hoskins. 1797.

31926   THE CENTINEL, & COUNTRY GAZETTE. VOL. I. No. 33. FRIDAY, JANUARY 6, [—
VOL. II. No. 84. FRIDAY, DECEMBER 29, 1797.]
George-Town. (On the Potomak.) From the Press of Green, English & Co.
1797. fol.

31927   THE CENTINEL OF FREEDOM. VOL. I. No. 14. WEDNESDAY, JANUARY 4, [— No.
13. VOL. II. TOTAL NUMB. 65. TUESDAY, DECEMBER 26, 1797.]
Newark, [New-Jersey.] Printed and published by Daniel Dodge & Co.
1797. fol.

With the issue for October 4th, the imprint became Aaron Pennington
& Daniel Dodge, Publishers.

31928   THE CENTINEL OF LIBERTY AND GEORGE-TOWN ADVERTISER. No. 63. VOL. I.
TUESDAY, JANUARY 3, [— No. 62. VOL. II. FRIDAY, DECEMBER 29, 1797.]
George-Town. (On the Potomak) From the Press of Green, English & Co. On
Tuesdays and Fridays. 1797. fol.

In July, the imprint was changed to the heading, and this motto added:
Liberty is a right of doing whatever the laws permit; and if a citizen
could do what they forbid, he would no longer be possessed of Liberty,
because all his fellow-citizens would have the same power.—Montesquieu.

31929   CHANDLER, SETH
AN ASTRONOMICAL DIARY: OR ALMANACK, FOR THE YEAR OF OUR LORD 1798: BEING
THE SECOND AFTER BISSEXTILE OR LEAP-YEAR, AND THE TWENTY SECOND OF THE
INDEPENDENCE OF THE UNITED STATES OF AMERICA; WHICH BEGAN JULY 4, 1776.
[Seven lines.] CALCULATED FOR THE MERIDIAN OF BOSTON, IN AMERICA, LATITUDE
42 DEGREES, 25M. NORTH. BY SETH CHANDLER, A STUDENT OF PHYSIC. [Four
lines of verse.]
Boston: Printed by Joseph Bumstead, for the Author. [1797.] pp. (24).
12mo.   AAS. LOC. NYPL.

To the reader is dated, July 12th, 1797.

31930   CHAPMAN, E.
A DISCOURSE ON THE PROPHECIES; MORE ESPECIALLY ON THOSE PROPHECIES WHICH
PREDICT THE RISE, CONTINUANCE AND DOWNFAL [*sic*] OF THOSE TWO GREAT ANTI-
CHRISTIAN EMPIRES FOUNDED BY THE POPE AND MOHAMMED: TOGETHER WITH THE
REMARKABLE AND GLORIOUS EVENTS WHICH WILL IMMEDIATELY FOLLOW: BEING THE
SUBSTANCE OF TWO SERMONS PREACHED AT BETHEL. BY E. CHAPMAN, V. D. M.
PUBLISHED BY DESIRE. [Quotation from] REV. 4TH, 1ST.
Printed at Portland by John K. Baker. 1797. pp. 39. 8vo.   AAS.

31931   CHARLESTON. SOUTH CAROLINA. BAPTIST ASSOCIATION.
MINUTES OF THE CHARLESTON BAPTIST ASSOCIATION, MET AT HIGH HILLS OF SANTEE,
NOVEMBER 4TH, 1797.
[Charleston: 1797.] pp. 8. 4to.   JCB.

31932   CHAUNCEY, CHARLES, JUNIOR   1777–1849
AN ORATION, DELIVERED BEFORE THE SOCIETY OF THE P B K; AT THEIR ANNI-
VERSARY MEETING IN THE CITY OF NEW-HAVEN, ON THE EVENING PRECEDING
COMMENCEMENT ANNO DOMINI 1797. BY CHARLES CHAUNCEY, JUN. PUBLISHED
AT THE REQUEST OF THE SOCIETY.
Printed by T. & S. Green, New-Haven. [1797.] pp. 34. 8vo.
AAS. BA. JCB. UTS. YC.

AUCTION
VALUES

31933   THE CHELSEA COURIER. NUMBER 6. WEDNESDAY, JANUARY 4, [—VOL. II. NUMBER 5. WEDNESDAY, DECEMBER 27, 1797.]
Norwich, (Chelsea Society): Printed by Thomas Hubbard. 1797. fol.   CHS. HC.

31934   THE CHESTER GARLAND, IN FOUR PARTS.
Rutland: Printed by Josiah Fay. 1797.

31935   CHURCH, JOHN   1774–1809
AN INAUGURAL DISSERTATION ON CAMPHOR: SUBMITTED TO THE EXAMINATION OF THE REV. JOHN EWING, S. S. T. P. PROVOST; THE TRUSTEES & MEDICAL FACULTY OF THE UNIVERSITY OF PENNSYLVANIA, ON THE 12TH OF MAY, 1797; FOR THE DEGREE OF DOCTOR OF MEDICINE. BY JOHN CHURCH, A. M. OF PHILADELPHIA, MEMBER OF THE PHILADELPHIA MEDICAL AND CHEMICAL SOCIETIES. VIDI SED NON VICI.
Printed by John Thompson, of Philadelphia. 1797. pp. 70. 8vo.
                                               AAS. BM. LOC. NYPL.

31936   CISH, JANE
THE VISION AND WONDERFUL EXPERIENCE OF JANE CISH, SHEWING HOW SHE WAS CONVERTED, AND HOW SHE FELL INTO A TRANCE, ON THE THIRD OF MAY, 1780. AND SAW HEAVEN AND HELL, WITH MANY OTHER STRANGE THINGS: BEING A COPY FROM HER OWN MOUTH, AND PUBLISHED AT THE REQUEST OF SEVERAL OF HER FRIENDS. COME HITHER ALL YE THAT LOVE THE LORD, AND I WILL TELL YE WHAT HE HATH DONE FOR MY SOUL.
Philadelphia: Printed in the year M,DCC,XCVII. pp. (15). 8vo.   AAS.

31937   CITY GAZETTE & [seal] DAILY ADVERTISER. [Motto.] VOL. XV. No. 2941. MONDAY, JANUARY 2, [— No. 3248. SATURDAY. DECEMBER 30, 1797.]
Charleston: Published by Freneau & Paine, Printers to the City, No. 47, Bay. . . . 1797. fol.

31938   CITY GAZETTE & DAILY TELEGRAPHE. NUM. 555. MONDAY, JANUARY 2, [— NUM. 683. WEDNESDAY, MAY 31, 1797.]
[Baltimore:] Printed and published (daily) by Clayland, Dobbin & Co., at the new Printing-Office, No. 36, Market-Street, opposite the Vendue Store. 1797. fol.
The firm of Clayland, Dobbin & Co. was dissolved 30 May, 1797. Thomas E. Clayland, and Thomas Dobbin continuing publication under the firm name of T. E. Clayland and T. Dobbin, and with the changed title of *The Telegraphe and Daily Advertiser.*

31939   CLARKE, JOHN   1755–1798
AN ANSWER TO THE QUESTION, "WHY ARE YOU A CHRISTIAN?" BY JOHN CLARKE, MINISTER OF A CHURCH IN BOSTON. THE FIFTH EDITION.
Printed by Samuel Hall, in Cornhill, Boston. 1797.

31940   —— — AN ANSWER TO THE QUESTION, "WHY ARE YOU A CHRISTIAN?" BY JOHN CLARKE, MINISTER OF A CHURCH IN BOSTON. THE SIXTH EDITION.
Boston: Published by Samuel Hall. October, 1797. pp. 80. 8vo.
With an advertisement signed T. Lindsey.   AAS. BM. JCB. MHS.

31941   CLAY, MATTHEW   1754–1815
[AN OPEN LETTER ON THE POSITION OF FRANCE SINCE THE JAY TREATY WITH ENGLAND IN 1795.]
Philadelphia: July 8, 1797. pp. (2). fol.

31942   CLAYPOOLE'S AMERICAN DAILY ADVERTISER. NUMBER 5570. MONDAY, JANUARY 2, [— NUMBER 5845. SATURDAY, DECEMBER 30, 1797.]
Philadelphia:—Printed by David C. and Septimus Claypoole, No. 48, Market-Street. 1797. fol.   AAS. BM. HSP.

31943   COBBETT, WILLIAM   1762–1835
AN ACCURATE PLAN OF THE BLOCKADE OF CADIZ. PUBLISHED BY PETER PORCUPINE.
PRICE 9D.
> *[Philadelphia: Published by William Cobbett, opposite Christ Church. 1797.]*

31944   —— DIE BLUT-FAHNE, AUSGESTECKET ZUR WARNUNG POLITISCHER WEGWEISER IN
AMERICA, ODER EINE GETREUE ERZÄHLUNG EINER GROSSEN AUZAHL HANDLUNGEN-
DER ABSCHENLICHSTEN GRAUSAMKEITEN, SOLCHE ALS NIE EIN AUGE GESEHEN NIE
EINE ZUNGE AUSGESPROCHEN, ODER DIE EINBILDUNGSKRAFT GEDACHT, EHE DIE
FRANZOISCHE REVOLUTION IHREN ANFANG GENOMMEN HAT. WELCHEN EIN UNTER-
RECHTENDER VERSUCH DER DIESEN SCHRECKLICHEN THATSACHEN BIS AUF IHREN
WAHREN URSPRUNG NACHFORSCHET BEYGEFÜGT IST. AUSGEZIENT MIT VIER TREF-
FENDEN KUPFERSTICHEN. VON PETER PORCUPINE. [Six lines] AUS DES ABT
MAURY'S REDE VOR DER NATIONALE-ASSEMBLIE.
> *Reading: Gedruckt bey Gottlob Jungmann und Comp.* 1797. pp. (2), (2), (2),
> (3), (3), (198), (2), frontispiece, 3 plates. 8vo.   AAS. HSP. LOC.

181st Pennsylvania District Copyright issued to Benjamin Davies, as
Proprietor, 1 June, 1797.

31945   —— A BONE TO GNAW, FOR THE DEMOCRATS; OR, OBSERVATIONS ON A PAMPHLET, EN-
TITLED, "THE POLITICAL PROGRESS OF BRITAIN." THE THIRD EDITION, REVISED.
[Two lines of French from] LA POMPADOUR.
> *Philadelphia: Printed by William Young, for William Cobbett. opposite
> Christ's Church,* 1797. pp. v, (66). 8vo.

Page 2 is misnumbered 41. Another "Third edition revised" was published by Thomas Bradford, in Philadelphia, in 1795.

31946   —— PORCUPINE'S POLITICAL CENSOR, FOR JAN. 1797. CONTAINING, REMARKS ON THE
PROCEEDINGS IN CONGRESS, PAGE 3, MR. PICKERING'S LETTER, 4 ATTACK ON THE
SAME BY SANS-CULOTTE BACHE, 5 OBSERVATIONS ON CITIZEN ADET'S COMPLAINTS
RESPECTING THE FRENCH FLAG AND THE ALMANACK-MAKERS, 8 AN ACCOUNT OF MR.
ADAMS'S ELECTION, WITH REMARKS ON THE CONDUCT OF THE FRENCH EMISSARIES
SUBSEQUENT THERETO, 15 THE FESTIVAL OF FOOLS. THEIR TOASTS, WITH REMARKS,
30 MR. ADAMS'S FAREWEL ADDRESS TO THE SENATE, WITH THE SENATE'S ANSWER.
> *Philadelphia: Published by William Cobbett, opposite Christ Church; where
> all letters to the Publisher are desired to be addressed, post-paid. Price one quar-
> ter of a dollar.* [1797.] pp. 51. 8vo.   JCB. LOC. NYHS. NYPL.

31947   —— PORCUPINE'S POLITICAL CENSOR, FOR MARCH, 1797. CONTAINING, AN INTEREST-
ING LETTER FROM A GENTLEMAN IN SWITZERLAND, TO HIS FRIEND IN AMERICA,
DESCRIBING THE SITUATION OF FRANCE, 53 NOAH WEBSTER'S ATTACK ON PORCU-
PINE, 75 PORCUPINE'S ANSWER, LETTER I. 79 LETTER II. 81 PORCUPINE'S LAST
WILL AND TESTAMENT, 10 INDEX TO THE GAZETTE FOR MARCH, 1797, 117
☞ THERE IS NO CENSOR FOR FEBRUARY, THIS YEAR.
> *Philadelphia: Published by William Cobbett, opposite Christ Church, where
> all letters to the Publisher are desired to be addressed, post paid. Price, one quar-
> ter of a dollar.* [1797.] pp. (2), (2), (53)–123. 8vo.   HC. JCB. LOC. NYHS. NYPL.

31948   —— PORCUPINE'S WORKS. VOL. I. [— II.] [Four line quotation.]
> *Philadelphia: Published by William Cobbett, opposite Christ Church.* [1797.]
> 2 vols. pp. (2), (1), (7); 88; (2). 91–160; [31]; (2), 66; (2), (5), (1), (77); (71);
> iv, (64). Vol. II. (2), (1), (1); (2), (37)–104; (2), (67)–134, plate; (2), (173)–
> (240); (23); (56); (2), (251)–327; (78); 64. 8vo.   NL. NYPL.

This is the second collected issue.

COBBETT, WILLIAM, continued.

Second title: OBSERVATIONS ON THE EMIGRATION OF DR. JOSEPH PRIESTLEY: TO WHICH IS ADDED, A COMPREHENSIVE STORY OF A FARMER'S BULL. [Four lines of French from] BOILEAU.

[Philadelphia: Printed by Richard Folwell, No. 33 Carter's Alley. February 8th, 1795.] pp. 88.

Second heading: THE SHORT BUT COMPREHENSIVE STORY OF A FARMER'S BULL. pp. (83)—88.

Copyright secured according to law. This is Bradford's second Philadelphia edition although not so marked.

Third title: A BONE TO GNAW, FOR THE DEMOCRATS; OR, OBSERVATIONS ON A PAMPHLET, ENTITLED, "THE POLITICAL PROGRESS OF BRITAIN." THE THIRD EDITION, REVISED. [Two lines of French from] LA POMPADOUR.

Philadelphia: Printed by William Young, for William Cobbett, opposite Christ's Church. 1797. pp. (2), (91)–(160).

Fourth title: A KICK FOR A BITE; OR, REVIEW UPON REVIEW; WITH A CRITICAL ESSAY ON THE WORKS OF MRS. S. ROWSON; IN A LETTER TO THE EDITOR, OR EDITORS, OF THE AMERICAN MONTHLY REVIEW. SECOND EDITION. BY PETER PORCUPINE. "AUTANTS DE TRAITS QUE D'ENNEMIS."

Philadelphia: Printed by Thomas Bradford. 1796. pp. [31.]

Fifth title: PART II. A BONE TO GNAW, FOR THE DEMOCRATS; CONTAINING, 1ST, OBSERVATIONS ON A PATRIOTIC PAMPHLET ENTITLED, "PROCEEDINGS OF THE UNITED IRISHMEN." 2DLY, DEMOCRATIC MEMOIRES; OR AN ACCOUNT OF SOME RECENT FEATS PERFORMED BY THE FRENCHIFIED CITIZENS OF THE UNITED STATES OF AMERICA. BY PETER PORCUPINE.

Philadelphia: Printed by William Young, for William Cobbett, opposite Christ's Church. 1797. pp. (2), (66).

Sixth title: A LITTLE PLAIN ENGLISH, ADDRESSED TO THE PEOPLE OF THE UNITED STATES, ON THE TREATY, NEGOCIATED WITH HIS BRITANNIC MAJESTY, AND ON THE CONDUCT OF THE PRESIDENT RELATIVE THERETO; IN ANSWER TO "THE LETTERS OF FRANKLIN." WITH A SUPPLEMENT CONTAINING AN ACCOUNT OF THE TURBULENT AND FACTIOUS PROCEEDINGS OF THE OPPOSERS OF THE TREATY. BY PETER PORCUPINE. SECOND EDITION. [Eight lines from] SHAKESPEARE.

Philadelphia: From the Free and Independent Political & Literary Press of Thomas Bradford, Printer, Bookseller & Stationer, No. 8, South Front Street. 1796. pp. (2), (5), (1), (77).

Seventh title: SECOND EDITION. A NEW YEAR'S GIFT TO THE DEMOCRATS; OR OBSERVATIONS ON A PAMPHLET, ENTITLED, "A VINDICATION OF MR. RANDOLPH'S RESIGNATION." BY PETER PORCUPINE. [Six lines from] SWIFT.

Philadelphia: Published by Thomas Bradford, Printer, Book-Seller & Stationer, No. 8, South Front-Street. 1796. pp. (71).

Eighth title: A PROSPECT FROM THE CONGRESS-GALLERY, DURING THE SESSION, BEGUN DECEMEER 7, 1795. CONTAINING, THE PRESIDENT'S SPEECH, THE ADDRESSES OF BOTH HOUSES, SOME OF TH *[sic]* DEBATES IN THE SENATE, AND ALL THE PRINCIPAL DEBATES IN THE HOUSE OF REPRESENTATIVES; EACH DEBATE BEING BROUGHT UNDER ONE HEAD, AND SO DIGESTED AND SIMPLIFIED AS TO GIVE THE READER THE COMPLETEST VIEW OF THE PROCEEDINGS WITH THE LEAST POSSIBLE FATIGUE. WITH OCCASIONAL REMARKS BY PETER PORCUPINE. THE SECOND EDITION.

Philadelphia: Published by Thomas Bradford, Printer, Bookseller & Stationer, No. 8, South Front-Street. 1796. pp. (iv), (64).

COBBETT, WILLIAM, continued.

Ninth title: PORCUPINE'S WORKS. VOL. II. [Four line quotation.]

Philadelphia: Published by William Cobbett, opposite Christ Church. [1797.]
pp. (2), (1), (1).

Tenth title: THE POLITICAL CENSOR, OR MONTHLY REVIEW OF THE MOST INTEREST-
ING POLITICAL OCCURRENCES, RELATIVE TO THE UNITED STATES OF AMERICA. [For
March, 1796.] BY PETER PORCUPINE. THE THIRD EDITION.

*Philadelphia: Printed for, and sold by, William Cobbett, No. 25, North Second
Street, opposite Christ Church.* M.DCC.XCVI. pp. (2), (37)–(104).

Eleventh title: PORCUPINE'S POLITICAL CENSOR, FOR APRIL, 1797 [*sic* 1796.] CON-
TAINING, DEBATES IN THE HOUSE OF REPRESENTATIVES CONTINUED 67 ON PAPERS
RELATIVE TO THE TREATY WITH GREAT BRITAIN 69 PRESIDENT'S MESSAGE TO
THE HOUSE OF REPRESENTATIVES IN REPLY TO THEIR REQUEST OF A COPY OF HIS
INSTRUCTIONS TO MR. JAY 73 PETER PORCUPINE'S REMARKS ON THE SAME 75
RESOLUTION BY WAY OF PROTEST AGAINST THE PRESIDENT'S MESSAGE, WITH RE-
MARKS 85 RESOLUTION FOR SETTING ASIDE THE BRITISH TREATY 100 PETER
PORCUPINE'S REMARKS ON THE SAME 101 TRAITEROUS ADVERTISEMENT OF THE
BANKRUPTS OF VIRGINIA 104 LOYAL ADDRESS OF THE VIRGINIANS TO THE KING
OF GREAT BRITAIN IN THE YEAR 1769 106 REVIEW OF MONSIEUR SWANWICK'S
TITLES AND HIS POETICAL WRITINGS 111 LORD GRENVILLE'S RECEPTION OF CITI-
ZEN GALLATIN, ENVOY EXTRAORDINARY TO THE COURT OF GREAT BRITAIN 120
LETTER FROM COUSIN HEDGE-HOG OF NEW-YORK TO PETER PORCUPINE 131

[*Philadelphia: Published by William Cobbett, opposite Christ Church.* 1797.]
pp. (2), (67)–134, plate.

Twelfth title: THE POLITICAL CENSOR, OR MONTHLY REVIEW OF THE MOST INTER-
ESTING POLITICAL OCCURRENCES, RELATIVE TO THE UNITED STATES OF AMERICA
[For May, 1796.] BY PETER PORCUPINE. THE THIRD EDITION.

*Philadelphia: Printed for, and sold by, William Cobbett, No. 25, North Second
Street, opposite Christ Church.* M.DCC.XCVI. pp. (2), (173)–(240).

Thirteenth title: THE SCARE-CROW; BEING AN INFAMOUS LETTER, SENT TO MR. JOHN
OLDDEN, THREATENING DESTRUCTION TO HIS HOUSE, AND VIOLENCE TO THE PERSON
OF HIS TENANT, WILLIAM COBBETT. WITH REMARKS ON THE SAME. BY PETER
PORCUPINE. THE SECOND EDITION.

*Philadelphia: Printed for, and sold by, William Cobbett, North Second Street,
opposite Christ Church.* M.DCC.XCVI. pp. (23).

Fourteenth title: THE LIFE AND ADVENTURES OF PETER PORCUPINE, WITH A FULL
AND FAIR ACCOUNT OF ALL HIS AUTHORING TRANSACTIONS; BEING A SURE AND IN-
FALLIBLE GUIDE FOR ALL ENTERPRISING YOUNG MEN WHO WISH TO MAKE A FORTUNE
BY WRITING PAMPHLETS. BY PETER PORCUPINE HIMSELF. [Two lines from]
SHAKESPEARE. SECOND EDITION.

*Philadelphia: Printed for, and sold by, William Cobbett, North Second Street,
opposite Christ Church.* Oct. 1796. pp. (56).

Fifteenth title: PORCUPINE'S POLITICAL CENSOR, FOR SEPT. 1796. CONTAINING,
THE LIFE OF TOM PAINE, INTERSPERSED WITH REMARKS AND REFLECTIONS 251
REMARKS ON "A ROASTER FOR PETER PORCUPINE" 301—"THE BLUE SHOP"
301—"PORCUPINE, A PRINT" 302—"HISTORY OF A PORCUPINE" 305 "A PILL
FOR PORCUPINE" 306—"THE IMPOSTOR DETECTED;" WITH ANECDOTES OF THE
FAMILY OF LORD BRADFORD, 309 [Second edition.]

*Philadelphia: Published by William Cobbett, opposite Christ Church; where all
letters to the Publisher are desired to be addressed, post-paid.* [1797.] pp. (2),
(251)–327.

COBBETT, WILLIAM, continued.
Sixteenth title: PORCUPINE'S POLITICAL CENSOR, FOR NOVEMBER, 1796. CONTAIN-
ING OBSERVATIONS ON THE INSOLENT AND SEDITIOUS NOTES, COMMUNICATED TO THE
PEOPLE OF THE UNITED STATES BY THE LATE FRENCH MIN STER ADET;

*Philadelphia: Printed for, and sold by, William Cobbett, opposite Christ
Church. Nov.* 1796. pp. (78).

Seventeenth title: PORCUPINE'S POLITICAL CENSOR, FOR DECEMBER, 1796. CON-
TAINING, REMARKS ON THE DEBATES IN CONGRESS, PARTICULARLY ON THE TIMIDITY
OF THE LANGUAGE HELD TOWARDS FRANCE. ALSO, A LETTER TO THE INFAMOUS
TOM PAINE IN ANSWER TO HIS BRUTAL ATTACK ON THE FEDERAL CONSTITUTION,
AND ON THE CONDUCT AND CHARACTER OF GENERAL WASHINGTON. THE SECOND
EDITION.

*Philadelphia: Published by William Cobbett, opposite Christ's Church. Price,
one quarter of a dollar.* [1797.] pp. (64).

31949 COBBY, JOHN
POETIC ESSAYS ON THE GLORY OF CHRIST, AND ON THE DIVINITY AND WORK OF THE
HOLY SPIRIT. BY JOHN COBBY. PRICE EIGHT CENTS.

New-York: Printed by John Tiebout, No. 358, Pearl-Street, for the Author.
1797. pp. (16). 8vo.   BM. LOC. NYHS.

31950 COCHRAN, JAMES
A [Metallic pocket] CALENDAR. JAMES COCHRAN, NEW-HAVEN.
Made and sold by James Cochran, Chapel-Street, New-Haven. 1797.

Connecticut District Copyright, issued to James Cochran, as Author,
8 February, 1797.

31951 COCHRUN, SIMON
THE EXTRAORDINARY LIFE AND CONFESSION OF CHARLES O'DONNELL, WHO WAS EX-
ECUTED ON THE 19TH DAY OF JUNE, 1797, AT MORGAN-TOWN, MONONGAHELA-
COUNTY, VIRG. FOR THE WILLFUL MURDER OF HIS SON. THIS ACCOUNT WAS TAKEN
FROM HIMSELF BY THE REV. SIMON COCHRUN, OF MONONGAHELA-COUNTY, TWO
DAYS BEFORE HIS EXECUTION, IN WHICH ARE RECOUNTED SOME OF THE MOST EX-
TRAORDINARY ACTS OF VILLANY AND CRUELTY EVER RECORDED.

Washington, (Pennsylvania): Printed by John Colerick. 1797.

31952 COLDEN, CADWALLADER   1688–1776
THE HISTORY OF THE SIX INDIAN NATIONS IN NORTH AMERICA: CONTAINING AN
ACCURATE ACCOUNT OF ALL THEIR TREATIES, AND BATTLES WITH THE EUROPEANS
AND OTHERS, AND ALL OTHER REMARKABLE TRANSACTIONS FROM THE YEAR 1601
TO THE PRESENT TIME; THE FORMER PART OF IT IS THE PRODUCTION OF CADWAL-
LADER COLDEN, ESQ. FORMERLY GOVERNOR OF THE STATE OF NEW-YORK. TO
WHICH IS ADDED, A HISTORY OF THE RAPID SETTLEMENT AND OF ALL THE LATE
DISCOVERIES OF THE MANY CURIOSITIES IN THE WESTERN COUNTRY, WITH A SKETCH
OF GENERAL SULLIVAN'S CAMPAIGN TO THE WESTWARD AGAINST THE INDIANS. BY
ELIJAH WARREN.

Troy: Printed? by Luther Pratt. 1797.

Proposals for printing the above were made by Luther Pratt at Troy,
New York.

31953   A COLLECTION OF POEMS, ON RELIGIOUS AND MORAL SUBJECTS. EXTRACTED FROM THE MOST CELEBRATED AUTHORS. COLLECTA REVIRESCUNT.

Elizabeth-Town: Printed by Shepard Kollock. for Cornelius Davis, No. 94, Water-Street, New-York. M,DCC,XCVII. pp. (2), 124: 39. 12mo.

AAS. BM. JCB. LOC. NYPL.

Contains,—The last epiphany,—On the general conflagration, and ensuing judgment, by Pomfret,—The day of judgment, by Watts,—The grave, by Blair,—An elegy in a country church-yard, by Gray,—The hermit, by Parnell,—The hermit, by Beattie,—On the shortness of human life.—The day of judgment, by Glynn,—Death, by Porteus.

Second title: THE LAST DAY. A POEM. IN THREE BOOKS. VENIT SUMMA DIES. VIRGIL. BY EDWARD YOUNG, L. L. D.

Elizabeth-Town: Printed by Shepard Kollock, for Cornelius Davis, No. 94, Water-Street, New-York. M,DCC,XCVII. pp. 39.

31954   COLMAN, GEORGE, JUNIOR   1762–1836
WHEN THE HOLLOW DRUM. SONG IN THE MOUNTAINEERS.

Baltimore: Published by I. Carr. 1797.

31955   THE COLUMBIAN ALMANAC FOR THE YEAR OF OUR LORD, 1798.

Printed for Mathew Carey, Philadelphia, by William and Robert Dickson, Lancaster. [1797.] pp. (40). 16mo.   LOC.

Contains, Curious adventures of a Hessian during the late war.

31956   THE COLUMBIAN ALMANAC: OR, THE NORTH-AMERICAN CALENDAR. FOR THE YEAR OF OUR LORD, 1798, BEING THE SECOND AFTER LEAP YEAR. [Cut of] ARMS OF THE UNITED STATES.

Wilmington: Printed and sold by Peter Brynberg, in Market-street. [1797.] pp. (36). 12mo.   LOC.

31957   COLUMBIAN [U.S.A. in Star] CENTINEL. NO. 35 OF VOL. XXVI. WHOLE NO. 2115. WEDNESDAY, JANUARY 4, [— NO. 34. OF VOL. XXVIII. SATURDAY, DECEMBER 30, 1797.]

Printed and published on Wednesdays and Saturdays, by Benjamin Russell, Printer to the United States, for the northern States. [south side] State-Street [next to the Coffee-House], Boston, (Massachusetts). 1797. fol.

AAS. BA. BM. EI. HC. LOC. MHS. NYHS.

31958   THE COLUMBIAN MIRROR AND ALEXANDRIA GAZETTE. VOL. V. NO. 584. TUESDAY, JANUARY 3, [—VOL. VI. NO. 737. SATURDAY, DECEMBER 30, 1797.]

Alexandria: Printed every Tuesday, Thursday, and Saturday, by Ellis Price and Henry Gird, jun. 1797. fol.   AAS.

With the issue for November 21st, Gird withdrew temporarily.

31959   THE COLUMBIAN MUSE, A SELECTION OF AMERICAN POETRY FROM VARIOUS AUTHORS OF ESTABLISHED REPUTATIONS, VIZ. BARLOW, HOPKINSON, LIVINGSTON, DWIGHT, TRUMBULL, FRENEAU, SMITH, HUMPHREYS, JAMES, PRICHARD, HOPKINS, LATHROP, DAWES, FENTHAM, LADD, BRADFORD, BAYARD, EVANS, DUNLAP, ALSOP, &C.

Philadelphia: Printed by James Carey, No. 83, North Second-Street. [1797.]

31960   COLUMBIAN MUSEUM & SAVANNAH ADVERTISER. [Motto.] VOL. I. No. 87. TUES-
DAY, JANUARY 3, [— VOL. II. No. 87. FRIDAY, DECEMBER 29, 1797.]
*Savannah—Published on Tuesday and Friday, by Powers & Seymour, in
Market-Square, opposite Mr. Hill's Tavern. . . .* 1797. fol.   AAS. GHS.

Titus Powers deceased July 26th, the issue for that date appearing in
heavy black borders, and publication was continued by Gurdon I. Seymour alone to the issue for December 13th, when Philip D. Woolhopter
was admitted to junior partnership under his own name. In April, the
Printing-Office was moved to "On the Bay."

31961   THE COLUMBIAN SONGSTER, A JOVIAL COMPANION: BEING A COLLECTION OF TWO
HUNDRED AND TWENTY CHOICE SONGS, SELECTED FROM VARIOUS VOLUMES AND DE-
TACHED PARCELS—OF WHICH NEAR FIFTY ARE AMERICAN PRODUCTIONS. MIRTH,
LOVE AND SENTIMENT ARE HERE HAPPILY BLENDED, THE CHASTE TO THE CHASTEST
EAR UNOFFENDED.
From Greenleaf's Press. New-York, 1797. pp. viii, 232. 16mo.   BPL.

31962   COMBS, MOSES N.
A COLLECTION OF ESSAYS ON A VARIETY OF SUBJECTS IN PROSE AND VERSE.
Newark: Printed by Daniel Dodge & Co. 1797. pp. 84. 8vo.   NJHS.

31963   —— A MAGAZINE: CONTAINING A VARIETY OF ESSAYS ON SCRIPTURE. [Eight lines of
Scripture texts.] [July—October, 1797.]
*Newark—-Printed by D. Dodge, & Co. For Moses N. Combs.—*1797.—pp. 96.
8vo.   NYHS.

31964   COMMERCIAL [cut of ship] ADVERTISER. VOL. I. NUMBER 1. MONDAY, OCTOBER
2, [— NUMBER 78. SATURDAY, DECEMBER 30, 1797.]
*[New-York:] Published (daily) at No. 40, Pine-Street, by Geo. F. Hopkins,
Printer of the Laws of the United States for the District of New-York.* 1797. fol.
   BA. LCP. LOC. NYHS.

In continuation of *The Minerva & Mercantile Evening Advertiser.* The
issue for October 2d. has been reproduced in facsimile.

31965   A COMPENDIOUS HISTORY OF ROME, WITH AN APPENDIX, CONTAINING SKETCHES OF
THE HISTORY OF CARTHAGE, MACEDON, SPAIN, PONTUS, CIMBRI, GAUL, NUMANTIA,
ENGLAND, GERMANY, PARTHIA, MUNDA, PHILIPPI, RHODES, SICILY, AND SYRACUSE.
AS CONNECTED WITH ROMAN HISTORY. VOL. I. [— II.]
*Philadelphia; Printed by Thomas Dobson, at the Stone-House, No. 41, S.
Second-Street.* 1797. 2vols. pp. (2), 360; (2), 428. 12mo.   AAS.

31966   THE COMPLETE FORTUNE TELLER; OR, AN INFALLIBLE GUIDE TO THE HIDDEN DE-
CREES OF FATE; BEING A NEW AND REGULAR SYSTEM FOR FORETELLING FUTURE
EVENTS, BY ASTROLOGY, PHYSIOGNOMY, PALMISTRY, MOLES, CARDS, DREAMS, &C.
Boston: 1797. frontispiece. 16mo.

31967   CONGREGATIONAL CHURCH IN CONNECTICUT.
AN ADDRESS OF THE GENERAL ASSOCIATION OF CONNECTICUT, TO THE DISTRICT
ASSOCIATIONS ON THE SUBJECT OF A MISSIONARY SOCIETY; TOGETHER WITH SUM-
MARIES AND EXTRACTS FROM LATE EUROPEAN PUBLICATIONS ON MISSIONS TO THE
HEATHEN.
*Norwich: Printed by Thomas Hubbard.—*1797.—pp. 32. 8vo.
   AAS. BM. HC. MHS. NYPL. UTS.

31968   CONGREGATIONAL CHURCH in Connecticut, continued.
—— A Continuation of the Narrative of the missions to the new settle-
ments, according to the appointment of the General Association of the
State of Connecticut: together with an account [*sic*] of the receipts and
expenditures of the money contributed for the support of the mission-
aries, agreeably to an Act of the General Assembly of the State.
New-Haven—Printed by T. &. S. Green. 1797. pp. (15.) 8vo.
AAS. JCB. MHS. NYPL. UTS.

31969   —— *Heading:* On the ordination of deacons. [The substance of certain manuscripts, read before the North Association of Litchfield County, 27 September,
1797.]
[*Litchfield: Printed by Thomas Collier.* 1797.] pp. 11. 12mo.   AAS.

31970   CONGREGATIONAL CHURCH in Vermont.
Articles of consociation, recommended to a number of churches in the
western districts of Vermont, and parts adjacent, by their Representatives met in Convention, at Rutland, June 6th, A. D. 1797.
Fairhaven. Printed by J. P. Spooner. 1797. pp. 15. 16mo.   AAS.

31971   CONNECTICUT. State.
[Seal,] Acts and laws, made and passed by the General Court or Assembly
of the State of Connecticut, in America, holden at Hartford, (in said
State) on the second Thursday of May, Anno Domini 1797. [Colophon:]
Hartford: Printed by Elisha Babcock. [1797.] pp. 455–468. 8vo.
This is the official issue.   CHS. JCB. PLA.

31972   —— — [Seal.] Acts and laws, made and passed in and by the General Court
or Assembly of the State of Connecticut, in America, holden at Hartford,
(in said State) on the second Thursday of May, Anno Domini 1797.
[*Hartford: Printed by Hudson and Goodwin.* 1797.] pp. 455–468. 8vo.
CHS. YC.

31973   —— —· [Seal.] Acts and laws, made and passed in and by the General Court
or Assembly of the State of Connecticut, in America, holden at New-
Haven, (in said State) on the second Thursday of October, Anno Domini
1797. [Colophon:]
Hartford: Printed by Elisha Babcock. [1797.] pp. 469–480. 8vo.
This the official issue.   CHS. JCB. PLA.

31974   —— — [Seal.] Acts and laws, made and passed in and by the General Court
or Assembly of the State of Connecticut, in America, holden at New-
Haven, (in said State) on the second Thursday of October, Anno Domini
1797.
[*Hartford: Printed by Hudson and Goodwin.* 1797.] pp. 469–480. 8vo.
CHS. CSL. YC.

31975   —— By his excellency Oliver Wolcott, esq. governor and commander in
chief of the State of Connecticut. A Proclamation. . . . , appoint Friday, the fourteenth day of April next, to be observed as a day of public
humiliation, fasting, and prayer throughout this State . . . All servile
labour on said day is forbidden. Given at Litchfield, this seventeenth
day of March, in the year of our Lord, one thousand seven hundred and
ninety-seven, and of the independence of the United States of America
the twenty first. Oliver Wolcott. By his excellency's command. Samuel
Wyllys, secretary.
[*Litchfield: Printed by Thomas Collier?* 1797.] Broadside. fol.

CONNECTICUT. STATE, continued.

31976 —— BY HIS EXCELLENCY OLIVER WOLCOTT, ESQUIRE, GOVERNOR AND COMMANDER IN CHIEF OF THE STATE OF CONNECTICUT. A PROCLAMATION. . . . APPOINT THURSDAY, THE SIXTEENTH DAY OF NOVEMBER NEXT, TO BE OBSERVED AS A DAY OF THANKSGIVING AND PRAISE TO ALMIGHTY GOD, THROUGHOUT THIS STATE . . . GIVEN AT LITCHFIELD, THIS 25TH DAY OF OCTOBER, IN THE YEAR OF OUR LORD ONE THOUSAND SEVEN HUNDRED AND NINETY SEVEN, AND OF THE INDEPENDENCE OF THE UNITED STATES OF AMERICA THE TWENTY-SECOND. OLIVER WOLCOTT. BY HIS EXCELLENCY'S COMMAND. SAMUEL WYLLYS, SECR'Y.

[Litchfield : Printed by Thomas Collier ? 1797.] Broadside. fol.

31977 THE CONNECTICUT COURANT. VOL. XXXII. NUMBER 1667. MONDAY, JANUARY 2, [— NUMBER 1718. MONDAY, DECEMBER 25, 1797.]

Hartford : Printed by Hudson & Goodwin, opposite the North Meeting-House. 1797. fol.   AAS. CHS. YC.

31978 —— GUILLOTINA, FOR 1797. ADDRESSED TO THE READERS OF THE CONNECTICUT COURANT. . . . [By Lemuel Hopkins.] HARTFORD, JANUARY 1, 1797.

Hartford : Printed by Hudson and Goodwin. 1797. pp. (2). fol.

31979 —— — GUILLOTINA, FOR JANUARY 1, 1797. ADDRESSED TO THE READERS OF THE CONNECTICUT COURANT. [By Lemuel Hopkins. Four columns.]

[Philadelphia : 1797.] Broadside. fol.   AAS.

31980 CONNECTICUT [arms] GAZETTE. QUI TRANSTULIT SUSTINET. VOL. XXXIII. NO. 1730. THURSDAY, JANUARY 5, [— VOL. XXXIV. NO. 1781. WEDNESDAY, DECEMBER 27, 1797.]

New-London :—Printed and published by Samuel Green, at his Office adjoining the Bank. 1797. fol.   CHS.

31981 CONNECTICUT JOURNAL. VOL. XXX. No. 1523. WEDNESDAY, JANUARY 4, [— No. 1574. THURSDAY, DECEMBER 28, 1797.]

New-Haven : Printed by Thomas and Samuel Green, opposite the Post-Office. 1797. fol.   AAS. LOC. YC.

31982 COOK, JAMES   1728–1779

CAPTAIN COOK'S THREE VOYAGES TO THE PACIFIC OCEAN. THE FIRST PERFORMED IN THE YEARS 1768, 1769, 1770 AND 1771: THE SECOND IN 1772, 1773, 1774 AND 1775: THE THIRD AND LAST IN 1776, 1777, 1778, 1779 AND 1780. FAITHFULLY ABRIDGED FROM THE QUARTO EDITIONS. CONTAINING A PARTICULAR RELATION OF ALL THE INTERESTING TRANSACTIONS DURING THE SEVERAL VOYAGES. TO WHICH IS PREFIXED, THE LIFE OF CAPTAIN COOK. COMPLETE IN TWO VOLUMES. VOL. I, [— II.] [ILLUSTRATED WITH EIGHT HANDSOME COPPERPLATE ENGRAVINGS.]

Printed at Boston, by Manning and Loring, for Thomas & Andrews and D. West. Jan. 1797. 2 vols. pp. 315, 4 plates; 351, 4 plates. 12mo. AAS. HC. LOC.

31983 —— — CAPTAIN COOK'S THREE VOYAGES TO THE PACIFIC OCEAN. THE FIRST PERFORMED IN THE YEARS 1768, 1769, 1770, AND 1771. THE SECOND IN 1772, 1773, 1774, AND 1775. THE THIRD AND LAST IN 1776, 1777, 1778, 1779, AND 1780. FAITHFULLY ABRIDGED FROM THE QUARTO EDITIONS. CONTAINING A PARTICULAR RELATION OF ALL THE INTERESTING TRANSACTIONS DURING THE SEVERAL VOYAGES. TO WHICH IS PREFIXED, THE LIFE OF CAPT. COOK. COMPLETE IN TWO VOLUMES. ILLUSTRATED WITH EIGHT HANDSOME COPPERPLATE ENGRAVINGS,

Philadelphia : Printed by James Carey, No. 83, North Second-Street. 1797. 2 vols.

81984   COOPER, SAMUEL
The History of North America. Containing, a review of the customs and manners of the original inhabitants, the first settlement of the British Colonies, their rise and progress, from the earliest period to the time of their becoming united, free and independent States. By the Rev. Mr. Cooper.

Philadelphia: Printed by Henry Schweitzer. 1797. pp.158. 12mo. BA. NYPL.

81985   COOPER, SAMUEL   1772–1798
A Dissertation on the properties and effects of the datura stramonium, or common thorn-apple; and on its use in medicine. By Samuel Cooper, member of the Chemical and Medical Societies of Philadelphia.

Philadelphia: Printed by Samuel H. Smith. M,DCC,XCVII. pp. 58. 8vo.
AAS. BM. LOC. 8GO.

81986   COOPER, WILLIAM
The Promised seed. A sermon, preached to God's ancient Israel the Jews, at Sion-Chapel, Whitechapel, London, August 28th, 1796. By a Young man completing that day his 20th year.

Boston: Printed by S. Hall, No. 52, Cornhill. 1797.

81987   —— — The Promised seed. A sermon preached to God's ancient Israel, the Jews, at Sion-Chapel, White Chapel, London on Sunday afternoon, August 28, 1796. By William Cooper. To which are added, the hymns that were sung, and the prayers that were offered up, before and after the sermon.

London, printed. Re-printed at Concord, (New Hampshire) by Geo. Hough, for Francis Mitchel, of Hopkinton. October—1797. pp. 30. 8vo. JCB.

81988   —— — The Promised seed. A sermon preached to God's ancient Israel the Jews, at Sion Chapel, Whitechapel, London, on Sunday afternoon, August 28, 1796. By William Cooper.

Newburyport: Printed by William Barrett. 1797.

81989   —— — The Promised seed. A sermon preached to God's ancient Israel, the Jews, at Sion Chapel, White-Chapel, London, August 28, 1796. By William Cooper. To which are added, the hymns that were offered up before and after the sermon.

Portsmouth, New-Hampshire: Printed by Charles Peirce. August, 12, 1797.

81990   —— — The Promised seed. A sermon preached to God's ancient Israel, the Jews, at Sion Chapel, White-Chapel, London, August 28, 1796. By William Cooper. To which are added, the hymns that were sung, and the prayers that were offered up before and after the sermon.

Portsmouth, New-Hampshire: Printed by Charles Peirce. September, 1797.

81991   —— — The Promised seed. A sermon preached to God's ancient Israel, the Jews, at Sion Chapel, White-Chapel, London. August 28, 1796. By William Cooper. To which are added, the hymns that were sung, and the prayers that were offered up before and after the sermon.

Portsmouth, New-Hampshire: Printed by Charles Peirce. October 14, 1797.

81992   —— — The Promised seed. A sermon preached to God's ancient Israel, the Jews, at Sion Chapel, White-Chapel, London. August 28, 1796. By William Cooper.

Windsor: Printed by Alden Spooner. 1797.

31993   A COPY OF A LETTER, WRITTEN BY OUR BLESSED LORD AND SAVIOUR, JESUS CHRIST, AND FOUND UNDER A GREAT STONE, 65 YEARS AFTER HIS CRUCIFIXION.
[Boston:] Printed at Russell's Office, near Liberty Pole. 1797. pp. 8. 16mo.

31994   —— A COPY OF A LETTER, WRITTEN BY OUR BLESSED LORD AND SAVIOR JESUS CHRIST, AND FOUND UNDER A GREAT STONE, SIXTY-FIVE YEARS AFTER HIS CRUCIFIXION. FAITHFULLY TRANSLATED FROM THE ORIGINAL HEBREW COPY, UNDER THE INSPECTION OF SEVERAL EMINENT CHRISTIANS AT MESOPOTAMIA.
Cooperstown: Printed by Elihu Phinney. 1797.

31995   CORRAN, WILLIAM   –1794
A SHOCKING NARRATIVE OF THE MURDER OF MR. JOSEPH PORTER, BY CAPT. WILLIAM CORRAN; ON BOARD OF THE BRIG FALMOUTH, THE 27TH DAY OF MAY, 1794. BEING ON A VOYAGE FROM PORT-ROYAL, IN JAMAICA, TO BELFAST, IN IRELAND. CONTAINING AN ACCOUNT OF THE CONDUCT OF THE CAPTAIN, PREVIOUS TO THE MURDER; ALSO, THE SECURING OF HIM BY THE PEOPLE AFTERWARDS; WHO THEN PUT INTO A PORT NEAR HALIFAX, WHERE THE CAPTAIN WAS SENT, TRIED, AND SENTENCED TO BE HANGED, WHICH SENTENCE WAS PUT IN EXECUTION ON MONDAY THE 21ST OF JULY, 1794.
Rutland: Printed by Josiah Fay, 1797.

31996   COURIER OF NEW HAMPSHIRE. NO. 48. VOL. VII. WHOLE NO. 360. TUESDAY, JANUARY 3, [— NO. 47. VOL. VIII. WHOLE NO. 411. TUESDAY, DECEMBER 26, 1797.]
Devoted to news and national politicks: Published by George Hough, at Concord. 1797. fol.

31997   COURRIER FRANÇAIS. (NUMÉRO 529) (ANNÉE IIIÉME) PHILADELPHIE, 13 NIVÔSE (LUNDI 2 JANVIER 1797, VIEUX STYLE) L'AN CINQUIÉME DE LA RÉPUBLIQUE FRANÇAISE UNE ET INDIVISIBLE. [—(NUMÉRO 218) ANNÉE IVME PHILADELPHIE, 10 NIVÔSE (SAMEDI 30 DÉCEMBRE 1797, VIEUX STYLE) L'AN SIXIEME DE LA RÉPUBLIQUE FRANÇAISE UNE ET INDIVISIBLE.
[A Philadelphie.] Publié et Imprimé par Parent, Rue Vine, No. 85. [1797.]
pp. (1357)–(1706); (1)–(876). fol.   NYPL.

In April, the office of publication was removed to Cinquième Rue Sud, No. 32.

31998   COUSTOS, JEAN
THE UNPARALLELED SUFFERINGS OF JOHN COUSTOS, WHO NINE TIMES UNDERWENT THE MOST CRUEL TORTURES INVENTED BY MAN, AND WAS SENTENCED TO THE GALLEY FOUR YEARS, BY COMMAND OF THE INQUISITORS AT LISBON, IN ORDER TO EXTORT FROM HIM THE SECRETS OF FREEMASONRY; FROM WHENCE HE WAS RELEASED BY THE INTERPOSITION OF THE KING OF GREAT BRITAIN. WITH AN ACCOUNT OF THE INQUISITION, A COLLECTION OF MASONIC SONGS, AND A LIST OF REGULAR LODGES.
New-London: Printed and sold by Charles Holt. 1797. pp. 280. 8vo.

31999   —— — FREE-MASONRY. UNPARALLELED SUFFERINGS OF JOHN COUSTOS, WHO NINE TIMES UNDERWENT THE MOST CRUEL TORTURES EVER INVENTED BY MAN, AND SENTENCED TO THE GALLEY FOUR YEARS, BY COMMAND OF THE INQUISITORS AT LISBON, IN ORDER TO EXTORT FROM HIM THE SECRETS OF FREE-MASONRY; FROM WHENCE HE WAS RELEASED BY THE GRACIOUS INTERPOSITION OF HIS LATE MAJESTY, KING GEORGE II. TO THIS EDITION IS ADDED, A SELECTION OF MASONIC SONGS, AND A COMPLETE LIST OF LODGES, FOREIGN AND DOMESTIC.
*New-York: Printed by Jacob S. Mott, for Charles Smith, No. 51, Maiden-Lane.—1797.—*pp. (4), ii, iv, 282. 12mo.   JCB.

32000   CRANE, ISAAC WATTS
     AN ORATION DELIVERED IN THE PRESBYTERIAN CHURCH, AT NEWARK, ON THE
     FOURTH OF JULY, 1797, AT THE REQUEST OF THE CITIZENS OF NEWARK, IT BEING
     THE TWENTY-FIRST ANNIVERSARY OF AMERICAN INDEPENDENCE. BY ISAAC WATTS
     CRANE, A. M. PUBLISHED AT THE REQUEST OF A RESPECTABLE NUMBER OF THE
     AUDITORS. [Two lines from] PUBLIUS.
        Newark: Printed by John Woods. 1797. pp. 24. 12mo.   NJHS.

32001   CRAWFORD, CHARLES
     THE DYING PROSTITUTE. A POEM. BY CHARLES CRAWFORD, ESQ. [Four lines from]
     WHOLE DUTY OF WOMAN. BY A LADY. A NEW EDITION.
        Philadelphia: 1797. pp. 12. 12mo.   BU.

32002   CRISP, STEPHEN   1628–1692
     A SHORT HISTORY OF A LONG TRAVEL FROM BABYLON TO BETHEL.
        Printed in New-Haven—1797. pp. (23). 8vo.   AAS.

32003   CROSS, JOHN C.
     THE PURSE; OR, BENEVOLENT TAR. A MUSICAL DRAMA, IN ONE ACT, AS PERFORMED
     AT THE BOSTON THEATRE, FEDERAL-STREET. BY J. C. CROSS. (THE MUSIC BY
     MR. REEVE.)
        Boston: Printed for W. Pelham, No. 59, Cornhill. 1797. pp. 24. 12mo.
                                                     AAS. BPL.

32004   CROUCH, NATHANIEL   1632–1725
     THE TRAVELS OF FOURTEEN ENGLISHMEN TO JERUSALEM. IN THE YEAR 1669.
        Keene—(Newhampshire): Compiled by, & Printed [by Henry Blake & Co.]
     for Amos Taylor. M,DCC,XCV pp. (20). 8vo.   AAS.
     In correction of X:28505.

32005   CUMBERLAND, RICHARD   1732–1811
     CALVARY; OR, THE DEATH OF CHRIST. A POEM, IN EIGHT BOOKS. BY RICHARD CUM-
     BERLAND.
        Philadelphia: Printed by H. Kammerer, jun. 1797.

32006   CUMINGS, HENRY   1737–1823
     A SERMON PREACHED AT BILLERICA, DECEMBER 15, 1796, BEING THE DAY APPOINTED
     BY AUTHORITY, TO BE OBSERVED THROUGHOUT THE COMMONWEALTH OF MASSACHU-
     SETTS, AS A DAY OF PUBLIC PRAISE AND THANKSGIVING. BY HENRY CUMINGS, A. M.
     PASTOR OF THE CHURCH THERE.
        Printed by Thomas Fleet, jun. Cornhill, Boston. MDCCXCVII. pp. (35).
     8vo.   AAS. BA. BM. CLA. HC. JCB. LOC. MHS. NYPL. YC.

32007   CUMMINGS, ABRAHAM   1755–1827
     A DISSERTATION ON THE INTRODUCTION AND GLORY OF THE MILLENNIUM. TO WHICH
     IS PREFIXED, A DISCOURSE ON THE TWO WITNESSES. BY ABRAHAM CUMMINGS, A. M.
     [Two lines from] JUSTIN MARTYR. PUBLISHED ACCORDING TO ACT OF CONGRESS.
        Boston: Printed by Manning & Loring. 1797. pp. 26; 118. 12mo.   AAS. JCB.

32008   CURTIS, JOHN
     A NEW COLLECTION OF HYMNS AND SPIRITUAL SONGS.
        Newark: Printed by Daniel Dodge & Co. 1797.

32009   CURTIS, SAMUEL
THE GENTLEMAN'S POCKET ALMANACK, FOR THE YEAR 1798: TO WHICH IS ADDED, A
REGISTER OF NEW-HAMPSHIRE, CONTAINING A LIST OF THE OFFICERS, EXECUTIVE,
LEGISLATIVE AND JUDICIARY IN THE SERVICE OF THE UNITED STATES, WITH MANY
OTHER COMMUNICATIONS, IN THIS STATE, BOTH USEFUL AND INTERESTING. [Orna-
ment.]
Printed at Exeter, by H. Ranlet, for the Compiler. 1797. pp.(108). 24mo. NL.

32010   CUSHING, JACOB   1730–1809
A DISCOURSE, OCCASIONED BY THE DEATH OF THE REVEREND MR. JOSEPH JACKSON,
LATE PASTOR OF THE CHURCH IN BROOKLINE, WHO DEPARTED THIS LIFE JULY 22,
1796, ÆTATIS 62, DELIVERED AT HIS INTERMENT, JULY 25, 1796. BY JACOB CUSH-
ING, A. M. PASTOR OF THE CHURCH IN WALTHAM. PUBLISHED AT THE DESIRE OF
THE PARISHIONERS IN BROOKLINE. [Ornaments.]
Printed by Samuel Hall, No. 53, Cornhill, Boston. 1797. pp. [23.] 8vo.
Title within mourning borders.   AAS. BM. HC. JCB. LOC. NYPL.

32011   CYNTHIA, WITH THE TRAGICAL ACCOUNT OF THE UNFORTUNATE LOVES OF ALMERIN
AND DESDEMONA: BEING A NOVEL. ILLUSTRATED WITH A VARIETY OF THE CHANCES
OF FORTUNE; MORALIZED WITH MANY USEFUL OBSERVATIONS, WHEREBY THE READER
MAY REAP BOTH PLEASURE AND PROFIT.
Hartford: Printed by J. Babcock. 1797. pp. 108. 12mo.   AAS. NYPL.

32012   DABOLL, NATHAN   1750–1818
THE NEW-ENGLAND ALMANAC, AND GENTLEMEN AND LADIES' DIARY, ENLARGED, FOR
THE YEAR OF OUR LORD CHRIST, 1798: BEING THE SECOND AFTER BISSEXTILE OR
LEAP-YEAR, AND THE 22D OF AMERICAN INDEPENDENCE. FITTED TO THE MERIDIAN
OF NEW-LONDON, LAT. 41° 25′ N. BUT WILL ANSWER, WITHOUT ANY ESSENTIAL
VARIATION FOR EITHER OF THE NEW-ENGLAND STATES. CONTAINING, BESIDES
THE ASTRONOMICAL CALCULATIONS, A GREAT VARIETY OF USEFUL AND ENTERTAIN-
ING MATTER. BY NATHAN DABOLL. [Eight lines of verse.]
New-London: From Springer's Press, for Samuel Green. [1797.] pp. (32).
12mo.   AAS. CHS. HSP. LOC. NYHS.

32013   ——— SHEET ALMANAC FOR THE YEAR 1798.
New-London: From Springer's Press, for Samuel Green. 1797. Broadside.

32014   DAGGETT, HERMAN   1766–1832
A DISCOURSE ON THE NATURE AND IMPORTANCE OF CHURCH DISCIPLINE; ADDRESSED
ORIGINALLY TO THE FIRST CHRISTIAN SOCIETY IN SOUTHHAMPTON, LONG ISLAND,
DECEMBER 28TH, 1794. BY HERMAN DAGGETT, PASTOR OF THAT CHURCH.
New-London: Printed by Samuel Green. 1797. pp. 31. 8vo.   NYPL.

32015   THE DAILY [N.Y. arms] ADVERTISER. VOL. XIII. NO. 3712. MONDAY, JANUARY 2,
[— NO. 4024. SATURDAY, DECEMBER 30, 1797.]
*New-York: Printed by William Robins, for the Proprietor, Printer to the
State, at the State Printing-Office, No. 71, Pine-Street.* 1797. fol.   NYHS.

32016   THE DAILY ADVERTISER. VOL. V. NO. 1. TUESDAY, FEBRUARY 7, [— NO. 125.
MONDAY, JULY 3. 1797.]
Philadelphia: Published by James Carey & John Markland. 1797. fol.
BM. HSP. LCP.

Established, as a daily, by James Carey, and John Markland, and continued by them to July 3, 1797, when Markland withdrew. James Carey
continued publication from July 5th, as *Carey's Daily Advertiser*, to
September 12th—the last number located.

32017   DARWIN, ERASMUS   1731–1802
        ZOONOMIA; OR, THE LAWS OF ORGANIC LIFE. PART SECOND. BY ERASMUS DARWIN,
        M. D. A NEW EDITION; WITH AN INTRODUCTORY ADDRESS, AND A SHORT APPENDIX,
        BY CHARLES CALDWELL, M. D. FELLOW OF THE COLLEGE OF PHYSICIANS OF PHIL-
        ADELPHIA, MEMBER OF THE AMERICAN PHILOSOPHICAL SOCIETY, &C. &C. VOL. I.
        [— II.]

           Philadelphia: Printed by T. Dobson, at the Stone House. No. 41, South Sec-
        ond Street. 1797. 2 vols. pp. xxiv, (2), 486; (2), (2), 539. 8vo.   AAS.

           Part one, Edited by Samuel L. Mitchill, was printed in New York, in
        1796.

32018   DAVIES, BENJAMIN
        THE AMERICAN REPOSITORY OF USEFUL INFORMATION: CONTAINING A CALENDAR OF
        THE PRESENT YEAR: AN ACCOUNT OF THE UNITED STATES, THEIR TERRITORY AND
        POPULATION; OF THE FEDERAL GOVERNMENT & COURTS OF JUSTICE. WITH VARIOUS
        OTHER INTERESTING MATTER. ORNAMENTED WITH 12 VIGNETTES, & A FRONTIS-
        PIECE, ENGRAVED BY I. SMITHER & E. TRENCHARD. TO BE CONTINUED ANNUALLY.

           Philadelphia: Printed for B. Davies, No. 68 High Street.—1797—*I. Smither,*
        sculpt. pp. (2), [84], frontispiece. 48mo.   AAS. HSP. LOC.

32019   DAY, THOMAS   1777–1855
        THE SUICIDE. A DIALOGUE EXHIBITED ON THE STAGE AT THE PUBLIC COMMENCE-
        MENT OF YALE-COLLEGE, SEPT. 13TH, M.DCC.XCVII.

           Litchfield: Printed by T. Collier. [1797.] pp. 20. 8vo.   BU. YC.

32020   DEANE, SAMUEL   1733–1814
        THE NEW-ENGLAND FARMER: OR GEORGICAL DICTIONARY: CONTAINING A COMPEND-
        IOUS ACCOUNT OF THE WAYS AND METHODS IN WHICH THE IMPORTANT ART OF
        HUSBANDRY, IN ALL ITS VARIOUS BRANCHES, IS, OR MAY BE, PRACTICED TO THE
        THE GREATEST ADVANTAGE IN THIS COUNTRY. BY SAMUEL DEANE, D. D. VICE-
        PRESIDENT OF BOWDOIN COLLEGE, AND FELLOW OF THE AMERICAN ACADEMY OF
        ARTS AND SCIENCES. THE SECOND EDITION, CORRECTED, IMPROVED AND ENLARGED
        BY THE AUTHOR. [Three lines of Latin from] VIRGIL.

           Printed at Worcester, Massachusetts, at the Press of Isaiah Thomas, by Leon-
        ard Worcester, for Isaiah Thomas. 1797. pp. viii, 396 [397.] 8vo.
                                                    AAS. JCB. LOC. NYHS. NYPL.

32021   DEARBORN, BENJAMIN   1755–1838
        THE VOCAL INSTRUCTOR, PUBLISHED IN NUMBERS. NO. 1. CONTAINING THE RULES
        OF VOCAL MUSIC, BY PRINCIPLE, IN QUESTIONS AND ANSWERS; AND HINTS FOR RE-
        COVERING ITS RESPECTABILITY. A MORNING AND EVENING HYMN, COMPOSED AND
        SET TO MUSIC, FOR THIS WORK; AND A SLIDING MUSIC SCALE, NEVER BEFORE PUB-
        LISHED; IN WHICH A MORE ABLE INDEX POINTS OUT THE NAMES AND DISTANCES OF
        THE NOTES IN ALL THEIR VARIATIONS. ☞ THE OTHER NUMBERS OF THE WORK
        WILL CONTAIN, SACRED, MORAL OR SENTIMENTAL PSALMS, HYMNS, SONGS, AND
        ADAPTED TO PARTICULAR AND GENERAL OCCASIONS, FOR THE IMPROVEMENT AND
        PLEASURE OF YOUTH. BY BENJAMIN DEARBORN.

           Boston: 1797.

           113th Massachusetts District Copyright, issued to Benjamin Dearborn,
        as Author, 28 February, 1797.

32022   DECALVES, ALONSO, pseudonym.
TRAVELS TO THE WESTWARD, OR UNKNOWN PARTS OF AMERICA. BEING A TOUR OF ALMOST FOURTEEN MONTHS. CONTAINING, AN ACCOUNT OF THE COUNTRY, UPWARDS OF TWO THOUSAND MILES WEST OF THE CHRISTIAN PARTS OF NORTH-AMERICA; WITH AN ACCOUNT OF WHITE INDIANS; THEIR MANNERS, HABITS, AND MANY OTHER PARTICULARS. BY DON ALONSO DECALVES. CONFIRMED BY THREE OTHER PERSONS. THE SECOND DOVER EDITION.
Dover, New-Hampshire: Printed by Samuel Bragg, jun. 1797.

32023   —— — TRAVELS TO THE WESTWARD, OR THE UNKNOWN PARTS OF AMERICA; IN THE YEARS 1786, AND 1787. CONTAINING AN ACCOUNT OF THE COUNTRY, TO THE WESTWARD OF THE RIVER MISSISIPPI, [*sic*] ITS PRODUCTIONS, ANIMALS, INHABITANTS, CURIOSITIES, &C. &C. BY ALONSO DECALVES.
From the Herald-Office, Rutland. Printed by Josiah Fay. M.DCC.XCVII. pp. 48. 12mo.

32024   —— — NEW TRAVELS TO THE WESTWARD, OR UNKNOWN PARTS OF AMERICA: BEING A TOUR OF ALMOST FOURTEEN MONTHS. CONTAINING, AN ACCOUNT OF THE COUNTRY, UPWARDS OF TWO THOUSAND MILES WEST OF THE CHRISTIAN PARTS OF NORTH AMERICA; WITH AN ACCOUNT OF WHITE INDIANS, THEIR MANNERS, HABITS, AND MANY OTHER PARTICULARS. THE WHOLE FORMING AN AGREEABLE, INSTRUCTIVE, AND ENTERTAINING NARRATIVE.
Schenectady: Printed by Cornelius P. Wyckoff. 1797.

32025   —— — TRAVELS TO THE WESTWARD, OR THE UNKNOWN PARTS OF AMERICA IN THE YEARS 1786 AND 1787. CONTAINING AN ACCOUNT OF THE COUNTRY TO THE WESTWARD OF THE MISSISSIPPI, TOGETHER WITH ITS PRODUCTIONS, ANIMALS, INHABITANTS, VEGETABLES, CURIOSITIES, &C. BY DON ALONZO DECALVES.
Windsor: Printed by Alden Spooner. 1797. pp. 36. 12mo.

32026   —— — TRAVELS TO THE WESTWARD, OR THE UNKNOWN PARTS OF AMERICA IN THE YEARS 1786 AND 1787. CONTAINING AN ACCOUNT OF THE COUNTRY TO THE WESTWARD OF THE MISSISSIPPI, TOGETHER WITH ITS PRODUCTIONS, ANIMALS, INHABITANTS, VEGETABLES, CURIOSITIES, &C. BY DON ALONZO DECALVES. [Second impression.]
Windsor: Printed by Alden Spooner. 1797. pp. 36. 12mo.

32027   DECAMBON, MARIA GEERTRUIDA VAN DE WERKEN
LETTERS AND CONVERSATIONS BETWEEN SEVERAL YOUNG LADIES, ON INTERESTING AND IMPROVING SUBJECTS. TRANSLATED FROM THE DUTCH OF MADAME DECAMBON, WITH ALTERATIONS AND IMPROVEMENTS. THIRD EDITION.
Philadelphia: Printed by Thomas Dobson, at the Stone-House, No. 41, *South Second Street.* 1797. pp. 318. 12mo.   AAS. JCB.

32028   DELAWARE. STATE.
JOURNAL OF THE HOUSE OF REPRESENTATIVES OF THE STATE OF DELAWARE.
New-Castle: Printed by Samuel and John Adams. 1797.

32029   —— JOURNAL OF THE SENATE OF THE STATE OF DELAWARE.
New-Castle: Printed by Samuel and John Adams. 1797.

32030   —— LAWS OF THE STATE OF DELAWARE, FROM THE FOURTEENTH DAY OF OCTOBER, ONE THOUSAND SEVEN HUNDRED, TO THE EIGHTEENTH DAY OF AUGUST, ONE THOUSAND SEVEN HUNDRED AND NINETY-SEVEN. IN TWO VOLUMES. VOLUME I. [—II.] PUBLISHED BY AUTHORITY.
New-Castle: Printed by Samuel and John Adams. M,DCC,XCVII. 2 vols. pp. 590, 101; (591)–1376, [2], 128. 4to.   AAS. BM. BU. NYHS. NYPL.
Edited by Chief Justice George Read? Volumes 3, and 4, were printed in 1816.

32031 DELAWARE. STATE, continued.
—— LAWS OF THE STATE OF DELAWARE, PASSED AT A SESSION OF THE GENERAL ASSEMBLY, WHICH WAS BEGUN AND HELD AT DOVER, ON TUESDAY, THE THIRD DAY OF JANUARY, AND ENDED ON TUESDAY, THE TWENTY-FOURTH DAY OF THE SAME MONTH, IN THE YEAR OF OUR LORD ONE THOUSAND SEVEN HUNDRED AND NINETY-SEVEN, AND OF THE INDEPENDENCE OF THE UNITED STATES OF AMERICA THE TWENTY-FIRST. PUBLISHED BY AUTHORITY.
New-Castle: Printed by Samuel & John Adams. 1797. pp. 57. 8vo.   LOC.

32032 THE DELAWARE AND EASTERN-SHORE ADVERTISER. No. 276. MONDAY, JANUARY 2, [— No. 379. THURSDAY, DECEMBER 28, 1797.]
Wilmington: Printed on Mondays and Thursdays, by Samuel & John Adams, corner of King and High-Streets, . . . 1797. fol.

32033 THE DELAWARE GAZETTE. No. 693. WEDNESDAY, JANUARY 4, [— No. 792. SATURDAY, DECEMBER 30, 1797.]
Printed (Wednesdays & Saturdays) by W. C. Smyth, two doors below Mr. Brinton's Tavern, High-Street, Wilmington. 1797. fol.

32034 DER DEUTSCHE WASHINGTON CORRESPONDENT.
Hagerstaun, Maryland. Gedruckt bey Johann Gruber, 1797. fol.

Scharffs "History of Western Maryland" says that the above was established in 1795, but as Johann Gruber was printing in Reading, Pennsylvania, in 1793-1796, and began printing in Hagerstown in 1797, this year is the earliest publication could have been made. No copies are known, and it is not improbable that the *Westliche Correspondenz*, established by Gruber, in Hagerstown, in June, 1799, is the publication meant.

32035 DEVENS, RICHARD, JUNIOR
A DISCOURSE, COMPOSED FOR AND DELIVERED TO THE STUDENTS IN DIVINITY, AT THE COLLEGE IN PRINCETON, NEW-JERSEY, IN THE YEAR 1771(?) BY RICHARD DEVENS, JUN. A. M. A TUTOR IN THE COLLEGE, AND AUTHOR OF THE PARAPHRASE OF A PART OF THE BOOK OF JOB.
Charlestown: Printed by J. Lamson, near the Bridge. 1797. pp. 16. 8vo.
AAS. BA.

32036 DE WITT, BENJAMIN   1774–1819
A CHEMICO-MEDICAL ESSAY TO EXPLAIN THE OPERATION OF OXIGENE, OR THE BASE OF VITAL AIR ON THE HUMAN BODY. BY BENJAMIN DE WITT, M. P. M. S. CITIZEN OF THE STATE OF NEW-YORK. [Eight lines of verse from] DARWIN.
Philadelphia: Printed by William Woodward, No. 17, Chesnut-Street. [Imprimatur, J. Woodhouse.] 1797. pp. 35. 8vo.   AAS. BM. JCB. SGO.

32037 D'HAPPART, JR. LEGER
APPEAL OF J. H. D'HAPPART TO THE PUBLIC, IN CONSEQUENCE OF HIS BUSINESS WITH MESSRS. WILLIAM, JAMES & NATHANIEL FELLOWS CUNNINGHAM, BOSTON.
Boston: Printed by Manning & Loring. 1797. pp. 16. 4to.   BA.

32038 THE DIARY. No. 1514. MONDAY, JANUARY 1, [— No. 1836. SATURDAY, DECEMBER 30, 1797.]
New-York: Published by Cornelius C. Van Alen & Co. 1797. fol.

With the issue for January 25th, publication was made for John I. Johnson, by John Crookes and Robert Saunders, as Crookes & Saunders. And, with the issue for March 20th, the title was changed to *Diary and Mercantile Advertiser*—the last two words of greatest prominence. With the issue for March 31st, publication was made by John Crookes, for John I. Johnson; and, after June 16th, by John Crookes, for the Proprietor.

32039   DIBDIN, CHARLES   1745–1814
    DIBDIN'S MUSEUM, BEING A COLLECTION OF THE NEWEST AND MOST ADMIRED SONGS.

    Philadelphia: Printed by R. Aitken, No. 22, Market-Street. For Joseph Charles. 1797. pp. 72. 8vo.   LCP.

32040   —— NANCY, OR THE SAILOR'S JOURNAL. AS SUNG BY MR. WILLIAMSON, AT THE HAYMARKET THEATRE.

    Boston: Printed and for sale by James White, Court-Street, and Eben Larkin, Cornhill. 1797.

32041   —— SWEET PASSION OF LOVE. SONG FROM THE PADLOCK.

    New-York: [1797.] 4to.   JCB.

32042   DICKINSON, JOHN   1732–1808
    THE LETTERS OF FABIUS, IN 1788, ON THE FEDERAL CONSTITUTION; AND IN 1797,
    ON THE PRESENT SITUATION OF PUBLIC AFFAIRS. COPY-RIGHT SECURED.

    From the Office of the Delaware Gazette, Wilmington, by W. C. Smyth. 1797.
    pp. (2), (2), (202), (1). 8vo.   AAS. HC. JCB. LOC. NYPL.

    (No. 2.) Delaware District Copyright issued to William Catherwood
    Smyth, as Proprietor, 20 September, 1797. "The first nine letters, appeared separately in news-papers, and have never been published together before this present edition."

32043   DICKINSON, JONATHAN   1688–1747
    FAMILIAR LETTERS TO A GENTLEMAN, UPON A VARIETY OF SEASONABLE AND IMPORTANT
    SUBJECTS IN RELIGION. BY JONATHAN DICKINSON, A. M. MINISTER OF THE GOSPEL
    AT ELIZABETH-TOWN, N. J. [Eleven lines of Scripture texts.]

    Newark, New-Jersey: Printed by John Woods. M:DCC:XCVII. pp. [416],
    (1). 12mo.   AAS. JCB. LOC. NPL. NYPL. PU.

    "The Printer some time since (1792), issued Proposals for printing this
    work by subscription—about the time he was preparing it for the Press,
    he was informed that an impression was then printing in Philadelphia;
    but as the whole of that impression has been sold off he has thought
    proper to execute his former plan of publishing the work, . . . Printing-office, January, 1797."

32044   DICKINSON, SAMUEL FOWLER   1775–1838
    AN ORATION, IN CELEBRATION OF AMERICAN INDEPENDENCE; DELIVERED AT BEL-
    CHERSTOWN. JULY, 4TH, 1797. BY SAMUEL F. DICKINSON, A. B. STUDENT AT LAW.
    AMHERST. [Four lines of quotations.]

    Printed at Northampton (Massachusetts) by William Butler. M,DCC,XC,VII.
    pp. [23.] 8vo.   AAS. LOC. NYPL.

32045   DICKSON, WILLIAM, and ROBERT
    DICKSON'S BALLOON ALMANAC, FOR THE YEAR OF OUR LORD, 1798. THE SECOND
    AFTER LEAPYEAR. CAREFULLY SUITED TO PENNSYLVANIA AND THE ADJOINING
    STATES. [Cut of balloon ascension.]

    *Lancaster, Printed and sold by W. & R. Dickson, in Queen-street, north of
    the Courthouse.* [1797.] pp. (40). 12mo.   HSP. LOC.

32046 DILWORTH, Thomas   –1780
A New guide to the English tongue. In five parts. Containing, i. Words, both common and proper, from one to six syllables: the several sorts of monosyllables in the common words, being distinguished by tables, into words of two, three and four letters, &c. The several sorts of polysyllables also, being ranged in proper tables, have their syllables divided, and directions placed at the head of each table for the accent, to prevent false pronunciation. ii. A large and useful table of words, which are the same in sound, but different in signification. iii. A short sketch of grammar of the English tongue, delivered in the most familiar and instructive method. iv. A useful collection of sentences in prose and verse, divine, moral and historical; together with a select number of fables, v. Forms of prayer for children. The whole being recommended by several clergymen and eminent schoolmasters. By Thomas Dilworth.
  Boston: Printed and sold by J. White, near Charles River Bridge. [1797.] pp. 107, portrait, 8 cuts. 12mo.   AAS.

32047 —— — A New guide to the English tongue. In five parts. Containing, i. Words both common and proper, from one to six syllables; . . . ii. A large and useful table of words, that are the same in sound, but different in signification; . . . iii. A short but comprehensive grammar of the English tongue. . . . iv. A useful collection of sentences in prose and verse. . . . And v. Forms of prayer for children, on several occasions. . . . By Thomas Dilworth.
  New-York: 1797. 12mo.

32048 —— The Schoolmaster's assistant. Being a compendium of arithmetic, both practical and theoretical. In five parts, Containing i. Arithmetic in whole numbers wherein all the common rules, having each of them a sufficient number of questions, with their answers, are methodically and briefly handled. ii. Vulgar fractions, wherein several things, not commonly met with, are distinctly treated of, and laid down in the most plain and easy manner. iii. Decimals, in which, among other things, are considered the extraction of roots; interest both simple and compound; annuities, rebate, and equation of payments. iv. A large collection of questions with their answers, serving to exercise the foregoing rules, together with a few others, both pleasant and diverting. v. Duodecimals, commonly called cross multiplication; wherein that sort of arithmetic is thoroughly considered, and rendered very plain and easy; together with the method of proving all the foregoing operations at once, by division of several denominations, without reducing them into the lowest terms mentioned. The whole being delivered in the most familiar way of question and answer, is recommended by several eminent mathematicians, accomptants and schoolmasters, as necessary to be used in schools by all teachers who would have their scholars thoroughly understand, and make a quick progress in arithmetic. To which is prefixt, an Essay on the education of youth; humbly offered to the consideration of parents. By Thomas Dilworth, author of the New guide to the English tongue; Young book-keeper's assistant, &c. &c. and schoolmaster in Wapping. The latest edition.
  New-London: Printed by Samuel Green, for Napthali Judah, New-York. 1797. pp. xvi, (6), 192, portrait. 12mo.   AAS. BPL.

32049 DILWORTH, W. H.
The Complete letter-writer. Containing familiar letters on the most common occasions in life. Also, a variety of elegant letters for the direction and embellishment of style. On business, duty, amusement, love, courtship, marriage, friendship, & other subjects. In four parts. Fourth edition.
  Salem: Printed by Thomas C. Cushing. 1797. pp. 251. 12mo. AAS. EI.

32050 A DISCOURSE CONCERNING FAITH AS THE CONDITION OF THE GOSPEL COVENANT, AND AS THE INSTRUMENT WHEREBY VALUATION IS WROUGHT IN THE HEART BY DIVINE POWER. WITH AN APPENDIX CONTAINING SOME REMARKS ON MR. LOCKE'S PARAPHRASE AND NOTES ON ST. PAUL'S EPISTLES. [Heavy line.]
George-Town: From the Press of Green, English & Co. M,DCC,XCVI. pp. (60). 8vo.   AAS.

32051 A DISCOURSE ON MASONRY. . . .
Philadelphia: Printed by D. Humphreys. M,DCC,XCVII. pp. 10. 8vo.

32052 DIVINE ORACLES THE TRUE ANTIDOTE AGAINST DEISM, AND FALSE CHRISTIANITY; OR, THE CLEAR LIGHT OF REVELATION CONTRASTED TO THE DARKNESS OF A BOASTED AGE OF REASON. IN LETTERS TO A SON. TO WHICH ARE PREFIXED, INTRODUCTORY STRICTURES ON SOME LATE WRITINGS.
Providence (R. I.) Printed by B. Wheeler, for D. Brewer, of Taunton, and sold at their respective Book-Stores. MDCCXCVII. pp. (44). 8vo.   AAS. JCB. RIHS.

32053 —— DIVINE ORACLES, THE TRUE ANTIDOTE AGAINST DEISM AND FALSE CHRISTIANITY: OR, THE CLEAR LIGHT OF REVELATION CONTRASTED TO THE DARKNESS OF A BOASTED AGE OF REASON. IN LETTERS TO A SON. TO WHICH ARE PREFIXED, INTRODUCTORY STRICTURES ON SOME LATE WRITINGS. TO WHICH IS ANNEXED, THE EVIDENCE AND IMPORT OF CHRIST'S RESURRECTION, VERSIFIED. SOME YEARS AGO, FOR THE HELP OF THE MEMORY.
Providence: Printed by B. Wheeler, for D. Brewer of Taunton, and sold at their respective Bookstores. MDCCXCVII. pp. (44); (12). 8vo.   AAS. BM. RIHS.

Second title: THE EVIDENCE AND IMPORT OF CHRIST'S RESURRECTION, VERSIFIED, SOME YEARS AGO, FOR THE HELP OF THE MEMORY. THE FORCE OF DIVINE TRUTH WHICH APPEARS IN THIS PLAIN SHORT POEM, MAY WELL STRIKE A TOTAL DAMP TO EVERY FAVOURABLE THOUGHT OF DEISM OR DEISTICAL CHRISTIANITY. [Ornaments.]
Providence (R. I.) Printed by B. Wheeler, for D. Brewer, of Taunton, and sold at their respective Bookstores. MDCCXCVII. pp. (12).

32054 DOBSON, THOMAS
FIRST LESSONS FOR CHILDREN. [VOLUME FIRST-SECOND.]
Philadelphia: Printed by Thomas Dobson, at the Stone House, No. 41, S. Second-Street. 1797. 2 vols. pp. (36); — 8vo.   NYPL.
174th and 175th Pennsylvania District Copyrights, issued to Thomas Dobson, as Author, 6 March, 1797.

32055 —— THE HOLIDAY, OR CHILDREN'S SOCIAL AMUSEMENT.
Philadelphia: Printed by Thomas Dobson, at the Stone House, No. 41, S. Second-Street. 1797.
177th Pennsylvania District Copyright, issued to Thomas Dobson, as Author, 23 March, 1797.

32056 —— PLEASING INSTRUCTIONS FOR YOUNG MINDS.
Philadelphia: Printed by Thomas Dobson, at the Stone House, No. 41, S. Second-Street. 1797.
180th Pennsylvania District Copyright, issued to Thomas Dobson, as Author, 30 May, 1797.

32057 DODDRIDGE, PHILIP   1702–1751
SERMONS ON THE RELIGIOUS EDUCATION OF CHILDREN: PREACHED AT NORTHAMPTON. BY PHILIP DODDRIDGE.
Amherst, Newhampshire: Printed and sold by Samuel Cushing, M,DCC,XCVII. pp. 108. 12mo.   AAS.

32058 DODGE, PAUL   1777–1886
A POEM: DELIVERED AT THE COMMENCEMENT OF RHODE-ISLAND COLLEGE, SEPTEMBER 6, A. D. 1797. BY PAUL DODGE, A. B.
Providence: Printed by Carter and Wilkinson. 1797. pp. 8. 8vo.
AAS. BA. BU. JCB. NYPL. RIHS.

32059 DODSLEY, ROBERT   1708–1764
THE CHRONICLE OF THE KINGS OF ENGLAND, FROM WILLIAM THE CONQUEROR, TO THE YEAR MDCCXCV. IN IMITATION OF THE HOLY WRITINGS. BY NATHAN BEN SADDI, A JEW.
New-York: Printed by J. Buel, for C. Davis. 1797. pp. 119. 18mo.   NYPL.

32060 —— THE ECONOMY OF HUMAN LIFE. TRANSLATED FROM AN INDIAN MANUSCRIPT, WRITTEN BY AN ANTIENT BRAMIN. TO WHICH IS PREFIXED AN ACCOUNT OF THE MANNER IN WHICH THE SAID MANUSCRIPT WAS DISCOVERED. IN A LETTER, FROM AN ENGLISH GENTLEMAN RESIDING IN CHINA, TO HIS FRIEND IN ENGLAND.
Printed at Leominster (Massachusetts) by Charles Prentiss. 1797. pp. 84. 12mo.
AAS. LOC.

32061 —— THE OECONOMY OF HUMAN LIFE. IN TWO PARTS. TRANSLATED FROM AN INDIAN MANUSCRIPT, WRITTEN BY AN ANCIENT BRAMIN. TO WHICH IS PREFIXED, AN ACCOUNT OF THE MANNER IN WHICH THE SAID MANUSCRIPT WAS DISCOVERED. IN A LETTER FROM AN ENGLISH GENTLEMAN RESIDING IN CHINA, TO THE EARL OF * * * * * * *.
Wilmington: Printed by Peter Brynberg. 1797.

32062 DOGGETT, SIMEON, JUNIOR   1765–1852
A DISCOURSE ON EDUCATION, DELIVERED AT THE DEDICATION AND OPENING OF BRISTOL ACADEMY, THE 18TH DAY OF JULY, A. D. 1796. BY SIMEON DOGGETT, JUN. A. M. PRECEPTOR OF THE ACADEMY. [Three lines from] THOMPSON.
Newbedford (Massa.)—Printed by J. Spooner. 1797. pp. 28. 8vo.
AAS. BM. HC. JCB. NYHS.

32063 DUCRAY-DUMÉNIL, FRANÇOIS GUILLAUME   1761–1819
ALEXIS: OR, THE COTTAGE IN THE WOODS. A NOVEL. FROM THE FRENCH. THE MANUSCRIPT FOUND ON THE BANKS OF THE ISERE. THE SECOND AMERICAN EDITION. [Vignette.]
Printed at Newburyport, by W. Barrett, for Thomas and Andrews. Sold at their Bookstore, No. 45, Newbury-street, Boston; by said Thomas in Worcester; by Thomas, Andrews & Penniman, Albany; and by Thomas, Andrews & Butler, Baltimore. 1797. pp. iv, 269. 12mo.
AAS. NYPL.

32064 DUFOUR, PHILIPPE SYLVESTRE called SYLVESTRE   1622–1687
MORAL INSTRUCTIONS OF A FATHER TO HIS SON, READY TO UNDERTAKE A LONG VOYAGE, . . . TRANSLATED FROM THE FRENCH OF SILVESTRE DU FOUR.
New-London: Printed by James Springer. 1797.

32065 DUNHAM, JOSIAH
DUNHAM AND TRUE'S SECOND YEAR'S ALMANAC, FOR THE YEAR OF OUR LORD, 1797: BEING THE FIRST AFTER BISSEXTILE OR LEAP YEAR, AND OF INDEPENDENCE OF THE UNITED STATES THE TWENTY-FIRST. CALCULATED FOR THE MERIDIAN OF HANOVER, LATITUDE 43 DEGREES 33 MINUTES NORTH; CONTAINING EVERY THING NECESSARY FOR AN ALMANAC, AND A VARIETY OF OTHER USEFUL AND ENTERTAINING MATTER. [Four lines of Scripture text.]
Printed at Hanover, by Dunham and True for Alden Spooner, of Windsor. Sold at his Office, whole sale & retail. [1797.] pp. (24). 12mo.   NHHS. NYHS.

32066 DUNLOP, WILLIAM   1766–1839
TELL TRUTH AND SHAME THE DEVIL; A COMEDY, IN TWO ACTS, AS PERFORMED BY
THE OLD AMERICAN COMPANY, IN NEW-YORK. JANUARY, 1797.
> *New-York: Printed by T. and J. Swords, No. 99, Pearl-street.* 1797.· pp.
> 45, (1). 12mo.   AAS. BPL. BU. HC. NYPL.

Based upon "Jerome Pointu," a French comedy, by Alexander B. Rob-
ineau, better known as Beaunoir.

32067 D'URFEY, THOMAS   1653–1723
'TWAS WITH IN A MILE OF EDINBURGH TOWN.
> *Boston:* [1797.]   JCB.

32068 DWIGHT, NATHANIEL
A SHORT BUT COMPREHENSIVE SYSTEM OF THE GEOGRAPHY OF THE WORLD: BY WAY
OF QUESTION AND ANSWER. PRINCIPALLY DESIGNED FOR CHILDREN, AND COMMON
SCHOOLS. BY NATHANIEL DWIGHT. THE FOURTH EDITION. PUBLISHED ACCORD-
ING TO ACT OF CONGRESS.
> *Boston: Printed by Manning & Loring, for David West, No. 56, Cornhill.*
> 1797. pp. 215, (1). 12mo.   AAS. JCB.

32069 DWIGHT, TIMOTHY   1752–1817
A DISCOURSE, PREACHED AT THE FUNERAL OF THE REVEREND ELIZUR GOODRICH, D. D.
PASTOR OF THE CHURCH IN DURHAM, AND ONE OF THE MEMBERS OF THE CORPO-
RATION OF YALE-COLLEGE; BY THE REVEREND TIMOTHY DWIGHT, D. D. PRESIDENT
OF YALE-COLLEGE; NOVEMBER 25TH, 1797. PRINTED AT THE REQUEST OF THE
CONGREGATION.
> *New-Haven: Printed by T. and S. Green.* [1797.] pp. (38). (1). 8vo.
>   AAS. BPL. CHS. JCB. LOC. NYHS. NYPL. UTS. YC.

32070 [Cut.] THE EAGLE: OR, DARTMOUTH CENTINEL. — DEDICATED TO POLITICS, AND
THE BELLES-LETTRES. — [Motto.] VOLUME IV. NUMBER XXIV. MONDAY, JANU-
ARY 2, [— VOLUME V. NUMBER XXIII. MONDAY, DECEMBER 25, 1797.]
> *Hanover, (Newhampshire) Printed and published at the Academy, by Dun-*
> *ham & True . . .* 1797. fol.   AAS.

In March, publication was made in the name of Benjamin True.

32071 EASTERN HERALD [cut] AND GAZETTE OF MAINE. MONDAY, JANUARY 2, [— MON-
DAY, DECEMBER 25, 1797.]
> *Published by John Kelse Baker, Fish Street, Portland.* [*District of Maine.*]
> [*Massachusetts.*] 1797. fol.   AAS.

With the issue for September 9th, a weekly issue was resumed.

32072 EDWARDS, JONATHAN   1703–1758
SINNERS IN THE HANDS OF AN ANGRY GOD. A SERMON, PREACHED AT ENFIELD, JULY
8, 1741, AT A TIME OF GREAT AWAKENINGS; AND ATTENDED WITH REMARKABLE
IMPRESSIONS ON MANY OF THE HEARERS. BY THE LATE REVEREND MR. JONATHAN
EDWARDS, PRESIDENT OF THE COLLEGE OF NEW-JERSEY.
> *New-York: Printed by G. Forman, opposite the Post-Office, for C. Davis, No.*
> *94, Water-street.* 1797. pp. 33, (1), (1). 18mo.   AAS. NYPL.

32073 EDWARDS, JONATHAN   1745–1801
A DISSERTATION CONCERNING LIBERTY AND NECESSITY; CONTAINING REMARKS ON THE
ESSAYS OF DR. SAMUEL WEST, AND ON THE WRITINGS OF SEVERAL OTHER AUTHORS,
ON THOSE SUBJECTS. BY JONATHAN EDWARDS, D. D.
> *Printed at Worcester, by Leonard Worcester.* 1797. pp. 234, errata. 8vo.
>   AAS. BA. BM. JCB. NYPL. PTS. PU.

32074   [Cut of] THE ELEPHANT, ACCORDING TO THE ACCOUNT OF THE CELEBRATED BUF-FON, IS THE MOST RESPECTABLE ANIMAL IN THE WORLD. [Nineteen lines.] *** A PLACE IS FITTED UP FOR HIM (SUITABLE TO RECEIVE GENTEEL COMPANY) IN A STORE BACK OF THE COFFEE-HOUSE; WHERE HE WILL REMAIN FOR A FEW DAYS ONLY, AS HE IS TO BE AT CAMBRIDGE AT THE APPROACHING COMMENCEMENT. ADMITTANCE, ONE QUARTER OF A DOLLAR — CHILDREN ONE EIGHTH OF A DOLLAR. [Colophon:]

> *Providence, June 27, 1797. Printed by Carter & Wilkinson.* Broadside. fol.
>
>   AAS. BU. JCB. RIHS.

     Another impression, without the cut, of the same day and date, was also printed. Reproduced in facsimile.

32075   —— [Cut of] THE ELEPHANT, ACCORDING TO THE ACCOUNT OF THE CELEBRATED BUFFON, IS THE MOST RESPECTABLE ANIMAL IN THE WORLD. . . . [Colophon:]

> *Boston: Printed by D. Bowen, at the Columbian Museum Press, Head of the Mall. [August 18th, 1797.]* Broadside. 4to.   EI.

32076   —— [Cut of] THE ELEPHANT, ACCORDING TO THE ACCOUNT OF THE CELEBRATED BUFFON, IS THE MOST RESPECTABLE ANIMAL IN THE WORLD. . . . ADMITTANCE ONE QUARTER OF A DOLLAR. CHILDREN ONE EIGHTH OF A DOLLAR. SALEM, AU-GUST 29, 1797.

> *[Salem: Printed by Thomas C. Cushing, 1797.]* Broadside.   EI.

32077   —— [Cut of] THE ELEPHANT, ACCORDING TO THE ACCOUNT OF THE CELEBRATED BUFFON, IS THE MOST RESPECTABLE ANIMAL IN THE WORLD. . . .

> *[Newburyport: Printed by William Barrett, September 21, 1797.]* Broad-side. 4to.   NYHS.

32078   ELIOT, JOHN   1754–1813
A SERMON, PREACHED IN MILTON, NOVEMBER 1, 1797, AT THE ORDINATION OF THE REV. MR. JOSEPH M'KEAN. BY JOHN ELIOT, A. M. PASTOR OF THE CHURCH IN NORTH STREET, BOSTON. [Ornaments.]

> *Printed [by Manning & Loring] at Boston.* 1797. pp. 54. 8vo.
>
>   AAS. BA. HC. JCB. MHS. NYHS. NYPL. UTS.

     The Charge, by the Rev. Jason Haven of Dedham; and the Right hand of fellowship, by Rev. Thaddeus Mason Harris, of Dorchester.

32079   ELLWOOD, THOMAS   1639–1713
DAVIDEIS; THE LIFE OF DAVID, KING OF ISRAEL: A SACRED POEM. IN FIVE BOOKS. BY THOMAS ELLWOOD. [One line of Latin from] HOR.

> *Wilmington: Printed by Johnson & Preston, No. 73, Market-Street.* 1797. pp. 159. 12mo.   AAS. JCB. NYPL. WiPL.

32080   ELY, JOHN
THE CHILD'S INSTRUCTOR: CONSISTING OF EASY LESSONS FOR CHILDREN; ON SUBJECTS WHICH ARE FAMILIAR TO THEM, IN LANGUAGE ADAPTED TO THEIR CAPACITIES. BY A TEACHER OF LITTLE CHILDREN IN PHILADELPHIA. VOLUME I. THE FOURTH EDITION. [One line from] ST. PAUL.

> *Mount-Pleasant: Printed by W. Durell, for R. Magell, J. Harrisson, C. Davis, N. Judah, E. Duyckinck and Co. T. Allen, B. Gomez, P. Mesier and Buel and Knox.* M,DCC,XCVII. *[Who has the privilege of Copy Right for the States of New-York and New-Jersey.]* pp. 108. 12mo.   AAS.

32081 | ELY, SAMUEL
THE DEFORMITY OF A HIDEOUS MONSTER, DISCOVERED IN THE PROVINCE OF MAINE,
BY A MAN IN THE WOODS, LOOKING AFTER LIBERTY.
[Boston:] Printed near Liberty tree, for the good of the Commonwealth. [1797.]
pp. [31.] 8vo. AAS.

32082 | EMERSON, JOHN 1745–1826
THE DIGNITY AND GLORY OF CHRIST'S CHURCHES AND MINISTERS. A DISCOURSE,
DELIVERED AT THE ORDINATION OF THE REV. JOEL BAKER, TO THE MINISTERIAL
OFFICE IN THE SECOND CHURCH OF GRANVILLE, JUNE 21ST, 1797. BY JOHN EM-
ERSON, A. M. PASTOR OF THE CONGREGATIONAL CHURCH IN CONWAY.
Springfield—(Massa.)—Printed by Francis Stebbins, for the Society. M,DCC,-
XCVII. pp. [24.] 8vo. AAS. JCB. LOC.

32083 | ——— ISAIAH'S MISSION CONSIDERED AND APPLIED. A SERMON, DELIVERED AT THE OR-
DINATION OF THE REV. JESSE EDSON, TO THE PASTORAL OFFICE IN HALIFAX, (VER.)
NOVEMBER 23, 1796; BY THE REV. JOHN EMERSON, A. M. PASTOR OF THE CONGRE-
GATIONAL CHURCH IN CONWAY. TOGETHER WITH THE CHARGE AND RIGHT HAND
OF FELLOWSHIP.
Brattleborough, Vermont: Printed by Benjamin Smead. 1797. pp. 35.
12mo. JCB.

32084 | EMMONS, NATHANAEL 1745–1840
A DISCOURSE, DELIVERED AT WARDSBOROUGH, VERMONT, NOVEMBER 4, 1795, AT THE
ORDINATION OF THE REVEREND JAMES TUFTS, TO THE PASTORAL OFFICE IN THAT
TOWN. BY NATHANIEL EMMONS, A. M. PASTOR OF THE CHURCH IN FRANKLIN.
Brattleborough, Vermont: Printed by Benjamin Smead. 1797. pp. [32.]
12mo. AAS. BPL. BU. JCB.

32085 | ——— AN EXTRACT FROM A DISCOURSE, DELIVERED AUGUST 10, 1795, AT THE FUNERAL
OF THE LATE REV. ELISHA FISH, A. M. PASTOR OF THE CHURCH IN UPTON; WHO DE-
PARTED THIS LIFE AUGUST 6, 1795, IN THE 76TH YEAR OF HIS AGE, AND 44TH OF HIS
MINISTRY. BY NATHANAEL EMMONS, A. M. PASTOR OF THE CHURCH IN FRANKLIN.
*New-York: Printed by T. & J. Swords, for C. Davis:—*1797.—pp. (24).
12mo. HC. JCB. NYPL. UTS. YC.

32086 | ——— NATIONAL PEACE THE SOURCE OF NATIONAL PROSPERITY. A SERMON, DELIVERED
AT FRANKLIN, ON THE DAY OF ANNUAL THANKSGIVING, DECEMBER 15TH, MDCCXCVI.
BY NATHANAEL EMMONS, A. M. PASTOR OF THE CHURCH IN FRANKLIN.
Printed at Worcester, by Leonard Worcester. MDCCXCVII. pp. 23. 8vo.
AAS. BA. BM. CLA. HC. JCB. LOC. UTS.

32087 | ——— A SERMON, DELIVERED AT SALEM, IN NEW-HAMPSHIRE, JANUARY 4, 1797, AT
THE ORDINATION OF THE REV. JOHN SMITH, A. B. TO THE WORK OF THE MINISTRY
IN THAT PLACE. BY NATHANIEL EMMONS, A. M. PASTOR OF THE CHURCH IN FRANK-
LIN, MASSACHUSETTS.
Printed by George Hough, at Concord. M.DCC.XCVII. pp. 44. 8vo.
AAS. BPL. BU. JCB. LOC.
The Charge. By the Rev. Gyles Merrill, minister of Plastow and part
of Haverhill. The Right hand of fellowship. By the Rev. Mr. Peabody,
of Atkinson.

32088   ENCYCLOPÆDIA; OR, A DICTIONARY OF ARTS, SCIENCES, AND MISCELLANEOUS LIT-
ERATURE; CONSTRUCTED ON A PLAN, BY WHICH THE DIFFERENT SCIENCES AND ARTS
ARE DIGESTED INTO THE FORM OF DISTINCT TREATISES OR SYSTEMS, COMPREHEND-
ING THE HISTORY. THEORY, AND PRACTICE, OF EACH, ACCORDING TO THE LATEST
DISCOVERIES AND IMPROVEMENTS; AND FULL EXPLANATIONS GIVEN OF THE VARIOUS
DETACHED PARTS OF KNOWLEDGE, WHETHER RELATING TO NATURAL AND ARTIFI-
CIAL OBJECTS, OR TO MATTERS ECCLESIASTICAL, CIVIL, MILITARY, COMMERCIAL, &C.
INCLUDING ELUCIDATIONS OF THE MOST IMPORTANT TOPICS RELATIVE TO RELIGION,
MORALS, MANNERS, AND THE OECONOMY OF LIFE: TOGETHER WITH A DESCRIPTION
OF ALL THE COUNTRIES, CITIES, PRINCIPAL MOUNTAINS, SEAS, RIVERS, &C. THROUGH-
OUT THE WORLD: A GENERAL HISTORY, ANCIENT AND MODERN, OF THE DIFFERENT
EMPIRES, KINGDOMS, AND STATES; AND AN ACCOUNT OF THE LIVES OF THE MOST
EMINENT PERSONS IN EVERY NATION. FROM THE EARLIEST AGES DOWN TO THE PRES-
ENT TIMES. COMPILED FROM THE WRITINGS OF THE BEST AUTHORS, IN SEVERAL
LANGUAGES; THE MOST APPROVED DICTIONARIES, AS WELL OF GENERAL SCIENCE AS
OF ITS PARTICULAR BRANCHES; THE TRANSACTIONS, JOURNALS, AND MEMOIRS, OF
VARIOUS LEARNED SOCIETIES, THE MS. LECTURES OF EMINENT PROFESSORS ON DIF-
FERENT SCIENCES; AND A VARIETY OF ORIGINAL MATERIALS, FURNISHED BY AN EX-
TENSIVE CORRESPONDENCE. THE FIRST AMERICAN EDITION, IN EIGHTEEN VOLUMES,
GREATLY IMPROVED. ILLUSTRATED WITH FIVE HUNDRED AND FORTY-TWO COPPER
PLATES. VOL. XVII. SCO–STR. INDOCTI DISCANT ET AMENT MEMINISSE PERITI.

> *Philadelphia: Printed by Thomas Dobson, at the Stone House, No.* 41, *South
> Second Street.* [1797.] pp. 827, (1), 37 plates (447–483). 4to.

     AAS. APS. LCP. LOC. MHS. NYHS. NYPL. WL.

32089   ERRA PATER, pseudonym.
THE BOOK OF KNOWLEDGE: TREATING OF THE WISDOM OF THE ANCIENTS. IN FOUR
PARTS. WRITTEN BY ERRA PATER, A JEW DOCTOR IN ASTRONOMY AND PHYSICK,
BORN IN BETHANY, NEAR MOUNT OLIVET IN JUDEA. MADE ENGLISH BY WILLIAM
LILLY, STUDENT IN PHYSICK AND ASTROLOGY.

> *Suffield: Printed by H. & O. Farnsworth.* 1797. 16mo.

32090   —— — THE BOOK OF KNOWLEDGE: TREATING OF THE WISDOM OF THE ANCIENTS.
IN FOUR PARTS. WRITTEN BY ERRA PATER, A JEW DOCTOR IN ASTRONOMY AND
PHYSIC, BORN IN BETHANY, NEAR MOUNT OLIVET IN JUDEA. MADE ENGLISH BY
W. LILLY, STUDENT IN PHYSIC AND ASTROLOGY.

> *Wilmington: Printed by Peter Brynberg.* 1797.

32091   ERSKINE, RALPH   1685–1752
SERMONS UPON THE MOST IMPORTANT AND INTERESTING SUBJECTS. BY THE LATE REV-
EREND RALPH ERSKINE, MINISTER AT THE GOSPEL AT DUNFERMLINE. THE FIRST
AMERICAN EDITION.

> *Philadelphia: Printed by John M'Culloch, No.* 1, *North Third-street.*
> M,DCC,XCVII. pp. 453, (1), (2), (4). 12mo.   AAS. JCB.

> Contains, two pages of Books for sale, by John M'Culloch; and a later
> list of four pages of Books for sale by his son William M'Culloch.

32092   ERSKINE, THOMAS, baron   1750–1823
CHRISTIANITY VINDICATED, IN THE ADMIRABLE SPEECH OF THE HON. THO. ERSKINE, IN
THE TRIAL OF J. [sic] WILLIAMS, FOR PUBLISHING PAINE'S "AGE OF REASON." 24TH
JUNE, 1797. FROM THE TWELFTH LONDON EDITION.

> *Philadelphia: Printed by J. Carey, No.* 83, *N. Second-Street, for G. Douglas,
> No.* 2 *South Third-Street.* 1797. pp. (15). 8vo.   LOC. MHS. NYPL.

ERSKINE, THOMAS, baron, continued.

32093 —— — THE SPEECHES OF THE HON. THOMAS ERSKINE, IN THE COURT OF KING'S
BENCH, JUNE 28 [*sic* 24] 1797, BEFORE THE RIGHT HON. LLOYD LORD KENYON,
AND A SPECIAL JURY, ON THE TRIAL THE KING VERSUS THOMAS WILLIAMS, FOR
PUBLISHING THE AGE OF REASON, WRITTEN BY THOMAS PAINE; TOGETHER WITH
MR. STEWART KYD'S REPLY, AND LORD KENYON'S CHARGE TO THE JURY.

Philadelphia: Printed for, and sold by William Cobbett, Nov. 1797. pp. 23.
8vo.   AAS. BA. JCB. NYHS. NYPL..

32094 —— A VIEW OF THE CAUSES & CONSEQENCES OF THE PRESENT WAR WITH FRANCE.
BY THE HON. THOMAS ERSKINE.

*Albany: Printed by Charles R. & George Webster, at their Bookstore, in the
White-House, corner of State and Pearl Streets.* 1797. pp. 153, (3). 12mo.   AAS.

Contains, a three-page list of Books for sale by the Websters.

32095 —— — A VIEW OF THE CAUSES AND CONSEQUENCES OF THE PRESENT WAR WITH
FRANCE. BY THE HONOURABLE THOMAS ERSKINE. FROM THE TWENTY-FOURTH
LONDON EDITION.

Boston: Printed for Adams & Larkin, Court-Street, and E. Larkin, No. 47
Cornhill. [1797.] pp. (2), (2), 100. 8vo.   AAS. BM. JCB. LOC.

32096 —— —— A VIEW OF THE CAUSES AND CONSEQUENCES OF THE PRESENT WAR WITH
FRANCE. BY THE HON. THOMAS ERSKINE. THE FIRST AMERICAN, FROM THE
TWENTY-FOURTH LONDON EDITION.

New-York: Printed by J. Buel, for C. Smith. M.DCC.XCVII. pp. (70).
8vo.   AAS. LOC. NYHS. NYPL.

32097 —— — A VIEW OF THE CAUSES AND CONSEQUENCES OF THE PRESENT WAR WITH
FRANCE, IN ANSWER TO MR. BURKE'S REGICIDE PEACE. BY THE HONOURABLE
THOMAS ERSKINE. WITH A DEDICATION TO THE AUTHOR, BY P. PORCUPINE; AND
AN APPENDIX, CONTAINING, THE CORRESPONDENCE BETWEEN MILES AND THE INFA-
MOUS LE BRUN, MINISTER OF WAR, AT THE TIME WHEN WAR WAS DECLARED AGAINST
GREAT BRITAIN; WHICH DEVELOPS THE REAL CAUSES OF THAT DECLARATION, ALL
THE SECRET STEPS WHICH THE FRENCH TOOK PREVIOUS TO IT, AND CLEARLY UN-
RAVELS THE THREAD OF THEIR AMBITIOUS PROJECTS.

Philadelphia: Printed by William Cobbett, opposite Christ Church. 1797.
pp. [73], [24.] 8vo.   AAS. BA. JCB. LOC. NYHS. NYPL.

32098 —— — A VIEW OF THE CAUSES AND CONSEQUENCES OF THE PRESENT WAR WITH
FRANCE. BY THE HON. THOMAS ERSKINE.

Philadelphia: Printed by Richard Folwell, for Robert Campbell & Co. No.
40, *South Second-Street.* 1797. pp. [77], (1). 8vo.   HSP. JCB. LOC. NYPL.

32099 —— — A VIEW OF THE CAUSES AND CONSEQUENCES OF THE PRESENT WAR WITH
FRANCE. BY THE HON. THOMAS ERSKINE. THE SECOND EDITION.

Philadelphia: Printed by Richard Folwell, for Robert Campbell & Co. No.
40, *South Second-Street.* 1797. pp. [77], (1). 8vo.   AAS. LOC.

32100   EVANGELICAL REFORMED CHURCH IN THE UNITED STATES OF AMERICA
DAS NEUE UND VERBESSERTE GESANG-BUCH, WORINNEN DIE PSALMEN DAVIDS SAMT
EINER SAMMLUNG ALTER UND NEUER GEISTREICHER LIEDER SOWOHL FÜR PRIVAT
UND HAUSSANDACHTEN, ALS AUCH FÜR DEN ÖFFENTLICHEN GOTTESDIENST ENTHAL-
TEN SIND. NEBST EINEM ANHANG DES HEYDELBERGISCHEN CATECHISMUS, WIE
AUCH ERBAULICHER GEBÄTER. NACH EINEM SYNODAL SCHLUSS ZUSAMMENGETRA-
GEN UND EINGERICHTET VOR DIE EVANGELISCH-REFORMIRTEN GEMEINEN IN DEN
VEREINIGTEN STAATEN VON AMERIKA.

     Philadelphia: Gedruckt bey Steiner und Kammerer und H. Kammerer, jun.
1797. pp. (2), (4), 148; (2), (6), 585, (10); (24); (9), frontispiece. 12mo.
                                            AAS. JCB.

     Second title: SAMMLUNG ALTER UND NEUER GEISTREICHER LIEDER, ZUR ÖFFENT-
LICHEN UND BESONDERN ERBAUUNG DER EVANGELISCH-REFORMIRTEN GEMEINEN
IN DEN VEREINIGTEN STAATEN VON AMERICA, AUF VERODNUNG DES SYNODS BE-
SAGTER GEMEINEN ZUSAMMENGETRAGEN VON EINIGEN DAZU ERWÄHLTEN GLIEDERN
DESSELBEN.

       Philadelphia: Gedruckt bey Steiner und Kammerer, und H. Kammerer, jun.
1797. pp. (2), (6), 585, (10).

     Third heading: CATECHISMUS ODER KURZER UNTERRICHT CHRISTLICHER LEHR,
WIE DERSELBE IN KIRCHEN UND SCHULEN DER EVANGELISCH-REFORMIRTEN GE-
MENDEN GELEHRET WIRD. pp. (22).

     Fourth heading: MORGEN-UND ABEND-GEBET. pp. (9).

     189th Pennsylvania District Copyright, issued to William Hendel, Presi-
dent of the Synod of the German Reformed Congregations in the United
States of America (for the use and on behalf of the Synod of the German
Reformed Congregations), 7 August, 1797.

32101   EVANS, JOHN   1767–1827
A SKETCH OF THE DENOMINATIONS INTO WHICH THE CHRISTIAN WORLD IS DIVIDED;
ACCOMPANIED WITH A PERSUASIVE TO RELIGIOUS MODERATION. TO WHICH IS PRE-
FIXED, A SHORT ACCOUNT OF ATHEISM, DEISM, JUDAISM, AND CHRISTIANITY. BY JOHN
EVANS, A. M. FOURTH EDITION, ENLARGED AND CORRECTED. [Four lines of quo-
tations.]

     Philadelphia: Printed for Griffiths and Rhees, by Lang and Ustick. 1797.
pp. 176. 18mo.   AAS.

32102   THE EXCELLING ELECTION: OR AN EXCELLENT NEW SONG, WRITTEN AND SUNG AT
RUTLAND, MARCH 3D, '97, BEING THE EVENING AFTER COL. LYON'S ELECTION.
     Rutland: Printed by Josiah Fay. 1797.

32103   THE EXPERIENCED CHRISTIAN'S MAGAZINE. [VOL. I. No. 9. JANUARY— No. 12.
APRIL, 1797.] EDITED BY WILLIAM PHŒBUS.
     New-York: Printed and sold by Wilson & Kirk, Printers and Booksellers,
No. 299, Broad-way. 1797. pp. 257–384. 8vo.   AAS. HSP. NYHS.

32104   FAIR ROSALIE. A FAVORITE SONG. SUNG BY MISS WESTRAY. THE MELODY BY CHARLES
DIGNUM.
     New-York: [1797.]   JCB.

32105   FAIRFAX, BRYAN. 8th baron   1727–1802
STRICTURES ON THE SECOND PART OF THE AGE OF REASON.
     Georgetown: From the Press of Green, English & Co. 1797. pp. 91. 12mo.
                                                  NYPL.

32106   THE FAMILY ALMANAC, FOR THE YEAR OF CHRISTIAN ERA 1798; BEING SECOND AFTER LEAP-YEAR. CALCULATED FOR THE MERIDIAN OF PORTSMOUTH, NEW-HAMPSHIRE, LAT. 43 DEG. 5 MIN. NORTH: BUT MAY SERVE FOR ANY OF THE NEW-ENGLAND STATES. CONTAINING EVERY THING NECESSARY FOR AN ALMANAC, WITH MANY USEFUL FAMILY MATTERS. [Eight lines of verse.]

       Portsmouth, New-Hampshire: Printed by Charles Peirce, No. 5, Daniel-street, sold by him, wholesale and retail, and by most of the shop-keepers in town and country. [1797.] pp. (24). 12mo.   NHHS.

32107   THE FARMER'S DAUGHTER OF ESSEX. CONTAINING AN ACCOUNT OF HER DISTRESS, WONDERFUL ADVENTURES, MANNER OF BEING COURTED AND SEDUCED BY A NOBLE-MAN IN LONDON, WHO AFTER LIVING WITH HER SOME YEARS, PARTED IN THE MOST DISHONORABLE MANNER.—WITH AN ACCOUNT OF HER MEETING HIM A SECOND TIME, AND MANY PARTICULAR OCCURRENCES THAT HAPPENED DURING THE REMAINDER OF THEIR LIVES. WRITTEN BY HERSELF.

       Hartford: Printed by J. Babcock. 1797. pp. [120]+ 12mo.   AAS.

32108   —— THE FARMER'S DAUGHTER OF ESSEX. CONTAINING AN ACCOUNT OF HER DIS-TRESS, WONDERFUL ADVENTURES, MANNER OF BEING COURTED AND SEDUCED BY A NOBLEMAN IN LONDON, WHO AFTER LIVING WITH HER SOME YEARS, PARTED IN THE MOST DISHONORABLE MANNER. WITH AN ACCOUNT OF HER MEETING HIM A SECOND TIME, AND MANY PARTICULAR OCCURRENCES THAT HAPPENED DURING THE REMAIN-DER OF THEIR LIVES. WRITTEN BY HERSELF.

       New-London: Printed by James Springer. 1797.

32109   THE FARMER'S JOURNAL, AND NEWTON ADVERTISER. VOL. I. NUMBER 50. FRI-DAY, JANUARY 6, [— VOL. II. NUMBER 101. WEDNESDAY, DECEMBER 27, 1797.]

       Newton: Printed by Eliot Hopkins, & Co. 1797. fol.

32110   THE FARMER'S LIBRARY. OR FAIRHAVEN TELEGRAPHE. [Motto.] VOL. II. NUM. 76. WEDNESDAY, JANUARY 4, [— NUM. 84. WEDNESDAY, MARCH 1, 1797.]

       Printed by Judah P. Spooner, at Fairhaven, Vermont. 1797. fol.   HC.

       The paper dwindled in matter to half sheets in January and February, and publication was discontinued at the above date. In November, Spooner resumed publication under the following title:

32111   THE FARMER'S LIBRARY. OR, VERMONT AND NEW-YORK INTELLIGENCER. A RE-PUBLICAN PAPER. GOD AND THE PEOPLE JOINING IN CONSENT—FORM THE TRUE BASIS OF JUST GOVERNMENT. VOL. I. NUM. 1. TUESDAY, NOVEMBER 14, [— NUM. 7. TUESDAY, DECEMBER 26, 1797.]

       Printed at Fairhaven, by Judah P. Spooner. 1797. fol.

32112   FARMER'S [cut] ORACLE. VOLUME I. NUMBER 1. TUESDAY, JANUARY 31, [— NUMBER 48. TUESDAY, DECEMBER 26, 1797.]

       Troy: (State New-York) Printed by Luther Pratt, & Co. near the Ferry, . . . 1797. fol.

       Established, as a weekly, in continuation of the *Farmer's Oracle, and Lansingburgh Weekly Gazette,* by Luther Pratt, and Daniel Curtiss, jun-ior, and continued into April, 1798, when it was probably discontinued owing to the competition of the *Northern Budget.*

32113 THE FARMER'S WEEKLY MUSEUM: NEWHAMPSHIRE AND VERMONT JOURNAL. [Motto.]
VOL. V. No. 209. TUESDAY, APRIL 4, [— VOL. V. No. 247. TUESDAY, DECEMBER
26, 1797.]
> *Printed at Walpole, Newhampshire, by David Carlisle, jun. in the Main
> Street . . . 1797.* fol. AAS.

In continuation of *The Newhampshire and Vermont Journal: or, the
farmer's weekly museum.* With the change of title the size of the paper
was enlarged to royal folio, with the motto: "Wouldst thou remember
From New-Year's day to the last of December, Then read" — Bunyan.
Following the death of the Printer's father in December, "junior"
was dropped from David Carlisle's name.

32114 FARMER'S ALMANACK, FOR THE YEAR OF OUR LORD, 1798: BEING THE SECOND YEAR
AFTER BISSEXTILE, OR LEAP YEAR: AND THE TWENTY SECOND OF AMERICAN INDE-
PENDENCE. ADAPTED TO THE DISTRICT OF MAINE. CALCULATED FOR THE MERID-
IAN OF PORTLAND, LAT. 23 DEG. 43 MIN. NORTH. BUT WILL ANSWER FOR ANY OF
THE NORTHERN STATES. [Four lines of verse from] ADDISON.
> *Printed at Portland by John Kelse Baker.* [1797.] pp. (36). 12mo. AAS.

32115 FAUCHET, JEAN ANTOINE JOSEPH   1761–1834
A SKETCH OF THE PRESENT STATE OF OUR POLITICAL RELATIONS WITH THE UNITED
STATES OF NORTH-AMERICA. BY JOSEPH FAUCHET, EX-MINISTER OF THE FRENCH
REPUBLIC AT PHILADELPHIA. TRANSLATED BY THE EDITOR OF THE AURORA. [Ben-
jamin Franklin Bache.]
> *Philadelphia: Printed by Benj. Franklin Bache, No. 112, Market-street.*
> M,DCC,XCVII. pp. [31.] 8vo. AAS. BA. BM. HSP. JCB. LOC. MHS. NL. NYHS. NYPL.

32116 FAUGERES, MARGARETTA V. BLEECKER   1771–180!
THE GHOST OF JOHN YOUNG THE HOMICIDE, WHO WAS EXECUTED THE 17TH OF AU-
GUST LAST, FOR THE MURDER OF ROBERT BARWICK, A SHERIF'S OFFICER. [Two-em
inverted rule.] THE FOLLOWING MONODY IS WRITTEN WITH A VIEW OF RESCUING
HIS MEMORY FROM OBLOQUY, AND SHEWING HOW INCONSISTENT SANGUINARY LAWS
ARE, IN A COUNTRY WHICH BOASTS OF HER FREEDOM AND HAPPINESS: BY MRS.
FAUGERES. [PRICE SIX PENCE.]
> *[New-York: 1797.]* pp. 6. 8vo. BU.

32117 FEDERAL [cut] GALAXY. GOD SAID, "LET THERE BE LIGHT AND THERE WAS LIGHT."
VOL. I. No. 1. FRIDAY, JANUARY 6, [— No. 52. TUESDAY, DECEMBER 26, 1797.]
> *For Windham County.—Published by Benjamin Smead, in Brattleborough,
> Vermont, for Dickman and Smead.* 1797. fol. AAS.

The cut of United States Arms is surrounded by thirteen stars. Established, as a weekly, by Thomas Dickman, and Benjamin Smead. The
partnership of Dickman and Smead was dissolved, by mutual consent,
July 1, 1797. Benjamin Smead continuing publication into January
1803, when he removed to Dansville, New York, returning subsequently
to Burlington, Vermont, where he published the Vermont Gazette from
1806 to 1811.

32118 FEDERAL GAZETTE & BALTIMORE DAILY ADVERTISER. VOL. V. No. 986. MONDAY,
JANUARY 2, [—VOL. VI. No. 1297. SATURDAY, DECEMBER 30, 1797.]
> *[Baltimore:] Printed and sold by Yundt and Brown, No. 3, Calvert-Street,
> near the Court-House.* 1797. fol.

32119 FEDERAL GAZETTEER. [Motto.] VOL. I. No. 41. WEDNESDAY, JANUARY 4, [—
No. 52? WEDNESDAY, MARCH 22? 1797.]
> *New-Haven: Printed and published by Edward O'Brien & Co.* 1797. fol.

Discontinued publication, probably, at the end of its first volume, in
March, 1797.

32120   THE FEDERAL Primer.
       Wilmington: Printed by Peter Brynberg. 1797.

32121   THE FEDERAL Spy. Vol. v. No. 212. Tuesday, January 3, [—Vol. vi. No. 263. Monday, December 25, 1797.]
       Published by Francis Stebbins—Springfield—Massachusetts. 1797. fol.

32122   FEMALE friendship, or the innocent suffer. A moral novel. Volume the first. [— second.] [Two lines of verse.]
       Hallowell: Printed by Howard S. Robinson, for Nathaniel Cogswell, [at the Hallowell Bookstore.] 1797. 2 vols. pp. 126; 120. 12mo.   AAS.

32123   FÉNELON, François de Salignac de La Mothe, archevêque de Cambray Les Aventures de Telemaque, fils d'Ulysse. Par messire François de Salignac de la Motte Fenelon, archeveque de Cambray. Nouvelle edition. Comparée soigneusement avec les meilleures editions Francoises; revue & corrigée, par Joseph Nancrede, maitre de langue Françoise, en l'Université de Cambridge. Tome premiere.
       A Boston: Chez Joseph Nancrede, Libraire, No. 49, Marlboro' Street. 1797. pp. iii, 371. 12mo.   AAS. JCB.

32124   —— — The Adventures of Telemachus, the son of Ulysses. By the archbishop of Cambray. In French and English. The original carefully compared with the best French editions, and revised and corrected by Joseph Nancrede, French instructor in the University of Cambridge. Vol. I. [— II.]
       Boston: Joseph Nancrede, No. 49, Marlboro'-Street. 1797. 2 vols. pp. (2), (2), 188; 188; (2),(2), 184; 184. 12mo.   JCB.
      French and English texts on opposite pages.

32125   —— — The Adventures of Telemachus, the son of Ulysses. By the archbishop of Cambray. In French and English. The original carefully compared with the best French editions, and revised and corrected by Joseph Nancrede, French instructor in the University of Cambridge. Vol. I.[—II.]
       Philadelphia: Printed for G. Decombaz, No. 48, North Third Street. 1797. 2 vols. pp. (2), (2), 188; 188; (2),(2), 184; 184, (1). 12mo.   AAS. NYPL.
      French and English texts on opposite pages.

32126   —— — The Adventures of Telemachus son of Ulysses From the French of Fenelon by the celebrated Jno. Hawkesworth ll.d. Corrected & revised by G. Gregory d. d. With a life of the Author and a complete Index historical and geographical. Embellished with engravings. In two volumes. Vol. 2.
       Printed for, & published by David Longworth, No. 11, Park, New-York. [1797.] pp. (2), 318, (1), frontispiece, 4 plates. 8vo.   AAS. MHS.
      The first volume was published in 1796. Both with engraved title-pages.

32127   FENNING, Daniel
      The Ready reckoner, or, trader's useful assistant, adapted to the use of all who deal by wholesale or retail; exhibiting at one view, the amount or value of any number or quantity of goods or merchandize, from one up to ten thousand. At the various prices from 1 farthing to 1 pound. To which are prefixed, i. A table of interest, at six per cent. ii. A table of the weight and value of coins as they pass in the respective States of the Union, with their sterling and federal value. iii. a table shewing the amount of cents, &c.
       York: Printed by Salomon Myer. M,DCC,XCVII. pp. 191. 12mo.   AAS.

32128   FIELDING, Henry   1707–1754
      The History of Tom Jones, a foundling. Abridged from the works of Henry
      Fielding, esq. Adorned with [six full-page] cuts. [Ornament.]
         Boston: Printed and sold by S. Hall, in Cornhill. 1797. pp. 131, 6 plates.
      24mo.   AAS.

32129   FINLAY'S American Naval and [cut] Commercial Register. No. 112. Tuesday,
      January 3, [— No. 189. Friday, December 29. 1797.]
         Philadelphia: Printed (Tuesday and Friday) by Samuel Finlay, No. 16,
      Chesnut-Street. 1797. fol.   LCP.

32130   FISH, Elisha   1719–1795
      Extract from a Discourse [at Worcester, March 28, 1795, at the desire of the
      Convention of Committees for the County of Worcester.] By rev. Elisha Fish.
      New-York: 1797. 18mo.

32131   FISHER, James
      An Inaugural dissertation on that grade of the intestinal state of fever
      known by the name of dysentery. Submitted to the examination of the
      rev. John Ewing, s. t. p. provost, the trustees and medical faculty of the
      University of Pennsylvania. On the 12th day of May, 1797. For the de-
      gree of doctor of medicine. By James Fisher, of Delaware, member of
      the Philadelphia Medical Society.
         Philadelphia: Printed by Ormrod & Conrad, 41, *Chesnut-Street.* [1797.]
      pp. (52). 8vo.   AAS. BM. SGO.

32132   FISKE, Oliver   1763–1837
      An Oration, pronounced at Worcester, on the anniversary of American inde-
      pendence; July 4, 1797. By dr. Oliver Fiske. . . .
         Printed at Worcester, Massachusetts, by Isaiah Thomas, jun.—July—A. D.—
      1797. pp. 15. 4to.   AAS. BM. JCB. MHS.

32133   FLANAGAN, Christopher
      The Conversation and conduct, of the late unfortunate John Young, who
      was executed for the murder of Robert Barwick (deputy sheriff), from
      the time of receiving sentence of death, to that of his execution. By
      Christopher Flanagan, preacher of the Gospel. Who frequently visited
      him, during that period. [Four lines of verse.]
         New-York: 1797. 8vo.

      52d New York District Copyright, issued to Christopher Flanagan, as
      Author, 28 August, 1797.

32134   FLEET, John, junior   –1813
      A Discourse relative to the subject of animation, delivered before the
      Humane Society of the Commonwealth of Massachusetts, at their semi-
      annual meeting June 13th, 1797. By John Fleet, jun. m. d. m. m. s. "Ars
      longa est." [Printers mark.]
         Boston: Printed by John and Thomas Fleet, Cornhill, 1797. pp. 25. 4to.
                           AAS. BA. BM. BPL. HC. JCB. MHS. NYHS. NYPL. SGO.

32135   FLEET, Thomas, and John
      Fleets' Register, and pocket Almanack for the year of our Lord 1798. Being
      the second after leap [*sic*] year, and twenty second of American inde-
      pendence, which began July 4th, 1776. Calculated chiefly for the use of
      the Commonwealth of Massachusetts, Boston, the metropolis, being in
      latitude 42 deg. 23 min. north. longitude 71 deg. 4 min. west from the
      Royal Observatory at Greenwich.
         Boston: Printed and sold by T. & J. Fleet, at the Bible and Heart in Corn-
      hill. [1797.] pp. (20), (147). 24mo.   AAS. BA. HC. LOC. MHS. NYHS.

32136 | FOLSOM, JOHN WEST
FOLSOM'S NEW POCKET ALMANAC, FOR THE YEAR 1798.
Boston: Printed by John W. Folsom. [1797.] pp. (36). 12mo.

32137 | —— — FOLSOM'S NEW POCKET ALMANAC, FOR THE YEAR 1798. SECOND EDITION.
Boston: Printed by John W. Folsom. [1797.] pp. (36). 12mo.

32138 | FOLWELL, RICHARD
SHORT HISTORY OF THE YELLOW FEVER, THAT BROKE OUT IN THE CITY OF PHILA-
DELPHIA, IN JULY, 1797; WITH A LIST OF THE DEAD; OF THE DONATIONS FOR THE
RELIEF OF THE POOR, AND A VARIETY OF OTHER INTERESTING PARTICULARS.
Philadelphia: Printed by Richard Folwell, No. 33, Carter's Alley. M.DCC.-
XCVII. pp. 64, (8). 8vo.   LOC. SGO.

197th Pennsylvania District Copyright, issued to Richard Folwell, as
Author, 4 January 1798.

32139 | FORBES, ELI   1726–1804
THE RIGHTEOUS AND THE MERCIFUL TAKEN AWAY FROM THE EVIL TO COME — OR
THEIR DEATH CONSIDERED AND IMPROVED IN A SERMON PREACHED AT THE FUNERAL
OF JOHN LOW, ESQUIRE, ON THE 6TH DAY OF NOVEMBER, 1796, BY ELI FORBES,
M. A. PASTOR OF THE FIRST CHURCH OF CHRIST IN GLOUCESTER. (AND NOW MADE
PUBLIC BY DESIRE.) [Two lines from] KING DAVID.
Printed at Newburyport, by Edmund M. Blunt——1797. pp. 21. 8vo.
AAS. BA. BPL. HC. JCB. MHS. NYHS. NYPL.

32140 | FORREST, MICHAEL
THE POLITICAL REFORMER: OR A PROPOSED PLAN OF REFORMATIONS IN THE LAWS AND
GOVERNMENTS OF THE UNITED STATES OF AMERICA: CALCULATED TO PROMOTE HU-
MAN HAPPINESS. TO WHICH ARE ADDED, STRICTURES ON JOHN ADAMS'S DEFENCE
OF THE CONSTITUTIONS OF GOVERNMENT OF THE UNITED STATES OF AMERICA.
[Signed, CAMILLUS.]
*Philadelphia: Printed for the Author, by W. W. Woodward, No. 17, Chesnut
Street.* 1797. pp. 73. 8vo.   BA. BPL. JCB. LOC. MHS. NYPL.

A corrected duplicate entry of "Camillus" this year.

32141 | FOSTER, DAN   1748–1810
TWENTY BIOGRAPHICAL AND CHARACTERISTICAL SERMONS, ON THE LIVES AND CHAR-
ACTERS OF PERSONS RECORDED IN SCRIPTURES, ON REMARKABLE PASSAGES IN SA-
CRED HISTORY, AND ON SEVERAL PARTICULAR VIRTUES AND VICES OF THE HUMAN
HEART. BY DAN FOSTER, A. M. PREACHER OF THE GOSPEL IN CHARLESTON.
Walpole: Printed (?) by David Carlisle, jun. 1797. pp. 400. 8vo.

Proposals for printing, as above, were made by David Carlisle, junior,
this year.

32142 | FOSTER, HANNAH WEBSTER   1759–1840
THE COQUETTE; OR, THE HISTORY OF ELIZA WHARTON: A NOVEL; FOUNDED ON FACT.
BY A LADY OF MASSACHUSETTS.
Boston: Printed by Samuel Etheridge, for E. Larkin, No. 47, Cornhill.
1797. pp. 261, (1). 12mo.   NYPL.

Based on the love affairs of Pierrepont Edwards, Joseph Buckminster,
and Elizabeth Whitman. 143d Massachusetts District Copyright, issued
to Ebenezer Larkin, as Proprietor, 11 July, 1798.

32143 FOSTER, JOEL   1755–1812
AN ORATION DELIVERED AT NEW SALEM, JULY 4TH, 1797; BEING THE ANNIVERSARY
OF THE INDEPENDENCE OF THE UNITED STATES OF AMERICA. BY JOEL FOSTER.
Northampton: Printed by William Butler. 1797. pp. 16. 8vo.
                                                AAS. BM. JCB. NYPL.

32144 FOSTER, NATHANIEL
THE YOUNG FREEMASON'S GUIDE; BEING, AN ADDRESS DELIVERED BEFORE THE MEM-
BERS OF ST. ALBAN'S LODGE, AT BROOKLYN THE 27TH DECEMBER 1797, BEING THE
ANNIVERSARY OF ST. JOHN THE EVANGELIST. BY BROTHER NATHANIEL FOSTER, J. W.
New-York: Printed by J. Buel, No. 74, William-Street. 1797. pp. [23.]
8vo.   BPL. LOC. NYHS. NYPL.

32145 FOWLER, JOHN
THE TRUTH OF THE BIBLE FAIRLY PUT TO THE TEST, BY CONFRONTING THE EVIDENCES
OF ITS OWN FACTS. BY JOHN FOWLER.
Alexandria: Printed for the Author, by Price and Gird. 1797. pp. v, (7)–
(161). 8vo.   JCB. LOC.

9th Virginia District Copyright, issued to John Fowler, as Author, 15
May, 1797.

32146 FRAISIER, J. C.
THE SCHOLAR'S COMPANION, CONTAINING A CHOICE COLLECTION OF COTILLIONS &
COUNTRY-DANCES. BY M. J. C. FRAISIER.
*Boston: Printed by D. Bowen, at the Columbian Museum Press, for the
Author.* 1796. pp. [16.] 16mo.   LOC.

32147 FRANKLIN, BENJAMIN   1706–1790
THE LIFE OF DR. BENJAMIN FRANKLIN. WRITTEN BY HIMSELF. FIRST ALBANY
EDITION.
*Albany: Printed and sold by Barber & Southwick, Faust's Statue, below the
Dutch Church, State Street.* 1797. pp. 177, (3). 12mo.   NYPL.

With a List of the firm's publications at the end.

32148 —— THE WORKS OF THE LATE DR. BENJAMIN FRANKLIN; CONSISTING OF ESSAYS, HU-
MOROUS, MORAL AND LITERARY; CHIEFLY IN THE MANNER OF THE SPECTATOR.
Printed by Bunce and Spencer, corner of Fleet and George-Street, New-Haven.—
1797—pp. 108. 18mo.   AAS.

32149 —— — THE WORKS OF THE LATE DR. BENJAMIN FRANKLIN. CONSISTING OF HIS
LIFE, WRITTEN BY HIMSELF. TOGETHER WITH ESSAYS, HUMOUROUS, MORAL AND
LITERARY; CHIEFLY IN THE MANNER OF THE SPECTATOR.
New-York: Printed for Phillip Arnold. 1797. 2 vols. pp. 182; 104, (2),
portrait. 12mo.

32150 —— —— THE WORKS OF THE LATE DR. BENJAMIN FRANKLIN; CONSISTING OF HIS
LIFE WRITTEN BY HIMSELF: TOGETHER WITH ESSAYS HUMOUROUS, MORAL, AND
LITERARY; CHIEFLY IN THE MANNER OF THE SPECTATOR.
New-York: Printed for Johnson and Manchester. 1797. 2 vols. pp. 184,
portrait; 104, (2). 12mo.   NYPL.

32151 THE FRANKLIN REPOSITORY. VOL. I. NO. 38. THURSDAY, JANUARY 5, [—VOL. II.
NO. 37. TOTAL NO. 89. THURSDAY, DECEMBER 28, 1797.]
Chambersburg: Published by Robert Harper. 1797. fol.

32152   FRANKS, WILLIAM
THE MAN IN IRON; OR THE SUBSTANCE OF A DISCOURSE, INTRODUCED BY AN ALLE-
GORY, FROM DAVID'S LAST WORDS. DELIVERED BY WILLIAM FRANKS.
     New-York: Printed by T. & J. Swords, No. 99 Pearl-street. 1797. pp. 16.
8vo.   BM. NYHS.

32153   FRASER, DONALD
THE RECANTATION; BEING AN ANTICIPATED VALEDICTORY ADDRESS OF THOMAS PAINE
TO THE FRENCH DIRECTORY.
     New-York: Printed for the Author. 1797. pp. (15). 8vo.   AAS. LOC. NYHS.

32154   —— — THE RECANTATION; BEING AN ANTICIPATED VALEDICTORY ADDRESS OF
THOMAS PAINE, TO THE FRENCH DIRECTORY.
     Lexington: Printed by James H. Stewart. 1797.

32155   FREDERICKTOWN. PENNSYLVANIA. LIBRARY COMPANY.
A CATALOGUE OF BOOKS BELONGING TO THE FREDERICKTOWN LIBRARY COMPANY
TO WHICH IS PREFIXED, THE OBJECTS, ARTICLES, AND CONDITIONS ON WHICH THE
SAID COMPANY IS INCORPORATED.
     Washington: Printed for the Company, by John Colerick. 1797. pp. (12).
12mo.   AAS.

32156   FREE AND ACCEPTED MASONS. GENERAL GRAND ROYAL ARCH CHAPTER.
CONSTITUTION OF THE GENERAL GRAND ROYAL ARCH CHAPTER OF THE NORTHERN
STATES OF AMERICA.
     Printed at Albany, for Spencer and Webb. 1797. 12mo.

32157   FREEMAN, SAMUEL   1743–1831
A VALUABLE ASSISTANT TO EVERY MAN: OR, THE AMERICAN CLERK'S MAGAZINE. CON-
TAINING THE MOST USEFUL AND NECESSARY FORMS OF WRITINGS, WHICH COMMONLY
OCCUR BETWEEN MAN AND MAN, UNDER THE NAMES OF ACQUITTANCES, AGREEMENTS,
ASSIGNMENTS. AWARDS, BARGAINS, BILLS, BONDS, COMPLAINTS, CONVEYANCES, COV-
ENANTS. DEEDS, FEOFFMENTS, FINE AND RECOVERY, GIFTS, AND GRANTS, INDEN-
TURES, LEASES, LEASE AND RELEASE, LETTERS OF ATTORNEY, MORTGAGES, NOTES,
PLEAS, RECEIPTS, RELEASES, SALES, SURRENDERS, WILLS, WRITS, AND DECLARATIONS,
&C. AND OTHER INSTRUMENTS. THE WHOLE OF WHICH ARE CALCULATED FOR THE
USE OF THE CITIZENS OF THE UNITED STATES, AND CONFORMABLE TO LAW. BY
SAMUEL FREEMAN, ESQ. COMPILER OF THE TOWN OFFICER, PROBATE AUXILIARY,
AND MASSACHUSETTS JUSTICE. THE THIRD EDITION, REVISED, ENLARGED, AND MUCH
IMPROVED. PUBLISHED ACCORDING TO ACT OF CONGRESS.
     *Printed at Boston, by I. Thomas and E. T. Andrews, and sold by them at
Faust's Statue, No. 45, Newbury-Street; by Thomas, Son & Thomas in Worcester;
by Thomas, Andrews & Penniman, Albany: and Thomas, Andrews & Butler, Balti-
more.—Feb.* 1797. pp. 297, (1). 12mo.   AAS. JCB.

32158   FREEMAN'S JOURNAL. [Motto.] VOL. I. NUMBER 30. SATURDAY, JANUARY 1. [—
VOL. II. NUMBER 28. SATURDAY, DECEMBER 30, 1797.]
     *Cincinnati: Printed by S. Freeman and Son; subscriptions are received at
Cincinnati by the Editors: Columbia, by John Armstrong, esq. Maj. B. Stites, and
Capt. E. Kibby: Calwell's Mill, by James Calwell: Hamilton, by Thomas M'Cullagh,
esq. Colerain, by James Barrett, esq. North Bend, by Maj. S. Howell: South Bend,
by George Callum, esq. Newport, by Wm. Freeman: Bank-Lick, by William Smith,
and at Deerfield, by Capt. B. Stites.* 1797. fol.

32159 FRENEAU, PHILIP   1752–1832
MEGARA AND ALTAVOLA. TO A FEMALE SATIRIST (AN ENGLISH ACTRESS) ON RECEIVING FROM HER NO. I. OF A VERY SATIRICAL AND BITING ATTACK.
[*Monmouth, N. J. Printed at the Press of Philip Freneau, at Mount-Pleasant, near Middletown-Point.* 1797.]
"Six copies only of this little Poem were printed and sent to the satirist."

32160 THE FRIENDLY INSTRUCTOR: OR, A COMPANION FOR YOUNG LADIES AND YOUNG GENTLEMEN. IN WHICH THEIR DUTY TO GOD, AND THEIR PARENTS, THEIR CARRIAGE TO SUPERIORS, AND SEVERAL OTHER USEFUL AND INSTRUCTIVE LESSONS ARE RECOMMENDED, IN PLAIN AND FAMILIAR DIALOGUES. BY A LADY.
Printed at Boston, by B. Edes, jun. for Samuel Hall, No. 53, *Cornhill.* M,DCC,XCVII. pp. 60+ 18mo.   JCB.

32161 FRIENDS, SOCIETY OF
THE EPISTLE FROM THE YEARLY MEETING, HELD IN LONDON, BY ADJOURNMENTS, FROM THE 22D TO THE 31ST OF THE FIFTH MONTH, 1797. TO THE QUARTERLY AND MONTHLY MEETINGS OF FRIENDS IN GREAT BRITAIN, IRELAND, AND ELSEWHERE.
[*Philadelphia:* 1797.] pp. (4). fol.   AAS.

32162 —— RULES OF DISCIPLINE AND CHRISTIAN ADVICES OF THE YEARLY MEETING OF FRIENDS FOR PENNSYLVANIA AND NEW JERSEY. FIRST HELD AT BURLINGTON IN THE YEAR 1681, AND FROM 1685 TO 1760, INCLUSIVE, ALTERNATELY IN BURLINGTON AND PHILADELPHIA: AND SINCE AT PHILADELPHIA. ALPHABETICALLY DIGESTED AND PRINTED BY DIRECTION OF THE SAID MEETING.
Philadelphia: Printed by Samuel Sansom, jun. 1797. pp. 142. 4to. AAS. BM.
An excellent example of good printing and book-making.

32163 —— TO THE SENATE AND HOUSE OF REPRESENTATIVES OF THE UNITED STATES IN CONGRESS ASSEMBLED. THE MEMORIAL AND ADDRESS OF THE PEOPLE CALLED QUAKERS, FROM THEIR YEARLY MEETING HELD IN PHILADELPHIA BY ADJOURNMENTS FROM THE 25TH OF THE 9TH MONTH, TO THE 29TH OF THE SAME INCLUSIVE, 1797: [Against slavery, horse racing, cock fighting, gaming, shews, plays, entertainments, etc.]
[*Philadelphia:* 1797.] pp. 9. fol.

32164 FROTHINGHAM'S LONG-ISLAND HERALD. [Motto.] VOL. V. NUMB. 215. WEDNESDAY, JANUARY 4, [—VOL. VI. NUMB. 266. MONDAY, DECEMBER 25, 1797.]
Sag-Harbor, Printed by David Frothingham. 1797. fol.

32165 FRY, BENJAMIN
AN ASTRONOMICAL DIARY OR ALMANAC FOR THE YEAR OF CHRISTIAN ERA 1798; BEING SECOND AFTER LEAP-YEAR. CALCULATED FOR THE MERIDIAN OF PORTSMOUTH, NEW-HAMPSHIRE, LAT. 43 DEG. 5 MIN. NORTH: BUT MAY SERVE FOR ANY OF THE NEW-ENGLAND STATES. CONTAINING, ECLIPSES; ASPECTS; JUDGMENT OF THE WEATHER; TIMES OF RISING AND SETTING OF THE SUN, MOON, AND OF SEVERAL STARS AND PLANETS; HIGH WATER AT PORTSMOUTH; FEDERAL AND STATE COURTS; INTEREST TABLE, DO. OF GOLD COINS; ALSO A TIDE TABLE; FRIENDS' MEETINGS; A SHORT DESCRIPTION OF THE SOLAR SYSTEM; LIST OF ROADS, WITH MANY OTHER USEFUL MATTERS. BY BENJAMIN FRY. [Seven lines of verse.]
Portsmouth, New-Hampshire: Printed by Charles Peirce, No. 5, *Daniel-Street, sold by him wholesale and retail, and by most of the shop-keepers in town and country.* [1797.] pp. (24). 12mo.   NHHS.

32166 THE FUNNY COMPANION.
Wilmington: Printed by Peter Brynberg. 1797.

32167   FURLONG, LAWRENCE

THE AMERICAN COAST PILOT CONTAINING THE COURSES AND DISTANCES BETWEEN THE PRINCIPAL HARBOURS, CAPES AND HEADLANDS FROM PASSAMAQUODDY THROUGH THE GULPH OF FLORIDA, WITH DIRECTIONS FOR SAILING INTO THE SAME, DESCRIBING THE SOUNDINGS AND BEARINGS OF THE LIGHT HOUSES AND BEACONS FROM THE ROCKS, SHOALS, LEDGES, &C. TOGETHER WITH THE COURSES AND DISTANCES FROM CAPE COD AND CAPE ANN TO GEORGE'S BANK THROUGH THE SOUTH AND EAST CHANNELS, AND SETTING OF THE CURRENTS WITH THE LATITUDES AND LONGITUDES OF THE PRINCIPAL HARBOURS ON THE COAST. TOGETHER WITH A TIDE TABLE. BY CAPT. LAWRENCE FURLONG. CORRECTED AND IMPROVED BY THE MOST EXPERIENCED PILOTS IN THE UNITED STATES. ALSO INFORMATION TO MASTERS OF VESSELS WHEREIN THE MANNER OF TRANSACTING BUSINESS AT THE CUSTOM HOUSES IS FULLY ELUCIDATED. THE WHOLE FORMING A BODY OF INFORMATION HIGHLY USEFUL TO ALL PERSONS IN MERCANTILE OR MARITIME EMPLOYMENT. [Second edition.]

Newburyport (Massachusetts) Printed by Edmund M. Blunt. 1797.

135th Massachusetts District Copyright, issued to Edmund March Blunt, as Proprietor, 21 November, 1797.

32168   GADSDEN, CHRISTOPHER   1723–1805

A FEW OBSERVATIONS ON SOME LATE PUBLIC TRANSACTIONS, IN AND OUT OF CONGRESS; PARTICULARLY ON THE DANGEROUS AND SEEMINGLY UNCONSTITUTIONAL MANNER THE LATE ELECTION FOR A CHIEF MAGISTRATE WAS CONDUCTED THROUGHOUT THE STATES OF THE UNION. MOST RESPECTFULLY RECOMMENDED TO THE SERIOUS CONSIDERATION OF THE CITIZENS OF ALL THE UNITED STATES. BY A MEMBER OF THE CONGRESS ON THE STAMP ACT, HELD AT NEW-YORK IN 1765, AND OF THE TWO FIRST AT PHILADELPHIA IN 1774 AND 1775. OBSTA PRINCIPIIS. [Signed, A STEADY FEDERALIST. CHARLESTON, JANUARY 30, 1797.]

Charleston: Printed by Freneau & Paine, No. 48, Bay. MDCCXCVII. pp. 27. 8vo.   BA.

32169   GAIFER, pseudonym.

THE CONVERSION OF A MAHOMETAN TO THE CHRISTIAN RELIGION, DESCRIBED IN A LETTER FROM GAIFER, IN ENGLAND, TO ALY-BEN-HAYTON, HIS FRIEND IN TURKEY. WE SPEAK THAT WE DO KNOW. THE TENTH EDITION—PRICE SEVEN-PENCE.

Concord: Printed by George Hough, for Francis Mitchel, of Hopkinton, N. H. MDCCXCVII. pp. (24). 12mo.   AAS. JCB.

32170   —— — THE CONVERSION OF A MAHOMETAN, TO THE CHRISTIAN RELIGION, DESCRIBED IN A LETTER FROM GAIFER IN ENGLAND TO ALI-BEN-HAYTON, HIS FRIEND IN TURKEY. WE SPEAK THAT WE DO KNOW.

Hallowell: Printed by Peter Edes. 1797. pp. 21. 12mo.

32171   GALES'S INDEPENDENT [cut] GAZETTEER. [Motto.] No. 1839. NEW SERIES. NO. 32. TUESDAY, JANUARY 3, [— No. 1911. NEW SERIES. No. 104. TUESDAY, SEPTEMBER 12, 1797.]

Philadelphia: Printed every Tuesday and Friday at noon, by Joseph Gales, No. 145, North Second-Street, where printing in general is executed, in a neat and correct manner. Subscriptions, advertisements, articles of intelligence, orders for printing, &c. are also received by Wm. Young Birch, at his Stationary-Store, No. 17, South Second-Street. ☞ *Price of the Independent Gazetteer four dollars per annum.* 1797. fol.   LCP.

With the issue for September 12th, publication ceased. Joseph Gales disposing of all his interests to Samuel Harrison Smith who established, in November, *The Universal Gazette.*

32172   GALLATIN, ABRAHAM ALBERT ALPHONSE   1761–1849
AN EXAMINATION OF THE CONDUCT OF THE EXECUTIVE OF THE UNITED STATES, TO-
WARDS THE FRENCH REPUBLIC; LIKEWISE AN ANALYSIS OF THE EXPLANATORY
ARTICLE OF THE BRITISH TREATY—IN A SERIES OF LETTERS. BY A CITIZEN OF
PENNSYLVANIA. "THERE'S SOMETHING ROTTEN IN THE STATE OF DENMARK!"
SHAKESPEARE.

    Philadelphia: Printed by Francis and Robert Bailey, at Yorick's-Head, No.
116, High-street. M,DCC,XCVII. pp. [vi], [72.] 8vo.

                        AAS. BA. HC. HSP. JCB. LOC. NYHS. VSL.

32173   THE GAMUT; OR SCALE OF MUSIC. FOR THE USE OF SCHOOLS.
    Troy: Printed and sold by Luther Pratt & Co. 1797.

32174   GAY, ANTHELME
NEW FRENCH PRONOUNCING SPELLING-BOOK, OR, PROSODICAL GRAMMAR, DESIGNED
FOR THE USE OF SUCH YOUNG LADIES AND GENTLEMEN AS MAY WISH TO ACQUIRE,
WITH FACILITY, A JUST AND ELEGANT PRONUNCIATION OF THAT POLITE AND USEFUL
LANGUAGE. BY A. GAY.

    Philadelphia: Printed by John Ormrod, No. 41, Chesnut-Street, 1797. pp.
202, xi. 12mo.   AAS.

32175   GAZETTE, FRANCAISE. NO. 129. LUNDI, 2 JANVIER, [— NO. 284. VENDREDI, 29
DECEMBRE, 1797.]

    Imprimée [par Claude Parisot] a New-York, Pearl-Street, No. 51. 1797.
4to.   HC.

32176   GAZETTE OF THE UNITED STATES, & PHILADELPHIA DAILY ADVERTISER. NUMBER
1348. MONDAY, JANUARY 2, [— NUMBER 1655. SATURDAY, DECEMBER 30, 1797.]

    [Philadelphia:] Printed by John Fenno,—No. 119, Chesnut-street. 1797.
fol.   AAS. BA. BPL. HC. LCP. LOC.

32177   DER GEMEINNÜTZIGE LANDWIRTHSCHAFTS CALENDER AUF DAS JAHR . . . 1798.
    Lancaster: Gedruckt bey Johann Albrecht u. Comp. [1797.]

32178   THE GENIUS OF LIBERTY; AND FREDERICKSBURG & FALMOUTH ADVERTISER. VOL.
I. No. 1. FRIDAY, OCTOBER 20, [— No. 11. FRIDAY, DECEMBER 29, 1797.]
    Fredericksburg, (Va.) Printed by Mercer & Carter. 1797. fol.

    Established, as a weekly, by Robert Mercer and George Carter, and con-
tinued by them into 1799, when Carter withdrew, and was succeeded by
—— Field, under the firm name of Mercer & Field. Mercer died 11
September, 1800, and the Printing-office passed into the possession of
James Walker, who established, in October, in continuation, *The Courier.*

32179   GENLIS, STÉPHANIE FÉLICITÉ BRULART DUCREST DE ST. AUBIN, comtesse DE
SACRED DRAMAS, WRITTEN IN FRENCH, BY MADAME LA COMTESSE DE GENLIS. TRANS-
LATED INTO ENGLISH BY THOMAS HOLCROFT. CONTENTS, THE DEATH OF ADAM,
HAGAR IN THE WILDERNESS, THE SACRIFICE OF ISAAC, JOSEPH MADE KNOWN TO HIS
BRETHREN, RUTH AND NAOMI, WIDOW OF SAREPTA, RETURN OF TOBIAS.

    Fredericksburg: Printed by L. A. Mullin, for the Rev. Mason L. Weems.
1797. pp. viii, 136. 12mo.   AAS. LOC. NYPL.

    The Widow of Sarepta, was omitted from this edition. See, also, No.
235, of the excellent "Weems Bibliography" by Emily Ellsworth Ford
Skeel.

32180   THE GENTLEMAN'S ANNUAL POCKET REMEMBRANCER, FOR THE YEAR 1798.
    Boston: Sold by David West, John West, and W. P. and Lemuel Blake. [1797.]

32181   THE GEORGETOWN CHRONICLE: AND SOUTH-CAROLINA WEEKLY ADVERTISER. VOL. VII. No. 304. TUESDAY, JANUARY 3, [—VOL. VII. No. 356. WEDNESDAY, NOVEMBER 1, 1797.]

       Georgetown: Printed by James Smylie. 1797. fol.

       Sometime this year publication was made semi-weekly, and "weekly" dropped from the title. The above is the last number located.

32182   GEORGIA. STATE.
     ACTS OF THE STATE OF GEORGIA, PASSED AT THE LAST SESSION OF THE LEGISLATURE.
       Augusta: Printed by John E. Smith, Printer to the State. 1797.

32183   —— THE REPRESENTATION AND REMONSTRANCE OF THE LEGISLATURE OF THIS STATE TO THE PRESIDENT, SENATE AND HOUSE OF REPRESENTATIVES OF THE UNITED STATES.
       Augusta: Printed by Alexander M'Millan, Printer to the State. 1797.

32184   GEORGIA. THE AUGUSTA CHRONICLE AND GAZETTE OF THE STATE. [Motto.] VOL. XI. No. 535. SATURDAY, JANUARY 7, [—VOL. XII. No, 586. SATURDAY, DECEMBER 30, 1797.]
       Augusta: Printed by John E. Smith, Printer to the State. 1797. fol. GHS.

32185   GEORGIA GAZETTE. No. 723. SATURDAY, SEPTEMBER 2, [— No. 740. FRIDAY, DECEMBER 29, 1797.]
       Savannah: Printed by N. Johnston and Co. 1797. fol.

       "Savannah, June 8, 1797. The publication of the Georgia Gazette having been suspended by the destruction of the office of James & Nicholas Johnston, in the calamitous fire, which happened on the 26th of November, 1796, and their partnership having terminated on the 1st of January last, the printing of the paper will again commence, at the office of Nicholas Johnston & Co., in Broughton-Street." Beginning with the issue for October 13th, the day of publication was changed from Saturday to Friday.

32186   DIE GERMANTAUNER ZEITUNG. NUM. 338. DIENSTAG DEN 4 JANUAR, [— NUM. 389. DIENSTAG, DEN 27 DECEMBER, 1797.]
       Diese Zeitung wird wochentlich Dienstag Nachmittags herausgegeben von Michael Billmeyer, Buchdrucker, zu Germantaun; . . . 1797. 4to.

32187   GESNER, SALOMON   1730–1787
     THE DEATH OF ABEL. IN FIVE BOOKS. ATTEMPTED FROM THE GERMAN OF MR. GESSNER. THE THIRTIETH EDITION.
       New-York: Printed by John Tiebout, for E. Duyckinck & Co. No. 110. Pearl-street. 1797. pp. iv, 140. 24mo.   AAS. NYPL.

32188   —— — DEATH OF ABEL, IN FIVE BOOKS. ATTEMPTED FROM THE GERMAN OF MR. GESSNER, BY MARY COLLYER.
       Wilmington, (Del.) Printed by Peter Brynberg. 1797. pp. 108. 12mo.

32189   GIFFORD, JOHN, assumed name of JOHN RICHARDS GREENE   1758–1818
     THE HISTORY OF FRANCE, FROM THE EARLIEST TIMES, TILL THE DEATH OF LOUIS SIXTEENTH. FROM THE FRENCH OF VEILLY, VILLART, GARNIER, MEZERAY, DANIEL, AND OTHER EMINENT HISTORIANS; WITH NOTES, CRITICAL AND EXPLANATORY; BY JOHN GIFFORD, ESQ. AND, CONTINUED FROM THE ABOVE PERIOD, UNTIL THE CONCLUSION OF THE PRESENT WAR, BY A CITIZEN OF THE UNITED STATES. [William Duane.] VOL. II.
       Philadelphia: Printed for James Stewart & Co. by Snowden & M'Corkle. 1797. pp. 567, 10 plates. 4to.   AAS. LOC.

GIFFORD, John, continued.

32190 —— — The History of France, FROM THE EARLIEST TIMES, TILL THE DEATH OF Lewis the sixteenth. From the French of Velly, Villaret, Garnier, Mezeray, Daniel, AND OTHER EMINENT HISTORIANS: WITH NOTES CRITICAL AND EXPLANATORY; BY John Gifford, ESQ. AND, CONTINUED FROM THE ABOVE PERIOD, UNTIL THE PRESENT DAY. BY A Citizen of the United States. [William Duane.] VOL. III.

Philadelphia: Printed by Stewart and Rowson, No. 9, Cherry-Street. 1797. pp. 568, (6), 8 plates. 4to.   AAS. LOC.

The first volume was published in 1796, and a fourth volume in 1798.

32191 —— A Letter to the hon. Thomas Erskine; CONTAINING SOME STRICTURES ON HIS View of the causes and consequences of the present war with France. By John Gifford, ESQ. AUTHOR OF A Letter to the earl of Lauderdale, &c. &c. [Two lines of French from] Voltaire.

Philadelphia: Published by William Cobbett, opposite Christ Church, November, 1797. pp. (4), 128. 8vo.   AAS. BA. LOC. MHS. NYPL. RIHS.

32192 GILDERSLEEVE, Cyrus   1769–1838
A Century sermon, delivered at Midway, January 1st, 1797. A copy of which BEING REQUESTED, BY THE SELECTMEN OF THE SOCIETY, IN ORDER TO BE PRINTED, WAS HANDED TO THEM BY THE Author. The rev. Cyrus Gildersleeve, A. M. PASTOR . . .

Savannah: Printed by Seymour & Woolhopter, on the Bay. [1797.] pp. 32. 16mo.   LOC. NYPL.

The above may have been printed with his New Year's Sermon, in 1798.

32193 GILL. John   1697–1771
Three sermons, ON THE PRESENT AND FUTURE STATE OF THE CHURCH. Preached TO THE SOCIETY, WHICH SUPPORT THE Wednesday's evening lecture in Cannon-street, London. Serm. I. The Watchman's answer to the question, What of.the night? From Isaiah XXI. 11, 12. Serm. II. The Practical improvement of the watchman's answer to the question, What of the night? From I Chron. XII. 32. Serm. III. The Glory of the church in the latter day, From Psalm LXXVII. By John Gill, D. D. The sixth edition.

Re-printed at Northampton, (Massachusetts) by William Butler. M,DCC,-XCVII. pp. 64. 8vo.   AAS. BA.

32194 GILPIN, William   1724–1804
An Account of a new poor-house, erected in the parish of Boldre, in New Forest, near Lymington.

Philadelphia: Printed by Thomas Dobson, at the Stone-House, No. 41, *South Second-Street*—1797. pp. (23). 12mo.   AAS.

32195 GIRAUD, Jean Jacques   1759–1839
Sel spécifique et universel du docteur Giraud pour les maladies vénéri-ennes. . . .

[Philadelphia: Imprimé par Pierre Parent. 1797.] pp. 8. 8vo.   NYPL.

"a Philadelphia, chez Parent . . . a New-York, chez M. Parisot . . . a Charleston, chez——— . . . . a Baltimore chez L' auteur."

32196   GLEASON, James   1723–1803
AN EXPOSITION OF THE THREE FIRST CHAPTERS ON GENESIS, EXPLAINED AND IM-
PROVED. WHEREIN THE FOUR DISPENSATIONS CONTAINED IN THE SCRIPTURES FROM
AGE TO AGE, ARE REVEALED. COMPRISING THE TRAVEL OF MYSTICAL AND POLITIC
BABYLON, AND THE DESTRUCTION THEREOF. OR THE GOSPEL GLASS, OR TRAVEL OF
ZION'S CHURCH IN THE WORLD, UNTIL THE OPENING OF THE LAST GREAT AND SEV-
ENTH SEAL, WHEN THE MYSTERY OF GOD IS FINISHED; AND THE JUBILEE TRUMP
PROCLAIM ALLELUIA AND SALVATION. BY DR. JAMES GLEASON, OF CONNECTICUT.
    Norwich: Printed by John Trumbull. M,DCC,XCVII. pp. 190, (1). 8vo.
                    BM. JCB. NYPL.

32197   GODWIN, William   1756–1836
THE ENQUIRER. REFLECTIONS ON EDUCATION, MANNERS, AND LITERATURE. IN A
SERIES OF ESSAYS. BY WILLIAM GODWIN. [Two lines of Latin from] OVID.
    Philadelphia: Printed for Robert Campbell & Co. by John Bioren. 1797.
pp. viii, 387. 8vo.   AAS. JCB. NYPL.

32198   GOETZ, Johann Nepomück
LIED DER FREUDE GESUNGEN AM FEIERLICHEN GEBURTSTAGE SEINER EXCELLENZ
GENERAL WASCHINGTON, WÜRDEGSTEN PRESIDENT DER VEREINIGTEN STAATEN
AMERICANS. VON JOHANN NEPOMUCK GOETZ.
    *Philadelphia: Gedruckt bey Henrich Schweitzer, No. 85 in der Rees-strasse
zwischen der Zweiten und Dritten-strasse.* 1797. pp. 7. 8vo.

32199   THE GOLDEN BALLS.
    Rutland: Printed by Josiah Fay. 1797.

32200   GOLDSMITH, Oliver   1728–1774
THE BEAUTIES OF GOLDSMITH: OR THE MORAL AND SENTIMENTAL TREASURY OF GEN-
IUS; [Three lines from] CITIZEN OF THE WORLD.
    *Philadelphia: Printed by Francis Bailey, at Yorick's-Head, No. 116, High-
Street.* M,DCC,XCVII. pp. xvii, (7), 244. 24mo.   AAS.

32201   THE GOSHEN REPOSITORY, AND WEEKLY INTELLIGENCER. VOL. VIII. No. 416. TUES-
DAY, JANUARY 3, [—VOL. IX. No. 467. TUESDAY, DECEMBER 26, 1797.]
    Published every Tuesday by William Hurtin, in Goshen (Orange County)
. . . 1797. fol.

32202   THE GRAFTON [cut] MINERVA, AND HAVERHILL WEEKLY BUD. [Motto.] VOL. I.
No. 43. THURSDAY, JANUARY 5, [— No. 46. MONDAY, JANUARY 23, 1797.]
    *Haverhill, (New Hampshire) Published on Thursdays, by Nathaniel Coverly,
directly opposite the Court-House.* 1797. fol.
    The above is the last number located.

32203   GRANGER, Gideon   1767–1822
AN ORATION SPOKEN ON TUESDAY, THE FOURTH OF JULY, 1797, AT THE EAST MEET-
ING-HOUSE IN SUFFIELD: BEING THE ANNIVERSARY OF AMERICAN INDEPENDENCE.
BY GIDEON GRANGER, ESQ.
    Suffield: Printed and for sale by Havila & Oliver Farnsworth, M,DCC,XCVII.
pp. 24. 8vo.   AAS. BM. CHS. NYPL. YC.

32204   GRATTAN, Henry   1746–1820
PRESENT STATE OF IRELAND! MR. GRATTAN'S ADDRESS TO HIS FELLOW-CITIZENS OF
DUBLIN, ON HIS RETIRING FROM PARLIAMENT. TO WHICH IS ADDED, HIS ANSWER
TO THE INDEPENDENT CITIZENS OF DUBLIN.
    *Philadelphia: Printed (from the tenth Dublin edition) by J. Carey, for M.
Carey, 118, Market-Street, G. Douglas, 2 S. Third-Street, and J. Carey, 83 N.
Second-Street.* 1797. pp. (44). 8vo.   BA. JCB. LOC. MHS.

32205   GREEN or GREENE, BENJAMIN   1764–1837
AN ORATION, DELIVERED BEFORE THE RIGHT WORSHIPFUL MASTER, WARDENS AND
BRETHREN OF THE PHILANTHROPIC LODGE OF FREE AND ACCEPTED MASONS, AT
THE SECOND MEETING-HOUSE IN MARBLEHEAD, ON THE FESTIVAL OF ST. JOHN THE
BAPTIST, JUNE 24, 5797. BY BROTHER BENJAMIN GREEN.
Printed at Salem, by Thomas C. Cushing. 1797. pp. [23.] 8vo. AAS. EI. HC. NYPL.

32206   GREEN, JACOB   1722–1790
A VISION OF HELL, AND A DISCOVERY OF SOME OF THE CONSULTATIONS AND DEVICES
THERE, IN THE YEAR 1767. BY THEODORUS VAN SHEMAIN. [Eleven lines of
Scripture texts.]
Amherst: Printed and sold by Samuel Preston. 1797. pp. (24). 12mo. AAS.

32207   GREEN, SAMUEL
GREEN'S ALMANACK AND REGISTER, FOR THE STATE OF CONNECTICUT; FOR THE
YEAR OF OUR LORD, 1798; BEING THE TWENTY-SECOND OF THE INDEPENDENCE OF
THE UNITED STATES.
New-London: Printed and sold by Samuel Green. [1797.] pp. 148. 24mo.
CHS. YC.

32208   GREENFIELD GAZETTE. OR, MASSACHUSETTS AND VERMONT TELEGRAPHE. NO. 50
OF VOL. V. WHOLE NO. 258. THURSDAY, JANUARY 5, [—NO. 49 OF VOL. VI. WHOLE
NO. 309. THURSDAY, DECEMBER 28, 1797.]
Printed at Greenfield, (Massachusetts) by Thomas Dickman . . . 1797. fol.
AAS.
In January, 1798, the title was changed to *Greenfield Gazette. An im-
partial register of the times.*

32209   —— NEW-YEAR'S ADDRESS OF THE CARRIERS OF THE GREENFIELD GAZETTE. [Five
six-line verses. BY SAMUEL ELLIOT, OF BRATTLEBORO' VERMONT.]
Greenfield: Printed by Thomas Dickman. 1797. Broadside.

32210   GREENLEAF'S NEW-YORK JOURNAL, & PATRIOTIC REGISTER. [Motto.] VOL. LI.
NUMB. 1. TOTAL NUMB. 3151. WEDNESDAY, JANUARY 4, [— NUMB. 104. TOTAL
NUMB. 3254. SATURDAY, DECEMBER 30, 1797.]
*New-York—Printed and published (on Wednesdays and Saturdays) by Thomas
Greenleaf, at his Printing-Office, No. 54, Wall-Street.* . . . 1797. fol.
AAS. NYHS. NYPL.

32211   GRIFFITH, WILLIAM   1766–1826
A TREATISE ON THE JURISDICTION AND PROCEEDINGS OF JUSTICES OF THE PEACE, IN
CIVIL SUITS; WITH AN APPENDIX, CONTAINING ADVICE TO EXECUTORS, ADMINISTRA-
TORS AND GUARDIANS—ALSO, AN EPITOME OF THE LAW OF LANDLORD AND TENANT.
THE WHOLE INTERSPERSED WITH PROPER FORMS, AND CALCULATED FOR GENERAL
INSTRUCTION. BY WM. GRIFFITH, ESQ, COUNSELLOR AT LAW. THE SECOND EDI-
TION, WITH IMPROVEMENTS, A NEW CHAPTER ON CONVEYANCING.
Newark, New-Jersey: Printed by John Woods, for the Author. 1797. pp.
12, 320, 21. 12mo.   NPL. NYHS. NYPL.

32212   —— THE SCRIVENER'S GUIDE; CONTAINING CONCISE PRECEDENTS OF ACQUITTANCES,
DEEDS OF SALE, PARTITION, &C. AGREEMENTS, INDENTURES OF APPRENTICE, ARBI-
TRATION AND AWARDS, LEASES, ASSIGNMENTS, LICENCE OF DEBTORS, ATTORNIES
LETTERS, &C. MORTGAGES, BILLS OF SALE, PROMISSORY NOTES, BILLS, &C. BONDS AND
CONDITIONS, RECOGNIZANCE, COMPOSITION WITH CREDITORS, WILLS AND CODICILS.
WITH PRACTICAL NOTES AND EXPLANATIONS. "MULTUM IN PARVO." BY WM.
GRIFFITH, ESQ, COUNSELLOR AT LAW.
Newark, New-Jersey: Printed by John Woods. MDCCXCVII. pp. 48. 8vo.
AAS. NPL. NYPL.
This is a re-paged reprint of pages 273–320 of the preceding title.

32213   GRIFFITHS, John
A Collection of the newest cotillions, and country dances. Principally compiled by J. Griffiths, dancing-master. To which is added, Rules for conversation, and instances of ill manners to be avoided by youth.

Hartford: Printed by Elisha Babcock, for John Babcock. 1797.

32214   GRIMKÉ, John Faucheraud   1752–1819
The Duty of executors and administrators; pointing out, in a plain and familiar manner, how executors are to proceed in the probate of wills, getting in the effects, and paying the debts and legacies of their testator: shewing also who are entitled by law to be the administrators of an intestate person: with full and clear directions to a man's relations how his estate will be distributed among them, according to the laws of South-Carolina. To which are prefixed, all the statutes and acts relative to these subjects, Mr. Blackstone's rules for interpreting wills and deeds, and a table of inheritance, with a concise and easy explanation thereof. To which is added, a variety of precedents of wills, codicils, &c. with instructions for every person to make, alter and republish his will; and likewise, all the forms made use of in the court of ordinary. [One line of Latin from] Cicero.

New-York: Printed by T. and J. Swords, No. 99, Pearl-street. 1797. pp. (xvii), 343, (2), 2 tables. 8vo.   AAS.

South Carolina District Copyright, issued to John Faucheraud Grimké, as Author, 20 January, 1798.

32215   GRISWOLD, Alexander Viets   1766–1843
A Discourse . . . at Harwinton, on the 5th day of January, 1797, occasioned by the death of Mr. Lent Munson, . . .

Litchfield: Printed by T. Collier. MDCCXCVII. pp. 16. 8vo.

32216   GUARDIAN; or, New-Brunswick Advertiser. Num. 10, of Vol. v. Whole num. 218. Tuesday, January 3, [— Num. 9. of Vol. vi. Whole num. 269. Tuesday, December 26, 1797.]

New-Brunswick, New-Jersey: Printed by Abraham Blauvelt, in Albany-Street. 1797. fol.   AAS.

32217   GUTHRIE, William   1620–1665
The Christian's great interest: in two parts. i. The trial of a saving interest in Christ. ii. The way how to attain it. By William Guthrie, minister of the Gospel at New-Kilmarnock, Scotland.—Also—the Life of the Author. [By Robert Trail.] [Nine lines of Scripture texts.]

New-Brunswick (New-Jersey:) Printed by Abraham Blauvelt, for John Smith.—1797. pp. (xii), (202). 12mo.   AAS. NYPL.

32218   HALL, Prince   1748–1807
A Charge, delivered to the African Lodge, June 24, 1797, at Menotomy. By the right worshipful Prince Hall.

[Boston: Printed by Benjamin Edes, for and sold at Prince Hall's Shop, opposite the Quaker Meeting-House, Quaker-Lane.] Published by the desire of the members of said Lodge.—1797.—pp. (18). 16mo.   AAS. BA. BPL. HC. MHS. NYPL.

32219 HALL'S WILMINGTON GAZETTE. VOL. I. NO. 1. THURSDAY, JANUARY 5, [— No. 52. THURSDAY, DECEMBER 28, 1797.]

Wilmington, N. C. Printed by Allmand Hall. 1797. fol.

Established, as a weekly, in continuation of *The Wilmington Chronicle,* by Allmand Hall, and continued by him into October, 1808, when William S. Hasell purchased his interests and became its publisher. In 1810, —— Magrath was admitted to partnership as Hasell & Magrath, but before 1812 Hasell again became sole publisher up to his death, October 6, 1815. He was succeeded by the firm of Macalester & Loring The earliest issue bearing their name, which is also the last number located, is for January 13, 1816. In 1799, the title was changed to *The Wilmington Gazette,* the "The" being dropped from 1802 to September, 1806; and became *Wilmington Gazette, commercial and political,* under its last owners.

32220 HAMILTON, ALEXANDER 1739–1802
OUTLINES OF THE THEORY AND PRACTICE OF MIDWIFERY. BY ALEXANDER HAMILTON, M. D. F. R. S. PROFESSOR OF MIDWIFERY IN THE UNIVERSITY, AND FELLOW OF THE ROYAL COLLEGE OF PHYSICIANS, EDINBURGH. ARTE NON VI. FROM THE LAST BRITISH EDITION, REVISED, CORRECTED, AND ENLARGED, BY THE AUTHOR. THE THIRD AMERICAN EDITION.

Printed at Northampton, by Wm. Butler, for Thomas & Andrews. Sold by them at their Book-Store in Boston; by Thomas, Andrews & Penniman, Albany; and by Thomas, Andrews & Butler, Baltimore. October, 1797. pp. 288. 12mo.
AAS. JCB. NYPL. 8GO.

32221 —— — OUTLINES OF THE THEORY AND PRACTICE OF MIDWIFERY. BY ALEXANDER HAMILTON, M. D. F. R. S. PROFESSOR OF MIDWIFERY IN THE UNIVERSITY, AND FELLOW OF THE ROYAL COLLEGE OF PHYSICIANS, EDINBURGH. A NEW EDITION.

Philadelphia: Printed by Thomas Dobson, at the Stone House, No 41, South Second-Street. 1797. pp. xv, 288; 98, 40 plates. 8vo. AAS. NYPL. 8GO.

Second title: A SET OF ANATOMICAL TABLES, WITH EXPLANATIONS, AND AN ABRIDGEMENT OF THE PRACTICE OF MIDWIFERY; WITH A VIEW TO ILLUSTRATE A TREATISE ON THAT SUBJECT, AND COLLECTION OF CASES. BY WILLIAM SMELLIE, M. D.

Philadelphia: Printed by Thomas Dobson, at the Stone House, No. 41, South Second-Street. 1797. pp. 98, 40 plates.

32222 HAMILTON, ALEXANDER 1757–1804
OBSERVATIONS ON CERTAIN DOCUMENTS CONTAINED IN NO. V. & VI. OF "THE HISTORY OF THE UNITED STATES FOR THE YEAR 1796," IN WHICH THE CHARGE OF SPECULATION AGAINST ALEXANDER HAMILTON, LATE SECRETARY OF THE TREASURY, IS FULLY REFUTED. WRITTEN BY HIMSELF.

Philadelphia: Printed for John Fenno, by John Bioren. 1797. pp. (37), lviii. 8vo. AAS. BA. BM. BU. HC. HSP. JCB. LCP. LOC. MHS. NYHS. NYPL.

188th Pennsylvania District Copyright, issued to John Fenno, as Proprietor, 26 July, 1797. Usually referred to as the "Reynold's pamphlet." An attempt was later made by Hamilton's family to destroy it; and it is not included in the edition of his works published in 1810, or in the one authorized by the Congress in 1850. Republished in Philadelphia, and in New York, in 1800; and, in an edition of seventy-five copies, for the Hamilton Club, in New York, in 1865.

32223 HAMILTON, ——
HAMILTONS VERSUS EATON: A CASE RESPECTING BRITISH DEBTS, LATELY DETERMINED IN THE CIRCUIT COURT OF THE UNITED STATES, FOR NORTH-CAROLINA DISTRICT, PRESIDED B C. J. ELLSWORTH. [Ornament.]

Newbern: Francois-Xavier Martin. 1797. pp. (2), 77. 8vo. LOC. NYPL.

32224   HAMLIN, Amos
THE REPUBLIC OF REASON: BEING AN ESSAY ON NATURE AND REASON. [Four lines of verse from] BARLOW. BY AMOS HAMLIN. WHO TAKES THE LIBERTY RESPECTFULLY TO DEDICATE THIS SMALL ESSAY TO THE UNBIGOTTED AND REASONABLE PART OF MANKIND OF EVERY SECT AND DENOMINATION IN THE UNITED STATES OF AMERICA, AND THE WORLD AT LARGE.
Albany: Printed for the Author. M,DCC,XCVII. pp. 12. 12mo.   BU.

32225   HAMPSHIRE GAZETTE. VOL. XI. NUMB. 549. WEDNESDAY, JANUARY 4, [— VOL. XII. NUMB. 591. WEDNESDAY, DECEMBER 27, 1797.]
Printed at Northampton, (Massachusetts), by William Butler. 1797. fol.
     AAS. MHS.

32226   HARPER, ROBERT GOODLOE   1765-1825
OBSERVATIONS ON THE DISPUTE BETWEEN THE UNITED STATES AND FRANCE, ADDRESSED BY ROBERT GOODLOE HARPER, OF SOUTH CAROLINA, TO HIS CONSTITUENTS, IN MAY, 1797.
Philadelphia: Printed & sold by Thomas Bradford, Book-seller & Stationer, No. 8, South Front-Street. 1797. pp. (2), 102. 8vo.
     AAS. BA. BM. CLS. HC. JCB. LCP. NYHS.

187th Pennsylvania District Copyright, issued to Thomas Bradford, as Proprietor, 24 June, 1797.

32227   —— — OBSERVATIONS ON THE DISPUTE BETWEEN THE UNITED STATES AND FRANCE. ADDRESSED BY ROBERT GOODLOE HARPER, OF SOUTH CAROLINA, TO HIS CONSTITUENTS, IN MAY, 1797. SECOND EDITION.
Philadelphia: Printed and sold by Thomas Bradford, Book-seller and Stationer, No. 8, South Front-Street. 1797. pp. 79. 8vo.   AAS. LCP.

Not less than fifteen editions of the Observations were printed in this country and Great Britain in this and the following years.

32228   HARRIS, THADDEUS MASON   1768-1842
A DISCOURSE, DELIVERED AT BRIDGEWATER NOVEMBER 8, 1797, AT THE REQUEST OF THE MEMBERS OF FELLOWSHIP LODGE, ON OCCASION OF THE CONSECRATION OF THE LODGE AND INSTALLATION OF THE OFFICERS. BY THE REVEREND BROTHER THADDEUS MASON HARRIS, CHAPLAIN TO THE GRAND LODGE OF MASSACHUSETTS. [Two lines of Latin quotations.] [Cut of crown.]
Boston: Printed by Samuel Hall. No. 53, Cornhill. 1797. pp. [20], [11.] 8vo.   AAS. HC. JCB. NYHS.

Second title: AN ORATION, DELIVERED NOVEMBER 8D, A. L. 5797, BY THE REQUEST OF FELLOWSHIP LODGE, IN BRIDGEWATER, AT THE CONSECRATION OF THE LODGE AND INSTALLATION OF OFFICERS; IN THE PRESENCE OF THE GRAND LODGE OF FREE AND ACCEPTED MASONS IN THE COMMONWEALTH OF MASSACHUSETTS, AND THE GRAND LODGE OF THE STATE OF RHODE-ISLAND. BY HECTOR ORR. [Cut of crown.]
Printed by Samuel Hall, No. 53, Cornhill, Boston. 1797. pp. [11.]

32229   —— — IGNORANCE AND PREJUDICE SHEWN TO BE THE ONLY ENEMIES TO FREE MASONRY —— THEIR OBJECTIONS CONSIDERED AND ANSWERED —— AND THE TRUE DESCRIPTION OF THE SOCIETY GIVEN IN A SERMON AT THE CONSECRATION OF SAINT PAUL'S LODGE IN GROTON, AND THE INSTALLATION OF ITS OFFICERS IN DUE FORM, AUGUST 9TH, A. L. 5797. BY THE REV. BROTHER THADDEUS M. HARRIS, CHAPLAIN TO THE GRAND LODGE OF MASSACHUSETTS. [Two lines of Scripture text.]
Leominster, Mass. Printed by brother Charles Prentiss. A. L. 5797 [1797]. pp. (28). 8vo.   AAS. BA. NYPL.

HARRIS, Thaddeus Mason, continued.

32230 —— A Sermon, preached at the ordination of the Rev. John Pierce, to the pastoral care of the church and christian society in Brookline, March 15th, 1797. By Thaddeus Mason Harris, pastor of the Congregational church and society in Dorchester. [Ornament.]

Boston: Printed by Manning & Loring. May, 1797. pp. 39, (1). 8vo.

AAS. BA. HC. JCB. MHS. UTS.

The Charge, by the Rev. Jacob Cushing, of Waltham. The Right hand of fellowship, by the Rev. Eliphalet Porter, of Roxbury.

32231 HARTFORD. Connecticut.
By-laws of the city of Hartford.

Hartford: Printed by Hudson & Goodwin. 1797. pp. 53, (2). 8vo.

32232 HARTFORD. Connecticut. Library Company.
Constitution, extracts from the By-laws, and a Catalogue of the books, in the Hartford Library Company.

Hartford: Printed by Hudson & Goodwin. 1797. pp. 20. 8vo.

32233 HARVARD UNIVERSITY.
Catalogus eorum qui in Universitate Harvardiana Cantabrigiæ, in Republica Massachusettensi, ab anno MDCXLII, ad annum MDCCXCVII. Alicujus gradûs laureâ donati sunt. Theologiæ professores et ecclesiarum pastores literis italicis exarantur. Qui ad imum classium à cæteris, lineâ interpositâ, separantur, alibi instituti fuerunt, vel apud nos gradu honorario donati.

Bostoniæ: Typis Johannes et Thomæ Fleet. MDCCXCVII. *Annoque Rerum-Publicarum Americæ Fœderatarum summæ potestatis* XXII. pp. 40. 8vo.

AAS. BA. HC. JCB. IOC. MHS. NL. NYPL.

32234 —— Illustrissimo Crescentio Sumner, armigero, gubernatori; honoratissimo Mosi Gill, armigero, vice gubernatori; consiliariis et senatoribus Reipublicæ Massachusettensis; reverendisque ecclesiarum in oppidis sex vicinis, presbyteris, Universitatis Harvardianæ curatoribus; reverendo Josepho Willard, s. t. d. ll. d. præsidi; [Four lines] Theses hasce, juvenes in artibus initiati, [Fifty-four names.] Humillimé dedicant. [Four columns.] Habita in comitiis Universitatis Cantabrigiæ, Massachusettensis, die Julii xix, anno salutis MDCCXCVII. Rerumque publicarum Fœderatarum Americæ potestatis xxii. [Colophon:]

Bostoniæ: Typis Manning & Loring. [1797.] Broadside. fol.

AAS. BPL. CHS. EI. HC. MHS. YC.

32235 —— Harvard University in Cambridge, Commonwealth of Massachusetts. The order of the exercises of commencement, July 19th, MDCCXCVII.

[Boston: Printed by J. and T. Fleet, 1797.] Broadside. fol.

AAS. BA. BPL. HC. NYHS.

32236 HASWELL, Anthony   1756–1816
Haswell's Federal and Vermont Register: together with an Almanac, for the year 1798.

Bennington: Printed by Anthony Haswell, [1797.] pp. (36). 12mo.

32237 HATFIELD. Massachusetts. House Joiners and Cabinet Makers.
Regulations ascertaining the work and wages of house-joiners and cabinet makers; agreed upon at Hatfield, in the County of Hampshire, March 2nd, 1796. A paper very useful both for the workmen and their employers.

Rutland: Printed by Josiah Fay. 1797.

32238   HAVRE DE GRACE. MARYLAND. HAVRE DE GRACE COMPANY.
ARTICLES OF ASSOCIATION OF THE HAVRE DE GRACE COMPANY.
     Philadelphia: Printed by Charles Cist, No. 104, North Second-Street,
M,DCC,XCVII. pp. 15. 8vo.   HC. LOC.

32239   HAWKINS, JOSEPH   1772–
A HISTORY OF A VOYAGE TO THE COAST OF AFRICA, AND TRAVELS INTO THE INTERIOR
OF THAT COUNTRY; CONTAINING PARTICULAR DESCRIPTIONS OF THE CLIMATE AND
INHABITANTS, AND INTERESTING PARTICULARS CONCERNING THE SLAVE TRADE. BY
JOSEPH HAWKINS OF NEW-YORK, WHO HAS SINCE BECOME BLIND; AND FOR WHOSE
BENEFIT IT IS NOW PUBLISHED BY HIS FRIENDS.
     Philadelphia: Printed for the Author, by S. C. Ustick, & Co. 1797. pp.
179, (1), (1), plate. 12mo.   AAS. BA. BPL. JCB. LCP. LOC. NYPL.
     163d Pennsylvania District Copyright, issued to Joseph Hawkins, as
Proprietor, 3 January, 1797.

32240   —— — A HISTORY OF A VOYAGE TO THE COAST OF AFRICA, AND TRAVELS INTO THE
INTERIOR OF THAT COUNTRY; CONTAINING PARTICULAR DESCRIPTIONS OF THE CLI-
MATE AND INHABITANTS, AND INTERESTING PARTICULARS CONCERNING THE SLAVE
TRADE. BY JOSEPH HAWKINS, OF NEW YORK, WHO HAS SINCE BECOME BLIND;
AND FOR WHOSE BENEFIT IT IS NOW PUBLISHED BY HIS FRIENDS. THE SECOND
EDITION.
     Troy: Printed for the Author, by Luther Pratt. 1797. pp. 180, frontispiece.
18mo.   BM. NYPL.
     With a Letter from Felix Pascalis Ouviere prefixed. Introduction
signed, A Student.

32241   HAYDN, FRANZ JOSEPH   1732–1809
OVERTURE, BY HAYDN. PRICE 75 CENTS.
     Printed by G. Willig, Market Street, Philadelphia. [1797.]

32242   HEIDELBERG CATECHISM.
THE HEIDELBERG CATECHISM, OR METHOD OF INSTRUCTION IN THE CHRISTIAN RE-
LIGION. AS THE SAME IS TAUGHT IN THE REFORMED CHURCHES AND SCHOOLS IN
HOLLAND. TOGETHER WITH THE ARTICLES OF FAITH, AND LITURGY OF SAID
CHURCH. TRANSLATED FOR THE USE OF THE REFORMED PROTESTANT DUTCH
CHURCH IN NEW YORK.
     New-Brunswick: Printed by A. Blauvelt. 1797. pp. 102. 18mo.   AAS.

32243   HEINS, H. A.
VON DEN WOHLTHATIGEN ABSICHTEN DER DEUTSCHEN GESELLSCHAFT VON PENNSYL-
VANIEN. REDE GEHALTEN DER 20. SEPTEMBER 1796.
     Philadelphia: Gedruckt bey Carl Cist. 1797.

32244   HELLENBROEK, ABRAHAM   1658–1731
SPECIMEN OF DIVINE TRUTHS, FITTED FOR THE USE OF THOSE, OF VARIOUS CAPACITIES,
WHO DESIRE TO PREPARE THEMSELVES FOR A DUE CONFESSION OF THEIR FAITH.
. . . TRANSLATED FROM THE DUTCH. . . .
     Wilmington: Printed by Peter Brynberg. 1797.

32245   HENFREY, BENJAMIN
A PLAN WITH PROPOSALS FOR FORMING A COMPANY TO WORK MINES IN THE UNITED
STATES; AND TO SMELT AND REFINE THE ORES WHETHER OF COPPER, LEAD, TIN,
SILVER, OR GOLD. BY BENJAMIN HENFREY. IS IT NOT THE INTEREST OF EVERY
CITIZEN OF AMERICA TO PROMOTE THE WORKING OF MINES; SINCE ALL THAT IS OB-
TAINED FROM THE BOWELS OF THE EARTH BECOMES AN ADDITION TO THE PUBLIC
STOCK. [Ornament.]
     Philadelphia: Printed by Snowden & M'Corkle, No. 47 North Fourth-Street.
1797. pp. (34), folded table. 8vo.   AAS. BA. LOC. MHS. NYHS. NYPL.

32246   THE HERALD; A GAZETTE FOR THE COUNTRY. VOL. III. NUMB. 268. WEDNESDAY,
JANUARY 4, [— VOL. IV. NUMB. 343. SATURDAY, SEPTEMBER 30, 1797.]
*Published (Wednesdays and Saturdays) by Hopkins, Webb & Co. No. 40,
Pine-Street, New-York.* 1797. fol.   AAS. BPL. HC. LOC. NYHS. NYPL.

Beginning June 24th, "Printers of the Laws of the United States for the
district of New-York," was added to the imprint. Beginning October
4th, a new series was begun under the same editor, and George F. Hopkins, alone, as publisher, under the title of *The Spectator.*

32247   THE HERALD OF THE TIMES; OR, THE LUZERNE IMPARTIAL GAZETTE. [Motto.]
VOL. I. No. 10. TUESDAY MORNING, JANUARY 3, [— No. 52. TUESDAY MORNING,
OCTOBER 31, 1797.]
*Wilkesbarre, County of Luzerne, (Pennsylvania). Published by M. Johnson
& B. Hall, near the Post Office.* 1797. fol.

With the issue for January 24, Micah Johnson withdrew, and publication was continued by Benajah Hall alone to the end of the first volume,
in October, when it was discontinued. In April, the title was shortened
to *The Herald of the Times.*

32248   HERALD OF THE UNITED STATES. No. 40 OF VOL. V. WHOLE NO. 249. SATURDAY,
JANUARY 7, [— No. 39 OF VOL. VI. WHOLE NO. 299. SATURDAY, DECEMBER 29,
1797.]
*Warren:—Published at the Post-Office, by Nathaniel Phillips, Printer to the
State.* 1797. pp. 988–1192. fol.   AAS. RIHS.

32249   HERVEY, JAMES   1714–1758
THE BEAUTIES OF HERVEY: OR DESCRIPTIVE, PICTURESQUE AND INSTRUCTIVE PAS-
SAGES, SELECTED FROM THE WORKS OF THIS DESERVEDLY ADMIRED AUTHOR, VIZ.
MEDITATIONS AMONGST THE TOMBS—REFLECTIONS ON A FLOWER GARDEN—DES-
CANT ON THE CREATION—CONTEMPLATIONS ON THE NIGHT—THE STARRY HEAVENS
—A WINTER PIECE—THE MOST IMPORTANT, INTERESTING, AND PICTURESQUE PAS-
SAGES FROM THERON AND ASPASIO—LETTERS AND SERMONS—MISCELLANEOUS
TRACTS—RELIGIOUS EDUCATION OF DAUGHTERS—AND—REMARKS ON LORD BOL-
INGBROKE'S LETTERS. TO WHICH ARE ADDED. MEMOIRS OF THE AUTHOR'S LIFE
AND CHARACTER; WITH AN ELEGIAC POEM ON HIS DEATH. [Signed, G. W.] [Four
lines of verse.]
Wilmington: Printed by Peter Brynberg. M,DCC,XCVII. pp, 226, (2), (4).
12mo.   AAS. DHS. NYPL.

With the exception that the title-page and preliminary leaves have been
entirely reset, the body of the work is identically the same as the edition
printed by V. Bonsal in 1796.

32250   —— MEDITATIONS AND CONTEMPLATIONS. IN TWO VOLUMES. CONTAINING, VOLUME I.
MEDITATIONS AMONG THE TOMBS. REFLECTIONS ON A FLOWER GARDEN: AND, A
DESCANT UPON CREATION. VOLUME II. CONTEMPLATIONS ON THE NIGHT. CONTEM-
PLATIONS ON THE STARRY HEAVENS: AND A WINTER-PIECE. BY JAMES HERVEY,
A. M. LATE RECTOR OF WESTON-FAVELL, NORTHAMPTONSHIRE. VOLUME I. [—II.]
Wilmington: Printed and sold by Peter Brynberg. M,DCC,XCVII. 2 vols.
in one. pp. 428. 12mo.   AAS. BM. DHS. JCB.

32251   HEYWOOD, JOSHUA   1761–1814
AN ORATION AT AMHERST, NEW-HAMPSHIRE, ON THE 4TH OF JULY, 1796. BY JOSHUA
HEYWOOD.
Amherst: Printed by Biglow and Cushing. 1796.

AUCTION
VALUES

32252   HILLARD, ISAAC
TO THE PUBLIC. [Statement of his reasons for instituting prosecutions against those who had kidnapped, sold, and sent out of the State free negroes.]
[Without place or Printer. 1797.] pp. 16. 8vo.

32253   HILLS, JOHN
THIS PLAN OF THE CITY OF PHILADELPHIA AND ITS ENVIRONS IS DEDICATED TO THE MAYOR, ALDERMEN AND CITIZENS THEREOF. BY JOHN HILLS, MAY 30, 1796.
[Philadelphia ? John Hills, 1797.] 37 x 27.
Republished by Samuel L. Smedley in 1881.

32254   THE HISTORY OF CONSTANTIUS & PULCHERA, OR CONSTANCY REWARDED. AN AMERICAN NOVEL. [Eight lines of verse.]
Printed at Leominster, (Mass.) by Charles Prentiss, for Robert B. Thomas, Sterling. 1797. pp. 102, (5). 24mo.   AAS. NYPL.
Contains, a five-page list of Books, for sale by Robert B. Thomas, in Sterling.

32255   THE HISTORY OF JANE SHORE, AND FAIR ROSAMOND.
Wilmington: Printed by Peter Brynberg. 1797.

32256   THE HISTORY OF LITTLE GOODY TWO SHOES. ORNAMENTED WITH [twenty] CUTS. [Vignette.]
Charlestown: Printed by J. Lamson, for Samuel Hall, in Cornhill, Boston. 1797. pp. 94, frontispiece. 48mo.

32257   —— THE HISTORY OF LITTLE GOODY TWO-SHOES. OTHERWISE CALLED MRS. MARGERY TWO-SHOES. WITH THE MEANS BY WHICH SHE ACQUIRED HER LEARNING AND WISDOM, AND IN CONSEQUENCE THEREOF HER ESTATE. SET FORTH AT LARGE FOR THE BENEFIT OF ALL THOSE PRETTY LITTLE BOYS AND GIRLS WHO WISH TO BE GOOD AND HAPPY.
Wilmington, Delaware: Printed by Peter Brynberg. 1796. pp. 128, frontispiece, and cuts in text. 64mo.

32258   THE HISTORY OF MARTIN AND JAMES, A MORAL TALE, IN WHICH VIRTUE AND VICE ARE CONTRASTED.
Boston: Printed and sold by William Spotswood, No. 55, Marlborough-Street. 1795.

32259   HITCHCOCK, ENOS   1744–1803
A NEW-YEAR'S SERMON; DELIVERED AT PROVIDENCE, JANUARY 1, 1797. BY ENOS HITCHCOCK, D. D. PUBLISHED BY REQUEST OF THE BENEVOLENT CONGREGATIONAL SOCIETY.
Providence: Printed by Carter and Wilkinson. 1797. pp. (12). 8vo.
         AAS. JCB, RIHS.

32260   THE HIVE. VOL. I. No. 1. WEDNESDAY, MAY 31, [— No. 31. WEDNESDAY, DECEMBER 27, 1797.]
Printed by W. Hamilton, King Street, Lancaster. 1797. pp. (124). 4to. LANHS.
Established, as a weekly literary periodical, by William Hamilton, and continued by him to the end of the first volume, May 23, 1798.

32261   HOARE, PRINCE   1755–1834
HEY DANCE TO THE FIDDLE & TABOR. A DIALOGUE IN THE LOCK & KEY. SUNG BY MRS. & MR. HODGKINSON.
New-York: Printed & sold at J. Hewitt's Musical Repository, No. 131, William Street. Sold also by B. Carr Philadelphia & J. Carr Baltimore. Price 25 cts. [1797.] pp. (2). 4to.   LOC.

32262 | DER HOCH-DEUTSCHE Americanische Calendar, Auf das Jahr 1798. Nach der Gnadenreichen Geburt unsers Herrn und Heylandes Jesu Christi, (welches in gemeines Jahr von 365 Tagen ist). [Eight lines.] Zum Vierzehntenmal heraus gegeben.
Germantown, gedruckt und zu finden bey Michael Billmeyer. [Six lines.] [1797.] pp. (40). 4to.   AAS. LOC.

32263 | HODGKINSON, John   1767–1806
A Narrative of his connection with the Old American Company, from the fifth of September, 1792, to the thirty-first of March, 1797. By John Hodgkinson.
New-York: Printed by J. Oram, No. 33, Liberty Street. 1797. pp. 28, (1), portrait. 8vo.   AAS. BA. NYHS. NYPL.

32264 | HOLLINSHEAD, William
An Oration . . . at the Orphan-House of Charleston . . . October 18, 1797. By the Rev. William Hollinshead, D. D.
Charleston: Printed by W. P. Young. 1797. pp. 22. 8vo.

32265 | HOLMES, Abraham
An Oration delivered in Middleborough, June 1, 1796, before the Philological Society, being their anniversary meeting. By Abraham Holmes.
Newbedford: Printed by John Spooner. 1797. pp. 14. 8vo.

32266 | HOLMES, Elkanah
A Church covenant; including a summary of the fundamental doctrines of the Gospel. Compiled by Elkanah Holmes. [Three lines of Scripture texts.]
New-York: Printed by John Tiebout, at Homer's Head, No. 358, Pearl-Street, for the Compiler. 1797. pp. (2), 82. 12mo.   AAS.
Contains a Collection of xi Hymns.

32267 | HOME, Henry, lord Kames.   1696–1782
The Culture of the heart; or, hints on education. By the late Henry Home, lord Kames.
Albany: 1797.

32268 | HOMES, John
Catalogue of books for sale at John Homes's Book and Stationery Store, opposite the north door of the State House, State Street, Boston.
Boston: Printed for John Homes. 1797. pp. 21. 12mo.

32269 | HONESTUS, pseudonym.
The Seventeenth jewel, of the United States of America: shining in its meridian splendor; in the latitude and longitude of the intended State of Maine. Or, the future intentional addition of its Constitution to the Federal Union. [Wood cut of Fame.]
n. p. Printed for the Author. 1797. pp. 35. 12mo.   AAS.
Signed, Honestus. Dated, Hancock County. Town of Milton, January 4, 1797.

32270 | HOOK, James   1746–1827
Alone by the light of the moon. A favourite song.
Boston: 1797.   BPL. JCB.

32271 | —— Donna donna donna Della. A favorite song. Composed by Mr. Hook.
New York: Printed & sold at J. Hewitt's Musical Repository No. 131 William Street. And at B. Carr's Philadelphia and J. Carr's Baltimore. [1797.] pp. (2). 4to.   LOC.

HOOK, JAMES, continued.

32272   —— HE LOVES HIS WINSOME KATE. A FAVORITE SCOTCH SONG. COMPOSED BY MR. HOOK.
New-York. Printed & sold at J. Hewitt's Musical Repository No. 131 William Street. Sold also by B. Carr Philadelphia & J. Carr, Baltimore. Pr. 25 cents. [1797.] 4to.   BPL. LOC.

32273   —— HERE'S THE PRETTY GIRL I LOVE. COMPOSED BY MR. HOOK.
New-York. Printed & sold at J. Hewitt's Musical Repository No. 131 William St. Sold also by B. Carr Philadelphia & J. Carr, Baltimore. Pr. 25 cents. [1797.] pp. (2). 4to.   BPL. LOC.

32274   —— HOOT AWA YOU LOON, A FAVOURITE SCOTS SONG. COMPOSED BY MR. HOOK.
New-York. Printed & sold at J. Hewitt's Musical Repository No. 131 William Str. Price 25 cents. [1797.] pp. (2). 4to.   LOC.

32275   —— I'M IN HASTE. COMPOSED BY MR. HOOK.
New-York: Printed for James Hewitt & sold at his Musical Repository William Street, at B. Carr's Philada. at J. Carr's Baltimore. [1797.] pp. (2). 4to.   LOC.

32276   —— IF A BODY LOVES A BODY. COMPOSED BY MR. HOOK.
New-York. Printed & sold at J. Hewitt's Musical Repository, No. 131 William St. Sold also by B. Carr Philadelphia & J. Carr Baltimore. [1797.] pp. (2). 4to.   LOC.

32277   —— THE LINNET. SONG.
New York. Printed & sold at J. Hewitt's Musical Repository, No. 131 William St. Sold also by B. Carr Philadelphia & J. Carr Baltimore. [1797.] pp. (2). 4to.   BPL.

32278   —— WHAT CAN A LASSY DO. SONG BY JAMES HOOK.
New York. Printed & sold at J. Hewitt's Musical Repository, No. 131 William St. Sold also by B. Carr Philadelphia. [1797.]   BPL.

32279   —— WHERE LIFFEY ROLLS ITS SILVER STREAM. A FAVORITE SONG IN THE OPERA OF JACK OF NEWBERRY. COMPOSED BY MR. HOOK.
New York. Printed and sold at J. Hewitt's Musical Repository No. 131 William Street. And at B. Carr's Philadelphia and at J. Carr's Baltimore. [1797.]   HSP.

32280   —— WHERE'S THE HARM OF THAT. A FAVORITE SONG COMPOSED BY MR. HOOK.
New York. Printed & sold at J. Hewitt's Musical Repository No. 131 William Street. Sold also by B. Carr Philadelphia & J. Carr Baltimore. Price 25 cts. [1797.] pp. (2). 4to.   HSP.

32281   HORNE, MELVILL
LETTERS ON MISSIONS; ADDRESSED TO THE PROTESTANT MINISTERS OF THE BRITISH CHURCHES. BY MELVILL HORNE, LATE CHAPLAIN OF SIERRA LEONE, IN AFRICA. [Six lines from] PHILIP. IV. 8.
Schenectady: Printed by C. P. Wyckoff, in State-Street. 1797. pp. xiii, 124, (2). 12mo.   AAS. NYPL.

Contains, a two-page list of Books for sale, by Cornelius P. Wyckoff, at his Book-Store, corner of State and Washington Streets, Schenectady. Reprinted in Andover in 1815.

32282   HOSACK, ALEXANDER, JUNIOR.   –1865
HISTORY OF THE YELLOW FEVER, AS IT APPEARED IN THE CITY OF NEW YORK, IN 1795. BY ALEXANDER HOSACK, JUN. M. D. OF NEW YORK.

Philadelphia: Printed by Thomas Dobson, at the Stone-House, No. 41, South Second-Street. 1797. pp. 36. 8vo.   JCB. NYHS. NYPL. 8GO.

32283   —— AN INAUGURAL ESSAY ON THE YELLOW FEVER, AS IT APPEARED IN THIS CITY IN 1795. SUBMITTED TO THE PUBLIC EXAMINATION OF THE FACULTY OF PHYSIC, UNDER THE AUTHORITY OF THE TRUSTEES OF COLUMBIA COLLEGE, IN THE STATE OF NEW-YORK, WILLIAM SAMUEL JOHNSON, LL. D. PRESIDENT FOR THE DEGREE OF DOCTOR OF PHYSIC, ON THE 3D OF MAY, 1797. BY ALEXANDER HOSACK, JUN. A. M. OF NEW-YORK.

New-York: Printed by T. and J. Swords, Printers to the Faculty of Physic of Columbia College, No. 99 Pearl-street.—1797.—pp. 40. 8vo.   AAS. NYPL. 8GO.

32284   HOUGHTON, ASA
THE GENTLEMEN'S AND LADIES' DIARY AND ALMANAC, WITH AN EPHEMERIS, FOR THE YEAR OF THE CREATION, ACCORDING TO SACRED WRIT, 5760, AND OF THE CHRISTIAN ERA. 1798. BEING THE SECOND AFTER BISSEXTILE. OR LEAP YEAR; AND THE TWENTY-SECOND YEAR OF THE INDEPENDENCE OF THE UNITED STATES OF AMERICA. [Five lines.] BY ASA HOUGHTON, PHILOM. [Eight lines of verse.]

Printed at Keene, New Hampshire. By C. Sturtevant, jun. & Co. Sold by them, and by most of the merchants in this and the adjacent States. [Price—7 dollars per gross—75 cents per dozen—10 cents single.] [1797.] pp. (48). 12mo.
                             AAS. MEHS. NYHS.

The Author's second Almanac. Dated, Bolton, August 28, 1797; but first in New Hampshire.

32285   HOWARD, THOMAS
THE HISTORY OF THE SEVEN WISE MISTRESSES OF ROME. CONTAINING MANY INGENIOUS AND ENTERTAINING STORIES; WHEREIN THE TREACHERY OF EVIL COUNSELLORS IS DISCOVERED, INNOCENCY CLEARED, AND THE WISDOM OF THE SEVEN WISE MISTRESSES DISPLAYED.

Boston: Printed and sold by William Spotswood, No. 55, Marlborough-Street. 1795. pp. 114, (2). 24mo.   AAS.

32286   —— — THE HISTORY OF THE SEVEN WISE MISTRESSES OF ROME. CONTAINING MANY INGENIOUS AND ENTERTAINING STORIES; WHEREIN THE TREACHERY OF EVIL COUNSELLORS IS DISCOVERED, INNOCENCY CLEARED, AND THE WISDOM OF THE SEVEN WISE MISTRESSES DISPLAYED.

Wilmington: Printed and sold by Peter Brynberg. 1797.

To the Reader. Signed, By Tho. Howard. In correction of X: 29492, and XI: 31176.

32287   HUDSON. NEW YORK. MASON HALL.
AN ACCOUNT OF THE PERFORMANCES AT THE DEDICATION OF MASON-HALL, HUDSON, ON THE FESTIVAL OF ST. JOHN THE EVANGELIST, ANNO LUCIS, 5796, CORRESPONDING TO DECEMBER 27, 1796, WITH A BRIEF RECORD OF THE ORIGIN OF THE LODGES IN THE COUNTY OF COLUMBIA, WITH THEIR PAST AND PRESENT OFFICERS. TO WHICH WILL BE AFFIXED, THE LIVES OF ST. JOHN THE BAPTIST, AND ST. JOHN THE EVANGELIST, EXTRACTED FROM THE ANCIENT WRITINGS, WITH NOTES AND OBSERVATIONS.

Hudson: Printed by Ashbel Stoddard, for the Authors, 1797. pp. [89.] 16mo.   AAS.

Contains, Poems, and Prayer, by John Frederick Ernst; and a Poetical Prayer of dedication, and an Oration, by Walter Clarke Gardiner.

32288   HUDSON Gazette. Vol. XII. Numb. 614. Monday, January 2, [—Vol. XIII. Numb. 665. Tuesday, December 26, 1797.]
[Hudson:] Printed by Ashbel Stoddard. 1797. fol.

32289   HUGER, Francis K.
An Inaugural dissertation on gangrene and mortification, submitted to the examination of the rev. John Ewing, s. t. p. provost; the trustees and medical faculty of the University of Pennsylvania, on the 12th day of May, 1797. For the degree of doctor of medicine. By Francis K. Huger, of South Carolina. [Two lines of Latin from] Hor.
Philadelphia: Printed by Stephen C. Ustick. 1797. pp. 31. 8vo.   AAS. BM. SGO.

32290   HUMPHREYS, Daniel   1740–1827
An Appeal to the Bible, on the controversy What is genuine christianity? and against the corruptions of that religion by the clergy; containing strictures on mr. Macclintock's ordination sermon, entitled, "Evidences of christianity." By Daniel Humphreys. [Eight lines of Scripture texts.]
Portsmouth: N. H. Printed by Charles Peirce, No. 5, Daniel-street, and for sale at his Bookstore.—1797. pp. 59. 8vo.   AAS. BPL.

32291   THE HUNTINGDON Courier and Weekly Advertiser. Vol. i. No. 1. Tuesday, July 4, [— No. 26. Tuesday, December 26, 1797.]
Huntingdon, Pennsylvania. Published by Michael Duffey. 1797. fol.

Established, as a weekly, by Michael Duffey, and continued by him into February, 1798, when it was discontinued.

32292   HUNTINGTON, Enoch   1739–1809
A Sermon preached at Haddam, June 14, 1797. On the day of the execution of Thomas Starr, condemned for the murder of his kinsman, Samuel Cornwell, by seven wounds given him, by a penknife, in the trunk of his body, July 26th, 1796, of which he languished a few days and died: with a sketch of the life and character of said Starr. By Enoch Huntington, a. m, pastor of the first church in Middletown. [Five lines of Scripture texts.]
Middletown: Printed by Moses H. Woodward. [1797.] *pp. 24. 12mo.*
AAS. BA. CHS. HC. NYHS. UTS. YC.

32293   —— Life and character of Thomas Starr, who was executed on the 14th [June] inst. for murder.
Middletown: Printed by Moses H. Woodward. 1797.

32294   —— A Sermon, preached at Middletown, June 28, 1797, on the celebration of the festival of St. John the Baptist, by St. John's Lodge, No. 2, Middletown. By Enoch Huntington, a. m. pastor of the first church in Middletown. [Two lines of Scripture texts.]
Middletown: Printed by Moses H. Woodward. [1797.] *pp. 16. 8vo.*   UTS.

32295   HUNTINGTON, William   1745–1813
God, the poor man's guardian, and the bank of faith; or, a display of the providences of God, which have at sundry periods of time attended the author. By William Huntington, minister of the Gospel at Providence chapel, &c. &c. To which is added, his Last will and testament. [Five lines of Scripture texts.]
Newburyport: Printed by Edmund M. Blunt.— 1797. pp. 180 ; [48.] *12mo.*   AAS.

Second title: The Last will and testament of William Huntington, a servant of Christ, and of the church for His sake. [Two lines of Scripture texts.] pp. [48.]

32296   HUTCHINS, GABRIEL
THE UNITED STATES ALMANAC, FOR THE YEAR OF OUR LORD, 1798: BEING THE SECOND AFTER LEAP-YEAR, AND THE XXIID OF AMERICAN INDEPENDENCE, 'TILL 4TH JULY; CONTAINING EVERY THING THAT IS USEFUL OR NECESSARY IN AN ALMANAC. ALSO, A VARIETY OF ENTERTAINING MATTER IN PROSE AND VERSE. BY GABRIEL HUTCHINS, MATHEMATICIAN.
     Elizabeth-Town: Printed by Shepard Kollock, for Samuel Campbell, No. 124, Pearl-Street, New-York. [1797.] pp. (36). 12mo.   AAS.
     Contains, Anecdotes. Geographical description of the Isle of Matrimony. The child trained up for the gallows. By the late Governor Livingston. The agreeable ghost. Absurd customs. By John Gregory, M. D. Let somebody else do it. The unfeeling father. Curious invention. Useful to sportsmen who are naturalists.

32297   HUTCHINS, JOHN NATHAN
HUTCHINS IMPROVED: BEING AN ALMANACK AND EPHEMERIS OF THE MOTIONS OF THE SUN AND MOON; THE TRUE PLACES AND ASPECTS OF THE PLANETS; THE RISING AND SETTING OF THE SUN; AND THE RISING, SETTING, AND SOUTHING OF THE MOON, FOR THE YEAR OF OUR LORD 1798: BEING THE 2D AFTER BISSEXTILE, OR LEAP-YEAR, AND THE 22D YEAR OF AMERICAN INDEPENDENCE, 'TILL 4TH JULY. [Five lines.] BY JOHN NATHAN HUTCHINS, PHILOM.
     New-York: Printed and sold by H. Gaine at his Printing-Office, at the Bible, in Pearl-Street, where may be had the New-York Pocket Almanack. [1797.] pp. (36). 12mo.   AAS. LOC. NJHS. NYHS. NYPL.

32298   ——   THE TOWN AND COUNTRY ALMANAC, FOR THE YEAR OF OUR LORD, 1798; BEING THE SECOND AFTER LEAP-YEAR, AND THE TWENTY-THIRD OF AMERICAN INDEPENDENCE, AFTER THE FOURTH OF JULY. CONTAINING THE LUNATIONS, CONJUNCTIONS, ECLIPSES, JUDGMENT OF THE WEATHER, RISING AND SETTING OF THE PLANETS, THE LENGTH OF DAYS AND NIGHTS, REMARKABLE OCCURRENCES AND IMPORTANT PERIODS, &C. TABLES OF ENGLISH, PORTUGUESE AND FRENCH GOLD COINS,—SHEWING THE AMOUNT OF WAGES OR EXPENCES—OF THE VALUE AND WEIGHTS OF COINS—INTEREST AT SEVEN PER CENT.—OF DISCOUNT PER CENT. BOARD MEASURE, COURTS, ROADS, &C. &C. TOGETHER WITH A GREATER VARIETY OF USEFUL ESSAYS, VALUABLE RECEIPTS, APHORISMS, ANECDOTES, &C. THAN ARE USUALLY FOUND IN WORKS OF THIS KIND. BY J. N. HUTCHINGS [*sic*] PHILOM.
     Newark: Printed by John Woods. [1797.] pp. (36). 12mo.   AAS.

32299   HYDE, ALVAN   1768–1833
A SERMON DELIVERED AT LEE, DECEMBER 15TH, 1796, BEING THE DAY APPOINTED BY AUTHORITY FOR A PUBLIC THANKSGIVING. BY ALVAN HYDE, A, M. PASTOR OF THE CHURCH IN LEE.
     Stockbridge: Printed by Rosseter & Willard. April, 1797. pp. 24. 8vo.
                                                  AAS BM. CHS. JCB. LOC. MHS.

32300   IMPARTIAL HERALD. VOL. IV. No. 297. TUESDAY, JANUARY 3, [—VOL. v. No. 380. FRIDAY, OCTOBER 27, 1797.]
     Newburyport—Published on Tuesdays and Fridays, by Angier March, at his Office, State-Street. Two dolls. fifty cents per ann. Delivered also by Edmund M. Blunt, at his Printing-Office and Bookstore, Sign of the Bible, State-Street, 1797. fol.   AAS.
     In February, the Printing-Office was removed to Middle-Street; and the title was divided by a cut of a flying herald, with scales—a new cut being substituted in the issue for March 21st. Beginning in April, publication was made on Tuesdays and Saturdays. On October 27th, William Barrett, and Angier March, announced the discontinuance of their newspapers, the "Political Gazette," and the "Impartial Herald:" and that they would, together, issue a new paper, under the title of *The Newburyport Herald and country gazette*, to be published twice a week, on Tuesdays and Fridays. In July, 1798, Angier March re-established the Impartial Herald, in Haverhill, Massachusetts.

32301   IMPARTIAL HERALD; A PERIODICAL REGISTER OF THE TIMES. VOL. I. NO. 1. WEDNES-
DAY, JUNE 14, [— NO. 29. WEDNESDAY, DECEMBER 27, 1797.]
Suffield, Connecticut: Published by H. & O. Farnsworth. 1797. fol.

Established, as a weekly, by Havila, and Oliver Farnsworth, and continued by them to July, 1798. Beginning with the issue for July 17,
1798, the paper was published by Edward Gray and Rescombe D, Albro, under the firm name of Gray & Albro, and a new numbering, with
that issue, was begun. At the end of the year 1798, Albro withdrew,
and beginning with the issue for January 1, 1799, the Herald was published by Edward Gray, alone, until publication ceased in June, 1799.

32302   THE IMPARTIAL OBSERVER: OR, SHEPHERD'S-TOWN, CHARLES-TOWN, & COUNTY
ADVERTISER. VOL. I. NO. 1. WEDNESDAY, JUNE 28, [— NO. 16. WEDNESDAY,
OCTOBER 11, 1797.]
Shepherd's-Town, Virginia: Printed by Philip Rootes & Charles Blagrove.
1797. fol.
Established, as a weekly, by Philip Rootes, and Charles Blagrove, and
continued by them to October 11, 1797—the last number located.

32303   THE IMPARTIAL READING HERALD. VOL. I. NO. 25. FRIDAY, JANUARY 6, [—
NO. 26. FRIDAY, JANUARY 13, 1797.]
Reading, Pennsylvania: Printed by J. Schneider and G. Gerrish. 1797. fol.

Publication was discontinued in January as above.

32304   INCHBALD, ELIZABETH SIMPSON   1753–1821
WIVES, AS THEY WERE, AND MAIDS AS THEY ARE: A COMEDY, IN FIVE ACTS. PER-
FORMED AT THE LONDON AND DUBLIN THEATRES WITH UNIVERSAL APPLAUSE—AND
AT GREENWICH-STREET, N. YORK. FIRST AMERICAN—FROM THE THIRD LONDON
EDITION.
New-York: Printed by R. Wilson, 1797. pp. 58. 12mo.   NYPL.

32305   —— — WIVES, AS THEY WERE, AND MAIDS AS THEY ARE. A COMEDY, IN FIVE ACTS.
Boston: Printed and sold by William Spotswood. 1797.

32306   THE INDEPENDENT [Mass. arms] CHRONICLE; AND THE UNIVERSAL ADVERTISER.
VOL. XXIX. NO. 1648. MONDAY, JANUARY 2, [— NO. 1749. THURSDAY, DECEM-
BER, 28, 1797.]
Boston, (Massachusetts):—Published on Mondays and Thursdays, by Adams &
Larkin, at their Printing-Office, directly opposite the Court-House, in Court-Street.
1797. fol.   AAS. LOC. MHS.
In July, the imprint was altered to read, "Printed and published", and
the word "directly" was dropped. On December 4th, Isaac Larkin, the
junior publisher died, aged twenty-six years, and after that date Thomas
Adams' name appears alone as Printer and Publisher.

32307   —— THE CARRIER OF THE INDEPENDENT CHRONICLE, TO HIS EVER GENEROUS AND
WORTHY PATRONS WISHES A HAPPY THRICE HAPPY NEW-YEAR. [Thirty-two lines
of verse.] THE CARRIER. [Colophon:]
[Boston: Printed by Adams & Larkin, January 1, 1797.] Broadside. fol.
HSP.

32308   THE INTERESTING TRIALS OF THE PIRATES, FOR THE MURDER OF WILLIAM LITTLE,
CAPTAIN OF THE SHIP AMERICAN EAGLE.
Newburyport: Re-printed [by Angier March] at the Herald Press, from a late
London publication. [1797.] pp. 59. 12mo.   BA.

32309   IVINS, SAMUEL
The COLUMBIAN ALMANAC, FOR THE YEAR OF OUR LORD, 1798; BEING THE SECOND
AFTER LEAP-YEAR, AND THE 23D OF AMERICAN INDEPENDENCE, AFTER THE 4TH
OF JULY. CONTAINING, (BESIDES THE ASTRONOMICAL CALCULATIONS, BY SAMUEL
IVINS.) [Fifteen lines.]
> *Philadelphia: Printed and sold by Stewart & Cochran, No. 34, South Second-
> Street.* [1797.] pp. (40). 12mo.   AAS. HSP. NYHS.

Contains, a Sketch of the life of George Washington. With portrait.

32310   —— FATHER ABRAHAM'S ALMANAC, FOR THE YEAR OF OUR LORD, 1798; BEING THE
SECOND AFTER LEAP-YEAR, AND THE 23D OF AMERICAN INDEPENDENCE, AFTER THE
4TH OF JULY. CONTAINING, (BESIDES THE ASTRONOMICAL CALCULATIONS, BY SAMUEL
IVINS,) [Seventeen lines.]
> *Philadelphia: Printed for H. & P. Rice, No. 16, South Second-Street, and No.
> 50, Market-Street.* [1797.] pp. (40). 12mo.   LOC.

With cut of George Washington on last page.

32311   —— THE PENNSYLVANIA, NEW-JERSEY, DELAWARE, MARYLAND AND VIRGINIA AL-
MANAC, FOR THE YEAR OF OUR LORD, 1798. BEING THE SECOND AFTER LEAP-YEAR,
AND THE 23D OF AMERICAN INDEPENDENCE, AFTER THE 4TH OF JULY. CONTAIN-
ING, (BESIDES THE ASTRONOMICAL CALCULATIONS, BY SAMUEL IVINS) JUDGMENT OF
THE WEATHER, LENGTH OF DAYS, FESTIVALS AND OTHER REMARKABLE DAYS, TABLES
OF INTEREST AT SIX AND SEVEN PER CENT., TABLES OF THE WEIGHT AND VALUE OF
COINS, TABLES OF DOLLARS AND CENTS, QUAKERS YEARLY MEETINGS, TIMES OF HOLD-
ING FEDERAL COURTS, AND COURTS FOR PENNSYLVANIA, NEW JERSEY, DELAWARE,
MARYLAND, AND VIRGINIA, LARGE LIST OF ROADS, &C. TIME OF HIGH WATER AT
PHILADELPHIA, FOR EVERY DAY IN THE YEAR, AND A GENERAL TIDE-TABLE FOR
THE UNITED STATES. ALSO, A VARIETY OF INSTRUCTING AND ENTERTAINING MAT-
TER, IN PROSE AND VERSE. CALCULATED FOR THE MERIDIAN OF PHILADELPHIA,
BUT MAY, WITHOUT SENSIBLE VARIATION, SERVE FOR ANY OF THE MIDDLE STATES.
> *Philadelphia: Printed and sold by Stewart & Cochran, No. 34, South Sec-
> ond-street.* [1797.] pp. (40). 12mo.   AAS.

The last page is a wood cut portrait, and sketch of Washington.

32312   JACKSON, JAMES   1757–1806
The CONTESTED ELECTION OF JAMES JACKSON AND ANTHONY WAYNE TO CONGRESS
FROM THE STATE OF GEORGIA, IN 1791.
> *Philadelphia: Sold by R. Campbell.* 1797.

32313   JAMES, W.
The LETTERS OF CHARLOTTE, DURING HER CONNEXION WITH WERTER. [Two lines
of Italian verse.] VOL. I. [— II.]
> *New-York: Printed by William A. Davis, for E. Duyckinck & Co. T. Allen,
> T. & J. Swords, T. Greenleaf, and J. Tiebout.* 1797. 2 vols. in one. pp. 240,
> frontispiece. 12mo.   AAS. NYPL.

32314   —— — THE LETTERS OF CHARLOTTE, DURING HER CONNEXION WITH WERTER.
[Two lines of Italian verse.] VOL. I. [— II.]
> *New-York: Printed by William A. Davis, for Benj. Gomez, Bookseller and
> Stationer, No. 97, Maiden-lane.* 1797. 2 vols. in one. pp. 240, frontispiece.
> 12mo.   AAS. JCB. YC.

The difference in the two impressions is in the imprints only.

32315   JANEWAY, James   1636–1674
A TOKEN FOR CHILDREN: BEING AN EXACT ACCOUNT OF THE CONVERSION, HOLY AND EXEMPLARY LIVES, AND JOYFUL DEATHS OF SEVERAL YOUNG CHILDREN. IN TWO PARTS. BY THE REVEREND JAMES JANEWAY. [Three lines from] LUKE X. 14.
    Elizabeth-Town: Printed by Shepard Kollock, for Cornelius Davis, No. 94, Water-Street, New-York. M,DCC,XCVII. pp. (2), iii, ix, 90. 18mo.   AAS.

32316   JAUDON, Daniel
A SHORT SYSTEM OF POLITE LEARNING: BEING A CONCISE INTRODUCTION TO THE ARTS AND SCIENCES. ADAPTED FOR SCHOOLS. [Four lines from] LOCKE.
    London Printed: Litchfield Re-printed by Thomas Collier. M,DCC,XCVII. pp. 112. 12mo.   AAS.

32317   JOHNSON, John   1706–1791
A MATHEMATICAL QUESTION, PROPOUNDED BY THE VICEGERENT OF THE WORLD; ANSWERED BY THE KING OF GLORY; ENIGMATICALLY REPRESENTED AND DEMONSTRATIVELY OPENED. BY JOHN JOHNSON, LATE OF LIVERPOOL, IN ENGLAND. [One line from] PSAL. XLIX. 4.
    Amherst, Newhampshire: Printed by Samuel Preston. 1797. pp. 132. 12mo.
     AAS.

32318   JOHNSON, John Barent   1769–1803
["Mr. Johnson's Sermon will be ready for Subscribers this week. April 4, 1797."]
    Printed by William M'Lean,—Whitestown, (Herkimer County). 1797.

JOHNSON, John I.
REFLECTIONS ON POLITICAL SOCIETY. AN ORATION DELIVERED ON THE TWELFTH DAY OF MAY BEFORE THE TAMMANY SOCIETY, OR COLUMBIAN ORDER, AT THEIR ANNIVERSARY. BY JOHN I. JOHNSON. [Ornament.]
    New-York: Printed by Freneau & Menut, for Napthali Judah, No. 47, Water-Street. 1797. pp. 19, (2). 12mo.   NYPL.

32319   JOHNSON, Joseph
AN EXPERIMENTAL INQUIRY INTO THE PROPERTIES OF CARBONIC ACID GAS OR FIXED AIR; ITS MODE OF OPERATION, USE IN DISEASES, AND MOST EFFECTUAL METHOD OF RELIEVING ANIMALS AFFECTED BY IT. BEING AN INAUGURAL THESIS, SUBMITTED TO THE EXAMINATION OF THE REV. JOHN EWING, S. T. P. PROVOST; THE TRUSTEES AND MEDICAL FACULTY OF THE UNIVERSITY OF PENNSYLVANIA, ON THE 12TH DAY OF MAY, 1797. FOR THE DEGREE OF DOCTOR OF MEDICINE. BY JOSEPH JOHNSON, OF CHARLESTON, (S. C.) MEMBER OF THE CHEMICAL, AND HONORARY MEMBER OF THE PHILADELPHIA MEDICAL SOCIETY. [Two lines of Latin from] HOR. DE ARTE POETA.
    Philadelphia: Printed for the Author, by Stephen C. Ustick. 1797. pp. 50. 8vo.   AAS. BM. RIMS. SGO.

32320   JOHNSTONE, Benjamin   –1797
THE ADDRESS OF ABRAHAM [sic Benjamin] JOHNSTONE, A BLACK MAN, WHO WAS HANGED AT WOODBURY, IN THE COUNTY OF GLOCESTER, AND STATE OF NEW-JERSEY, ON SATURDAY, THE THE [sic] 8TH DAY OF JULY LAST; TO THE PEOPLE OF COLOUR. TO WHICH IS ADDED HIS DYING CONFESSION OR DECLARATION, ALSO A COPY OF A LETTER TO HIS WIFE, WRITTEN THE DAY PREVIOUS TO HIS EXECUTION.
    Philadelphia: Printed [by Robert Bell,] for the Purchasers. 1797. pp. 47. 12mo.   BA. BM. HC. NYPL.

32321   THE JOHNSTOWN Gazette. VOL. II. NUMB. 78. WEDNESDAY, JANUARY 4, [— VOL. III. NUMB. 129. WEDNESDAY, DECEMBER 27, 1797.]
    Johnstown, (State of New-York:) Printed by Jacob Dockstader. 1797. fol.

32322   JOHONNET, JACKSON
THE REMARKABLE ADVENTURES OF JACKSON JOHONNET, OF MASSACHUSETTS. WHO SERVED AS A SOLDIER IN THE WESTERN EXPEDITION, UNDER GENERAL HARMAR. CONTAINING AN ACCOUNT OF HIS CAPTIVITY, SUFFERINGS, AND ESCAPE FROM THE KICKAPOO INDIANS.
Schenectady: Printed by Cornelius P. Wyckoff. 1797.

32323   JONES, EDWARD THOMAS
JONES'S ENGLISH SYSTEM OF BOOK-KEEPING, BY SINGLE OR DOUBLE ENTRY.
Printed by G. Forman, opposite the Post Office, New York City. 1797. 4to.

32324   JONES, SAMUEL
AN INAUGURAL DISSERTATION ON HYDROCELE. SUBMITTED TO THE EXAMINATION OF THE REV. JOHN EWING, S. T. P. PROVOST; THE TRUSTEES AND MEDICAL FACULTY OF THE UNIVERSITY OF PENNSYLVANIA, ON THE 12TH DAY OF MAY, 1797. FOR THE DEGREE OF DOCTOR OF MEDICINE. BY SAMUEL JONES, A. M. MEMBER OF THE MEDICAL AND CHEMICAL SOCIETIES OF PHILADELPHIA.
Philadelphia: Printed by Stephen C. Ustick. 1797. pp. 27. 8vo.
AAS. BM. 8GO.

32325   JUDAS ISCARIOT
THE BIRTH, LIFE, AND CHARACTER OF JUDAS ISCARIOT. [Ornament.]
Amherst—Printed by S. Preston. MDCCXCVII. pp. 23. 12mo.   AAS.

32326   JUNG called STILLING, JOHANN HEINRICH   1740–1817
DIE GESCHICHTE FLORENTIUS V. FAHLENDORN. EINE LEHRREICHE UND ANMUTHIGE BEGEBENHEIT. VON HEINRICH STILLING. IN DREY THEIL. [Ornament.] ERSTER [— DRITTER] THEIL.
Reading: Gedruckt bey Jacob Schneider und Comp. Im Jahr 1797. 3 vols. in one. pp. (2), (2), 128; 97; 105. 12mo.   AAS. NYPL.

32327   KEACH, BENJAMIN   1640–1704
THE TRAVELS OF TRUE GODLINESS, FROM THE BEGINNING OF THE WORLD, TO THIS PRESENT DAY. IN AN APT AND PLEASANT ALLEGORY. SHEWING WHAT TRUE GODLINESS IS: ALSO, THE TROUBLES, OPPOSITIONS, REPROACHES, AND PERSECUTION HE HATH MET WITH IN EVERY AGE. TOGETHER WITH THE DANGER AND SAD DECLINING STATE HE IS IN AT THIS PRESENT TIME, BY ERRORS, HERESIES, AND UNGODLINESS, OR OPEN PROFANENESS. BY BENJAMIN KEACH, AUTHOR OF A BOOK CALLED, WAR WITH THE DEVIL; AND SION IN DISTRESS.
Wilmington: Printed by Peter Brynberg, for John Boggs, minister of the Gospel. 1797. pp. 234. 18mo.   AAS. DHS. NYPL. WiPL.

32328   KEATE, GEORGE   1729–1797
AN ACCOUNT OF THE PELEW ISLANDS, IN THE WESTERN PART OF THE PACIFIC OCEAN, AND THE SHIPWRECK OF THE ANTELOPE, EAST-INDIA PACKET THERE.
Printed in Catskill, by M. Croswell—1797. pp. 101, frontispiece, and cuts. 18mo.   AAS. NYPL.

32329   —— —— AN ACCOUNT OF THE PELEW ISLANDS, SITUATED IN THE GREAT SOUTH SEA. COMPOSED FROM THE JOURNALS OF CAPTAIN HENRY WILSON AND HIS OFFICERS: WHO, IN AUGUST, 1783, WERE THERE SHIPWRECKED IN THE ANTELOPE PACKET. [Motto.]
Printed at Rutland, Vt. by Josiah Fay, for S. Williams & Co. MDCCXCVII. pp. 96. 12mo.

32330   KEATINGE, George
        The Maryland Ahiman Rezon, of Free & Accepted Masons; containing the
        history of masonry, from the establishment of the Grand Lodge to the
        present time; with their ancient charges, addresses, prayers, lectures,
        prologues, epilogues, songs, &c. Corrected from their old records, faith-
        ful traditions, & lodge-books. Compiled by order of the Grand Lodge of
        Maryland, by brother G. Keatinge, w. m. b. l.
            Baltimore: Printed by W. Pechin—for George Keatinge's Book-store. 1797.
        pp. (4), 9–272. 8vo.   AAS. BA. LOC.

32331   KELLOGG, Elijah   1761–1842
        A Thanksgiving sermon, delivered in Portland, November 30, 1797. By Eli-
        jah Kellogg, a. m. pastor of a Congregational church and society in that
        place. Published by request of the hearers.
            Portland: Printed by John K. Baker, 1797. pp. 20. 8vo.   AAS. BM.

32332   KELLY, John   1763–1848
        The Gentleman and lady's Angloamerican grammar: founded on the genius of
        the language upon a new plan partly original. Designed for the use of
        schools and academies, as well as of private families. By John Kelly, a. m.
            Concord, New-Hampshire: Printed? by Russell & Davis. 1797.

        Proposals for printing the above were made July 28, 1797.

32333   KENDAL or Kendall, David   –1853
        The Young lady's arithmetic; containing an epitome of definitions, rules,
        and examples, which explain in a familiar, concise, & easy manner, the
        first principles, & common use of numbers. Calculated in federal money;
        and published by request of several young ladies, desirous of adding to
        their other mental accomplishments the pleasing & useful science of fig-
        ures. By David Kendal, a. m. Published according to Act of Congress.
            Printed at Leominster, (Massachusetts) by Charles Prentiss, for the Author.
        1797. pp. 44, errata. 16mo.   AAS. NYPL.

        121st Massachusetts District Copyright, issued to David Kendall, as
        Author, 12 August, 1797.

32334   [U. S. arms.] KENNEBECK Intelligencer. [Seal of District of Maine.] [Motto.]
        Vol. ii. No. 59. Saturday, January 7, [— Vol. iii. No. 109. Tuesday, De-
        cember 26, 1797.]
            *[District of Maine.] Published by Peter Edes, near the Court-House, in
        Hallowell.* . . . 1797. fol.   AAS.

        Following the division of the town of Hallowell, with the issue for March
        18th, the place of publication in the imprint appears as Harrington; and,
        when this name was changed in June, the place of publication is given
        as Augusta.

32335   KENRICK, William   1725–1779
        The Whole duty of woman, comprised in the following sections; viz. 1
        Introduction. 2 Curiosity. 3 Reflection. 4 Vanity. 5 Knowledge. 6 Reputa-
        tion. 7 Applause. 8 Censure. 9 Insinuation. 10 Affectation. 11 Modes-
        ty. 12 Chastity. 13 Complacence. 14 Acquaintance. 15 Friendship. 16
        Elegance. 17 Frugality. 18 Employment. 19 Virginity. 20 Marriage.
        21 Education. 22 Authority. 23 Widowhood. 24 Religion. By a Lady.
        Written at the desire of a noble lord.
            *Printed at Walpole, Newhampshire, by David Carlisle, jun. and sold at his
        Bookstore.* 1797. pp. 68. 16mo.   AAS. LOC.

32336 | KENTUCKY. State.
ACTS PASSED AT THE FIRST SESSION OF THE FIFTH GENERAL ASSEMBLY FOR THE COMMONWEALTH OF KENTUCKY: BEGUN AND HELD AT THE CAPITAL, IN THE TOWN OF FRANKFORT, ON MONDAY THE SEVENTH OF NOVEMBER, IN THE YEAR OF OUR LORD, ONE THOUSAND SEVEN HUNDRED AND NINETY-SIX, AND IN THE FIFTH YEAR OF THE COMMONWEALTH, [— 17 DECEMBER, 1796.]
Lexington: Printed by James H. Stewart, Printer to the Commonwealth. [1797.] pp. (141). fol. LOC. NYPL.

32337 | —— ACTS PASSED AT THE SECOND SESSION OF THE FIFTH GENERAL ASSEMBLY FOR THE COMMONWEALTH OF KENTUCKY: BEGUN AND HELD AT THE CAPITAL, IN THE TOWN OF FRANKFORT, ON   FEBRUARY, IN THE YEAR OF OUR LORD ONE THOUSAND SEVEN HUNDRED AND NINETY-SIX, AND IN THE FIFTH YEAR OF THE COMMONWEALTH. [— 1 MARCH, 1797.]
[Lexington: Printed by James H. Stewart, 1797.] pp. (143)–221, (1). fol. LOC. NYPL.

32338 | THE KENTUCKY ALMANAC, FOR THE YEAR OF OUR LORD 1798: BEING THE SECOND AFTER BISSEXTILE OR LEAP YEAR—THE TWENTY SECOND YEAR OF AMERICAN INDEPENDENCE—THE TENTH OF OUR FEDERAL GOVERNMENT—AND THE SEVENTH OF THIS COMMONWEALTH. CONTAINING THE LUNATIONS, ECLIPSES, JUDGMENT OF THE WEATHER, REMARKABLE DAYS, LENGTH OF DAYS AND NIGHTS, TIME COURTS ARE HELD, &C. TOGETHER WITH A VARIETY OF ENTERTAINING PIECES IN PROSE AND VERSE. CALCULATED FOR THE LATITUDE OF 37° NORTH. AND A MERIDIAN OF 15′ WEST OF PHILADELPHIA; AND WILL SERVE WITHOUT ANY SENSIBLE ERROR, FOR THE TERRITORY NORTH-WEST OF THE OHIO, ST. VINCENTS, THE TERRITORY SOUTH OF THE OHIO, AND THE WESTERN PARTS OF VIRGINIA.
Lexington: Printed and sold (wholesale and retail) by J. Bradford, on Main Street. [1797.] pp, (32). 16mo. AAS.
Contains, Origin of tobacco, by Dr. Franklin. Death. Darby and Joan. Information to aid people how they may preserve the eye sight, by James Calder. On gaming. Story of a sagacious bear. Account of a remarkable fall in Connecticut River.

32339 | THE KENTUCKY GAZETTE. VOLUME X. NUMBER 485. WEDNESDAY, JANUARY 4, [—VOLUME XI. NUMBER 588. SATURDAY, DECEMBER 30, 1797.]
Lexington:—Printed [on Wednesdays and Saturdays] by J. Bradford, on Main-Street; . . . 1797. fol. AAS.

32340 | DIE KINDER IM WALDE.
Ephrata: Gedruckt bey Benjamin Meyer. 1797. pp. 15. 16mo.

32341 | KLINE'S CARLISLE WEEKLY GAZETTE. VOL. XII. NO. 570. WEDNESDAY, JANUARY 4, [—VOL. XIII. NO. 621. WEDNESDAY, DECEMBER 27, 1797.]
Carlisle: (State of Pennsylvania) Printed by George Kline. 1797. fol. AAS.

32342 | KNOX, SAMUEL   1756–1832
THE SCRIPTURAL DOCTRINE OF FUTURE PUNISHMENT VINDICATED, IN A DISCOURSE FROM THESE WORDS, "AND THESE SHALL GO AWAY INTO EVERLASTING PUNISHMENT, BUT THE RIGHTEOUS INTO LIFE ETERNAL." MATH. XXV. & 46TH. TO WHICH ARE PREFIXED SOME PREFATORY STRICTURES ON THE LATELY GROWED RELIGIOUS PRINCIPLES OF JOSEPH PRIESTLEY, LL. D. F. R. S. &C. &C. PARTICULARLY IN A DISCOURSE DELIVERED BY HIM IN THE CHURCH OF THE UNIVERSALISTS, IN PHILADELPHIA, AND PUBLISHED IN 1796,—ENTITLED "UNITARIANISM EXPLAINED AND DEFENDED" &C. BY SAMUEL KNOX, M. A. MINISTER OF THE GOSPEL, AT BLADENSBURGH, MARYLAND. [Four lines from] II EP. OF PETER CHAP. II V. 1.
George-Town: Printed by Green, English, & Co. [1797.] pp. 25, (1), [23.] 8vo. AAS.

32343   KURZGEFASSTES ARZNEY-BÜCHLEIN, FÜR MENSCHEN UND VIEH, DARINNEN CXXX
AUSERLESENE RECEPTEN.
> *Ephrata, zum siebensten mal gedruckt bey Benjamin Meyer.* 1797. pp. 23.
> 12mo.

32344   THE LADY'S MUSICAL MISCELLANY.
> *Boston: Published? by P. A. von Hagen.* 1797.
> Advertised April 7, 1797, to be published monthly—the first number to
> appear as soon as the subscription is found adequate to the expense—
> each number to consist of three songs and a music piece, and every
> twelfth number a title page, index and list of subscribers.

32345   THE LADY'S POCKET LIBRARY. CONTAINING, 1. MISS MORE'S ESSAYS. 2. DR. GREG-
ORY'S LEGACY TO HIS DAUGHTERS. 3. LADY PENNINGTON'S UNFORTUNATE MOTHER'S
ADVICE TO HER DAUGHTERS. 4. RUDIMENTS OF TASTE, BY THE COUNTESS OF CAR-
LISLE. 5. MRS. CHAPONE'S LETTER ON THE GOVERNMENT OF THE TEMPER. 6.
SWIFT'S LETTER TO A YOUNG LADY NEWLY MARRIED. 7. MOORE'S FABLES. FOR
THE FEMALE SEX. THIRD AMERICAN EDITION, IMPROVED.
> *Chambersburg: Printed by Dover & Harper, for Mathew Carey, Philadelphia.*
> M,DCC,XCVII. pp. 312, (2), (2). 12mo.   AAS. BA. JCB. LOC.

32346   LAFITTE DU COURTEIL, AMABLE-LOUIS-ROSE DE
PROPOSAL TO DEMONSTRATE THE NECESSITY OF A NATIONAL INSTITUTION IN THE
UNITED STATES OF AMERICA, FOR THE EDUCATION OF CHILDREN OF BOTH SEXES.
TO WHICH IS JOINED, A PROJECT OF ORGANIZATION, &C. BY AMABLE-LOUIS-ROSE
DE LAFITTE DU COURTEIL, PROFESSOR OF THE FRENCH LANGUAGE, MATHEMATICS,
GEOGRAPHY, HISTORY, &C. MASTER OF DRAWING AT THE ACADEMY OF BORDENTOWN.
> *Philadelphia: Printed for G. Decombaz, Bookseller, No. 48, North Third
> Street.* 1797. pp. [59.] 8vo.   LOC. NYPL.

32347   LAMBERT, ANNE THÉRÈSE, marquise DE   1647–1733
THE FAIR SOLITARY; OR FEMALE HERMIT. FROM THE FRENCH OF THE MARCHIONESS
DE LAMBERT.
> *New-London: Printed by James Springer.* 1797.

32348   LANCASTER COUNTY. PENNSYLVANIA.
ADDRESS. FELLOW CITIZENS AND BROTHER FARMERS OF THE COUNTY OF LANCASTER.
THE CALAMITY, WITH WHICH IT HAS PLEASED GOD TO VISIT THE CITY OF PHILADEL-
PHIA, HAS REDUCED MANY INDUSTRIOUS FAMILIES TO THE UTMOST DISTRESS, AND
CALLS LOUDLY FOR THE BENEVOLENT AID OF THE CHARITABLE AND WELL DISPOSED
IN EVERY QUARTER OF THE STATE. [Fourteen lines.] EDWARD HAND. LAMPETER
TOWNSHIP. OCT. 10TH, 1797. THE REVEREND GENTLEMEN OF THE CLERGY OF
EVERY DENOMINATION IN LANCASTER COUNTY ARE RESPECTFULLY DESIRED TO GIVE
ALL THE PUBLICITY IN THEIR POWER TO THE FOREGOING ADDRESS. [Twelve lines.]
PAUL ZANTZINGER, CHAIRMAN.
> *Lancaster, [Printed by William Hamilton,] Oct. 11th.* 1797. Broadside.
> 4to.   HSP.

32349   THE LANCASTER JOURNAL. [Motto.] VOL. III. NO. 30. FRIDAY, JANUARY 6, [—
VOL. IV. NO. 32. SATURDAY, DECEMBER 30, 1797.]
> *Lancaster: Printed by William Hamilton, at Euclid's Head, in King-Street,
> nearly opposite Mr. Stofft's,* . . . 1797. fol.

32350   THE LAND WE LIVE IN; OR DEATH OF MAJOR ANDRE.
> [*Boston: Printed for Francis Marriott.* 1797.]
> 108th Massachusetts District Copyright, issued to Francis Marriott, as
> Proprietor, 30 January, 1797.

32351   LANGDON, Timothy   1758–1801
The Pleasure and advantages of church music. A sermon, preached at a concert of vocal and instrumental music, in Danbury, on Wednesday, April 5, 1797. By Timothy Langdon, a. m. pastor of the first church in Danbury.
     Danbury: Printed by Douglas & Nichols. 1797. pp. 10. 8vo.   NYPL.

32352   A LARGE collection of cotillions and country dances.
     Rutland: Printed by Josiah Fay. 1797.

32353   THE LAST confession and dying speech of Peter Porcupine, with an account of his dissection.
     Philadelphia, Printed [by William T. Palmer] and sold by the Booksellers, May 22, 1797. pp. [32.] 8vo.   AAS. LOC. RIHS.
     Title within mourning borders.

32354   —— The Last confession and dying speech of Peter Porcupine, with an account of his dissection. Second edition.
     Philadelphia, Printed [by William T. Palmer] and sold by the Booksellers, May 27, 1797. pp. 32. 8vo.   LOC. NYPL.
     Title within mourning borders.

32355   —— The Last confession and dying speech of Peter Porcupine, with an account of his dissection. The second edition.
     Philadelphia, Printed [by William T. Palmer] and sold by the Booksellers, June, 1797. pp. (36). 8vo.   LOC.
     Title within mourning borders.

32356   —— The Last confession and dying speech of Peter Porcupine, with an account of his dissection.
     New-York: Printed and sold—Price one shilling. 1797. pp. 28. 8vo.
                                                 BM. NYHS.

32357   A LAST speech, confession and dying words of a deist.
     Newark: Printed by Daniel Dodge & Co. 1797.

32358   LATHROP, John   1740 1816
God our protector and refuge in danger and trouble. A discourse, delivered at the public lecture in Boston, on Thursday, March 16, 1797. By John Lathrop, d. d. a. a. s. With an appendix, containing an account of several daring attempts to set fire to the town and rob the inhabitants; together with hints tending to the security of populous towns and cities, against the evils to which they are more particularly exposed.
     Boston: Printed by Manning & Loring. 1797. pp. 30. 8vo.
                   AAS. BA. BM. HC. JCB. LOC. MHS. NYPL. UTS.

32359   LATHROP, Joseph   1731–1820
A Funeral sermon, delivered October 25, 1796, at the interment of mrs. Mary Gay, relict of the reverend doctor Gay, pastor of the first church in Suffield. By Joseph Lathrop, d. d. pastor of the first church in West-Springfield.
     Suffield: From the Press of H. & O. Farnsworth. M,DCC,XCVII. pp. 23. 8vo.
                   AAS. BM. CHS JCB. MHS. NYPL. UTS.

32360   —— God's challenge to infidels, to defend their cause, illustrated and applied in a sermon, delivered in West-Springfield, May 4, 1797, being the day of general fast. By Joseph Lathrop, d. d. minister of the first parish in said town. [Ornament.]
     West-Springfield: Printed by Edward Gray. [1797.] pp. [36.] 12mo.
                 AAS. BA. BM. CHS. CLA. JCB. NYHS. UTS.

32361 LATHROP, JOSEPH, continued.

—— A SERMON PREACHED AT RUTLAND, IN THE STATE OF VERMONT, FEBRUARY 1, 1797, AT THE ORDINATION OF THE REVEREND HEMAN BALL, TO THE WORK OF THE GOSPEL MINISTRY IN THAT PLACE. BY JOSEPH LATHROP, D.D. PASTOR OF THE FIRST CHURCH IN WEST-SPRINGFIELD, MASSACHUSETTS.

—*Rutland:—Printed by Josiah Fay.* M,DCC,XCVII.—pp. (2), 34. 12mo.

AAS. CHS. JCB. UTS.

32362 —— STEDFASTNESS IN RELIGION, EXPLAINED AND RECOMMENDED IN A SERMON, DELIVERED IN THE FIRST PARISH IN WEST-SPRINGFIELD, BY JOSEPH LATHROP, D.D. MINISTER OF SAID PARISH. ON THE 25TH DAY OF AUGUST, IN THE YEAR 1796. IT BEING THE DAY WHICH CLOSED THE 40TH YEAR OF HIS MINISTRY; AND THE YEAR, WHICH COMPLETED A CENTURY FROM THE INCORPORATION OF SAID PARISH.

West-Springfield: Printed by Edward Gray. M,DCC,XCVII. pp. [34.] 12mo.

AAS. BA. BM. CHS. JCB. NYPL. UTS.

32363 LAUS DEO. THE WORCESTER COLLECTION OF SACRED HARMONY. CONTAINING I. THE RULES OF VOCAL MUSIC, IN A CONCISE AND PLAIN MANNER. II. A LARGE AND CHOICE COLLECTION OF PSALM TUNES, ANTHEMS, &C. PROPER FOR DIVINE WORSHIP MANY OF WHICH ARE ENTIRELY NEW. THE WHOLE COMPILED FOR THE USE OF SCHOOLS AND SINGING SOCIETIES. THE SIXTH EDITION, ALTERED, CORRECTED AND REVISED, WITH ADDITIONS, BY OLIVER HOLDEN.

Printed typographically at Boston, by Isaiah Thomas & Ebenezer T. Andrews. August, 1797. pp. 144. obl. 8vo.

AAS. BPL.

128th Massachusetts District Copyright, issued to Isaiah Thomas and Ebenezer T. Andrews, as Proprietors, 12 September, 1797.

32364 LAWS, JOHN

AN INAUGURAL DISSERTATION ON THE RATIONALE OF THE OPERATION OF OPIUM ON THE ANIMAL ECONOMY; WITH OBSERVATIONS ON ITS USE IN DISEASE.

Wilmington: Printed by W. C. Smyth? 1797. pp. 12. 8vo.

SGO.

32365 LEAVITT, DUDLEY   1772–1851

THE NEW ENGLAND CALENDAR: OR ALMANACK FOR THE YEAR OF OUR LORD 1797: BEING THE FIRST AFTER BISSEXTILE OR LEAP-YEAR AND THE 21ST OF AMERICAN INDEPENDENCE. CALCULATED FOR THE MERIDIAN OF CONCORD, LATITUDE 43° 14″ N. LONGITUDE 72° 45″ W. AND WITH BUT LITTLE VARIATION WILL ANSWER FOR ANY OF THE NEWENGLAND STATES. BY DUDLEY LEAVITT. [Cut.]

From the Mirror Press of Russell & Davis, Printers, Concord, Newhampshire. [1797.] pp. (24). 12mo.

LOC. NHHS.

32366 LEE, CHAUNCEY   1763–1842

THE AMERICAN ACCOMPTANT; BEING A PLAIN, PRACTICAL AND SYSTEMATIC COMPENDIUM OF FEDERAL ARITHMETIC; IN THREE PARTS: DESIGNED FOR THE USE OF SCHOOLS, AND SPECIALLY CALCULATED FOR THE COMMERCIAL MERIDIAN OF THE UNITED STATES OF AMERICA. BY CHAUNCEY LEE, A. M.

Lansingburgh: Printed by William W. Wands. M,DCC,XCVII. pp. 297, (15,) frontispiece. 12mo.   AAS. BM. BU. JCB. LOC. NYPL. YC.

Contains a twelve-page list of subscribers. It is claimed that this work was the first to use the dollar mark, $. 6th Vermont District Copyright, issued to Chauncey Lee, as Author, 8 February, 1797.

32367 —— AN ORATION, DELIVERED AT LANSINGBURGH, ON THE FOURTH OF JULY, A.D. 1797, IN CELEBRATION OF THE TWENTY-FIRST ANNIVERSARY OF AMERICAN INDEPENDENCE. BY CHAUNCEY LEE, A. M.

Lansingburgh: Printed by R. Moffitt & Co. 1797. pp. 16. 8vo.   JCB. RIHS.

32368   LEE, RICHARD
SONGS FROM THE ROCK TO HAIL THE APPROACHING DAY; SACRED TO TRUTH, LIBERTY
AND PEACE. INSCRIBED TO THE SOVEREIGN PEOPLE. BY THE AUTHOR OF FLOWERS
FROM SHARON. [Two lines from] ISAIAH.
Philadelphia: Printed for Richard Lee. 1796.

32369   LE GUEN, LEWIS
SPECIAL VERDICT, IN THE CASE OF LEWIS LE GUEN AND ISAAC GOUVERNEUR AND
PETER KEMBLE, IN THE SUPREME COURT OF THE STATE OF NEW-YORK, 1797.
New-York: Printed at the Argus Office. 1797. pp. 61. 8vo.   BPL. NYHS.

Alexander Hamilton was attorney for Le Guen.

32370   LEONARD, DAVID AUGUSTUS   1771–1818
THE LAWS OF SIASCONSET: A BALLAD. PROPOSED, WITH A PIPE OF TOBACCO, AS AN
EVENING'S AMUSEMENT TO THE FISHERMEN. [TO THE TUNE "VICAR OF BRAY."]
BY A FRIEND TO NATIVE SIMPLICITY. EMBELLISHED WITH A COPPER-PLATE.
Printed at New Bedford, (Massachusetts) By John Spooner—1797. pp. (8),
plate. 4to.   AAS. BU.

32371   —— AN ORATION, PRONOUNCED AT NANTUCKET, DECEMBER 27, 1796, AT THE CELE-
BRATION OF THE FESTIVAL OF ST. JOHN THE EVANGELIST. BY DAVID LEONARD,
A. B. [Five lines from] JESUS CHRIST. [Ornament.]
Newbedford—Printed by John Spooner. M,DCC,XCVII. pp. 23. 8vo.   AAS.

32372   LE SAGE, ALAIN RENE   1668–1747
THE COMICAL AND ENTERTAINING ADVENTURES OF GIL BLAS OF SANTILLANE.
*Boston: Printed and sold by William Spotswood, No. 55. Marlborough-Street.
1795.*

32373   LESLIE, CHARLES   1650–1722
A SHORT AND EASY METHOD WITH THE DEISTS; WHEREIN THE CERTAINTY OF THE
CHRISTIAN RELIGION IS DEMONSTRATED; IN A LETTER TO A FRIEND. BY MR. CHARLES
LESLIE. TO WHICH ARE ADDED, AN APOLOGY FOR CHRISTIANITY, AND AN APOLOGY
FOR THE BIBLE. BY R. WATSON, D. D. F. R. S. LORD BISHOP OF LANDAFF, AND RE-
GIUS PROFESSOR OF DIVINITY IN THE UNIVERSITY OF CAMBRIDGE.
Lancaster, Printed and sold by W. & R. Dickson, in Queenstreet, 1797. pp. 32;
78; 118. 8vo.   JCB.

Half title: PAGE 1 (2ND SERIES), AN APOLOGY FOR CHRISTIANITY. LETTER I.
[Lancaster, Printed and sold by W. & R. Dickson, 1796.] pp. 78.

Third title: PAGE 1 (3RD SERIES). AN APOLOGY FOR THE BIBLE; IN A SERIES OF
LETTERS, ADDRESSED TO THOMAS PAINE, AUTHOR OF A BOOK, ENTITLED, THE AGE
OF REASON, PART THE SECOND; BEING AN INVESTIGATION OF TRUE AND OF FABU-
LOUS THEOLOGY. BY R. WATSON, D. D. F. R. S. LORD BISHOP OF LANDAFF, AND RE-
GIUS PROFESSOR OF DIVINITY IN THE UNIVERSITY OF CAMBRIDGE.
*Lancaster, Printed and sold by W. & R. Dickson, and W. Hamilton, King-
street, 1796.* pp. 118.

32374   LESUEUR, JEAN FRANCOIS   1763–1837
THE WRETCHED SLAVE. SUNG IN THE NEW OPERA OF PAUL AND VIRGINIA.
New-York. [1797.]   JCB.

32375   A LETTER to Thomas Paine, in answer to his scurrilous epistle addressed to our late worthy President Washington: and containing comments and observations on his life, political and deistical writings, &c. &c. Intended as an alarm to the good people of these States, from being led astray by the sophistical reasonings of mr. Paine. By an American Citizen, in whose heart the *amor patriæ* holds the highest place.

New-York: Printed for the Author by John Bull, No. 115, Cherry-Street. 1797. pp. (2), 24. 8vo.   AAS. LOC. NL. NYHS.

32376   LEVI, David   1740–1799
A Defence of the Old Testament, in a series of letters, addressed to Thomas Paine, author of a book, entitled, The Age of reason, part the second, being an investigation of true and of fabulous theology. By David Levi, author of Letters to dr. Priestley, in answer to his to the Jews, &c. &c. &c. [Two lines of Scripture texts.]

New-York: Printed by William A. Davis, 26 Moore street, for Naphtali Judah, Bookseller No. 47, Water street. 1797. pp. 239. 12mo.

AAS. BA. BM. JCB. NYPL.

32377   LEWIS, Isaac   1746–1840
The Political advantages of Godliness. A sermon, preached before his excellency the governor, and the honorable Legislature of the State of Connecticut, convened at Hartford on the anniversary election. May 11, 1797. By Isaac Lewis, d. d. pastor of a church in Greenwich. [Printer's mark.]

Hartford: Printed by Hudson & Goodwin. 1797. pp. 31. 8vo.

AAS. BA. BM. CHS. JCB. LOC. MHS. NYPL. YC.

32378   LEWIS, Samuel
Map of the United States: compiled chiefly from the State maps, and other authentic information, by Sam'l Lewis.

Engraved for and sold by Mathew Carey, Philadelphia. [1797.] 36 x 25½.

32379   THE LIFE and death of mr. John Bunyan, . . . late preacher at Bedford.
Newburyport: Printed by A. March. [1797.] pp. 28. 12mo.

32380   THE LIFE of don Pedro Aguilio, containing love intrigues, duels, hair-breadth escapes, together with many surprising and perilous adventures, both by sea and land.
Cooperstown: Printed by Elihu Phinney. 1797.

32381   THE LITERARY museum, or monthly magazine, for January [—June] 1797.
West-Chester: Printed by Derrick & Sharples. And sold by the principal Booksellers in Philadelphia. [1797.] pp. 336, 3 plates. 8vo.   AAS. HSP. LOC. NYHS. NYPL.

32382   LOGAN, George   1753–1821
Fourteen agricultural experiments, to ascertain the best rotation of crops: addressed to the "Philadelphia Agricultural Society." By George Logan, m. d.

Philadelphia: Printed by Francis and Robert Bailey, at Yorick's Head, No. 116 *High-Street.* M,DCC,XCVII. pp. (4), 41. 8vo.   BA. NYPL.

164th Pennsylvania District Copyright, issued to Francis Bailey, as Proprietor, 11 January, 1797.

32384   LONDON. ENGLAND. MISSIONARY SOCIETY.
SERMONS, PREACHED IN LONDON, AT THE FORMATION OF THE MISSIONARY SOCIETY,
SEPTEMBER 22, 23, 24, 1795. TO WHICH ARE PREFIXED, MEMORIALS, RESPECTING
THE ESTABLISHMENT AND FIRST ATTEMPTS OF THAT SOCIETY. [Seven lines from]
ISAIAH. BY ORDER OF THE DIRECTORS. PUBLISHED FOR THE BENEFIT OF THE
SOCIETY.
> *London—Printed: Newburyport—Re-printed, by Barrett & March, Market-*
> *Square.—1797. pp. 246, (5). 12mo.*   AAS.
>> Contains: An Introductory memorial respecting the formation of the
>> Missionary Society. The Apostolic commission, preached at the Spa
>> Field's Chapel, September 22, 1795. By the Rev. T. Haweis. A Mission
>> to the heathen, founded upon the moral law. Delivered at Haberdasher's
>> Hall Meeting-House, Sept 23, 1795. By Samuel Greathead. The Ful-
>> ness of times. Preached at the Tabernacle, September 23, 1795. By John
>> Hey. Glorious displays of Gospel grace. Preached at Surry Chapel,
>> September 24, 1795. By the Rev. Rowland Hill. Objections against
>> a mission to the heathen, stated and considered. Preached at Totten-
>> ham Court Chapel. 24 September, 1795. By David Bogue. A Memoir,
>> on the most eligible part to begin a mission. Delivered in Surry-Street
>> Chapel, September 24, 1795. By the Rev. T. Haweis. Subscribers names.

32385   LONG, ROBERT
TO THE HONORABLE ALEXANDER CONTEE HANSON, ESQUIRE, CHANCELLOR OF THE
STATE OF MARYLAND. [Statement of claim against Boulding's flour mill on Gun-
powder River, for investments made 1794–1797.]
> *Baltimore: Printed by Samuel Sower, Fayette-Street.* [1797.] pp. (36). 12mo.

32386   LONGWORTH, DAVID
LONGWORTH'S AMERICAN ALMANACK, NEW-YORK REGISTER, AND CITY DIRECTORY,
FOR THE TWENTY-SECOND YEAR OF AMERICAN INDEPENDENCE. CONTAINING MOST
THINGS USEFUL IN A WORK OF THE KIND. EMBELLISHED WITH A VIEW OF THE
NEW THEATRE.
> *New-York: Printed for the Editor, by T. & J. Swords, No. 99. Pearl-Street.*
> —1797.—pp. (6), (15), (14)—340, plate. 16mo.   AAS. HC. NYHS. NYPL.
> *Second title:* ASTRONOMICAL CALCULATIONS FOR THE TWENTY-SECOND YEAR OF
> AMERICAN INDEPENDENCE, COMMENCING, A. D. THE FOURTH OF JULY, 1797. CON-
> TAINING THE RISING, SETTING, PLACES, AND ECLIPSES OF THE SUN AND MOON; THE
> PHASES OF THE MOON; ALSO THE RISING, SETTING, AND SOUTHING OF THE MOST CON-
> SPICUOUS PLANETS AND FIXED STARS; THE EQUATION OF TIME; AND TIME OF HIGH
> WATER AT NEW-YORK, &C. ALSO, THE INCREASE, DECREASE, AND LENGTH OF DAYS;
> WITH THE FESTIVALS, &C. CALCULATED FOR THE LATITUDE AND MERIDIAN OF NEW-
> YORK, BY ABRAHAM SHOEMAKER.
> *[New-York:] From the Press of T. & J. Swords.* [1797.] pp. (15).

32387   LOUISIANA. PROVINCE.
AN OFFICIAL ACCOUNT OF THE SITUATION, CLIMATE, SOIL, PRODUCE, &C. OF THAT PART
OF LOUISIANA, WHICH LIES BETWEEN THE MISSOURI AND NEW MADRID, OR L'ANSE
A LA GRAISE, AND ON THE WEST SIDE OF THE MISSISSIPPI. TOGETHER WITH AN
ABSTRACT OF THE SPANISH GOVERNMENT.
> *Lexington: Printed by John Bradford.* 1796.

32388   LOUVET DE COUVRAY, JEAN BAPTISTE   1760–1797
LOVE AND PATRIOTISM! OR, THE EXTRAORDINARY ADVENTURES OF M. DUPORTAIL,
LATE MAJOR-GENERAL IN THE ARMIES OF THE UNITED STATES. INTERSPERSED
WITH MANY SURPRISING INCIDENTS IN THE LIFE OF THE LATE COUNT PULASKI.
> *Philadelphia: Printed by Carey & Markland.* 1797. pp. 120. 12mo.
>   AAS. BM. HC. JCB. LOC. NYPL.
> From the Author's "Les Amours du Chevalier de Faublas."

32389   LOVE, Christopher   1618–1651
PROPHECIES OF THE REVEREND CHRISTOPHER LOVE; AND HIS LAST WORDS ON THE SCAFFOLD; WHO WAS BEHEADED AT TOWER HILL, LONDON, AUGUST, 22, 1751.
> *Exeter: Printed by Henry Ranlet.* 1797. 12mo.

> Contains, A Prophecy found in Paris, engraved on a flagstone two yards square in Hebrew characters.

32390   LOVE TRIUMPHANT, OR, CONSTANCY REWARDED. FOR THE AMUSEMENT AND INSTRUCTION OF YOUTH: IN LANGUAGE SUITED TO THEIR CAPACITIES. TO WHICH IS ADDED A POETICAL APPENDIX. BY A FRIEND TO YOUTH.
> *Troy: Printed by Luther Pratt & Co.* 1797. pp. 122, frontispiece. 24mo.
>   AAS.

32391   LOW, Nathanael   1740–1808
[Low's.] AN ASTRONOMICAL DIARY: OR ALMANACK, FOR THE YEAR OF CHRISTIAN ÆRA 1798. BEING THE SECOND AFTER BISSEXTILE, OR LEAP-YEAR, AND THE TWENTY-SECOND OF THE INDEPENDENCE OF THE UNITED STATES OF AMERICA, WHICH BEGAN JULY 4TH, 1776. [Nine lines.] BY NATHANAEL LOW. COPY RIGHT SECURED. [Six lines from] POPE.
> *Boston: Printed and sold by John & Thomas Fleet, at the Bible and Heart, Cornhill. Where may be had their Register & Pocket Almanack, for 1798.* [1797.] pp. [24.] 12mo.   AAS. LOC. NYPL.

32392   —— A SHEET ALMANACK, WITH LOW'S CALCULATIONS FOR THE YEAR 1798. VERY CONVENIENT FOR MERCHANTS, COMPTING-ROOMS, PUBLIC OFFICES, SHOPS, &C. &C.
> *Boston: Printed and sold by J. & T. Fleet, at the Bible and Heart, in Cornhill.* [1797.] Broadside. fol.

32393   LOWELL, John   1769–1840
THE ANTIGALLICAN; OR, THE LOVER OF HIS OWN COUNTRY: IN A SERIES OF PIECES PARTLY HERETOFORE PUBLISHED AND PARTLY NEW, WHEREIN FRENCH INFLUENCE, AND FALSE PATRIOTISM, ARE FULLY AND FAIRLY DISPLAYED. BY A CITIZEN OF NEW ENGLAND.
> *Philadelphia: Published by William Cobbett, opposite Christ Church. December,* 1797. pp. (82); [84.] 8vo.   AAS. BA. BM. HC. JCB. MHS. NYHS. NYPL.

> The Numbers, I–XII. Signed Leonidas. The Pseudo patriot, No. 1.–10, signed Ascanius.

32394   LYMAN, Joseph   1749–1828
A SETTLED MINISTRY, AN INSTITUTION OF THE CHRISTIAN CHURCH. A SERMON PREACHED AT NEW BRAINTREE, OCTOBER 26, A. D. 1796. AT THE INSTALLATION OF THE REV. JOHN FISKE, TO THE PASTORAL CARE OF THE CHURCH AND CONGREGATION IN THAT TOWN. BY JOSEPH LYMAN, A. M. PASTOR OF THE CHURCH IN HATFIELD.
> *Printed at Northampton, (Massachusetts) by William Butler.* M,DCC,XCVII, pp. 24. 8vo.   AAS. BA. BM. BU. CHS. JCB. MHS. UTS. YC.

32395   LYNCHBURG WEEKLY MUSEUM. VOL. I. No. 1. MONDAY, JUNE 5, [— No. 30. MONDAY, DECEMBER 25, 1797.]
> *Lynchburg, (Va.) Printed by John Davis, & Co.* 1797. fol.

> Established, as a weekly, by John Davis, & Company, and continued by them into May, 1798, when it was evidently succeeded, in June, by the *Lynchburg Weekly Gazette.*

32396   LYTTELTON, GEORGE, 1st baron   1709–1773
         DIALOGUES OF THE DEAD, BY THE LATE LORD (GEORGE) LYTTELTON. [*sic*]. FIRST
         AMERICAN EDITION, FROM THE FIFTH LONDON EDITION, CORRECTED. [Vignette.]
             *Printed at Worcester, Massachusetts, by Thomas, Son & Thomas. Sold by
             them, and in Boston, by Thomas & Andrews. April—1797.* pp. (2), (vii)–268.
             12mo.   AAS. BA. NYPL.

32397   MACCLINTOCK, SAMUEL   1732–1804
         AGUR'S CHOICE. A SERMON DELIVERED AT DOVER, BEFORE THE PISCATAQUA ASSOCIA-
         TION AUGUST 9TH, 1797. BY SAMUEL MACCLINTOCK, D.D. PASTOR OF THE CHURCH
         IN GREENLAND. [Two lines from] YOUNG. [Heavy line.]
             Dover, (N. H.) Printed at the Sun Office, for Subscribers. M,DCC,XCVII.
             pp. 24. 4to.   AAS. JCB.

32398   —— EVIDENCES OF CHRISTIANITY. A SERMON, DELIVERED AT THE ORDINATION OF
         THE REV. JESSE APPLETON, TO THE PASTORAL CARE OF THE CONGREGATIONAL SO-
         CIETY IN HAMPTON, FEBRUARY 22D, 1797. BY SAMUEL MACCLINTOCK, D. D. PAS-
         TOR OF THE CHURCH IN GREENLAND.
             Printed at the Oracle-Press, in Portsmouth, N. H. by Charles Peirce. 1797.
             pp. 24. 8vo.   AAS. BA. BM. JCB. LOC.

32399   M'CULLOCH, JOHN
         A CONCISE HISTORY OF THE UNITED STATES, FROM THE DISCOVERY OF AMERICA TILL
         1795: WITH A CORRECT MAP OF THE UNITED STATES. [Arms.] THE SECOND EDI-
         TION.
             *Philadelphia: Printed and sold by John M'Culloch. No. 1, North Third-
             Street.—1797. [Entered according to Act of Congress.]* pp. 272, map. 12mo. AAS.

32400   —— M'CULLOCH'S POCKET ALMANAC, FOR THE YEAR 1798. BEING THE SECOND
         AFTER LEAP YEAR, AND 22–23 OF AMERICAN INDEPENDENCE. [Thirteen lines.]
             Philadelphia: Printed and sold by J. M'Culloch, No. 1, North Third-Street.
             [1797.] pp. (32). 32mo.   AAS. NYPL.

32401   M'DONALD, PHILIP
         A SURPRISING ACCOUNT OF THE CAPTIVITY AND ESCAPE OF PHILIP M'DONALD & ALEX
         M'CLOUD, OF VIRGINIA, FROM THE CHICKKEMOGGA INDIANS, AND OF THE GREAT
         DISCOVERIES IN THE WESTERN WORLD, FROM JUNE 1779, TO JANUARY 1786, WHEN
         THEY RETURNED IN HEALTH TO THEIR FRIENDS, AFTER AN ABSENCE OF SIX YEARS
         AND A HALF. WRITTEN BY THEMSELVES.
             Printed at Rutland, Vermont, by Josiah Fay, for S. Williams & Co. MDCC-
             XCVII. pp. 14. 8vo.   BM.

32402   M'FARLAND, ASA   1769–1827
         WISDOM OF GOD, AS EXHIBITED IN CREATION. A SERMON; DELIVERED AT HANOVER,
         BEORE THE FRANKLIN LODGE OF FREE AND ACCEPTED MASONS, ON THE FESTIVAL
         OF ST. JOHN THE BAPTIST. BY ASA M'FARLAND, A. M. TUTOR IN DARTMOUTH
         UNIVERSITY. PUBLISHED BY DESIRE OF THE CRAFT. ANNO DOMINI 1797. ANNO
         LUCIS 5797.
             Hanover, (N. H.) Printed by Benjamin True; 1797. pp. [16.] 8vo.
                                                          AAS. JCB. NYHS.

32403   MACGOWAN, JOHN   1726–1780
         INFERNAL CONFERENCE: OR, DIALOGUES OF DEVILS. BY THE LISTENER.
             Printed at Worcester, Massachusetts, by Leonard Worcester, for Isaiah Thomas.
             MDCCXCVII.

32404   MACGOWAN, JOHN, continued.
—— THE LIFE OF JOSEPH, THE SON OF ISRAEL. IN EIGHT BOOKS, CHIEFLY DESIGNED TO ALLURE YOUNG MINDS TO A LOVE OF THE SACRED SCRIPTURES. BY JOHN MACGOWAN.

Portsmouth, New-Hampshire: Printed by Charles Peirce. 1797. 16mo.

32405   —— — THE LIFE OF JOSEPH, THE SON OF ISRAEL. IN EIGHT BOOKS. CHIEFLY DESIGNED TO ALLURE YOUNG MINDS TO A LOVE OF THE SACRED SCRIPTURES. BY JOHN MACGOWAN. [Ornament.]

Windham: (Connecticut) Printed by John Byrne. 1797. pp. 166. 12mo.   AAS.

32406   MACHIAS. DISTRICT OF MAINE. CHURCH.
PROCEEDINGS OF THE CHURCH AND CONGREGATION AT MACHIAS, RELATIVE TO THE SETTLEMENT OF THE REV. CLARK BROWN, AS THEIR GOSPEL MINISTER. PUBLISHED BY DESIRE. LET ALL THINGS BE DONE IN ORDER. INSPIRATION.

—New-Bedford:—Printed by John Spooner. M,DCC,XCVII. pp. 20. 8vo. AAS.

32407   MACKENZIE, COLIN
AN INAUGURAL DISSERTATION ON THE DYSENTERY. SUBMITTED TO THE EXAMINATION OF THE REV. JOHN EWING, S. S. T. P. PROVOST, THE TRUSTEES AND MEDICAL FACULTY OF THE UNIVERSITY OF PENNSYLVANIA. ON THE 12TH DAY OF MAY, 1797. FOR THE DEGREE OF DOCTOR OF MEDICINE. BY COLIN MACKENZIE, OF BALTIMORE, MEMBER OF THE PHILADELPHIA MEDICAL AND CHEMICAL SOCIETIES. [Three lines of Latin from] QUINTILLIAN.

Philadelphia: Printed by Ormrod & Conrad, 41, Chesnut-Street. [1797.] pp. (47). 8vo.   AAS. SGO.

32408   MACKENZIE, RODERICK
READING NO PREACHING; OR, A LETTER TO A YOUNG CLERGYMAN, FROM A FRIEND IN LONDON, CONCERNING THE UNWARRANTABLE PRACTICE OF READING THE GOSPEL, INSTEAD OF PREACHING IT. [Three lines from] LUKE IV. 20, 21, 22. [Printer's mark.]

Norwich: Printed by T. Hubbard.—1797—pp. [24.] 12mo.   AAS.

32409   M'KINNEY, JAMES
A VIEW OF THE RIGHTS OF GOD AND MAN, IN SOME SERMONS. BY THE REV. JAMES M'KINNEY. [Ten lines of quotations.]

Philadelphia: Printed for the Author, at Franklin's Head, No. 41, Chesnut-Street. 1797. pp. (64). 8vo.   AAS. NYHS.

"The remainder will be published with all convenient speed."

32410   MACKINTOSH, DUNCAN
ESSAI RAISONNÉ SUR LA GRAMMAIRE ET LA PRONONCIATION ANGLOISE, À L'USAGE DES FRANÇAIS QUI DÉSIRENT D'APPRENDRE L'ANGLOIS. PAR DUNC'AN MACK'INTOSH ET SES DEUX FILLES. N.B. CHAQUE EXEMPLAIRE DE CET OUVRAGE SERA NUMERATÉ ET SIGNÉ PAR MR. MACKINTOSH.

Boston: Printed by Manning & Loring. 1797. pp. (3), 192, folded table. 8vo.   HC. JCB.

124th Massachusetts District Copyright, issued to Duncan Mac Intosh and his two daughters, as Authors, 1 September, 1797.

MACKINTOSH, DUNCAN, continued.

32411 —— A PLAIN, RATIONAL ESSAY ON ENGLISH GRAMMAR: THE MAIN OBJECT OF WHICH IS TO POINT OUT A PLAIN, RATIONAL AND PERMANENT STANDARD OF PRONUNCIATION. TO WHICH IS GIVEN, A GAMUT OR KEY, STILL MORE SIMPLE, PLAIN AND EASY. THAN THAT GIVEN TO MUSIC, POINTING OUT THE QUANTITY AND QUALITY OF EVERY SYLLABLE AND WORD, ACCORDING TO THE PRESENT MODE AMONG POLITE SCHOLARS. LONG SYLLABLES ARE DISTINGUISHED FROM SHORT ONES, BY AUTHORITY OF LEGAL ACCENT; AND THE SOUNDS OF BOTH CLEARLY POINTED OUT, BY TYPOGRAPHICAL MARKS OR CHARACTERS, AND ILLUSTRATED BY SUCH RULES AND EXAMPLES AS RENDER THE WHOLE SO VERY INTELLIGIBLE AND EASY, EVEN TO THE WEAKEST CAPACITY, THAT FOREIGNERS, AS WELL AS NATIVES, MAY LEARN TO READ ENGLISH PROPERLY, IN A FEW WEEKS. THIS PLAN, HITHERTO UNATTEMPTED, IS RESPECTFULLY INSCRIBED TO BRITISH AND AMERICAN LADIES AND GENTLEMEN, WHOSE GENEROUS CRITICISM AND ASSISTANCE IS HUMBLY REQUESTED BY THEIR DEVOTED HUMBLE SERVANTS, DUNC'AN MACK'INTOSH AND HIS TWO DAUGHTERS. MARTINI'CO, THE 4TH OF JULY, 1797.

> *Boston: Printed by Manning & Loring.* 1797. pp. 239, 2 folded tables. 8vo.
> BM. HC. JCB.

> 125th Massachusetts District Copyright, issued to Duncan Mackintosh and his two daughters, as Authors, 1 September, 1797.

32412 **MACLEAN, JOHN** 1771–1814
TWO LECTURES ON COMBUSTION: SUPPLEMENTARY TO A COURSE OF LECTURES ON CHEMISTRY, READ AT NASSAU-HALL. CONTAINING AN EXAMINATION OF DR. PRIESTLEY'S CONSIDERATIONS ON THE DOCTRINE OF PHLOGISTON, AND THE DECOMPOSITION OF WATER. BY JOHN MACLEAN, PROFESSOR OF MATHEMATICS AND NATURAL HISTORY IN THE COLLEGE OF NEW-JERSEY.

> *Philadelphia: Printed by T. Dobson.* 1797. pp. 71. 8vo.
> NYHS. NYPL. RIMS. SGO.

32413 **MAGAW, SAMUEL** 1740–1812
A DISCOURSE OCCASIONED BY THE MOURNFUL CATASTROPHE, THROUGH FIRE, WHICH OVERWHELMED AND DESTROYED MR. ANDREW BROWN, HIS WIFE, AND THREE CHILDREN. DELIVERED IN ST. PAUL'S CHURCH, SUNDAY AFTERNOON, FEBRUARY 5, 1797. BY SAMUEL MAGAW, D. D.

> *Philadelphia: Printed by Ormrod & Conrad, 41, Chesnut Street, for the benefit of the two young women, Mr. Brown's domestics, sufferers by the fire.* [1797.] pp. 22; (13). 12mo.
> AAS. JCB. NYPL.

> The "Appendix" gives a Sketch of the life of Andrew Brown, owner, editor and publisher of the "Federal Gazette."

32414 **MAILLET, BENOIT DE** 1656–1738
TELLIAMED; OR, THE WORLD EXPLAIN'D: CONTAINING DISCOURSES BETWEEN AN INDIAN PHILOSOPHER AND A MISSIONARY, ON THE DIMINUTION OF THE SEA—THE FORMATION OF THE EARTH—THE ORIGIN OF MEN & ANIMALS: AND OTHER SINGULAR SUBJECTS, RELATING TO NATURAL HISTORY & PHILOSOPHY.—A VERY CURIOUS WORK.—

> *Baltimore: Printed by W. Pechin, No. 15, Market-Street—for D. Porter, at the Observatory, Federal-Hill.* 1797. pp. [268.] 8vo. AAS. BA. LOC. SGO.

> "This curious work was written by de Maillet, whose name is concealed in the word Telliamed. It is supposed to have suggested to Mr Darwin his celebrated theory."—Sabin.

32415   MALHAM, John   1747–1821
THE NAVAL GAZETTEER; OR, SEAMAN'S COMPLETE GUIDE. BEING A COMPLETE GEO-
GRAPHICAL DICTIONARY, CONTAINING A FULL AND ACCURATE ACCOUNT, ALPHABET-
ICALLY ARRANGED, OF ALL THE COUNTRIES AND ISLANDS IN THE KNOWN WORLD;
SHEWING THEIR LATITUDE, LONGITUDE, SOUNDINGS, AND STATIONS FOR ANCHORAGE;
WITH A PARTICULAR DESCRIPTION OF THE SEVERAL BAYS, CAPES, CHANNELS, COVES,
CREEKS, CURRENTS, GULFS, HARBOURS, HAVENS, LAKES, OCEANS, RACES, RIVERS,
ROADS, ROCKS, SANDS, SHOALS, SOUNDS, STRAITS, TIDES, VARIATION OF THE COMPASS,
&C. TOGETHER WITH A PARTICULAR RELATION OF THE SHAPE AND APPEARANCE AT
SEA, OF THE SEVERAL HEADLANDS, ISTHMUSES, PENINSULAS, POINTS, PROMONTORIES,
AND WHATEVER IS OF USE OR IMPORTANCE TO THE MASTER, PILOT, COMMANDER OR
SEAMAN OF ANY SHIP OR VESSEL, IN NAVIGATING THE WATERY ELEMENT. ALSO,
COMPREHENDING AMPLE DIRECTIONS FOR SAILING INTO OR OUT OF THE DIFFERENT
PORTS, STRAITS, AND HARBOURS OF THE FOUR QUARTERS OF THE WORLD; AND FOR
AVOIDING DANGERS ON THE VARIOUS AND EXTENDED COAST; IN WHICH MORE THAN
TWELVE THOUSAND DISTINCT NAMES OF PLACES, &C. ARE TREATED OF AND EX-
PLAINED. BY THE REV. JOHN MALHAM. ILLUSTRATED WITH A CORRECT SET OF
CHARTS FROM THE LATEST AND BEST SURVEYS. FIRST AMERICAN EDITION. IN
TWO VOLUMES. VOL. I. [— II.]

> *Boston: Printed [by Samuel Etheridge] for and sold by W. Spotswood and
> J. Nancrede*, 1797. 2 vols. pp. xlvi, 7–436; 573, (1), 17 charts. 8vo.
>
>   AAS. BA. BPL. JCB. NYHS. NYPL.

32416   MANN, ELIAS   1750–1825
THE NORTHAMPTON COLLECTION OF SACRED HARMONY. IN THREE PARTS. CONTAIN-
ING, I. A PLAIN AND CONCISE INTRODUCTION TO THE GROUNDS OF MUSIC. II. A
LARGE NUMBER OF PSALM TUNES, SELECTED FROM THE MOST APPROVED AND EMI-
NENT AUTHORS. ADAPTED TO ALL THE DIFFERENT METRES AND KEYS USED IN THE
CHURCHES. III. A NUMBER OF LENGTHY PIECES OF SEVERAL VERSES EACH, MANY
OF WHICH ARE COMPOSITIONS NEVER BEFORE PUBLISHED, AND CALCULATED FOR THE
USE OF CHURCHES AND OTHER OCCASIONS;—WITH A NUMBER OF UNIVERSALLY AP-
PROVED ANTHEMS. BY ELIAS MANN, [Eight lines from] MILTON. PUBLISHED
ACCORDING TO ACT OF CONGRESS.

> *Printed, typographically, at Northampton, by Daniel Wright & Co. Sold by
> them in Northampton; by the principal Booksellers in Boston; and by Nathaniel
> Patten in Hartford.*—1797. pp. iv, 139, (1). obl. 12mo.   LOC. NL.

132d Massachusetts District Copyright, issued to Elias Mann, as Author,
3 November, 1797.

32417   MANN, HERMAN   1772–1833
THE FEMALE REVIEW: OR, MEMOIRS OF AN AMERICAN YOUNG LADY; WHOSE LIFE
AND CHARACTER ARE PECULIARLY DISTINGUISHED—BEING A CONTINENTAL SOLDIER,
FOR NEARLY THREE YEARS, IN THE LATE AMERICAN WAR. DURING WHICH TIME,
SHE PERFORMED THE DUTIES, OF EVERY DEPARTMENT, INTO WHICH SHE WAS CALLED
WITH PUNCTUAL EXACTNESS, FIDELITY AND HONOR, AND PRESERVED HER CHASTITY
INVIOLATE BY THE MOST ARTFUL CONCEALMENT OF HER SEX. WITH AN APPENDIX,
CONTAINING CHARACTERISTIC TRAITS, BY DIFFERENT HANDS: HER TASTE FOR ECON-
OMY, PRINCIPLES OF DOMESTIC EDUCATION, &C. BY A CITIZEN OF MASSACHUSETTS.

> *Dedham: Printed by Nathaniel and Benjamin Heaton, for the Author.*
> M,DCC,XCVII. pp. 258, (6), portrait. 12mo.   AAS. JCB. NYPL.

Contains a List of subscribers' names. Reprinted in Boston in 1866.
127th Massachusetts District Copyright, issued to Herman Mann, as
Author, 11 September, 1797. An account of the experiences of Deborah
Sampson, afterwards Mrs. Benjamin Gannet, who served under the name
of Robert Shurtlieff.

32418 MARCHANT, William
An Oration, pronounced at Newport, in the State of Rhode-Island, on the fourth of July, A. D. 1797. By William Marchant. [Two lines of Latin.]
Newport: Printed by Henry Barber. 1797. pp. 18. 4to. AAS. BM. RIHS.

32419 MARKHAM, Gervase 1568-1637
The Citizen and countryman's experienced farrier. Containing, I. The most best approved method of ordering, dieting, exercising, purging, scowring, and cleaning of horses: also choice restoratives to clear the heart, procure an appetite, and to clear the lungs and pipes, so as to strengthen wind, and give large breath to the running or race-horse. II. A certain sure method to know the true state of any horse's body, as to sickness or health. III. The true shape of a horse explained; with choice directions for buying. IV. An experienced and approved method for raising of horses, as to ordering, keeping, &c. Also mares, colts and stallions. V. A sure and certain rule to know the age of any horse, from one year to ten, with good observations as he further advances in years. VI. The best and experienced way of keeping the common hackney, or hunting horse, so as to keep him lively, chearful, free from colds, strains, windgalls, and gross humours. VII. An approved method of purging, bleeding and feeding cattle; with choice approved receipts for the diseases they are incident to: with signs to know the disease, and directions for the use of medicines. To all which is added: a valuable and fine collection of the surest and best receipts in the known world for the cure of all maladies and distempers that are incident to horses of what kind soever, with directions to know what is the ailment, or disease. By J. Markham, G. Jefferies, and discreet Indians.
Baltimore: Printed by Samuel Sower, M,DCC,XCVII. pp. 317.. 12mo.
 AAS. JCB. 8GO.

32420 MARMONTEL, Jean François 1723-1799
The Shepherdess of the Alps. A moral tale. Translated from the French of Monsieur Marmontel. Second American edition.
Baltimore: Printed by John Hayes, for George Keatinge's wholesale and retail Book-store. 1797. pp. 71, (1). 12mo. AAS.
Printed on heavy laid paper.

32421 —— The Widow of the village. Or, the adventures of innocence, a moral tale, by the celebrated Marmontel. Translated from the original French, by mr. Heron. To which is added, The Error of a good father.
Hartford: Printed by John Babcock. 1797. pp. 108. 12mo. AAS. NYPL.

32422 THE MARRIAGE: an epic poem. Written by an Eminent American poet.
Rutland: Printed by Josiah Fay. 1797.

32423 THE MARRIAGE of a deceased wife's sister vindicated. In a letter from a Citizen to a friend.
New-York: Printed by T. and J. Swords, No. 99, Pearl-street.—1797—pp. 30. 8vo. AAS. JCB. NYHS. NYPL.

32424 MARSH, John 1743-1821
A Sermon, delivered at the installation of the Rev. William Lockwood, in the pastoral office over the first church in Glastenbury, August 30, 1797. By John Marsh, a.m. pastor of the first church in Wethersfield. To which are annexed The Charge by the rev. dr. Dana, and the Right hand of fellowship, by the rev. mr. Atwater. Published at the request of the society in Glastenbury.
Hartford: Printed by Hudson and Goodwin. [1797.] pp. 35. 8vo.
 AAS. HC. JCB. NYPL. UTS.

32425 MARTEL, MICHEL
MARTEL'S ELEMENTS; CONTAINING A CHOICE OF THE MOST INTERESTING TRAITS IN
ANCIENT & MODERN HISTORY, PARALLELS OF PHILOSOPHERS, STATESMEN & HEROES,
A COLLECTION OF THOUGHTS FROM THE BEST AUTHORS, IN PROSE, AND A GREAT
VARIETY OF EXAMPLES OF ALL SORTS OF POETRY IN FRENCH, WITH THE LATIN,
ITALIAN, SPANISH, OR ENGLISH, WHEN IT IS AN IMITATION, THE WHOLE PROPER TO
FORM, AT THE SAME TIME, THE HEART AND THE JUDGMENT, THE MIND AND THE
STYLE, OF CHILDREN OF BOTH SEXES, AND THEREFORE, PROPOSED FOR THE USE OF
SCHOOLS. TEQUE TUASQUE DECET. HORACE. VOL. II.
New-York: Printed for the Author. 1797. pp. (2), (2), 139–680. 12mo.
AAS. NYPL.

32426 MARTIN, FRANÇOIS XAVIER   1764–1846
NOTES OF A FEW DECISIONS IN THE SUPERIOR COURTS OF THE STATE OF NORTH-
CAROLINA, AND IN THE CIRCUIT COURT OF THE U. STATES, FOR NORTH-CAROLINA
DISTRICT. TO WHICH IS ADDED A TRANSLATION OF LATCHS'S CASES.
Newbern: [Printed by] Francois –Xavier Martin. 1797. pp. (2), (2), (3),
78; 83, (5), (1); (2), (2), (2), (2), (215), (4), (15), (1). 8vo.   HC. JCB. NYPL.

Second title: CASES DETERMINED IN THE COURT OF KING'S BENCH: DURING THE
I. II. & III. YEARS OF CHARLES I. COLLECTED BY JOHN LATCH, OF THE MIDDLE
TEMPLE, ESQUIRE, FIRST PUBLISHED, IN NORMAN-FRENCH, [1661,] BY EDWARD
WALPOOLE, OF GRAY'S INN, ESQUIRE. TRANSLATED INTO THE ENGLISH LANGUAGE,
BY FRANCOIS—XAVIER MARTIN.
Newbern: From the Translator's Press. 1793. pp. (2), (2), (2), (2), (215),
(4), (15), (1).

The unsold copies of Latchs's Cases, published in 1793, were used by
the Translator and Publisher in this way, though called, by Allibone,
a second edition.

32427 MARTINET, JOHANNES FLORENTIUS   1729–1795
THE CATECHISM OF NATURE. FOR THE USE OF CHILDREN. BY DOCTOR MARTINET,
PROFESSOR OF PHILOSOPHY AT ZUTPHEN. TRANSLATED FROM THE DUTCH. READ
NATURE—NATURE IS A FRIEND TO TRUTH. YOUNG.
*Printed for Cornelius Davis, No. 96, Water-Street, New-York—*1797. pp.
107, (1). 24mo.   JCB.

32428 —— — THE CATECHISM OF NATURE; FOR THE USE OF CHILDREN. BY DR. MARTINET,
PROFESSOR OF PHILOSOPHY AT ZUTPHEN. TRANSLATED FROM THE DUTCH. . . .
Wilmington: Printed and sold by Peter Brynberg. 1797. 24mo.

32429 MARYLAND. STATE.
ACTS PASSED AT DIFFERENT SESSIONS OF THE GENERAL ASSEMBLY OF THE STATE OF
MARYLAND. . . . CONCERNING THE NAVIGATION OF THE RIVER SUSQUEHANNA,
FROM THE LINE OF THE STATE TO TIDE-WATER.
Baltimore: Printed by W. Pechin. 1797. pp. 37. 8vo.   HC.

32430 —— LAWS OF MARYLAND, MADE AND PASSED AT A SESSION OF ASSEMBLY, BEGUN AND
HELD AT THE CITY OF ANNAPOLIS ON MONDAY THE SEVENTH OF NOVEMBER, IN
THE YEAR OF OUR LORD ONE THOUSAND SEVEN HUNDRED AND NINETY-SIX. [— 31
DECEMBER, 1796.]
Annapolis: Printed by Frederick Green, Printer to the State. [1797.] pp.
(154). fol.   LOC. NYPL.

With the Presidents' Address to the people of the United States. And
the Testamentary System. In Council, February 14, 1797. And, System
of education.

MARYLAND. STATE, continued.

32431 —— TESTAMENTARY SYSTEM. IN COUNCIL, FEBRUARY 14, 1797. ORDERED, THAT THE TESTAMENTARY SYSTEM REPORTED BY THE CHANCELLOR, IN PURSUANCE OF THE REQUEST OF THE LEGISLATURE, BE PRINTED FOR CONSIDERATION, WITH THE ACTS OF ASSEMBLY OF THE LAST SESSION, AGREEABLY TO A REPORT OF A COMMITTEE ON THAT SUBJECT. BY ORDER, N. PINKNEY, CLK. COUNCIL.
[Annapolis: Printed by Frederick Green. 1797.] pp. (38+) fol.   MDL.

32432 —— VOTES AND PROCEEDINGS OF THE HOUSE OF DELEGATES OF THE STATE OF MARY-LAND. NOVEMBER SESSION, 1796. BEING THE FIRST SESSION OF THIS ASSEMBLY. [9 NOVEMBER, — 31 DECEMBER, 1796.]
[Annapolis: Printed by Frederick Green, 1797.] pp. 117. fol.   LOC. NYPL.

32433 THE MARYLAND & VIRGINIA ALMANAC, FOR THE YEAR 1798. CONTAINING, BESIDES EVERYTHING NECESSARY IN AN ALMANAC, A VARIETY OF PIECES IN PROSE AND VERSE.
Elizabeth (Hager's) Town: Printed and sold by Thomas Grieves, near the Court-House. [1797.]
Contains, A Sermon in praise of cursing and swearing in common conversation.

32434 THE MARYLAND GAZETTE. LIIND. YEAR. NO. 2608. THURSDAY, JANUARY 5, [— LIIID. YEAR. NO. 2659. THURSDAY, DECEMBER 28, 1797.]
Annapolis: Printed by Frederick and Samuel Green. 1797. fol.   MDHS.

32435 THE MARYLAND HERALD, AND EASTERN SHORE INTELLIGENCER. VOL. VII. NO. 343. TUESDAY, JANUARY 3, [— VOL. VIII. NO. 394. TUESDAY, DECEMBER 26, 1797.]
Easton: Printed by James Cowan. 1797. fol.   MDHS.

32436 THE MARYLAND HERALD, AND ELIZABETH-TOWN ADVERTISER. VOL. I. No. 1. THURSDAY, MARCH 2, [— No. 44. THURSDAY, DECEMBER 28, 1797.]
Elizabeth-Town, (Maryland) Printed and published by Tho. Grieves. 1797. fol.   MDHS.
Established, as a weekly, by Thomas Grieves, attorney for John D. Cary, administrator of the estate of Stewart Herbert, deceased, Printer of *The Washington Spy,* in continuation of that paper, and published continuously beyond the period of this work. In April, 1797. the Printing-Office was removed to "the Shop lately occupied by Mr. Frederick Millar, apothecary, next door to Dr. R. Pindel's near the Court-House, Elizabeth-Town." Beginning in June, 1797. the imprint was made a part of the heading, and reads: Elizabeth (Hager's) Town: Printed (every Thursday) by Thomas Grieves, near the Court-House, and so continued. With the issue for February 26, 1801, the title was changed to *The Maryland Herald, and Elizabeth-Town Weekly Advertiser.* And, with the issue for February 22, 1804, "Hager's-Town" replaced Elizabeth-Town in both the title, and the imprint. With the issue for March 10, 1813, Stewart Herbert, son of the founder of the press, became associated in the publication under the firm name of Thomas Grieves & Stewart Herbert. They continued the paper until after 1820.

32437 MARYLAND JOURNAL & BALTIMORE DAILY ADVERTISER. NO. 2261. MONDAY, JANUARY 2, [— No. 2399. SATURDAY, JULY 1, 1797.]
Baltimore: Printed by D. Finchete Freebairn. 1797. fol.
Publication was suspended with the issue for February 28th, when Freebairn withdrew. Philip Edwards resumed publication with the issue for March 21st, shortening the title to *Maryland Journal,* and finally discontinuing its publication with the issue for July 1, 1797.

32438   MASON, John Mitchell   1770–1829
Hope for the heathen: a sermon, preached in the old Presbyterian church, before the New-York Missionary Society, at their annual meeting, November 7, 1797. By John M. Mason, a. m. pastor of the Scots Presbyterian church in the city of New-York.
> New-York: Printed by T. & J. Swords, No. 99 Pearl-street.—1797.—pp. 49. 8vo.   AAS. BA. BM. HC. JCB. MHS. NYHS. NYPL. UTS.

Contains, Report of the directors of the New York Missionary Society, for 1797.

32439   MASONIC. Songs, orations, odes, anthems, prologues, and toasts: adapted to the different degrees of masonry.
> Waterford [New-York]: Compiled, Printed, & published, by brother James Lyon, in the year of light VMDCCXCVII [1797.] pp. vii, [5]–[140.] 48mo. LOC.

32440   MASSACHUSETTS. State.
[Arms.] Acts and laws, passed by the General Court of Massachusetts: begun and held at Boston, in the County of Suffolk, on Wednesday, the twenty-fifth day of January, Anno Domini, 1797. [Colophon:]
> Boston: Printed by Young & Minns, Printers to the State. [1797.] pp. 41–120. fol.   AAS. LOC. NYPL.

32441   —— — [Arms.] Acts and laws, passed by the General Court of Massachusetts: begun and held at Boston, in the County of Suffolk, on Tuesday, the thirty-first day of May, Anno Domini, 1797. [Colophon:]
> Boston: Printed by Young & Minns, Printers to the State. [1797.] pp. 121–154. fol.   AAS. LOC. NYPL.

32442   —— [Arms.] Commonwealth of Massachusetts. By the governor. A Proclamation for a day of solemn fasting & prayer. . . . Thursday, the fourth day of May next, ensuing . . . Given at the council-chamber, in Boston, this twentieth day of March, in the year of our Lord, one thousand seven hundred and ninety-seven, and in the twenty-first year of the independence of the United States of America. Samuel Adams. Attest, John Avery, secretary. God save the Commonwealth of Massachusetts. [Colophon:]
> Printed by Young & Minns, Printers to the State. [1797.] Broadside. fol.   AAS. BPL.

32443   —— [Arms.] Commonwealth of Massachusetts. By his excellency Increase Sumner, esquire, governor of the Commonwealth of Massachusetts, A Proclamation for a day of public thanksgiving. . . . Thursday, the thirtieth of November next. . . . Given at the council chamber, in Boston, this twenty-third day of October, in the year of our Lord, one thousand seven hundred and ninety-seven; and in the twenty-second year of the independence of the United States of America. Increase Sumner. Attest, John Avery, secretary. God save the Commonwealth of Massachusetts. [Colophon:]
> Printed by Young and Minns, State Printers. [1797.] Broadside. fol.   AAS. BPL. MHS.

32444   —— Commonwealth of Massachusetts. In the year of our Lord, one thousand seven hundred and ninety-seven. An Act dividing this Commonwealth into districts, and providing for a more speedy, prompt and satisfactory administration of justice.
> [Boston:] Printed by Young and Minns, Printers to the State. [1797.] pp. 4. fol.   AAS. EI. NYPL.

MASSACHUSETTS. STATE, continued.

32445 —— [Arms.] COMMONWEALTH OF MASSACHUSETTS. IN THE YEAR OF OUR LORD, ONE THOUSAND, SEVEN HUNDRED AND NINETY-SEVEN. AN ACT, IN ADDITION TO THE SEVERAL ACTS NOW IN FORCE, RESPECTING HIGHWAYS. FEBRUARY 28, 1797. [Colophon:]
Boston: Printed by Young and Minns, State Printers. [1797.] Broadside. fol.　　　　　　　　　　　　　　　　　　　　　　　　MHS. NYPL.

32446 —— COMMONWEALTH OF MASSACHUSETTS. TO THE HON. SENATE AND HOUSE OF REPRESENTATIVES, IN GENERAL COURT ASSEMBLED. THE PETITION AND MEMORIAL OF THE SUBSCRIBERS, A COMMITTEE IN BEHALF OF THE TOWN OF FRANKLIN. . . . [Regarding the redemption of treasury notes.]
[Boston: Printed by Young and Minns. 1797.] pp. 3. fol.　　　　AAS.

32447 —— GENERAL ORDERS. HEAD-QUARTERS, BOSTON, JUNE 13TH, 1797. . . . [Signed, William Donnison, adjutant general.]
[Boston: Printed by Young and Minns. 1797.] pp. (2).　　　　NYHS.

32448 —— GENERAL ORDERS. HEAD-QUARTERS, BOSTON, AUGUST 22, 1797. . . . [Signed, William Donnison, adjutant-general.]
[Boston: Printed by Young and Minns. 1797.] pp. (3).　　　　EI.

32449 —— [Arms.] RESOLVES OF THE GENERAL COURT OF THE COMMONWEALTH OF MASSACHUSETTS: TOGETHER WITH THE MESSAGES, &C. OF HIS EXCELLENCY THE GOVERNOR, TO THE SAID COURT: BEGUN AND HELD AT BOSTON, IN THE COUNTY OF SUFFOLK, ON WEDNESDAY, THE TWENTY-FIFTH DAY OF JANUARY, ANNO DOMINI, 1797. [—11 MARCH, 1797.] [Colophon:]
Boston: Printed by Young & Minns, Printers to the State. [1797.] pp. (45)-88. fol.　　　　　　　　　　　　　　　　　　AAS. LOC. NYPL.

32450 —— —— RESOLVES OF THE GENERAL COURT OF THE COMMONWEALTH OF MASSACHUSETTS. TOGETHER WITH THE GOVERNOR'S MESSAGES, &C. TO THE COURT. BEGUN AND HELD AT BOSTON, IN THE COUNTY OF SUFFOLK, ON WEDNESDAY THE THIRTY-FIRST DAY OF MAY, ANNO DOMINI—M,DCC,XCVII. [—23 JUNE, 1797.] [Arms.]
Boston: Printed by Young & Minns, Printers to the honorable the General Court. [1797.] pp. 30. fol.　　　　　　　　　AAS. LOC. NYPL.

32451 —— RESOLVE APPOINTING COMMISSIONERS, TO SETTLE DIFFERENCES WITH RESIDENTS ON THE WALDO CLAIM, &C. MARCH 9, 1797.
[Boston:] Printed by Young & Minns, Printers to the State. [1797.] Broadside.　　　　　　　　　　　　　　　　　　　　MHS.

32452 —— TAX NO. FOURTEEN. [Arms.] COMMONWEALTH OF MASSACHUSETTS. IN THE YEAR OF OUR LORD, ONE THOUSAND, SEVEN HUNDRED AND NINETY-SEVEN. AN ACT FOR APPORTIONING AND ASSESSING A TAX, OF ONE HUNDRED AND THIRTY-THREE THOUSAND, THREE HUNDRED AND EIGHTY ONE DOLLARS, AND FIFTY THREE CENTS; AND PROVIDING FOR THE REIMBURSEMENT OF TEN THOUSAND, THREE HUNDRED AND SIXTY EIGHT DOLLARS, PAID OUT OF THE PUBLIC TREASURY TO THE MEMBERS OF THE HOUSE OF REPRESENTATIVES FOR THEIR ATTENDANCE THE LAST TWO SESSIONS OF THE GENERAL COURT. [Colophon:]
Boston: Printed by Young & Minns, Printers to the State. [1797.] pp. 20. fol.　　　　　　　　　　　　　　　　　　AAS. HSP. LOC.

AUCTION VALUES

32453   MASSACHUSETTS HISTORICAL SOCIETY.
BOSTON, DECEMBER, 1797. PROPOSAL FOR PRINTING BY SUBSCRIPTION, THE COLLEC-
TIONS OF THE MASSACHUSETTS HISTORICAL SOCIETY, FOR THE YEAR 1798; . . .
     [*Boston:* 1797.] Broadside.   MHS.

32454   MASSACHUSETTS [arms] MERCURY. NO. 1. OF VOL. IX. TOTAL NO. 443. TUES-
DAY, JANUARY 3, [— NO. 52 OF VOL. X. FRIDAY, DECEMBER 29, 1797.]
     *Boston: Printed by Young and Minns, Printers to the honorable the General
Court.* 1797. fol.   AAS. BA. BPL. MHS.

32455   MAURY, JEAN SIFFREIN, cardinal   1746–1817
THE PRINCIPLES OF ELOQUENCE; ADAPTED TO THE PULPIT AND THE BAR. BY THE
ABBE MAURY. THE FIRST AMERICAN EDITION. TRANSLATED FROM THE FRENCH;
WITH ADDITIONAL NOTES, BY JOHN NEAL LAKE, A. M. [Nine lines of quotations.]
     *Albany: Printed by Loring Andrews & Co. For Thomas, Andrews & Pen-
niman, sold at their Book store, No. 45, State-Street, Albany; by I. Thomas, in
Worcester; by Thomas & Andrews, in Boston; and by Thomas, Andrews & Butler,
in Baltimore.*—1797. pp. xii, 239. 12mo.   AAS. BA. HC. JCB. NYPL.

32456   MAXCY, JONATHAN   1768–1820
A SERMON PREACHED IN BOSTON, AT THE ANNUAL CONVENTION OF THE WARREN ASSO-
CIATION, IN THE REV. DR. STILLMAN'S MEETING-HOUSE, SEPTEMBER 12, A. D. 1797.
BY JONATHAN MAXCY, A. M. PRESIDENT OF RHODE-ISLAND COLLEGE. PUBLISHED
BY REQUEST.
     Boston: Printed by Manning & Loring. 1797. pp. 22. 8vo.
                    AAS. BA. BU. JCB. NYHS. NYPL. RIHS.

32457   MEAD, MATTHEW   1630–1699
THE ALMOST CHRISTIAN DISCOVERED: OR, THE FALSE PROFESSOR TRIED AND CAST.
BEING THE SUBSTANCE OF SEVEN SERMONS, FIRST PREACHED AT SEPULCHRES IN
LONDON, 1661, AND AT THE IMPORTUNITY OF FRIENDS MADE PUBLIC. BY MATTHEW
MEAD. LUKE XVI, 14, 15. [Six lines.]
     *Albany: Printed by Fry and Southwick, at the Chronicle Office, corner of
Dock Street and Mark Lane.* 1797. pp. 167. 12mo.   AAS.

32458   MEAD, SAMUEL   –1832
PUBLIC WORSHIP A PLEASURE TO A PIOUS MAN. A SERMON. DELIVERED AT HAVER-
HILL, MARCH 1, 1797, AT THE ORDINATION OF THE REV. ISAAC TOMPKINS, A. M.
TO THE WORK OF THE MINISTRY IN THAT PLACE. BY THE REV. SAMUEL MEAD, A. M.
PASTOR OF A CHURCH IN DANVERS. (PUBLISHED BY DESIRE OF THE HEARERS.)
     Printed at Newburyport by Edmund M. Blunt—1797. pp. (31). 8vo.
                    AAS. BM. JCB.

32459   MEDICAL COMMENTARIES, FOR THE YEAR 1795. EXHIBITING A CONCISE VIEW OF THE
LATEST AND MOST IMPORTANT DISCOVERIES IN MEDICINE AND MEDICAL PHILOSOPHY.
COLLECTED AND PUBLISHED BY ANDREW DUNCAN, M, D. F. R. & A. SS. ED. PHYSI-
CIAN TO HIS ROYAL HIGHNESS THE PRINCE OF WALES FOR SCOTLAND; FELLOW OF
THE ROYAL COLLEGE OF PHYSICIANS, EDINBURGH; MEMBER OF THE ROYAL SOCI-
ETIES OF PARIS, COPENHAGEN, EDINBURGH, &C. AND PROFESSOR OF THE INSTITU-
TIONS OF MEDICINE IN THE UNIVERSITY OF EDINBURGH. [Two lines of Latin
from] BAGLIVIUS. VOLUME TENTH [*sic* ELEVENTH.]
     *Philadelphia: Printed by Thomas Dobson, at the Stone-House, No 41, South
Second-Street.* M.DCC.XCVII. pp. xii, 218, (2). 8vo.   RIMS. 8GO.

32460   THE MEDICAL REPOSITORY. CONDUCTED BY S. L. MITCHELL, E. MILLER, AND ELIHU H. SMITH. VOL. I. No. 1. JULY 26, 1797 [— OCTOBER, 1797.]
New-York: Printed by T. & J. Swords. 1797. 8vo.

AAS. BA. BPL. LCP. NYPL. SGO. YC.

The first Journal of its kind in the United States. Continued quarterly through the year 1824. The prospectus and circular address is dated November 15, 1796. Following his death in 1798, Elihu H. Smith's name was dropped after the second volume, Beginning with volume 4, the words, "and Review of American publications on Medicine, Surgery, and the auxiliary branches of Philosophy" were added to the title. With volume 16, E. Miller's connection ceased, and the names of Felix Pascalis, and Samuel Akerly substituted. The title was then altered to: "The Medical Repository of original essays and intelligence relative to Physic, Surgery, Chemistry and Natural History", and with volume 20, Samuel Akerly's name was dropped. The first volume was reprinted in 1800, and again in 1804. The second volume in 1800, and again in 1805. And the fourth volume in 1808. Vol. I. No. 1. 50th New York District Copyright, issued to Samuel Latham Mitcel, Edward Miller, Elihu Hubbard Smith, as Proprietors, 29 July, 1797. No. II. 56th New York District Copyright, (to the same) 9 November, 1797. No. IV. 58th New York District Copyright, (to the same) 30 January, 1798.

32461   THE MEDLEY or NEWBEDFORD MARINE JOURNAL. NUMBER 10 OF VOLUME V. WHOLE NUMBER 218. FRIDAY, JANUARY 6, [— NUMBER 9 OF VOLUME VI. WHOLE NUMBER 268. FRIDAY, DECEMBER 29, 1797.]
Newbedford (Massachusetts) Printed and published by John Spooner, at his Office, corner of Union and Sixth Streets. 1797. fol.   AAS.

32462   MELLEN, JOHN, JUNIOR   1752–1828
A SERMON, DELIVERED BEFORE HIS EXCELLENCY THE GOVERNOR, AND THE HONOURABLE LEGISLATURE, OF THE COMMONWEALTH OF MASSACHUSETTS, ON THE ANNUAL ELECTION MAY 31, 1797. BY JOHN MELLEN, JUN. ONE OF THE MINISTERS OF BARNSTABLE.
Printed at Boston, by Young & Minns, Printers to the State. 1797. pp. 36. 8vo.   AAS. BA. BM. BPL. HC. JCB. MHS. NYHS. NYPL.

32463   —— A SERMON, DELIVERED AT YARMOUTH, NOVEMBER 13, 1796, OCCASIONED BY THE SUDDEN DEATH OF MRS. SARAH ALDEN, CONSORT OF THE REVEREND TIMOTHY ALDEN. BY JOHN MELLEN, JUN. MINISTER OF THE EAST CHURCH IN BARNSTABLE. [Ornament.]
Printed by S. Hall, No. 53, Cornhill, Boston. 1797. pp. [28.] 12mo.
AAS. BA. HC. MHS. NYPL.

Contains a genealogical Appendix. By Timothy Alden, junior.

32464   MELSHEIMER, FRIEDRICH VALENTINE   1749–1814
GESPRÄCHE ZWISCHEN EINEM PROTESTANTEN UND RÖMISCHEN PRIESTER.
Hanover, York County, Pennsylvania: Gedruckt bey Stellingius und Lepper. 1797.

32465   MENDON. MASSACHUSETTS. MENDON ASSOCIATION.
EVIDENCES OF REVEALED RELIGION. BY MENDON ASSOCIATION, (MASSACHUSETTS.) [Ornament.]
Printed at Worcester, by Leonard Worcester. 1797. pp. 163. 8vo.
AAS. BA. JCB. NYPL.

32466 THE MERCHANTS' DAILY ADVERTISER. VOL. I. NO. 1. MONDAY, JANUARY 16, [— VOL. II. NO. 299. SATURDAY, DECEMBER 30, 1797.]

  [Philadelphia: Published] By Thomas Bradford, No. 8, South Front-Street. 1797. fol.   AAS. HC. HSP.

  Established, as a daily, by Thomas Bradford. With the issue for June 4, 1798, Thomas Bradford was succeeded as publisher, by his Son, Samuel F. Bradford, who discontinued publication with the issue for June 30, 1798, and established on July 2d, in continuation, *The True American and Commercial Advertiser.*

32467 MERCIER, LOUIS SÉBASTIEN   1740–1814

  SERAPHINA; A NOVEL. FROM THE FRENCH OF M. MERCIER. TO WHICH IS ADDED, AUGUSTE AND MADELAINE. A REAL HISTORY. BY MISS HELEN MARIA WILLIAMS.

  Wiscasset, (District of Maine.) Printed ? by Henry Hoskins & John W. Scott. 1797.

32468 MERRILL, R.

  THE MUSICAL PRACTITIONER, OR AMERICAN PSALMODY. IN TWO PARTS. CONTAINING I. A NUMBER OF PSALM, HYMN TUNES AND ANTHEMS. II. A NUMBER OF THE MOST MODERN AND CELEBRATED AMERICAN AND ENGLISH SONGS. THE WHOLE ENTIRELY NEW. COMPOSED BY R. MERRILL, OF HOPKINTON, NEW-HAMPSHIRE.

  Newburyport: Printed by William Barrett? 1797.

32469 MERRY, ROBERT   1755–1798

  THE PAINS OF MEMORY. A POEM. BY ROBERT MERRY, A. M. [Eight lines of verse from] GOLDSMITH.

  Boston: Printed by Manning & Loring, for David West, No. 56, Cornhill. 1797. pp. 39. 4to.   AAS. BA. BU. HC. NYPL.

32470 THE MERRY-FELLOWS COMPANION; OR AMERICAN JEST BOOK. CONTAINING A CHOICE SELECTION OF ANECDOTES, BON MOTS, JESTS, REPARTEES, STORIES, &C. &C.

  Printed at Harrisburgh, by John Wyeth, for Mathew Carey, of Philadelphia. 1797. pp. 96, frontispiece. 12mo.   AAS. LOC.

32471 METHODIST EPISCOPAL CHURCH IN THE UNITED STATES OF AMERICA.

  ARTICLES OF ASSOCIATION, OF THE TRUSTEES OF THE EUND [sic] FOR THE RELIEF AND SUPPORT OF THE ITINERANT, SUPERANNUATED, AND WORN-OUT MINISTERS AND PREACHERS OF THE METHODIST EPISCOPAL CHURCH, IN THE UNITED STATES OF AMERICA, THEIR WIVES AND CHILDREN, WIDOWS AND ORPHANS.

  Philadelphia.—Printed by Henry Tuckniss—and may be had, gratis, of John Dickins, No. 50, North Second-Street. 1797. pp. 12. 8vo. AAS.

32472 —— THE DOCTRINES AND DISCIPLINE OF THE METHODIST EPISCOPAL CHURCH IN AMERICA, REVISED AND APPROVED AT THE GENERAL CONFERENCE HELD AT BALTIMORE IN THE STATE OF MARYLAND, IN NOVEMBER 1792: IN WHICH THOMAS COKE AND FRANCIS ASBURY PRESIDED: TO WHICH ARE ADDED THE MINUTES OF THE GENERAL CONFERENCE HELD AT BALTIMORE OCTOBER 20TH 1796. THE NINTH EDITION.

  Philadelphia: Printed by Henry Tuckniss, and sold by John Dickins, No. 50 North Second Street, near Arch Street. 1797. pp. 208, (4). 12mo.

METHODIST EPISCOPAL CHURCH, continued.

32473 —— Minutes taken at the several annual conferences of the Methodist Episcopal Church in America, for the year 1797.

Philadelphia: Printed by Henry Tuckniss, and sold by John Dickins. 1797.

32474 —— A Pocket hymn-book, designed as a constant companion for the pious. Collected from various authors. The twenty-first edition. Psalm civ. 33. [Three lines.]

Philadelphia: Printed by Henry Tuckniss, No. 25, Church-Alley, and sold by John Dickins, No. 50, North Second-Street, near Arch-Street. 1797. [Price half a dollar.] pp. (2), 285, (1), (10), (2). 24mo.   AAS.

Contains, a two-page list of Books, for the use of Methodist Societies.

32475 THE METHODIST Magazine, for [January — December] the year 1797. Containing, original sermons, experiences, letters, and other religious pieces; together with instructive and useful extracts from different authors. Volume I.

Philadelphia: Printed by Henry Tuckniss: Sold by John Dickins, No. 50, North Second Street, Philadelphia, and by the Methodist ministers and preachers throughout the United States. [1797.] pp. (570), (5). 8vo.   AAS. LCP. NYHS.

32476 MIDDLESEX Gazette. Vol. XII. Numb. 581. Friday, January 6, [— Vol. XIII. Numb. 632. Friday, December 29, 1797.]

Printed by M. H. Woodward, in Middletown. 1797. fol.   AAS. CHS.

With the issue for October 6th, Woodward disposed of his interests to Tertius Dunning, and moved to New Haven, where he engaged in bookselling—occupying Abel Morse's old Bookstore. His readers being prepared for the change by the reduced size and poor quality of paper. The imprint was changed to Middletown—(Connecticut)—Printed and published every Friday, by T. Dunning.

32477 MILLER Samuel   1769–1850
A Discourse, delivered April 12, 1797, at the request of and before the New-York Society for promoting the manumission of slaves, and protecting such of them as have been or may be liberated. By Samuel Miller, a.m. one of the ministers of the United Presbyterian churches in the city of New-York, and member of said Society.

New-York: Printed by T. and J. Swords, No. 99 Pearl-Street.—1797.—pp. 36. 8vo.   AAS. HC. JCB. MHS. NYHS. NYPL.

32478 MILLOT, Claude François Xavier, l'abbé   1726–1785
Elements of ancient history. Translated from the French of the abbe Millot. In two volumes. Vol. I. [— II.]

New-York: Printed and sold by [Jacob S. Mott.] No. 70, Vesey-Street.—1797—2 vols. pp. viii, 504; (2), viii, 519. 8vo.   AAS.

32479   MILNS, WILLIAM   1761–1801
THE AMERICAN ACCOUNTANT; OR, A COMPLETE SYSTEM OF PRACTICAL ARITHMETIC.
CONTAINING, I. WHOLE NUMBERS PARTICULARLY ADAPTED TO THE AMERICAN AND
BRITISH COMMERCE. II. VULGAR FRACTIONS; IN WHICH THE RULES ARE SO SIMPLE
AND THE CONTRACTIONS SO OBVIOUS; AS TO RENDER THE OPERATIONS REMARKABLY
SHORT AND EASY. III. DECIMALS, WITH CONCISE METHODS OF MANAGING ALL KINDS
OF SIMPLE AND COMPOUND REPETENDS; THE EXTRACTION OF ROOTS; INTEREST, AN-
NUITIES, &C. &C. IV. DUODECIMALS; OR MULTIPLICATION OF FEET AND INCHES.
V. CURIOUS, USEFUL AND ENTERTAINING QUESTIONS, WITH THEIR SOLUTIONS; &C. &C.
THE WHOLE CALCULATED TO EASE THE TEACHER AND ASSIST THE PUPIL; IT WILL
BE FOUND LIKEWISE EXTREMELY USEFUL TO AMERICAN MERCHANTS, &C. GENERAL
RULES AND COMPACT TABLES BEING GIVEN TO CHANGE THE CURRENCIES, STERLING,
FRENCH AND DUTCH MONIES INTO EACH OTHER. BY WILLIAM MILNS, MEMBER OF
ST. MARY-HALL IN THE UNIVERSITY OF OXFORD; AUTHOR OF THE WELL-BRED
SCHOLAR, PENMAN'S REPOSITORY, &C. &C. [One line of Latin from] SEN.

*New-York: Printed by J. S. Mott, for the Author, and sold by him No. 29
Gold-Street, sold also by C. Smith, No. 51 Maiden-lane, and by the principal Booksellers in the United States. 1797. Copy-right secured.* pp.(2),(3),(3) 320. 16mo.

54th New York District Copyright, issued to William Milns, as Author,   AAS.
21 September, 1797.

32480   —— *Engraved title:* THE COLUMBIAN LIBRARY CONTAINING A CLASSICAL SELECTION
OF BRITISH LITERATURE, VOL. I. THE WELL-BRED SCHOLAR. [Vignette.]
New-York: Printed & Published by W. Milns. No. 29 Gold St. 1797.

Title: THE WELL-BRED SCHOLAR, OR PRACTICAL ESSAYS ON THE BEST METHODS OF
IMPROVING THE TASTE, AND ASSISTING THE EXERTIONS OF YOUTH IN THEIR LITER-
ARY PURSUITS. BY WILLIAM MILNS, MEMBER OF ST. MARY HALL, IN THE UNIVER-
SITY OF OXFORD; AUTHOR OF THE AMERICAN ACCOUNTANT, PENMAN'S REPOSITORY,
&C. &C. [Six lines from] AKENSIDE. SECOND EDITION, WITH ALTERATIONS AND
REVISIONS.

New-York: Printed at the Literary Printing Office, No. 29 Gold Street. 1797.
(*Copy Right secured.*) pp. (2), viii, (1), 284. 16mo.   AAS. BM. JCB. NYPL.

Dedication. To the Superintendants of schools. Dated, Dec. 4, 1797.
"A few copies will be printed on an English wove paper, of the very
finest quality, with which will be given proof impressions of the plates,
for the accomodation of the curious." 57th New York District Copyright. issued to William Milns, as Author, 2 December, 1797.

32481   —— PENMAN'S REPOSITORY. TEXT, ROUND AND RUNNING HAND COPIES.
New-York: Complete sets for sale by the Author, No. 29, Gold-Street. 1797.

32482   —— SONGS &C. IN THE COMET; OR, HE WOULD BE A PHILOSOPHER. A COMEDY IN FIVE
ACTS, AS PERFORMED BY THE OLD AMERICAN COMPANY NEW YORK. WRITTEN BY
WILLIAM MILNS. THE MUSIC BY J. HEWITT.
New-York: Printed for the Author. 1797. 12mo.

46th New York District Copyright, issued to William Milns, as Author,
30 January, 1797.

32483   THE MINERVA. VOLUME I. NUMBER 13. TUESDAY, JANUARY 3, [— VOLUME II.
NUMBER 64. THURSDAY, DECEMBER 28, 1797.]
*Dedham, (Massachusetts) Printed and published by Nathaniel and Benjamin
Heaton, about 60 rods east of the Cou -House, . . .* 1797. fol.   AAS.

With the issue for December 7th, the name of Herman Mann took the
place of the junior partner in the imprint, and at the end of the year
Nathaniel Heaton also withdrew.

32484 THE MINERVA & MERCANTILE EVENING ADVERTISER. VOL. IV. NUMB. 1030. MONDAY, JANUARY 2, [—VOL. IV. No. 1162. SATURDAY, SEPTEMBER 30, 1797.]

Published (daily) by Hopkins, Webb & Co. at No. 40, Pine-Street, New-York. 1797. fol.   AAS. BA. LCP. LOC. NYHS. NYPL.

With the issue for May 15th, Joseph D. Webb withdrew after a disagreement, and Webster and Hopkins continued as Hopkins & Co. With the issue for October 2d, the title was changed to *Commercial Advertiser.*

32485 THE MIRROR. VOL. V. No. 259. TUESDAY, OCTOBER 10, [— VOL. VI. No. 269. TUESDAY, DECEMBER 26, 1797.]

[Printed and published] By Russell and Davis, Concord, [New Hampshire.] 1797. fol.   AAS.

In continuation of the successive numbering of *The Federal Mirror. Republican Gazetteer. Russel & Davis' Republican Gazetteer. The New Star.* With the issue for October 26th, Elijah Russell withdrew to Fryeburg, Maine, and publication was continued in the name of Moses Davis only.

32486 THE MIRROR. VOL. I. No. 1. MONDAY, OCTOBER 2, [— No. 13. MONDAY, DECEMBER 25, 1797.]

Newburgh. [N. Y.] Published by Philip Van Horne. 1797. fol.

Established, as a weekly, by Philip Van Horne, and continued by him to November, 1798, when he disposed of his interests to Joseph W. Barber, who continued publication to November ? 1799, when its publication was merged in *The Orange County Gazette.*

32487 THE MIRROR. FIRM, FREE, AND TEMPERATE. VOL. I. No. 1. SATURDAY, SEPTEMBER 16, [— No 16. SATURDAY, DECEMBER 30, 1797.]

Washington, (Kentucky) Printed and published (weekly) by Hunter & Beaumont. . . . 1797. fol.   UOC.

Established, as a weekly, by William Hunter, and William H. Beaumont, and continued by them until the dissolution of partnership in December, 1799, when publication ceased. In August, 1798, the firm established at Frankfort, The Palladium, which Hunter conducted there. while Beaumont conducted The Mirror, at Washington, both printed and published by Hunter and Beaumont.

32488 MITCHILL, SAMUEL LATHAM   1764–1831
THE PRESENT STATE OF MEDICAL LEARNING IN THE CITY OF NEW-YORK.

New-York: Printed by T. and J. Swords, Printers to the Faculty of Physic of Columbia College, No. 99, Pearl-Street. July, 1797. pp. 16. 8vo.

HC. MHS. NYHS. SGO.

32489 THE MOHAWK MERCURY. VOL. III. No. 108. TUESDAY, JANUARY 3, [— VOL. IV. No. 159. TUESDAY, DECEMBER 26, 1797.]

Schenectady, (on the Banks of the Mohawk). Printed by Cornelius P. Wyckoff, corner of State & Washington Streets. 1797. fol.   AAS.

32490 MONITEUR DE LA LOUISIANE. No. 12. SAMEDI, 7 JANVIER, [— No. 63. SAMEDI, 30 DÉCEMBRE, 1797.]

Nouvelle Orleans: 1797. 4to.

32491　MONROE, James　　　　　　　　　　　　　　　　　1758–1831
A View of the conduct of the executive, in the foreign affairs of the
United States, connected with the missions to the French Republic, during
the years 1794, 5, and 6. By James Monroe, late minister plenipotentiary
to the said Republic. Illustrated by his instructions and correspondence
and other authentic documents.
Philadelphia: Printed by and for Benj. Franklin Bache. MDCCXCVII. pp.
(4), lxvi, 407. 8vo.　　　　　AAS. BA. BM. BPL. HC. JCB. MHS. NL. NYHS. VSL.
195th Pennsylvania District Copyright, issued to Benjamin Franklin
Bache, as Proprietor, 21 December 1797. Reprinted in London, in 1798.

32492　THE MONTHLY Military Repository. Respecfully [*sic*] inscribed to the military of the United States of America. By Charles Smith. Vol. ii. [Vignette.]
New-York: Printed by John Buel, for the Author, No. 51, Maiden-Lane.—
1797.—pp. 215, (1), portrait of Wayne. 8vo.　　AAS. JCB. LOC. NYHS. NYPL. WHS.

32493　MOORE, John　　　　　　　　　　　　　　　　　1729–1802
A Journal during a residence in France, from the beginning of August, to
the middle of December, 1792, to which is added, an account of the most
remarkable events that happened at Paris from that time to the death
of the late King of France. By John Moore, m.d. In two volumes. Vol. i.
[— ii.] [Two lines of Latin from] Tacit.
*Chambersburg: Printed by Andrew Dover, for Mathew Carey, No. 118, Mar-
ket-Street, Philadelphia.* M,DCC,XCVII. 2 vols. pp. 233, map; — —12mo. AAS.
Title of map: A Map of general Dumourier's campaign on the Meuse. Engraved for Berry, Rogers & Berrys edition.

32494　MOORE, John Hamilton　　　　　　　　　　　　　　–1807
The Young gentleman and lady's monitor, and English teacher's assistant:
being a collection of select pieces from our best modern writers : calculated to eradicate vulgar prejudices and rusticity of manners; improve
the understanding; rectify the will; purify the passions; direct the minds
of youth to the pursuit of proper objects; and to facilitate their reading, writing, and speaking the English language, with elegance and propriety. Particularly adapted for the use of our eminent schools and
academies, as well as private persons, who have not an opportunity of
perusing the works of those celebrated authors, from whence this collection is made. Divided into small portions for the ease of reading in
classes. By J. Hamilton Moore.
Printed by George Bunce — New-Haven. M.DCC.XCVII. pp. 312; (27), 4
plates; (3). 12mo.　　　　　　　　　　　　　　　　　　　AAS.
Contains, Walker's Elements of gesture, pp. (27).

32495　——　—　The Young gentleman and lady's monitor, and English teacher's
assistant ; being a collection of select pieces from our best modern writers:
calculated to eradicate vulgar prejudices and rusticity of manners; improve the understanding; rectify the will.; purify the passions; direct
the minds of youth to the pursuit of proper objects; and to facilitate
their reading, writing, and speaking the English language, with elegance and propriety. Particularly adapted for the use of our eminent
schools and accademies [*sic*], as well as private persons, who have not an
opportunity of perusing the works of those celebrated authors, from
whence the collection is made. Divided into small portions for the ease
of reading in classes. The latest edition. By J. Hamilton Moore. Author
of the Practical Navigator, and Seamen's New daily assistant.
Wilmington: Printed and sold by Peter Brynberg. 1797. pp. 392, 4, 4 plates.
12mo.　　　　　　　　　　　　　　　　　　　　　　AAS. LOC.
Contains, Walker's Elements of gesture. pp. (359)–392, 4 plates.

32496 MOORE, Thomas
ORATION DELIVERED AT WHITESTOWN, JULY 4, 1797. BY THOMAS MOORE.
Whitestown, New-York. Printed by Lewis & Webb. 1797.

32497 MOORE, Thomas, pseudonym.
GAINE'S NEW-YORK POCKET ALMANACK, FOR THE YEAR 1798. BEING THE 2D AFTER
LEAP-YEAR, AND 22D OF AMERICAN INDEPENDENCE 'TILL 4TH JULY. CALCULATED
FOR THIS AND THE NEIGHBOURING STATES. . . . BY THOMAS MOORE, PHILO.
New-York: Printed by H. Gaine, at the Bible, in Pearl-Street. [1797.] pp.
(96). 48mo.   AAS. NYHS.

32498 MOORE, Zephaniah Swift   1770–1823
A THANKSGIVING SERMON, DELIVERED AT PETERBOROUGH, IN NEW HAMPSHIRE,
NOVEMBER 17, 1796. BY ZEPHANIAH S. MOORE, A.M.
Keene, New Hampshire: Printed by C. Sturtevant, jun. & Co. 1797. pp. 36.
12mo.   CHS. CLA. NYPL.

32499 MORAL & INSTRUCTIVE TALES FOR THE IMPROVEMENT OF YOUNG LADIES; CALCULATED
TO AMUSE THE MIND, AND FORM THE HEART TO VIRTUE. FIRST AMERICAN EDITION.
[Ornament.]
Printed at Leominster, Mass. By Charles Prentiss. 1797. pp. 124. 24mo.
AAS.

32500 THE MORAL STORY TELLER. UNITING PLEASURE WITH INSTRUCTION. NOTHING IS
INSERTED THAT HAS NOT ITS FOUNDATION IN TRUTH.
Hartford: Printed by John Babcock. 1797. pp. 69 [sic 96.] 12mo.
AAS. NYPL.

32501 MORE, Hannah   1745–1833
[The History of] THE TWO SHOEMAKERS. [PARTS I.–IV.] [Vignette.]
[Printed and] Published by B. Johnson No. 247 Market St. Philadelphia.
[1797.] pp. (2), 36; 36, plate; 36, plate; 36, plate. 12mo.   JCB.

Title-page engraved. Contains Ode to Content; Verses supposed to be
written by Alexander Selkirk. By William Cowper. Originally published in London as one of the Cheap Repository Tracts, in six parts.

32502 ——— SEARCH AFTER HAPPINESS: A PASTORAL DRAMA. BY MISS HANNAH MORE. AS
PERFORMED BY SOME YOUNG LADIES OF BRISTOL IN ENGLAND. — ALSO AT THE
ACADEMIES IN MASSACHUSETTS. . . .
Worcester: From the Press of Isaiah Thomas, jun.—1797. pp. 35. 12mo. AAS.

32503 ——— THOUGHTS ON THE IMPORTANCE OF THE MANNERS OF THE GREAT TO GENERAL
SOCIETY. YOU ARE THE MAKERS OF MANNERS.—SHAKESPEARE. FIFTH EDITION.
Worcester: Printed by Isaiah Thomas, jun.—July—1797.—pp. 84. 12mo.
AAS. LOC. MHS.

32504 MOREAU DE ST.-MÉRY, Médéric Louis Elie   1750–1819
DESCRIPTION TOPOGRAPHIQUE, PHYSIQUE, CIVILE, POLITIQUE ET HISTORIQUE DE LA
PARTIE FRANÇAISE DE L'ISLE SAINT-DOMINGUE. AVEC DES OBSERVATIONS GÉN-
ÉRALES SUR SA POPULATION, SUR LE CARACTÈRE & LES MŒURS DE SES DIVERS HAB-
ITANS; SUR SON CLIMAT, SA CULTURE, SES PRODUCTIONS, SON ADMINISTRATION . . .
ACCOMPAGNÉES DES DÉTAILS LES PLUS PROPRES À FAIRE CONNAITRE L'ETAT DE
CETTE COLONIE À L'ÉPOQUE DU 18 OCTOBRE 1789 . . . D'UNE NOUVELLE CARTE
DE LA TOTALITÉ DE L'ISLE. PAR M. L. E. MOREAU DE SAINT-MÉRY. TOME 1.
a Philadelphie: Imprime et s'y trouve chez l'Auteur, 1797. pp. xix, (1), 788,
map. 4to.   BM. HC. NYPL.

32505   MOREAU DE ST.-MÉRY, continued.

—— A GENERAL VIEW OR ABSTRACT OF THE ARTS AND SCIENCES, ADAPTED TO THE CAPACITY OF YOUTH. PUBLISHED BY M. L. E. MOREAU DE SAINT-MERY; AND TRANSLATED FROM THE FRENCH BY MICHAEL FORTUNE. [Three lines of Latin from] CICERO.

Philadelphia: Printed by the Editor, Printer, at the corner of Front and Callow-Hill street. October, 1797. pp. xii, 363, (6). 12mo.   AAS.

194th Pennsylvania District Copyright, issued to M. L. E. Moreau de Saint Mery, as Proprietor, 30 November, 1797.

32506   MORHOUSE, ABRAHAM

THE WRITINGS OF A PRETENDED PROPHET, (IN SIX LETTERS), WHO ASSUMED THE TITLE OF A "FAITHFUL SERVANT OF JESUS CHRIST" OFFICIALLY COMMISSIONED BY ALMIGHTY GOD, TO DEMAND AND RECEIVE OF ABRAHAM MOREHOUSE, ESQR. OF JOHNSTOWN, (N. Y.) TWO THOUSAND POUNDS: WITH TERRIBLE DENUNCIATIONS, IN CASE OF REFUSAL. TO WHICH IS ADDED, HIS RECANTATION: OR, FOUR LETTERS, WRITTEN BY THE PROPHET, AFTER HIS DETECTION.

Rutland: Printed by Williams & Fay. 1797.

32507   MORRIS, THOMAS

QUASHY, OR, THE COAL-BLACK MAID. A TALE. BY CAPTAIN THOMAS MORRIS.

London, Printed. Philadelphia: Re-printed and sold by James Humphreys, No. 74, North Third-Street. 1797. pp. (2), [13], (1). 12mo.   AAS.

32508   MORRIS COUNTY GAZETTE. [Motto.] VOL. I. NO. 1. WEDNESDAY, MAY 24, [— No. 32. WEDNESDAY, DECEMBER 27, 1797.]

Morris-Town: Printed by E. Cooper & Co. 1797. fol.

Established, as a weekly, by Elijah Cooper, and Caleb Russell. For a few months, it was published by Cooper alone, and, beginning in November, by Russell, alone. With the issue for January 2, 1798, it was published by Jacob Mann, and so continued to the end of the first volume in May, 1798, when Mann established in continuation, with a new serial numbering, and continuing its advertisements, *The Genius of Liberty.*

32509   MORSE, JEDIDIAH   1761–1826

THE AMERICAN GAZETTEER, EXHIBITING, IN ALPHABETICAL ORDER, A MUCH MORE FULL AND ACCURATE ACCOUNT, THAN HAS BEEN GIVEN, OF THE STATES, PROVINCES, COUNTIES, CITIES, TOWNS, VILLAGES, RIVERS, BAYS. HARBOURS, GULFS, SOUNDS, CAPES, MOUNTAINS, FORTS, INDIAN TRIBES, & NEW DISCOVERIES. ON THE AMERICAN CONTINENT, ALSO OF THE WEST-INDIA ISLANDS, AND OTHER ISLANDS APPENDANT TO THE CONTINENT, AND THOSE NEWLY DISCOVERED IN THE PACIFIC OCEAN: DESCRIBING THE EXTENT, BOUNDARIES, POPULATION, GOVERNMENT, PRODUCTIONS, COMMERCE, MANUFACTURES, CURIOSITIES, &C. OF THE SEVERAL COUNTRIES, AND OF THEIR IMPORTANT CIVIL DIVISIONS—AND THE LONGITUDE AND LATITUDE THE BEARINGS AND DISTANCES, FROM NOTED PLACES, OF THE CITIES, TOWNS, AND VILLAGES; — WITH A PARTICULAR DESCRIPTION OF THE GEORGIA WESTERN TERRITORY. THE WHOLE COMPRISING UPWARDS OF SEVEN THOUSAND DISTINCT ARTICLES. COLLECTED AND COMPILED FROM THE BEST AUTHORITIES, AND ARRANGED WITH GREAT CARE, BY AND UNDER THE DIRECTION OF, JEDIDIAH MORSE, D. D. AUTHOR OF THE AMERICAN UNIVERSAL GEOGRAPHY. FELLOW OF THE AMERICAN ACADEMY OF ARTS AND SCIENCES, AND MEMBER OF THE MASSACHUSETTS HISTORICAL SOCIETY. ILLUSTRATED WITH SEVEN NEAT AND NEW MAPS. PUBLISHED ACCORDING TO ACT OF CONGRESS.

Printed in Boston, at the presses of S. Hall. and Thomas & Andrews, and sold by E. Larkin, and the other Book-sellers in Boston; by Gaine & Ten Eyck, and S. Campbell, New-York; M. Carey, and W. Young. Philadelphia; by Messrs. Web-

MORSE, JEDIDIAH, continued.
sters, and Thomas, Andrews & Penniman, Albany: and Thomas, Andrews & Butler, Baltimore. 1797. pp. viii, (619), 7 maps. 8vo.

AAS. BA. BM. BU. HC. JCB. LOC. MHS. NYPL. UTS. YC.

117th Massachusetts District Copyright, issued to Jedidiah Morse, as Author, 29 May, 1797.

32510 —— A DESCRIPTION OF THE SOIL, PRODUCTIONS, COMMERCIAL, AGRICULTURAL AND LOCAL ADVANTAGES OF THE GEORGIA WESTERN TERRITORY: TOGETHER WITH A SUMMARY AND IMPARTIAL VIEW OF THE CLAIMS OF GEORGIA AND OF THE UNITED STATES TO THIS TERRITORY, AND OF THE PRINCIPAL ARGUMENTS ADDUCED BY THE PURCHASERS AGAINST THESE CLAIMS. COLLECTED AND STATED FROM VARIOUS AUTHENTIC DOCUMENTS. EXTRACTED AND PUBLISHED IN THIS FORM, (BY PERMISSION) FROM REV. DR. MORSE'S AMERICAN GAZETTEER, A NEW WORK. ILLUSTRATED WITH A NEW AND CORRECT MAP.

Boston: Printed by Thomas & Andrews. 1797. pp. 24, map. 8vo.

AAS. BA. JCB. MHS. NYPL.

32511 MORSE, SAMUEL BENJAMIN   –1798
SCHOOL DIALOGUES. A NEW SELECTION OF DIALOGUES, FROM A VARIETY OF THE BEST PLAYS IN THE ENGLISH LANGUAGE. DESIGNED FOR THE USE OF SCHOOLS AND ACADEMIES. CALCULATED TO PROMOTE AN EASY AND ELEGANT MODE OF CONVERSATION AMONG THE YOUNG MASTERS AND MISSES OF THE UNITED STATES. BY SAMUEL B. MORSE, A. M. PUBLISHED ACCORDING TO ACT OF CONGRESS.

Printed at Boston, by Manning & Loring, for Thomas & Andrews, Faust's Statue, No. 45, Newbury-Street. Sold by them; by Thomas, Son & Thomas, Worcester; Thomas, Andrews & Penniman, Albany; Thomas, Andrews & Butler, Baltimore; and other Booksellers in the United States. Jan. 1797. pp. 140, (2). 24mo.

111th Massachusetts District Copyright, issued to Isaiah Thomas and   AAS.
Ebenezer T. Andrews, as Proprietors, 11 February, 1797.

32512 MORTON, SARAH WENTWORTH APTHORP   1759–1846
BEACON HILL. A LOCAL POEM. HISTORIC AND DESCRIPTIVE. BOOK I. PUBLISHED ACCORDING TO ACT OF CONGRESS. [Ornament.]
Boston: Printed by Manning & Loring for the Author. 1797. pp. 56. 4to.

AAS. BA. BM. HC. JCB. LOC. MHS. NYPL.

126th Massachusetts District Copyright, issued to Perez Morton, as Proprietor for the benefit of the Author, 19 September, 1797. All that was published.

32513 MOSHEIM, JOHANN LORENZ VON   1694–1755
AN ECCLESIASTICAL HISTORY, ANCIENT AND MODERN, FROM THE BIRTH OF CHRIST, TO THE BEGINNING OF THE PRESENT CENTURY; IN WHICH THE RISE, PROGRESS, AND VARIATIONS OF CHURCH POWER ARE CONSIDERED IN THEIR CONNEXION WITH THE STATE OF LEARNING AND PHILOSOPHY, AND THE POLITICAL HISTORY OF EUROPE DURING THAT PERIOD. BY THE LATE LEARNED JOHN LAWRENCE MOSHEIM, D. D. AND CHANCELLOR OF THE UNIVERSITY OF GÖTTINGEN. TRANSLATED FROM THE ORIGINAL LATIN, AND ACCOMPANIED WITH NOTES, AND CHRONOLOGICAL TABLES, BY ARCHIBALD MACLAINE, D. D. IN SIX VOLUMES. TO THE WHOLE IS ADDED AN ACCURATE INDEX. FIRST AMERICAN EDITION. VOLUME I.

Philadelphia: Printed by Stephen C. Ustick. 1797. pp. xxiii, xvii–xxxi, 420. 8vo.

Volumes II–VI, were printed in 1798, and 1799.

AUCTION
VALUES

32514   THE MOTHER'S GIFT, OR PRETTY TOY.
> *Boston: Printed and sold by William Spotswood, No. 55, Marlborough-Street.*
> *1797.*

32515   THE MOVING MARKET, OR NEW LONDON CRIES.
> *Boston: Printed and sold by William Spotswood, No. 55, Marlborough-Street.*
> *1795.*

32516   NEAL, MOSES LEAVITT   –1829
     "THE PRESBYTERIAD," A POEM.
> *Dover: Printed by Samuel Bragg, jun. 1797.*

32517   —— — THE PRESBYTERIAD. WITH NOTES CRITICAL AND EXPLANATORY. [Two
lines of Latin from] OVID.
> *Rutland: Printed by Williams & Fay. 1797.*

32518   NELSON, JOHN   –1766
A LETTER TO THE PROTESTANT-DISSENTERS IN THE PARISH OF BALLY KELLY, IN IRE-
LAND; OCCASIONED BY THEIR OBJECTIONS AGAINST THEIR LATE MINISTER. IN THIS
LETTER THERE IS AN ATTEMPT, UPON SCRIPTURAL AND PROTESTANT PRINCIPLES, TO
SHOW WHAT REGARD IS DUE TO HUMAN ARTICLES OF FAITH: AND ALSO, TO EXPLAIN
SEVERAL PARTICULARS RELATIVE TO THE DOCTRINES OF ORIGINAL SIN AND ELEC-
TION, . . . THE SECOND [third] AMERICAN EDITION.
> *Newburyport: Printed by Barrett & March. 1797.* 12mo.   HC.

32519   DER NEUE, GEMEINNÜTZIGE LANDWIRTHSCHAFTS CALENDER, AUF DAS JAHR, NACH
DER HEILBRINGENDEN GEBURT UNSERS HERRN JESU CHRISTI, 1798. WELCHES
EIN GEMEINES JAHR VON 365 TAGEN IST. [Nine lines.] ZUM ELFTENMAL HER-
AUSGEGEBEN.
> *Lancaster: Gedruckt und zu haben bey Johann Albrecht und Comp. in der*
> *neuen Buchdruckerey in der Prinz-strasse, das 2te Haus nördlich vom Gesängniss.*
> [1797.] pp. (44). 4to.   AAS. LOC. NYPL.

> The cover gives a full-page cut of a farming scene, and the title as:
> Neuer Lancästerscher Calender, 1798.

32520   DER NEUE HOCH-DEUTSCHE AMERICANISCHE CALENDER, AUF DAS JAHR CHRISTI,
1798. . . .
> *Baltimore, gedruckt und zu finden bey Samuel Saur. . . .* [1797.] pp.
> 40. 4to.

> The cover title is a full-page woodcut view of Baltimore. With two
> vignettes, and a view of Boston Meeting House; and the title: Samuel
> Saur's Calendar, auf das Jahr 1798. Contains, The Life of David Rit-
> tenhouse. The Captivity of the Manheim family.

32521   DER NEUE NORD-AMERICANISCHE STADT UND LAND CALENDER. AUF DAS JAHR UN-
SERES HEYLANDES JESU CHRISTI 1798. ZUM ERSTENMAL HERAUSGEGEBEN.
> *Hagerstown, Maryland. Gedruckt bey Johann Gruber.* [1797.] 4to.

> The cover leaf, bears an emblematical design, engraved by J. F. Reiche,
> Philadelphia, and the title: Der Volksfreund und Hägerstauner Cal-
> ender auf 1798.

32522   DER NEUE UNPARTHEYISCHE BALTIMORE [cut] BOTE UND MÄRYLÄNDER STAATS-
REGISTER. NUM. 94. MITWOCHS, DEN 4 JANUAR. [— DEZEMBER, 1797.]
> *Diese Zeitung wird erstlich alle Mittwochen heraus gegeben von Samuel Saur,*
> *Buchdrucker in der Fayettestrasse zu Baltimore.* 1797. fol.

32523   NEUE, UNPARTHEYISCHE LÄNCÄSTER ZEITUNG UND ANZEIGS-NACHRICHTEN. NUM.
493. MITWOCH, DEN 4 JANUAR, [—NUM. 544. MITWOCH, DEN 27 DEZEMBER 1797.]
     Lancaster: Gedruckt bey Johann Albrecht & Comp. 1797. fol.
     In the following year the title was altered to: *Der Deutsche Porcupein
und Lancaster Anzeige-nachrichten.*

32524   NEUE UNPARTHEYISCHE READINGER ZEITUNG UND ANZEIGS-NACHRICHTEN. MIT-
WOCH DEN 4 JANUAR, [— MITWOCH DEN 27 DEZEMBER, 1797.]
     Reading: Gedruckt bey Jungmann und Gruber. 1797. fol.
     Sometime this year Johann Gruber withdrew, to Hagerstown, and the
firm name was changed to Gottlob Jungmann and Company.

32525   NEUER HAUSWIRTHSCHAFTS CALENDER, AUF DAS GNADENREICHE JAHR, NACH DER
HEILBRINGENDEN GEBURT UNSERS HERRN UND HEYLANDES JESU CHRISTI, 1798,
WELCHES EIN GEMEIN JAHR VON 365 TAGEN IST. [Six lines.] ZUM ERSTENMAL
HERAUSGEGEBEN.
     *Reading: Gedruckt und zu haben bey Gottlob Jungmann und Comp. in der
Deutsch-und Englischen Buchdruckerey, in der Callowhill-strasse, sud von dem
Courthaus.* [1797.] pp. (44). 4to.   AAS.
     The cover is a full-page woodcut of the: Südwestlicher prospect von
Reading.

32526   NEUER UNPARTHEYISCHER EASTONER BOTHE, UND NORTHAMPTONER KUNDSCHAFTER.
NUM. 174. MITWOCHS DEN 4 JANUAR, [— NUM. 223. DIENSTAGS DEN 26 DEZEM-
BER, 1797.]
     *Diese Zietung wird alle Mitwoch [Dienstag] morgens herausgegeben von Jacob
Weygandt und Sohn, in der Neuen Buchdruckerey zu Easton . . .* 1797. fol.

32527   THE NEW-ENGLAND PRIMER AMENDED AND IMPROVED; BY THE AUTHOR OF THE
GRAMMATICAL INSTITUTE [NOAH WEBSTER, JUNIOR.] CONTAINING BESIDES WHAT IS
USUALLY PUT IN A PRIMER, A LARGE NUMBER OF MORAL AND ENTERTAINING LESSONS
FOR CHILDREN; PROVERBS AND MAXIMS; A RELIGIOUS DIALOGUE; A VARIETY OF
ENTERTAINING STORIES. ADORN'D WITH EMBLEMATICAL ENGRAVINGS, SPIRITUAL
SONGS, &C. &C. &C.
     Hartford: Printed by Elisha Babcock, for John Babcock. 1797.

32528   —— THE NEW-ENGLAND PRIMER FOR THE MORE EASY ATTAINING THE TRUE READ-
ING OF ENGLISH. TO WHICH IS ADDED, THE ASSEMBLY OF DIVINES SHORTER
CATECHISM. ALSO SOME SHORT AND EASY QUESTIONS FOR CHILDREN, &C. &C. &C.
     *New York: Printed and sold, wholesale and retail, by John Harrisson, at his
Printing Office and Book Store, No. 3, Peck-Slip.* 1797. Price six cents. pp. (71).
24mo.   LOC.
     A portrait of George Washington forms the first page.

32529   —— THE NEW ENGLAND PRIMER (ENLARGED AND MUCH IMPROVED) FOR THE MORE
EASY ATTAINING THE TRUE READING OF ENGLISH. TO WHICH IS ADDED THE ASSEM-
BLY'S CATECHISM.
     *Philadelphia: Printed by Charles Cist, No. 104, in Second-street, near Race-
street,* 1796. pp. (76). 32mo.

32530   —— THE NEW-ENGLAND PRIMER; MUCH IMPROVED. CONTAINING, A VARIETY OF
EASY LESSONS, FOR ATTAINING THE TRUE READING OF ENGLISH.
     *Philadelphia: Printed by T. Dobson, at the Stone House, No. 41, S. Second
Street.* 1797. pp. (72). 24mo.   AAS. BPL. EI. WL.

32531   —— THE NEW-ENGLAND PRIMER, OR AN EASY AND PLEASANT GUIDE TO THE ART OF
READING.
     Wilmington: Printed by Peter Brynberg. 1797.

32532   NEW HAMPSHIRE. STATE.
Half title: PROCEEDINGS OF THE HON. SENATE.
Title: A JOURNAL OF THE PROCEEDINGS OF THE HONORABLE SENATE, OF THE STATE OF NEW-HAMPSHIRE, AT A SESSION OF THE GENERAL-COURT, HOLDEN AT CONCORD, NOVEMBER, 1796. [— 16 DECEMBER, 1796.] [Arms.]
State of New-Hampshire: Portsmouth: Printed by John Melcher, Printer to the State. 1797. pp. 89. 8vo.   AAS. LOC.

32533   —— *Half title:* PROCEEDINGS OF THE HOUSE OF REPRESENTATIVES.
Title: A JOURNAL OF THE PROCEEDINGS OF THE HON. HOUSE OF REPRESENTATIVES, OF THE STATE OF NEW-HAMPSHIRE, AT THEIR SESSION, BEGUN AND HOLDEN AT CONCORD, THE 23D NOVEMBER, 1796. [— 15 DECEMBER, 1796.] [Arms.]
State of New-Hampshire: Portsmouth: Printed by John Melcher, Printer to the State. 1797. pp. 141. 8vo.   AAS. LOC.

32534   —— *Half title:* PROCEEDINGS OF THE HOUSE OF REPRESENTATIVES.
Title: A JOURNAL OF THE PROCEEDINGS OF THE HON. HOUSE OF REPRESENTATIVES, OF THE STATE OF NEW-HAMPSHIRE, AT THEIR SESSION, BEGUN AND HOLDEN AT CONCORD, THE 7TH DAY OF JUNE, 1797. [— 22 JUNE, 1797.] [Arms.]
State of New-Hampshire: Portsmouth: Printed by John Melcher, Printer to the State. 1797. pp, 96. 8vo.   AAS. LOC.

32535   —— THE LAWS OF THE STATE OF NEW-HAMPSHIRE, PASSED AT A SESSION OF THE HONORABLE GENERAL-COURT, BEGUN AND HOLDEN AT CONCORD, DECEMBER, 1796. PRINTED FROM ATTESTED COPIES.
Portsmouth—New-Hampshire: Printed by John Melcher, Printer to the State, 1797. pp. 22. 8vo.   AAS. LOC.

32536   —— THE LAWS OF THE STATE OF NEW-HAMPSHIRE, THE CONSTITUTION OF THE STATE OF NEW-HAMPSHIRE, AND THE CONSTITUTION OF THE UNITED STATES, WITH ITS PROPOSED AMENDMENTS. PRINTED BY ORDER OF THE HONORABLE THE GENERAL-COURT.
State of New-Hampshire: Portsmouth: Printed by John Melcher, Printer to the State. 1797. pp. 492. 8vo.   AAS. HC. NYPL.

32537   —— THE LAWS OF THE STATE OF NEW-HAMPSHIRE, PASSED AT A SESSION OF THE HONORABLE GENERAL-COURT, BEGUN AND HOLDEN AT CONCORD, JUNE 1797. PRINTED FROM ATTESTED COPIES.
Portsmouth—New-Hampshire: Printed by John Melcher, Printer to the State. 1797. pp. (2), 493–498. 8vo.   AAS. LOC.

32538   NEW HAMPSHIRE BAPTIST ASSOCIATION.
MINUTES OF THE NEW-HAMPSHIRE ASSOCIATION, HELD AT TEE [*sic*] BAPTIST MEETING-HOUSE IN WATERBOROUGH: WEDNESDAY AND THURSDAY, JUNE 14TH AND 15TH, 1797.
Portsmouth, New-Hampshire. Printed by Charles Peirce, No. 5, Daniel-street. —1797. pp. 11. 8vo.   AAS.

32539   THE NEWHAMPSHIRE AND VERMONT JOURNAL: OR, THE FARMER'S WEEKLY MUSEUM. [Motto.] VOL. IV. No. 196. TUESDAY, JANUARY 3, [—VOL. IV. No. 208. TUESDAY, MARCH 28, 1797.]
Printed at Walpole, New-Hampshire, by David Carlisle, jun. in the Main-Street . . . 1797. fol.   AAS.

With the issue for April 4th, the title was transposed to *The Farmer's Weekly Museum: New-Hampshire and Vermont Journal.*

32540   THE NEW HAMPSHIRE AND VERMONT MAGAZINE, AND GENERAL REPOSITORY.
No. 1. FOR JULY, 1797. [— No. 4. FOR OCTOBER, 1797.] [Edited by Josiah
Dunham.]
> *[Windsor: Printed by Alden Spooner? 1797.]* pp. 160, plate. 8vo.   DC. LOC.

All that was published.

32541   THE NEW HAMPSHIRE GAZETTE. [Motto.] VOL. XLI. NUMB. 2093. SATURDAY,
JANUARY 7, [—VOL. XLII. NUMB. 2144. WEDNESDAY, DECEMBER 27, 1797.]
> *Portsmouth: (New-Hampshire)—Published every Saturday morning by John
> Melcher, Printer to the State, at his Office, corner of Market Street . . . 1797.*
> fol.   AAS. BA.

In May, the Gazette was printed from a new and handsome type, imported from England; and publication was made every Tuesday; and,
in December, every Wednesday. In October, the motto was changed
to, "—Our country's good our constant aim.—"

32542   NEW-HAMPSHIRE SPY. VOL. I. No. 16. SATURDAY, JANUARY 7, [— No. 26. SAT-
URDAY, MARCH 18, 1797.]
> *Exeter, (New-Hampshire) Published on Saturdays, by Henry Ranlet, in
> Main-Street, . . . 1797.* fol.   AAS.

Discontinued with the above issue, for want of support.

32543   A NEW HISTORY OF A TRUE BOOK, [The Bible] IN VERSE. [Ornament.]
> *[Newburyport:] For sale at A. March's Bookstore; price 6 cents single, and
> to those who buy to give away, 2 dols. pr. hundred.* [1797.] pp. (12). 12mo.
> AAS. NYPL.

32544   NEW JERSEY. STATE.
ACTS OF THE TWENTY-FIRST GENERAL ASSEMBLY OF THE STATE OF NEW-JERSEY.
AT A SESSION BEGUN AT TRENTON ON THE TWENTY-FIFTH DAY OF OCTOBER, SEVEN-
TEEN HUNDRED AND NINETY-SIX, AND CONTINUED BY ADJOURNMENTS. BEING THE
SECOND SITTING. [Arms.]
> *Trenton: Printed by Matthias Day, Printer to the State.* M,DCC,XCVII.
> pp. (2), (129)–238. fol.   LOC.

32545   —— — ACTS OF THE TWENTY-SECOND GENERAL ASSEMBLY OF THE STATE OF NEW-
JERSEY. AT A SESSION BEGUN AT TRENTON ON THE TWENTY-FOURTH DAY OF
OCTOBER, SEVENTEEN HUNDRED AND NINETY-SEVEN, AND CONTINUED BY ADJOURN-
MENTS. BEING THE FIRST SITTING. [Arms.]
> *Trenton: Printed by Matthias Day, Printer to the State.* M,DCC,XCVII.
> pp. (2), 241–256, ix, (1). fol.   LOC. NYLI.

32546   —— VOTES AND PROCEEDINGS OF THE TWENTY-FIRST GENERAL ASSEMBLY OF THE
STATE OF NEW-JERSEY, AT A SESSION BEGUN AT TRENTON ON THE TWENTY-FIFTH
DAY OF OCTOBER, SEVENTEEN HUNDRED NINETY-SIX, AND CONTINUED BY ADJOURN-
MENTS. BEING THE SECOND SITTING. [25 January, — 10 March, 1797.]
> *Trenton: Printed by Matthias Day, Printer to the State.* M,DCC,XCVII. pp.
> (72). fol.   NYPL.

32547   NEW-JERSEY HARMONY; BEING THE BEST SELECTION OF PSALM TUNES EVER YET
PUBLISHED. TOGETHER WITH PLAIN AND CONCISE RULES FOR LEARNERS.
> *Philadelphia: Printed by John M'Culloch, No. 1, North Third-Street, De-
> cember, 1797.* pp. 80. obl. 32mo.   NYPL.

32548   THE NEW-JERSEY JOURNAL. VOL. XIV. No. 69¹. WEDNESDAY, JANUARY 4, [— VOL. XV. No. 742. TUESDAY, DECEMBER 26, 1797.]
     Elizabeth-Town: Printed and published by Shepard Kollock, every Wednesday. 1797. fol.   AAS.
     In December, the day of publication was changed to Tuesday.

32549   A NEW METHOD OF KEEPING BILL-BOOKS ADAPTED FOR THE EASE AND CONVENIENCE OF MERCHANTS IN GENERAL BUT PARTICULARLY FOR THOSE WHO ARE EXTENSIVELY CONCERNED IN TRADE EXHIBITING AT ONE VIEW ALL THE BILLS WHICH A MERCHANT MAY HAVE TO RECEIVE OR PAY IN THE COURSE OF THE WHOLE YEAR FOR EACH MONTH SEPARATELY AND THEREBY PREVENTING THE TROUBLE AND INCONVENIENCE ATTENDANT ON THE MODE NOW IN USE OF SELECTING THE BILLS DUE IN EACH MONTH FROM THE PROMISCUOUS ENTRIES OF SEVERAL MONTHS. TO WHICH IS PREFIXED A TABLE SHEWING THE NUMBER OF DAYS FROM ANY DAY OF ANY MONTH TO THE SAME DAY IN ANY OTHER MONTH.
     Philadelphia: Printed for Robert Campbell and Company. 1797.
     163d Pennsylvania District Copyright, issued to Robert Campbell and Company, as Proprietors, 30 December, 1796.

32550   THE NEW STAR. NUMB. 1. TUESDAY, APRIL 11, [— NUMB. 26. TUESDAY, OCTOBER 3, 1797.]
     Printed by Russel & Davis, Concord, Newhampshire. 1797. pp. (208; 208). 8vo.   AAS. HC. NHHS. NYPL.
     Established, as a weekly, by Elijah Russell and Moses Davis, in continuation of *Russel & Davis' Republican Gazetteer.* Two editions were simultaneously issued, each of eight pages, octavo, with the same title, number, date, and paging, one, "a Republican paper" devoted to general news — the other, "a Republican miscellaneous and literary paper" devoted wholly to literature. Because of "the decided disapprobation of a large majority of our patrons to it book wise," publication was discontinued after twenty-six numbers had been issued. The publishers resuming, in folio form, the publication of *The Mirror.*

32551   THE NEW-WINDSOR GAZETTE. VOL. I. No. 1. TUESDAY, NOVEMBER 14, [— No. 7. TUESDAY, DECEMBER 26, 1797.]
     New-Windsor: [New-York.] Printed by Jacob Schultz & Abraham Lott. 1797. fol.
     Established. as a weekly, by Jacob Schultz, and Abraham Lott, and continued by them to the end of the second volume, in November, 1799, when they removed to Newburgh, and established, with a new numbering, *The Orange County Gazette.*

32552   THE NEW WORLD. VOL. II. No. 171. MONDAY, JANUARY 2, [— VOL. III. No. 365. WEDNESDAY, AUGUST 16, 1797.]
     Philadelphia: Printed by Samuel Harrison Smith, No. 118, Chesnut Street. 1797. fol.   LCP. WHS.
     Discontinued on the above date. And succeeded in November by *The Universal Gazette.*

32553   NEW YORK. STATE.
   JOURNAL OF THE ASSEMBLY OF THE STATE OF NEW-YORK; AT THEIR TWENTIETH SESSION, THE FIRST MEETING BEGAN AND HELD AT THE CITY OF NEW-YORK, THE FIRST DAY OF NOVEMBER, 1796; AND THE SECOND, AT THE CITY OF ALBANY, THE THIRD DAY OF JANUARY, 1797. [— 3 APRIL, 1797.]
     Albany: Printed by Charles R. & George Webster, at their Bookstore, in the White House, corner of State and Pearl-streets, for John Morton, Printer to the State. [1797.] pp. 218. fol.   LOC. NYPL.
     Contains, Washington's Farewell Address.

NEW YORK. STATE, continued.

32554 —— JOURNAL OF THE SENATE, OF THE STATE OF NEW-YORK; AT THEIR TWENTIETH SESSION, THE FIRST MEETING BEGAN AND HELD AT THE CITY OF NEW-YORK, THE FIRST DAY OF NOVEMBER, 1796; AND THE SECOND, AT THE CITY OF ALBANY, THE THIRD DAY OF JANUARY, 1797. [— 3 APRIL, 1797.]

Albany: Printed by Charles R. & George Webster, at their Bookstore, in the White House, corner of State and Pearl-streets, for John Morton, Printer to the State. [1797.] pp. 136. fol.   NYPL.

Contains, Washington's Farewell Address.

32555 —— LAWS OF THE STATE OF NEW-YORK, COMPRISING THE CONSTITUTION, AND THE ACTS OF THE LEGISLATURE, SINCE THE REVOLUTION, FROM THE FIRST TO THE TWENTIETH SESSION, INCLUSIVE. [Arms.] IN THREE VOLUMES. VOLUME III. [Three lines of Latin quotations.]

*New-York—Printed by Thomas Greenleaf—*M,DCC,XCVII. pp. (2), (2), 98. (3), 99–100; 8, 107–160; [159]–258, (3); [259]–354, (2); [355]–506, index, [507]–525. 8vo.   BA. IIC. JCB. NYHS.

Originally issued in five parts, with table of contents to each part, to supplement Greenleaf's two volumes issued in 1792, and containing the sixteenth — twentieth sessions.

32556 —— LAWS OF THE STATE OF NEW-YORK, PASSED AT THE TWENTIETH SESSION OF THE LEGISLATURE, BEGUN AT THE CITY OF NEW-YORK, AND HELD BY ADJOURNMENT AT THE CITY OF ALBANY. [Arms.]

New-York:—Printed by William Robins, for the Printer to the State. 1797. pp. 340, (4). 8vo.   LOC.

32557 —— THE ROAD-ACT PASSED INTO A LAW, AT ALBANY, MARCH 21, 1797, AT THE SECOND MEETING OF THE TWENTIETH SESSION OF THE LEGISLATURE OF THE STATE OF NEW-YORK.

City of Albany: (by authority) Printed by Charles R. and George Webster, at their Bookstore, in the White House, corner of State and Pearl-streets; where may be had the School, Militia, Ten Pound and Tavern Acts; also all the forms of Military Returns, as drawn up and approved by the Adjutant General—Deeds, Mortgages, Leases, Bonds, Bills of Sale, Indentures, Warrants, Powers of Attorney and Justices Blanks of all kinds. [1797.] pp. 20. 8vo.   NYHS.

32558 —— — THE NEW ROAD LAW.

Albany: Printed by Barber & Southwick. 1797.

32559 —— — THE ROAD ACT. TO WHICH IS ADDED, EXTRACTS FROM THE SCHOOL ACT.

Cooperstown: Printed by Elihu Phinney. 1797.

32560 —— — THE ROAD ACT.

New-York: Printed by Thomas Greenleaf. 1797.

32561 NEW YORK. CITY.

CITY OF NEW YORK SS. AT A COMMON COUNCIL HELD ON THURSDAY THE 9TH DAY OF NOVEMBER, 1797. . . . A LAW TO REGULATE CARTS AND CARTMEN IN THE CITY OF NEW YORK. [Three columns.] GIVEN UNDER MY HAND AND SEAL THIS TENTH DAY OF NOVEMBER, ONE THOUSAND SEVEN HUNDRED AND NINETY SEVEN. RICHARD VARICK.

[New-York: Printed by George Forman. 1797.] Broadside. fol.   LOC.

NEW YORK. City, continued.

32562 —— Laws and ordinances, ordained and established by the mayor, aldermen and commonalty of the city of New-York, in Common Council convened; for the good rule and government of the inhabitants and residents of the said city. Passed and published the first day of May, 1797. in the eighth year of the mayoralty of Richard Varick, esquire.
New-York: Printed by George Forman, opposite the Post-Office. 1797. pp. (67), (1). 8vo. AAS. NYHS.

32563 —— List of foremen of the respective classes of cartmen, with their places of residence. [Twenty lines.] Richard Varick, mayor.
[New-York: Printed by George Forman. December 1, 1797.] Broadside. 4to. LOC.

32564 NEW YORK. City. Association of Tallow Chandlers and Soap Makers.
The Case of the manufacturers of soap and candles in the city of New-York, stated and examined. To which are prefixed, the Laws of the State of New-York, concerning infectious diseases, with an addition, in form of an appendix; containing, several documents and papers, relative to these subjects. Published by the Association of Tallow chandlers and Soap makers.
New-York: Printed by John Buel, for the Association. MDCCXCVII. pp. [62.] 8vo. HC. LOC. MHS. NYHS. SGO.

32565 NEW YORK. City. Baptist Association.
Minutes of the New York Baptist Association.
[New-York: 1797.] 4to.

32566 NEW YORK. City. Dispensary.
Charter and ordinances of the New-York Dispensary.
New-York: Printed by Hopkins, Webb & Co. Pine-Street. 1797. pp. 80, (1). 8vo. NYHS. NYPL.
Contains a nine-page List of the names of the contributors to the Dispensary.

32567 NEW YORK. City. English Evangelical Lutheran Church.
A Collection of [299] Evangelical hymns from various authors: for the use of the English Evangelical Lutheran Church in New York. To which are added, The Liturgy, Gospels and Epistles of the English Evangelical Church in New York. Compiled by Rev. George Strebeck.
New-York: 1797.

32568 NEW YORK. City. Militia.
A Statement, explanatory of the resignations of the officers of the regiment of Artillery, of the city & County of New-York.
New-York: Printed by William A. Davis, 1797. pp. 32. 8vo.
In correction of X: 29203. JCB. NYHS. NYPL.

32569 NEW YORK. City. Society Library.
Additional Catalogue of books belonging to the New-York Society Library.
New-York: Printed by T. and J. Swords? 1797.

32570 THE NEW-YORK Gazette and General Advertiser. Numb. 2506. Monday, January 2, [— Numb. 2844. Saturday, December 30, 1797.]
Published (daily) by M'Lean, and Lang, Franklin's Head, No. 116, Pearl-Street, nearly opposite the New-York Bank. 1797. fol.
With the issue for January 3d, John Lang was admitted to partnership as M'Lean and Lang.

32571 THE NEW-YORK MAGAZINE, OR LITERARY REPOSITORY, [January — December]
1797. NEW SERIES. — VOL. II. [Ornament.]
New-York: Printed and sold by T. and J. Swords, No. 99, Pearl-street.
1797. pp. viii, 672, 12 plates. 8vo.
AAS. BA. BPL. HC. HSP. JCB. LCP. LOC. NYHS. NYPL. WHS. YC.

32572 THE NEW-YORK PRICES CURRENT. VOL. II. NO. 54. MONDAY, JANUARY 2, [—
NO. 75. SATURDAY, MAY 27, 1797.]
New-York: Published weekly by James Oram. 1797. 4to.   NYHS.

With the issue for June 3d, the title was changed to *Oram's New-York
Price-Current, and Marine Register.*

32573 THE NEW-YORK WEEKLY MAGAZINE; OR, MISCELLANEOUS REPOSITORY: FORMING
AN INTERESTING COLLECTION OF ORIGINAL AND SELECT LITERARY PRODUCTIONS, IN
PROSE AND VERSE: CALCULATED FOR INSTRUCTION AND RATIONAL ENTERTAINMENT
—THE PROMOTION OF MORAL AND USEFUL KNOWLEDGE—AND TO ENLARGE AND COR-
RECT THE UNDERSTANDING OF YOUTH. VOLUME II. [WEDNESDAY, JULY 6, 1796
— WEDNESDAY, JUNE 28, 1797.] [Two lines of verse. Ornament.]
*New-York: Printed for the Proprietors, at Homer's-Head, No. 358, Pearl-
Street.* 1797. pp. viii, 416, frontispiece. 4to.   LOC.

The Colophons variously read: "Printed by Thomas Burling, No. 115,
Cherry-Street." . . . And at, "No. 33 Oliver-Street." "Thomas Burl-
ing, jun. & Co. No. 115 Cherry Street." . . . And, "at the Circulating
Library of Mr. J. Fellows, No. 60, Wall-Street." "Pine-Street." "Printed
by John Tiebout, No. 358, Pearl-Street, for Thomas Burling, jun. & Co."
Continued as the *Sentimental & Literary Magazine.*

32574 NEWARK. NEW JERSEY. NEWARK FIRE ASSOCIATION.
ARTICLES OF ASSOCIATION AND SYSTEMS OF ORGANIZATION AND REGULATIONS OF THE
NEWARK FIRE ASSOCIATION.
Newark: Printed by Daniel Dodge & Co. 1797. pp. 24. 12mo.   NYHS.

32575 NEWARK [cut] GAZETTE AND NEW-JERSEY ADVERTISER. VOLUME I. NO. 1. WEDNES-
DAY, NOVEMBER 8, [— NO. 8. TUESDAY, DECEMBER 26, 1797.]
Newark: Printed by John Woods for the Proprietors. 1797. fol.   AAS.

In continuation, with a new numbering, of *Woods's Newark Gazette and
New-Jersey Advertiser.*

32576 THE NEWBURGH PACKET. VOL. V. NO. 162. MONDAY, JANUARY 2, [— NO. 184.
MONDAY, JUNE 5, 1797.]
Newburgh, [N. Y.] Printed by D. Denniston. 1797. fol.

The issue for June 5th. has a supplement. How much longer publication
was continued is not known; but it was discontinued before October,
as it was succeeded by *The Mirror* in that month.

32577 NEWBURYPORT. MASSACHUSETTS. UNION SOCIETY.
NEWBURY PORT. [September 25, 1797.] NOTICE OF A MEETING OF THE UNION SO-
CIETY.
[Newburyport: Engraved. 1797.] Broadside.   EI.

AUCTION VALUES

32578   THE NEWBURYPORT HERALD AND COUNTRY GAZETTE. VOL. I. NO. 1. TUESDAY, OCTOBER 31, [— NO. 18 OF VOL. I. FRIDAY, DECEMBER 29, 1797.]
Published on Tuesdays and Fridays, by Barrett & March, west corner of Market-Square. 1797. fol.   AAS.

Established, as a semi-weekly, upon the discontinuance of the *Impartial Herald*, published by Angier March, and the *Political Gazette*, published by William Barrett. With the issue for December 22, 1797, William Barrett withdrew. Angier March continued publication alone, except from April to October, 1800, when it was published by Chester Stebbins for the Proprietor, to August, 1801, when, owing to failing health, he disposed of his interests to Ephraim W. Allen and Jeremiah Stickney. With the issue for June 18, 1802, Stickney disposed of his interests to John Barnard. With the issue for March 4, 1803, the title was shortened to *Newburyport Herald*. With the issue for July 8, 1803, Barnard withdrew. E. W. Allen continued publication, except, from April to December, 1805, when it was published by Wm. B. Allen for E. W. Allen; from April to October, 1815, when it was published by Henry Small; from February to March, 1816, when it was published by Benjamin W. Folsom for E. W. Allen; from February, 1817, to February, 1818, when it was published by William Hastings for E. W. Allen, and for the Proprietors; and from June, 1819 to February, 1820, when Henry R. Stickney's name appears as Printer, to beyond the period of this work. With the issue for December 3, 1811, the title was changed to *Newburyport Herald. And country gazette.* With the issue for April 18, 1815, this was changed to *Newburyport Herald, and commercial gazette.* With the issue for April 25, 1817, this was changed to *Newburyport Herald, commercial and country gazette.* . And, with the issue for February 4, 1818, this was changed to *Newburyport Herald.*

32579   THE NEWPORT MERCURY. NO. 1811. TUESDAY, JANUARY 3, [— NO. 1862. TUESDAY, DECEMBER 26, 1797.]
Newport: (Rhode-Island) Published by Henry Barber, near the State-House. 1797. fol.   AAS. LOC. NHS. RIHS. RL.

32580   NEWTON, JOHN   1725–1807
General title: LETTERS AND SERMONS, WITH A REVIEW OF ECCLESIASTICAL HISTORY, AND HYMNS. BY JOHN NEWTON, RECTOR OF ST. MARY, WOOLNOTH, LONDON. IN SIX VOLUMES. VOL. VI. [— VIII.]
Philadelphia: Printed by William Young, Bookseller, No. 52, Second-Street, the corner of Chesnut-Street. M,DCC,XCVI. 3vols. pp. (2), 348; (2), (2), 336; vi, (31); (10); (2), xi, (14), (6), 335. 12mo.   AAS.

Second title: OLNEY HYMNS, IN THREE BOOKS: BOOK I. ON SELECT TEXTS OF SCRIPTURE. BOOK II. ON OCCASIONAL SUBJECTS. BOOK III. ON THE PROGRESS AND CHANGES OF THE SPIRITUAL LIFE. BY THE REV. JOHN NEWTON, LONDON. [Eight lines of quotations.]
Philadelphia: Printed by William Young, Bookseller [sic] *No. 52, Second-Street, the corner of Chesnut-Street.* M,DCC,XCVII. pp. (2), 348.

Third title: LETTERS TO A WIFE. BY JOHN NEWTON, AUTHOR OF OMICRON'S LETTERS, ECCLESIASTICAL HISTORY, &c. [Three lines of quotations.]
Philadelphia: Printed by William Young, Bookseller, No. 52, Second-Street, corner of Chesnut-Street. M,DCC,XCVII. pp. (2), (2), 336; vi, (31), (10).

In all copies seen, pages 13–48 are missing.

Fourth title: A MONUMENT TO THE PRAISE OF THE LORD'S GOODNESS, AND TO THE MEMORY OF DEAR ELIZA CUNNINGHAM. PUBLISHED FOR THE BENEFIT OF A CHARITABLE INSTITUTION. [Two lines of quotations.]
Philadelphia: Printed by William Young, No. 52, South Second-Street, corner of Chesnut-Street. 1797. pp. vi, (31); (10).

NEWTON, John, continued.

Fifth heading: EBENEZER: A MEMORIAL OF THE UNCHANGEABLE GOODNESS OF GOD UNDER CHANGING DISPENSATIONS. No. I. [— II. And other] POEMS. pp. (10).

The American Antiquarian Society also has a variant edition of "Ebenezer," reset, and of later printing, pp. (12), appended to "Olney Hymns."

Sixth title: MESSIAH. FIFTY EXPOSITORY DISCOURSES, ON THE SERIES OF SCRIPTURAL PASSAGES, WHICH FORM THE SUBJECT OF THE CELEBRATED ORATORIO OF HANDEL. PREACHED IN THE YEARS 1784 AND 1785, IN THE PARISH-CHURCH OF ST. MARY, WOOLNOTH, LOMBARD-STREET. BY JOHN NEWTON, RECTOR. IN TWO VOLUMES. VOL. I. [Three lines of quotations.]

Philadelphia: Printed by William Young, Bookseller, No. 52, *Second-Street, corner of Chesnut-Street.* M,DCC,XCVII. pp. (2), xi, (14), (6), 335.

32581 —— LETTERS TO A WIFE. BY JOHN NEWTON, AUTHOR OF OMICRON'S LETTERS, ECCLESIASTICAL HISTORY, &C. [Three lines of quotations.]

Whitehall: Printed by William Young, Bookseller and Stationer, No. 52. *South Second-Street, Philadelphia.* M,DCC,XCVII. pp. (2), 336; vi, (31); (10). 12mo. AAS. JCB. NYPL.

In all copies seen, pages 13–48 are missing.

Second title: A MONUMENT TO THE PRAISE OF THE LORD'S GOODNESS, AND TO THE MEMORY OF DEAR ELIZA CUNNINGHAM. PUBLISHED FOR THE BENEFIT OF A CHARITABLE INSTITUTION. [Two lines of quotations.]

Philadelphia: Printed by William Young, No. 52, *South Second-Street, corner of Chesnut-Street.* 1797. pp. vi, (31); (10).

Third heading: EBENEZER: A MEMORIAL TO THE UNCHANGEABLE GOODNESS OF GOD UNDER CHANGING DISPENSATIONS. No. I. [— II. And other] POEMS. pp. (10).

32582 NEWTON, ROGER 1737–1816
A DISCOURSE, DELIVERED ON THE ANNIVERSARY OF AMERICAN INDEPENDENCE, THE 4TH OF JULY, 1797. BY THE REV. ROGER NEWTON.

Greenfield: Printed by Thomas Dickman. 1797.

32583 NICHOLS, FRANCIS
A TREATISE OF PRACTICAL ARITHMETIC, AND BOOKKEEPING, CONTAINING ALL THE RULES OF ARITHMETIC, WHICH ARE GENERALLY USEFUL IN TRANSACTING BUSINESS WHEN ARITHMETIC IS REQUIRED. FOR THE USE OF STUDENTS. BY F. NICHOLS. PUBLISHED ACCORDING TO ACT OF CONGRESS.

Boston: Printed by Manning & Loring, for David West, No. 56, *Cornhill. July,* 1797. pp. 103. 12mo. AAS. BM.

122d Massachusetts District Copyright, issued to F. Nichols, as Author, 12 August, 1797.

32584 THE NIGHTINGALE OF LIBERTY: OR DELIGHTS OF HARMONY. A CHOICE COLLECTION OF PATRIOTIC, MASONIC, & ENTERTAINING SONGS. TO WHICH ARE ADDED TOASTS AND SENTIMENTS, MORAL, HUMOROUS, AND REPUBLICAN. THOU SWEETEST SONGSTER OF THE FEATHER'D TRIBE, CAROL, WITH NOTES HARMONIOUS, SONGS TO LIBERTY.

New-York: Printed by John Harrisson, and sold at his Book-Store, No. 3 *Peck-Slip.* 1797. pp. 83, frontispiece. 12mo. LOC.

The engraved frontispiece represents, at the left, the seated, full dressed figure of America; and, at the right, a standing figure of Liberty holding a pole with a Liberty cap on the top, with an oval bust portrait of Washington, between them, while standing in the branches of laurel over them is a Nightingale.

32585 THE NOBLE SLAVES. BEING AN ENTERTAINING HISTORY OF SURPRIZING ADVENTURES
AND REMARKABLE DELIVERANCES FROM ALGERINE SLAVERY OF SEVERAL SPANISH
NOBLEMEN AND LADIES OF QUALITY.
  Boston: 1797.
  "Four editions already printed in Boston."

32586 —— THE NOBLE SLAVES. BEING AN ENTERTAINING HISTORY OF THE SURPRISING
ADVENTURES AND REMARKABLE DELIVERANCES, FROM ALGERINE SLAVERY, OF
SEVERAL SPANISH NOBLEMEN AND LADIES OF QUALITY.
  Danbury: Printed by Douglas & Nichols. 1797.

32587 —— THE NOBLE SLAVES. BEING AN ENTERTAINING HISTORY OF SURPRIZING ADVEN-
TURES AND REMARKABLE DELIVERANCES FROM ALGERINE SLAVERY OF SEVERAL
SPANISH NOBLEMEN AND LADIES OF QUALITY.
  New-Haven: Printed by Geo. Bunce. 1797. pp. 216. 12mo.

32588 NORFOLK. VIRGINIA.
  THE CHARTER OF NORFOLK BOROUGH.
  Norfolk: Printed by Willett and O'Connor. 1797.

32589 THE NORFOLK HERALD, & PUBLIC ADVERTISER. VOL. 3. No. 210. MONDAY,
JANUARY 2, [VOL. 4. No. 363. SATURDAY, DECEMBER 30, 1797.]
  *Norfolk: Published on Mondays, Thursdays and Saturdays, by Willett and
O'Connor, near the Market.* 1797. fol.   LOC.

32590 THE NORFOLK WEEKLY JOURNAL, AND COUNTRY INTELLIGENCER. VOL. I. No. 1.
WEDNESDAY, SEPTEMBER 6, [—— —— 1797.]
  Norfolk: Printed by Willett and O'Connor, near the Market. 1797. fol.

  Established, as a weekly edition of *The Norfolk Herald, & Public Advertiser,* for the country, by Charles Willett and James O'Connor, but
apparently the project was abandoned with the first number.

32591 NORMAN, WILLIAM, publisher.
  THE MUSICAL REPOSITORY, CONTAINING A VARIETY OF THE MOST MODERN AND FA-
VORITE SONGS, AS PERFORMED ON THE STAGE IN EUROPE AND AMERICA. No. 3–4.
  *Boston: Published by William Norman, at his Book Store, No. 75, Newbury-
Street, nearly opposite the Sign of the Lamb.* [1797.]

32592 NORTH, EDWARD
  AN INAUGURAL DISSERTATION, ON THE RHEUMATIC STATE OF FEVER; SUBMITTED TO
THE EXAMINATION OF THE REV. JOHN EWING, S. T. P. PROVOST; THE TRUSTEES AND
MEDICAL FACULTY OF THE UNIVERSITY OF PENNSYLVANIA; ON THE 12TH MAY,
1797. FOR THE DEGREE OF DOCTOR OF MEDICINE. BY EDWARD NORTH, OF SOUTH
CAROLINA, MEMBER OF THE PHILADELPHIA MEDICAL SOCIETY.
  Philadelphia: Printed by William W. Woodward, No. 17, Chesnut Street.
1797. pp. 37. 8vo.   AAS. BM. 8GO.

32593 NORTH CAROLINA. STATE.
  JOURNAL OF THE HOUSE OF COMMONS OF THE GENERAL ASSEMBLY OF NORTH-CAR-
OLINA, 1796.
  [*Halifax: Printed by Hodge & Wills.* 1797.]

32594 —— JOURNAL OF THE SENATE OF THE GENERAL ASSEMBLY OF NORTH-CAROLINA.
  [*Halifax: Printed by Hodge & Wills,* 1797.]

32595   NORTH CAROLINA. STATE, continued.
—— LAWS OF NORTH-CAROLINA. AT A GENERAL ASSEMBLY, BEGUN AND HELD AT
THE CITY OF RALEIGH, ON THE TWENTY-FIRST DAY OF NOVEMBER, IN THE YEAR OF
OUR LORD ONE THOUSAND SEVEN HUNDRED AND NINETY-SIX, AND IN THE TWENTY-
FIRST YEAR OF THE INDEPENDENCE OF THE SAID STATE: BEING THE FIRST SESSION
OF THE SAID ASSEMBLY. [— 25 DECEMBER, 1796.]
        [Edenton: Printed by Hodge and Wills, 1797.] pp. 45 [sic 43.] fol. NYPL.
        Pages 41, 42, 43, are mispaged 43, 44, 45.

32596   —— —— LAWS OF NORTH-CAROLINA. AT A GENERAL ASSEMBLY, BEGUN AND HELD
AT THE CITY OF RALEIGH, ON THE TWENTY-FIRST DAY OF NOVEMBER, IN THE YEAR
OF OUR LORD ONE THOUSAND SEVEN HUNDRED AND NINETY-SIX, AND IN THE TWENTY-
FIRST YEAR OF THE INDEPENDENCE OF THE SAID STATE: BEING THE FIRST SESSION
OF THE SAID ASSEMBLY. [— 25 DECEMBER, 1796.] [Colophon:]
        Halifax: Printed by Hodge & Wills, Printers to the State. [1797.] pp. 68.
        fol.   LOC.

32597   NORTH-CAROLINA GAZETTE. VOL. XII. No. 573. SATURDAY, JANUARY 7, [—VOL.
XII. No. 603. SATURDAY, AUGUST 5, 1797.]
        Newbern: Printed by Francois X. Martin. 1797. fol.
        The above is the last number located.

32598   THE NORTH-CAROLINA JOURNAL. No. 233. MONDAY, JANUARY 2, [— No. 284.
MONDAY, DECEMBER 25, 1797.]
        Halifax: Printed by Abraham Hodge, joint Printer to the State with H. Wills.
        1797. fol.   HSP. LOC.

32599   THE NORTH-CAROLINA MINERVA, AND FAYETTEVILLE ADVERTISER, VOL. I.
NUMB. 43. SATURDAY, JANUARY 7, [— VOL. II. NUMB. 94. SATURDAY, DECEM-
BER 30, 1797.]
        Fayetteville: Published every Saturday by Hodge & Boylan. 1797. fol.

32600   THE NORTHERN BUDGET. VOL. I. No. 1. TUESDAY, JUNE 20, [— No. 28. TUES-
DAY, DECEMBER 26, 1797.]
        Lansingburgh: Published by Robert Moffitt & Co. 1797. fol.   AAS.

        Established, as a weekly, by Robert Moffitt and Jesse Buel, and con-
        tinued by them, as Robert Moffitt & Co., to July, 1801. With the issue
        for July 11, 1797, the title was shortened to *Northern Budget.* In Novem-
        ber, 1797, a cut of Franklin divided the title, with his motto added:
        Where Liberty dwells there is my Country. In May, 1798, the Print-
        ing-Office was removed to Troy, New York, and publication continued
        there under the same title, and numbering. With the issue for July 7,
        1801, Jesse Buel withdrew, and was succeeded by Zebulon Lyon, under
        the firm name of Moffitt & Lyon. Robert Moffitt died May 4, 1807, and
        publication was continued in the name of Oliver Lyon to 1815, owing
        to a fire no issues were made from March to June, 1810. In January,
        1815, Ebenezer Hill, succeeded Lyon as publisher to September, 1817,
        when his name gave place to Zephaniah Clark, who continued publica-
        tion beyond the period of this work.

32601   NORTHERN MISSIONARY SOCIETY IN THE STATE OF NEW YORK.
        THE CONSTITUTION OF THE NORTHERN MISSIONARY SOCIETY IN THE STATE OF NEW-
        YORK. TO WHICH IS ANNEXED THE ADDRESS OF THE SOCIETY TO THE PUBLIC.
        Schenectady: Printed by C. P. Wyckoff, in State-Street. 1797. pp. (19).
        8vo.   AAS. HC. NYPL.

32602   THE NORWICH PACKET. VOL. XXIII. NO. 1190. THURSDAY, JANUARY 5, [— VOL. XXIV. NO. 1242. TUESDAY, DECEMBER 26, 1797.]

Norwich, (Connecticut)—Published by John Trumbull, a few rods west of the Meeting-House. 1797. fol.

In July, the day of publication was changed from Thursday to Tuesday.

32603   NOTT, ELIPHALET   1773–1866

FEDERAL MONEY; BEING A SKETCH OF THE MONEY OF ACCOUNT OF UNITED AMERICA. BY ELIPHALET NOTT, A.M. PRINCIPAL OF CHERRY-VALLEY ACADEMY. FOR THE USE OF SCHOOLS.

Cooperstown: Printed by Elihu Phinney. 1797.

32604   NOYES, JAMES   1608–1656

A SHORT CATECHISM. COMPOSED BY MR. JAMES NOYES, LATE TEACHER OF THE CHURCH OF CHRIST IN NEWBURY, IN NEW ENGLAND. FOR THE USE OF THE CHILDREN THERE. *Newburyport: Printed by Barrett & March. 1797. pp. 13. 16mo.*

Reprinted in Coffin's History of Newbury. pp. 287–291.

32605   NOYES, JAMES

THE FEDERAL ARITHMETIC; OR, A COMPENDIUM OF THE MOST USEFUL RULES OF THAT SCIENCE, ADAPTED TO THE CURRENCY OF THE UNITED STATES. FOR THE USE OF SCHOOLS AND PRIVATE PERSONS. PUBLISHED AGREEABLY TO ACT OF CONGRESS. BY JAMES NOYES.

Printed at Exeter, by Henry Ranlet, for the Author. M,DCC,XCVII. pp. 128. 16mo.   LOC.

32606   NOYES, NATHANIEL   1735–1810

MAN ON PROBATION FOR THE WORLD TO COME. TWO SERMONS, PREACHED AT SOUTH-HAMPTON, MARCH 12, 1797. BY NATHANIEL NOYES, A. M. PASTOR OF THE CHURCH IN THAT TOWN. PUBLISHED AT THE DESIRE OF THE HEARERS.

Newburyport—From the Press of William Barrett, Market-Square. 1797. pp. 19. 8vo.   BA. JCB.

32607   NOYES, THOMAS   1769–1837

A DISCOURSE DELIVERED AT FITCHBURG, ON THE DEATH OF CAPTAIN JOSEPH FOX, FEBRUARY 28, 1797. BY THOMAS NOYES.

Leominster: Printed by Charles Prentiss. 1797. 8vo.

32608   OBSERVATIONS ON ACCIDENTAL FIRES: WITH AN ACCOUNT OF THOSE THAT HAVE LATELY HAPPENED IN THE UNITED STATES. BY A CITIZEN OF NEW-YORK.

Printed at New-York, by J. Oram. 1797. pp. 40. 8vo.   NYPL.

32609   THE OBSERVATORY; OR, A VIEW OF THE TIMES. VOL. I. NO. 1. MONDAY, JULY 3, [— NO. 52. THURSDAY, DECEMBER 28, 1797.]

Richmond: Printed Mondays and Thursdays by John Dixon. 1797. fol.

Established, as a semi-weekly, by John Dixon, and continued by him to September 13, 1798, when he changed its title to *Dixon's Observatory* under which it was continued to November 26, 1798. On December 3, 1798, Dixon joined with Meriwether Jones in establishing *The Examiner.*

32610   O'CONNOR, afterwards CONDORCET O'CONNOR, ARTHUR   1763–1852
ADDRESS TO THE FREE ELECTORS OF THE COUNTY OF ANTRIM. BY ARTHUR O'CON-
NOR, MEMBER OF THE IRISH HOUSE OF COMMONS.
     *Philadelphia: From the Press of Snowden & M'Corkle, No. 47, North Fourth-
Street.* 1797. pp. (12). 12mo.   LOC.

32611   O'KEEFFE, JOHN   1747–1833
THE HIGHLAND REEL: A COMIC OPERA, IN THREE ACTS. AS PERFORMED WITH UNI-
VERSAL APPLAUSE, AT THE THEATRE FEDERAL-STREET. BY JOHN O'KEEFE, ESQ.
AUTHOR OF THE AGREEABLE SURPRISE, FARMER, YOUNG QUAKER, WORLD IN A
VILLAGE, &C.
     *Boston: Printed by Joseph Bumstead, for Wm. P. and L. Blake, at the Boston
Book-store, Cornhill.* 1797. pp. 68, (1), (2). 12mo.   AAS. BPL. LCP. NYPL.

32612   THE OLD BACHELOR'S MASTERPIECE: TO WHICH ARE ADDED SEVERAL PIECES OF
POETRY, NEVER BEFORE PUBLISHED.
     Fairhaven: Printed by J. P. Spooner. 1797. pp. 47. 16mo.   AAS.

32613   ON JOSEPH'S MAKING HIMSELF KNOWN TO HIS BRETHREN. [Fourteen four-line verses.]
[Colophon:]
     Boston: Printed and sold next Liberty-Pole. 1797. Broadside. nar. fol.
                           AAS. BPL.

32614   ON THE DEATH OF [cut] POLLY GOOLD. [Colophon:]
     [Boston:] Printed at Russell's Office, Liberty-Pole. [1797.] Broadside. fol.
                           NYHS.

32615   ONTARIO GAZETTE. VOL. I. NUMB. 4. FRIDAY, JANUARY 6, [— NUMB. 52? FRIDAY,
DECEMBER 8,? 1797.]
     *Published every Friday by Lucius Cary in Geneva, County of Ontario, State
of New-York.* 1797. fol.

     It is probable that early in the following year Cary removed his Print-
ing-Press to Canandaigua, and, in April, 1798, began there with a con-
tinuous numbering, his *Ontario Gazette.*

32616   THE ORACLE OF DAUPHIN. AND HARRISBURGH ADVERTISER. VOL. V. NO. 11,
WEDNESDAY, JANUARY 4, [— VOL. VI. NO. 11. WEDNESDAY, DECEMBER 27.
1797.]
     Harrisburgh: Published by John Wyeth. 1797. fol.

32617   THE ORACLE OF THE DAY. [Mottoes.] NO. 11. OF VOL. VII. WEDNESDAY, JANUARY
4, [— NO. 11, OF VOL. VIII. SATURDAY, DECEMBER 30, 1797.]
     *[Printed and] published every Wednesday [Saturday] morning by Charles
Peirce, in Court [Daniel] Street, Portsmouth, New-Hampshire.* 1797. fol.   AAS.

     A second motto: Reason and truth impartial guide the way, was added
this year to the heading.

32618   ORAM'S NEW-YORK PRICE CURRENT, AND MARINE REGISTER. NO. 76. SATURDAY,
JUNE 3, [— NO. 106. SATURDAY, DECEMBER 30, 1797.]
     New-York: Published weekly by James Oram. 1797. 4to.   NYHS.

     In continuation of *The New-York Prices Current.*

32619   ORANGE Nightingale, and New-Hampshire Advertiser. Vol. i. No. 34. Monday, January 2, [—Vol. ii. No. 18. Monday, September 4, 1797.]
Newbury, (Vermont): Printed by Nathaniel Coverly, jun'r. 1797. fol.

The above is the last number located.

32620   ORIENTAL [cut] Trumpet. Vol. i. No. 4. Thursday, January 5, [— Vol. 2. No. 55. Thursday, December 28, 1797.]
Portland—(Dist. of Maine)—Published by John Rand, at his Office in Middle-Street, near the head of Fish-Street. 1797. fol.   AAS.

32621   OSGOOD, David   1747–1822
The Uncertainty of life, illustrated in a discourse, delivered April 2, 1797. The Sabbath after the funeral of a child [Joseph Teel], whose death had been occasioned by the accidental discharge of a gun. By David Osgood, a. m. pastor of the church in Medford. [Ornament.]
Printed by Samuel Hall, No. 53, Cornhill, Boston. 1797. pp. [22.] 8vo.
            AAS. BA. BPL. JCB. MHS.

32622   OTSEGO Herald: or, Western Advertiser. [Motto.] Vol. ii. Numb. 93. Thursday, January 5, [— Vol. iii. Numb. 144. Thursday, December 28, 1797.]
Cooperstown: Printed and published by Elihu Phinney, first door east of the Court-House. 1797. fol.

32623   OULTON, Walley Chamberlain   1770–1820
The Wonderful story-teller; or pocket library of agreeable entertainment. Containing a miscellaneous collection of remarkable stories, surprising narratives, wonderful occurrences, singular events, whimsical tales, striking anecdotes, miraculous and heroic adventures in human life, odd sayings, supernatural visions, unaccountable appearances, absurd characters, memorable exploits, astonishing deliverances from death and various other dangers, amusing histories, strange accidents, extraordinary memoirs, &c. in the wonderful phenomena of nature. The whole interspersed with choice extracts from the most celebrated historians, ancient and modern; and including many wonderful stories entirely original, and founded on well-attested facts. By Walley C. Oulton, esq. [Eight lines of verse.]
Boston: Printed by Joseph Bumstead. Sold by Thomas & Andrews, E. Larkin, Wm. P. & L. Blake, J. Nancrede, and J. Bumstead. 1797. pp. 321, (3). 12mo.
            AAS. JCB. NYPL.

32624   OXFORD County. District of Maine.
Petition to the Senate and House of Representatives of Massachusetts. [For clearing the Androscoggin River. Signed by forty-four names.]
[Augusta: Printed by Peter Edes. June 12th 1797.] pp. (3). fol.

32625   PACKARD, Hezekiah   1761–1849
The Rational method of preaching exemplified by the great Apostle of the Gentiles is evangelical, and recommended to christian ministers of every denomination in a discourse delivered June 28th, 1797; at the ordination of the Rev. Andrew Beattie, to the pastoral care of the church and christian society in the west parish of Salisbury. By Hezekiah Packard, minister of Chelmsford. Together with the Charge by the Rev. Nathaniel Noyes, of South-Hampton: and the Right hand of fellowship, by the rev. Thomas Cary, of Newburyport. [Two lines of Scripture text.]
Printed at Newburyport by E. M. Blunt.—1797. pp. (36). 8vo.
            AAS. BA. BM. JCB. NYHS. NYPL.

32626 PAGE, John   1744–1808
An Address to the citizens of the district of York, in Virginia, by their
Representative, John Page, of Rosewell.
[Philadelphia: 1797.] pp. (40). 8vo.   AAS. HSP.

Dated, Rosewell, Gloucester County, June 20th, 1794; but not printed,
according to its postscript, until 1797.

32627 PAIN, William   1730–1790
The Carpenter's pocket directory; containing the best methods of framing
timber buildings of all figures and dimensions, with their several parts.
. . . With the plan and sections of a barn. Engraved on twenty-four
plates, with explanations. . . . By William Pain. . . .
Philadelphia: Published by J. H. Dobelbower, and J. Thackara. 1797. pp.
68, 24 plates. sm. 4to.

32628 —— The Practical house carpenter; or, youth's instructor. . . . The whole
illustrated, and made perfectly easy, by one hundred and forty-eight
copper-plates, with explanations to each. By William Pain. The sixth
edition, with additions.
Philadelphia: Printed by Thomas Dobson, at the Stone-House, No. 41, *South
Second Street.* 1797. pp. v, 15, 148 plates. 4to.   NYPL.

32629 PAINE, Thomas   1737–1809
Agrarian justice, opposed to agrarian law, and to agrarian monopoly, being
a plan for meliorating the condition of man, by creating in every nation
a national fund, to pay to every person, when arrived at the age of
twenty-one years, the sum of fifteen pounds sterling, to enable him or
her to begin the world! And also, ten pounds sterling per annum during
life to every person now living of the age of fifty years, and to all others
when they shall arrive at that age to enable them to live in old age
without wretchedness, and go decently out of the world. By Thomas Paine,
author of Common sense, Rights of man, Age of reason, &c.
Baltimore: Printed for George Keatinge's Book-store. 1797. pp. (34). (2).
8vo.   LOC. NYPL.

32630 —— —— Agrarian justice, opposed to agrarian law, and to agrarian monopoly. Being a plan for meliorating the condition of man, by creating in
every nation, a national fund, to pay to every person, when arrived at
the age of twenty-one years. The sum of fifteen pounds sterling, to enable him or her to begin the world! And also, ten pounds sterling
per annum during life to every person now living of the age of fifty
years, and to all others when they shall arrive at that age, to enable
them to live in old age without wretchedness, and go decently out of
the world. By Thomas Paine, author of Common sense, Rights of man, Age
of reason, &c. &c.
Philadelphia: Printed by R. Folwell, for Benjamin Franklin Bache. [1797.]
pp. (32). 8vo.   AAS. BA. BM. JCB. LOC. NYPL.

32631 —— Thomas Paine's Letter to George Washington, president of the United
States. [Dated, Paris, July 30th, 1796.]
Baltimore, printed. 1797. pp. 36. sm. 4to.   NYPL.

32632 —— A Letter to the hon. Thomas Erskine, on the prosecution of Thomas
Williams, for publishing the Age of reason. With his Discourse on the
Society of the Theophilanthropists.
Newburgh: Printed by D. Denniston. [1797.] pp. 48, 8vo.

32633

PAINE, Thomas, continued.

—— The Works of Thomas Paine, secretary for foreign affairs, to the Congress of the United States, in the late war. In two volumes. Vol. i. [— ii.]

Philadelphia: Printed by James Carey, No. 83, North Second-street. 1797. 2 vols. pp. vi, (2), 391, (1); (2), (2), (2), (2), 368; 148; (2), 80. 8vo.

AAS. BPL. JCB. LOC. NYPL.

Contains: Vol. I. Common sense. — Epistle to Quakers.—The Crisis, No. i — xiv. Crisis extraordinary. Two supernumary Crisis.— Public good.—Letter to Abbe Raynal.—Dissertations on Government, the Affairs of the Bank, and Paper-money.—Miscellaneous pieces, in prose and verse. "These were all issued during the Author's residence in America, and the last four, with two numbers of The Crisis, have never appeared in any previous edition of his works." Vol. II. Prospects on the Rubicon. — Rights of man, Part i. — Part ii. —Letter to the Authors of the Republican.— Letter to Abbe Syeyas.— Address to the Addressers.—Two Letters to Lord Onslow.—Dissertation on First Principles of Government.—Letter to Mr. Secretary Dundas.— The decline and fall of the English system of finance. — Letter to the people of France. — Reasons for preserving the life of Louis Capet, as delivered to the National Convention.—The Age of Reason, Part i.— Part ii.

The Editor says: He believes this volume contains the whole of Paine's European publications, except his Letter to General Washington, which, being a copy-right, could not legally be published by him. As several have expressed a wish that the Age of Reason be omitted, that treatise has been separately paged at the end. "To accomodate persons who wish to read both sides of every interesting question, some sets are bound up with Dr. Watson's Apology for the Bible annexed. And to gratify those who disapprove of Paine's theological works, a number of sets are bound up without the Age of Reason."

Third title: The Age of reason. Being an investigation of true and of fabulous theology. By Thomas Paine, secretary for foreign affairs, to the Congress of the United States, in the late war.

Philadelphia: Printed by James Carey, No. 83, North Second-Street. [1797.] pp. 148.

Fourth title: An Apology for the Bible, in a series of letters, addressed to Thomas Paine, author of a book entitled, The Age of reason, part the second, being an investigation of true and of fabulous theology. By R. Watson, d. d. f. r. s. lord bishop of Landaff, and regius professor of divinity in the University of Cambridge. Carey's third Philadelphia edition.

Philadelphia: Printed by James Carey, No. 83, North Second-Street. 1797. *[Price three-eighths of a dollar.]* pp. (2), (80).

See, also, No. 243 of the excellent "Weems Bibliography," by Emily Ellsworth Ford Skeel.

32634

PAINE, Thomas, afterwards Robert Treat, junior   1773–1811
The Ruling passion: an occasional poem. Written by the appointment of the society of the P B K, and spoken on their anniversary, in the chapel of the University, Cambridge, July 20, 1797. By Thomas Paine, a. m.

Boston: Printed by Manning & Loring, for the Author. 1797. pp. 32. 4to.

AAS. BA. BM. BU. HC. JCB. MHS. NYHS. NYPL.

119th Massachusetts District Copyright, issued to Thomas Paine, as Author, 2 August, 1797.

32635 PALMER, ELIHU   1764–1806
AN ENQUIRY RELATIVE TO THE MORAL & POLITICAL IMPROVEMENT OF THE HUMAN
SPECIES. AN ORATION, DELIVERED IN THE CITY OF NEW-YORK ON THE FOURTH OF
JULY, BEING THE TWENTY-FIRST ANNIVERSARY OF AMERICAN INDEPENDENCE. BY
ELIHU PALMER.
  New-York: Printed by John Crookes. 1797. pp. (35). 12mo.
          AAS. BA. LOC. NYHS. NYPL.

32636 PALMER, STEPHEN   1766–1821
A SERMON, DELIVERED AT ROWLEY, SECOND PARISH, JUNE 7, 1797. AT THE ORDINA-
TION OF THE REV. ISAAC BRAMAN, TO THE PASTORAL CARE OF THE SECOND CHURCH
AND SOCIETY IN THAT TOWN. BY STEPHEN PALMER, A. M. PASTOR OF A CHURCH IN
NEEDHAM.
  Printed at Dedham, by Nathaniel and Benjamin Heaton. M,DCC,XCVII. pp.
(35). 8vo.   AAS BM. JCB. NYPL.
  The inducting Address. By the Rev. Mr. Cleaveland, of Ipswich. The
  Charge. By the Rev. Mr. Dana, of Ipswich. The Right hand of fellow-
  ship. By the Rev. Mr. Bradford, of Rowley.

32637 PANTHER, ABRAHAM
A VERY SURPRISING NARRATIVE OF A YOUNG WOMAN DISCOVERED IN A ROCKY CAVE;
AFTER HAVING BEEN TAKEN BY THE SAVAGE INDIANS OF THE WILDERNESS, IN THE
YEAR 1777, AND SEEING NO HUMAN BEING FOR THE SPACE OF NINE YEARS. IN A
LETTER FROM A GENTLEMAN TO HIS FRIEND.
  *Putney, (Vermont): Printed [by Cornelius Sturtevant jun. & Co.] for the
Purchaser.* M,DCC,XCVII. pp. 12. 12mo.

32638 ——— A SURPRISING NARRATIVE OF A YOUNG WOMAN, WHO WAS DISCOVERED IN A
CAVE, AFTER HAVING BEEN TAKEN BY THE INDIANS, IN THE YEAR 1777, AND SEE-
ING NO HUMAN BEING FOR THE SPACE OF NINE YEARS. IN A LETTER FROM A GEN-
TLEMAN TO HIS FRIEND.
  Rutland: Printed by Josiah Fay. 1797.

32639 PATTERSON, ROBERT   1743–1824
TABLE OF LATITUDE AND DEPARTURE.
  Philadelphia: 1797. 16mo.

32640 PEABODY, STEPHEN   1741–1819
A SERMON, DELIVERED AT CONCORD, BEFORE THE HONOURABLE GENERAL COURT OF
THE STATE OF NEW-HAMPSHIRE, AT THE ANNUAL ELECTION, HOLDEN ON THE FIRST
WEDNESDAY IN JUNE, 1797. . . . PUBLISHED BY ORDER OF THE GENERAL COURT.
  Concord: Printed by George Hough. M,DCC,XCVII. pp. 23. 8vo.
         AAS. BA. BM. JCB. LOC. NYHS.

32641 PEAK, JOHN   1761–1842
A SERMON, PREACHED AT THE ORDINATION OF THE REV. WILLIAM BATCHELDER, TO
THE PASTORAL CARE OF THE BAPTIST CHURCH OF CHRIST IN BERWICK, NOV. 30TH
1796. BY JOHN PEAK, PASTOR OF THE BAPTIST CHURCH OF CHRIST IN NEWTOWN,
N. H.
  Printed at Exeter, by Henry Ranlet, M,DCC,XCVII. pp. 28. 8vo. AAS.
  A second edition was printed in Exeter in 1823.

32642 PEALE, CHARLES WILLSON   1741–1827
AN ESSAY ON BUILDING WOODEN BRIDGES. BY CHARLES W. PEALE PROPRIETOR OF
THE MUSEUM IN PHILADELPHIA.
  Philadelphia: 1797. plates.
  176th Pennsylvania District Copyright, issued to Charles Wilson Peale,
  as Author, 16 March, 1797.

32643 PEDDLE, MRS. ———
RUDIMENTS OF TASTE. IN A SERIES OF LETTERS FROM A MOTHER TO HER DAUGHTERS. BY THE AUTHOR OF THE LIFE OF JACOB.
Chambersburg: Printed by Dover & Harper, for Mathew Carey, Philadelphia. M,DCC,XCVII. pp. 52. 12mo. AAS. JCB.

32644 PEIRCE, JOHN, JUNIOR
THE NEW AMERICAN SPELLING-BOOK: IN THREE PARTS. CONTAINING I. TABLES OF COMMON WORDS, FROM ONE TO FIVE SYLLABLES; . . . II. A COLLECTION OF WORDS OF TWO, THREE, AND FOUR SYLLABLES, DIVIDED INTO THREE TABLES; III. A VERY PLAIN AND EASY INTRODUCTION TO ENGLISH GRAMMAR, PARTICULARLY ADAPTED TO THE CAPACITIES OF YOUTH, AND INTENDED FOR THE USE OF SCHOOLS. COMPILED BY JOHN PEIRCE, JUN. THE THIRD EDITION.
Philadelphia: Printed by Joseph Crukshank. 1797.

32645 PENN, WILLIAM   1644–1718
NO CROSS, NO CROWN: A DISCOURSE SHEWING THE NATURE AND DISCIPLINE OF THE HOLY CROSS OF CHRIST; AND THAT THE DENIAL OF SELF, AND DAILY BEARING OF CHRIST'S CROSS, IS THE ALONE WAY TO THE REST AND KINGDOM OF GOD. TO WHICH ARE ADDED, THE LIVING AND DYING TESTIMONIES OF MANY PERSONS OF FAME AND LEARNING, BOTH OF ANCIENT AND MODERN TIMES, IN FAVOUR OF THIS TREATISE. IN TWO PARTS. BY WILLIAM PENN. [Four lines of Scripture texts.]
Philadelphia: Printed by Benjamin & Jacob Johnson, No. 147, High-Street.— 1797. pp. (6), 358. 8vo. AAS. HC. NYPL.

32646 PENNSYLVANIA. STATE.
ACCOUNTS OF THE TREASURY OF PENNSYLVANIA, FROM THE FIRST OF JANUARY TO THE THIRTY-FIRST OF DECEMBER [1796] INCLUSIVE. [Ornament.]
Philadelphia: Printed by Zachariah Poulson, junior, number eighty, Chesnut-Street. 1797. pp. (12). fol. LOC.

32647 ——— AN ACT [IN FORM OF A BILL FROM THE SENATE] TO PROVIDE FOR THE INSTRUCTION OF YOUTH BY ESTABLISHING SCHOOLS THROUGHOUT THIS COMMONWEALTH SO THAT THE POOR MAY BE TAUGHT GRATIS.
Philadelphia: Printed by Zachariah Poulson, junior, February 9, 1797. pp. [12.] fol. AAS.

32648 ——— ACTS OF THE GENERAL ASSEMBLY OF THE COMMONWEALTH OF PENNSYLVANIA, PASSED AT A SESSION, WHICH WAS BEGUN AND HELD AT THE CITY OF PHILADELPHIA ON TUESDAY, THE SIXTH DAY OF DECEMBER, IN THE YEAR ONE THOUSAND SEVEN HUNDRED AND NINETY-SIX, AND OF THE INDEPENDENCE OF THE UNITED STATES OF AMERICA THE TWENTY-FIRST. [— 14 February, 1797.] PUBLISHED BY AUTHORITY.
Philadelphia: Printed by Hall and Sellers, No. 51, Market-Street. M,DCC,-XCVII. pp. (2), (93)-[182.] fol. LOC.

32649 ——— ——— ACTS OF THE GENERAL ASSEMBLY OF THE COMMONWEALTH OF PENNSYLVANIA, PASSED AT A SESSION, WHICH WAS BEGUN AND HELD AT THE CITY OF PHILADELPHIA ON MONDAY, THE TWENTY-EIGHTH DAY OF AUGUST, IN THE YEAR ONE THOUSAND SEVEN HUNDRED AND NINETY-SEVEN, AND OF THE INDEPENDENCE OF THE UNITED STATES OF AMERICA THE TWENTY-SECOND. [— 29th August, 1797.] PUBLISHED BY AUTHORITY.
Philadelphia: Printed by Hall and Sellers, No. 51, Market-Street. M.DCC.-XCVII. pp. (2), (185)-(186). fol. LOC.

32650 ——— NO. XLV. IN GENERAL ASSEMBLY. WEDNESAY [*sic*] FEBRUARY 8, 1797. AN ACT TO ESTABLISH A SYSTEM OF BANKRUPTCY WITHIN THIS COMMONWEALTH.
[*Philadelphia: Printed by Hall and Sellers,* 1797.] pp. (39). fol. LOC.

PENNSYLVANIA. STATE, continued.

32651 —— JOURNAL OF THE FIRST SESSION OF THE SEVENTH HOUSE OF REPRESENTATIVES OF THE COMMONWEALTH OF PENNSYLVANIA. 1796–1797.

Philadelphia: 1797. pp. 440; 18.

32652 —— TAGEBUCH DES SIEBENTEN HAUSES DER REPRÄSENTANTEN DER REPUBLIK PENNSYLVANIEN. 1796–1797.

Philadelphia: Gedruckt bey Steiner und Kammerer. 1797.

32653 —— JOURNAL OF THE SENATE OF THE COMMONWEALTH OF PENNSYLVANIA. COMMENCING ON TUESDAY, THE SIXTH DAY OF DECEMBER, IN THE YEAR OF OUR LORD ONE THOUSAND SEVEN HUNDRED AND NINETY-SIX, AND OF THE INDEPENDENCE OF THE UNITED STATES OF AMERICA THE TWENTY-FIRST. [— 29 AUGUST, 1797.] VOLUME VII. [Ornament.]

Philadelphia: Printed by Zachariah Poulson, junior, number eighty, Chesnut-Street. 1796. [1797.] pp. (319). fol. LOC.

32654 —— TAGEBUCH DES SENATS DER REPUBLIK PENNSYLVANIEN. 1796–1797.

Germantown: Gedruckt bey Michael Billmeyer. 1797.

32655 —— LAWS OF THE COMMONWEALTH OF PENNSYLVANIA, FROM THE FOURTEENTH DAY OF OCTOBER, ONE THOUSAND SEVEN HUNDRED, TO THE FIRST DAY OF OCTOBER, ONE THOUSAND SEVEN HUNDRED AND EIGHTY-ONE. REPUBLISHED, UNDER THE AUTHORITY OF THE LEGISLATURE, BY ALEXANDER JAMES DALLAS. VOL. I.

Philadelphia: Printed by Hall and Sellers. MDCCXCVII. pp. (2), (2), (2), [913], [64], [iv], (22). fol. AAS. HC. HSP. JCB. LOC. NYHS.

The second volume was published in Philadelphia in 1798. The third volume in Philadelphia in 1795. And the fourth volume in Lancaster in 1801.

32656 —— THE NAMES AND PLACES OF ABODE OF THE MEMBERS AND OFFICERS OF THE SENATE OF PENNSYLVANIA. [Twenty-nine lines.]

[Philadelphia:] Zachariah Poulson, junior, Printer, No. 80, Chesnut-Street. [1797.] Broadside. fol. AAS. HSP.

32657 —— REPORT OF THE REGISTER-GENERAL OF THE STATE OF THE FINANCES OF PENNSYLVANIA, FOR THE YEAR 1796.

Philadelphia: Printed by Zachariah Poulson, junior, number eighty, Chesnut-Street. [1797.] pp. (19). fol. LOC.

32658 THE PENNSYLVANIA GAZETTE. NUMBER 3468. WEDNESDAY, JANUARY 4, [— NUMBER 3519. WEDNESDAY, DECEMBER 27, 1797.]

Philadelphia: Printed by Hall and Sellers, at the new Printing-Office, near the Market. 1797. fol. AAS. HC. LCP.

32659 THE PENNSYLVANIA HERALD, AND YORK GENERAL ADVERTISER. VOL. VIII. NO. 48. TOTAL NO. 412 WEDNESDAY, JANUARY 4, [— VOL. IX. NO. 47. TOTAL NO. 463. WEDNESDAY, DECEMBER 27, 1797.]

York: Printed every Wednesday, by John Edie. 1797. fol. YHS.

32660 PENNSYLVANIA LAND COMPANY.
PLAN OF ASSOCIATION OF THE PENNSYLVANIA LAND COMPANY, ESTABLISHED MARCH 1797.

Philadelphia: Printed by R. Aitken, Market Street. M,DCC,XCVII. pp. (15), (12), (3). 8vo. LOC.

32661   PENNSYLVANIA PROPERTY COMPANY.
        PLAN OF ASSOCIATION OF THE PENNSYLVANIA PROPERTY COMPANY.
        Philadelphia: 1797. pp. 16. 8vo.

32662   THE PENNSYLVANIA, MARYLAND, AND VIRGINIA ALMANACK, FOR THE YEAR 1798.
        *Frederick-Town: Printed by Matthias Bartgis, at his English & German
        Printing-Office.* [1797.]

32663   DIE PENNSYLVANISCHE CORRESPONDENZ. NUM. 1. DIENSTAG, OKTOBER 10,
        [— NUM. 24. FREITAG, DEZEMBER 29, 1797.]
            *Philadelphia: Gedruckt bey Henrich Schweitzer, corner Fourth and Rees-
        Strasse. 1797. fol.*

            Established, as a semi-weekly, by Heinrich Schweitzer, and continued
            by him probably not longer than the issue for April 27, 1798, when it
            was apparently consolidated with the *Philadelphische Correspondenz.*

32664   DIE PENNSYLVANISCHE WOCHENSCHRIFT. NUM. 1. APRIL [—DEZEMBER 1797.]
            *Hanover, York County, Pennsylvania: Gedruckt bey Stellingius & Lepper.
        1797. fol.*

            Established, as a weekly, by E. Stellingius, and William Daniel Lepper.
            Before 1802, Stellingius (or Stettinius) withdrew and Lepper continued
            publication alone into February, 1805, when it was discontinued.

32665   PENNSYLVANISCHER KALENDER. AUF DAS 1798STE JAHR CHRISTI.
            Ephrata: Gedruckt bey Salomon Mayer. 1797. pp. (42). 4to.   AAS.

32666   PERCIVAL, THOMAS   1740–1804
        A FATHER'S INSTRUCTIONS; CONSISTING OF MORAL TALES, FABLES, AND REFLECTIONS;
        DESIGNED TO PROMOTE THE LOVE OF VIRTUE, A TASTE FOR KNOWLEDGE, AND AN
        EARLY ACQUAINTANCE WITH THE WORKS OF NATURE: BY THOMAS PERCIVAL,
        M.D.F.R.S. AND A.S. LOND. F.R.S. AND R.M.S. EDINB. PRESIDENT OF THE LITERARY
        AND PHILOSOPHICAL SOCIETY OF MANCHESTER, AND MEMBER OF VARIOUS FOREIGN
        SOCIETIES. THE NINTH EDITION.
            *Philadelphia: Printed by T. Dobson, No. 41, S. Second-Street. 1797. pp.
        xii, 219. 12mo.*   AAS.

32667   PERKINS, ELISHA   1740–1810
        EVIDENCES OF THE EFFICACY OF DOCTOR PERKINS'S PATENT METALLIC INSTRUMENTS.
            New-Haven: [1797.] 8vo.   AAS.

32668   —— — EVIDENCES OF THE EFFICACY OF DOCTOR PERKINS'S PATENT METALLIC
        INSTRUMENTS. [Dated, Plainfield, January 2, 1797.]
            New-London: From S. Green's Press. [1797.] pp. [32.] 8vo.
                                          AAS. BM. NYHS. NYPL. SGO.

32669   —— — EVIDENCES OF THE EFFICACY OF DOCTOR PERKINS'S PATENT METALLIC
        INSTRUMENTS.
            Newburyport: Printed by Edmund M. Blunt, [1797.] pp. 24. 8vo.
                                          BA. BM. MHS. RIMS. SGO.

32670   —— — EVIDENCES OF THE EFFICACY OF DOCTOR PERKINS'S PATENT METALLIC
        INSTRUMENTS. [Dated, Plainfield, June, 1797.]
            Philadelphia: Printed by Richard Folwell. [1797.] pp. 36. 12mo. BA. NYPL.

32671 PERKINS, JOSEPH   1772–1803
AN ORATION UPON GENIUS, PRONOUNCED AT THE ANNIVERSARY COMMENCEMENT OF
HARVARD UNIVERSITY, IN CAMBRIDGE, JULY 19, 1797. BY JOSEPH PERKINS, A.M.
[Ornament.]

*Boston: Printed by Manning & Loring, for Joseph Nancrede, No. 49, Marl-
bro' Street.* 1797. pp. [22.] 12mo.   AAS. BA. HC. JCB. MHS. NYHS. NYPL.

32672 PERRY, WILLIAM
THE ONLY SURE GUIDE TO THE ENGLISH TONGUE: OR, NEW PRONOUNCING SPELLING
BOOK. UPON THE SAME PLAN AS PERRY'S ROYAL STANDARD ENGLISH DICTIONARY,
NOW MADE USE OF IN ALL THE CELEBRATED SCHOOLS IN GREATBRITAIN, IRELAND
AND AMERICA. TO WHICH IS ADDED, A GRAMMAR OF THE ENGLISH LANGUAGE; AND
A SELECT NUMBER OF MORAL TALES AND FABLES, FOR THE INSTRUCTION OF YOUTH.
WITH AN APPENDIX. CONTAINING, DIRECTIONS FOR THE DIFFERENT SOUNDS OF THE
CONSONANTS BEFORE ALL THE VOWELS, WITH EVERY EXCEPTION THAT IS TO BE MET
WITH IN OUR LANGUAGE, FROM SUCH GENERAL RULES: ALSO, A COMPLETE LIST OF
ALL THE WORDS IN WHICH E FINAL DOES NOT LENGTHEN THE SYLLABLE: LIKEWISE,
SEVERAL VALUABLE APHORISMS RESPECTING THE SOUNDS OF THE VOWELS IN THE
LAST SYLLABLE OF WORDS ENDING WITH E. AND, A COMPLETE LIST OF ALL THE
WORDS IN THE ENGLISH LANGUAGE, WHICH, THOUGH WRITTEN DIFFERENTLY HAVE
A SIMILARITY OF SOUND.—OF THOSE SUBSTANTIVES AND VERBS, OF THE SAME OR-
THOGRAPHY, BUT OF A DIFFERENT ACCENT.—OF THOSE SUBSTANTIVES AND VERBS,
WHICH VARY IN THEIR SOUND EITHER BY A DIFFERENT CONSONANT, OR BY CHANG-
ING THE HARD SOUND OF THAT CONSONANT INTO THE SOFT SOUND.—OF THOSE AD-
JECTIVES AND VERBS ALIKE IN ORTHOGRAPHY, BUT DIFFERENTLY ACCENTED.—OF
THE SUBSTANTIVES AND ADJECTIVES CHANGING THE SEAT OF THE ACCENT. BY W.
PERRY, LECTURER ON THE ENGLISH LANGUAGE IN THE ACADEMY, EDINBURGH.
TENTH WORCESTER EDITION, ILLUSTRATED WITH [twelve] CUTS. CAREFULLY RE-
VISED BY PERRY'S ROYAL STANDARD ENGLISH DICTIONARY, BY ISAIAH THOMAS.
AND CORRECTED OF THE NUMEROUS ERRORS, WHICH ARE IN ALL OTHER EDITIONS
BOTH BRITISH AND AMERICAN.

*Printed at Worcester, Massachusetts, by Isaiah Thomas, jun. Sold wholesale
and retail, at his Bookstore in Worcester, and at the Worcester Bookstore. Sold
also by Thomas and Andrews, and other Booksellers in Boston.* MDCCXCVII. pp.
180, frontispiece. 12mo.   AAS.

32673 PETERS, RICHARD   1744–1828
AGRICULTURAL ENQUIRIES ON PLAISTER OF PARIS. ALSO, FACTS, OBSERVATIONS AND
CONJECTURES ON THAT SUBSTANCE [sic], WHEN APPLIED AS MANURE. COLLECTED,
CHIEFLY FROM THE PRACTICE OF FARMERS IN PENNSYLVANIA, AND PUBLISHED AS
MUCH WITH A VIEW TO INVITE, AS TO GIVE INFORMATION. BY RICHARD PETERS.

*Philadelphia: Printed by Charles Cist, No. 104, North Second-Street, and
John Markland, No. 91, South Front Street. [Entered according to Act of Congress.]* 1797. pp. (2), 111, (1), (2). 8vo.   AAS. BA. BM. LOC. NYPL.

169th Pennsylvania District Copyright, issued to Charles Cist and John
Markland, as Proprietors, 20 January, 1797. Prepared, at the request
of and dedicated to George Washington.

32674 THE [cut] PHENIX; OR WINDHAM HERALD. VOL. VI. NUMB. 305. SATURDAY, JANU-
ARY 7, [— VOL. VII. NUMB. 356. THURSDAY, DECEMBER 28, 1797.]

Windham: Printed by John Byrne, in the lower room of the Court-House.
1797. fol.   AAS. CHS. NYHS.

32675 PHILADELPHIA. PENNSYLVANIA.
THE COMMITTEE APPOINTED TO EXAMINE INTO THE TITLE OF THE CORPORATION TO THE NORTH EAST PUBLIC SQUARE, AND THE BOUNDARIES OF THE SAME; AND ALSO TO ENQUIRE, WHETHER ANY, AND WHAT, ENCROACHMENTS HAVE BEEN MADE THEREUPON, REPORT, . . . JOS. HOPKINSON [and two others.] FEBRUARY 4TH, 1797. [With Plan of Square.]
[Philadelphia:] [Printed by Zachariah Poulson, junior, February, 22. 1797.] pp. (2). fol. HSP.

32676 PHILADELPHIA. PENNSYLVANIA. AMERICAN SOCIETY OF UNITED IRISHMEN.
DECLARATION AND CONSTITUTION OF THE AMERICAN SOCIETY OF UNITED IRISHMEN, *Philadelphia: Printed for the Society, August* 8, 1797.

32677 PHILADELPHIA. PENNSYLVANIA. BAPTIST ASSOCIATION.
MINUTES OF THE PHILADELPHIA BAPTIST ASSOCIATION, HELD AT LOWER DUBLIN, PHILADELPHIA COUNTY, STATE OF PENNSYLVANIA, OCTOBER 3D, 4TH, AND 5TH, 1797. [Colophon:]
Southampton: Printed by Stephen C. Ustick. [1797.] pp. 8. 4to. AAS. BU. NYPL.

32678 PHILADELPHIA. PENNSYLVANIA. BRICKLAYERS CORPORATION.
CHARTER ARTICLES AND BYE LAWS, OF THE BRICKLAYERS CORPORATION. FOUNDED . . . 1790. INCORPORATED . . . 1797.
Northern Liberties: Printed by B. Scheffler & Co. M,DCC,LXXXXVII. pp. 23. 12mo.

32679 PHILADELPHIA. PENNSYLVANIA. CHURCHES.
AN ACCOUNT OF THE BAPTISMS AND BURIALS IN THE UNITED CHURCHES OF CHRIST CHURCH AND ST. PETER'S.
Philadelphia: 1797. Broadside. fol. I.CP.

32680 PHILADELPHIA. PENNSYLVANIA. HOSPITAL.
THE COMMITTEE, APPOINTED TO PREPARE AN ACCOUNT OF THE MONIES RECEIVED FROM THE LEGISLATURE OF PENNSYLVANIA, TOWARDS ERECTING ADDITIONAL BUILDINGS TO THE PENNSYLVANIA HOSPITAL, AND FINISHING THE SAME AND OF THE EXPENDITURES OF THE SAID BUILDINGS—REPORT, . . . SAMUEL COATES, SECRETARY. [Colophon:]
[Philadelphia:] Printed by John Fenno. [1797.] Broadside. fol. AAS.

32681 PHILADELPHIA. PENNSYLVANIA. MEDICAL SOCIETY.
ACT OF INCORPORATION, AND LAWS OF THE PHILADELPHIA MEDICAL SOCIETY.
Philadelphia: 1797. 8vo.

32682 PHILADELPHIA. PENNSYLVANIA. SCHUYLKILL RIVER BRIDGE.
PLAN FOR THE ESTABLISHMENT OF A COMPANY, TO BE INCORPORATED BY THE LEGISLATURE OF PENNSYLVANIA (IF SUCH INCORPORATION SHALL TO THAT LEGISLATURE SEEM PROPER) BY THE NAME AND TITLE OF "THE COMPANY FOR ERECTING A BRIDGE OVER THE RIVER SCHUYLKILL, AT OR NEAR THE CITY OF PHILADELPHIA." . . . [Followed by:] THE MEMORIAL OF THE SUBSCRIBERS. . . .
Philadelphia, January 25, 1797. pp. (2). fol. HSP.

32683 PHILADELPHIA. PENNSYLVANIA. SOCIETY OF THE SONS OF ST. GEORGE.
RULES AND CONSTITUTIONS OF THE SOCIETY OF THE SONS OF ST. GEORGE, ESTABLISHED AT PHILADELPHIA, FOR THE ADVICE AND ASSISTANCE OF ENGLISHMEN IN DISTRESS. [With list of members.]
Philadelphia: Printed by William Cobbett, opposite Christ Church. 1797. pp. (25). 8vo. LOC. NYPL. SGO.

32684 PHILADELPHIA, January 31, 1797. Sir, I have noticed that one of the objects proposed to Congress as a fit subject for additional taxation, is that of white cotton goods imported into this country.—[Asking for the exception of printed calicoes.] A Friend to the useful arts.
[Philadelphia: 1797.] Broadside. fol. AAS.

32685 THE PHILADELPHIA Gazette & universal daily advertiser. [Motto.] Vol. xiv. No. 2556. Monday, January 1, [— No. 2377. Saturday, December 30, 1797.]
Printed and published by Andrew Brown, at Washington's Head, in Chesnut Street,—No. 29—between Front and Second Streets. 1797. fol. BM. LCP. WHS.
Andrew Brown died February 4th, from the effects of a fire which destroyed his Printing Office January 27th, and was succeeded by his son, Andrew Brown.

32686 —— Brown's Gazette extra. Wednesday evening, July 5. Symptoms of treason! [In order to appease the anxiety of the citizens on the subject of the following important letter, we have taken the liberty of laying it before them at this untimely hour.] [Letter, dated April 21, 1797, from William Blount.] With a "brief analysis of the circumstances relative to this extraordinary business" . . . The official documents, we are informed will appear in a contemporary print to-morrow morning.
[Philadelphia: Printed by Andrew Brown. 1797.] Broadside. fol. AAS.

32687 THE PHILADELPHIA Minerva. — Utile dulci — No, 49, of Vol. ii. Whole no. 101. Saturday, January 7, [— No. 48, of Vol. iii. Whole no. 152. Saturday, December 30, 1797.]
[Philadelphia:] Printed and published (every Saturday) by John Turner, in Chesnut-Street, between Nos. 72 and 74. (Price two dollars per annum). 1797. 4to. AAS. HC. HSP. LOC. NYHS. WHS.
Beginning with the third volume, on February 4th, John Turner relinquished control to William T. Palmer, who removed his Printing Office, in March, to No. 18, North Third-Street.

32688 PHILADELPHISCHE [cut] Correspondenz. [Motto.] Num. 575. Dienstag den 3 Januar, [— Num. 657. Dienstag den 17 October, 1797.]
Diese Zeitung wird alle Dienstag und Freytag heraus gegeben von Steiner und Kammerer, in der Rees-Strasse, zwischen der Zweyten-und Dritten-Strasse, No. 85; . . . 1797. fol.
Publication was suspended at the above date, and resumed in May, 1798, by Henrich and Joseph K. Kammerer, junior.

32689 PHILLIPS, Nathaniel
Phillips's United States diary; or an Almanack, for the year of our Lord, 1798: being the second after leap-year and twenty second of American independence. [Eight lines. U. S. & R. I. arms. Four lines of verse.]
Printed at Warren (R. I.) by Nathaniel Phillips. Great encouragement given to wholesale purchasers. [1797.] pp. (24). 12mo. AAS. LOC. RIHS.

32690 PHILOMATHES, pseudonym.
Franklin's Legacy; or, the Lansingburgh Almanack, for the year of our Lord, 1798: the 2d after leap-year; and of American independence, part of the 22d and 23d years. [Cut of Franklin.] Where Liberty dwells there is my country. This is the basis of Liberty. dr. Benj. Franklin. [Five lines of verse.] By Philomathes.
[Lansingburgh:] Printed by R. Moffitt & Co. and sold by them, by the gross, dozen or single. [1797.] pp. (86). 12mo. AAS.

32691　PICKMAN, Benjamin, junior　　　　1763–1843
An Oration, pronounced, February 22, 1797, before the inhabitants of the town of Salem, in Massachusetts, assembled to commemorate the birth-day of George Washington, president of the United States of America. By Benjamin Pickman, jun. [Four lines from] Pope.
　Printed at Salem, by Thomas C. Cushing. 1797. pp. 22. 8vo.
　　　　　　　　　　AAS. BA. BM. HC. JCB. NYHS.

32692　PIKE, Nicholas　　　　1743–1819
A New and complete system of arithmetic. Composed for the use of the citizens of the United States. By Nicolas [*sic*] Pike, a.m. [Three lines of Latin from] Cicero. Second edition, enlarged. Revised and corrected, by Ebenezer Adams, a. m. preceptor of Leicester Academy.
　Printed at Worcester, Massachusetts, at the Press of Isaiah Thomas, by Leonard Worcester, for said Thomas. Sold by Thomas, Son & Thomas, in Worcester; by Thomas & Andrews, D. West, E. Larkin, S. Hall, J. White, and J. West, in Boston, and by all the Booksellers in the United States. 1797. pp. 516. 8vo.
　　　　　　　　　　AAS. BA. JCB. NYPL.

32693　PINKHAM, Paul
A Chart of George's Bank including Cape Cod, Nantucket, and the shoals lying on their coast, with directions for sailing over the same &c. Survey'd by capt. Paul Pinkham.
　Newburyport: Printed by Edmund M. Blunt. 1797.
　130th Massachusetts District Copyright, issued to Edmund M. Blunt, as Proprietor, 28 September, 1797.

32694　THE PITTSBURGH Gazette. Vol. xi. No. 540. Saturday, January 7, [— Vol. 12. No. 591. Saturday, December 30, 1797.]
　Pittsburgh: Printed by John Scull, in Front Street, next door to the corner of Market Street. 1797. fol.
　Beginning in January the old type text of the heading was resumed, and the imprint made a part of the heading.

32695　PLUMMER, Jonathan, junior
To sir Timothy Dexter, on his returning to Newburyport, after residing a long time at Chester, in Newhampshire. A congratulatory ode. By Jonathan Plummer, jun. poet laureat to his lordship. [Eleven six-line verses.]
　Newburyport: Printed by William Barrett. 1797. Broadside.

32696　POIVRE, Pierre　　　　1719–1786
Travels of a philosopher; or, observations on the manners and arts of various nations in Africa and Asia. By m. Le Poivre, late emissary to the King of Cochin-China.
　Augusta (Kennebeck) Re-printed by Peter Edes. 1797. pp. 94. 12mo. NYPL.

32697　POLAR Star and [cut] Boston Daily Advertiser. Vol. i. No. 75. Monday, January 2, [— No. 102. Thursday, February 2, 1797.]
　Printed by Alexander Martin, for the Proprietors, No. 71, State-Street, opposite the Custom-House, Boston—(Mass.) 1797. fol.　　　　BA.
　Discontinued with the issue for February 2d, as above, probably.

32698　POLITICAL Gazette. Vol. ii. No. 37. Total no. 89. Friday, January 6, [— Vol. iii. No. 27. Total no. 123. Friday, October 27. 1797.]
　Newburyport (Massachusetts) Published on Fridays [Thursdays], by William Barrett, west corner of Market Square. . . . 1797. fol.
　In the issue for October 27th. William Barrett, and Angier March, announced that, owing to the great expense of publishing three papers in

POLITICAL GAZETTE, continued.

Newburyport, rendering them unprofitable, they had determined to discontinue the publication of the "Impartial Herald," and of the "Political Gazette," and to combine and issue a new paper, under the title of *The Newburyport Herald and country gazette*, to be published twice a week on Tuesdays and Fridays,

32699   POOR WILL'S ALMANACK, FOR THE YEAR OF OUR LORD, 1798: BEING THE SECOND AFTER BISSEXTILE OR LEAP-YEAR. [Seventeen lines.] ALSO THE ACT LAYING DUTIES ON STAMPED VELLUM, PARCHMENT, AND PAPER.

Philadelphia: Printed for, and sold by, Joseph and James Crukshank, No. 87, High-Street. [1797.] pp. (36). 12mo.   AAS. HSP. LOC. NYPL.

32700   POOR WILL'S POCKET ALMANACK, FOR THE YEAR 1798; BEING THE SECOND AFTER BISSEXTILE OR LEAP-YEAR. [Eighteen lines.]

Philadelphia: Printed for, and sold by, Joseph & James Crukshank, No. 87, High-Street. [1797.] pp. (48). 48mo.   AAS. HSP. LOC.

32701   POPE, ALEXANDER   1688–1744
AN ESSAY ON MAN. IN FOUR EPISTLES TO H. ST. JOHN, LORD BOLINGBROKE. BY ALEXANDER POPE.

Re-printed at Fairhaven by Judah P. Spooner. 1797. 12mo.

32702   —— — AN ESSAY ON MAN.: IN FOUR EPISTLES TO H. ST. JOHN, LORD BOLINGBROKE. TO WHICH IS ADDED, THE UNIVERSAL PRAYER. BY ALEXANDER POPE, ESQ.

Printed at Worcester, Massachusetts: by Thomas, Son & Thomas. Sold by them and the Booksellers in Boston.—1797—pp. 59. 12mo.   AAS. NYPL.

32703   POPE, JOSEPH   1745–1826
THE LOSS OF CHRISTIAN FRIENDS A WARRANTABLE CAUSE OF GRIEF AND SORROW. A SERMON, PREACHED AT BRIMFIELD, NOVEMBER 30, MDCCXCVI: AT THE FUNERAL OF THE REV. NEHEMIAH WILLIAMS. BY JOSEPH POPE, A. M. PASTOR OF A CHURCH IN SPENCER.

Printed at Worcester, by Leonard Worcester. MDCCXCVII. pp. 23. 8vo.
                                                        AAS. JCB. NYPL.

32704   PORCUPINE'S GAZETTE AND UNITED STATES DAILY ADVERTISER. VOL. I. NO. 1. SATURDAY EVENING, MARCH 4TH, [— NO. 257. SATURDAY, DECEMBER 30, 1797.]
Published by William Cobbett, opposite Christ Church, Philadelphia. 1797. fol.   AAS. BA. HSP. LCP. LOC. MDHS. NYPL. PSL.

Established, as a daily, by William Cobbett, and continued by him, ably but offensively, and with varying fortunes, until he returned to England in 1800. Beginning April 24, 1797, the sub-title was dropped; and on July 1st, a cut of a porcupine was added, and divided the heading. From August 29 to October 11th, 1799, the Gazette was printed at Bustleton, on account of the yellow fever epidemic in Philadelphia. No. 777, for October 10th, was issued in duodecimo form, pp. 1–24, and the editor curtly instructs his subscribers to "cut it open, or it can be used for wrapping up snuff and tobacco, as it is." Also, giving notice that he expects to remove his office to Philadelphia, in November. No. 778, for October 26th, is in the same form, signature B. pages 25–48. No. 779. Signature C. pages 49–72, was printed: New-York— Published by Wm. Cobbett.—Jan. 13, 1800, contains his farewell "To the subscribers to this Gazette," in which he gives acrimonious opinions of Thomas McKean, the new Governor of Pennsylvania: and of Benjamin Rush, who had gained a verdict of five thousand dollars against him, for libel. A tri-weekly edition was also published from March 5, 1798 to August 28, 1799, entitled *The Country Porcupine.*

32705 THE POTOMAK GUARDIAN, & BERKELEY ADVERTISER. VOL. VII. No. 319. THURS-
DAY, JANUARY 5, [—VOL. VIII. No. 370. THURSDAY, DECEMBER 28, 1797.]
*Martinsburgh, Virginia: Printed and published, every Thursday, by N. Willis,
Burke-Street. 1797. fol.*

32706 THE POUGHKEEPSIE JOURNAL. TOTAL NUM. 597. WEDNESDAY, JANUARY 4, [—
TOTAL NUM. 649. TUESDAY, DECEMBER 26, 1797.]
*Poughkeepsie, Dutchess County—Published by Nicholas Power, at the Post-
Office. 1797. fol.*   AAS.
In August the day of publication was changed to Tuesday.

32707 PRENTISS, CHARLES   1774–1820
THE AMERICAN BEE; A COLLECTION OF ENTERTAINING HISTORIES, SELECTED FROM
DIFFERENT AUTHORS, AND CALCULATED FOR AMUSEMENT AND INSTRUCTION. THE
FIRST EDITION.
Leominster. (Massachusetts): Printed by and for Charles Prentiss. 1797. pp.
249. 12mo.   AAS. BM. LOC. NYPL.

32708 —— A COLLECTION OF FUGITIVE ESSAYS, IN PROSE AND VERSE. WRITTEN BY CHARLES
PRENTISS. . . . PUBLISHED ACCORDING TO ACT OF CONGRESS.
Leominster (Massachusetts): Printed by and for the Author. 1797. pp. 204,
errata. 12mo.   BU. NYPL.
118th Massachusetts District Copyright, issued to Charles Prentiss, as
Author, 22 July, 1797.

32709 PRESBYTERIAN CHURCH IN PENNSYLVANIA.
ACT OF THE ASSOCIATE PRESBYTERY OF PENNSYLVANIA, AGAINST OCCASIONAL COM-
MUNION. TO WHICH IS ADDED, A JUSTIFICATION OF THE DOCTRINE OF THIS ACT,
. . . TOGETHER WITH AN APPENDIX, CONTAINING A VINDICATION OF THE ASSO-
CIATE PRESBYTERY FROM THE MISREPRESENTATIONS OF DR. LINN IN AN APPENDIX
TO HIS SERMONS ON THE SIGNS OF THE TIMES. BY A MEMBER OF SAID PRESBYTERY.
Philadelphia: Printed by David Hogan. 1797. pp. iv, 55, (1). 8vo.   NYPL.

32710 PRESBYTERIAN CHURCH IN THE UNITED STATES OF AMERICA.
ACTS AND PROCEEDINGS OF THE GENERAL ASSEMBLY OF THE PRESBYTERIAN CHURCH,
IN THE UNITED STATES OF AMERICA. MAY 18, 1797.
Philadelphia: Printed by William W. Woodward, No. 17, Chesnut-Street.
1797. pp. [8.] 8vo.   AAS. JCB. NYPL. PHS. PTS.

32711 —— THE CONSTITUTION OF THE PRESBYTERIAN CHURCH IN THE UNITED STATES OF
AMERICA CONTAINING THE CONFESSION OF FAITH, THE CATECHISMS, THE GOVERN-
MENT AND DISCIPLINE, AND THE DIRECTORY FOR THE WORSHIP OF GOD. RATIFIED
AND ADOPTED BY THE SYNOD OF NEW-YORK AND PHILADELPHIA, HELD AT PHILA-
DELPHIA MAY THE 16TH 1788, AND CONTINUED BY ADJOURNMENTS UNTIL THE 28TH
OF THE SAME MONTH.
Philadelphia: Printed by Robert Aitken, No. 22, Market Street. MDCC-
XCVII. pp. vii, 468. 12mo.   AAS. HC. JCB. PHS. UTS.

32712 PRICE, NATHANIEL
THE TRIAL OF NATHANIEL PRICE, FOR COMMITTING A RAPE ON THE BODY OF UNICE
[*sic*] WILLIAMSON, A CHILD BETWEEN 10 AND 11 YEARS OF AGE. AT BROOKLYN
IN KING'S COUNTY, IN MAY 1797. ☞ THIS CAUSE WHICH HAD MUCH EXCITED
THE PUBLIC ATTENTION, WAS TRIED AT A COURT OF OYER AND TERMINER, HELD
BY THE HON. JUDGE HOBART, AT FLAT-BUSH COURT-HOUSE, ON THE 29TH OF
AUGUST 1797.
New-York: Printed for Elijah Weedg. [1797.] pp. 8. 8vo.   NYHS.

32713   PRIESTLEY, JOSEPH   1733–1804
AN ADDRESS TO THE UNITARIAN CONGREGATION AT PHILADELPHIA, DELIVERED ON
SUNDAY, MARCH 5, 1797. BY JOSEPH PRIESTLEY. . . .

Philadelphia: Printed by Joseph Gales. 1797. pp. 24. 8vo.   BM. NYPL.

32714   —— THE CASE OF POOR EMIGRANTS RECOMMENDED, IN A DISCOURSE, DELIVERED AT
THE UNIVERSITY HALL IN PHILADELPHIA, ON SUNDAY, FEBRUARY 19, 1797. BY
JOSEPH PRIESTLEY, L.L.D.F.R.S. &C.

*Philadelphia: Printed by Joseph Gales, No. 145, North Second Street; and
sold by W. Y. Birch at his Stationary Store, No. 17, South Second Street; and by
the Booksellers in Philadelphia, New-York, and Baltimore. 1797. pp. (32). 8vo.*

BM. JCB. LCP. LOC.

32715   —— DISCOURSES RELATING TO THE EVIDENCES OF REVEALED RELIGION, DELIVERED
IN PHILADELPHIA. BY JOSEPH PRIESTLEY, LL. D. F. R. S. &C. &C. VOL. II. [Two lines
from] 1 PET. III, 15.

*Philadelphia: Printed by Thomas Dobson, at the Stone-House, No. 41, South
Second-Street. 1797. pp. xi, 474, (2). 8vo.*   AAS. BA. BM.

Volume I. was published in 1796.

32716   —— DR. PRIESTLEY HAVING CONTINUED HIS HISTORY OF THE CHRISTIAN CHURCH
FROM THE FALL OF THE WESTERN ROMAN EMPIRE TO THE REFORMATION BY
LUTHER, IS DESIROUS OF PUBLISHING IT. [Asking subscriptions for the work.]
[Philadelphia: Printed by Thomas Dobson.] 22d February, 1797. Broad-
side. fol.   AAS.

32717   —— AN HISTORY OF THE CORRUPTIONS OF CHRISTIANITY, IN TWO VOLUMES. BY JOSEPH
PRIESTLEY, LL. D. F. R. S. THE THIRD EDITION. [Two lines from] MATT. XIII. 27.
VOL. I. [— II.]

*Boston: Printed by William Spotswood. 1797. 2 vols. pp. xii, 245, (1);
316. 12mo.*   AAS. BA. BU. HC. JCB.

32718   —— LETTERS TO MR. VOLNEY, OCCASIONED BY A WORK OF HIS ENTITLED RUINS, AND
BY HIS LETTER TO THE AUTHOR. BY JOSEPH PRIESTLEY, LL. D. F. R. S. &C. [One
line of Latin from] OVID.

*Philadelphia: Printed by Thomas Dobson, at the Stone-House, No. 41, South
Second-Street. 1797. pp. 28. 8vo.*   AAS. BA. BM. BPL. LOC. NYHS. NYPL.

32719   —— OBSERVATIONS ON THE DOCTRINE OF PHLOGISTON AND THE DECOMPOSITION OF
WATER. PART THE SECOND. BY JOSEPH PRIESTLEY, LL.D.F.R.S. &C. &C.

*Philadelphia: Printed by Thomas Dobson, at the Stone-House, No. 41, South
Second Street. 1797. pp. 38. 8vo.*   JCB. SGO.

32720   —— — RÉFLEXIONS SUR LA DOCTRINE DU PHLOGISTIQUE ET LA DÉCOMPOSITION DE
L'EAU. PAR JOSEPH PRIESTLEY. OUVRAGE TRADUIT DE L'ANGLAIS ET SUIVI D'UNE
RÉPONSE PAR P.-A. ADET.

*Philadelphie: Imprimé par L. E. Moreau de St.-Méry, au coin de la Première
rue Sud & de Walnut No. 84. 1797. pp. 96. 8vo.*   RIMS. SGO.

32721   —— OBSERVATIONS ON THE INCREASE OF INFIDELITY. BY JOSEPH PRIESTLEY, L.L.D,
F. R. S. &C. &C. THE THIRD EDITION. TO WHICH ARE ADDED, ANIMADVERSIONS ON
THE WRITINGS OF SEVERAL MODERN UNBELIEVERS, AND ESPECIALLY THE RUINS OF
MR. VOLNEY. [Three lines of French from] BONNET.

*Philadelphia: Printed [by John Thompson] for Thomas Dobson, No. 41, South
Second-Street. 1797. pp. xxvi, 179. 8vo.*   AAS. BA. JCB. NYPL.

32722 PRIESTLEY, Joseph, continued.
—— An Outline of the evidences of revealed religion. By Joseph Priestley, LL.D.F.R.S. &c. [Three lines of French from] Bonnet.
Philadelphia: Printed by T. Dobson, No. 41, S. Second-Street. 1797. pp. viii, 30, (2). 8vo.   BM. JCB. NYPL.

32723 PRINDLE, Chauncey   1753–1833
A Discourse, delivered in Christ's church in Watertown, on Friday, March 3, 1797, at the funeral of mr. Ethel Porter. By Chauncy Prindle, a. m. rector of said church.
Litchfield: Printed by Tho. Collier. [1797.] pp. 30. 8vo.   JCB.

32724 PROTESTANT EPISCOPAL CHURCH in Maryland.
An Abstract of the proceedings of the Corporation for the relief of the widows and children of the clergy of the Protestant Episcopal Church in Maryland.
Baltimore: Printed by Philip Edwards, No. 1, Light-street. 1797. pp. [12.] 12mo.   MDL.

32725 PROTESTANT EPISCOPAL CHURCH in New Jersey.
Proceedings of a Convention of the Protestant Episcopal Church, in the State of New-Jersey. Held at Trenton, the seventh of June, 1797.
Philadelphia: Printed by Ormrod & Conrad, No. 41, Chesnut-street. 1797. pp. (2), (82)–(89), (1), (15). 8vo.   AAS. NYHS.
The appendix consists of the Constitution, Rules, Canons, Recommendations.

32726 PROTESTANT EPISCOPAL CHURCH in New York.
Journal of the proceedings of a Convention of the Protestant Episcopal Church in the State of New-York, held in Trinity church, in the city of New-York, from Tuesday, October 3d, to Thursday, October 5th, one thousand seven hundred and ninety-seven.
New-York: Printed by Hugh Gaine, at the Bible, Pearl-street.—1797.—pp. [7], (1). 8vo.   AAS.

32727 PROTESTANT EPISCOPAL CHURCH in the United States of America.
The Book of common prayer, and administration of the sacraments and other rites and ceremonies of the Church, according to the use of the Protestant Episcopal Church in the United States of America: together with the Psalter, or Psalms of David.
New-York: Printed for T. Allen. 1797. pp. 185, (1); 168, (ii). 12mo.   AAS. LCP. LOC.

Second title: The Whole Book of Psalms, in metre, with hymns, suited to the feasts and fasts of the Church and other occasions of public worship.
New-York: Printed for T. Allen. 1797. pp. 168, (ii).

32728 —— Protestant Episcopal Church Catechism; with some questions, to try, whether children repeat it merely by rote; to engage their attention, and to imprint the sense of it on their minds. [Heavy lines.]
Johnstown: Printed by Jacob Dockstader, M,DCC,XCVII. pp. 32. 32mo. NYHS.

32729   PROUD, ROBERT   1728–1813
THE HISTORY OF PENNSYLVANIA, IN NORTH-AMERICA, FROM THE ORIGINAL INSTITU-
TION AND SETTLEMENT OF THAT PROVINCE, UNDER THE FIRST PROPRIETOR, AND
GOVERNOR WILLIAM PENN, IN 1681, 'TILL AFTER THE YEAR 1742; WITH AN INTRO-
DUCTION, RESPECTING THE LIFE OF W. PENN, PRIOR TO THE GRANT OF THE PROV-
INCE, AND THE RELIGIOUS SOCIETY OF THE PEOPLE CALLED QUAKERS;—WITH THE
FIRST RISE OF THE NEIGHBORING COLONIES, MORE PARTICULARLY OF WEST-NEW-
JERSEY, AND THE SETTLEMENT OF THE DUTCH AND SWEDES ON DELAWARE. TO
WHICH IS ADDED, A BRIEF DESCRIPTION OF THE SAID PROVINCE, AND OF THE GEN-
ERAL STATE, IN WHICH IT FLOURISHED, PRINCIPALLY BETWEEN THE YEARS 1760
AND 1770. THE WHOLE INCLUDING A VARIETY OF THINGS, USEFUL AND INTEREST-
ING TO BE KNOWN, RESPECTING THAT COUNTRY IN EARLY TIME, &C. WITH AN AP-
PENDIX. WRITTEN PRINCIPALLY BETWEEN THE YEARS 1776 AND 1780, BY ROBERT
PROUD. [Four lines of quotations.] VOLUME I.

> *Philadelphia: Printed and sold by Zachariah Poulson, junior, number eighty,*
> *Chesnut-Street.* 1797. pp. 508, portrait of Penn. 8vo.
>
> AAS. BA. BM. BPL. BU. HC. HSP. JCB. LOC. MHS. NL. NYHS. NYPL.

171st Pennsylvania District Copyright, issued to Robert Proud, as
Author, 17 February, 1797.

32730   THE PROVIDENCE GAZETTE. VOL. XXXIV. No. 1723. SATURDAY, JANUARY 7, [—
No. 1774. SATURDAY, DECEMBER 30, 1797.]

> *Printed and published by Carter and Wilkinson, at the Post-Office, opposite the*
> *Market; . . .* 1797. fol.   AAS. BU. JCB. LOC. RIHS. RL.

32731   PUGLIA, SANTIAGO FELIPE
THE DISAPPOINTMENT, OR PETER PORCUPINE IN LONDON: A COMEDY IN THREE ACTS.
WRITTEN BY JAMES QUICKSILVER, AUTHOR OF THE BLUE SHOP, POLITICAL MAS-
SACRE, &C.

> *Philadelphia: Printed ? by Moreau de St. Méry, No.* 84, *corner of Front &*
> *Walnut Streets.* 1797.

32732   PURVES, JAMES   1734–1795
OBSERVATIONS ON DOCTOR PRIESTLEY'S DOCTRINES OF PHILOSOPHICAL NECESSITY AND
MATERIALISM. BY JAMES PURVES.

> *Philadelphia: Printed by Thomas Dobson, at the Stone House No.* 41 *South*
> *Second-Street.* 1797. pp. 244. 12mo.   AAS. NYPL. PTS. WIPL.

32733   RADCLIFFE, ANN WARD   1764–1822
THE CASTLES OF ATHLIN AND DUNBAYNE, A HIGHLAND STORY. BY ANN RADCLIFFE,
AUTHOR OF THE SICILIAN ROMANCE, ROMANCE OF THE FOREST, &C. &C.

> *Boston: Sold by David West.* 1797.

32734   —— THE ITALIAN, OR THE CONFESSIONAL OF THE BLACK PENITENTS. A ROMANCE.
BY MRS. ANN RADCLIFFE.

> *Boston: Printed ? by Samuel Etheridge.* 1797.

Proposals were made July 18, 1797, by Samuel Etheridge, Boston: "The
three volumes to be comprised in six numbers, containing at least 144
pages each, with an engraving by an American artist in the last number.

32735   —— – THE ITALIAN; OR, THE CONFESSIONAL OF THE BLACK PENITENTS. A ROMANCE.
BY ANN RADCLIFFE, AUTHOR OF THE MYSTERIES OF UDOLPHO, &C.

> *Mount-Pleasant, New-York: Printed by William Durell.* 1797. 2vols. 12mo.

32736   —— — THE ITALIAN; OR, THE CONFESSIONAL OF THE BLACK PENITENTS. A ROMANCE.
BY ANN RADCLIFFE.

> *New-York: Printed by Thomas Greenleaf.* 1797. 2vols. 12mo.

32737   RADCLIFFE, ANN WARD, continued.
—— — THE ITALIAN; OR, THE CONFESSIONAL OF THE BLACK PENITENTS. A ROMANCE. BY ANN RADCLIFFE, AUTHOR OF THE ROMANCE OF THE FOREST, &C. &C. [Five lines of verse.]
> *Philadelphia: Printed for Mathew Carey, No. 118, Market-Street. 1797.* 2vols. 12mo.

32738   —— — THE ITALIAN, OR, THE CONFESSIONAL OF THE BLACK PENITENTS. A ROMANCE. BY ANN RADCLIFFE, AUTHOR OF THE MYSTERIES OF UDOLPHO, &C. &C. [Five lines of verse.] IN TWO VOLUMES. VOL. I. [— II.]
> *Philadelphia: Printed by Richard Folwell, for H. and P. Rice, and Robert Campbell and Co.* M,DCC,XCVII. 2 vols. pp.——; 363, (1). 12mo.   AAS.

32739   RANLET, HENRY
THE GENTLEMAN'S POCKET ALMANACK, FOR . . . 1798 TO WHICH IS ADDED A REGISTER OF NEW-HAMPSHIRE.
> *Printed at Exeter by H. Ranlet.* [1797.] pp. (108). 12mo.   NHSL.

32740   RASPE, RUDOLF ERICH   1737–1794
GULLIVER REVIVED; CONTAINING SINGULAR TRAVELS, CAMPAIGNS, VOYAGES AND ADVENTURES, IN RUSSIA, ICELAND, TURKEY, EGYPT, GIBRALTAR, UP THE MEDITERRANEAN, AND THE ATLANTIC OCEAN: ALSO AN ACCOUNT OF A VOYAGE INTO THE MOON, WITH MANY EXTRAORDINARY PARTICULARS RELATIVE TO THE COOKING ANIMALS IN THAT PLANET, WHICH ARE HERE CALLED THE HUMAN SPECIES. BY BARON MUNCHAUSEN.
> *New-York: 1797.* 18mo.

32741   A REAL TREASURE FOR THE PIOUS MIND. COMPILED BY A LADY OF CONNECTICUT. FROM THE COLLECTIONS AND WRITINGS OF THE COUNTESS OF HUNTINGDON, MRS. ROWE, MISS HARVEY, MR. PERIN, AND MR. SMITH.
> *Hartford: Printed by John Babcock.* 1797. pp. 96. 12mo.   AAS. JCB. NYPL.

32742   REEVE, CLARA   1729–1807
THE OLD ENGLISH BARON, A GOTHIC STORY. FIRST AMERICAN EDITION.
> *Philadelphia: Printed and sold by Stewart & Cochran, No. 34, South Second-street.* M,DCC,XCVII. pp. 213, (3). 12mo.   AAS.

Contains, a three-page list of Books for sale by Stewart and Cochran.

32743   REEVE, JOHN   1608–1658
A TRANSCENDENT SPIRITUAL TREATISE UPON SEVERAL HEAVENLY DOCTRINES, FROM THE HOLY SPIRIT OF THE MAN JESUS, SENT UNTO ALL HIS ELECT . . . BY THE HAND OF HIS OWN PROPHET . . . THE SECOND AMERICAN EDITION.
> *New-London: Printed by James Springer, for Isaac Walden, Carter's Island.* 1797. pp. 38. 16mo.

A few lines, by way of advertisement, are prefixed by Walden,—who was a basket-maker by trade, living on an island in the Thames River below Norwich, a half recluse, and a devout Muggletonian.

32744   REFLECTIONS ON THE PROPOSITION TO COMMUNICATE, BY A NAVIGABLE CANAL, THE WATERS OF CHESAPEAKE WITH THOSE OF DELAWARE BAY, ADDRESSED TO THE CITIZENS OF MARYLAND. TO WHICH IS PREFIXED THE BILL, AS PUBLISHED FOR CONSIDERATION BY ORDER OF THE HOUSE OF DELEGATES.
> *Annapolis: Printed by Frederick Green, Printer to the State.* [1797.] pp. 50. 8vo.

32745   REFORMED DUTCH CHURCH IN THE UNITED STATES OF AMERICA.
ACTS AND PROCEEDINGS OF THE GENERAL SYNOD OF THE REFORMED DUTCH CHURCH
IN THE UNITED STATES OF AMERICA.
     New-York: 1797.

32746   RELF, SAMUEL   1776–1823
INFIDELITY, OR THE VICTIMS OF SENTIMENT. A NOVEL, IN A SERIES OF LETTERS.
[One line from] YOUNG.
     Philadelphia: Printed by W. W. Woodward, No. 17, Chesnut-street. 1797.
pp. 190, (1). 12mo.   AAS.
     172d Pennsylvania District Copyright, issued to Samuel Relf, as Author,
21 February, 1797. Contains, a list of Subscribers' names.

32747   THE REMEMBRANCER, FOR LORD'S DAY EVENING, DESIGNED TO BE CONTINUED
FOR TWO YEARS. BY JOSEPH BROWN, PASTOR OF THE SECOND CHURCH IN EXETER,
NEW-HAMPSHIRE. No. 1. FOR LORD'S DAY EVENING, JANUARY 1, 1797. [— No. 8.
FOR LORD'S DAY EVENING, MARCH 20, 1797.]
     *Exeter: Printed by Henry Ranlet. [To be sold by Thomas and Andrews, and
David West, Boston.]* 1797. pp. 64. 8vo.   BA.
     An original weekly periodical work, each number of eight pages, two
hundred copies, certainly continued to No. 8, for March 20, 1797, when
advance subscriptions of one dollar were solicited to continue the work.

32748   THE REPUBLICAN CITIZEN, AND FARMER AND PLANTER'S CHRONICLE. [Motto.]
VOL. I. NUMB. XXVI. WEDNESDAY, JANUARY 4, [—VOL. II. NUMB. 55. WEDNES-
DAY, JUNE 14, 1797.]
     *Fredericksburg, (Va.): Published [every Wednesday] by Lancelot A. Mullin.
[Market-Street, west corner of the upper Tobacco Inspection.]* 1797. fol.
     The above is the last number located.

32749   REPUBLICAN GAZETTEER. [Motto.] VOL. I. NUMB. 7. TUESDAY, JANUARY 3, [—
NUMB. 9. TUESDAY, JANUARY 17, 1797.]
     Printed by Moses Davis, Concord, Newhampshire. 1797. fol.
     With the issue for January 24th, Elijah Russell re-entered the firm, and
the title was changed to *Russel & Davis' Republican Gazetteer.*

32750   REPUBLICAN JOURNAL. [Motto.] VOL. I. No. 14. MONDAY, JANUARY 2, [—VOL. II.
No. 62. MONDAY, DECEMBER 25, 1797.]
     *Printed, & published by Douglas & Nichols, near the Court-House, in Dan-
bury.* 1797. fol.   AAS.

32751   RHODE ISLAND. STATE.
FEBRUARY, 1797. AT THE GENERAL ASSEMBLY OF THE GOVERNOR AND COMPANY OF
THE STATE OF RHODE-ISLAND, AND PROVIDENCE-PLANTATIONS, BEGUN AND HOLDEN,
BY ADJOURNMENT, AT EAST-GREENWICH, WITHIN AND FOR THE STATE AFORESAID,
ON THE LAST MONDAY IN FEBRUARY, IN THE YEAR OF OUR LORD ONE THOUSAND
SEVEN HUNDRED AND NINETY-SEVEN, AND IN THE TWENTY-FIRST YEAR OF INDE-
PENDENCE. [Colophon:]
     Warren (Rhode-Island): Printed by Nathaniel Phillips, Printer to the State.
[1797.] pp. 42. fol.   AAS. JCB. LOC. RIHS.

32752   —— MAY, 1797. AT THE GENERAL ASSEMBLY OF THE GOVERNOR AND COMPANY OF
THE STATE OF RHODE-ISLAND, AND PROVIDENCE PLANTATIONS, BEGUN AND HOLDEN,
AT NEWPORT, WITHIN AND FOR THE STATE AFORESAID, ON THE FIRST WEDNESDAY
IN MAY, IN THE YEAR OF OUR LORD ONE THOUSAND SEVEN HUNDRED AND NINETY-
SEVEN, AND IN THE TWENTY-FIRST YEAR OF INDEPENDENCE. [Colophon:]
     Warren (Rhode-Island): Printed by Nathaniel Phillips, Printer to the State.
[1797.] pp. 27. fol.   AAS. JCB. LOC. RIHS.

RHODE ISLAND, STATE, continued.

32753 —— JUNE, 1797. AT THE GENERAL ASSEMBLY OF THE GOVERNOR AND COMPANY OF THE STATE OF RHODE-ISLAND, AND PROVIDENCE-PLANTATIONS, BEGUN AND HOLDEN, BY ADJOURNMENT, AT NEWPORT, WITHIN AND FOR THE STATE AFORESAID, ON THE FOURTH MONDAY IN JUNE, IN THE YEAR OF OUR LORD ONE THOUSAND SEVEN HUNDRED AND NINETY-SEVEN, AND IN THE TWENTY-FIRST YEAR OF INDEPENDENCE. [Colophon:]
Warren (Rhode-Island): Printed by Nathaniel Phillips, Printer to the State. [1797.] pp. 20. fol.   AAS. JCB. LOC. RIHS.

32754 —— OCTOBER, 1797. AT THE GENERAL ASSEMBLY OF THE GOVERNOR AND COMPANY OF THE STATE OF RHODE-ISLAND, AND PROVIDENCE-PLANTATIONS, BEGUN AND HOLDEN, AT SOUTH-KINGSTOWN, WITHIN AND FOR THE STATE AFORESAID, ON THE LAST WEDNESDAY IN OCTOBER, IN THE YEAR OF OUR LORD ONE THOUSAND SEVEN HUNDRED AND NINETY-SEVEN, AND IN THE TWENTY-SECOND YEAR OF INDEPENDENCE. [Colophon:]
Warren (Rhode-Island): Printed by Nathaniel Phillips, Printer to the State. [1797.] pp. 32. fol.   AAS. JCB. LOC. RIHS.

32755 —— STATE OF RHODE ISLAND, &c. IN GENERAL ASSEMBLY. OCTOBER SESSION, A. D. 1797. AN ACT FOR FURNISHING THE QUOTA OF THIS STATE OF THE DETACHMENT OF MILITIA, ORDERED BY CONGRESS. [Colophon:]
Providence: Printed by Carter and Wilkinson. [1797.] Broadside.   RIHS.

32756 —— STATE OF RHODE ISLAND, &c. IN GENERAL ASSEMBLY. OCTOBER SESSION, A. D. 1797. AN ACT FOR GRANTING AND APPORTIONING A TAX OF TWENTY THOUSAND DOLLARS, UPON THE INHABITANTS OF THIS STATE. [Colophon:]
Warren (Rhode Island.) Printed by Nathaniel Phillips, Printer to the State. [1797.] Broadside.   RIHS.

32757 —— STATE OF RHODE ISLAND, &c. NOVEMBER 6, 1797. THE FOLLOWING ARE THE ALLOWANCES TO BE MADE TO THE OFFICERS AND SOLDIERS OF THIS STATE'S QUOTA OF THE MILITIA, ORDERED BY AN ACT OF THE GENERAL ASSEMBLY, PASSED AT OCTOBER SESSION LAST, AS THIS STATE'S PROPORTION OF MILITIA DIRECTED TO BE HOLDEN IN READINESS BY AN ACT OF CONGRESS, PASSED JUNE 24TH, A. D. 1797, IN CASE THIS SAID STATE'S QUOTA SHALL BE CALLED INTO ACTUAL SERVICE, TO WIT: [Thirty-one lines.] Witness, HENRY WARD, SEC'RY. [Colophon:]
[Providence:] Printed by Carter and Wilkinson. [1797.] Broadside. fol.   AAS. RIHS.
Reproduced in facsimile.

32758 —— BY HIS EXCELLENCY ARTHUR FENNER, ESQUIRE, GOVERNOR, CAPTAIN-GENERAL, AND COMMANDER IN CHIEF OF THE STATE OF RHODE-ISLAND, AND PROVIDENCE-PLANTATIONS. A PROCLAMATION. WHEREAS THE GENERAL ASSEMBLY . . . [Appointing, "Thursday, the thirtieth day of November a day of thanksgiving."] GIVEN UNDER MY HAND, AND THE SEAL OF THE SAID STATE, AT PROVIDENCE, THIS THIRTIETH DAY OF OCTOBER, IN THE YEAR OF OUR LORD ONE THOUSAND SEVEN HUNDRED AND NINETY-SEVEN. [Colophon:]
Warren: Printed by Nathaniel Phillips, Printer to the State. [1797.] Broadside. fol.   JCB. RIHS.

32759 —— STATE OF RHODE ISLAND AND PROVIDENCE PLANTATIONS. TO THE FREEMEN OF THE STATE AFORESAID, JULY 24, 1797. [Resignation of Elisha R. Potter, as a member of the Congress.]
[Providence: Printed by Carter and Wilkinson. 1797.] Broadside. 4to. RIHS.

32760 RHODE ISLAND. College of, now Brown University.
Commencement of Rhode-Island College, September 6, 1797. Order of the day.
[*Providence:*] *Printed by Carter and Wilkinson.* [1797.] Broadside. fol. BU.

32761 —— Illustrissimo Jabez Bowen, armigero Collegii Rhod-Insulæ quod Providentiæ est, cancellario; reverendo Jonathani Maxcy. s. t. p. præsidi; [Three lines.] Hæcce philosophemata juvenes in artibus initiati, [Twenty-three names] humillimè dedicant. [Three columns.] [Colophon:]
Habita in Solennibus Academicis Providentiæ Rep. Ins. Rhod. et Prov. Plant. die sexto Septembris, A.D. M,DCC,XCVII. *Rerumque publicarum fœderatarum Americæ summæ potestatis* xxii. *Providentiæ: Typis Carter et Wilkinson.* Broadside. fol. AAS. BU.
Reproduced in facsimile.

32762 RICHARD, Old Father, pseudonym.
Poor Richard revived: or Barber & Southwick's Almanack, for the year of our Lord, 1798; calculated for the meridian of the State of New-York, but will answer for the neighbouring States of Vermont, Connecticut, &c. &c. By Old Father Richard, mathemat.
Albany: Printed and sold by Barber & Southwick. [1797.] pp. (36). 12mo. AAS. HC.

32763 RICHARDSON, Samuel. 1689–1761
The History of Pamela; or, virtue rewarded. Abridged from the works of Samuel Richardson, esquire. Adorned with [six full-page] cuts. [Ornament.]
Boston: Printed and sold by S. Hall, in Cornhill. 1797. pp. 142. 24mo. AAS.

32764 —— The History of sir Charles Grandison. Abridged from the works of Samuel Richardson.
Suffield, Connecticut: Printed by H. & O. Farnsworth. 1797. 12mo.

32765 RICHMOND. Virginia. St. John's Lodge.
By-laws of St. John's Lodge, no. 36. Passed unanimously, October 7, A. L. 5737,—A. D. 1797. Printed by order of the Lodge, October, 1797. [Ornament.]
Richmond: Printed by Thomas Nicolson. M,DCC,XCVII. pp. 11, (1). 12mo. LOC.

32766 RIGG, Edward
The New American Latin grammar. By Edward Rigg, teacher of a grammar school in New-York.
New-York: Printed and sold by Hugh Gaine, at the Bible, in Pearl-Street. 1797. 12mo.

32767 THE RIGHTS of man. For the use and benefit of all mankind.
Philadelphia: 1797. pp. iv, 56. 8vo. BM.

32768 RIGHTS of man:—By John Winter. Vol. iii. No. 155. Wednesday, January 4, [— Vol. iv. No. 206. Wednesday, December 27, 1797.]
Frederick-Town (Maryland): Printed by John Winter, at his Office, in Patrick-Street. . . . 1797. fol.

32769   RIGHTS OF MAN, OR THE KENTUCKY MERCURY. VOL. I. No. 1. WEDNESDAY, MAY 31, [— No. 31. WEDNESDAY, DECEMBER 27, 1797.]
Paris: Printed by Darius Moffett. 1797. fol.   HC.
Established, as a weekly, by Darius Moffett and continued by him to January 10, 1798—the last number located.

32770   RISING SUN. VOL. IV. No. 172. FRIDAY, JANUARY 6, [— VOL. V. No. 223. SATURDAY, DECEMBER 30, 1797.]
Kingston, (Ulster County). Printed by William Copp and Samuel Freer. 1797. fol.

32771   THE RISING SUN. [Motto.] VOL. II. No. 22. WHOLE NO. 74. TUESDAY, JANUARY 3, [—VOL. III. No. 21. WHOLE NO. 125. SATURDAY, DECEMBER 30, 1797.]
[Printed and published] By Cornelius Sturtevant jun. & Co. Keene, (New-hampshire). 1797. fol.   AAS.
In August the day of publication was changed to Saturday.

32772   ROBBINS, CHANDLER   1738–1799
A SERMON, PREACHED AT THE ORDINATION OF THE REV. WARD COTTON, TO THE PASTORAL CARE OF THE FIRST CHURCH AND SOCIETY IN BOYLSTON, JUNE 6, 1797. BY CHANDLER ROBBINS, D. D. PASTOR OF A CHURCH IN PLYMOUTH.
Printed at Worcester, Massachusetts, at the Press of Isaiah Thomas, by Leonard Worcester, for said Thomas. 1797. pp. 34. 8vo.
      AAS. BA. BM. BPL. BU. JCB. NYPL. YC.
The Charge, by the Rev. Mr. Whitney, of Northborough. The Right hand of fellowship, by the Rev. Aaron Bancroft, of Worcester.

32773   ROCHAMBEAU, MARIE JOSEPH DONATIEN DE VIMEUR, vicomte de DONATIEN, called RÉPONSE DU GÉNÉRAL ROCHAMBEAU, A L'ARRÊTÉ DES AGENS PARTICULIERS DU DIRECTOIRE EXECUTIF À ST. DOMINGUE. [Dated at end, Bordeaux, le 9 Pluviose, an V de la R. F. une et indivisible.]
a Philadelphie, De L'Imprimerie de Parent, Cinquieme rue Sud No. 32, [1797.] pp. (2), 10. 8vo.   JCB.

32774   ROCK, EDMUND
ESSAY, POEMS AND LETTERS. BY EDMUND ROCK, SECRETARY FOR THE SOCIETY FOR THE ENCOURAGEMENT OF AGRICULTURE, ARTS, MANUFACTURE, AND COMMERCE, AND TO THE PHILOSOPHICAL SOCIETY LATELY INSTITUTED AT BATH, ENGLAND, AND AUTHOR OF MENTOR'S LETTERS TO YOUTH.
Wiscasset, (District of Maine). Printed by Henry Hoskins. 1797. pp. 500. 8vo.
Proposals for printing the above were made in February 1797.

32775   ROCKWELL, SAMUEL
AN ORATION, DELIVERED AT THE CELEBRATION OF AMERICAN INDEPENDENCE, AT SALISBURY, FOURTH JULY, NINETY-SEVEN. BY DR. SAMUEL ROCKWELL. PUBLISHED AT THE REQUEST OF THE COMMITTEE.
Litchfield: Printed by T. Collier. [1797.] pp. 16. 8vo.   LOC. NYPL.

32776   ROGERS, TIMOTHY   1658–1728
THE RIGHTEOUS MAN'S EVIDENCE FOR HEAVEN: OR, A TREATIES SHEWING HOW EVERY ONE, WHILE HE LIVES HERE, MAY CERTAINLY KNOW WHAT SHALL BECOME OF HIM AFTER HIS DEPARTURE OUT OF THIS LIFE. BY TIMOTHY ROGERS. PREACHER OF GOD'S WORD IN ESSEX. [Six lines of Scripture texts.]
West-Springfield: Printed by Edward Gray, for Nathaniel Patten; sold by said Patten, at his Bookstore in Hartford, and by E. Gray, in West-Springfield. 1797. pp. 132, (1). 24mo.   AAS.

32777 ROMAN CATHOLIC CHURCH.
NOUVELLES ÉTRENNES SPIRITUELLES SELON L'USAGE DE ROME. [In Latin and French.]
a Philadelphie: Imprime par Moreau de St.-Mery. 1797. 12mo.

32778 ROSCOE, WILLIAM 1753–1831
STRICTURES ON MR. BURKE'S TWO LETTERS, ADDRESSED TO A MEMBER OF THE PRESENT
PARLIAMENT: ON THE PROPOSALS FOR PEACE WITH THE "REGICIDE DIRECTORY OF
FRANCE." PART THE FIRST.
*Philadelphia: Printed by John Thompson, and sold by the Booksellers of
Philadelphia, New York, and Baltimore.* 1797. pp. iv, [50.] 8vo. LOC. NYHS.

32779 ROULSTONE'S KNOXVILLE GAZETTE, AND WEEKLY ADVERTISER. NO. 10. MONDAY,
JANUARY 2, [— NO. 34. MONDAY, JUNE 19, 1797.]
Knoxville, [State of Tennessee.] Published by George Roulstone. 1797. fol.
The above is the last number located. Succeeded in June, 1798, by *The
Knoxville Register.*

32780 ROUSSEAU, JEAN JACQUES 1711–1778
A DISSERTATION ON POLITICAL ECONOMY; TO WHICH IS ADDED, A TREATISE ON THE
SOCIAL COMPACT; OR, THE PRINCIPLES OF POLITIC LAW. BY JEAN JACQUES ROUS-
SEAU, CITIZEN OF GENEVA. THE FIRST AMERICAN EDITION. COMPILED FROM THE
WORKS OF THE AUTHOR.
*Albany: Printed and sold by Barber & Southwick, at Faust's Statue, State
Street.* 1797. pp. 72; 214, (2), portrait. 12mo. NYPL.
Contains a List of Subscribers.

32781 ROWSON, SUSANNA HASWELL 1762–1824
CHARLOTTE TEMPLE. A TALE OF TRUTH. BY MRS. ROWSON, LATE OF THE NEW THE-
ATRE, PHILADELPHIA; AUTHOR OF VICTORIA, THE INQUISITOR, FILLE DE CHAMBRE,
&C. TWO VOLUMES IN ONE. [Seven lines of quotations.] VOL. I. [— II.] THIRD
AMERICAN EDITION.
Philadelphia: Printed for Mathew Carey, by Stephen C. Ustick. August 24,
1797. 2 vols. in one. pp. 204. 12mo. AAS. LOC.

32782 RUDDOCK, SAMUEL A.
VALUABLE TABLES; SHEWING THE VALUE OF ANY NUMBER OF CENTS FROM ONE TO ONE
HUNDRED, IN SHILLINGS, PENCE AND FARTHINGS; AND FOR SHEWING THE VALUE OF
FRENCH, SPANISH, ENGLISH AND PORTUGUESE GOLD, IN DOLLARS, CENTS, AND MILLS.
ALSO, A TABLE OF SIMPLE INTEREST, AT SIX PER CENT. PER ANN. FOR ANY SUM FROM
ONE HALF DOLLAR, TO ONE THOUSAND, IN DOLLARS, DIMES, CENTS AND MILLS.
Putney, Vermont: Printed by Cornelius Sturtevant jun. & Co. 1797.

32783 THE RURAL REPOSITORY. [Motto.] VOL. II. NO. 64. THURSDAY, JANUARY 5, [—
VOL. II. NO. 78. THURSDAY, APRIL 13, 1797.]
*Published every Thursday by Charles Prentiss, south of the meeting house, in
Leominster (Massachusetts.)* 1797. fol. AAS.
Discontinued in April, as above, for want of support.

32784 RUSH, BENJAMIN 1745–1813
MEDICAL INQUIRIES AND OBSERVATIONS. BY BENJAMIN RUSH, M. D. PROFESSOR OF
THE INSTITUTES OF MEDICINE, AND OF CLINICAL PRACTICE IN THE UNIVERSITY OF
PENNSYLVANIA. VOLUME II. A NEW [second American] EDITION.
*Philadelphia: Printed by Thomas Dobson, at the Stone House, No. 41, South
Second-Street.* M,DCC,XCVII. pp. vii, (1), 322, (2). 8vo. AAS. NYPL.
The first volume of this edition was published in Philadelphia, in 1794.

32785   RUSHTON, EDWARD   1756–1814
AN EXPOSTULATORY LETTER TO GEORGE WASHINGTON, OF MOUNT VERNON. BY ED-
WARD RUSHTON, OF LIVERPOOL, FEBRUARY 20, 1797. [On the inconsistency of
Washington being a slave owner.]
     Lexington: Printed by John Bradford. 1797.

32786   —— — EXPOSTULATORY LETTER TO GEORGE WASHINGTON, OF VIRGINIA. BY ED-
WARD RUSHTON, OF LIVERPOOL, FEBRUARY 20, 1797. [An appeal to the moral
sentiments of mankind, on the subject of absolute slavery, and the inconsistency
of Washington being a slave owner.]
     [New-York? 1797.] Broadside. fol.   BM. NYPL.

32787   RUSSEL, ROBERT
SEVEN SERMONS; VIZ. I. OF THE UNPARDONABLE SIN AGAINST THE HOLY GHOST; OR,
THE SIN UNTO DEATH. II. THE SAINT'S DUTY AND EXERCISE: IN TWO PARTS. BEING
AN EXHORTATION TO, AND DIRECTION FOR PRAYER. III. THE ACCEPTED TIME AND
DAY OF SALVATION. IV. THE END OF TIME, AND BEGINNING OF ETERNITY. V. JOSHUA'S
RESOLUTION TO SERVE THE LORD. VI. THE WAY TO HEAVEN MADE PLAIN. VII. THE
FUTURE STATE OF MAN; OR, A TREATISE ON THE RESURRECTION. BY ROBERT RUS-
SEL, AT WADHURST, IN SUSSEX. [Ornament.]
     *Leominster, (Massachusetts). Printed by Charles Prentiss, for Robert B.
Thomas, Sterling. 1797.* pp. 152. 16mo.   AAS. JCB.

32788   —— — SEVEN SERMONS, VIZ. I. OF THE UNPARDONABLE SIN AGAINST THE HOLY
GHOST; OR, THE SIN UNTO DEATH. II. THE SAINT'S DUTY AND EXERCISE; IN TWO
PARTS. BEING AN EXHORTATION TO, AND DIRECTION FOR PRAYER. III. THE AC-
CEPTED TIME AND DAY OF SALVATION. IV. THE END OF TIME, AND BEGINNING
OF ETERNITY. V. JOSHUA'S RESOLUTION TO SERVE THE LORD. VI. THE WAY TO
HEAVEN MADE PLAIN. VII. THE FUTURE STATE OF MAN; OR, A TREATISE ON THE
RESURRECTION. BY ROBERT RUSSEL, AT WADHURST, IN SUSSEX.
     Wilmington, Delaware: Printed by Peter Brynberg. 1797. 18mo.

32789   RUSSEL & DAVIS' REPUBLICAN GAZETTEER. [Motto.] VOL. I. NUMB. 10. TUESDAY.
JANUARY 24, [— NUMB. 20. TUESDAY, APRIL 4, 1797.]
     Printed by Russel & Davis, Concord, Newhampshire. 1797. fol.

     With the issue for April 11th, the publishers changed the form, and the
title to *The New Star.*

32790   RUSSELL, JOHN MILLER   –1840
AN ORATION, PRONOUNCED AT CHARLESTOWN, JULY 4, 1797. AT THE REQUEST OF
THE SELECTMEN, ARTILLERY COMPANY, AND TRUSTEES OF THE SCHOOL IN SAID
TOWN, IN COMMEMORATION OF THE ANNIVERSARY OF AMERICAN INDEPENDENCE.
[Ornament.] BY JOHN MILLER RUSSELL.
     Charlestown: Printed by J. Lamson, at his Office, near the Bridge. [1797.]
pp. 16. 8vo.   AAS. BM. HC. JCB. LOC. MHS.

32791   —— — AN ORATION, PRONOUNCED AT CHARLESTOWN, JULY 4, 1797. AT THE RE-
QUEST OF THE SELECTMEN, ARTILLERY COMPANY, AND TRUSTEES OF THE SCHOOL IN
SAID TOWN, IN COMMEMORATION OF THE ANNIVERSARY OF AMERICAN INDEPEN-
DENCE. BY JOHN MILLER RUSSELL. THE SECOND EDITION.
     Philadelphia: Printed by William Cobbett, opposite Christ Church. 1797. pp.
15. 8vo.   BA. MHS.

32792   THE RUTLAND HERALD: A REGISTER OF THE TIMES. [Motto.] VOL. III. No. 5.
MONDAY, JANUARY 2, [— VOL. IV. No. 4. MONDAY, DECEMBER 25, 1797.]
    *Rutland, Vermont:—Printed by John S. Hutchins, for S. Williams & Co. a
few rods south of the State House.* 1797. fol.   AAS.

> In January, the partnership of Doctor Samuel Williams, and Samuel
> Williams, esquire, was dissolved by mutual consent, the latter withdraw-
> ing. On February 21st, Hutchins was succeeded by Josiah Fay, as
> printer, who formed a partnership on that day with Doctor Samuel Wil-
> liams. In March, the paper was "Printed by Josiah Fay, for Williams
> & Fay." Which was changed, in September, to "Printed by Josiah Fay,
> for S. Williams & Co.

32793   RYCAUT, Sir PAUL   –1700
THE COUNTERFEIT MESSIAH; OR FALSE CHRIST, OF THE JEWS AT SMYRNA; IN THE
YEAR 1666. WRITTEN BY AN ENGLISH PERSON OF QUALITY THERE RESIDENT; SOON
AFTER THE AFFAIR HAPPENED.
    Putney, Vermont: Printed by Cornelius Sturtevant jun. & Co. 1797. pp. 36.
12mo.

32794   SAINT LAMBERT, JEAN FRANÇOIS DE   1716–1803
THE STORY OF SARAH PHILLIPS. A NOVEL. BY M. DE SAINT LAMBERT.
    Wiscasset, (District of Maine). Printed? by Henry Hoskins & John W. Scott.
1797.

32795   SAINT PIERRE, JACQUES HENRI BERNARDIN DE   1737–1814
BOTANICAL HARMONY DELINEATED: OR, APPLICATIONS OF SOME GENERAL LAWS OF
NATURE TO PLANTS. ILLUSTRATED WITH PLATES.—BY JAMES HENRY BERNARDIN
DE SAINT PIERRE, AUTHOR OF THE STUDIES OF NATURE. TRANSLATED BY HENRY
HUNTER, D. D. MINISTER OF THE SCOTS CHURCH, LONDON WALL. FIRST AMERI-
CAN EDITION.
    *Worcester: Printed [by Thomas, Son & Thomas] for J. Nancrede, No. 49,
Marlborough Street.* 1797. pp. 179. 12mo.   AAS. BA. BM. BPL. NYPL.

> Colophon: Printed at Worcester, Massachusetts, by Thomas, Son &
> Thomas. In this separate form, the three plates which illustrate it in
> 'Studies of Nature' are omitted.

32796   —— STUDIES OF NATURE. BY JAMES HENRY BERNARDIN DE ST. PIERRE. MISERIS
SUCCURRERE DISCO. TRANSLATED BY HENRY HUNTER, D.D. MINISTER OF THE SCOTS
CHURCH, LONDON WALL. FIRST AMERICAN EDITION. IN THREE VOLUMES. VOL. I.
    *Worcester: Printed [by Thomas, Son & Thomas] for J. Nancrede, Marlbor-
ough Street, Boston.* 1797. pp. (2), lxiii, 395, frontispiece. 8vo.
                                                AAS. BM. BPL. HC. NYPL.

32797   —— A VINDICATION OF DIVINE PROVIDENCE; DERIVED FROM A PHILOSOPHIC AND
MORAL SURVEY OF NATURE AND OF MAN. BY JAMES HENRY BERNARDIN DE SAINT
PIERRE. AUTHOR OF THE STUDIES OF NATURE.—MISERIS SUCCURRERE DISCO.
TRANSLATED BY HENRY HUNTER, D. D. MINISTER OF THE SCOTS CHURCH, LONDON
WALL. FIRST AMERICAN EDITION. VOL. I. [— II.]
    *Worcester: Printed [by Thomas, Son & Thomas] for J. Nancrede, No. 49,
Marlborough Street, Boston.* 1797. 2 vols. pp. (2), 331, 2 plates; 432, 3 plates.
8vo.   AAS. JCB. NYPL.

> "Compiled from those parts of the 'Studies of Nature' which relate to
> the subject of religion."

32798   SALAS BARBADILLO, ALONSO JERÓNIMO   1580–1635
THE LUCKY IDIOT: OR, FOOLS HAVE FORTUNE. VERIFIED IN THE LIFE OF D. PEDRO DE CENUDO. WHOSE FOLLIES HAD GENERALLY A PROSPEROUS EVENT: BUT WHEN HE PRETENDED TO BE WISE WAS USUALLY UNFORTUNATE. IMPROVED WITH VARIETY OF MORAL REMARKS, AND DIVERTING AMUSEMENTS. WRITTEN IN SPANISH BY DON QUEVEDO DE ALCALA. [Two lines of Latin quotation.]
> *Worcester, Massachusetts: Printed for the Purchasers.* 1797. pp. 144. 24mo.
> AAS. NYPL.

32799   SALEM. MASSACHUSETTS. AQUEDUCT.
RULES AND REGULATIONS OF THE PROPRIETORS OF THE SALEM AND DANVERS AQUEDUCT, 1797.
> [*Salem: Printed by Thomas C. Cushing,* 1797.] Broadside.   EI.

32800   SALEM. MASSACHUSETTS. SOCIAL LIBRARY.
BYLAWS AND REGULATIONS OF THE INCORPORATED PROPRIETORS OF THE SOCIAL LIBRARY IN SALEM. [With Catalogue.]
> [*Salem: Printed by Thomas C. Cushing.* 1797.] pp. 32. 8vo.   BA. EI. HC.

32801   THE SALEM GAZETTE. VOLUME XI. NUMBER 565. TUESDAY, JANUARY 3, [— NUMBER 668. FRIDAY, DECEMBER, 29, 1797.]
> *Printed and published every Tuesday and Friday, by William Carlton, Essex-Street, between Washington and Market-Streets, Salem, Massachusetts.* 1797. fol.
> AAS. EI. HC. LOC.

     On July 28th, without any editorial announcement of the change, Thomas C. Cushing resumed the printing and publishing of the Gazette.

32802   SAMPSON, EZRA   1749–1823
A SERMON ON THE DEATH OF MISS OLIVE SOULE, . . . OF PLYMPTON, WHO DEPARTED THIS LIFE, JANUARY 30TH, 1795, IN THE 19TH YEAR OF HER AGE.
> *New-Bedford: Printed by John Spooner.* 1797. pp. 11. 8vo.   BM.

32803   SANDABAD or SINDBAD.
HISTORY OF THE SEVEN WISE MASTERS OF ROME, CONTAINING MANY INGENIOUS AND ENTERTAINING STORIES, WHEREIN THE TREACHERY OF EVIL COUNSELLORS IS DISCOVERED, INNOCENCY CLEARED, AND THE WISDOM OF THE SEVEN WISE MASTERS DISPLAYED.
> *Wilmington: Printed by Peter Brynberg.* 1797.

32804   SAUNDERS, DANIEL, JUNIOR
A JOURNAL OF THE TRAVELS AND SUFFERINGS OF DANIEL SAUNDERS, JUN. A MARINER ON BOARD THE SHIP COMMERCE, OF BOSTON, SAMUEL JOHNSON, COMMANDER, WHICH WAS CAST AWAY NEAR CAPE MOREBET, ON THE COAST OF ARABIA, JULY 10, 1792.
> *Leominster, (Massachusetts): Printed by Charles Prentiss, for Robert B. Thomas, Sterling.* 1797. pp. 104, 21. 18mo.   AAS. BPL. HC. JCB. NYPL.

     Dated, Salem, November, 1794. The Appendix is separately paged, and contains An Account of the manners and customs of the Arabs and "Bedoweens" or wild Arabs. Reprinted in Salem in 1824, and in a sixth edition in Exeter, New Hampshire, in 1830.

32805   SAUNDERS, WILLIAM   1743–1817
A TREATISE ON THE STRUCTURE, ECONOMY, AND DISEASES OF THE LIVER; TOGETHER WITH AN INQUIRY INTO THE PROPERTIES AND COMPONENT PARTS OF THE BILE AND BILIARY CONCRETIONS. BY WILLIAM SAUNDERS, M. D. F. R. S. FELLOW OF THE COLLEGE OF PHYSICIANS, AND SENIOR PHYSICIAN TO GUY'S HOSPITAL. FIRST AMERICAN, FROM SECOND LONDON EDITION, WITH CONSIDERABLE ADDITIONS.
> *Boston: Printed for W. Pelham, No. 59, Cornhill.* 1797. [Price one dollar.]
> pp. XX, 231. 12mo.   AAS. JCB. NYPL. SGO.

32806   SAVANNAH. GEORGIA.
THE FIRE ORDINANCE, AND PATROL LAW.
Savannah: Printed by N. Johnston and Co. [1797.]

32807   SAVERY, WILLIAM   1750–1804
THREE SERMONS PREACHED AT THE MEETING-HOUSE OF THE PEOPLE COMMONLY CALLED
QUAKERS, IN HOUNSDITCH, ON TUESDAY EVENING, JULY 19, 1796. THE TWO FIRST
BY WILLIAM SAVERY, AND THE LAST BY GEORGE DILLWYN, OF NORTH-AMERICA.
TAKEN IN SHORT-HAND BY JOB SIBLY. THE THIRD EDITION.
London, Printed; and New-York, Re-printed and sold by Isaac Collins, No.
189, Pearl-Street. 1797. pp. (55). 8vo.   AAS.

Second title: A SERMON PREACHED AT THE MEETING-HOUSE OF THE PEOPLE CALLED
QUAKERS, PETER'S-COURT, ST. MARTIN'S-LANE, ON THE LORD'S-DAY-EVENING, JULY
25TH, 1796. BY WILLIAM SAVERY, OF NORTH-AMERICA. TAKEN IN SHORT-HAND
BY JOB SIBLY.
London, Printed; and New-York, Reprinted and sold by Isaac Collins, No.
189, Pearl-Street. 1797. pp. (2), (21)–(36).

Third title: A SERMON, PREACHED BEFORE THE PEOPLE COMMONLY CALLED QUAK-
ERS, AT THE BOROUGH NEW-MARKET, ON THE LORD'S-DAY-EVENING, JULY 31ST,
1796. WITH THE PRAYER, BEFORE THE SERMON; BY WILLIAM SAVERY, OF NORTH-
AMERICA. TAKEN IN SHORT-HAND BY JOB SIBLY.
London, Printed; and New-York, Re-printed and sold by Isaac Collins, No.
189, Pearl-Street. 1797. pp. (2), (39)–(55).

32808   SCHNEIDER, PETER
MERKWÜRDIGE PROPHEZEYUNG EINES EINSIEDLERS, WELCHER 15 JAHRE ALLEIN IN
DER WÜSTEN-GEWOHNET. ENTDECKT VON DR. PETER SCHNEIDER. FÜNFTE AUF-
LAGE.
Ephrata: Gedruckt bey Salomon Mayer. 1797.

32809   EINE SCHÖNE SAMMLUNG DER NEUESTEN LIEDER ZUM GESELLSCHAFTLICHEN VERG-
NÜGEN.
Reading: Gedruckt bey Jungmann und Comp. 1797.
165th Pennsylvania District Copyright, issued to Gottlob Jungmann,
as Proprietor, 17 January, 1797.

32810   SCOTT, JOB   1751–1793
JOURNAL OF THE LIFE, TRAVELS AND GOSPEL LABOURS, OF THAT FAITHFUL SERVANT
AND MINISTER OF CHRIST, JOB SCOTT.
New-York: Printed and sold by Isaac Collins, No. 189, Pearl-Street. 1797.
pp. xii, (2), 360. 12mo.   AAS. BU. JCB. NYPL.

32811   —— — JOURNAL OF THE LIFE, TRAVELS AND GOSPEL LABOURS OF THAT FAITHFUL
SERVANT AND MINISTER OF CHRIST, JOB SCOTT.
Wilmington: Printed and sold by Bonsal & Niles. 1797. pp. x, (2), 324.
12mo.   WIPL.

32812   SCOTT, SARAH ROBINSON   –1795
THE MAN OF [real] SENSIBILITY: OR, THE HISTORY OF SIR GEORGE ELLISON. FOUNDED
ON FACT. [Five lines from] STERNE.
Philadelphia: Printed by H. Kammerer, jun. M,DCC,XCVII. pp. 92, (2).
12mo.   LOC.

AUCTION VALUES

32813   SCOTT, Thomas   1747–1821
A VINDICATION OF THE DIVINE INSPIRATION OF THE HOLY SCRIPTURES, AND OF THE DOCTRINES CONTAINED IN THEM: BEING AN ANSWER TO THE TWO PARTS OF MR. T. PAINE'S AGE OF REASON. BY THOMAS SCOTT, CHAPLAIN TO THE LOCK HOSPITAL, LONDON. [Five lines of Scripture texts.]
London, Printed: New-York, Re-printed by G. Forman, for C. Davis, Bookseller, No. 94, Water-Street.—1797.—pp. 202, (2). 12mo.   AAS. BU. JCB. NYPL.

32814   SCOTT, William
LESSONS IN ELOCUTION: OR A SELECTION OF PIECES, IN PROSE AND VERSE, FOR THE IMPROVEMENT OF YOUTH IN READING AND SPEAKING. BY WILLIAM SCOTT. THE SEVENTH AMERICAN EDITION. TO WHICH ARE PREFIXED, ELEMENTS OF GESTURE. ILLUSTRATED BY FOUR ELEGANT COPPER-PLATES; AND RULES FOR EXPRESSING, WITH PROPRIETY, THE VARIOUS PASSIONS AND EMOTIONS OF THE MIND. [By John Walker.]
Wilmington: Printed and sold by Peter Brynberg. M,D,CC,XCVII. pp. 383, 4 plates. 12mo.   AAS.

32815   SEABURY, Samuel   1729–1796
AN ADDRESS TO THE MINISTERS AND CONGREGATIONS OF THE PRESBYTERIAN AND INDEPENDENT PERSUASIONS IN THE UNITED STATES OF AMERICA. BY A MEMBER OF THE EPISCOPAL CHURCH.
Boston: Printed by Manning & Loring. 1797. pp. 56. 12mo.   NYPL.

32816   SEAMAN, Valentine   1770–1817
AN ACCOUNT OF THE EPIDEMIC YELLOW FEVER, AS IT APPEARED IN THE CITY OF NEW-YORK IN THE YEAR 1795. CONTAINING BESIDES ITS HISTORY, &c. THE MOST PROBABLE MEANS OF PREVENTING ITS RETURN AND OF AVOIDING IT IN CASE IT SHOULD AGAIN BECOME EPIDEMIC. BY VALENTINE SEAMAN, M. D. ONE OF THE PHYSICIANS OF THE HEALTH COMMITTEE OF NEW-YORK IN 1795. . . . [Second edition.]
New-York: Printed by Hopkins, Webb & Co. No. 40, Pine-Street.—1797— pp. ix, 246. 8vo.

32817   SEARSON, John   1750–
POEMS ON VARIOUS SUBJECTS AND DIFFERENT OCCASIONS, CHIEFLY ADAPTED TO RURAL ENTERTAINMENT IN THE UNITED STATES OF AMERICA. BY JOHN SEARSON, FORMERLY OF PHILADELPHIA, MERCHANT. [Six lines from] THOMPSON'S [*sic*] SEASONS, BOOK IV.
Philadelphia: Printed by Snowden & M'Corkle, No. 47, North Fourth-Street, 1797. pp. 94, (8), (1). 8vo.   AAS. BA. BU. NYPL.

Dedicated, with an acrostic, to His Excellency John Adams, President of the United States. Contains an eight-page list of Subscribers' names.

32818   A SELECTION OF SACRED HARMONY: CONTAINING LESSONS EXPLAINING THE GAMUT, KEYS, AND CHARACTERS USED IN VOCAL MUSIC; AND A RICH VARIETY OF TUNES.
Philadelphia: Printed for W. Young, Mills & Son. 1797. obl. 4to.

32819   SENTIMENTAL & LITERARY MAGAZINE. VOL. III. NO. 105. WEDNESDAY, JULY 5, [— NO. 112. WEDNESDAY, AUGUST 23, 1797.]
New-York: Printed (weekly) by John Tiebout, No. 358 Pearl-Street, for Thomas Burling, jun. & Co. Subscriptions for this Magazine (at three dollars per annum) are taken in at the Printing-Office; and at the Book-store of Mr. J. Fellows, Pine-Street. 1797. pp. 64. 4to.   LOC. NYHS.

In continuation of *The New York Weekly Magazine*. Discontinued on the above date.

32820   SERMONS ON IMPORTANT SUBJECTS; COLLECTED FROM A NUMBER OF MINISTERS, IN SOME OF THE NORTHERN STATES OF AMERICA. [Printers mark.]

Printed by Hudson & Goodwin, Hartford. MDCCXCVII. pp. (2), (2), 516. 8vo.   AAS. JCB. NYPL.

Contains: The Religious sentiments of Christ. Exhibited in two sermons, by Samuel J. Mills, of Torrington, Connecticut.—The Testimony of God to the truth of christianity. By Stephen West, of Stockbridge.— The Church of Christ essentially the same, in all ages. By John Stevens, of New-Marlborough.—A Future state of existence and the immortality of the soul, illustrated from the light of Scripture and reason. By Jonathan Edwards, of Colebrook. — Absolute dependence: or, the regeneration and salvation of sinners the effects, solely, of the eternal purpose, and free grace of God. Two sermons, by Eliphalet Steele, of Paris, New-York. — The Doctrine of divine sovereignty, a motive of morality. By Jacob Catlin, of New-Marlborough. On the first promise of the Saviour in the Scriptures. By Ephraim Judson, of Sheffield.—The Necessity of atonement for sin, in order to the pardon of the sinner. By Stephen West, of Stockbridge.—The Purpose of God displayed in abasing the pride of nations. By Alvan Hyde, of Lee.—The Divine sincerity, in the free and indiscriminate offer of salvation to sinners, together with their moral liberty and accountableness, consistent with distinguishing, efficacious grace. By Asahel Hooker, of Goshen, Connecticut.—Religion the one thing needful. By Jeremiah Day, of New-Preston.—True obedience to the Gospel, harmonious and entire, By Samuel Austin, of Worcester.—The Nature and importance of covenanting with God. By Peter Starr, of Warren, Connecticut. — Calamity coming on the wicked. By Ammi R. Robbins, of Norfolk.—On the judgment of the great day. By Ephraim Judson, of Sheffield. — On the endless torments of the finally impenitent. By David Porter, of Spencertown.—True christianity the safety of this world. By Alexander Gillet, of Torrington.—The Character and claims of Christ vindicated. By Jacob Catlin, of New-Marlborough.—The Wicked, on account of worldly prosperity, and unbelief of a future state, openly reject and despise the Almighty. By Jacob Catlin, of New-Marlborough.

In 1794, the Litchfield North Association of Ministers requested Reverend Ephraim Judson—one of the contributors — to collect manuscript sermons for publication and this volume is the result of their action.

32821   SERMONS TO CHILDREN; TO WHICH ARE ADDED, SHORT HYMNS, SUITED TO THE SUBJECTS. BY A LADY.

Boston: Printed and sold by Samuel Hall, No. 53, Cornhill. Jan. 1797. pp. 105. 24mo.   AAS. JCB.

32822   SEWALL, DANIEL   1755–1842

AN ASTRONOMICAL DIARY, OR ALMANAC, FOR THE YEAR OF CHRISTIAN ÆRA, 1798; BEING SECOND AFTER BISSEXTILE OR LEAP-YEAR. CALCULATED FOR THE MERIDIAN OF PORTSMOUTH, NEW-HAMPSHIRE, LAT. 43 DEG. 5 MIN. NORTH. AND DESIGNED CHIEFLY FOR THE STATE OF NEW-HAMPSHIRE AND DISTRICT OF MAINE. CONTAINING EVERY THING NECESSARY FOR AN ALMANAC, WITH A VARIETY OF ENTERTAINING AND USEFUL MATTERS. BY DANIEL SEWALL. [Seven lines of verse.]

Portsmouth, New-Hampshire: Printed by Charles Peirce, No. 5, Daniel-Street. Sold by him wholesale and retail, also, by the Author at his Office in York, and by most of the shopkeepers in town and country. [1797.] pp. (24). 12mo.

          AAS. BM. LOC. NHHS. NYHS.

AUCTION VALUES

32823 SEWALL, JONATHAN MITCHELL   1748–1808
VERSES OCCASIONED BY READING THE ANSWER OF THE PRESIDENT OF THE UNITED
STATES, TO THE HOUSE OF REPRESENTATIVES, REQUESTING CERTAIN PAPERS REL-
ATIVE TO THE TREATY WITH GREAT-BRITAIN.
Boston: Printed in the year 1797. pp. 7. 16mo.   BU. MHS.

Reprinted in his "Miscellaneous Poems," in 1801, under the title of
"The Inflexible Patriot."

32824 SHAFTSBURY. VERMONT. BAPTIST ASSOCIATION.
MINUTES OF THE SHAFTSBURY ASSOCIATION, AT THEIR ANNUAL CONVENTION, HELD IN
BOTTSKILL, 1797.
[*Without Place or Printer.* 1797.]

32825 SHARP, JOSHUA
THE COLUMBIAN ALMANAC FOR THE YEAR 1798. CONTAINING ASTRONOMICAL CALCU-
LATIONS BY JOSHUA SHARP.
Philadelphia? [1797.] pp. 36. 12mo.

32826 —— FATHER TAMMANY'S ALMANAC, FOR THE YEAR 1798: BEING THE SECOND AFTER
LEAP-YEAR. CONTAINING, (BESIDES THE ASTRONOMICAL CALCULATIONS, BY JOSHUA
SHARP,) A VARIETY OF PIECES IN PROSE AND VERSE. [Cut of Indian hunting deer.]
*Philadelphia: Printed for William Young, Bookseller, No. 52, Second-Street,
corner of Chesnut-Street.* [1797.] pp. (36). 12mo.   AAS. BM.

32827 —— POOR ROBIN'S ALMANAC, FOR THE YEAR 1798: BEING THE SECOND AFTER LEAP-
YEAR. CONTAINING, (BESIDES THE ASTRONOMICAL CALCULATIONS, BY JOSHUA SHARP,)
A HYMN FOR THE NEW-YEAR. POLITICAL ARITHMETIC. WHERE TO FIND GOLD.
OBSERVATIONS ON THE BEST METHOD TO RESTORE WORN-OUT FIELDS WITHOUT
MANURE. HINTS ON THE USES TO WHICH ASHES MAY BE APPLIED. WONDERFUL
APE OF MARSEILLES. AN USEFUL HINT. LINES ON A PRESENT OF A PENKNIFE.
CURIOUS ADVERTISEMENT. WOMEN HAVE NO SOULS: A SCOTS ANECDOTE. CURIOUS
SERMON IN PRAISE OF THIEVING. BY ROBIN GOODFELLOW.
*Philadelphia: Printed and sold by John M'Culloch, No. 1, North Third-
Street.* [1797.] pp. (36). 12mo.   AAS.

32828 SHERWIN, THOMAS
DIVINE BREATHINGS; OR, A PIOUS SOUL THIRSTING AFTER CHRIST, IN A HUNDRED
PATHETICAL MEDITATIONS. THE THIRD EDITION. PSALM LXXIII. 25. [Two lines.]
*Elizabeth-Town: Printed by Shepard Kollock, for Cornelius Davis, No. 94,
Water-Street, New-York.* M,DCC,XCVII. pp. 103. 18mo.   AAS.

To the christian reader, signed, Christopher Perin—the editor.

32829 THE SHIPMASTER'S ASSISTANT AND OWNER'S MANUAL: CONTAINING COMPLETE IN-
FORMATION TO MERCHANTS, MASTERS OF SHIPS, AND PERSONS EMPLOYED IN THE
MERCHANT SERVICE, RELATIVE TO THE MERCANTILE AND MARITIME LAWS AND
CUSTOMS.
Salem: Printed by Thomas C. Cushing. 1797.

32830 THE SHIPPENSBURGH MESSENGER. VOL. I. No. 1. WEDNESDAY, MAY 24. [—
No. 6. WEDNESDAY, JUNE 28, 1797.]
Shippensburgh, Pennsylvania: Printed by Henry & Benjamin Grimler. 1797.
fol.

Established, as a weekly, by Henry, and Benjamin Grimler, and continued by them to the issue for June 28, 1797—the first, and only number located.

32833 SHOEMAKER, ABRAHAM
THE NEW-JERSEY AND PENNSYLVANIA ALMANAC, FOR THE YEAR 1798; BEING THE
SECOND AFTER LEAP-YEAR, AND THE TWENTY-THIRD OF AMERICAN INDEPENDENCE,
AFTER THE FOURTH OF JULY. [Sixteen lines.] CALCULATED FOR THE LATITUDE
AND MERIDIAN OF PHILADELPHIA. BY ABRAHAM SHOEMAKER.

Trenton: Printed and sold, wholesale and retail, by Matthias Day. [1797.]
pp. (40). 12mo. LOC. NJSL. NYHS.

32834 —— POULSON'S TOWN AND COUNTRY ALMANAC, FOR THE YEAR OF OUR LORD, 1798;
BEING THE SECOND AFTER LEAP-YEAR. [Three lines. Constellations. Three lines.]

*—Philadelphia:—Printed and sold by Zachariah Poulson, junior, No. 80,
Chesnut-Street, eight doors below Third-Street.* [1797.] pp. (48). 12mo. . LOC.

"The astronomical calculations of this Almanac, by Abraham Shoemaker, of New-York." Contains, The picture of life. Description of
the Banyan tree. Anecdote of a sailor; a footman; of Czar Ivan; a
prisoner. The twin brothers of Mezzorania. Account of the secret tribunal of Westphalia. Address, To the free Africans and other free
people of colour in the United States. Advice to farmers. Receipts.
Tables. Courts. Roads.

32835 A SHORT INTRODUCTION TO LATIN GRAMMAR, FOR THE USE OF THE UNIVERSITY AND
ACADEMY OF PENNSYLVANIA, IN PHILADELPHIA. [Two lines from] HORACE. FIFTH
EDITION, CAREFULLY REVISED.

Philadelphia: Printed by Charles Cist, in Second-Street, near Race-Street.
M,DCC,LXXXXVII. pp. iv, 116. 12mo. AAS.

32836 THE SIAMESE TALES: BEING A COLLECTION OF STORIES TOLD TO THE SON OF THE
MANDARIN SAM-SIB, FOR THE PURPOSE OF ENGAGING HIS MIND IN THE LOVE OF
TRUTH AND VIRTUE. WITH AN HISTORICAL ACCOUNT OF THE KINGDOM OF SIAM.
TO WHICH ARE ADDED THE PRINCIPAL MAXIMS OF THE TALAPOINS. TRANSLATED
FROM THE SIAMESE. FROM MENAM'S ORIENT STREAM THAT NIGHTLY SHINES WITH
INSECT LAMPS. THOMSON,

*Baltimore: Printed for Henry S. Keatinge's Book-store by T. E. Clayland &
T. Dobbin.* 1797. pp. 178, (1), (1). 18mo. AAS. JCB.

32837 SIBLY, JOB
THE TRIAL OF RICHARD PARKER, COMPLETE; PRESIDENT OF THE DELEGATES, FOR
MUTINY, &C. ON BOARD THE SANDWICH, AND OTHERS OF HIS MAJESTY'S SHIPS, AT
THE NORE, IN MAY, 1797. BEFORE A COURT MARTIAL, HELD ON BOARD THE NEP-
TUNE, OF 98 GUNS. LAYING OFF GREENHITHE, NEAR GRAVESEND, ON THURSDAY,
JUNE 22, 1797, AND FOLLOWING DAYS. TAKEN IN SHORT HAND ON BOARD THE
NEPTUNE, BY JOB SIBLY.

*Boston: Printed by Samuel Etheridge, for William T. Clap, Fish-street, corner
Proctor's Lane.* 1797. pp. [60.] 12mo. AAS. JCB. NYPL.

32838 SIMONS, JAMES
A NEW PRINCIPLE OF TACTICS PRACTISED BY THE ARMIES OF THE REPUBLIC OF
FRANCE; ILLUSTRATED, AND RECOMMENDED TO BE PRACTISED BY THE REGULAR AND
MILITIA ARMIES OF THE UNITED STATES. BY JAMES SIMONS, BRIGADE INSPECTOR.

Charleston: From the Press of Timothy & Mason, M,DCCXCVII. pp. (2), 12,
plate. 12mo. AAS. BA. BM. CLS.

Copyright secured.

32839   THE SKY-LARK: OR GENTLEMEN AND LADIES' COMPLETE SONGSTER. BEING A COLLECTION OF THE MOST MODERN AND CELEBRATED AMERICAN, ENGLISH AND SCOTCH SONGS. TOGETHER WITH AN APPENDIX; CONTAINING A NUMBER OF CELEBRATED MASONIC SONGS, COTILLIONS AND COUNTRY DANCES. BEING THE SECOND EDITION GREATLY ENLARGED AND IMPROVED.

Worcester: From the Press of Isaiah Thomas, jun. 1797. pp. 310. 18mo.

32840   SLACK, Mrs. ——

THE INSTRUCTOR: OR, YOUNG MAN'S BEST COMPANION. CONTAINING SPELLING, READING, WRITING AND ARITHMETIC, IN AN EASIER WAY THAN ANY YET PUBLISHED; AND HOW TO QUALIFY ANY PERSON WITHOUT THE HELP OF A MASTER. INSTRUCTIONS TO WRITE A VARIETY OF HANDS, WITH COPIES BOTH IN PROSE AND VERSE. HOW TO WRITE LETTERS ON BUSINESS OR FRIENDSHIP, FORMS OF INDENTURES, BONDS, BILLS OF SALE, RECEIPTS, WILLS, LEASES, RELEASES, &C. ALSO MERCHANTS ACCOMPTS. AND A SHORT AND EASY METHOD OF SHOP AND BOOK-KEEPING. TOGETHER WITH THE METHOD OF MEASURING CARPENTERS' JOINERS,' SAWYERS,' BRICKLAYERS,' PLAISTERERS,' PLUMBERS,' MASONS,' GLAZIERS,' AND PAINTERS' WORK HOW TO UNDERTAKE EACH WORK, AND AT WHAT PRICE; THE RATES OF EACH COMMODITY; AND THE COMMON WAGES OF JOURNEYMEN: WITH THE DESCRIPTION OF GUNTER'S LINE AND COGGESHALL'S SLIDING-RULE. LIKEWISE THE PRACTICAL GAUGER MADE EASY: THE ART OF DIALING, AND HOW TO ERECT AND FIX DIALS; WITH INSTRUCTIONS FOR DYING, COLOURING AND MAKING COLOURS; AND SOME GENERAL OBSERVATIONS FOR GARDENING EVERY MONTH IN THE YEAR. TO WHICH ARE ADDED, THE FAMILY'S BEST COMPANION; AND A COMPENDIUM OF GEOGRAPHY AND ASTRONOMY: ALSO SOME USEFUL INTEREST TABLES. BY GEORGE FISHER, ACCOMPTANT.

Wilmington: Printed and sold by Peter Brynberg. M,DCC,XCVII. pp. iv, 360. 12mo.   AAS. DHS. WIFL.

32841   SMITH, CHARLES   1768–1808

THE AMERICAN GAZETTEER, OR GEOGRAPHICAL COMPANION. CONTAINING A GENERAL AND CONCISE ACCOUNT, ALPHABETICALLY ARRANGED OF THE STATES, PRINCIPAL CITIES, POST-TOWNS, PORTS OF ENTRY, HARBOURS, RIVERS, BAYS, CAPES, LAKES, &C. OF THE AMERICAN UNION.

New-York: Printed by Alexander Menut, for Charles Smith, No. 51, *Maiden lane.* 1797. pp. (53), (1), map. 24mo.   AAS.

"Preparing for publication by subscription. An Historical print of the United States, from an entire original drawing, which will be exhibited at Charles Smith's Bookstore, in a few days."

32842   —— THE AMERICAN WAR, FROM 1775 TO 1783, WITH PLANS. BY CHARLES SMITH.

New-York: Printed for C. Smith, Bookseller and Stationer, No. 51 *Maiden Lane.*—1797.—pp. 183. 2 portraits, 7 folded plans. 8vo.   BA. JCB. NYPL.

Originally printed in Smith's Monthly Military Repository, in 1796 and 1797. Although mostly reset some of the signatures retain the mark. Vol. II, as originally published.

32843   SMITH, ELIHU HUBBARD   1771–1798

EDWIN AND ANGELINA, OR, THE BANDITTI. AN OPERA, IN THREE ACTS. [Ornament.]

New-York. Printed by T. & J. Swords, No. 99 *Pearl-Street.*—1797.—pp. 72, plate. 8vo.   AAS. BA. BPL. BU. JCB. LCP. LOC. MHS. NYHS. YC.

Based upon Goldsmith's Edwin and Angelina. Opera composed by Victor Pelissier. Performed for the first, and last time at New York, December 19, 1796. 47th New York District Copyright, issued to Elihu Hubbard Smith, as Author, 24 February, 1797. Dedicated to his parents. Printed on thick paper.

32844 SMITH, EUNICE
A DIALOGUE OR, DISCOURSE BETWEEN MARY & MARTHA. [Cut.] BY EUNICE SMITH,
OF ASHFIELD,
> *Boston: Printed and sold at Russell's Office, Essex-Street, near Liberty-Pole,*
1797. pp. 16. 8vo.   BPL. JCB. LOC.
"Some arguments against worldly-mindedness, and needless care and
trouble. With some other useful instructions, represented in this Dialogue or discourse between two, called by the names of Mary and
Martha." "The rapid sale of a late edition of this useful and ingenious
pamphlet, has encouraged this impression. This is the fourth edition
from this press, and waits the reception of its former favours."

32845 SMITH, JOHN   1766-1831
THE COMING OF THE SON OF MAN: A SERMON, DELIVERED AT SALEM, NEW HAMP-
SHIRE, JULY 30, 1796. BY JOHN SMITH, A. B. PASTOR OF THE CHURCH IN SALEM.
[Six lines of Scripture texts.]
> *Concord: Printed by Geo. Hough, for the Subscribers.* M,DCC,XCVII. pp. 34.
8vo.   AAS.

32846 ⸺ A SERMON, PREACHED IN SALEM, (NEW-HAMPSHIRE) ON THE ANNIVERSARY
THANKSGIVING, NOVEMBER 17, 1796. BY JOHN SMITH, A. B. PASTOR OF THE CHURCH
IN SALEM. [Two lines from] DAVID. PUBLISHED AT THE REQUEST OF THE HEARERS.
> *Amherst: From the Press of Samuel Preston.* 1797. pp. 32. 8vo. AAS. CLA. NHHS.

32847 SMITH, JOHN BLAIR   1756-1799
THE ENLARGEMENT OF CHRIST'S KINGDOM, THE OBJECT OF A CHRISTIAN'S PRAYERS
AND EXERTIONS. A DISCOURSE, DELIVERED IN THE DUTCH CHURCH, IN ALBANY;
BEFORE THE NORTHERN MISSIONARY SOCIETY IN THE STATE OF NEW-YORK, AT
THEIR ORGANIZATION, FEB. 14, 1797. BY JOHN BLAIR SMITH, D. D. PRESIDENT OF
UNION-COLLEGE, AT SCHENECTADY.
> *Schenectady: Printed by C. P. Wyckoff, in State-Street.* 1797. pp. [42.]
8vo.   BA. JCB. NYHS. NYPL. PU.

32848 SMITH, JOSHUA   -1795
DIVINE HYMNS, OR SPIRITUAL SONGS, FOR THE USE OF RELIGIOUS ASSEMBLIES, AND
PRIVATE CHRISTIANS: BEING A COLLECTION BY JOSHUA SMITH AND SAMUEL SLEEPER.
THE SEVENTH EXETER EDITION.
> *Exeter: Printed by Henry Ranlet.* 1797. 12mo.

32849 ⸺ ⸺ DIVINE HYMNS, OR SPIRITUAL SONGS; FOR THE USE OF RELIGIOUS ASSEM-
BLIES AND PRIVATE CHRISTIANS: BEING A COLLECTION BY JOSHUA SMITH ⸺ AND
OTHERS.
> *New-London: From Springer's Press, for J. Springer and J. Trumbull.*
1797. pp. 216. 12mo.   AAS.

32850 ⸺ ⸺ DIVINE HYMNS, OR SPIRITUAL SONGS; FOR THE USE OF RELIGIOUS ASSEM-
BLIES AND PRIVATE CHRISTIANS: BEING A COLLECTION BY JOSHUA SMITH ⸺ AND
OTHERS. EIGHTH EDITION. WITH LARGE ADDITIONS AND ALTERATIONS: BY WIL-
LIAM NORTHUP, V. D. M.
> *Norwich: Printed and sold by John Sterry & Co.* M,DCC,XCVII. pp. 216.
12mo.   AAS. CHS. JCB.

32851 SMITH, SAMUEL STANHOPE   1750-1819
A DISCOURSE DELIVERED ON THE 22D OF FEBRUARY, 1797, AT THE FUNERAL OF THE
REV. GILBERT TENNENT SNOWDEN, PASTOR OF THE PRESBYTERIAN CHURCH OF
CRANBERRY, IN THE STATE OF NEW-JERSEY. BY THE REV. SAMUEL STANHOPE
SMITH, D. D. PRESIDENT OF THE COLLEGE OF NEW-JERSEY.
> *Philadelphia: Printed for John Ormrod, No. 41, Chesnut-Street, by Ormrod*
> *& Conrad.* [1797.] pp. 37. 8vo.   AAS. BM. MHS. NYPL. PU.

32852   SMITH, STEPHEN   –1797
[Cuts.] LIFE, LAST WORDS AND DYING SPEECH OF STEPHEN SMITH. A BLACK MAN WHO WAS EXECUTED AT BOSTON THIS DAY BEING THURSDAY, OCTOBER 12, 1797, FOR BURGLARY. [Two columns within mourning borders.]

     [Boston: 1797.] Broadside. fol.   BPL.

32853   SMITH, WILLIAM LOUGHTON   1758–1812
THE PRETENSIONS OF THOMAS JEFFERSON TO THE PRESIDENCY EXAMINED; AND THE CHARGES AGAINST JOHN ADAMS REFUTED. ADDRESSED TO THE CITIZENS OF AMERICA IN GENERAL; AND PARTICULARLY TO THE ELECTORS OF THE PRESIDENT. [Part first – second.]

     Philadelphia: Published complete and for sale by William Cobbett, opposite Christ Church. 1797.

32854   SMOLLETT, TOBIAS GEORGE   1721–1771
THE HISTORY OF ENGLAND, FROM THE REVOLUTION TO THE END OF THE AMERICAN WAR, AND PEACE OF VERSAILLES IN 1783. IN SIX VOLUMES. DESIGNED AS A CONTINUATION OF MR. HUME'S HISTORY. BY T. SMOLLETT, M. D. AND OTHERS. VOL. III. [— IV.] A NEW EDITION, WITH CORRECTIONS AND IMPROVEMENTS.

     Philadelphia: Printed for Robert Campbell & Co. by Henry Sweitzer. M.DCC.XCVII. 2 vols. pp. 586, portrait of George II; 584, portrait of George III, Index. 8vo.   AAS. LCP. NYPL.

32855   SMYTH, ALEXANDER   1765–1830
LETTERS OF ALEXANDER SMYTH TO FRANCIS PRESTON.

     Richmond: Printed by Samuel Pleasants, jun. for Prichard and Davidson. 1797.

32856   SOUTH CAROLINA. STATE.
ACTS AND RESOLUTIONS OF THE GENERAL ASSEMBLY, OF THE STATE OF SOUTH-CAROLINA. PASSED IN DECEMBER, 1796. [Arms.]

     Charleston: Printed by W. P. Young & D. Faust, State printers. Jan. 1797. (2), (61)–102, (2); (89)–132, (2). fol.   LOC.

32857   THE SOUTH-CAROLINA AND GEORGIA ALMANAC, FOR THE YEAR OF OUR LORD, 1798: BEING THE SECOND AFTER LEAP YEAR, AND (TILL THE 4TH OF JULY) THE TWENTY-SECOND OF AMERICAN INDEPENDENCE. [Seventeen lines.]

     Charleston: Printed by S. J. Elliott, No. 47, Bay. [1797.] pp. (44). 12mo. LOC.

32858   THE SOUTH-CAROLINA STATE GAZETTE, AND GENERAL ADVERTISER. FRIDAY, JANUARY 6, [—FRIDAY, DECEMBER 29, 1797.]

     Columbia, South-Carolina: Published by Young & Faust. 1797. fol.

32859   SOUTH-CAROLINA [cut] STATE GAZETTE AND TIMOTHY & MASON'S DAILY ADVERTISER. [Motto.] VOL. LVI. No. 5253. MONDAY, JANUARY 2, [—VOL. LVI. No. 5713. SATURDAY, DECEMBER 30, 1797.]

     Charleston: Printed by Timothy & Mason. 1797. fol.

     William Mason junior withdrew at the end of this year.

32860 SOUTH-CAROLINA WEEKLY MUSEUM; AND COMPLETE MAGAZINE OF ENTERTAINMENT
AND INTELLIGENCE. [Vignette cut of] GEO. WASHINGTON, ESQ. VOL. I. No. 1.
SATURDAY, JANUARY 14, [— VOL. II. NO. 51. SATURDAY, DECEMBER 30, 1797.]
Charleston: Printed and published by W. P. Harrison & Co. 1797. pp. 836,
viii; 750 ? 4to.

From the scattering numbers known of this Magazine, it would appear
that publication, as above, was begun by William Primrose Harrison
and Company, and continued to the end of the third volume, July 7,
1798, by Thomas Bartholomew Bowen, his former partner. Each number contained thirty pages, enclosed in printed wrappers, with a medal-
lion portrait of Geo. Washington, Esq. following the title.

32861 SOUTHERN CENTINEL, AND GAZETTE OF THE STATE. VOL. IV. NUMB. 187. THURS-
DAY, JANUARY 5, [— VOL. V. NUMB. 238. THURSDAY, DECEMBER 28, 1797.]
Augusta: Printed by Alexander M'Millan, Printer to the State. 1797. fol.

32862 THE SOUTHWARK GAZETTE, AND PHILADELPHIA CHRONICLE. VOL. I. No. 1.
SATURDAY, JULY 15, [— No. 8. TUESDAY, AUGUST 1, 1797.]
Philadelphia: Published by Timothy Mountford. 1797. fol.

Established, as a tri-weekly, by Timothy Mountford and continued by
him to August 1st.—the last number located.

32863 SPAIN. KINGDOM.
A LETTER TO TIMOTHY PICKERING, ESQ. SECRETARY OF STATE, FROM THE CHEVALIER
DE YRUJO, MINISTER PLENIPOTENTIARY OF HIS CATHOLIC MAJESTY, &C. &C. DATED
JULY 11, 1797. [Signed, Carlos Martinez de Yrujo.]
[Philadelphia: 1797.] pp. (15). 8vo.   AAS. BA. HSP.

32864 SPALDING, LYMAN   1775–1821
AN INAUGURAL DISSERTATION ON THE PRODUCTION OF ANIMAL HEAT; READ AND DE-
FENDED AT A PUBLIC EXAMINATION, HELD BY THE MEDICAL PROFESSORS, BEFORE
THE REV. JOSEPH WILLARD . . . AND THE GOVERNORS OF HARVARD COLLEGE,
FOR THE DEGREE OF BACHELOR IN MEDICINE, JULY 10, 1797. BY LYMAN SPALD-
ING.
Walpole, Newhampshire: Printed by David Carlisle, jun. 1797. pp. 30. 8vo.
AAS. BA. LOC. MHS. NYHS. NYPL.

32865 THE SPECTATOR. VOL. I. NUMBER 1. WEDNESDAY, OCTOBER 4, [— NUMBER 26.
SATURDAY, DECEMBER 30, 1797.]
*New-York, No. 40 Pine-Street: Published (Wednesdays and Saturdays) by
George F. Hopkins, Printer of the Laws of the United States for the district of New-
York.* 1797. fol.   AAS. BA. BPL. LOC. MHS. NYHS. NYPL. WHS. YC.

In continuation of *The Herald; a gazette for the country.* Edited by Noah
Webster, junior, to December, 1802. Issued, from the same Office, as
the semi-weekly edition of the "Commercial Advertiser."

32866 SPOONER'S VERMONT JOURNAL. VOLUME XIV. NUMBER 702. FRIDAY, JANUARY 6,
[— VOLUME XV. NUMBER 753. WEDNESDAY, DECEMBER 27, 1797.]
*[Windsor:] Printed and published by Alden Spooner on the west side of the
Main Street.* 1797. fol.   AAS.

32867 SPRINGER'S WEEKLY ORACLE. VOL. II. No. 53. SATURDAY, OCTOBER 21, [— No.
63. SATURDAY, DECEMBER 30, 1797.]
*New-London: Printed and published by James Springer, at his Printing-Of-
fice, Beach-Street.* 1797. fol.

In continuation of the *Weekly Oracle.*

32868 STAFFORD, Cornelius William

THE PHILADELPHIA DIRECTORY, FOR 1797: CONTAINING THE NAMES, OCCUPATIONS, AND PLACES OF ABODE OF THE CITIZENS; ARRANGED IN ALPHABETICAL ORDER: ALSO, A REGISTER OF THE EXECUTIVE, LEGISLATIVE, AND JUDICIAL MAGISTRATES OF THE UNITED STATES—THE CONSTITUTION OF THE UNITED STATES—OFFICERS OF THE COMMONWEALTH OF PENNSYLVANIA—AND THE MAGISTRATES OF THE CITY: WITH AN ACCURATE TABLE OF THE DUTIES ON GOODS, WARES, AND MERCHANDIZE; TOGETHER WITH A GENERAL ABSTRACT FROM THE REVENUE LAWS, RELATIVE TO THE DUTY OF MASTERS OF VESSELS—OF THE OWNERS OR CONSIGNEES OF GOODS—OF OFFICERS OF THE CUSTOMS—OF PAYMENT OF DUTIES, &C.—AND THE FORM OF ENTRY AT THE CUSTOM HOUSE ON THE IMPORTATION OF GOODS. TO ALL WHICH ARE ADDED, AN ACCOUNT OF THE POST OFFICE ESTABLISHMENT,—THE BANKS,—TABLES OF MONIES, &C.—WITH AN ALPHABETICAL LIST OF THE STREETS, LANES, AND ALLEYS. BY CORNELIUS WILLIAM STAFFORD.

Printed for the Editor, by William W. Woodward, No. 17, Chesnut Street. 1797. pp. (2), (2), (4), (5)-[203], [76], plan. 8vo.   AAS. HC. LCP.

32869 STANDFAST, Richard

A DIALOGUE BETWEEN A BLIND MAN AND DEATH. BY RICHARD STANDFAST, LATE MINISTER OF THE GOSPEL IN BRISTOL. [Colophon:]

Printed and sold at the Printing-Office, Fairhaven . . . and sold very low, wholesale or retail, by the Travelling Booksellers. 1797. pp. 8. 16mo.

32870 STANIFORD, Daniel

A SHORT BUT COMPREHENSIVE GRAMMAR, RENDERED SIMPLE AND EASY, BY FAMILIAR QUESTIONS AND ANSWERS,—ADAPTED TO THE CAPACITY OF YOUTH, AND DESIGNED FOR THE USE OF SCHOOLS AND PRIVATE FAMILIES. TO WHICH IS ADDED AN APPENDIX, COMPREHENDING A LIST OF VULGARISMS AND GRAMMATICAL IMPROPRIETIES, USED IN COMMON CONVERSATION, BY PERSONS OF DIFFERENT SOCIETIES. BY DANIEL STANIFORD, A. M.

Boston: 1797.

110th Massachusetts District Copyright, issued to Daniel Staniford, 2 February, 1797.

32871 STANTON, Samuel

ANSWER TO THOMAS PAINE'S LETTER TO GENERAL WASHINGTON PRESIDENT OF THE UNITED STATES ON AFFAIRS PUBLIC AND PRIVATE. BY SAMUEL STANTON, ESQ., AN OFFICER (OF TWENTY YEARS STANDING) IN THE BRITISH ARMY. AUTHOR OF MISCELLANEOUS LETTERS ON EVERY SUBJECT FROM THE PRINCE TO THE PEASANT. THE PRINCIPLES OF DUELLING. A TREATISE ON THE SLAVE TRADE. SENTIMENTS AND INFORMATION RESPECTING THE SLAVE TRADE, DELIVERED IN WRITING TO THE BRITISH HOUSE OF COMMONS, AND AFTERWARDS PRINTED BY BILL. DUELLING EXPLAINED FROM PHILANTHROPIC MOTIVES. TWO ELEGIAC POEMS, &C. THE CHARACTER OF THE ILLUSTRIOUS WASHINGTON IS HERE JUSTLY DEFENDED FROM MOTIVES OF THE STRICTEST HONOUR VIZ. THE VENERATION AND RESPECT THE AUTHOR HAS EVER HAD FOR GEORGE WASHINGTON.

Philadelphia: 1797.

178th Pennsylvania District Copyright, issued to Samuel Stanton, as Author, 1 April, 1797.

32872 THE STATE GAZETTE & NEW-JERSEY ADVERTISER. INDEPENDENCE 21ST YEAR. FEDERAL GOVERNMENT 8TH YEAR. NO. 18 OF VOL. V. WHOLE NO. 226. TUESDAY, JANUARY 3, [—NO. 17 OF VOL. VI. WHOLE NO. 277. TUESDAY, DECEMBER 26, 1797.]

Printed by Matthias Day, Trenton. 1797. fol.   AAS.

32873　STATE GAZETTE OF NORTH CAROLINA. VOL. XI. NUMB. 572. THURSDAY, JANUARY 5, [— VOL. XII. NUMB. 623. THURSDAY, DECEMBER 28, 1797.]

> *Edenton: Printed by Henry Wills, joint Printer to the State with A. Hodge.* 1797. fol.

> In November, Henry Wills was succeeded by his brother, James Wills, as Printer and publisher.

32874　STAUGHTON, WILLIAM　　　　　　　　　　　　　　　　　1770–1829
A DISCOURSE, OCCASIONED BY THE SUDDEN DEATH OF THREE YOUNG PERSONS, BY DROWNING. DELIVERED ON THE 28TH OF MAY, 1797, AT THE BAPTIST MEETING HOUSE IN BORDENTON, NEW JERSEY. BY THE REV. WILLIAM STAUGHTON, PRINCIPAL OF BORDENTON ACADEMY. TO WHICH IS ANNEXED, AN ORATION, DELIVERED THE PRECEDING EVENING AT THE INTERMENT OF THE BODIES, BY THE REV. BURGISS [*sic*] ALLISON, A. M.

> *Philadelphia: Printed by Stephen C. Ustick.* 1797. pp. 37. 8vo.

> Title within mourning borders.　　　　　　　　　　AAS. JCB. NYPL.

32875　STAUNTON GAZETTE. VOL. I. No. 50. WEDNESDAY, JANUARY 4, [—VOL. II. No. 30? FRIDAY, AUGUST 25? 1797.]

> *Staunton: Printed by Wise & Adams.* 1797. fol.

> About the above date, —— Adams withdrew, and John Wise continued publication alone, changing the title in October, to *Virginia Gazette, and Staunton Weekly Advertiser.*

32876　STEARNS, CHARLES　　　　　　　　　　　　　　　　　1753–1826
THE LADIES' PHILOSOPHY OF LOVE. A POEM, IN FOUR CANTOS. WRITTEN IN 1774. BY CHARLES STEARNS, A. B. SINCE PASTOR OF THE CHURCH, AND PRECEPTOR OF THE LIBERAL SCHOOL IN LINCOLN. NOW FIRST PUBLISHED—ACCORDING TO ACT OF CONGRESS.

> *Leominster, Mass. Printed by John Prentiss, & Co. for the Author.* 1797. pp. 76. 4to.　　　　　　　　　　　　　　　AAS. BA. BM. BU. NYPL.

> The preface states: "When the poem was written the author was in his twenty-second year and under no obligation to any of the fair; since that time he has been a lover, a husband, a father of a numerous family, a pastor, and a preceptor for many years to youth of both sexes. His experience has not disproved, but confirmed his principles." 133d Massachusetts District Copyright, issued to Charles Stearns. as Author, 11 November, 1797.

32877　STEVENS, JAMES WILSON
AN HISTORICAL AND GEOGRAPHICAL ACCOUNT OF ALGIERS; COMPREHENDING A NOVEL AND INTERESTING DETAIL OF EVENTS RELATIVE TO THE AMERICAN CAPTIVES. BY JAMES WILSON STEVENS.

> *Philadelphia: Printed by Hogan & M'Elroy, George-Street, third door below South-Street. August,* 1797. pp. 304, (6), (2), frontispiece. 12mo.
> 　　　　　　　　　　　　　　　　　AAS. JCB. NYPL. WiPL.

> Contains, a six-page list of Subscriber's names. 190th Pennsylvania District Copyright, issued to Hogan and McElroy, as Proprietors, 7 August, 1797.

32878   STEVENS, WILLIAM
A SYSTEM FOR THE DISCIPLINE OF THE ARTILLERY OF THE UNITED STATES OF
AMERICA, OR, THE YOUNG ARTILLERIST'S POCKET COMPANION. IN THREE PARTS.
PART I. CONTAINING: THE FORMATION OF A CORPS OF ARTILLERY, AND THE DUTY
AND PRACTICE OF LIGHT FIELD ARTILLERY &C. PART II. CONTAINING: THE THEORY
AND PRACTICE OF HEAVY ARTILLERY, IN GARRISON AND ON BOARD THE NAVY: AND
AN EXTRACT OF A TREATISE ON THE ORIGIN AND PRINCIPLES OF COURTS MARTIAL.
PART III. CONTAINING; LABORATORY DUTY; A GREAT VARIETY OF DIRECTIONS FOR
COMPOSITIONS, AND THE METHOD OF MAKING ARTIFICIAL FIRE-WORKS, WITH THE
FORMATION OF AMMUNITION NECESSARY FOR THE DIFFERENT KINDS OF ORDNANCE.
IN THREE VOLUMES. BY WILLIAM STEVENS. AN OFFICER IN THE AMERICAN
ARTILLERY THROUGH THE WHOLE OF THE LATE REVOLUTION, AND SINCE IN THE
MILITIA. [VOL. I.]
> *New-York: Printed by William A. Davis, No. 26, Moore-Street, for the
> Author.—1797.—pp. 260, 24 plates. 12mo.*   AAS. BM. JCB. NYPL.

> Apparently all that was published. 49th New York District Copyright,
> issued to William Stevens, as Author, 8 July, 1797.

32879   STEWART, JOHN   1778–1797
THE CONFESSION. LAST WORDS, AND DYING SPEECH OF JOHN STEWART, A NATIVE OF
IRELAND. TAKEN FROM HIMSELF, AT HIS OWN PARTICULAR REQUEST. [Two col-
umns.] JOHN STEWART. BOSTON JAIL. APRIL 6, 1797.
> *[Boston: 1797.] Broadside. fol.*   AAS. NYHS.

> Enclosed in heavy borders, with a cut of a coffin, at the top. Reproduced
> in facsimile.

32880   —— — THE CONFESSION, LAST WORDS, AND DYING SPEECH OF JOHN STEWART,
A NATIVE OF IRELAND, WHO WAS EXECUTED AT BOSTON, THE 6TH [April] INSTANT
FOR HOUSE-BREAKING.
> *Harrington, (District of Maine): Printed by Peter Edes.* 1797.

32881   STEWART'S KENTUCKY HERALD. VOLUME II. NUMB. 99. TUESDAY, JANUARY 3, [—
VOL. III. NO. 150. TUESDAY, DECEMBER 26, 1797.]
> *Lexington: Printed by James H. Stewart; . . .* 1797. fol.

32882   STILLMAN, SAMUEL   1737–1807
A GOOD MINISTER OF JESUS CHRIST. A SERMON, PREACHED IN BOSTON, SEPTEMBER
15, 1797, AT THE ORDINATION OF THE REV. MR. STEPHEN SMITH NELSON. BY
SAMUEL STILLMAN, D. D. PASTOR OF THE FIRST BAPTIST CHURCH IN BOSTON. TO
WHICH ARE ADDED, THE CHARGE, BY THE REV. MR. ISAAC BACKUS, OF MIDDLE-
BOROUGH; AND THE RIGHT HAND OF FELLOWSHIP, BY THE REV. MR. THOMAS BALD-
WIN, OF BOSTON.
> *Boston: Printed by Manning & Loring.* 1797. pp. 20. 8vo.   AAS. BA. BM. JCB.

32883   STOCK, JOHN EDMONDS
AN INAUGURAL ESSAY ON THE EFFECTS OF COLD UPON THE HUMAN BODY. SUBMITTED
TO THE EXAMINATION OF THE REV. JOHN EWING, S. T. P PROVOST, THE MEDICAL
PROFESSORS AND TRUSTEES, OF THE UNIVERSITY OF PENNSYLVANIA, FOR THE DE-
GREE OF DOCTOR OF MEDICINE, ON THE 12TH DAY OF MAY, 1797. BY JOHN ED-
MONDS STOCK, OF GLOUCESTERSHIRE, ENGLAND; MEMBER OF THE MEDICAL AND
NATURAL HISTORY SOCIETIES OF EDINBURGH.
> *Philadelphia: Printed by Joseph Gales, between Nos. 126 and 128, North
> Second Street.* 1797. pp. iii, (43). 8vo.   AAS. BM. SGO.

32884   STODDARD, AMOS   1762–1813
A MASONIC ADDRESS, DELIVERED BEFORE THE WORSHIPFUL MASTER, OFFICERS AND
BRETHREN OF THE KENNEBECK LODGE, IN THE NEW MEETING HOUSE, HALLOWELL,
MASSACHUSETTS; JUNE 24TH, ANNO LUCIS 5797. [Eight lines of verse.] BY
BROTHER AMOS STODDARD.
> *Hallowell: Printed by brother Howard S. Robinson, A. D.* 1797—*A. L.* 5797.
> pp. 20. 4to.   AAS. NYPL.

32885 STONINGTON. Connecticut. Baptist Association.
Minutes of the Stonington Association. 1797.
New-London: 1797.

32886 STOUT, Benjamin
Narrative of the loss of the ship Hercules, commanded by captain Benjamin Stout, on the coast of Caffraria, the 16th of June, 1796; also a circumstantial detail of his travels through the southern deserts of Africa, and the colonies, to the Cape of Good Hope. With an introductory address to the rt. hon. John Adams, president of the Continental Congress of America.
New-York: Printed for James Chevalier. [1797.] pp. liii, 113. 8vo. NYHS.

32887 STRONG, Nathan   1748–1816
A Sermon, preached at the annual thanksgiving, November 16th, 1797. By Nathan Strong, minister of the North Presbyterian church in Hartford. The copy was given to several of the hearers, who by permission have published it. [Printers mark.]
Hartford: Printed by Hudson & Goodwin. 1.797. pp. 16. 8vo.
        AAS. BA. BM. CHS. CLA. LOC. UTS. YC.

32888 —— A Sermon, preached in Hartford, June 10th, 1797, at the execution of Richard Doane. By Nathan Strong, minister of the North Presbyterian church in Hartford. To which is added, a Short account of his life, as given by himself, also of the state of his mind during the time of iiis confinement, and at his death.
Hartford: Printed by Elisha Babcock. 1797. pp. 21. 8vo.
        AAS. BM. CHS. LOC. YC.
Connecticut District Copyright, issued to Elisha Babcock, as Proprietor, 22 June, 1797.

32889 —— — A Sermon, preached in Hartford, June 10th, 1797, at the execution of Richard Doane. By Nathan Strong, minister of the North Presbyterian church in Hartford, To which is added, a Short account of his life, as given by himself, also of the state of his mind during the time of his confinement, and at his death. Second edition.
Hartford: Printed by Elisha Babcock. 1797. pp. 21. 8vo.

32890 STRONG, Nehemiah   1729–1807
An Astronomical diary, calendar, or Almanack, for the year of our Lord, 1798: and from the creation of the world, 5747, and till July 4th, the 22d of American independence. Being the second after bissextile, or leap-year. Containing, all things necessary for such a composition. Calculated for the meridian and horizon at Hartford, lat. 41 deg. 56 min. north; longit. 72 deg. 56 min. west. By Nehemiah Strong, late professor of mathematicks, and natural philosophy of Yale College. [Six lines of verse.]
Hartford: Printed by Elisha Babcock. [With privilege of copy-right.] [1797.] pp. (24). 12mo. AAS. CHS. YC.
Contains, A Short account of the life of Richard Doane, who was executed June 10th, 1797, for the murder of David M'Iver, as given by himself. Babcock advertised 10,000 genuine Almanacks, at one dollar and fifty cents per gross. Nathaniel Patten then advertised, in Babcock's newspaper, that he would sell 10,000 Strong's (spurious) Almanacks for 1798, as cheap as ever.

STRONG, Nehemiah, continued.

32891   —— Sheet Almanac for the year 1798.

       Hartford: Printed by Elisha Babcock. 1797. Broadside.

32892   —— Stafford's Almanack, for the year of our Lord 1798, and from the creation of the world five thousand seven hundred and forty-seven, and the 22d of American independence. Being the second after bissextile or leap year. Containing all things necessary for such a composition, adapted to the horizon and meridian of New Haven, [Seventeen lines.]

       New-Haven: Printed by Thomas and Samuel Green. [1797.] pp. [24.] 12mo.
           AAS. LOC. NYPL. YC.

32893   —— Sheet Almanac for the year 1798.

       New-Haven: Printed by Thomas & Samuel Green. 1797. Broadside.

32894   —— Strong's Astronomical diary, calendar or Almanack, for the year of our Lord, 1798: from the creation of the world, 5747. And till July 4th, the 22d of American independence, being the second after bissextile or leap-year. [Sixteen lines.]

       West-Springfield: Printed by Edward Gray. [1797.] pp. (24). 12mo.
       Spurious.   AAS. LOC. YC.

32895   THE [cut] SUN. Dover Gazette, and County Advertiser. [Motto.] Number 18 of vol. II. Whole number 70. Wednesday, January 4, [— Number 17 of vol. 3. Whole number 121. Wednesday, December 27, 1797.]

       Published on Wednesdays—By Samuel Bragg, jun. at his Printing-Office, Dover. . . . 1797. fol.   AAS.

32896   THE SUNBURY and Northumberland Gazette. Vol. v. No. 28. Saturday, January 7, [—Vol. vi. No. 27. Saturday, December 30, 1797.]

       Northumberland—Printed by George Schusler. 1797. fol.

32897   SWANWICK, John   1760–1798
       Heading: (Circular.) Philadelphia, September 22, 1797. Sir, Previous to my entering on a detail of what relates to my own transactions, which will form the subject of this letter, it may not be amiss to premise some observations on the state of the commerce of the United States in general in 1796 . . . [Messrs. John & Francis Baring & Co. of London, in account with John Swanwick, of Philadelphia.]

       [Philadelphia: 1797.] pp. 13, folded table. 8vo.   JCB.

32898   —— Poems on several occasions. By John Swanwick, esq. one of the representatives in the Congress of the United States, from the State of Pennsylvania.

       Philadelphia: Printed by F. and R. Bailey, at Yorick's Head, No. 116, *High-Street.* MDCCXCVII. pp. (2), (2), 174. 24mo.   AAS. BM. BU. NYPL.

       A dainty volume of admirable typography.

32899 SWEETING, Whiting   –1791
THE NARRATIVE OF WHITING SWEETING, WHO WAS EXECUTED AT ALBANY, THE 26TH
OF AUGUST, 1791. CONTAINING. AN ACCOUNT OF HIS TRIAL BEFORE THE SUPREME
COURT OF JUDICATURE OF THE STATE OF NEW-YORK, AT THE JULY TERM, 1791,
FOR THE MURDER OF DARIUS QUIMBY—THE SUBSTANCE OF THE CHARGE OF HIS
HONOR THE CHIEF JUSTICE TO THE JURY, WITH THE SENTENCE OF DEATH ON THE
PRISONER—AN ADDRESS TO THE PUBLIC, ON THE FATAL CONSEQUENCES OF A LIFE
SPENT IN SIN, INSTANCED IN HIS OWN CONDUCT; SETTING FORTH THE GREAT NECES-
SITY OF REMEMBERING OUR CREATOR IN THE DAYS OF OUR YOUTH AND PRACTISING
RELIGION AND VIRTUE IN OUR WHOLE LIVES—AN ADDRESS TO HIS PARENTS, TO HIS
BROTHERS AND SISTERS, AND TO HIS WIFE AND CHILDREN; WITH A MORAL INSTRUC-
TION, BY WAY OF QUESTION AND ANSWER, PARTICULARLY ADDRESSED TO THEM—AN
ADDRESS TO THE PARENTS OF HIS WIFE; TO HIS BROTHERS AND SISTERS BY MAR-
RIAGE—A FEW LINES ON HIS SENSE OF GRATITUDE TO MR. OSTRANDER THE GOALER
—HIS APPEAL TO THE HIGH COURT OF HEAVEN FOR THE TRUTH OF HIS DECLARA-
ATION *that the murder was committed without malice prepense*—WITH A SKETCH OF
THE PROCEEDINGS WHICH LED TO HIS BEING TAKEN—THE WARRANT, &C.—A FEW
WORDS ON THE GREAT IMPROPRIETY OF FALSE-SWEARING, OR GIVING A FALSE
COLOURING TO TESTIMONY BEFORE A COURT, IN NOT RELATING THE *whole* TRUTH—
HIS REASON FOR HIS ESCAPING FROM PRISON—HIS ACKNOWLEDGMENT TO THE
GENTLEMEN OF THE CLERGY, FOR THEIR ATTENTION TO HIM DURING HIS CONFINE-
MENT—HIS SENTIMENTS OF FREE GRACE, FREE WILL, &C. &C. WRITTEN BY HIM-
SELF, AND PUBLISHED FOR THE BENEFIT OF PRECIOUS SOULS, AT HIS PARTICULAR
AND DYING REQUEST. TO WHICH ARE ADDED, AN ACCOUNT OF THE BEHAVIOUR OF
THE UNHAPPY SUFFERER, FROM HIS CONFINEMENT TO EXECUTION, AND THE SUB-
STANCE OF HIS ADDRESS AT THE GALLOWS. BY ONE WHO HAD FREE ACCESS TO,
AND FREQUENT CONVERSATION WITH HIM. [William Carter.]

   Windham: Printed [by John Byrne] for Mr. James Huntington. 1797. pp.
47. 8vo.   AAS. BM. NYPL.

32900 SYMMES, William   1762–1807
AN ORATION, DELIVERED BEFORE THE CITIZENS OF PORTLAND, AND THE SUPREME
JUDICIAL COURT OF MASSACHUSETTS, ON THE FOURTH OF JULY, A. D. 1797. BEING
THE ANNIVERSARY OF THE INDEPENDENCE OF THE UNITED STATES OF AMERICA.
BY WILLIAM SYMMES.

   Printed at Portland, by John K. Baker. 1797. pp. 19. 8vo.   JCB.

32901 THE SYREN, OR VOCAL ENCHANTRESS: BEING A COLLECTION OF THE NEWEST AND
MOST ADMIRED MISCELLANEOUS,—PATHETIC. AND PASSIONATE,—ANACREONTIC AND
JOVIAL,—COMIC, INGENIOUS, AND WITTY,—SEA, HUNTING, AND MASONIC SONGS. SE-
LECTED FROM THE MOST APPROVED SENTIMENTAL, HUMOROUS, AND INGENIOUS PUB-
LICATIONS; INCLUDING ALL THE BEST SONGS OF DIBDIN, EDWIN, &C.

   *Wilmington: Printed [by Bonsal & Niles] for and sold by James Wilson,
Book-seller and Stationer, No. 5, High Street, opposite the upper Market-House.*
1797. pp. 38, 36, 24, 48, 28, (6). 12mo.   WIPL.

32902 THE TABLET; AND WEEKLY ADVERTISER. VOL. I. No. 1. WEDNESDAY, OCTOBER
25, [— No. 10. WEDNESDAY, DECEMBER 27, 1797.]

   New-York: Published by Tiebout & Burling. 1797. fol.

   Established, as a weekly, by John Tiebout and Thomas Burling, junior.
In April, 1798, Burling withdrew. Tiebout continued publication alone,
as the *Tablet*, into June, 1798, when, apparently, it was discontinued.

32903   TABLET OF THE TIMES. VOL. I. NO. 1. THURSDAY, JANUARY 5, [— NO. 35. THURS-
DAY, AUGUST 31, 1797.]
Bennington: Printed by Merrill & Langdon. 1797. fol.   VTSL.

Established, as a weekly, by Orsamus C. Merrill and Reuben Langdon,
and printed from the Office of, and in continuation of *The Vermont
Gazette.* In May, discouraged by financial conditions, Reuben Langdon
retired; and, in August, Orsamus C. Merrill, considering the conditions
hopeless, quit. Anthony Haswell, who had sold one-half of his printing establishment to them for their experiment, determined, once more,
to strive to conduct a paper successfully in Bennington; and, with a
new numbering, on September 5, 1797, revived *The Vermont Gazette.*

32904   TANGUY DE LA BOISSIÈRE, C. C.
OBSERVATIONS SUR LA DÉPÊCHE ÉCRITE LE 16 JANVIER, 1797, PAR M. PICKERING,
SECRÉTAIRE D'ETAT DES ETATS-UNIS DE L'AMÉRIQUE, À M. PINKNEY, MINISTRE
PLÉNIPOTENTIAIRE DES ETATS-UNIS PRÈS LA RÉPUBLIQUE FRANÇAISE.
Philadelphie: Imprimé par Moreau de St.-Méry, au coin du Front et Walnut.
1797 pp. 50. 8vo.   BA. BM. MHS. RIHS.

32905   —— —— OBSERVATIONS ON THE DISPATCH WRITTEN THE 16TH JANUARY 1797, BY
MR. PICKERING, SECRETARY OF STATE OF THE UNITED STATES OF AMERICA, TO MR,
PINKNEY, MINISTER PLENIPOTENTIARY OF THE UNITED SATES [*sic*] NEAR THE
FRENCH REPUBLIC. BY C. C. TANGUY DE LA BOISSIÈRE. TRANSLATED FROM THE
FRENCH BY SAMUEL CHANDLER. [Vignette.]
*Philadelphia: Printed and sold by Moreau de Saint-Mery, Book-seller and
Printer, corner of Front and Walnut Streets.* 1797. pp. (50). 8vo.
AAS. BA. BM. HSP. JCB. LOC. NYHS. NYPL.

173d Pennsylvania District Copyright, issued to C. C. Tanguy de La
Boissiere, as Author, 1 March, 1797.

32906   TAPLIN, WILLIAM   –1807
A COMPENDIUM OF PRACTICAL AND EXPERIMENTAL FARRIERY, ORIGINALLY SUGGESTED
BY REASON AND CONFIRMED BY PRACTICE. EQUALLY ADAPTED FOR THE CONVENI-
ENCE OF THE GENTLEMAN, THE FARMER, THE GROOM AND THE SMITH. INTERSPERSED
WITH SUCH REMARKS, AND ELUCIDATED WITH SUCH CASES AS EVIDENTLY TEND TO
INSURE THE PREVENTION AS WELL AS TO ASCERTAIN THE CURE OF DISEASE. BY
WILLIAM TAPLIN, SURGEON, AUTHOR OF THE GENTLEMAN'S STABLE DIRECTORY, 2
VOLS., THE TWELFTH EDITION OF WHICH IS NOW PUBLISHED.
*Wilmington: Printed by Bonsal & Niles, for Robert Campbell, Bookseller,
Philadelphia.* M,DCC,XCVII. pp. viii, 296, (6), plate, (12). 12mo.
AAS JCB. NYPL. WiPL.

The appended twelve pages in the copy in the Wilmington Public
Library contain "A Catalogue of books printed for and sold by John
Conrad, & Co. No. 30, Chesnut Street, Philadelphia. M. & J. Conrad,
& Co. No. 140, Market Street, Baltimore; and Rapin, Conrad, & Co.
near the Capital, Washington City," of a date later by four or five years,
and consisting principally of Robert Campbell remainders.

32907   TAPPAN, DAVID   1752–1803
A SERMON, DELIVERED BEFORE THE ANNUAL CONVENTION OF THE CONGREGATIONAL
MINISTERS OF MASSACHUSETTS, IN BOSTON, JUNE 1, 1797. BY DAVID TAPPAN, D.D.
PROFESSOR OF DIVINITY IN HARVARD COLLEGE. [Ornament.]
Printed by Samuel Hall, No. 53, Cornhill, Boston, 1797. pp. [34.] 8vo.
AAS BA. BM. HC. JCB. LOC. MHS. NYHS. NYPL UTS.

32908   TAYLOR, Christopher   –1686
AN ACCOUNT OF A DIVINE VISITATION AND BLESSING, ATTENDING THE RELIGIOUS CARE
AND EXERCISE OF THE TEACHERS OF WALTHAM ABBEY SCHOOL; WITH THE GRACIOUS
DEALINGS OF THE ALMIGHTY TOWARDS SOME OTHERS IN TENDER YEARS. ALSO SEV-
ERAL SELECT POEMS. [Edited by M. [artha] R. [outh].]
     Philadelphia: Printed by Samuel Sansom, jun. No. 27, Mulberry-Street.
1797. pp. 60. 8vo.   NYPL.

     Printed in London in 1799.

32909   TAYLOR, Jeremy   1613–1667
THE LIVES OF THE HOLY EVANGELISTS AND APOSTLES; WITH THEIR MARTYRDOMS,
FOR PREACHING THE GOSPEL OF OUR LORD JESUS CHRIST. BY J. TAYLOR, B. D.
[Ornament.]
     Printed at Leominster, (Massachusetts) by Charles Prentiss. 1797. pp. 48.
12mo.   AAS. JCB.

     An abridgment from William Cave.

32910   TAYLOR, Raynor   1747–1825
DIVERTIMENTI, OR FAMILIAR LESSONS FOR THE PIANOFORTE, TO WHICH IS PREFIXED
A GROUND FOR THE IMPROVEMENT OF YOUNG PRACTITIONERS, COMPOSED BY R.
TAYLOR, MUSIC PROFESSOR.
     *Philadelphia: Printed for the Author, No. 96, North Sixth-Street, and sold
at Carr's Musical Repositories Philadelphia and New-York.* 1797.

32911   —— SONATA FOR THE PIANOFORTE, WITH AN ACCOMPANIMENT FOR THE VIOLIN. COM-
POSED BY R. TAYLOR.
     *Philadelphia: Printed for the Author No. 96 North Sixth, and to be had at
the music stores.* 1797.

32912   THE TELEGRAPHE AND DAILY ADVERTISER. NUM. 684. THURSDAY, JUNE 1, [—
NUM. 830. SATURDAY, DECEMBER 30, 1797.]
     *Baltimore: Printed and published by T. E. Clayland and T. Dobbin, at the
New Printing-Office, No. 36, Market-Street, opposite the Vendue Store.* 1797. fol.

     In continuation of the *City Gazette & Daily Telegraphe.* Thomas E. Clay-
land died December 4, 1797, but the firm name, as above, continued
to the end of 1798.

32913   TENNESSEE. State.
ACTS PASSED AT THE FIRST SESSION OF THE SECOND GENERAL ASSEMBLY OF THE
STATE OF TENNESSEE, BEGUN AND HELD AT KNOXVILLE ON MONDAY THE EIGHT-
EENTH DAY OF SEPTEMBER ONE THOUSAND SEVEN HUNDRED AND NINETY-SEVEN.
[—28 OCTOBER, 1797.]
     Knoxville: Printed by George Roulstone, Printer to the State. 1797. pp.
(120). 8vo.   LOC.

32914   THACHER, Peter   1752–1802
A SERMON, PREACHED AT DORCHESTER, JUNE 24, 1797, BEFORE THE ANCIENT AND
HONORABLE SOCIETY OF FREE MASONS. BY PETER THACHER, D. D. PASTOR OF A
CHURCH IN BOSTON. [Ornament.]
     Printed by Samuel Hall, No. 53, Cornhill, Boston. 1797. pp. 21, (1). 8vo.
                                                  AAS. BA. BM. JCB. MHS. NYPL.

     Contains, A Hymn, sung at the consecration of Union Lodge, in Dor-
chester. Written by Rev. Brother Thaddeus Mason Harris.

32915   THAYER, NATHANIEL   1769–1840
THE CHARACTER OF ST. JOHN THE BAPTIST, DELINEATED IN A DISCOURSE, DELIVERED JUNE 24, 1797: BEFORE THE RIGHT WORSHIPFUL MASTERS, OFFICERS AND BRETHREN OF TRINITY, MORNING STAR, & ST. PAUL'S LODGES, OF FREE AND ACCEPTED MASONS. BY NATHANIEL THAYER, A. M. MINISTER OF THE CHURCH IN LANCASTER.
    Leominster: Printed by brother Charles Prentiss. A. L. 5797 [1797.] pp. (15). 8vo.   AAS. BA.

32916   THE THEOLOGICAL MAGAZINE, OR SYNOPSIS OF MODERN RELIGIOUS SENTIMENT. ON A NEW PLAN. [Seven lines of quotations.] VOL. II. [No. 1. SEPTEMBER AND OCTOBER, 1796 — No. 6. AUGUST AND SEPTEMBER, 1797.]
    New-York: Printed by T. and J. Swords, for Cornelius Davis. 1797. pp. viii, 480. 8vo.   AAS. BA. BPL. JCB. LOC. MHS. NYHS. NYPL. NYSL. PTS.. YC.

32917   THOMAS, ALEXANDER, JUNIOR   1775–1809
THE ORATOR'S ASSISTANT; BEING A SELECTION OF DIALOGUES FOR SCHOOLS AND ACADEMIES, TAKEN FROM SOME OF THE BEST DRAMATIC WRITINGS IN THE ENGLISH LANGUAGE. TO WHICH ARE ADDED A FEW HIGHLY ESTEEMED PIECES FOR DECLAMATION. INTENDED FOR YOUTH OF BOTH SEXES TO AID IN FORMING AN EASY, READY AND GRACEFUL ELOCUTION. BY ALEXANDER THOMAS, JUN. A.M. ORATOR FIT.
    *Worcester, Massachusetts: Printed at the Press of, and for Isaiah Thomas, jun. [at the Sign of Johnson's Head.]—October—*1797.—pp. 216. 12mo.
       AAS. BU. JCB. NYPL.
    123d Massachusetts District Copyright, issued to Isaiah Thomas, junior, as Proprietor, 17 August, 1797.

32918   THOMAS, ANDREWS AND PENNIMAN.
CATALOGUE OF BOOKS FOR SALE EITHER BY WHOLESALE OR RETAIL, BY THOMAS, ANDREWS & PENNIMAN, AT THE ALBANY BOOKSTORE, No. 45, STATE-STREET; WHERE CATALOGUES WILL BE DELIVERED GRATIS TO ANY PERSON WHO WILL CALL OR SEND FOR THEM. ORDERS FROM THE COUNTRY EXECUTED WITH THE UTMOST CARE, AND ATTENTION; AND A LARGE DISCOUNT MADE TO THOSE WHO PURCHASE TO SELL AGAIN.
    Albany: Printed by Loring Andrews & Co. for Thomas, Andrews & Penniman. [1797.] pp. 35. 12mo.   AAS.

32919   THOMAS'S MASSACHUSETTS, CONNECTICUT, RHODE-ISLAND, NEWHAMPSHIRE & VERMONT ALMANACK, WITH AN EPHEMERIS, FOR THE YEAR OF OUR LORD 1798: BEING THE SECOND AFTER BISSEXTILE, OR LEAP YEAR, AND TWENTY-SECOND OF THE INDEPENDENCE OF UNITED COLUMBIA. FROM CREATION, ACCORDING TO THE SCRIPTURES, 5760. [Six lines. Cut. Five lines of verse.]
    Printed at Worcester, Massachusetts: by Isaiah Thomas. Sold by him and by I. Thomas, jun. in Worcester; by Thomas & Andrews, S. Hall, B. Larkin, D. West, E. Larkin, J. Boyle, W. Spotswood, J. Nancrede, and at the Boston Bookstore in Boston; by Thomas, Andrews and Penniman, Albany; and by all the Booksellers in town and country. Price 7¼ *dols. per gross—*75 *cents doz.—*10 *cents single.* [1797.] pp. [48.] 12mo.   AAS. LOC. MHS.

32920   ——   SECOND EDITION. ISAIAH THOMAS'S MASSACHUSETTS, CONNECTICUT, RHODE-ISLAND, NEWHAMPSHIRE & VERMONT ALMANACK, WITH AN EPHEMERIS, FOR THE YEAR OF OUR LORD 1798: BEING THE SECOND AFTER BISSEXTILE, OR LEAP YEAR, AND TWENTY-SECOND OF THE INDEPENDENCE OF UNITED COLUMBIA. FROM CREATION, ACCORDING TO THE SCRIPTURES, 5760. [Six lines. Cut. Five lines of verse.]
    Printed at Worcester, Massachusetts, by Isaiah Thomas. Sold by him, and by I. Thomas, jun. in Worcester; by Thomas & Andrews, S. Hall, B. Larkin, D. West, E. Larkin, J. Boyle, W. Spotswood, J. Nancrede, and at the Boston Bookstore, in Boston; by Thomas, Andrews and Penniman, Albany; and by all the Booksellers, in town and country; . . . [1797.] pp. [48.] 12mo.   AAS. NYPL.
    Contains, An Act laying duties on stamped vellum, parchment, and paper.

32921 THOMAS'S MASSACHUSETTS SPY: OR, THE WORCESTER GAZETTE. [Mottos.] VOL. XXV. No. 1238. WEDNESDAY, JANUARY 4, [— VOL. XXVI. No. 1289. WEDNESDAY, DECEMBER 27, 1797.]

Printed at Worcester, (Massachusetts) by Leonard Worcester, at his Office, near the South Meeting House, for Isaiah Thomas. . . . 1797. fol.   AAS.

32922 THOMAS, ROBERT BAILEY   1766–1846
No. VI. THE FARMER'S ALMANACK, CALCULATED ON A NEW AND IMPROVED PLAN, FOR THE YEAR OF OUR LORD, 1798. BEING THE SECOND AFTER BISSEXTILE, OR LEAP-YEAR AND TWENTY-SECOND OF THE INDEPENDENCE OF AMERICA. [Six lines.] BY ROBERT B. THOMAS. [Cut. Four lines of verse from] THOMSON.

Boston: Printed by Manning & Loring, for John West, Proprietor of the copyright, and for sale at his Book-Store, No. 75 Cornhill, and by the other Booksellers in Boston. Sold also by the Booksellers in Salem, Newburyport, &c. by the Author at Sterling, and at various other places. [Price 7½ dollars per groce, 75 cents per dozen, and 10 cents single.] [1797.] pp. (48). 12mo.   AAS. LOC. MHS.

32923 THOMAS, WILLIAM
HODGE'S NORTH-CAROLINA ALMANACK, FOR THE YEAR OF OUR LORD 1798; BEING THE SECOND AFTER BISSEXTILE OR LEAP-YEAR, AND THE 22D–23D OF AMERICAN INDEPENDENCE. CALCULATED FOR THE STATE OF NORTH-CAROLINA, BEING PRE-CISELY ADAPTED TO THE MERIDIAN AND LATITUDE OF THE CITY OF RALEIGH; BUT WILL SERVE WITHOUT SENSIBLE ERROR FOR ANY OF THE STATES ADJACENT. . . .

Halifax: Printed by Abraham Hodge. [1797.]

32924 THOMPSON, JOHN
THE LOST AND UNDONE SON OF PERDITION: OR THE BIRTH, LIFE, AND CHARACTER OF JUDAS ISCARIOT. FAITHFULLY COLLECTED FROM SEVERAL ANCIENT AUTHORS OF UNDOUBTED CREDIT. BY J. THOMPSON.

Amherst, New-Hampshire: Printed by Samuel Preston. 1797. 12mo.

32925 THOMPSON, OTIS   1776–1859
A FUNERAL ORATION, DELIVERED IN THE CHAPEL OF RHODE-ISLAND COLLEGE, ON WEDNESDAY THE 29TH OF MARCH, 1797; OCCASIONED BY THE DEATH OF MR. ELIAB KINGMAN, A MEMBER OF THE JUNIOR CLASS. BY OTIS THOMPSON, CLASS-MATE OF THE DECEASED. [Four lines from] THOMPSON. PUBLISHED BY REQUEST OF THE STUDENTS.

Printed at Providence, by Carter and Wilkinson. M.DCC.XCVII. pp. (14). 4to.   AAS. JCB. NYPL. RIHS.

Contains, a Catalogue of members of the Junior Class in Rhode-Island College.

32926 THOMPSON, ——
HOMEWARD BOUND. A SONG. BY MICHAEL ARNE. THE WORDS BY CAPTAIN THOMPSON. PRICE 20 CENTS.

Printed and sold by B. Carr's Musical Repositories in New York and Philadelphia & J. Carr's Baltimore. 1797.   YC.

32927 THOMSON, JAMES   1700–1748
THE SEASONS. BY JAMES THOMSON. [Ten lines of verse.] STAFFORD'S EDITION. [With Life.]

Philadelphia: Printed by W. W. Woodward, No. 17. Chesnut St. 1797. pp. (2), (2), xxiv, 200, 4 plates. 12mo.   AAS. JCB. NYPL.

32928 THOUGHTS ON CONVERSATION AND MANNERS.
Augusta: Printed and sold by John E. Smith. 1797.

32929   THOUGHTS ON THE CHRISTIAN RELIGION. IN A LETTER TO A FRIEND. [Ornament.]
      Boston: Printed and sold by Samuel Hall, No. 53, Cornhill. 1797. pp. [14.]
8vo.   AAS. JCB.
      Dated, Dublin, 1796.

32930   THE THREE BROTHERS, A MORAL TALE; THE THREE SISTERS, A MORAL TALE; AND COUR-
AGE INSPIRED BY FRIENDSHIP, A MORAL TALE. EMBELLISHED WITH ENGRAVINGS.
      Boston: Printed and sold by William Spotswood, No. 55, Marlborough-Street.
1795.

32931   THUMB, THOMAS, pseudonym.
THE HISTORY OF THOMAS THUMB, WITH HIS WONDERFUL ADVENTURES AND SOME
ANECDOTES RESPECTING GRUMBO, THE GREAT GIANT.
      Wilmington: Printed by James Adams, north side of the upper Market House.
MDXXXCVII. pp. 30, wrappers. 32mo.

      Contains a three-page List of books for sale, by James Adams.

32932   THURBER, LABAN
THE YOUNG LADIES' & GENTLEMEN'S PRECEPTOR; OR EIGHTEEN MORAL RULES. BY
LABAN THURBER, MINISTER OF THE GOSPEL IN ATTLEBOROUGH. [COPY-RIGHT SE-
CURED ACCORDING TO LAW.]
      Warren, (Rhode-Island): Printed and sold by Nathaniel Phillips. M,DCC,-
XCVII. pp. 58. 12mo   AAS. BM. RIHS.

32933   THE TICKLER: BEING A SERIES OF PERIODICAL PAPERS, DESCRIPTIVE OF LIFE AND
MANNERS.
      New-York: Printed by George F. Hopkins. 1797.

      55th New York District Copyright, issued to George Foliot Hopkins,
as Proprietor, 2 October, 1797.

32934   THE TIME PIECE, AND LITERARY COMPANION. VOL. I. No. 1. MONDAY, MARCH 13,
[—VOL. II. No. 46. FRIDAY, DECEMBER 29, 1797.]
      *New-York: Printed on Monday, Wednesday and Friday mornings; at the
Office of P. Freneau, and A. Menut, No. 89, Beekman Street* . . . 1797. fol.
                                       BA. LOC. NYHS. NYPL..

      Established, as a tri-weekly, by Philip Freneau, and Alexander Menut,
and published until its publication ceased in August, 1798. In May, the
Printing-office was removed to No. 123 Fly-Market. On September 13th,
the partnership of Freneau and Menut, was dissolved by mutual consent: Freneau assuming all debts incurred during the first six months
of publication. And, beginning with the issue for September 15th, at
the commencement of the second volume, Matthew L. Davis was admitted
to partnership, and the sub-title dropped from the heading, appearing
as *The Time piece.* Published on Mondays, Wednesdays, & Fridays, by
P. Freneau & M. L. Davis, No. 26 Moore-Street, near Whitehall. With
the issue for March 14th, 1798, at the end of the first year of publication, Philip Freneau's connection ceased. The third volume being published by M. L. Davis & Co. into June, 1798, when it was published for
a short time by Robert Saunders, for the Proprietors, John Daly Burk,
and James Smith, at No. 25, Maiden-Lane, up to the issue for July 11th.
when Saunder's name ceased to appear, and no publisher appears up to
the issue for August 30, 1798, when publication apparently ceased.

32935   THE TIMES. [and] ALEXANDRIA [cut] ADVERTISER. [Motto.] VOL. I. No. 1. MON-
DAY, APRIL 10, [— No. 228. SATURDAY, DECEMBER 30, 1797.]
> *Printed daily, by Thomas and Westcott, Royal-Street, between the Post-Office
> and Coffee-House, Alexandria.* 1797. fol.   AAS. LOC.
>> Established, as a daily, by John V. Thomas and James D. Westcott, and
>> continued by them into April, 1799, when Thomas withdrew, and was
>> succeeded by John Westcott as J. & J. D. Westcott, up to May, 1802, when
>> John Westcott withdrew. James D. Westcott continued publication to
>> July 31, 1802, when it was discontinued, and established a tri-weekly
>> newspaper called *The Columbian Advertiser.* With the issue for April
>> 17, 1799, the title was altered to *The Times: and District of Columbia
>> Daily Advertiser.*

32936   TO THE ELECTORS OF DUTCHESS COUNTY. [Colophon:]
> *Poughkeepsie: Printed by N. Power.* 13 *April,* 1797. Broadside. fol.

32937   THE TOCSIN. SATURDAY, JANUARY 7, [— FRIDAY, AUGUST 25, 1797.]
> *Published by Benjamin Poor, at the Hook, Hallowell, [District of Maine.]
> [Massachusetts.]* 1797. fol.   AAS.
>> Discontinued, probably, in August, as above.

32938   TOWNSEND, SHIPPIE
OBSERVATIONS ON THE RELIGIOUS EDUCATION OF CHILDREN: IN A LETTER TO MR.
HEZEKIAH PACKARD MINISTER OF CHELMSFORD. WITH REMARKS ON HIS CATE-
CHISM. DESERVING HIS SERIOUS ATTENTION. RECOMMENDED TO HIM, AND THE
LEARNED GENTLEMEN, WHO HAVE PUBLICKLY PATRONIZED HIS WELL-MEANT PER-
FORMANCE, TO RE-EXAMINE AND COMPARE IT WITH THE SCRIPTURES. BY SHIPPIE
TOWNSEND. [Two lines from] PSALM CXIX. 105.
> *Printed by B. Edes, Kilby-Street, Boston.*—1797. *Sold by S. Hall, No. 53, Corn-
> hill.—J. Folsom, No. 30, Union-Street.—J. West, No. 75, Cornhill.* pp. 7. 8vo.   AAS.

32939   TRAVELS BEFORE THE FLOOD. AN INTERESTING, ORIGINAL RECORD OF MEN AND
MANNERS IN THE ANTEDILUVIAN WORLD, INTERPRETED IN FOURTEEN EVENING CON-
VERSATIONS BETWEEN THE CALIPH OF BAGDAD AND HIS COURT. TRANSLATED FROM
THE ARABIC.
> *London printed: Carlisle: Re-printed for A. Loudon, by George Kline.* 1797.
> 2 vols. pp. 164; 151. 12mo.

32940   TREZIULNEY, ——
LETTER TO GEORGE WASHINGTON PRESIDENT OF THE UNITED STATES: CONTAINING
STRICTURES ON HIS ADDRESS OF THE SEVENTEENTH OF SEPTEMBER, 1796, NOTIFY-
ING HIS RELINQUISHMENT OF THE PRESIDENTIAL OFFICE. BY JASPER DWIGHT, OF
VERMONT.
> *Baltimore: Printed for George Keatinge's Book-Store.* 1797. pp. (44). 8vo.
>   LOC.
>> This diatribe is usually ascribed to William Duane, *alias* Jasper Dwight,
>> of Vermont; who, born on the shores of Lake Champlain, left this coun-
>> try when ten years of age, during the troubles of the Green Mountain
>> Boys with their New York aggressors; lived in his mother's house in
>> Ireland a turbulous youth, marrying out of his church before he was of
>> age, a Presbyterian; then went to India, and engaged in journalism,
>> against the government, until he was shanghaied out of the country by
>> the authorities; when he arrived in England, the East India Company
>> sent him to Parliament, as a sop, and the Parliament promptly refused
>> to receive him; and, after again drifting into journalism, he came to
>> Philadelphia in 1795. With this career as a background, within a year,
>> he used this work of an employee, as a medium, to falsify opinions of
>> men and events in this country to meet his own, and his employer's ends.
>> See No. 31315 of this volume.

32941   TRUE, BENJAMIN
AN ALMANAC, FOR THE YEAR OF OUR LORD, 1798; BEING THE SECOND AFTER BIS-
SEXTILE OR LEAP YEAR, AND OF THE INDEPENDENCE OF THE UNITED STATES THE
TWENTY-SECOND. CALCULATED, FOR THE MERIDIAN OF HANOVER, NEWHAMPSHIRE,
LATITUDE 43 DEGREES, 35 MINUTES, NORTH; BUT WILL SERVE WITHOUT ANY
ESSENTIAL VARIATION FOR THE ADJACENT STATES. CONTAINING THE COMMON
ASTRONOMICAL CALCULATIONS, AND A VARIETY OF OTHER MATTERS INSTRUCTIVE &
ENTERTAINING. [Three lines of quotation.]
*Printed at Hanover, Newhampshire, by Benjamin True, and sold at his Office,
wholesale and retail.* [1797.] pp. (24). 12mo.   AAS. NHHS.

32942   TRUMBULL, BENJAMIN   1735–1820
A COMPLETE HISTORY OF CONNECTICUT, CIVIL AND ECCLESIASTICAL, FROM THE EMIGRA-
TION OF ITS FIRST PLANTERS FROM ENGLAND IN MDCXXX, TO MDCCXIII. BY BENJAMIN
TRUMBULL, D.D. VOL. I. PUBLISHED IN CONFORMITY TO ACT OF CONGRESS.
Hartford: Hudson & Goodwin. 1797. pp. xix, 587, portraits of John Dav-
enport, John Winthrop, Gurdon Saltonstall, map. 8vo.
     AAS. BA. BM. BU. CHS. HC. JCB. NL. NYHS. NYPL. UTS. YC.
Title of Map: A CORRECT MAP OF CONNECTICUT FROM ACTUAL SURVEY. ENGRAVED
BY A. DOOLITTLE NEWHAVEN 1797.

Reprinted, with a second volume, in New Haven, in 1818; and, in New
London, in 1898.

32943   TRUMBULL, JOHN   1750–1831
THE PROGRESS OF DULNESS, OR THE RARE ADVENTURES OF TOM BRAINLESS. BY THE
CELEBRATED AUTHOR OF MC.FINGAL.
Printed at Carlisle, for Archibald Loudon, Bookseller, by George Kline. 1797.
pp. 72. 12mo.   BU.

32944   TURNER, NATHANIEL
A FUNERAL ORATION, DELIVERED ON THE DEATH OF BENJAMIN FRENCH, A MEMBER
OF THE SOPHOMORE CLASS IN WILLIAMS COLLEGE. AUGUST 29TH, 1796. BY NA-
THANIEL TURNER, CLASSMATE OF THE DECEASED.
Stockbridge: Printed by Loring Andrews. 1797. pp. (21). 8vo.   AAS.

32945   TYLER, ROYALL   1757–1826
THE ALGERINE CAPTIVE; OR THE LIFE AND ADVENTURES OF DOCTOR UPDIKE UNDER-
HILL: SIX YEARS A PRISONER AMONG THE ALGERIANS. DEDICATED TO HIS EXCEL-
LENCY DAVID HUMPHREYS, ESQ; AND PUBLISHED ACCORDING TO ACT OF CONGRESS.
[Three lines of verse.]
Walpole, Newhampshire: Printed by David Carlisle, jun. 1797. 2 vols. pp.
428. 12mo.   AAS. BA. BM. HC. JCB. NYPL.

New Hampshire District Copyright, issued to David Carlisle, junior, as
Proprietor, 18 July, 1797. Reprinted in London in 1802; and in Hartford in 1816.

32946   —— THE GEORGIA SPEC; OR, LAND IN THE MOON. A COMEDY, IN THREE ACTS.
Boston: 1797. 8vo.

32947   UNION COLLEGE.
SONGS SUNG AT THE FIRST COMMENCEMENT OF UNION COLLEGE. MAY 3, 1797.
Schenectady: Printed by Cornelius P. Wyckoff. 1797. Broadside.

32948   UNITED BRETHREN, OR MORAVIANS.
TÄGLICHEN LOOSUNGEN, UND LEHRTEXTE DER BRÜDERGEMEINDE FÜR DAS JAHR 1798.
Lancaster: Gedruckt bey Johann Albrecht & Comp. 1797. 8vo.

32949   UNITED CHRISTIAN FRIENDS.
HYMNS FOR THE USE OF THE SOCIETY OF UNITED CHRISTIAN FRIENDS, WITH THEIR
CONSTITUTION ANNEXED.
New-York: 1797.

32950   UNITED STATES OF AMERICA.
ACTS PASSED AT THE SECOND SESSION OF THE FOURTH CONGRESS OF THE UNITED STATES
OF AMERICA: BEGUN AND HELD AT THE CITY OF PHILADELPHIA, IN THE STATE OF
PENNSYLVANIA, ON MONDAY THE FIFTH OF DECEMBER, ONE THOUSAND SEVEN HUN-
DRED AND NINETY-SIX [— 3 MARCH, 1797], AND OF THE INDEPENDENCE OF THE
UNITED STATES, THE TWENTY-FIRST.
Richmond: Printed by Aug: Davis, Printer for the Public. M,DCC,XCVII.
pp. (2), (57)–[84.] fol.   NYPL.

32951   —— ACTS PASSED AT THE FIRST SESSION OF THE FIFTH CONGRESS OF THE UNITED
STATES OF AMERICA: BEGUN AND HELD AT THE CITY OF PHILADELPHIA, IN THE
STATE OF PENNSYLVANIA, ON MONDAY THE FIFTEENTH OF MAY, ONE THOUSAND
SEVEN HUNDRED AND NINETY-SEVEN, AND OF THE INDEPENDENCE OF THE UNITED
STATES, THE TWENTY-FIRST. PUBLISHED BY AUTHORITY.
Philadelphia: Printed by William Ross, near Congress-Hall, 1797. pp. (46),
(2). 8vo.   AAS. JCB.

32952   —— — ACTS PASSED AT THE FIRST SESSION OF THE FIFTH CONGRESS OF THE UNITED
STATES OF AMERICA, BEGUN AND HELD AT THE CITY OF PHILADELPHIA, IN THE
STATE OF PENNSYLVANIA, ON MONDAY THE FIFTEENTH OF MAY IN THE YEAR
M,DCC,XCVII. AND OF THE INDEPENDENCE OF THE UNITED STATES, THE TWENTY-
FIRST.
Philadelphia: Printed by Richard Folwell, No. 33, Carter's Alley. [1797.]
pp. [50.] 8vo.   AAS. JCB.

32953   —— AN ACT AUTHORISING A DETACHMENT FROM THE MILITIA OF THE UNITED STATES.
[Forty-three lines.] APPROVED, JUNE 24TH, 1797. JOHN ADAMS, PRESIDENT OF
THE UNITED STATES.
[Philadelphia: Printed by William Ross. 1797.] Broadside. fol.   HSP.

32954   —— FIFTH CONGRESS OF THE UNITED STATES: AT THE FIRST SESSION, BEGUN AND
HELD AT THE CITY OF PHILADELPHIA, IN THE STATE OF PENNSYLVANIA, ON MON-
DAY THE FIFTEENTH DAY OF MAY, ONE THOUSAND SEVEN HUNDRED AND NINETY-
SEVEN. AN ACT IN ADDITION TO . . . "AN ACT . . . REGISTERING . . .
SHIPS." APPROVED JUNE TWENTY-SEVENTH, 1797.
[Philadelphia: Printed by William Ross. 1797.] pp. (2). fol.

Another Act added in printing.

32955   —— AN ACT LAYING DUTIES UPON STAMPED VELLUM, PARCHMENT, AND PAPER. PASSED
JULY 6, 1797.
[Alexandria: Printed by Thomas and Westcott, 1797.] Broadside. fol.

32956   —— STAMP ACT. AN ACT LAYING DUTIES ON STAMPED VELLUM, PARCHMENT,
AND PAPER. [Four columns.] APPROVED—JULY 6, 1797. JOHN ADAMS, PRESI-
DENT OF THE UNITED STATES. [Colophon:]
New-York: Printed by J. Oram, No. 33, Liberty-street. [1797.] Broadside.
fol.   LOC.

32957   —— AN ACT LAYING DUTIES ON STAMPED VELLUM, PARCHMENT, AND PAPER.
APPROVED BY THE PRESIDENT OF THE UNITED STATES, JULY 8TH, 1797.
Walpole, New-Hampshire: Printed by David Carlisle, jun. 1797.

AUCTION
VALUES

UNITED STATES, continued.

32958 —— FIFTH CONGRESS OF THE UNITED STATES: AT THE FIRST SESSION, BEGUN AND HELD AT THE CITY OF PHILADELPHIA, IN THE STATE OF PENNSYLVANIA, ON MONDAY THE FIFTEENTH DAY OF MAY, ONE THOUSAND SEVEN HUNDRED AND NINETY-SEVEN. AN ACT PROHIBITING EXPORTATION OF ARMS. . . . APPROVED, JUNE FOURTEEN, 1797.
[*Philadelphia: Printed by William Ross.* 1797.] Broadside. 4to.

32959 —— AN ACT RELATIVE TO THE COMPENSATIONS . . . CERTAIN OFFICERS EMPLOYED IN THE COLLECTION OF IMPORT. PASSED THE HOUSE OF REPRESENTATIVES FEBRUARY 24, 1797.
[*Philadelphia:*] *Printed by John Fenno.* [1797.] pp. (3). fol.

32960 —— AN ACT REPEALING IN PART "THE ACT CONCERNING THE DUTIES ON SPIRITS DISTILLED WITHIN THE UNITED STATES," PASSED THE EIGHTH OF MAY, ONE THOUSAND SEVEN HUNDRED AND NINETY-TWO, AND IMPOSING CERTAIN DUTIES ON THE CAPACITY OF STILLS OF A PARTICULAR DESCRIPTION. . . . APPROVED MARCH 3D 1797. GO. WASHINGTON, PRESIDENT OF THE UNITED STATES.
[*Philadelphia: Printed by William Ross.* 1797.] pp. (2). fol.   LOC.

32961 —— AN ADDRESS IN ANSWER TO THE SPEECH OF THE PRESIDENT OF THE UNITED STATES TO BOTH HOUSES OF CONGRESS, AT THE COMMENCEMENT OF THE PRESENT SESSION, REPORTED BY A SELECT COMMITTEE ON MONDAY, NOVEMBER 27, 1797.
Philadelphia: Printed by Joseph Gales. [1797.] pp. 6. 8vo.

32962 —— A BILL PROHIBITING FOR A LIMITED TIME, THE EXPORTATION OF ARMS. [June 8, 1797.]
[Philadelphia:] Printed by John Fenno. [1797.] fol.

32963 —— A BILL TO PREVENT CITIZENS OF THE UNITED STATES PRIVATEERING. [June 9, 1797.]
[*Philadelphia:*] *Printed by John Fenno.* [1797.] fol.

32964 —— 12TH DECEMBER, 1797. COMMITTED TO A COMMITTEE OF THE WHOLE HOUSE, TO-MORROW. A BILL FOR THE RELIEF OF THE REPRESENTATIVES OF WILLIAM CARMICHAEL, DECEASED. [Twenty-one lines.]
[*Philadelphia: Printed by William Ross.* 1797.] Broadside. fol.   LOC.

32965 —— THE DEBATES AND INTERESTING SPEECHES IN THE FIFTH CONGRESS OF THE U. STATES AT THEIR FIRST SESSION, BEGUN AND HELD AT PHILADELPHIA, ON THE 15TH DAY OF MAY, 1797. BEING AN HISTORICAL RELATION OF THEIR PROCEEDINGS COMPILED FROM THE REPORTS, BILLS, AND JOURNALS.
Newburgh: Printed by David Denniston. 1797. 8vo.

32966 —— [RECEIVED AND READ 19TH MAY.] DOCUMENTS. REFERRED TO IN THE PRESIDENT'S SPEECH TO BOTH HOUSES OF THE FIFTH CONGRESS, ON THE SIXTEENTH MAY, 1797. PUBLISHED BY ORDER OF THE HOUSE OF REPRESENTATIVES.
Philadelphia: Printed by W. Ross, near Congress-Hall. [1797.] pp. 72, (1). 8vo.   AAS. BA. HSP. JCB.

32967 —— IN SENATE OF THE UNITED STATES, MARCH 1ST, 1797. MR. HILLHOUSE, FROM THE COMMITTEE TO WHOM WAS REFERRED THE LETTER AND ENCLOSURES FROM THE GOVERNOR OF NORTH CAROLINA, RELATIVE TO THE EXTINGUISHMENT OF THE INDIAN TITLE TO LANDS GRANTED TO T. GLASGOW & CO. BY THE STATE OF NORTH CAROLINA—THE ADDRESS OF THE LEGISLATURE OF THE STATE OF TENNESSEE, ON THE SAME SUBJECT—AND ALSO THE PETITION OF J. GLASGOW AND OTHERS, RELATIVE TO LANDS ENTERED IN THE OFFICE OF JOHN ARMSTRONG, ESQ. AND SINCE CEDED TO THE UNITED STATES—REPORTED: . . .
[*Philadelphia: Printed by John Fenno.* 1797.] pp. 3. 8vo.   AAS.

UNITED STATES, continued.

32968 —— IN SENATE OF THE UNITED STATES, MARCH 2D, 1797. THE COMMITTEE TO
WHOM WAS REFERRED THE RESOLUTIONS OF THE SENATE RESPECTING THE SOUTH-
ERN AND WESTERN BOUNDARY OF GEORGIA, HAVING HAD THE SAME UNDER CON-
SIDERATION BEG LEAVE TO SUBMIT THE FOLLOWING REPORT—
[Philadelphia: Printed by John Fenno. 1797.] pp. (4). 8vo.　　　AAS.

32969 —— JOURNAL OF THE HOUSE OF REPRESENTATIVES OF THE UNITED STATES, AT THE
SECOND SESSION OF THE FOURTH CONGRESS. [5TH December] ANNO M,DCC,XCVI.
[— 3D MARCH, 1797.] AND OF THE INDEPENDENCE OF THE UNITED STATES THE
TWENTY-FIRST.
Philadelphia: Printed by William Ross, near Congress-Hall. 1796. [1797.]
pp. 299, (27). 8vo.　　　AAS. BA.

Also, apparently, issued in thirty-seven folio parts, of four pages each,
a day or so apart, during the session.

32970 —— JOURNAL OF THE HOUSE OF REPRESENTATIVES OF THE UNITED STATES, AT THE
FIRST SESSION OF THE FIFTH CONGRESS. THE TWENTY-FIRST YEAR OF THE INDE-
PENDENCE OF THE UNITED STATES. [15 May – 10 July, 1797.]
Philadelphia: Printed by W. Ross, near Congress-Hall. 1797. pp. 140, xii.
8vo.　　　AAS. BA. JCB.

32971 —— JOURNAL OF THE SENATE OF THE UNITED STATES OF AMERICA, BEING THE
SECOND SESSION OF THE FOURTH CONGRESS, BEGUN AND HELD AT THE CITY OF
PHILADELPHIA, DECEMBER 5TH, 1796, [— 3d March, 1797] AND IN THE TWENTY-
FIRST YEAR OF THE SOVEREIGNTY OF THE SAID UNITED STATES.
*Philadelphia: Printed by John Fenno, Printer to the Senate of the United
States.* M,DCC,XCVI. [1797.] pp. 175, iv, 18. 8vo.　　　AAS. BA. JCB. NYPL.

32972 —— JOURNAL OF THE SENATE OF THE UNITED STATES OF AMERICA. BEING THE
FIRST SESSION OF THE FIFTH CONGRESS, BEGUN AND HELD AT THE CITY OF PHILA-
DELPHIA, MAY 15TH, 1797 [— 10 July, 1797] AND IN THE TWENTY-FIRST YEAR OF
THE SOVEREIGNTY OF THE SAID UNITED STATES.
*Philadelphia: Printed by John Fenno, Printer to the Senate of the United
States.* 1797. pp. 115, xvii, x. 8vo.　　　AAS. BA. JCB. MHS.

32973 —— THE LAWS OF THE UNITED STATES OF AMERICA. IN THREE VOLUMES. VOL. III.
PUBLISHED BY AUTHORITY.
Philadelphia: Printed by Richard Folwell, No. 33, Carter's Alley. 1796.
[1797.] pp. 478; 130. 8vo.　　　JCB. MHS.
A fourth volume was published in 1799.

32974 —— THE LAWS OF THE UNITED STATES OF AMERICA. CONTAINING, ACTS OF THE
SECOND SESSION OF THE FOURTH CONGRESS. [5 December, 1796 — 3 March, 1797.]
PUBLISHED BY AUTHORITY.
Philadelphia: Printed by Richard Folwell, No. 33, Carter's Alley. 1797. pp.
(2), (143)–[240], 8. 8vo.　　　AAS.

32975 —— A LIST OF THE NAMES AND PLACES OF RESIDENCE, OF THE MEMBERS OF THE SEN-
ATE AND HOUSE OF REPRESENTATIVES OF THE UNITED STATES. [Three columns.]
[Philadelphia: Printed by John Fenno. 1797.] Broadside. fol.　　　AAS.

32976 —— MEMORIAL OF THE ILLINOIS AND WABASH LAND COMPANY, 13TH JANUARY,
1797, REFERRED TO MR. JEREMIAH SMITH, MR. KITTERA, AND MR. BALDWIN.
PUBLISHED BY ORDER OF THE HOUSE OF REPRESENTATIVES.
[Philadelphia: Printed by William Ross. 1797.] pp. 8. 8vo.　　　AAS. BA.

AUCTION
VALUES

UNITED STATES, continued.

32977 —— — MEMORIAL OF THE ILLINOIS AND WABASH LAND COMPANY. 13TH JANUARY, 1797. REFERRED TO MR. JEREMIAH SMITH. MR. KITTERA, AND MR. BALDWIN. PUBLISHED BY ORDER OF THE HOUSE OF REPRESENTATIVES.
Philadelphia: Printed by Richard Folwell. [1797.] pp. (26). 8vo.
CI.S. HC. JCB. LOC. NYPL. RIHS.

32978 —— MR. HARPER'S MOTION. 9TH FEBRUARY, 1797, COMMITTED TO A COMMITTEE OF THE WHOLE HOUSE, ON MONDAY NEXT. PUBLISHED BY ORDER OF THE HOUSE OF REPRESENTATIVES. [PHILADELPHIA. PRINTED BY ORDER OF THE HOUSE OF REPRESENTATIVES.]
[Philadelphia: Printed by William Ross. 1797.] pp. 4. 8vo.   AAS. BA.

32979 —— MR. WILLIAM SMITH'S MOTION TO AMEND THE CONSTITUTION OF THE UNITED STATES. 6TH JANUARY 1797. PUBLISHED BY ORDER OF THE HOUSE OF REPRESENTATIVES.
[Philadelphia: Printed by William Ross. 1797.] pp. (4). 8vo.   AAS. BA.

32980 —— THE REMONSTRANCE AND PETITION OF THE LEGISLATURE OF THE STATE OF TENNESSEE TO THE SENATE OF THE UNITED STATES. [October 20, 1797.]
Printed by John Fenno, Printer to the Senate of the United States. 1797. pp. (12). 8vo.   AAS. BA. JCB.
Against the extension of the boundary between the United States and the Cherokee Indians.

32981 —— REMONSTRANCE AND PETITION OF THE LEGISLATURE OF THE STATE OF TENNESSEE. 4TH DECEMBER, 1797. REFERRED TO MR. PINCKNEY, MR. VENABLE, MR. NATHANIEL SMITH, MR. WM. C. C. CLAIBORNE, AND MR. BAYARD. 20TH DECEMBER, 1797, REPORT MADE, AND COMMITTED TO A COMMITTEE OF THE WHOLE HOUSE, ON MONDAY NEXT. [PUBLISHED BY ORDER OF THE HOUSE OF REPRESENTATIVES.]
[Philadelphia: Printed by William Ross. 1797.] pp. (2), (177)–201. 8vo.
AAS. BA.

32982 —— REPORT OF THE COMMITTEE, APPOINTED ON THE TWENTY-FOURTH ULTIMO, TO ENQUIRE WHETHER ANY, AND WHAT ALTERATIONS ARE NECESSARY IN THE LAW, INTITULED "AN ACT REGULATING FOREIGN COINS; AND FOR OTHER PURPOSES." 11TH DECEMBER, 1797, CONSIDERATION POSTPONED UNTIL WEDNESDAY NEXT. [PUBLISHED BY ORDER OF THE HOUSE OF REPRESENTATIVES.]
[Philadelphia: Printed by William Ross. 1797.] pp. (91)–93. 8vo. AAS. BA.

32983 —— REPORT OF THE COMMITTEE APPOINTED TO PREPARE AN ADDRESS TO THE PRESIDENT OF THE UNITED STATES, IN ANSWER TO HIS SPEECH TO BOTH HOUSES OF CONGRESS. 12TH DECEMBER, 1796, READ, AND ORDERED TO BE COMMITTED TO A COMMITTEE OF THE WHOLE HOUSE, TO-MORROW. PUBLISHED BY ORDER OF THE HOUSE OF REPRESENTATIVES.
[Philadelphia: Printed by William Ross. 1797.] pp. 6. 8vo.   AAS. BA.

32984 —— REPORT OF THE COMMITTEE APPOINTED TO ENQUIRE WHETHER ANY, AND WHAT ALTERATIONS OUGHT TO BE MADE IN THE COMPENSATIONS ALLOWED BY LAW, TO THE OFFICERS OF THE UNITED STATES. 9TH JANUARY, 1797, COMMITTED TO A COMMITTEE OF THE WHOLE HOUSE, ON THURSDAY NEXT. PUBLISHED BY ORDER OF THE HOUSE OF REPRESENTATIVES.
[Philadelphia: Printed by William Ross. 1797.] pp. (4). 8vo.   AAS. BA.

UNITED STATES, continued.

32985 —— REPORT OF THE COMMITTEE APPOINTED TO ENQUIRE WHETHER ANY, AND WHAT AMENDMENTS MAY BE NECESSARY IN THE ACT "TO ASCERTAIN AND FIX THE MILITARY ESTABLISHMENT OF THE UNITED STATES." 13TH JANUARY 1797, COMMITTED TO A COMMITTEE OF THE WHOLE HOUSE, ON TUESDAY NEXT. PUBLISHED BY ORDER OF THE HOUSE OF REPRESENTATIVES.

[Philadelphia: Printed by William Ross. 1797.] pp. 4. 8vo. AAS. BA.

32986 —— REPORT OF THE COMMITTEE APPOINTED TO ENQUIRE INTO THE STATE OF THE NAVAL EQUIPMENT, ORDERED BY FORMER ACTS OF CONGRESS; AND WHETHER ANY, AND WHAT OTHER NAVAL FORCE IS NECESSARY FOR THE PROTECTION OF THE COMMERCE OF THE UNITED STATES, AND THE SUPPORT OF THEIR FLAG. 25TH JANUARY, 1797, COMMITTED TO A COMMITTEE OF THE WHOLE HOUSE, ON MONDAY NEXT. PUBLISHED BY ORDER OF THE HOUSE OF REPRESENTATIVES.

[Philadelphia: Printed by William Ross. 1797.] pp. 6. 8vo. AAS. BA.

32987 —— REPORT OF THE COMMITTEE APPOINTED ON THE FIFTH INSTANT, TO ENQUIRE INTO THE PROGRESS MADE IN CARRYING INTO EFFECT, THE ACT, INTITULED "AN ACT PROVIDING FOR THE SALE OF THE LANDS OF THE UNITED STATES, IN THE TERRITORY NORTH WEST OF THE RIVER OHIO, AND ABOVE THE MOUTH OF KENTUCKY RIVER." 30TH JANUARY, 1797, COMMITTED TO A COMMITTEE OF THE WHOLE HOUSE, ON WEDNESDAY NEXT. PUBLISHED BY ORDER OF THE HOUSE OF REPRESENTATIVES.

[Philadelphia: Printed by William Ross. 1797.] pp. 7. 8vo. AAS. BA. JCB.

32988 —— REPORT OF THE COMMITTEE APPOINTED THE SIXTEENTH OF DECEMBER LAST, TO ENQUIRE INTO THE ACTUAL STATE OF THE FORTIFICATIONS OF THE PORTS AND HARBOURS OF THE UNITED STATES; AND WHETHER ANY, AND WHAT PROVISION IS NECESSARY TO BE MADE ON THAT SUBJECT. 10TH FEBRUARY. 1797, ORDERED TO LIE ON THE TABLE. 11TH FEBRUARY, 1797, COMMITTED TO A COMMITTEE OF THE WHOLE HOUSE, ON WEDNESDAY NEXT. PUBLISHED BY ORDER OF THE HOUSE OF REPRESENTATIVES.

[Philadelphia: Printed by William Ross. 1797.] pp. 4. 8vo. AAS. BA.

32989 —— REPORT OF THE COMMITTEE APPOINTED TO ENQUIRE INTO THE OPERATION OF THE ACT FOR THE RELIEF AND PROTECTION OF AMERICAN SEAMEN, AND REPORT WHAT AMENDMENTS ARE NECESSARY TO BE MADE THERETO. 28TH FEBRUARY, 1797, COMMITTED TO A COMMITTEE OF THE WHOLE HOUSE, TO-MORROW. PUBLISHED BY ORDER OF THE HOUSE OF REPRESENTATIVES.

[Philadelphia: Printed by William Ross. 1797.] pp. 25. 8vo. AAS. BA. JCB.

32990 —— REPORT OF THE COMMITTEE OF CLAIMS, ON THE PETITION OF HENRY HILL. 26TH MAY, 1796. COMMITTED TO A COMMITTEE OF THE WHOLE HOUSE TO-MORROW. 9TH DECEMBER, 1796. COMMITTED TO A COMMITTEE OF THE WHOLE HOUSE, ON MONDAY NEXT. PUBLISHED BY ORDER OF THE HOUSE OF REPRESENTATIVES.

[Philadelphia: Printed by William Ross. 1797.] pp. 4. 8vo. AAS. BA.

32991 —— — REPORT OF THE COMMITTEE OF CLAIMS, TO WHOM WERE RE-COMMITTED THE PETITION OF HENRY HILL; AND SEVERAL REPORTS THEREON. 13TH JANUARY, 1797, COMMITTED TO A COMMITTEE OF THE WHOLE HOUSE, ON MONDAY NEXT. PUBLISHED BY ORDER OF THE HOUSE OF REPRESENTATIVES.

[Philadelphia: Printed by William Ross. 1797.] pp. 6. 8vo. AAS. BA. UTS.

32992 —— REPORT OF THE COMMITTEE OF CLAIMS, ON THE PETITION OF J. GIBBONS. 22 DECEMBER, 1796.

[Philadelphia: Printed by William Ross. 1796.] BA.

UNITED STATES, continued.

32993 —— REPORT OF THE COMMITTEE OF CLAIMS, ON THE PETITION OF WILLIAM PARSONS, BY STEPHEN PARSONS, HIS ATTORNEY. 26TH DECEMBER, 1796, ORDERED TO LIE ON THE TABLE. 27TH DECEMBER, 1796, COMMITTED TO A COMMITTEE OF THE WHOLE HOUSE, TO-MORROW. PUBLISHED BY ORDER OF THE HOUSE OF REPRESENTATIVES.
[Philadelphia: Printed by William Ross. 1797.] pp. (4). 8vo.   AAS. BA.

32994 —— REPORT OF THE COMMITTEE OF CLAIMS ON COPIES OF THE PROCEEDINGS OF THE ACCOUNTING OFFICERS OF THE TREASURY UPON CERTAIN CLAIMS NOT ADMITTED TO BE VALID.   29 DECEMBER, 1796.
[Philadelphia: Printed by William Ross. 1796.]   BA.

32995 —— REPORT OF THE COMMITTEE OF CLAIMS, ON THE PETITION OF GILBERT DENCH, 4TH JANUARY, 1797, COMMITTED TO A COMMITTEE OF THE WHOLE HOUSE, TO-DAY. PUBLISHED BY ORDER OF THE HOUSE OF REPRESENTATIVES.
[Philadelphia: Printed by William Ross. 1797.] pp. 4. 8vo.   AAS. BA.

32996 —— REPORT OF THE COMMITTEE OF CLAIMS, ON THE PETITION OF JAMES ORE. 12TH JANUARY, 1797, COMMITTED TO A COMMITTEE OF THE WHOLE HOUSE, ON WEDNESDAY NEXT. PUBLISHED BY ORDER OF THE HOUSE OF REPRESENTATIVES.
[Philadelphia: Printed by William Ross. 1797.] pp. 4. 8vo.   AAS. BA.

32997 —— REPORT OF THE COMMITTEE OF CLAIMS, ON THE PETITION OF OLIVER POLLOCK. 26TH MAY 1796, COMMITTED TO A COMMITTEE OF THE WHOLE HOUSE, TO-MORROW, 12TH JANUARY 1797, COMMITTED TO A COMMITTEE OF THE WHOLE HOUSE, ON MONDAY NEXT. PUBLISHED BY ORDER OF THE HOUSE OF REPRESENTATIVES.
[Philadelphia: Printed by William Ross. 1797.] pp. 4. 8vo.   AAS. BA.

32998 —— —— REPORT OF THE COMMITTEE OF CLAIMS, ON THE PETITION OF OLIVER POLLOCK. 26TH MAY, 1796, COMMITTED TO A COMMITTEE OF THE WHOLE HOUSE, TO-MORROW. 12TH JANUARY, 1797, COMMITTED TO A COMMITTEE OF THE WHOLE HOUSE, ON MONDAY NEXT. 18TH DECEMBER, 1797, COMMITTED TO A COMMITTEE OF THE WHOLE HOUSE, ON WEDNESDAY NEXT. [PUBLISHED BY ORDER OF THE HOUSE OF REPRESENTATIVES.]
[Philadelphia: Printed by William Ross. 1797.] pp. (2), (149)–150. 8vo.   AAS. BA.

32999 —— REPORT OF THE COMMITTEE OF CLAIMS, ON THE PETITION OF THE WIDOW OF THE LATE SCOLACUTTAW, OR HANGING MAN, ONE OF THE CHIEFS OF THE CHEROKEE NATION OF INDIANS. 17TH JANUARY, 1797, REFERRED TO THE COMMITTEE OF THE WHOLE HOUSE, TO WHOM IS COMMITTED THE REPORT OF THE COMMITTEE OF CLAIMS ON THE PETITION OF JAMES ORE. PUBLISHED BY ORDER OF THE HOUSE OF REPRESENTATIVES.
[Philadelphia: Printed by William Ross. 1797.] pp. 4. 8vo.   AAS. BA.

33000 —— REPORT OF THE COMMITTEE OF CLAIMS, ON THE PETITION OF EDWARD ST. LOE LIVERMORE. 24TH JANUARY, 1797, COMMITTED TO A COMMITTEE OF THE WHOLE HOUSE, TO-MORROW. PUBLISHED BY ORDER OF THE HOUSE OF REPRESENTATIVES.
[Philadelphia: Printed by William Ross. 1797.] pp. 4. 8vo.   AAS. BA.

33001 —— REPORT OF THE COMMITTEE OF CLAIMS, ON THE PETITION OF ANNA WELSH. 7TH FEBRUARY, 1797, COMMITTED TO A COMMITTEE OF THE WHOLE HOUSE, ON MONDAY NEXT. PUBLISHED BY ORDER OF THE HOUSE OF REPRESENTATIVES.
[Philadelphia: Printed by William Ross. 1797.] pp. 6. 8vo.   AAS. BA.

UNITED STATES, continued.

33002 —— Report of the committee of claims, on the Petition of Comfort Sands, and others. 9th February 1797, committed to a committee of the whole House, on Tuesday next. Published by order of the House of Representatives.

[Philadelphia: Printed by William Ross. 1797.] pp. 6. 8vo.   AAS. BA.

33003 —— Report of the committee of claims, on the Petition of the corporation of Rhode-Island College. 11th February 1797, committed to a committee of the whole House, on Wednesday next. Published by order of the House of Representatives.

[Philadelphia: Printed by William Ross. 1797.] pp. 4. 8vo. AAS. BA. RIHS.

33004 —— —— Report of the committee of claims on the Petition of the corporation of Rhode-Island College, 11th February, 1797, committed to a committee of the whole House, on Wednesday next. 12th December, 1797, committed to a committee of the whole House, to-morrow. [Published by order of the House of Representatives.]

[Philadelphia: Printed by William Ross. 1797.] pp. (2), (97)–101. 8vo.
AAS. BA. RIHS.

33005 —— Report of the committee of claims, on the Petitions of Samuel Abbot and others, of John Bennet, in behalf of himself and Abraham Sutton, of Samuel Edy, of Francis Guillow, of Thomas Roche, of Samuel Snow, of Joshua Whitney, by Timothy Winn, his agent, and of Thomas Wells. 21st February 1797, committed to a committee of the whole House, to-morrow.

[Philadelphia: Printed by William Ross. 1797.] pp. 4. 8vo.   AAS. BA.

33006 —— Report of the committee of claims, to whom it was referred, on the 20th of December last, to enquire into, and report on the expediency or inexpediency of designating certain claims against the United States, to be excepted from the operation of the acts of limitation. 24th February 1797, committed to a committee of the whole House, on Monday next. Published by order of the House of Representatives.

[Philadelphia: Printed by William Ross. 1797.] pp. 12. 8vo.   AAS. BA.

33007 —— —— Report of the committee of claims, to whom it was referred, on the 20th of December last, to enquire into, and report on the expediency or inexpediency of designating certain claims against the United States, to be excepted from the operation of the acts of limitation. 24th February, 1797, committed to a committee of the whole House, on Monday next. 6th December, 1797, committed to a committee of the whole House, on Friday next. [Published by order of the House of Representatives.]

[Philadelphia: Printed by William Ross. 1797.] pp. (51)–62. 8vo. AAS. BA.

33008 —— Report of the committee of claims on the Petition of John Carr. 8 December, 1797.

[Philadelphia: Printed by William Ross. 1797.]   BA.

33009 —— Report of the committee of claims to whom was referred, on the fifth instant, the Petition of Azar Bagley. 22d December, 1797, committed to a committee of the whole House, on Tuesday next. [Published by order of the House of Representatives.]

[Philadelphia: Printed by William Ross. 1797.] pp. (2), (165)–174. 8vo.
AAS.

UNITED STATES, continued.

33010 —— REPORT OF THE COMMITTEE OF COMMERCE AND MANUFACTURES, ON THE MEMO-
RIALS OF SUNDRY MANUFACTURERS OF CHOCOLATE. 8TH FEBRUARY 1797, REFERRED
TO THE COMMITTEE OF THE WHOLE HOUSE, TO WHOM IS COMMITTED THE REPORT
OF THE COMMITTEE OF WAYS AND MEANS, OF THE 3D ULTIMO, ON THE SUBJECT OF
FURTHER REVENUES. PUBLISHED BY ORDER OF THE HOUSE OF REPRESENTATIVES.
[Philadelphia: Printed by William Ross. 1797.] pp. 4. 8vo. AAS. BA. UTS.

33011 —— REPORT OF THE COMMITTEE OF COMMERCE AND MANUFACTURES, ON THE MEMO-
RIALS OF SUNDRY MANUFACTURERS OF SOAP AND CANDLES, IN PHILADELPHIA, NEW-
YORK, BOSTON AND BALTIMORE; OF SUNDRY MANUFACTURERS OF CORDAGE, IN NEW-
PORT; AND OF STEPHEN ADDINGTON, CALLICO PRINTER, IN GERMAN-TOWN. 23D
FEBRUARY, 1797, READ THE FIRST AND SECOND TIME, AND COMMITTED TO A COM-
MITTEE OF THE WHOLE HOUSE, TO-MORROW. PUBLISHED BY ORDER OF THE HOUSE
OF REPRESENTATIVES.
/ Philadelphia: Printed by William Ross. 1797.] pp. 4. 8vo. AAS. BA. HSP.

33012 —— REPORT OF THE COMMITTEE OF COMMERCE AND MANUFACTURES, ON THE PETI-
TION OF SAMUEL LEGARÉ, JAMES THEUS, AND SAMUEL PRIOLEAU. 27TH DECEM-
BER 1796. CONSIDERATION POSTPONED UNTIL TUESDAY NEXT. PUBLISHED BY
ORDER OF THE HOUSE OF REPRESENTATIVES.
[Philadelphia: Printed by William Ross. 1797.] pp. (4). 8vo. AAS. BA.

33013 —— REPORT OF THE COMMITTEE OF COMMERCE AND MANUFACTURES, ON THE PETI-
TION OF NORTH AND VEZEY, MERCHANTS IN CHARLESTON, SOUTH CAROLINA. 23D
FEBRUARY 1797, COMMITTED TO A COMMITTEE OF THE WHOLE HOUSE, TO-MORROW.
PUBLISHED BY ORDER OF THE HOUSE OF REPRESENTATIVES.
[Philadelphia: Printed by William Ross. 1797.] pp. 4. 8vo. AAS. BA.

33014 —— —— REPORT OF THE COMMITTEE OF COMMERCE & MANUFACTURES, ON THE PE-
TITION OF NORTH AND VESEY, MERCHANTS, IN CHARLESTON, SOUTH-CAROLINA. 23D
FEBRUARY 1797, COMMITTED TO A COMMITTEE OF THE WHOLE HOUSE TO-MORROW.
22D NOVEMBER 1797, COMMITTED TO A COMMITTEE OF THE WHOLE HOUSE ON
TUESDAY NEXT. [PUBLISHED BY ORDER OF THE HOUSE OF REPRESENTATIVES.]
[Philadelphia: Printed by William Ross. 1797.] pp. (2), 49–50. 8vo.
AAS. BA.

33015 —— REPORT OF THE COMMITTEE OF COMMERCE & MANUFACTURES ON THE PETITIONS
OF ORCHARD COOK AND ABIEL WOOD, JUNR. AND OF ROBERT HOOPER. 18TH DE-
CEMBER, 1797, READ, AND ORDERED TO BE RE-COMMITTED TO THE COMMITTEE OF
COMMERCE AND MANUFACTURES. 29TH DECEMBER, 1797, REPORT MADE, AND COM-
MITTED TO A COMMITTEE OF THE WHOLE HOUSE, ON WEDNESDAY NEXT. [PUBLISHED
BY ORDER OF THE HOUSE OF REPRESENTATIVES.]
/ Philadelphia: Printed by William Ross. 1797.] pp.(2),(225)–232. 8vo. AAS.

33016 —— REPORT OF THE COMMITTEE OF REVISAL AND UNFINISHED BUSINESS, ON BILLS,
AND REPORTS, DEPENDING AND UNDETERMINED UPON, AT THE LAST SESSION OF
CONGRESS. 9TH DECEMBER, 1796, ORDERED TO LIE ON THE TABLE. PUBLISHED
BY ORDER OF THE HOUSE OF REPRESENTATIVES.
[Philadelphia: Printed by William Ross. 1797.] pp. 8. 8vo. AAS. BA.

33017 —— REPORT OF THE COMMITTEE OF REVISAL AND UNFINISHED BUSINESS, ON BILLS,
REPORTS, AND OTHER MATTERS OF BUSINESS DEPENDING AND UNDETERMINED UPON
AT THE SECOND SESSION OF THE FOURTH CONGRESS, AND AT THE LAST SESSION. 20TH
NOVEMBER, 1797, ORDERED TO LIE ON THE TABLE. [PUBLISHED BY ORDER OF
THE HOUSE OF REPRESENTATIVES.]
[Philadelphia: Printed by William Ross. 1797.] pp. 15. 8vo. AAS. BA.

UNITED STATES, continued.

33018 —— REPORT OF THE COMMITTEE OF REVISAL AND UNFINISHED BUSINESS IN PART ON SUCH LAWS AS ARE NEAR EXPIRING, . . .

[Philadelphia: Printed by William Ross. 1797.] BA.

33019 —— REPORT OF THE COMMITTEE OF WAYS AND MEANS, ON THE MEASURES WHICH OUGHT TO BE TAKEN RELATIVE TO THE BALANCES FOUND BY COMMISSIONERS FOR SETTLING ACCOUNTS BETWEEN THE UNITED STATES AND THE INDIVIDUAL STATES TO BE DUE FROM CERTAIN STATES TO THE UNITED STATES. 26TH DECEMBER 1796, COMMITTED TO A COMMITTEE OF THE WHOLE HOUSE, ON THURSDAY NEXT. PUBLISHED BY ORDER OF THE HOUSE OF REPRESENTATIVES.

[Philadelphia: Printed by William Ross. 1797.] pp. 4. 8vo. AAS. BA.

33020 —— REPORT OF THE COMMITTEE OF WAYS AND MEANS, TO WHOM IT WAS REFERRED, TO TAKE INTO CONSIDERATION, THE SUBJECT OF FURTHER REVENUES, AND THE PROVISIONS REQUISITE FOR IMPROVING, AND MORE EFFECTUALLY SECURING THE INTERNAL REVENUES. 3D JANUARY 1797, COMMITTED TO A COMMITTEE OF THE WHOLE HOUSE, ON MONDAY NEXT. PUBLISHED BY ORDER OF THE HOUSE OF REPRESENTATIVES.

[Philadelphia: Printed by William Ross. 1797.] pp. (4). 8vo. AAS. BA.

33021 —— REPORT OF THE COMMITTEE OF WAYS AND MEANS, TO WHOM WAS REFERRED, A RESOLUTION OF THE HOUSE, OF THE TENTH INSTANT, RELATIVE TO THE PROPRIETY AND EXPEDIENCY OF LAYING A TAX UPON ALL THEATRICAL EXHIBITIONS; ALSO OF IMPOSING ADDITIONAL DUTIES, ON ARTICLES OF FOREIGN GROWTH OR MANUFACTURE, IMPORTED INTO THE UNITED STATES, AND ON ARTICLES MANUFACTURED OR USED WITHIN THE UNITED STATES. 23D JANUARY, 1797, COMMITTED TO A COMMITTEE OF THE WHOLE HOUSE, ON MONDAY NEXT. PUBLISHED BY ORDER OF THE HOUSE OF REPRESENTATIVES.

[Philadelphia: Printed by William Ross. 1797.] pp. 7. 8vo. AAS. BA.

33022 —— REPORT OF THE COMMITTEE OF WAYS AND MEANS, INSTRUCTED TO ENQUIRE "WHETHER ANY, AND WHAT ALTERATIONS MAY BE NECESSARY IN THE LAW INTITULED "AN ACT LAYING DUTIES ON STAMPED VELLUM, PARCHMENT, AND PAPER." 11TH DECEMBER, 1797, ORDERED TO LIE ON THE TABLE. [PUBLISHED BY ORDER OF THE HOUSE OF REPRESENTATIVES.]

[Philadelphia: Printed by William Ross. 1797.] pp. (2), (85)–88. 8vo.
AAS. BA. JCB.

33023 —— REPORT OF THE COMMITTEE OF WAYS AND MEANS, ON THE PETITION OF WILLIAM TOMLINSON AND OTHERS, CITIZENS OF THE STATE OF VIRGINIA. 18TH DECEMBER, 1797, COMMITTED TO A COMMITTEE OF THE WHOLE HOUSE, TO-MORROW. [PUBLISHED BY ORDER OF THE HOUSE OF REPRESENTATIVES.]

[Philadelphia: Printed by William Ross. 1797.] pp. (143)–146. 8vo.
AAS. BA. JCB.

33024 —— REPORT OF THE COMMITTEE TO WHOM WERE RE-COMMITTED THE PETITION OF HUGH LAWSON WHITE, AND THE REPORT OF THE SECRETARY OF WAR THEREON. 17TH JANUARY, 1797, COMMITTED TO A COMMITTEE OF THE WHOLE HOUSE, ON MONDAY NEXT. PUBLISHED BY ORDER OF THE HOUSE OF REPRESENTATIVES.

[Philadelphia: Printed by William Ross. 1797.] pp. 12. 8vo. AAS. BA.

UNITED STATES, continued.

33025 —— REPORT OF THE COMMITTEE, TO WHOM WAS RE-COMMITTED, ON THE FIFTH ULTIMO, A REPORT OF THE ATTORNEY-GENERAL, RELATIVE TO THE CONTRACT ENTERED INTO BETWEEN THE UNITED STATES AND JOHN CLEVES SYMMES: TOGETHER WITH THE DOCUMENTS ACCOMPANYING THE SAME. 9TH FEBRUARY, 1797, COMMITTED TO A COMMITTEE OF THE WHOLE HOUSE ON MONDAY NEXT. PUBLISHED BY ORDER OF THE HOUSE OF REPRESENTATIVES.

[Philadelphia: Printed by William Ross. 1797.] pp. 10. 8vo.   AAS. BA.

33026 —— REPORT OF THE COMMITTEE, TO WHOM WAS RE-COMMITTED ON THE SIXTEENTH INSTANT, THEIR REPORT, ON A RESOLUTION OF THE SENATE, "FOR OBTAINING INFORMATION RELATIVE TO THE AMENDMENT PROPOSED BY CONGRESS TO THE CONSTITUTION OF THE UNITED STATES, CONCERNING THE SUABILITY OF STATES." 21ST FEBRUARY, 1797, COMMITTED TO A COMMITTEE OF THE WHOLE HOUSE, TO-MORROW. PUBLISHED BY ORDER OF THE HOUSE OF REPRESENTATIVES.

[Philadelphia: Printed by William Ross. 1797.] pp. 6. 8vo.   AAS. BA.

33027 —— REPORT OF THE COMMITTEE TO WHOM WAS RECOMMITTED, ON THE SIXTH INSTANT, THE MOTION OF THE 24TH ULTIMO, RELATIVE TO THE METHOD OF TAKING EVIDENCE, TO BE ADDUCED IN THE TRIAL OF CONTESTED ELECTIONS OF THE MEMBERS OF THIS HOUSE. 15TH DECEMBER. 1797, COMMITTED TO A COMMITTEE OF THE WHOLE HOUSE, ON MONDAY NEXT. PUBLISHED BY ORDER OF THE HOUSE OF REPRESENTATIVES.

[Philadelphia: Printed by William Ross. 1797.] pp. (2), (109)–112. 8vo.
AAS. BA.

33028 —— REPORT OF THE COMMITTEE ON FURTHER PROVISION FOR THE FORTIFICATION OF THE PORTS AND HARBOURS OF THE UNITED STATES, JUNE 10, 1797.

[Philadelphia: Printed by William Ross. 1797.] pp. 8. 8vo.   BA. MHS.

33029 —— REPORT OF THE COMMITTEE ON THE MEMORIAL OF THE COMMISSIONERS APPOINTED UNDER THE ACT "FOR ESTABLISHING THE TEMPORARY AND PERMANENT SEAT OF THE GOVERNMENT OF THE UNITED STATES," AND ON SO MUCH OF THE PRESIDENT'S SPEECH AS RELATES TO THE ESTABLISHMENT OF A NATIONAL UNIVERSITY. 21ST DECEMBER 1796, COMMITTED TO A COMMITTEE OF THE WHOLE HOUSE, ON MONDAY NEXT. PUBLISHED BY ORDER OF THE HOUSE OF REPRESENTATIVES.

[Philadelphia: Printed by William Ross. 1797.] pp. 6. 8vo.   AAS. BA. UTS.

33030 —— REPORT ON THE PETITION OF JOHN CARR. 22D APRIL 1794, ORDERED TO LIE ON THE TABLE. 27TH MAY 1796, COMMITTED TO A COMMITTEE OF THE WHOLE HOUSE, TODAY. 5TH JANUARY 1797, COMMITTED TO A COMMITTEE OF THE WHOLE HOUSE ON TUESDAY NEXT. PUBLISHED BY ORDER OF THE HOUSE OF REPRESENTATIVES.

[Philadelphia: Printed by William Ross. 1797.] pp. (4). 8vo.   AAS. BA. JCB.

33031 —— REPORT OF THE COMMITTEE TO WHOM WAS REFERRED SO MUCH OF THE SPEECH OF THE PRESIDENT OF THE UNITED STATES, TO BOTH HOUSES OF CONGRESS AS RELATES TO THE PROMOTION OF AGRICULTURE. 11TH JANUARY 1797, COMMITTED TO A COMMITTEE OF THE WHOLE HOUSE, ON MONDAY NEXT. PUBLISHED BY ORDER OF THE HOUSE OF REPRESENTATIVES.

[Philadelphia: Printed by William Ross. 1797.] pp. 8. 8vo.   AAS.

33032 —— REPORT OF THE COMMITTEE, TO WHOM WAS REFERRED, ON THE 13TH ULTIMO, THE MEMORIAL OF THE ILLINOIS AND WABASH LAND COMPANY, BY JAMES WILSON, THEIR PRESIDENT. 3D FEBRUARY, 1797, ORDERED TO LIE ON THE TABLE. PUBLISHED BY ORDER OF THE HOUSE OF REPRESENTATIVES.

[Philadelphia: Printed by William Ross. 1797.] pp. 4. 8vo.   BA. UTS.

UNITED STATES, continued.

33033 —— REPORT OF THE COMMITTEE TO WHOM WAS REFERRED THE MEMORIAL OF ANNA DE NEUFVILLE, WIDOW OF JOHN DE NEUFVILLE, DECEASED. 7TH FEBRUARY 1797, REFERRED TO A COMMITTEE OF THE WHOLE HOUSE, ON FRIDAY NEXT. PUBLISHED BY ORDER OF THE HOUSE OF REPRESENTATIVES.

[Philadelphia: Printed by William Ross. 1797.] pp. (4). 8vo.   AAS BA.

33034 —— REPORT OF THE COMMITTEE TO WHOM WAS REFERRED, ON THE TWENTIETH OF DECEMBER LAST, A LETTER FROM THE SECRETARY OF STATE, INCLOSING A RE- PORT OF THE DIRECTOR OF THE MINT, SUGGESTING THE EXPEDIENCY OF SOME ALTERATIONS IN ITS ESTABLISHMENT, TO RENDER IT LESS EXPENSIVE TO THE PUBLIC, AND MORE ACCOMMODATING TO DEPOSITORS. 13TH FEBRUARY 1797, COM- MITTED TO A COMMITTEE OF THE WHOLE HOUSE, ON MONDAY NEXT. PUBLISHED BY ORDER OF THE HOUSE OF REPRESENTATIVES.

[Philadelphia: Printed by William Ross. 1797.] pp. 6. 8vo.   AAS. BA.

33035 —— —— REPORT OF THE COMMITTEE TO WHOM WAS REFERRED, ON THE TWEN- TIETH OF DECEMBER LAST, A LETTER FROM THE SECRETARY OF STATE, INCLOS- ING A REPORT OF THE DIRECTOR OF THE MINT, SUGGESTING THE EXPEDIENCY OF SOME ALTERATIONS IN ITS ESTABLISHMENT, TO RENDER IT LESS EXPENSIVE TO THE PUBLIC, AND MORE ACCOMODATING TO DEPOSITORS. 13TH FEBRUARY, 1797, COM- MITTED TO A COMMITTEE OF THE WHOLE HOUSE, ON MONDAY NEXT. 8TH DECEM- BER, 1797, COMMITTED TO A COMMITTEE OF THE WHOLE HOUSE, ON WEDNESDAY NEXT. [PUBLISHED BY ORDER OF THE HOUSE OF REPRESENTATIVES.]

[Philadelphia: Printed by William Ross. 1797.] pp. (2), (117)–120. 8vo.
AAS. BA.

33036 —— REPORT OF THE COMMITTEE TO WHOM WAS REFERRED THE RESOLUTIONS OF THE SENATE RESPECTING THE SOUTHERN AND WESTERN BOUNDARY OF GEORGIA. 2 MARCH, 1797.

[Philadelphia: Printed by William Ross. 1797.]   BA.

33037 —— REPORT OF THE COMMITTEE TO WHOM IT WAS REFERRED TO PREPARE AN ANSWER TO THE SPEECH OF THE PRESIDENT OF THE UNITED STATES, COMMUNICATED TO BOTH HOUSES OF CONGRESS, ON TUESDAY THE 16TH MAY, 1797. 19TH MAY, 1797, COMMITTED TO A COMMITTEE OF THE WHOLE HOUSE ON MONDAY NEXT.

[Philadelphia:] Printed by Joseph Gales, No. 126, North Second-street. [1797.] pp. (7). 8vo.   AAS. BA.

33038 —— REPORT OF THE COMMITTEE TO WHOM WAS REFERRED THE REMONSTRANCE AND PETITION OF THE LEGISLATURE OF THE STATE OF TENNESSEE. 20TH DECEM- BER, 1797, COMMITTED TO A COMMITTEE OF THE WHOLE HOUSE, ON MONDAY NEXT. [PUBLISHED BY ORDER OF THE HOUSE OF REPRESENTATIVES.]

[Philadelphia: Printed by William Ross. 1797.] pp. (2), (161)–162. 8vo.
AAS. BA. JCB.

33039 —— REPORT OF THE COMMITTEE TO WHOM WAS REFERRED, ON THE TWENTY-NINTH ULTIMO, SO MUCH OF THE PRESIDENT'S SPEECH, AS RELATES TO THE PROTECTION OF COMMERCE, AND THE DEFENCE OF THE COUNTRY. 26TH DECEMBER, 1797, COM- MITTED TO A COMMITTEE OF THE WHOLE HOUSE, ON THE FIRST MONDAY IN FEB- RUARY NEXT. [PUBLISHED BY ORDER OF THE HOUSE OF REPRESENTATIVES.]

[Philadelphia: Printed by William Ross. 1797.] pp. (2), (205)–209. 8vo.
AAS. BA.

UNITED STATES, continued.

33040   —— REPORT FROM THE COMMITTEE TO WHOM WAS REFERRED, ON THE TWENTY-SECOND INSTANT, THE MEMORIAL OF JUSTINE ADELAIDE MAXIME DE GRASSE AND MELANIE VERONIQUE MAXIME DE GRASSE, IN BEHALF OF THEMSELVES, AND THEIR ABSENT SISTERS, AMELIE AND SILVIE DE GRASSE, DAUGHTERS OF THE LATE COMPTE DE GRASSE. TOGETHER WITH THE SAID MEMORIAL, AND A FORMER MEMORIAL, PRESENTED THE 13TH FEB. 1795, WITH THE REPORT THEREON. DECEMBER 27, 1797. COMMITTED TO A COMMITTEE OF THE WHOLE HOUSE ON MONDAY NEXT.

Philadelphia: Printed by Joseph Gales, No. 126, North Second Street. [1797.] pp. (2), (213)–222. 8vo.   AAS. BA. JCB.

33041   —— REPORTS OF COMMITTEES, ON THE PETITIONS OF SUNDRY REFUGEES FROM CANADA AND NOVA-SCOTIA. 12TH DECEMBER 1796, COMMITTED TO A COMMITTEE OF THE WHOLE HOUSE, ON THURSDAY NEXT. PUBLISHED BY ORDER OF THE HOUSE OF REPRESENTATIVES.

Philadelphia: Printed by William Ross. 1797.] pp. (8). 8vo.   AAS.

33042   —— RULES AND ORDERS OF THE HOUSE OF REPRESENTATIVES OF THE UNITED STATES. *Philadelphia: Printed by Joseph Gales.* 1797. pp. 15. 8vo.

33043   —— *Heading:* [XXIX] RULES FOR CONDUCTING BUSINESS IN THE SENATE. *[Philadelphia: Printed by John Fenno.* 1797.] pp. 7. 8vo.

By Thomas Jefferson. The first publication of his frequently reprinted Manual of Parliamentary practice.

33044   —— THE CONSTITUTIONS OF THE SIXTEEN STATES, WHICH COMPOSE THE CONFEDERATED REPUBLIC OF AMERICA, ACCORDING TO THE LATEST AMENDMENTS. TO WHICH ARE PREFIXED, THE DECLARATION OF INDEPENDENCE; ARTICLES OF CONFEDERATION; THE DEFINITIVE TREATY OF PEACE WITH GREAT-BRITAIN; AND, THE CONSTITUTION OF THE UNITED STATES, WITH ALL THE AMENDMENTS.

Boston: Printed by Manning & Loring, for S. Hall, W. Spotswood, J. White, Thomas & Andrews, D. West, E. Larkin, W. P. & L. Blake, and J. West. 1797. pp. 300. 12mo.   AAS. BA. JCB. MdHS.

33045   —— TREATIES OF AMITY AND COMMERCE, AND OF ALLIANCE EVENTUAL AND DEFENSIVE, BETWEEN HIS MOST CHRISTIAN MAJESTY AND THE THIRTEEN UNITED STATES OF AMERICA; THE DEFINITIVE TREATY BETWEEN GREAT-BRITAIN AND THE THIRTEEN UNITED STATES OF AMERICA; AND THE TREATY OF AMITY, COMMERCE, AND NAVIGATION, BETWEEN HIS BRITANNIC MAJESTY AND THE UNITED STATES OF AMERICA.

Boston: Printed and sold by Samuel Hall, No. 53, Cornhill. 1797. pp. 71. 8vo.   JCB. NYPL.

33046   —— BY THE PRESIDENT OF THE UNITED STATES OF AMERICA. A PROCLAMATION. [For a national fast, on the ninth of May.] JOHN ADAMS. BY THE PRESIDENT. TIMOTHY PICKERING, SECRETARY OF STATE.

[Philadelphia: 1797.] Broadside. fol.

33047   —— BY THE PRESIDENT OF THE UNITED STATES OF AMERICA. A PROCLAMATION. [Convening Congress, in extra session on the fifteenth of May, 1797.] JOHN ADAMS. BY THE PRESIDENT. TIMOTHY PICKERING, SECRETARY OF STATE.

[Philadelphia: 1797.] Broadside. fol.   LOC.

UNITED STATES, continued.

33048 —— A Message from the President of the United States of America, to Congress; relative to the French Republic; delivered January 19, 1797, with [*sic*] the papers therein referred to. Published by order of the House of Representatives.

Philadelphia: Printed by W. Ross, near Congress-Hall. [1797.] pp. (92); 22. 8vo. AAS. CLS. LOC.

Second title: Reports of the Secretary of State, and of the Secretary of the Treasury, relative to the present situation of affairs with the Dey and Regency of Algiers. Accompanying a Confidential Message from the President of the United States, received the 19th of January, 1797.

[*Philadelphia: Printed by W. Ross..* 1797.] pp. 22.

33049 —— — A Message from the President of the United States of America, to Congress: relative to the French Republic; delivered January 19, 1797, with [*sic*] the papers therein referred to. Published by order of the House of Representatives.

Philadelphia: Printed by W. Ross, near Congress-Hall. [1797.] pp. 92; Appendix. Translations No. 1–163: pp. (56), 16, (380); French originals: pp. 207, (11), (1). 8vo. AAS. BA. CLS. JCB. MHS.

33050 —— Congress of the United States. In Senate, January the 20th, 1797. The following Message from the President of the United States, was read, communicating the copy of a Letter from the secretary for the Department of State to the minister plenipotentiary from the United States to the Republic of France.

[*Philadelphia: Printed by John Fenno.* 1797.] pp. 104. 8vo. BA.

Printed with wide margins.

33051 —— Message from the President of the United States, accompanying an Official statement of the expenditure, to the end of the year 1796, from the sums heretofore granted to defray the contingent charges of the government. 15th February 1797, ordered to lie on the table. 16th February 1797, referred to the committee of the whole House, to whom was committed, on the third instant, the bill making appropriations, for the support of government, and a partial appropriation for the military establishment, for the year one thousand seven hundred and ninety-seven. Published by order of the House of Representatives.

[*Philadelphia: Printed by William Ross.* 1797.] pp. 8. 8vo. AAS. BA.

33052 —— Message from the President of the United States, transmitting a Report, and sundry documents, from the Secretary of State, relative to the proceedings of the commissioner for running the boundary line between the United States and East and West-Florida. June 12th, 1797, ordered to lie on the table. Published by order of the House of Representatives.

[*Philadelphia: Printed by William Ross.* 1797.] pp. 36. 8vo. AAS. BA.

33053 —— Message from the President of the United States, transmitting a Report and sundry documents, from the Secretary of State, of the depredations committed on the commerce of the United States, since the first of October, 1796; in pursuance of a Resolution of the House of the tenth instant. June 22, 1797, ordered to lie on the table. Published by order of the House of Representatives.

Philadelphia: Printed by W. Ross, near Congress-Hall. [1797.] pp. 10, (148). 8vo. AAS. BA. JCB.

UNITED STATES, continued.

33054 —— CONFIDENTIAL MESSAGE FROM THE PRESIDENT OF THE UNITED STATES, INCLOS-
ING SUNDRY DOCUMENTS FROM THE DEPARTMENTS OF STATE AND WAR, RELATIVE
TO THE INTERCOURSE OF THE UNITED STATES WITH FOREIGN NATIONS. JULY 3,
1797, REFERRED TO MR. SITGREAVES, MR. BALDWIN, MR. DANA, MR. DAWSON, AND
MR. HINDMAN. PUBLISHED BY ORDER OF THE HOUSE OF REPRESENTATIVES.
> *Philadelphia: Printed by W. Ross, near Congress-Hall.* [1797.] pp. 8,(23);
> 23. 8vo.   AAS. BA.

Second title: REPORT OF THE SECRETARY OF WAR, [ACCOMPANYING A CONFIDEN-
TIAL MESSAGE FROM THE PRESIDENT OF THE UNITED STATES.] [RECEIVED THE 3D
OF JULY, 1797.]
> *[Philadelphia: Printed by William Ross.* 1797.] pp. 23.

33055 —— —— MESSAGE CONFIDENTIAL DU PRESIDENT DES ETATS-UNIS, RENFERMANT PLU-
SIEURS DOCUMENTS DES DÉPARTEMENS DE L'ETAT ET DE LA GUERRE, RELATIFS AUX
RELATIONS DES ETATS-UNIS AVEC LES NATIONS ÉTRANGÉRES 3 JUILLET 1797. REN-
VOYÉ À M. SITGREAVES, M. BALDWIN, M. DANA, M. DAWSON, ET M. HINDMAN. PUBLIÉ
PAR ORDRE DE LA CHAMBRE DES REPRÉSENTANS.
> *Philadelphie: Imprimé par W. Ross, Sixieme Rue Sud.* [1797.] pp. [85.]
> 8vo.   LOC.

33056 —— SPEECH OF THE PRESIDENT OF THE UNITED STATES, TO BOTH HOUSES OF CON-
GRESS, ON TUESDAY, MAY 16TH, 1797.
> *[Philadelphia: Printed by William Ross.* 1797.] pp. 12. 8vo.   AAS.

33057 —— —— SPEECH OF THE PRESIDENT OF THE UNITED STATES, TO BOTH HOUSES OF
CONGRESS, MAY 16, 1797.
> *[Without place or printer.* 1797.] Broadside. fol.

33058 —— THE SPEECH OF THE PRESIDENT OF THE UNITED STATES TO BOTH HOUSES OF
CONGRESS, DELIVERED IN THE REPRESENTATIVE CHAMBER ON THURSDAY NOV. 23,
1797. HOUSE OF REPRESENTATIVES, NOV. 23, 1797, ORDERED TO BE COMMITTED
TO A COMMITTEE OF THE WHOLE HOUSE, TO-MORROW.
> *Philadelphia: Printed by Joseph Gales, No. 126, North Second-Street.* [1797.]
> pp. (8). 8vo.   AAS.

33059 —— —— SPEECH OF THE PRESIDENT OF THE UNITED STATES TO BOTH HOUSES OF
CONGRESS, NOVEMBER 23, 1797. [Two columns.] JOHN ADAMS. UNITED STATES,
NOVEMBER 22, 1797.
> *[Philadelphia:* 1797.] Broadside. fol.   AAS.

33060 —— —— FROM THE MERCURY-OFFICE. PRESIDENT'S SPEECH. MERCURY OFFICE,
NOV. 29, 11 O'CLOCK A. M. BY TWO GENTLEMEN FROM NEW-YORK, WE ARE FA-
VORED . . .
> *[Boston: Printed by Young and Minns.* 1797.] Broadside. fol.   MHS.

33061 —— LETTER FROM THE ATTORNEY GENERAL, INCLOSING HIS REPORT ON THE ME-
MORIAL OF JOHN HOBBY, MARSHAL FOR THE DISTRICT OF MAINE, IN THE STATE
OF MASSACHUSETTS. 27TH FEBRUARY, 1797, COMMITTED TO A COMMITTEE OF THE
WHOLE HOUSE. TO-MORROW. PUBLISHED BY ORDER OF THE HOUSE OF REPRE-
SENTATIVES.
> *[Philadelphia: Printed by William Ross.* 1797.] pp. (4). 8vo. AAS. BA.

33062 —— LETTER FROM THE ATTORNEY-GENERAL, ACCOMPANYING HIS REPORT ON THE
PETITION OF FANNY FORSYTH, WIDOW AND ADMINISTRATRIX OF ROBERT FORSYTH,
DECEASED. 13TH JANUARY 1797, COMMITTED TO A COMMITTEE OF THE WHOLE
HOUSE, ON MONDAY NEXT. PUBLISHED BY ORDER OF THE HOUSE OF REPRE-
SENTATIVES.
> *[Philadelphia: Printed by William Ross.* 1797.] pp. 7. 8vo.   AAS. BA.

UNITED STATES, continued.

33063 —— LETTER FROM THE SECRETARY OF STATE TO CHARLES C. PINCKNEY, ESQ. IN ANSWER TO THE COMPLAINTS OF THE FRENCH MINISTER AGAINST THE GOVERNMENT OF THE UNITED STATES, CONTAINED IN HIS NOTES TO THE SECRETARY OF STATE, DATED THE 27TH OF OCTOBER, AND 15TH OF NOVEMBER, 1796.
New-York: Printed by Hopkins, Webb & Co. No. 40, Pine-street.—1797.—pp. (54). 8vo. JCB. LOC. NYHS. NYPL.

33064 —— — A LETTER FROM MR. PICKERING, SECRETARY OF STATE, TO MR. PINCKNEY, MINISTER PLENIPOTENTIARY AT PARIS, IN ANSWER TO THE COMPLAINTS COMMUNI-' CATED BY MR. ADET. MINISTER OF THE FRENCH REPUBLIC, AGAINST THE UNITED STATES OF AMERICA.
Richmond: Printed and sold by T. Nicolson. [1797.] pp. [93.] 8vo. JCB. LOC.

33065 —— — A LETTER FROM MR. PICKERING, SECRETARY FOR THE DEPARTMENT OF STATE OF THE UNITED STATES—TO MR. PINCKNEY, MINISTER PLENIPOTENTIARY OF THE UNITED STATES OF AMERICA AT PARIS.
Stockbridge, (Massachusetts:) Printed by Rosseter & Willard. 1797. pp. (98), (6). 8vo.
Contains, an eight-page list of Subscribers' names.

33066 —— — REVIEW OF THE ADMINISTRATION OF THE GOVERNMENT OF THE UNITED STATES OF AMERICA; SINCE THE YEAR NINETY-THREE. OR; THE CORRESPONDENCE BETWEEN THE SECRETARY OF STATE; AND THE FRENCH MINISTER, ON THAT SUBJECT. [Three lines from] GEORGE WASHINGTON.
Printed for general information—1797. *By Benjamin Russell, State-Street— Boston.* pp. [87.] 8vo. JCB. MHS. NYHS. NYPL.

33067 —— LETTER FROM MR. PICKERING, SECRETARY OF STATE, TO THE CHEVALIER DE YRUJO, ENVOY EXTRAORDINARY AND MINISTER PLENIPOTENTIARY OF HIS CATHOLIC MAJESTY TO THE UNITED STATES OF AMERICA. AUGUST 8TH, 1797.
[Trenton: Printed by Matthias Day. 1797.] pp. 37. 8vo. BA. CLS. MHS. NYHS.
Printed at the instance of Mr. Pickering, but not published.

33068 —— LETTER FROM THE SECRETARY OF STATE, INCLOSING A REPORT OF THE DIRECTOR OF THE MINT, SUGGESTING THE EXPEDIENCY OF SOME ALTERATIONS IN ITS ESTABLISHMENT, TO RENDER IT LESS EXPENSIVE TO THE PUBLIC, AND MORE ACCOMODATING TO DEPOSITORS. 20TH DECEMBER, 1796, REFERRED TO MR. PAGE, MR. HAVENS, AND MR. GOODRICH. 13TH FEBRUARY, 1797. COMMITTED TO A COMMITTEE OF THE WHOLE HOUSE, ON MONDAY NEXT. 8TH DECEMBER, 1797, COMMITTED TO A COMMITTEE OF THE WHOLE HOUSE, ON WEDNESDAY NEXT. [PUBLISHED BY ORDER OF THE HOUSE OF REPRESENTATIVES.]
[Philadelphia: Printed by William Ross. 1797.] pp. (2),(125)–(141). 8vo. AAS. BA. JCB.

33069 —— REPORT OF THE SECRETARY OF STATE, ON THE MEMORIAL OF ANTONIA CARMICHAEL, WIDOW OF WILLIAM CARMICHAEL, DECEASED. 23D FEBRUARY, 1797, COMMITTED TO A COMMITTEE OF THE WHOLE HOUSE TO-MORROW. [PUBLISHED BY ORDER OF THE HOUSE OF REPRESENTATIVES.]
[Philadelphia: Printed by William Ross. 1797.] pp. 8. 8vo. AAS. BA.

33070 —— — REPORT OF THE SECRETARY OF STATE, ON THE MEMORIAL OF ANTONIA CARMICHAEL, WIDOW OF WILLIAM CARMICHAEL, DECEASED. 23D FEBRUARY, 1797, COMMITTED TO A COMMITTEE OF THE WHOLE HOUSE TOMORROW. 22D NOVEMBER, 1797, COMMITTED TO A COMMITTEE OF THE WHOLE HOUSE ON MONDAY NEXT. [PUBLISHED BY ORDER OF THE HOUSE OF REPRESENTATIVES.]
[Philadelphia: Printed by William Ross. 1797.] pp. 8. 8vo. AAS. LOC.

UNITED STATES, continued.

33071 —— REPORT OF THE SECRETARY OF STATE, ON THE MEMORIAL OF SUNDRY CITIZENS
OF THE UNITED STATES, RESIDING IN THE CITY OF PHILADELPHIA, REFERRED TO
HIM, BY ORDER OF THE HOUSE, ON THE SEVENTH OF MAY LAST. 27TH FEBRUARY,
1797, ORDERED TO LIE ON THE TABLE. [PUBLISHED BY ORDER OF THE HOUSE OF
REPRESENTATIVES.]
[Philadelphia: Printed by William Ross. 1797.] pp. 9, (57). 8vo.
AAS. BA. CLS. JCB.

33072 —— TO THE EDITOR OF THE UNITED STATES GAZETTE, DEPARTMENT OF STATE,
PHILADELPHIA, MARCH 9, 1797. SIR, I INCLOSE THE COPY OF A LETTER WHICH I
RECEIVED THE 3D INSTANT, FROM THE LATE PRESIDENT OF THE UNITED STATES.
THE LETTER ITSELF WILL SATISFY YOU OF THE PROPRIETY OF ITS BEING PUB-
LISHED. THE ORIGINAL, AS DESIRED, IS DEPOSITED IN THIS OFFICE. I AM, SIR,
YOUR OBEDIENT SERVANT, TIMOTHY PICKERING.

Followed by: LETTER, FROM GEORGE WASHINGTON, DECLARING THE LETTERS AT-
TRIBUTED TO HIM IN 1777 TO BE FORGED LETTERS, AND THAT HE NEVER SAW
OR HEARD OF THEM UNTIL THEY APPEARED IN PRINT.
[Philadelphia: Printed by John Fenno. 1797.] Broadside. 8vo.   AAS.

33073 —— ACCOUNT OF RECEIPTS AND EXPENDITURES OF THE UNITED STATES, COMMENC-
ING ON THE FIRST DAY OF APRIL, 1796, AND ENDING ON THE THIRTY-FIRST OF
MARCH, 1797. PUBLISHED BY ORDER OF THE HOUSE OF REPRESENTATIVES.
[Philadelphia: Printed by William Ross. 1797.] pp. 15. 8vo.
AAS. BA. JCB. MHS.

33074 —— ACCOUNTS OF THE TREASURER OF THE UNITED STATES, OF PAYMENTS AND RE-
CEIPTS OF PUBLIC MONIES, COMMENCING THE FIRST OF JANUARY, AND ENDING THE
THIRTY-FIRST OF DECEMBER 1796. ALSO, HIS ACCOUNT OF RECEIPTS AND EX-
PENDITURES OF THE WAR DEPARTMENT, FROM THE FIRST OF JANUARY TO THE
THIRTY-FIRST OF DECEMBER 1796.
[Philadelphia: Printed by William Ross. 1797.] pp. (2), 154. 8vo.
AAS. BA. JCB. MHS. UTS.

33075 —— LETTER FROM THE SECRETARY OF THE TREASURY, ACCOMPANIED WITH HIS REPORT
AND ESTIMATES OF THE SUMS NECESSARY TO BE APPROPRIATED FOR THE SERVICE
OF THE YEAR 1798; ALSO, A STATEMENT OF RECEIPTS AND EXPENDITURES AT THE
TREASURY OF THE UNITED STATES, FOR ONE YEAR, PRECEDING THE FIRST OF
OCTOBER, 1797. 11TH DECEMBER, 1797, REFERRED TO THE COMMITTEE OF WAYS
AND MEANS. PUBLISHED BY ORDER OF THE HOUSE OF REPRESENTATIVES.
Philadelphia: Printed by Zachariah Poulson, jun. & W. Young. 1797. pp.
47. 8vo.   AAS. BA. HSP. JCB.

Second title: REPORT OF THE SECRETARY OF THE TREASURY, ACCOMPANIED WITH
ESTIMATES OF THE SUMS NECESSARY TO BE APPROPRIATED FOR THE SERVICE OF
THE YEAR 1798; ALSO, A STATEMENT OF RECEIPTS AND EXPENDITURES AT THE
TREASURY OF THE UNITED STATES, FOR ONE YEAR, PRECEDING THE FIRST OF OC-
TOBER, 1797; ACCOMPANYING A LETTER OF THE SECRETARY OF THE TREASURY.
11TH DECEMBER, 1797, REFERRED TO THE COMMITTEE OF WAYS AND MEANS.
PUBLISHED BY ORDER OF THE HOUSE OF REPRESENTATIVES.
Philadelphia: Printed by Zachariah Poulson, jun, & W. Young. 1797. pp. 47.

33076 —— LETTER FROM THE SECRETARY OF THE TREASURY, ACCOMPANYING A PLAN FOR
LAYING AND COLLECTING DIRECT TAXES, BY APPORTIONMENT, AMONG THE SEVERAL
STATES AGREEABLY TO THE RULE PRESCRIBED BY THE CONSTITUTION, IN PURSU-
ANCE OF A RESOLUTION OF THE HOUSE, OF THE FOURTH OF APRIL, 1796. PRE-
SENTED DECEMBER 19, 1796. PUBLISHED BY ORDER OF THE HOUSE OF
REPRESENTATIVES.
[Philadelphia: Printed by William Ross. 1797.] pp. 68. fol. AAS. BA. JCB.

UNITED STATES, continued.

33077 —— LETTER FROM THE SECRETARY OF THE TREASURY, ACCOMPANYING A REPORT AND SUNDRY STATEMENTS AND PAPERS, RELATIVE TO THE APPLICATION AND EXPENDITURE OF THE SUMS APPROPRIATED FOR EXPENSES ATTENDING THE INTERCOURSE BETWEEN THE UNITED STATES AND FOREIGN NATIONS, IN PURSUANCE OF THE RESOLUTIONS OF THE HOUSE, OF THE 9TH AND 10TH INSTANT. 16TH FEBRUARY 1797, REFERRED TO THE COMMITTEE OF THE WHOLE HOUSE, TO WHOM WAS COMMMITTED, ON THE THIRD INSTANT, THE BILL MAKING APPROPRIATIONS FOR THE SUPPORT OF GOVERNMENT, AND A PARTIAL APPROPRIATION FOR THE MILITARY ESTABLISHMENT FOR THE YEAR ONE THOUSAND SEVEN HUNDRED AND NINETY-SEVEN. PUBLISHED BY ORDER OF THE HOUSE OF REPRESENTATIVES.

[Philadelphia: Printed by William Ross. 1797.] pp. 20. 8vo.   AAS. BA.

33078 —— LETTER FROM THE SECRETARY OF THE TREASURY, ACCOMPANYING A REPORT FROM THE COMMISSIONERS OF THE CITY OF WASHINGTON, IN THE DISTRICT OF COLUMBIA, AND SUNDRY STATEMENTS MARKED A, B, C, D AND E, EXHIBITING A VIEW OF THE RECEIPTS AND EXPENDITURES OF ALL MONIES ENTRUSTED TO THEM; ALSO, OF THE PROGRESS AND STATE OF THE BUSINESS, AND OF THE FUNDS UNDER THEIR ADMINISTRATION, FROM THE 18TH OF MAY, TO THE 18TH OF NOVEMBER 1797. 14TH DECEMBER 1797, ORDERED TO LIE ON THE TABLE. PUBLISHED BY ORDER OF THE HOUSE OF REPRESENTATIVES.

[Philadelphia:] Printed by William Ross. [1797.] pp. 10. 8vo.   BA. JCB.

33079 —— LETTER FROM THE SECRETARY OF THE TREASURY, ACCOMPANYING A STATEMENT EXHIBITING THE AMOUNT OF DRAWBACKS PAID UPON THE DUTIABLE ARTICLES EXPORTED FROM THE UNITED STATES, IN THE YEARS 1793, 1794, AND 1795, MADE IN PURSUANCE OF A RESOLUTION OF THE HOUSE, OF THE FIRST OF JUNE LAST. 16TH DECEMBER 1796, ORDERED TO LIE ON THE TABLE. PUBLISHED BY ORDER OF THE HOUSE OF REPRESENTATIVES.

[Philadelphia: Printed by William Ross. 1797.] pp. (4), folded sheet. 8vo.
AAS. BA. JCB.

33080 —— LETTER FROM THE SECRETARY OF THE TREASURY, ACCOMPANYING A STATEMENT OF GOODS, WARES AND MERCHANDIZE [*sic*], EXPORTED FROM THE UNITED STATES, DURING ONE YEAR, PRIOR TO THE THIRTIETH OF SEPTEMBER, 1796, 9TH FEBRUARY 1797, READ AND ORDERED TO BE REFERRED TO THE COMMITTEE OF WAYS AND MEANS. PUBLISHED BY ORDER OF THE HOUSE OF REPRESENTATIVES.

[Philadelphia: Printed by William Ross. 1797.] pp. 10. 8vo.   AAS. BA.

33081 —— LETTER FROM THE SECRETARY OF THE TREASURY, ACCOMPANYING AN ABSTRACT OF THE OFFICIAL EMOLUMENTS AND EXPENDITURES OF THE OFFICERS OF THE CUSTOMS FOR 1796, ... 17 FEBRUARY, 1797.

[Philadelphia: Printed by William Ross. 1797.]   BA.

33082 —— LETTER FROM THE SECRETARY OF THE TREASURY, ACCOMPANYING HIS REPORT, AND TWO ESTIMATES OF THE SECRETARY AT WAR, OF THE SUMS REQUIRED TO BE APPROPRIATED FOR THE USE OF THE NAVAL DEPARTMENT; AND THE FORTIFICATIONS ERECTING FOR THE DEFENCE OF THE PORTS AND HARBOURS OF THE UNITED STATES. 19TH JANUARY 1797. SO MUCH OF THE SAID REPORT AND ESTIMATES AS RELATES TO THE NAVAL DEPARTMENT, REFERRED TO THE COMMITTEE APPOINTED ON THE 16TH ULTIMO, TO ENQUIRE INTO THE STATE OF THE NAVAL EQUIPMENT. SUCH OTHER PARTS OF THE SAID REPORT AND ESTIMATES AS RELATE TO THE FORTIFICATIONS OF THE PORTS AND HARBOURS OF THE UNITED STATES, REFERRED TO THE COMMITTEE APPOINTED ON THE 16TH ULTIMO, TO ENQUIRE INTO THE ACTUAL STATE OF THE SAID FORTIFICATIONS. PUBLISHED BY ORDER OF THE HOUSE OF REPRESENTATIVES.

[Philadelphia: Printed by William Ross. 1797.] pp. 7. 8vo.   AAS. BA. JCB.

UNITED STATES, continued.

33083 —— LETTER FROM THE SECRETARY OF THE TREASURY, ACCOMPANYING HIS REPORT, WITH AN ESTIMATE OF THE SECRETARY AT WAR, OF THE SUM NECESSARY TO BE APPPROPRIATED [*sic*] TO MAKE GOOD DEFICIENCIES IN THE APPROPRIATIONS FOR THE SERVICE OF THE MILITARY DEPARTMENT, IN THE YEAR 1796. 15TH FEBRUARY, 1797, ORDERED TO LIE ON THE TABLE. PUBLISHED BY ORDER OF THE HOUSE OF REPRESENTATIVES.

[Philadelphia: Printed by William Ross. 1797.] pp. 4. 8vo.   AAS. BA.

33084 —— LETTER FROM THE SECRETARY OF THE TREASURY, ACCOMPANYING SUNDRY STATEMENTS IN RELATION TO THE ANNUAL EXPENDITURES OF THE WAR DEPARTMENT, FROM THE COMMENCEMENT OF THE PRESENT GOVERNMENT, TO THE 31ST OF DECEMBER, 1795; ALSO, AN EXPLANATORY LETTER FROM THE REGISTER OF THE TREASURY THEREON. 12TH DECEMBER, 1796, ORDERED TO LIE ON THE TABLE. PUBLISHED BY ORDER OF THE HOUSE OF REPRESENTATIVES.

[Philadelphia: Printed by William Ross. 1797.] pp. [7], folded table, (2), folded table, [15], 19. 8vo.   AAS. BA. JCB. RIHS. UTS.

Second title: [No. 2.] STATEMENT OF THE MONIES EXPENDED, FOR THE MILITARY ESTABLISHMENT FOR EACH YEAR, FROM THE COMMENCEMENT OF THE PRESENT GOVERNMENT TO THE 1ST JANUARY, 1796. ACCOMPANYING A LETTER FROM THE SECRETARY OF THE TREASURY, RECEIVED THE 12TH OF DECEMBER, 1796. pp. (2), folded table.

Third title: [No. 3.] STATEMENT BY THE ACCOUNTANT OF THE WAR DEPARTMENT, OF THE EXPENDITURE AT THE WAR OFFICE FOR THE MILITARY ESTABLISHMENT, FROM THE COMMENCEMENT OF THE PRESENT GOVERNMENT, TO THE 1ST OF JANUARY, 1796. ACCOMPANYING A LETTER FROM THE SECRETARY OF THE TREASURY, RECEIVED THE 12TH OF DECEMBER, 1796. pp. [15.]

Fourth title: A STATEMENT OF THE AGGREGATE OF THE APPROPRIATIONS MADE BY LAW, AND THE ACTUAL EXPENDITURES OF THE UNITED STATES FOR THE WAR DEPARTMENT, FROM THE COMMENCEMENT OF THE PRESENT GOVERNMENT TO THE 1ST JANUARY, 1796. pp. 19.

33085 —— LETTER FROM THE SECRETARY OF THE TREASURY, TRANSMITTING A COPY OF A LETTER FROM THE COMMISSIONERS OF THE CITY OF WASHINGTON, IN THE DISTRICT OF COLUMBIA; INCLOSING SUNDRY DOCUMENTS MARKED A, B, C, D, AND E, EXHIBITING A VIEW OF THE RECEIPTS AND EXPENDITURES OF ALL MONIES INTRUSTED TO THEM; AND ALSO OF THE PROGRESS AND STATE OF THE BUSINESS, AND OF THE FUNDS UNDER THEIR ADMINISTRATION, FROM THE 18TH OF NOVEMBER 1796, TO THE 18TH OF MAY 1797. 3D OF JUNE, 1797. ORDERED TO LIE ON THE TABLE. PUBLISHED BY ORDER OF THE HOUSE OF REPRESENTATIVES.

[Philadelphia: Printed by William Ross. 1797.] pp. 10. 8vo.   AAS. BA.

33086 —— LETTER FROM THE SECRETARY OF THE TREASURY, TRANSMITTING THE COPY OF A LETTER FROM THE COMMISSIONER APPOINTED UNDER THE ACT, "FOR ESTABLISHING THE TEMPORARY AND PERMANENT SEAT OF THE GOVERNMENT OF THE UNITED STATES," WITH SUNDRY DOCUMENTS, MARKED A. B. C. D. E. AND F: EXHIBITING A VIEW OF THE RECEIPTS AND EXPENDITURES OF ALL MONIES INTRUSTED TO THEM; AND ALSO, OF THE PROGRESS AND STATE OF THE BUSINESS, AND OF THE FUNDS UNDER THEIR ADMINISTRATION, FROM THE 17TH OF MAY, TO THE 18TH OF NOVEMBER, 1796. 29TH DECEMBER, 1796, ORDERED TO LIE ON THE TABLE.

[Philadelphia: Printed by William Ross. 1797.] pp. [26], folded table. 8vo.   AAS. JCB. LOC.

UNITED STATES, continued.

33087 —— LETTER FROM THE SECRETARY OF THE TREASURY, TRANSMITTING A REPORT AND SUNDRY STATEMENTS EXHIBITING A VIEW OF THE DEBTS OF THE UNITED STATES, ON THE FIRST DAY OF JANUARY, IN THE YEARS 1790, 1791, AND 1796, IN PURSUANCE OF A RESOLUTION OF THE HOUSE, OF THE FIRST OF JUNE, 1796. 29TH DECEMBER, 1796, READ, AND ORDERED TO BE REFERRED TO THE COMMITTEE OF WAYS AND MEANS. [PUBLISHED BY ORDER OF THE HOUSE OF REPRESENTATIVES.]
[Philadelphia: Printed by William Ross. 1797.] pp. [39.] 8vo. AAS. BA. JCB.

33088 —— LETTER FROM THE SECRETARY OF THE TREASURY, TRANSMITTING A REPORT, TOGETHER WITH AN ESTIMATE FOR A SUPPLEMENTARY APPROPRIATION, FOR THE SERVICES OF THE YEAR 1797. JUNE 24TH, 1797, ORDERED TO LIE ON THE TABLE. [PUBLISHED BY ORDER OF THE HOUSE OF REPRESENTATIVES.]
[Philadelphia: Printed by William Ross. 1797.] pp. 8. 8vo. AAS.

33089 —— REPORT OF THE COMMISSIONERS OF THE SINKING FUND; INCLOSING A REPORT TO THEM, FROM THE SECRETARY OF THE TREASURY; AND SUNDRY OFFICIAL STATEMENTS OF THE ACCOUNTING OFFICERS OF THE TREASURY DEPARTMENT. RELATIVE TO THE MEASURES WHICH HAVE BEEN AUTHORIZED BY THE SAID COMMISSIONERS FOR PURCHASING THE PUBLIC DEBT, SUBSEQUENT TO THEIR REPORTS OF THE 16TH OF DECEMBER, 1796, AND 25TH OF JANUARY, 1797. 5TH DECEMBER, 1797: ORDERED TO LIE ON THE TABLE. PUBLISHED BY ORDER OF THE HOUSE OF REPRESENTATIVES.
Philadelphia: Printed by Zachariah Poulson, jun. & W. Young. 1797. pp. 25. 8vo. AAS. BA. HSP. JCB.

33090 —— REPORT OF THE COMMISSIONERS OF THE SINKING FUND, RELATIVE TO THE SALE OF A PART OF THE CAPITAL STOCK OF THE BANK OF THE UNITED STATES, BELONGING TO THE UNITED STATES, IN PURSUANCE OF THE ACT "MAKING PROVISION FOR THE PAYMENT OF CERTAIN DEBTS OF THE UNITED STATES." 26TH OF JANUARY, 1797, REFERRED TO THE COMMITTEE OF WAYS AND MEANS. PUBLISHED BY ORDER OF THE HOUSE OF REPRESENTATIVES.
[Philadelphia: Printed by William Ross. 1797.] pp. 15. 8vo. AAS. BA. UTS.

33091 —— LETTER FROM THE DIRECTOR OF THE MINT, ACCOMPANYING A REPORT, AND SUNDRY STATEMENTS, NUMBERED, 1, 2, 3 AND 4, MADE IN PURSUANCE OF A RESOLUTION OF THE HOUSE OF THE 18TH INSTANT. DECEMBER 17, 1797. PRINTED BY ORDER OF THE HOUSE OF REPRESENTATIVES.
Philadelphia: Printed by Joseph Gales, No. 126, North Second Street. [1797.] pp. 8. 8vo. AAS. BA. JCB.

33092 —— LETTER FROM THE SECRETARY OF WAR, INCLOSING HIS REPORT ON THE PETITION OF HUGH LAWSON WHITE. 26TH DECEMBER, 1796. READ, AND ORDERED TO BE COMMITTED TO A COMMITTEE OF THE WHOLE HOUSE, ON WEDNESDAY NEXT.
[Philadelphia: Printed by William Ross. 1797.] pp. 8. 8vo. AAS. BA.

33093 —— LETTER FROM THE SECRETARY OF WAR, RELATIVE TO EXPENSE OF BUILDING AND EQUIPPING CERTAIN VESSELS OF WAR. 2 JANUARY, 1797.
[Philadelphia: Printed by William Ross. 1797.] BA.

33094 —— LETTER FROM THE SECRETARY AT WAR, TO THE CHAIRMAN OF THE COMMITTEE ON THE NAVAL EQUIPMENT; INCLOSING SUNDRY STATEMENTS RELATIVE TO THE SUBJECT. ACCOMPANYING A REPORT OF THE COMMITTEE APPOINTED ON THE 16TH ULTIMO, TO ENQUIRE INTO THE STATE OF THE NAVAL EQUIPMENT. 25TH JANUARY, 1797, COMMITTED TO A COMMITTEE OF THE WHOLE HOUSE, ON MONDAY NEXT. PUBLISHED BY ORDER OF THE HOUSE OF REPRESENTATIVES.
[Philadelphia: Printed by William Ross. 1797.] pp. 11, folded sheet. 8vo.)
AAS. BA.

UNITED STATES, continued.

33095 —— LETTER FROM THE SECRETARY AT WAR, TRANSMITTING AN EXPLANATORY LETTER, FROM THE SECRETARY OF THE TREASURY; ALSO, SUNDRY STATEMENTS RELATIVE TO THE EXPENDITURES IN THE MILITARY DEPARTMENT, FOR THE YEAR 1796, IN PURSUANCE OF A RESOLUTION OF THE HOUSE, OF THE FIFTEENTH INSTANT. 20TH FEBRUARY, 1797, ORDERED TO LIE ON THE TABLE. PUBLISHED BY ORDER OF THE HOUSE OF REPRESENTATIVES.

[Philadelphia: Printed by William Ross. 1797.] pp. 8. 8vo.   AAS. BA.

33096 —— LETTER FROM THE SECRETARY OF WAR, TRANSMITTING SUNDRY STATEMENTS RELATIVE TO THE FRIGATES, UNITED STATES, CONSTITUTION AND CONSTELLATION, JUNE 17, 1797. PUBLISHED BY ORDER OF THE HOUSE OF REPRESENTATIVES.

Philadelphia: Printed by Zachariah Poulson, junior, number eighty, Chesnut-Street. 1797. pp. 10, folded table. 8vo,   BA. JCB.

33097 —— REGULATIONS TO BE OBSERVED IN THE DELIVERY AND DISTRIBUTION OF FUEL AND STRAW TO THE GARRISONS ON THE SEA COAST, AND RECRUITING PARTIES. [TWO columns.] GIVEN AT THE WAR OFFICE OF THE UNITED STATES IN PHILADELPHIA, THIS TWENTY-SIXTH DAY OF DECEMBER, A. D. 1797. BY ORDER OF THE PRESIDENT. [Signed, James McHenry, Secy. of War.]

[Philadelphia: Printed by William Ross. 1797.] Broadside. fol.   LOC.

33098 —— 19TH JUNE, 1797, COMMITTED TO A COMMITTEE OF THE WHOLE HOUSE, THIS DAY. REPORT OF THE SECRETARY OF WAR [on the corps of artillerists and engineers.] PUBLISHED BY ORDER OF THE HOUSE OF REPRESENTATIVES.

[Philadelphia: Printed by William Ross. 1797.] pp. (4). 8vo.   AAS. BA.

33099 —— REPORT OF THE SECRETARY OF WAR, ON THE PETITION OF MONSIEUR POIREY, FORMERLY SECRETARY AID-DE-CAMP TO THE MARQUIS DE LA FAYETTE. 5TH APRIL 1796, ORDERED TO LIE ON THE TABLE. 5TH JANUARY 1797. COMMITTED TO A COMMITTEE OF THE WHOLE HOUSE, TO-MORROW. PUBLISHED BY ORDER OF THE HOUSE OF REPRESENTATIVES.

[Philadelphia: Printed by William Ross. 1797.] pp. 4. 8vo.   AAS. BA. JCB.

33100 —— UNIFORM FOR THE NAVY OF THE UNITED STATES OF AMERICA. [Two columns.] JAMES M'HENRY, SECRETARY OF WAR. WAR-OFFICE, AUGUST 24, 1797.

[Philadelphia: Printed by William Ross. 1797.] Broadside. fol.   AAS.

33101 THE UNITED STATES ALMANAC, OR THE NORTH AMERICAN CALENDER FOR THE YEAR OF OUR LORD 1798; BEING THE SECOND AFTER LEAP-YEAR. [Two lines of verse.] ARMS OF THE UNITED STATES.

Wilmington: Printed and sold wholesale; by James Adams, north-side of the Upper Market. [1797.] pp. (36). 12mo.   AAS. LOC.

33102 [U. S. arms.] UNITED STATES CHRONICLE. [R. I. arms.] VOLUME XIV. NUMBER 677. THURSDAY, JANUARY 5, [— NUMBER 728. THURSDAY, DECEMBER, 28, 1797.]

Published by B. Wheeler, at his Office in Westminster Street, a few rods westward of the Great Bridge, Providence. 1797. fol.   AAS. HC. LOC. RIHS.

33103 THE UNIVERSAL DREAM-BOOK.

Wilmington: Printed by Peter Brynberg. 1797.

33104 THE UNIVERSAL GAZETTE. VOL. I. No. 1. THURSDAY, NOVEMBER 16, [— No. 7. THURSDAY, DECEMBER 28, 1797.]

Philadelphia: Printed by Samuel Harrison Smith. 1797. fol.   AAS. BA. LOC.

Established, as a weekly, by Samuel Harrison Smith, and continued by him up to his removal to the City of Washington in September, 1800.

33105   UNIVERSAL SPELLING-BOOK.
Wilmington: Printed by Peter Brynberg. 1797.

33106   UNIVERSALISTS.
THE ELDERS AND MESSENGERS FROM THE VARIOUS SOCIETIES BELIEVING THE DOC-
TRINE OF THE UNIVERSAL LOVE OF GOD IN CHRIST TO THE CHILDREN OF MEN; MET
IN CONVENTION AT MILFORD, IN THE STATE OF MASSACHUSETTS, SEPTEMBER 20,
1797. . . . SHIPPIE TOWNSEND, MODERATOR. HOSEA BALLON [*sic*] CLERK.
[Boston: 1797.] pp. (2). fol.   AAS.

33107   DER UNPARTHEYISCHER READINGER ADLER. NO. 2. DIENSTAG, JANUAR 3, [—
NO. 53. DIENSTAG, DEZEMBER 26, 1797.]
*Herausgegeben von Jacob Schneider und Comp. in der Deutsch-und Englischen
Buchdruckerey in Reading in der Pennstrasse.* 1797. fol.   AAS.

33108   DIE UNPARTHEYISCHE YORK GAZETTE. NO. 46. DIENSTAG, JANUAR 3, [—NO.
74. DIENSTAG, JULI 18, 1797.]
York: Gedruckt und Herausgegeben von Salomon Mayer. 1797. fol.   YHS.

The above is the last number located.

33109   VAILL, JOSEPH   1751–1838
NOAH'S FLOOD: A POEM, IN TWO PARTS. PART I. CONTAINS AN HISTORICAL ACCOUNT
OF THE DELUGE, TAKEN FROM THE BIBLE; INTERSPERSED WITH CONJECTURAL OB-
SERVATIONS. PART II. IS DESIGNED AS A MORAL IMPROVEMENT OF THE SUBJECT.
TO WHICH ARE ADDED THE FOLLOWING PIECES OF POETRY; VIZ. YOUTH'S CAUTIONER
AGAINST VICE. ON HAPPINESS. A NEW YEARS HYMN. BY JOSEPH VAIL, A.M.
PASTOR OF THE THIRD CHURCH IN EAST-HADDAM.
Hartford: Printed and sold by Hudson & Goodwin, and by the Author. 1797.

33110   VALENTINE AND ORSON.
THE HISTORY OF VALENTINE AND ORSON, THE TWO SONS OF THE EMPEROR OF GREECE.
Wilmington: Printed by Peter Brynberg. 1797.

33111   VAN BUSKIRK, LAWRENCE
SIX SERMONS, PREACHED BY THE LATE MR LAWRENCE V. BUSKIRK, B.A. CANDIDATE
FOR THE HOLY MINISTRY. EPITAPH OF THE DECEASED AUTHOR, TO BE SEEN IN THE
LUTHERAN CHURCH YARD OF THIS CITY. "I STOOD AMIDST A CROWD, PREPAR'D FOR
DIFFERENT VINEYARD-STAGES: BUT LO! TO ME THE OWNER CAME, AND SAID RE-
CEIVE THY WAGES." [Edited by Johann Christoff Kunze.]
New-York: Printed and sold by T. Kirk, 112, *Chatham-Street.* 1797. pp.
viii, 123. 12mo.   BM. HC. LCP.

33112   VAUGHAN, JOHN   1775–1807
OBSERVATIONS ON ANIMAL ELECTRICITY. IN EXPLANATION OF THE METALLIC OPERA-
TION OF DOCTOR PERKINS. BY JOHN VAUGHAN, M.P.M.S. FELLOW OF THE MEDICAL
SOCIETY OF DELAWARE. "WHO SHALL DECIDE, WHEN DOCTORS DISAGREE?" DRYDEN.
Wilmington: — From the Office of the Delaware Gazette, by W. C. Smyth.
1797. pp. (32). 8vo.   AAS. NYPL. RIMS. SGO. UTS.

First Delaware District Copyright, issued to John Vaughan, as Author,
21 July, 1797.

33113   DER VERBESSERTE HOCH DEUTSCHE AMERICANISCHE LAND UND STAATS CALEN-
DAR. AUF DAS JAHR . . . 1798. DER VIERZEHNTEN MAL HERAUSGEGEBEN.
Friedrich-Stadt, Maryland: Gedruckt bey Matthias Bartgis. [1797.]

33114   E PLURIBUS UNUM. DER VEREINIGTEN Staaten Calender, auf das Jahr Jesu
Christi, 1798. Ein gemeines Jahr von 365 Tagen.
> *Philadelphia: Gedruckt bey H. Kammerer, jun. und Comp. No. 24, in der
> Dritten-Strasse, zwischen der Markt-und Arch-Strasse.* [1797.] pp. (34). 4to.

As customary with all German Almanacs the title is enclosed in a full- AAS.
page woodcut—this having a view of Philadelphia. In continuation of
the Haus und Wirthschafts Calender.

33115   VERMONT. STATE.
AN ACT ASSESSING A TAX OF ONE CENT ON EACH ACRE OF LAND IN THIS STATE, FOR
SUPPORT OF GOVERNMENT DURING THE YEAR 1797 AND FOR OTHER PURPOSES. . . .
PASSED NOVEMBER 10TH, 1797. Attest, ROSWELL HOPKINS, SECRETARY.
> *[Bennington: Printed by Anthony Haswell.* 1797.] pp. (2). fol.

33116   —— AN ACT FOR REGULATING AND GOVERNING THE MILITIA OF THE STATE OF VER-
MONT. PASSED BY THE LEGISLATURE AT THEIR ADJOURNED SESSION AT RUTLAND,
MARCH 10TH, 1797.
> *Bennington: Printed by Anthony Haswell.* MDCC.XCVII. pp. [58.] 8vo.   BM.

33117   —— ACTS AND LAWS, PASSED BY THE LEGISLATURE OF THE STATE OF VERMONT, AT
THEIR ADJOURNED SESSION HOLDEN AT RUTLAND, FEBRUARY, A. D. ONE THOUSAND
SEVEN HUNDRED AND NINETY-SEVEN. [— 10 MARCH, 1797.]
> *Bennington: Printed by Anthony Haswell.* 1797. pp. [100]. 8vo.   LOC.

33118   —— ACTS AND LAWS, PASSED BY THE LEGISLATURE OF THE STATE OF VERMONT, AT
THEIR SESSION AT WINDSOR, OCTOBER, ONE THOUSAND SEVEN HUNDRED AND NINETY-
SEVEN. [— 9 NOVEMBER, 1797.] PUBLISHED BY AUTHORITY.
> *Prined* [sic] *at Rutland, by Josiah Fay, for the hon. Legislature.* M,DCC,-
> XCVII. pp. (2), (110). 8vo.   LOC.

33119   —— A JOURNAL OF THE PROCEEDINGS OF THE GENERAL ASSEMBLY OF THE STATE OF
VERMONT BEGUN AND HELD AT RUTLAND, IN THE COUNTY OF RUTLAND, OCTOBER
THIRTEENTH, ONE THOUSAND SEVEN HUNDRED AND NINETY-SIX.
> *Bennington: Printed by Anthony Haswell.* M,DCC,XCVII. pp. 184. 4to. vtsL.

33120   —— BY HIS EXCELLENCY THOMAS CHITTENDEN, ESQ. GOVERNOR, CAPTAIN GENERAL
AND COMMANDER IN CHIEF, IN AND OVER THE STATE OF VERMONT. A PROCLAMA-
TION. . . . APPOINT WEDNESDAY, THE NINETEENTH DAY OF APRIL NEXT, TO BE
OBSERVED AS A DAY OF PUBLIC HUMILIATION, FASTING, & PRAYER THROUGHOUT THIS
STATE. GIVEN UNDER MY HAND AT WILLISTON, THIS TENTH DAY OF MARCH, IN
THE YEAR OF OUR LORD, ONE THOUSAND SEVEN HUNDRED AND NINETY-SEVEN; AND
OF OUR INDEPENDENCE, THE TWENTY-FIRST. THOMAS CHITTENDEN. BY HIS EX-
CELLENCY'S COMMAND, TRUMAN SQUIER, SECRETARY. GOD SAVE THE PEOPLE.
> *[Burlington: Printed by Robert Donnelly?* 1797.] Broadside. fol.

33121   —— BY HIS EXCELLENCY ISAAC TICHENOR, CAPTAIN GENERAL, GOVERNOR, AND COM-
MANDER IN CHIEF, IN AND OVER THE STATE OF VERMONT. A PROCLAMATION. . . .
APPOINT THURSDAY, THE SEVENTH DAY OF DECEMBER NEXT TO BE OBSERVED
AS A DAY OF PUBLIC THANKSGIVING AND PRAISE, THROUGHOUT THIS STATE. . . .
GIVEN UNDER MY HAND IN COUNCIL CHAMBER AT WINDSOR, THIS 24TH DAY OF
OCTOBER, 1797. ISAAC TICHENOR. BY HIS EXCELLENCY'S COMMAND TRUMAN
SQUIER, SECRETARY.
> *[Windsor: Printed by Aiden Spooner.* 1797.] Broadside. fol.

33122 THE VERMONT GAZETTE. WE HERE THE TIDINGS OF THE WORLD PROCLAIM—
CANDOR OUR GUIDE, IMPARTIAL TRUTH OUR AIM. VOL. I. NUMBER 1. TUESDAY,
SEPTEMBER 5, [— NUMBER 17. TUESDAY, DECEMBER 26TH, 1797.]
Printed and published at Bennington, by Anthony Haswell, 1797. fol.

Re-established, as a weekly, by Anthony Haswell, in continuation of the
Tablet of the Times, an unsuccessful newspaper venture, printed from his
Office, by Merrill & Langdon, earlier in this year; as a revival of *The Vermont Gazette,* which was discontinued in December, 1796, and continued
with varying fortunes of changes in title, ownership, and lapses in publication, to beyond the period of this work.

33123 THE VILLAGE HARMONY, OR YOUTH'S ASSISTANT TO SACRED MUSICK. CONTAINING A
CONCISE INTRODUCTION TO THE GROUNDS OF MUSICK, WITH SUCH A COLLECTION OF
THE MOST APPROVED PSALM TUNES, ANTHEMS, AND OTHER PIECES, IN THREE, AND
FOUR PARTS, AS ARE MOST SUITABLE FOR DIVINE WORSHIP. DESIGNED FOR THE USE
OF SCHOOLS AND SINGING SOCIETIES. THE THIRD EDITION.
Printed at Exeter, by H. Ranlet, and sold at his Book-Store. 1797.

33124 VILLAGE MESSENGER. [Motto.] No. 1 OF VOL. 2. TUESDAY, JANUARY 7, [— No.
52 OF VOL. II. SATURDAY, DECEMBER 27, 1797.]
[*Printed and published*] *By Samuel Cushing, Amherst, Newhampshire.*
1797. fol.
AAS.

With the issue for April 18th, Cushing disposed of his interests to Samuel Preston who changed the motto to, "Old things shall pass away—
and all things become new."

33125 VIRGILIUS MARO, PUBLIUS   70–19 B. C.
M. MARTEL'S LITERAL TRANSLATION OF THE WORKS OF VIRGIL IN WHICH THE ORDER
OF CONSTRUCTION TO THE LATIN TEXT IS NOT ONLY TRANSLATED LITERALLY INTO
ENGLISH, BUT EVERY WORD IS COMPLETELY PARSED EXPLAINED AND ILLUSTRATED
BY CRITICAL HISTORICAL GEOGRAPHICAL MYTHOLOGICAL AND CLASSICAL NOTES, IN
ENGLISH, FROM THE BEST COMMENTATORS BOTH ANCIENT AND MODERN. THE EN-
GLISH TO THE LATIN WORDS IS IN ITALIC, AND THE WORDS WHICH HAVE BEEN ADDED
TO RENDER THE SENSE MORE INTELLIGIBLE, THE ENGLISH LESS UNFASHIONABLE,
STIFF AND AWKWARD, AND HAVE NOW TO ANSWER THEM IN THE ORIGINAL, ARE IN
A DIFFERENT CHARACTER. THERE IS ALSO IN THE BEGINNING OF THIS WORK A
SUFFICIENCY OF DECLENSIONS AND CONJUGATIONS TO ENABLE THE LEARNER TO PRO-
CEED TO TRANSLATE. AFTER A COUPLE OF WEEKS TUITION, A MOTHER CAN, WITH
THIS BOOK, TEACH LATIN TO HER CHILD, WHO WILL STUDY WITH ADVANTAGE AND
PLEASURE, BECAUSE HE CAN STUDY THEN, ALL THE DISHEARTENING DIFFICULTIES
BEING REMOVED. LET US HAVE NO MORE OF THAT CROSS, CRABBED, BARBAROUS AND
TREMENDOUS GO AND LOOK IT, INVENTED BY PEDANTS TO COVER THEIR IGNORANCE.
LET US RATHER AFFECTIONATELY SMILING ON THE ENQUIRING CHILD, RENEW FOR
HIM THE AGE WHEN SCHOOL AND PLAY WERE SYNONYMOUS.
New - York: 1797.

48th New York District Copyright, issued to Michael Martel, as Author,
20 March, 1797.

33126 VIRGINIA. STATE.
ACTS PASSED AT A GENERAL ASSEMBLY OF THE COMMONWEALTH OF VIRGINIA. BE-
GUN AND HELD AT THE CAPITOL, IN THE CITY OF RICHMOND, ON TUESDAY, THE
EIGHTH DAY OF NOVEMBER, ONE THOUSAND SEVEN HUNDRED AND NINETY-SIX.
[— 29 DECEMBER 1796.] [Ornament.]
Richmond: Printed by Augustine Davis, Printer for the Public. M,DCC,-
XCVII. pp. [48.] fol.
HSP. LOC. NYPL. VSL.

VIRGINIA. STATE, continued.

33127 —— IN COUNCIL JANUARY THE 16TH, 1797. GENTLEMEN, THE EXECUTIVE DEEM IT ESSENTIALLY NECESSARY, THAT AN ACCURATE STATE OF THE COMMISSION OF THE PEACE IN EACH COUNTY, SHOULD BE KNOWN TO THEM. [Fifteen lines. Signed, James Wood.] CIRCULAR.
[Richmond: Printed by Augustine Davis. 1797.] Broadside. 4to.   LOC.

33128 —— JOURNAL OF THE HOUSE OF DELEGATES OF THE COMMONWEALTH OF VIRGINIA, BEGUN AND HELD AT THE CAPITOL, IN THE CITY OF RICHMOND, ON TUESDAY, THE EIGHTH DAY OF NOVEMBER, ONE THOUSAND SEVEN HUNDRED AND NINETY-SIX. [— 27 DECEMBER, 1796.]
Richmond: Printed ? by Augustine Davis. 1797.
No printed copy is known to be extant. The manuscript record is in the Virginia State Library.

33129 —— JOURNAL OF THE SENATE OF THE COMMONWEALTH OF VIRGINIA, BEGUN AND HELD AT THE CAPITOL, IN THE CITY OF RICHMOND, ON TUESDAY, THE EIGHTH DAY NOVEMBER, ONE THOUSAND SEVEN HUNDRED AND NINETY-SIX. [— 27 DECEMBER, 1796.]
Richmond: Printed ? by Thomas Nicolson. 1797.
No copy in manuscript, or in print, is known.

33130 —— LIST OF PENSIONERS CONTINUED BY THE HONORABLE THE EXECUTIVE FOR THE YEAR 1796, TO BE PAID OUT OF THE REVENUE FOR THAT YEAR. [Fifty-one pensioners, and allowances.] SAMUEL SHEPARD, AUDITOR. AUDITOR'S-OFFICE. FEBRUARY 1, 1797.
[Richmond: Printed by Augustine Davis. 1797.] Broadside. fol.   LOC.

33131 THE VIRGINIA ALMANAC, FOR THE YEAR OF OUR LORD, 1798, BEING THE SECOND AFTER BISSEXTILE OR LEAP YEAR. THE TWENTY-SECOND OF AMERICAN INDEPENDENCE, AND THE TENTH YEAR OF OUR FEDERAL GOVERNMENT — WHICH MAY THE GOVERNOR OF THE WORLD PROSPER. CONTAINING THE MOTIONS OF THE SUN AND MOON; THE TRUE PLACES AND ASPECTS OF THE PLANETS; THE RISING AND SETTING OF THE SUN AND MOON; ALSO, THE LUNATIONS, CONJUNCTIONS, ECLIPSES, JUDGMENTS OF THE WEATHER, REMARKABLE DAYS, LENGTH OF DAYS AND NIGHTS, TIMES COURTS ARE HELD IN VIRGINIA, MARYLAND AND PENNSYLVANIA, ROADS, &C. LIKEWISE, A VARIETY OF ESSAYS IN PROSE & VERSE. THE WHOLE CALCULATED FOR GENERAL UTILITY AND ENTERTAINMENT. BY THE NORTH-MOUNTAIN PHILOSOPHER.
Winchester: Printed and sold by Richard Bowen, opposite the Episcopal Church in Loudoun street. [1797.] pp. (38). 12mo.   AAS.

33132 THE VIRGINIA & N. CAROLINA ALMANACK, FOR THE YEAR 1798; CONTAINING AMONG A VARIETY OF OTHER INTERESTING MATTER, THE STAMP ACT WHICH IS TO TAKE PLACE THE FIRST DAY OF JANUARY [1798] AND WHICH EVERY MAN IN BUSINESS OUGHT TO HAVE BY HIM.
Norfolk: Printed and sold by Willett & O'Connor. [1797.]

33133 VIRGINIA [cut] ARGUS. VOL. IV. No. 75. WHOLE NO. 386. TUESDAY, JANUARY 3, [— VOL. V. No. 74. WHOLE NO. 489. FRIDAY, DECEMBER 29, 1797.]
Richmond, (Virg.)— Printed (on Tuesdays and Fridays) by Samuel Pleasants jun. near the Vendue-Office. 1797. fol.
In the summer changed to *The Virginia Argus.*

33134 THE VIRGINIA GAZETTE, AND GENERAL ADVERTISER. VOL. XI. NUMB. 548. WEDNESDAY, JANUARY 4, [— NUMB. 599. WEDNESDAY, DECEMBER 27, 1797.]
Richmond: Printed by Aug. Davis. 1797. fol.

33135   VIRGINIA GAZETTE, & PETERSBURG INTELLIGENCER. NUMBER 756. TUESDAY, JAN-
UARY 3, [— NUMBER 859. FRIDAY, DECEMBER 29, 1797.]
Published every Tuesday and Friday by William Prentis. 1797. fol.

In March, & in the title was changed to and.

33136   VIRGINIA GAZETTE, AND STAUNTON WEEKLY ADVERTISER. VOL. II. NO. 31. FRI-
DAY, OCTOBER 6, [— VOL. II. NO. 43. FRIDAY, DECEMBER 29, 1797.]
Staunton: Printed by John Wise. 1797. fol.

33137   VIRGINIA GAZETTE AND WEEKLY ADVERTISER. NUMBER 724. MONDAY, JANUARY 2,
[— NUMBER 737. SATURDAY, APRIL 8, 1797.]
Richmond: Published by Thomas Nicolson, two doors above the Eagle-Tavern.
1797. fol.

The above is the last number located.

33138   THE VIRGINIA HERALD, AND FREDERICKSBURG & FALMOUTH ADVERTISER. VOL. IX.
NUMB. 587. TUESDAY, JANUARY 3, [— VOL. X. NUMB. 690. FRIDAY, DECEMBER
29, 1797.]
Fredericksburg, (Va). Published on Tuesdays and Fridays by T. Green.
1797. fol.

In August, the title was shortened to *The Virginia Herald.*

33139   VIVIAN, THOMAS
THREE DIALOGUES BETWEEN A MINISTER AND ONE OF HIS PARISHIONERS; ON THE TRUE
PRINCIPLES OF RELIGION, AND SALVATION FOR SINNERS BY JESUS CHRIST, THE ONLY
REDEEMER AND SAVIOUR OF MANKIND. BY THOMAS VIVIAN. THE TWENTIETH
EDITION.
*Bennington: Re-printed by Anthony Haswell, and sold by him, whole-sale or
retail.* M,DCC,XCVII. pp. 24. 12mo.   BA.

33140   VOLNEY, CONSTANTIN FRANÇOIS CHASSEBŒUF BOISGIVAIS, comte DE   1757–1820
VOLNEY'S ANSWER TO DOCTOR PRIESTLEY, ON HIS PAMPHLET ENTITLED "OBSERVATIONS
UPON THE INCREASE OF INFIDELITY, WITH ANIMADVERSIONS UPON THE WRITINGS OF
SEVERAL MODERN UNBELIEVERS, AND ESPECIALLY THE RUINS OF MR. VOLNEY, WITH
THIS MOTTO; "MINDS OF LITTLE PENETRATION REST NATURALLY ON THE SURFACE
OF THINGS. THEY DO NOT LIKE TO PIERCE DEEP INTO THEM, FOR FEAR OF LABOUR
AND TROUBLE; SOMETIMES STILL MORE FOR FEAR OF TRUTH—[One line of French
from] RACINE, ATHALIE ACT 2.
*Philadelphia: Printed for the Author—and sold at the Office of the Aurora, No.
112, Market-Street.* 1797. pp. (15). 8vo.   BA. BPL. HC. JCB. LOC. NYPL.

33141   —— THE LAW OF NATURE, OR PRINCIPLES OF MORALITY, DEDUCED FROM THE PHYS-
ICAL CONSTITUTION OF MANKIND AND THE UNIVERSE. BY C–F. VOLNEY. "FOR
MODES OF FAITH, LET GRACELESS ZEALOTS FIGHT; HIS CAN'T BE WRONG, WHOSE LIFE
IS IN THE RIGHT." POPE.
Philadelphia: Printed in the year 1797. pp. 56. 8vo.   JCB.

33142   DIE WAHRE BRANTWEIN BERENNERUNG ODER BRANTWEIN GIN UND CORDIALMACH-
ERKUNST WIE AUCH DIE ÄCHTE FÄRBE KUNST WIE MAN ALLE COULEUREN AUF SEIDE
LEINEN UND WOLLE FÄRBEN KAN.
York: Gedruckt bey Salomon Mayer. 1797.

179th Pennsylvania District Copyright, issued to Salomon Mayer, as
Proprietor, 19 May, 1797.

33143 WALKER, JAMES
An INQUIRY INTO THE CAUSES OF STERILITY IN BOTH SEXES; WITH ITS METHOD OF CURE.
BY JAMES WALKER, M.P.M.S. CITIZEN OF THE STATE OF VIRGINIA. [Three lines
of Latin from] GENESIS, CAP. I. VER. 28.
        Philadelphia: Printed by E. Oswald, No. 179, South Second-Street M,DCC,-
XCVII. pp. 22. 8vo.   AAS. RIMS.

33144 WALKER, ROBERT   1716–1783
SERMONS ON PRACTICAL SUBJECTS. BY ROBERT WALKER, LATE ONE OF THE MINIS-
TERS OF THE HIGH CHURCH OF EDINBURGH. TO WHICH IS PREFIXED, AN ACCOUNT
OF THE AUTHOR'S LIFE, AND A CHARACTER OF HIM: BY HUGH BLAIR, D.D. THE
FIRST AMERICAN EDITION. IN TWO VOLUMES. VOL. II.
        Albany: Printed by John M'Donald. MDCCXCVII. pp. vii, 278. 8vo.
        The first volume was published in 1796.   AAS. HC.

33145 WARNER, GEORGE JAMES
Half title: ORATION, DELIVERED BEFORE THE GENERAL SOCIETY OF MECHANICS AND
TRADESMEN THE TAMMANY SOCIETY, OR COLUMBIAN ORDER, THE DEMOCRATIC AND
NEW-YORK COOPER SOCIETIES AND OTHER CITIZENS, JULY 4TH, 1797.

Title: MEANS FOR THE PRESERVATION OF PUBLIC LIBERTY. AN ORATION DELIV-
ERED IN THE NEW DUTCH CHURCH, ON THE FOURTH OF JULY, 1797. BEING THE
TWENTY-FIRST ANNIVERSARY OF OUR INDEPENDENCE. BY G. J. WARNER. [Ten
lines from] FRENEAU.
        *New-York: Printed at the Argus Office, for Thomas Greenleaf and Naphtali
Judah.* 1797. pp. (2), 22. 8vo.   AAS. BPL. JCB. LOC. NYPL.

        Contains, Ode (composed for the occasion, by P. Freneau). The musick
performed by the Uranian Musical Society.

33146 WARREN. RHODE ISLAND. BAPTIST ASSOCIATION.
MINUTES OF THE WARREN ASSOCIATION, HELD AT THE FIRST BAPTIST MEETING-HOUSE
IN BOSTON, SEPTEMBER 12 AND 13, 1797.
        Boston: Printed by Manning and Loring. M,DCC,XCVII. pp. 12. 12mo.
                                                        AAS. BM. JCB. NYPL.

33147 WARWICK. NEW YORK. BAPTIST ASSOCIATION.
MINUTES OF THE WARWICK BAPTIST ASSOCIATION, HELD IN NEW YORK, MAY 30, 1797.
        [New-York: 1797.] 4to.

33148 WASHINGTON, GEORGE   1732–1799
AMERICA'S LEGACY: BEING THE ADDRESS OF G. WASHINGTON, ON HIS DECLINING A
RE-ELECTION TO THE PRESIDENCY. TO THE PEOPLE OF THE UNITED STATES.
        Printed in Hudson, by A. Stoddard. M,DCC,XCVII. pp. 200. 24mo.
                                                              LOC. NYPL.

Second title: A CIRCULAR LETTER FROM HIS EXCELLENCY GEORGE WASHINGTON,
COMMANDER IN CHIEF OF THE ARMIES OF THE UNITED STATES OF AMERICA, TO THE
GOVERNORS OF THE SEVERAL STATES.
        Printed at Hudson, by A. Stoddard. M,DCC,XCVII. pp. (2), 103–164.

Third heading: FAREWEL [*sic*] ORDERS OF GENERAL WASHINGTON, TO THE ARMIES
OF THE UNITED STATES. pp. 165–188.

Fourth heading: THE ANSWER TO HIS EXCELLENCY GENERAL WASHINGTON, COM-
MANDER IN CHIEF OF THE ARMIES OF THE UNITED STATES OF AMERICA. pp. 189–200.

WASHINGTON, George, continued.

33149   —— — The Legacy of the Father of his Country. Address of George Washington, President of the United States, to his Fellow Citizens, on declining
being considered a candidate for their future suffrages. "It is a legacy
worthy such a father," Shakespeare.
> *Printed at Northampton, (Massachusetts.) By William Butler.* 1797. pp. 24.
> 12mo.   NYPL.

33150   —— — Address and resignation of his excellency George Washington, esq.
President of the United States of America.
> *Troy: Printed by Luther Pratt & Co.* 1797.

33151   THE WASHINGTON [cut] Gazette. Number 55 of Volume I. From Saturday,
December 31, to Wednesday, January 4, [— Number 24, Volume II. From
Saturday, December 16, to Saturday, December 23, 1797.]
> *City of Washington: Published by Benjamin More, every Wednesday and
> Saturday, price 4 dollars per ann. at the house next west of the Hotel, where sub-
> scriptions will be thankfully received.—Handbills, &c. printed at the shortest notice.*
> 1797. fol.   AAS. HC. LOC.

With the issue for July 26th, publication was temporarily suspended
"until the publication is attended with some profit to the Publisher."
With the issue for September 16th, publication was resumed, as a weekly,
published on Saturdays, the cut being dropped from the heading. The
issue for December 23d, announced that the succeeding number "would
not appear until the week after Christmas."

33152   THE WASHINGTON Spy. No. 335. Wednesday, January 4, [— No. 342. Wednesday, February 22, 1797.]
> *Elizabeth (Hager's) Town, (Maryland): Printed at the Office of the Washing-
> ton Spy.* 1797. fol.

Discontinued in February. In March, Thomas Grieves, attorney for John
D. Cary, administrator of the estate of Stewart Herbert, founder of the
Spy, established, in continuation, *The Maryland Herald, and Elizabeth-
Town Advertiser.*

33153   WATSON, Richard   1737–1816
An Address to young persons after confirmation. By Richard Watson, lord
bishop of Landaff. First American edition.
> *Boston: Printed and sold by W. Spotswood; sold also by F. Nichols.* 1797. pp.
> 102, (2). 18mo.   BA.

"Copy-right secured agreeably to law." "As the celebrated Author
intended this Address particularly for the use of members of the
Church of England, it was thought expedient to alter or expunge a few
expressions in order to make it more generally useful to Christians of
all denominations in this country.—The two Prayers at the end were
communicated by a Friend." Contains, two pages of Books printed by
and for sale by W. Spotswood.

33154   —— An Apology for the Bible, in a series of letters, addressed to Thomas
Paine, author of a book entitled, The Age of Reason, part the second,
being an investigation of true and of fabulous theology. By R. Watson,
d.d. f.r.s. lord bishop of Landaff, and regius professor of divinity in the
University of Cambridge.
> *Chambersburg: Printed by Dover & Harper, for Riddle & Lane.* M,DCC,-
> XCVII. pp. (2), [80.] 8vo.   NYPL.

WATSON, RICHARD, continued.

33155   —— — AN APOLOGY FOR THE BIBLE, IN A SERIES OF LETTERS, ADDRESSED TO THOMAS PAINE, AUTHOR OF A BOOK ENTITLED, "THE AGE OF REASON," PART THE SECOND, BEING AN INVESTIGATION OF TRUE AND OF FABULOUS THEOLOGY. BY R. WATSON, D. D. F. R. S. LORD BISHOP OF LANDAFF, AND REGIUS PROFESSOR OF DIVINITY IN THE UNIVERSITY OF CAMBRIDGE.

     Lexington: Printed by John Bradford. 1797. pp. 94, (2). 8vo.   NYPL.

33156   —— — AN APOLOGY FOR THE BIBLE, IN A SERIES OF LETTERS, ADDRESSED TO THOMAS PAINE, AUTHOR OF A BOOK ENTITLED, THE AGE OF REASON," PART THE SECOND, BEING AN INVESTIGATION OF TRUE AND OF FABULOUS THEOLOGY. BY R. WATSON, D. D. F. R. S. LORD BISHOP OF LANDAFF, AND REGIUS PROFESSOR OF DIVINITY IN THE UNIVERSITY OF CAMBRIDGE.

     Re-printed at Litchfield, by T. Collier. 1797. pp. 230. 16mo.

                                 AAS. JCB. NYPL.

33157   —— — AN APOLOGY FOR THE BIBLE, IN A SERIES OF LETTERS, ADDRESSED TO THOMAS PAINE, AUTHOR OF A BOOK ENTITLED, THE AGE OF REASON, PART THE SECOND, BEING AN INVESTIGATION OF TRUE AND OF FABULOUS THEOLOGY. BY R. WATSON, D. D. F. R. S. LORD BISHOP OF LANDAFF, AND REGIUS PROFESSOR OF DIVINITY IN THE UNIVERSITY OF CAMBRIDGE. CAREY'S THIRD PHILADELPHIA EDITION.

     Philadelphia: Printed by James Carey, No. 83, North Second-Street, 1797. [Price three-eighths of a dollar.] pp. (2), (80). 8vo.   JCB. LOC.

33158   —— — CHRISTIAN PANOPLY; CONTAINING AN APOLOGY FOR THE BIBLE; IN A SERIES OF LETTERS, ADDRESSED TO THOMAS PAINE, AUTHOR OF A BOOK ENTITLED THE AGE OF REASON, PART THE SECOND. BY R. WATSON, D. D F. R. S. LORD BISHOP OF LANDAFF, AND REGIUS PROFESSOR OF DIVINITY IN THE UNIVERSITY OF CAMBRIDGE: AN ADDRESS TO THE SCOFFERS AT RELIGION. BY THE SAME AUTHOR: AND A BRIEF VIEW OF THE HISTORICAL EVIDENCES OF CHRISTIANITY. BY WILLIAM PALEY, M. A. ARCH DEACON OF CARLYSLE. [*sic.*]

     Shepherd's-Town:—1797. *Printed by P. Rootes & C. Blagrove.* pp. 332. 12mo.   AAS. JCB. LOC. NYPL. VSL.

     Second title: THE AUTHENTICITY OF THE BOOKS OF THE NEW TESTAMENT. BY WILLIAM PALEY. pp. 173-248.

     Third title: THE SOPHIST UNMASKED; IN A SERIES OF LETTERS, ADDRESSED TO THOMAS PAINE, AUTHOR OF A BOOK, ENTITLED THE AGE OF REASON. BY PHILO-BIBLIUS. OUT OF THINE OWN MOUTH WILL I JUDGE THEE. BIBLE. pp. 249-332.

     "The profits of this publication are appropriated to the purpose of supporting missionaries to preach the Gospel; or some pious and public use, under the direction of the Synod of Virginia."

33159   WATTERS, JAMES
A NEW PERIODICAL PUBLICATION. PROPOSAL OF JAMES WATTERS, FOR PUBLISHING BY SUBSCRIPTION, A NEW WORK, ENTITLED THE WEEKLY MAGAZINE. . . .

     Philadelphia, [Printed by James Watters] 13*th of December,* 1797. Broadside. fol.   HSP.

33160   —— SIR, BEING ON THE POINT OF COMMENCING THE PUBLICATION OF A LITERARY WEEKLY MAGAZINE, I AM LED TO SOLICIT, IN A PARTICULAR MANNER, THE PATRONAGE OF GENTLEMEN DISTINGUISHED BY SITUATION AND AN ATTACHMENT TO SCIENCE: I TRUST THEREFORE, YOU WILL PARDON THE LIBERTY I SHALL TAKE IN WAITING ON YOU FOR YOUR SIGNATURE. SIR, WITH RESPECT I AM YOUR MOST OBEDIENT, JAMES WATTERS.

     Philadelphia: [Printed by James Watters] December 18*th,* 1797. Broadside. 4to.   HSP.

33161   WATTS, ISAAC   1674–1748
THE BEAUTIES OF THE LATE REVEREND DR. ISAAC WATTS: CONTAINING THE MOST STRIKING AND ADMIRED PASSAGES IN THE WORKS OF THAT JUSTLY CELEBRATED DIVINE, PHILOSOPHER, MORALIST, AND POET: EQUALLY CALCULATED FOR THE COMMUNICATION OF POLITE AND USEFUL KNOWLEDGE, AND THE INCREASE OF WISDOM AND HAPPINESS.—TO WHICH IS ADDED—THE LIFE OF THE AUTHOR.
Printed at Newburyport, by Edmund M. Blunt, for Mathew Carey, Philadelphia. 1797. pp. 239. 12mo.   AAS. JCB.

33162   ——— DIVINE SONGS, ATTEMPTED IN EASY LANGUAGE, FOR THE USE OF CHILDREN. BY ISAAC WATTS, D.D. [Two lines from] MATTHEW XXI. 16. (THE SIXTY-FOURTH EDITION.)
Haverhill: Printed and sold by N. Coverly, 1797. [Price nine pence.] pp. 36. 12mo.   NYPL.

33163   ——— — DIVINE SONGS, ATTEMPTED IN EASY LANGUAGE, FOR THE USE OF CHILDREN. BY I. WATTS, D.D. [Two lines from] MATT. XXI. 16. TO WHICH ARE ADDED, THE PRINCIPLES OF THE CHRISTIAN RELIGION, EXPRESSED IN PLAIN AND EASY VERSE. BY P. DODDRIDGE. D.D.
*—Newark:— Printed by Pennington & Dodge, for Cornelius Davis, New-York.—*1797.—pp. 72. 24mo.   AAS.

33164   ——— — DIVINE SONGS, ATTEMPTED IN EASY LANGUAGE, FOR THE USE OF CHILDREN. BY I. WATTS, D.D.
Rutland: Printed by Josiah Fay, 1797.

33165   ——— A GUIDE TO PRAYER: OR, A FREE AND RATIONAL ACCOUNT OF THE GIFT, GRACE, AND SPIRIT OF PRAYER; WITH PLAIN DIRECTIONS HOW EVERY CHRISTIAN MAY ATTAIN THEM. BY. I. WATTS, D.D. LORD TEACH US TO PRAY. LUKE IX. I.
Elizabeth-Town: Printed and sold by Shepard Kollock. M,DCC,XCVII. pp. (2), 235. (3). 12mo.   AAS. JCB. NYPL.

33166   ——— A SHORT VIEW OF THE WHOLE SCRIPTURE HISTORY; WITH A CONTINUATION OF THE JEWISH AFFAIRS FROM THE OLD TESTAMENT, TILL THE TIME OF CHRIST; AND AN ACCOUNT OF THE CHIEF PROPHECIES THAT RELATE TO HIM: REPRESENTED IN A WAY OF QUESTION AND ANSWER. ILLUSTRATED WITH VARIOUS REMARKS ON THE HISTORY AND THE RELIGION OF THE PATRIARCHS, JEWS, AND CHRISTIANS; AND ON THE LAWS, GOVERNMENT, SECTS, CUSTOMS AND WRITINGS OF THE JEWS. BY I. WATTS, D.D. FROM THE SIXTEENTH LONDON EDITION.
Carlisle: Printed by George Kline, M,DCC,XCVII. pp. (2), 298. 12mo.
          AAS. JCB. NYPL.

33167   ——— DR. WATTS'S PLAIN AND EASY CATECHISMS FOR CHILDREN, AND PRESERVATIVE FROM THE SINS AND FOLLIES OF CHILDHOOD AND YOUTH. TO WHICH IS ADDED THE SHORTER CATECHISM, WITH EXPLANATORY NOTES. ALSO, SOME SHORT PRAYERS FOR CHILDREN.
Newburyport: Printed and sold by Edmund M. Blunt, at the Newburyport Book-Store. 1797.

33168   WEATHERWISE, ABRAHAM, pseudonym.
THE TOWN AND COUNTRY ALMANACK, FOR THE YEAR OF OUR LORD, 1798. [Cut.]
Boston: Printed by J. White, near Charles-river Bridge. [1797.] pp. (24). 12mo.

WEATHERWISE, ABRAHAM, continued.

33169　—— WEATHERWISE'S ALMANACK, FOR THE YEAR OF OUR LORD 1798: BEING THE
SECOND AFTER BISSEXTILE OR LEAP YEAR, AND THE TWENTY SECOND OF THE INDE-
PENDENCE OF THE UNITED STATES OF AMERICA; WHICH BEGAN JULY 4, 1776.
CONTAINING ECLIPSES, ASPECTS, JUDGMENT OF THE WEATHER, SUN AND MOON'S
RISING AND SETTING; TIME OF HIGH WATER AT BOSTON; VULGAR NOTES; MOON'S
PLACE; AN EPHEMERIS; RISING, SETTING, AND SOUTHING OF SOME OF THE MOST
PLANETS; COURTS; A TABLE OF INTEREST; FEMALE COURTSHIP; ANECDOTES;
ROADS TO THE TOWNS, &C. CALCULATED FOR THE MERIDIAN OF BOSTON, IN AMER-
ICA. LATITUDE 42 DEGREES, 25 M. NORTH. [Four lines of verse.]

*Printed at Boston. Sold by B. Larkin, E. Larkin, S. Hall, C. Bingham, D.
West, W. P. and L. Blake. J. Nancrede, J. Bumstead, and other Booksellers, in
town and country.* [1797.] pp. (24). 12mo.　　　　　　　　AAS.

33170　—— WEATHERWISE'S ALMANACK, FOR THE YEAR OF CHRISTIAN ÆRA, 1798: BEING
THE SECOND AFTER BISSEXTILE, OR LEAP-YEAR, AND OF THE INDEPENDENCE OF
AMERICA THE TWENTY-SECOND. CALCULATED FOR THE SEVERAL NEW-ENGLAND
STATES. CONTAINING EVERYTHING NECESSARY FOR AN ALMANACK, WITH A VARI-
ETY OF USEFUL AND ENTERTAINING MATTER. [Cut.]

Exeter: Printed and sold [by Henry Ranlet] at the Printing-Office. [1797.]
pp. (24). 12mo.　　　　　　　　LOC.

33171　—— WEATHERWISE'S GENUINE ALMANACK FOR THE YEAR OF OUR LORD 1798: BEING
THE SECOND AFTER BISSEXTILE OR LEAP-YEAR, AND THE TWENTY-SECOND OF THE
INDEPENDENCE OF THE UNITED STATES OF AMERICA; WHICH BEGAN JULY 4, 1776.
[Seven lines.] CALCULATED FOR THE MERIDIAN OF BOSTON, IN AMERICA. LATI-
TUDE 42 DEGREES, 25 MIN. NORTH. [Six lines of verse.]

*Printed at Boston. At Russell's Office, near Liberty Pole. Sold wholesale and
retail.* [1797.] pp. (24). 12mo.　　　　　　　　NYHS.

33172　WEATHERWISE, ANTHONY, pseudonym.
THE FARMER'S CALENDAR; OR, FRY AND SOUTHWICK'S ALMANACK, FOR THE YEAR OF
OUR LORD 1798: BEING THE SECOND AFTER BISSEXTILE, OR LEAP-YEAR, AND THE
TWENTY-SECOND OF AMERICAN INDEPENDENCE, TO THE FOURTH OF JULY. CALCU-
LATED FOR THE MERIDIAN [*sic*] OF THE STATE OF NEW-YORK, BUT MAY SERVE FOR
THE ADJACENT STATES. CONTAINING, BESIDES THE USUAL ASTRONOMICAL CALCULA-
TIONS, A GREAT VARIETY OF USEFUL AND ENTERTAINING MATTER. BY ANTHONY
WEATHERWISE, PHILO. MATH.

*Albany: Printed by J. Fry and H. C. Southwick, at the Chronicle-Office, cor-
ner of Dock-Street and Mark-Lane. Very liberal allowance made to retailers.* [1797.]
pp. (32). 12mo.　　　　　　　　AAS. NHS.

33173　WEBB, THOMAS SMITH　　　　　　　　1771–1819
THE FREEMASON'S MONITOR; OR, ILLUSTRATIONS OF MASONRY: IN TWO PARTS. PART I.
CONTAINING—ILLUSTRATIONS OF THE DEGREES OF ENTERED APPRENTICE; FELLOW
CRAFT; MASTER MASON; MASTER MARK MASON; PASSING THE CHAIR; MOST EXCEL-
LENT MASTER; ROYAL ARCH MASON; KNIGHTS TEMPLARS & KNIGHTS OF MALTA; WITH
THE CHARGES, &C. OF EACH DEGREE. ALSO A SKETCH OF THE HISTORY OF MASONRY
IN AMERICA. PART II. CONTAINING — AN ACCOUNT OF THE INEFFABLE DEGREES
OF MASONRY, VIZ. SECRET MASTER; PERFECT MASTER; ILLUSTRIOUS SECRETARY;
PROVOST AND JUDGE; INTENDANTS OF THE BUILDINGS; OR MASTER IN ISRAEL;
ELECTED KNIGHTS; ELECTED GRAND MASTER; ILLUSTRIOUS KNIGHTS; OR SUBLIME
KNIGHTS ELECTED; GRAND MASTER ARCHITECTS; KNIGHTS OF THE NINTH, OR ROYAL

WEBB, Thomas Smith, continued.
ARCH; GRAND, ELECT, PERFECT AND SUBLIME, OR ULTIMATE DEGREE OF MASONRY;
TOGETHER WITH THE HISTORY AND CHARGES APPERTAINING TO EACH DEGREE. BY
A ROYAL ARCH MASON, K.T.K. OF M. &C. &C.

*Printed at Albany. [by Fry and Southwick?] for Spencer & Webb, and sold
at their Book store in Market-Street.* 1797. pp. (12), 284. 12mo. AAS. BA. JCB.

With an appendix of masonic songs. Reprinted as No. 1. of the Publications of the Masonic Historical Society of New York, in 1899. 53d
New York District Copyright, issued to Spencer and Webb, as Proprietors, 12 September, 1797.

33174 WEBSTER, Noah, junior   1758–1843
AN AMERICAN SELECTION OF LESSONS, IN READING AND SPEAKING, CALCULATED TO
IMPROVE THE MINDS AND REFINE THE TASTE OF YOUTH. AND ALSO, TO INSTRUCT
THEM IN THE GEOGRAPHY, HISTORY, AND POLITICS OF THE UNITED STATES. TO
WHICH IS PREFIXED, RULES IN ELOCUTION, AND DIRECTIONS FOR EXPRESSING THE
PRINCIPAL PASSIONS OF THE MIND. BEING THE THIRD PART OF A GRAMMATICAL
INSTITUTE OF THE ENGLISH LANGUAGE. BY NOAH WEBSTER, JUN. ESQUIRE. [Two
lines from] MIRABEAU. THE THIRD ALBANY EDITION.

*Printed by Charles R. and George Webster, (with privilege of copy-right) at
their Book-store, in the White House, corner of State and Pearl-streets, opposite the
City-Tavern, Albany,* 1797. *Sold at said Bookstore, by wholesale and retail.* pp.
236, 4. 12mo.   AAS.

33175 —— — AN AMERICAN SELECTION OF LESSONS IN READING AND SPEAKING. CALCU-
LATED TO IMPROVE THE MINDS AND REFINE THE TASTE OF YOUTH. AND ALSO TO
INSTRUCT THEM IN THE GEOGRAPHY, HISTORY, AND POLITICS OF THE UNITED STATES.
TO WHICH IS PREFIXED, RULES IN ELOCUTION, AND DIRECTIONS FOR EXPRESSING
THE PRINCIPAL PASSIONS OF THE MIND. BEING THE THIRD PART OF A GRAMMAT-
ICAL INSTITUTE OF THE ENGLISH LANGUAGE. TO WHICH IS ADDED, AN APPENDIX,
CONTAINING SEVERAL NEW DIALOGUES. BY NOAH WEBSTER, JUN. ESQUIRE, AUTHOR
OF "DISSERTATIONS ON THE ENGLISH LANGUAGE," "COLLECTION OF ESSAYS AND
FUGITIVE WRITINGS," &C. THOMAS AND ANDREWS' NINTH EDITION. WITH MANY
CORRECTIONS AND IMPROVEMENTS, BY THE AUTHOR. [Two lines from] MIRABEAU.

*Printed at Boston, by Isaiah Thomas and Ebenezer T. Andrews, at Faust's
Statue, No.* 45, *Newbury Street. Sold, wholesale and retail, at their Bookstore; by
Thomas, Son & Thomas, in Worcester; by Thomas, Andrews & Butler, in Baltimore; and by Thomas, Andrews & Penniman, Albany—Dec.* 1797. pp. [240],
portrait. 12mo.   EI. NYPL.

Portrait headed: Part III. Ninth edition.—1797.

33176 —— — AN AMERICAN SELECTION OF LESSONS IN READING AND SPEAKING. CALCU-
LATED TO IMPROVE THE MINDS AND REFINE THE TASTE OF YOUTH. AND ALSO TO
INSTRUCT THEM IN THE GEOGRAPHY, HISTORY, AND POLITICS OF THE UNITED STATES.
TO WHICH ARE PREFIXED, RULES IN ELOCUTION, AND DIRECTIONS FOR EXPRESSING
THE PRINCIPAL PASSIONS OF THE MIND. BEING THE THIRD PART OF A GRAMMAT-
ICAL INSTITUTE OF THE ENGLISH LANGUAGE. TO WHICH IS ADDED, AN APPENDIX,
CONTAINING SEVERAL NEW DIALOGUES. BY NOAH WEBSTER, JUN. ESQUIRE, AUTHOR
OF "DISSERTATIONS ON THE ENGLISH LANGUAGE," "COLLECTION OF ESSAYS AND
FUGITIVE WRITINGS," &C. THOMAS AND ANDREWS' TENTH EDITION. WITH MANY
CORRECTIONS AND IMPROVEMENTS, BY THE AUTHOR. [Two lines from] MIRABEAU.

*Printed at Boston, by Isaiah Thomas and Ebenezer T. Andrews, at Faust's
Statue, No.* 45, *Newbury Street. Sold, wholesale and retail, at their Bookstore; by
said Thomas, in Worcester; by Thomas, Andrews & Penniman, in Albany; and by
Thomas, Andrews & Butler, in Baltimore.* - - - 1797. pp. 240, (2), portrait.
12mo.   AAS.

WEBSTER, Noah, junior, continued.

33177 — — — [There is a variant of Thomas and Andrews' tenth edition, with the following imprint:]
Printed at Boston, by Isaiah Thomas and Ebenezer T. Andrews, at Faust's Statue, No. 45, Newbury Street. Sold wholesale and retail, at their Bookstore; by said Thomas, in Worcester; by Thomas, Andrews & Butler, in Baltimore; and by Thomas, Andrews & Penniman, in Albany. - - - 1797. pp. 240, portrait. 12mo.

33178 — — An American selection of lessons in reading and speaking. Calculated to improve the minds and refine the taste of youth. And also to instruct them in the geography, history, and politics of the United States. To which are prefixed, rules in elocution, and directions for expressing the principal passions of the mind. Being the third part of a Grammatical institute of the English Language. To which is added, an appendix, containing several new dialogues. By Noah Webster, jun. esquire, author of "Dissertations on the English language," "Collection of essays and fugitive writings, &c. Thomas and Andrews' eleventh edition. With many corrections and improvements, by the Author. [Two lines from] Mirabeau.
Printed at Boston, by Isaiah Thomas and Ebenezer T. Andrews, at Faust's Statue, No. 45, Newbury Street. Sold, wholesale and retail, at their Bookstore; by said Thomas, in Worcester; by Thomas, Andrews & Penniman, in Albany; and by Thomas, Andrews & Butler, in Baltimore. - - 1797. pp. 240, portrait. 12mo.
                                   AAS. JCB. LOC. RIHS.
Other copies of Thomas and Andrews' eleventh edition are dated 1799, and 1800.

33179 — — An American selection of lessons in reading and speaking. Calculated to improve the minds and refine the taste of youth. To which are prefixed, rules in elocution, and directions for expressing the principal passions of the mind. Being the third part of a Grammatical institute of the English language. By Noah Webster, jun. Author of 'Dissertations on the English language,' 'Collection of essays and fugitive writings,' 'The Prompter,' &c. The twelfth edition.
Hartford: Printed by Hudson & Goodwin, [With the privilege of copy right.]
[1797.] pp. 261, (2). 12mo.   AAS. HC. NYPL. WL.

33180 — The American spelling book: containing an easy standard of pronunciation. Being the first part of a Grammatical institute of the English language. To which is now first added, an appendix containing a Moral catechism and a Federal catechism. By Noah Webster, jun. esquire. Author of "Dissertations on the English language," "Collection of essays and fugitive writings," &c. Thomas & Andrews' fifteenth edition. With many corrections and improvements by the Author.
Printed at Boston, by Isaiah Thomas and Ebenezer T. Andrews, Faust's Statue, No. 45, Newbury Street. Sold wholesale and retail, at their Bookstore; by said Thomas, at his Bookstore in Worcester; and by the Booksellers in town and country. MDCCXCVII. pp. 156, portrait. 12mo.

33181 — — The American spelling book: containing an easy standard of pronunciation. Being the first part of a Grammatical institute of the English language. To which is now first added, an appendix containing a Moral catechism and a Federal catechism. By Noah Webster, jun. esquire. Author of "Dissertations on the English language," "Collection of essays and fugitive writings," &c. Thomas & Andrews' sixteenth edition. With many corrections and improvements by the Author.
Printed at Boston, by Isaiah Thomas and Ebenezer T. Andrews, Faust's Statue, No. 45, Newbury Street. Sold wholesale and retail, at their Bookstore; by said Thomas, at his Bookstore in Worcester; and by the Booksellers in town and country. MDCCXCVII. pp. 156, portrait. 12mo.

WEBSTER, NOAH, JUNIOR, continued.

33182 —— — THE AMERICAN SPELLING BOOK: CONTAINING AN EASY STANDARD OF PRO-
NUNCIATION. BEING THE FIRST PART OF A GRAMMATICAL INSTITUTE OF THE ENGLISH
LANGUAGE. IN THREE PARTS. BY NOAH WEBSTER, JUNR. ESQUIRE. THE NINE-
TEENTH CONNECTICUT EDITION.

Hartford: Printed by Hudson & Goodwin. [With the privilege of copy right.]
[1797.] pp. 165, (1). 12mo.   AAS.

33183 —— — THE AMERICAN SPELLING-BOOK: CONTAINING AN EASY STANDARD OF PRO-
NUNCIATION. BEING THE FIRST PART OF A GRAMMATICAL INSTITUTE OF THE ENGLISH
LANGUAGE. IN THREE PARTS. BY NOAH WEBSTER, JUNR. NINETEENTH EDITION.

*New-York: Printed by W. A. Davis, No. 26, Moore-Street. For T. Allen, E.
Duyckinck, & Co. N. Judah, P. S. Mesier, and D. Dunham.* 1797. pp. 165, (1).
12mo.

33184 —— A GRAMMATICAL INSTITUTE OF THE ENGLISH LANGUAGE; COMPRISING AN EASY,
CONCISE AND SYSTEMATIC METHOD OF EDUCATION. DESIGNED FOR THE USE OF
ENGLISH SCHOOLS IN AMERICA. IN THREE PARTS. PART SECOND. CONTAINING A
PLAIN AND COMPREHENSIVE GRAMMAR, GROUNDED ON THE TRUE PRINCIPLES AND
IDIOMS OF THE LANGUAGE. BY NOAH WEBSTER, JUN. ESQUIRE. AUTHOR OF "DIS-
SERTATIONS ON THE ENGLISH LANGUAGE," "COLLECTION OF ESSAYS AND FUGITIVE
WRITINGS," &C. THOMAS AND ANDREWS' FIFTH EDITION. WITH MANY CORRECTIONS
AND IMPROVEMENTS, BY THE AUTHOR.

*Printed at Boston, by Isaiah Thomas and Ebenezer T. Andrews. At Faust's
Statue, No. 45, Newbury Street. Sold. wholesale and retail, at their Bookstore; by
said Thomas at his Bookstore in Worcester; by Thomas, Andrews & Penniman, in
Albany; and by Thomas, Andrews & Butler, in Baltimore.—July,* 1797. pp. 116,
(2), portrait. 12mo.   LOC.

33185 —— THE PROMPTER; OR A COMMENTARY ON COMMON SAYINGS AND SUBJECTS, WHICH
ARE FULL OF COMMON SENSE, THE BEST SENSE IN THE WORLD. "TO *see* ALL *others*
FAULTS, AND *feel* OUR *own*." PUBLISHED ACCORDING TO ACT OF CONGRESS. THE
FIFTH EDITION.

*Printed at Boston, by I. Thomas and E. T. Andrews, at Faust's Statue, No.
45, Newbury Street. Aug.* 1797. pp. 84, (2). 24mo.   NYPL.

33186 —— — THE PROMPTER; OR A COMMENTARY ON COMMON SAYINGS & SUBJECTS, WHICH
ARE FULL OF COMMON SENSE, THE BEST SENSE IN THE WORLD. "TO *see* ALL *others'*
FAULTS AND *feel* OUR *own*. SECOND LEOMINSTER EDITION.

[Leominster:] Printed by Charles Prentiss. Sept. 1797. pp. 91, 2, (7). 12mo.
AAS. LOC.

33187 —— — THE PROMPTER; OR, A COMMENTARY ON COMMON SAYINGS AND SUBJECTS,
WHICH ARE FULL OF COMMON SENSE, THE BEST SENSE IN THE WORLD. "TO *see* ALL
others FAULTS AND *feel* OUR OWN."

New-Brunswick: Printed by Abraham Blauvelt. 1797. pp. 84. 24mo. NYPL.

33188 WEEDON, J.
A SET OF ROUND HAND COPIES, WRITTEN BY J. WEEDON, W M: BRENTFORD. EN-
GRAVED BY S. HILL.

Published by David West, No. 56, Cornhill, Boston. [1797.] pp. (32). obl.
32mo.   AAS.

33189   THE WEEKLY ADVERTISER, OF READING, IN THE COUNTY OF BERKS. No. 36. SAT-
URDAY, JANUARY 7, [— No. 87. SATURDAY, DECEMBER 30, 1797.]

     *This paper is published every Saturday by Jungmann and Company in the
Printing-Office of Reading, at the rate of one dollar per annum, one half dollar to
be paid at subscribing and half a dollar at the expiration of every six months.*
1797. 4to.

33190   WEEKLY MONITOR. VOL. 13. No. 596. WEDNESDAY, JANUARY 4, [—VOL. 13. No.
647. WEDNESDAY, DECEMBER 27, 1797.]

     Litchfield, (Connecticut): Printed by Thomas Collier. 1797. fol.

33191   THE WEEKLY MUSEUM. VOL. IX. NUMBER 452. SATURDAY, JANUARY 7, [—VOL. X.
NUMBER 503. SATURDAY, DECEMBER 30, 1797.]

     *New-York: Printed and published by John Harrisson, at his Printing-Office
(Yorick's Head) No. 3, Peck-Slip.* 1797. 4to.   AAS. LOC. NYHS. NYPL. WHS.

33192   —— ADDRESS OF THE CARRIER OF THE WEEKLY MUSEUM TO HIS PATRONS, WITH THE
COMPLIMENTS OF THE SEASON. [Seven four-line verses.]

     [*New-York: Printed by John Harrisson,* 1797.] Broadside. fol.

33193   THE WEEKLY MUSEUM. VOL. I. No. 1. SUNDAY, JANUARY 8. [— No. 6. SUNDAY,
FEBRUARY 12, 1797.]

     Baltimore: Printed by John Smith and Christopher Jackson. 1797. pp. 48.
8vo.   HC.

     Established, as a weekly, Sunday, paper, in paged, octavo form, by John
Smith, and Christopher Jackson, and continued by them to February
12th,—the last number located.

33194   WEEKLY [seal] ORACLE. VOL. I. No. 12. SATURDAY, JANUARY 7, [— No. 52. SAT-
URDAY, OCTOBER 14, 1797.]

     *New-London: Printed and published by James Springer, at his Printing-
Office, Beach-Street.* 1797. 4to.

     After the above date, the size of the paper was enlarged to folio, and the
title changed to *Springer's Weekly Oracle.*

33195   WELLES, ARNOLD, JUNIOR   1761–1827
AN ADDRESS, TO THE MEMBERS OF THE MASSACHUSETTS CHARITABLE FIRE SOCIETY,
AT THEIR ANNUAL MEETING, JUNE 2, 1797. BY ARNOLD WELLES, JUN. A. M. [Five
lines from] OGILVIE'S PROVIDENCE.

     Boston: Printed by Samuel Etheridge. 1797. pp. 26, (1). 4to.
     AAS. BA. BM. JCB. MHS. NYPL.

33196   WELLS, WILLIAM   1744–1827
A SERMON DELIVERED AT PUTNEY, VERMONT, ON THE SIXTEENTH DAY OF NOVEMBER,
1797; AT THE FUNERAL OF THE REV. JOSIAH GOODHUE. BY THE REV. WILLIAM
WELLS, . . .

     From the Press of C. Sturtevant, jun. & Co. Putney, Vermont. [1797.] pp.
12. 12mo.   AAS.

WELLS, WILLIAM, continued.

33197 —— A SERMON, DELIVERED BY THE REV. WILLIAM WELLS, AT THE INTERMENT OF
MESS. PARDON TAYLOR, AND EDWARD PALMER, WHO WERE DROWNED IN CONNECTI-
CUT RIVER, JULY 2, 1797. PREFACED WITH THE MELANCHOLY CIRCUMSTANCES OF
THE EXIT OF THE YOUNG MEN, TOGETHER WITH SKETCHES OF THEIR RESPECTIVE
CHARACTERS.

From the Press of C. Sturtevant jun. & Co. Putney, Vermont. 1797.

33198 WESLEY, JOHN   1703–1791
A SERMON PREACHED ON OCCASION OF THE DEATH OF THE REV. MR. JOHN FLETCHER,
VICAR OF MADELY, SRHOPSHIRE [*sic*]. BY JOHN WESLEY, A.M.

*London; Printed: Re-printed by Francis Stebbins, Springfield, (Massachu-
setts.) M,DCC,XCVII. pp. [16.] 8vo.* AAS.

33199 WEST, BENJAMIN   1730–1813
BICKERSTAFF'S GENUINE ALMANACK, FOR THE YEAR OF OUR LORD 1798; BEING THE
SECOND AFTER BISSEXTILE OR LEAP-YEAR, AND THE TWENTY-SECOND OF THE INDE-
PENDENCE OF THE UNITED STATES OF AMERICA: WHICH BEGAN JULY 4, 1776.
[Fifteen lines.]

*Printed at Boston. At Russell's Office, near Liberty Pole. Sold wholesale and
retail.* [1797.] pp. (24). 12mo.   AAS. BPL. LOC.

33200 —— BICKERSTAFFS GENUINE ALMANACK, FOR THE YEAR OF OUR LORD, 1798. [Cut
of astronomer taking an observation.] BEING SECOND AFTER BISSEXTILE, OR LEAP-
YEAR; AND THE 22D OF THE INDEPENDENCE OF AMERICA.

*Boston: Printed and sold by J. White, near Charles-river Bridge, and by
most of the Booksellers.* [1797.] pp. (24). 16mo.   AAS.

33201 —— THE NEW-ENGLAND ALMANACK, OR LADY'S AND GENTLEMAN'S DIARY, FOR THE
YEAR OF OUR LORD CHRIST 1798: BEING THE SECOND AFTER BISSEXTILE, OR LEAP-
YEAR, AND THE TWENTY-SECOND OF AMERICAN INDEPENDENCE, WHICH COMMENCED
JULY 4, 1776. [Sixteen lines.] BY ISAAC BICKERSTAFF, ESQ; PHILOM.

*Printed at Providence (R. I.) by Carter and Wilkinson, and sold, wholesale
and retail, at their Book and Stationary Store, opposite the Market. Great allowance made to those who purchase in quantities.* [1797.] pp. (24). 12mo.
                                                          AAS. HSP. LOC. RIHS.

33202 —— THE RHODE-ISLAND CALENDAR: OR, AN ALMANACK FOR THE YEAR OF OUR LORD
1798: BEING THE SECOND AFTER BISSEXTILE, OR LEAP-YEAR, AND THE TWENTY-
THIRD OF AMERICAN INDEPENDENCE, AFTER THE 4TH OF JULY. CONTAINING, BE-
SIDES THE ASTRONOMICAL CALCULATIONS, MUCH AMUSING MATTER. CALCULATED
FOR THE MERIDIAN OF THE STATE OF RHODE-ISLAND. BY ISAAC BICKERSTAFF,
ESQ. PHILOM.

*Printed [by Carter and Wilkinson] for and sold by Joseph J. Todd, at his
Book Stores in Providence and Newport.* [1797.] pp. (24). 12mo.   AAS. RIHS.

33203 —— THE TOWN AND COUNTRY ALMANACK, FOR THE YEAR OF OUR LORD 1798. BEING
THE SECOND AFTER BISSEXTILE, OR LEAP YEAR, AND THE TWENTY-SECOND OF THE
INDEPENDENCE OF AMERICA. FITTED TO THE TOWN OF NORWICH, BUT WILL SERVE
FOR ANY OF THE NEW-ENGLAND STATES. CONTAINING ALL THE ASTRONOMICAL
CALCULATIONS THAT IS NECESSARY FOR AN ALMANACK, TOGETHER WITH MANY OTHER
MATTERS THAT IS CURIOUS, ENTERTAINING AND USEFUL. BY ISAAC BICKERSTAFF,
ASTRONOMER.

*Norwich, (Connecticut), Printed by John Trumbull, and sold in large or small
quantities at his Printing-Office and Book-Shop, a few rods west from the Court
House; also, by Mr. James Springer, at his Printing-Office, New-London; and by
several other people in town & country.* [1797.] pp. [24.] 12mo.   NYPL. WL.

33204   WEST, Benjamin, continued.
—— Wheeler's North-American calendar, or an almanack, for the year of our Lord 1798: being the 2d after bissextile, or leap year, and the twenty-second of American independence. [U. S. Arms.]

Printed at Providence, and sold by B. Wheeler, at his Book-Store, No. 1, West-minster Street. [1797.] pp. (24). 12mo.   AAS. LOC. RIHS.

33205   WEST, John
Catalogue of books. Published in America and for sale at the Bookstore of John West, No. 75 Cornhill.

Boston: Printed by Samuel Etheridge, 1797. pp. 36. 12mo.   JCB.

33206   WESTERN Centinel. Vol. iv. No. 1. Wednesday, January 4, [— No. 52. Wednesday, December 27, 1797.]

Printed by Oliver P. Easton, near the Post-Office, in Whitestown, State of New-York. 1797. fol.

About this year Easton was succeeded as printer by Lewis & Webb.

33207   WESTERN INLAND NAVIGATION COMPANY.
Rates of toll. The Directors of the Western Inland Lock Navigation Company, order, that the following rates of toll be received at the canal, at the Little-Falls, on the Mohawk-river. . . . By order of the board, Gerard Walton, v. pres. New-York, March 1, 1797. [Colophon:]

Printed by C. R. & G. Webster, in the White House, corner of State and Pearl-Streets, Albany. [1797.] Broadside. fol.   NYPL.

33208   —— Rates of toll to be received at Fort-Schuyler. The Directors of the Western Inland Lock Navigation Company, order that the following rates of toll be received by the collector at the canal at this place, for all boats or vessels passing up the Mohawk River and down the Wood Creek, or up the Wood Creek and down the Mohawk River, through the canal, at the following rates, . . . By order of the board, Gerard Walton, v. pres. New-York, August 18, 1797.

[Albany: Printed by C. R. & G. Webster, in the White House, corner of State and Pearl-Streets. 1797.] Broadside. fol.   NYPL.

33209   THE WESTERN [cut] Star. No. 16 of Vol. viii. Whole no. 380. Monday, March 6, [— No. 6 of Vol. ix. Whole no. 422. Monday, December 25, 1797.]

Printed at Stockbridge, (Mass.) by Rosseter & Willard. 1797. fol.   AAS.

In continuation of *Andrews's Western Star.*

33210   THE WESTERN Telegraphe, and Washington Advertiser. Free, but not licentious. Vol. ii. No. 73. Tuesday, January 3, [—Vol. iii. No. 124. Tuesday, December 26, 1797.]

Washington (Pennsylvania): Printed by John Colerick.—Subscriptions and advertisements taken in at Washington, by the Editor; Union Town, by Samuel King; Brownsville, by Jacob Bowman; Pittsburgh, by Jeremiah Barker; M'Kee's Port, by John Speir; Charlestown, (Mouth of Buffaloe) by Richard Speer; West Liberty, by William M'Kinley and Wm. Skinner; in Morgan-Town, by Hugh M'Neely; in Frederick-Town, by Isaac Jenkinson; in Middletown, by Samuel Urie; in Marietta, by Joseph Lincoln; and in Greensburgh, by John Badollet. 1797. fol.

33211   WESTMINSTER ASSEMBLY OF DIVINES.
THE SHORTER CATECHISM COMPOSED BY THE REVEREND ASSEMBLY OF DIVINES.
WITH THE SCRIPTURE-PROOFS IN WORDS AT LENGTH. CAREFULLY REVISED AND
CORRECTED BY A MINISTER OF THE GOSPEL.
Newburyport: Printed by Edmund M. Blunt. 1797. pp. 58. 18mo.   AAS.

33212   ——— THE SHORTER CATECHISM, COMPOSED BY THE ASSEMBLY OF DIVINES, AT
WESTMINSTER. CONTAINING THE PRINCIPLES OF THE CHRISTIAN RELIGION; WITH
SCRIPTURE PROOFS. TO WHICH IS ADDED A FORM OF PRAYER, IN SCRIPTURE
EXPRESSIONS, ON A NEW PLAN; DESIGNED AS A GUIDE TO YOUTH IN THEIR FIRST
ATTEMPTS IN THIS IMPORTANT DUTY.
Troy: Printed by Luther Pratt. 1797.

33213   WHEATON, LEVI   1761–1851
AN ORATION, DELIVERED TO THE SOCIETY OF BLACK FRIARS, NOVEMBER 10TH, 1796.
BY LEVI WHEATON, A.M.
*New-York: Printed by M'Lean and Lang, Franklin's Head, No. 116, Pearl-
Street.* 1797. pp. (22). 8vo.   LOC. RIMS.

33214   WHEN THE MIND IS IN TUNE. SUNG BY MISS BROADHURST. PRICE 20 CENTS.
*Printed & sold at B. Carr's Musical Repositories New York and Philadel-
phia & J. Carr's Baltimore.* [1797.] pp. (2). 4to.   HSP.

33215   WHITE, JAMES
A CATALOGUE OF BOOKS, CONSISTING OF A LARGE COLLECTION OF THE VARIOUS
BRANCHES OF LITERATURE, ALPHABETICALLY DISPOSED UNDER SEVERAL HEADS; TO
WHICH ARE ADDED, A GREAT VARIETY OF STATIONARY AND OTHER ARTICLES, FOR
SALE, WHOLESALE OR RETAIL, AT JAMES WHITE'S BOOK AND STATIONARY-STORE,
FRANKLIN'S HEAD, OPPOSITE THE PRISON, COURT-STREET, BOSTON.
[Boston: Printed for James White, 1797.] pp. 48. 12mo.   AAS.

33216   WHITE, WILLIAM CHARLES   1777–1818
ORLANDO; OR, PARENTAL PERSECUTION. A TRAGEDY, IN FIVE ACTS: BY WILLIAM
CHARLES WHITE. AS PERFORMED AT THE THEATRE, FEDERAL STREET, BOSTON.
Boston: Printed by John Russell, Quaker Lane. 1797. pp. 64, portrait, plate.
12mo.   AAS. BM. BU.

115th Massachusetts District Copyright, issued to William Charles White,
as Author, 18 March, 1797.

33217   WHITEFIELD, GEORGE   1714–1770
EIGHTEEN SERMONS PREACHED BY THE LATE REV. GEORGE WHITEFIELD, A. M. ON THE
FOLLOWING SUBJECTS: SERMON I. A FAITHFUL MINISTER'S PARTING BLESSING.
II. CHRIST, THE BELIEVER'S REFUGE. III. SOUL PROSPERITY. IV. THE GOSPEL,
A DYING SAINT'S TRIUMPH. V. REPENTANCE AND CONVERSION. VI. THE BE-
LOVED OF GOD. VII. THE FURNACE OF AFFLICTION. VIII. THE LORD OUR LIGHT.
IX. GLORIFYING GOD IN THE FIRE, OR THE RIGHT IMPROVEMENT OF AFFLICTION.
X. SELF-ENQUIRY CONCERNING THE WORK OF GOD. XI. THE BURNING BUSH. XII.
SOUL DEJECTION. XIII. SPIRITUAL BAPTISM. XIV. NEGLECT OF CHRIST THE KILL-
ING SIN. XV. ALL MENS PLACE. XVI. GOD, A BELIEVER'S GLORY. XVII. JACOB'S
LADDER. XVIII. THE GOOD SHEPHERD. TAKEN VERBATIM IN SHORT-HAND, AND
FAITHFULLY TRANSCRIBED BY JOSEPH GURNEY. REVISED BY ANDREW GIFFORD, D.D.
Printed at Newburyport, by Edmund M. Blunt. 1797. pp. (2), (6), 368, (3),
(2). 12mo.   AAS. BA. NYPL.

Contains a three-page list of Newburyport Subscribers' names.

33218 WHITEFIELD, GEORGE, continued.
—— TEN SERMONS PREACHED ON VARIOUS IMPORTANT SUBJECTS. BY GEORGE WHITE-
FIELD, A.B. CAREFULLY CORRECTED AND REVISED ACCORDING TO THE BEST LONDON
EDITION.

Portsmouth, New-Hampshire: Printed for Charles Peirce & S. Larkin, sold
by them at their respective Bookstores in Portsmouth, and by the principal Book-
sellers in the United States.—1797.—pp. 206. 12mo.   AAS. NYPL.

33219 WHITESTOWN GAZETTE. VOL. I. No. 31. TUESDAY, JANUARY 3, [—VOL. II. No.
82. TUESDAY, DECEMBER 26, 1797.]

Published by William M'Lean—Whitestown (Herkimer County), opposite the
Meeting-House. 1797. fol.

33220 WHITING, SAMUEL   1749–1819
A DISCOURSE, DELIVERED BEFORE HIS HONOR, PAUL BRIGHAM, ESQUIRE, LIEUTENANT
GOVERNOR, THE HONORABLE COUNCIL, AND HOUSE OF REPRESENTATIVES, OF THE
STATE OF VERMONT, AT WINDSOR, OCTOBER XII, MDCCXCVII. BEING THE DAY OF
GENERAL ELECTION. BY SAMUEL WHITING, A.M. PASTOR OF A CHURCH IN ROCK-
INGHAM.

Printed at Rutland, by Josiah Fay, for the hon. Legislature. M,DCC,XCVII.
pp. 23. 8vo.   AAS. BA. BM.

33221 WHITMAN, BENJAMIN   1768–1840
AN INDEX TO THE LAWS OF MASSACHUSETTS: FROM THE ADOPTION OF THE CONSTI-
TUTION [1780] TO THE YEAR MDCCXCVI. BY BENJAMIN WHITMAN, ATTORNEY AT
LAW.
Printed at Worcester, according to Act of Congress, by Thomas, Son & Thomas,
1797. pp. 152. 8vo.   AAS. BA. BM. JCB. MHS. MSL. NL. RIHS.

109th Massachusetts District Copyright, issued to Isaiah Thomas, as
Proprietor, 31 January, 1797. "A complete index to the Laws contained in the folio volume, printed by order of the General Court, and
in the octavo volume, published by I. Thomas, and all those since
printed in folio pamphlets, by direction of the General Court."

33222 WHITMAN, SAMUEL   1752–1827
A DISSERTATION ON THE ORIGIN OF EVIL. SECTION I. ON THE NATURE OF EVIL,
AND THE IMPOSSIBILITY OF GOD'S BEING ITS FONTAL CAUSE. † SECTION II. ON
THE SENSE OF THE PROPOSITION, THE LORD DOTH EVIL, DEDUCED FROM AMOS III, 6.
‡ SECTION III. ON THE CONSEQUENCES FROM THE FACT, THAT THE CONDUCT OF
DIVINE PROVIDENCE IS THE EFFICIENT, BUT NOT THE FONTAL CAUSE OF EVIL. BY
SAMUEL WHITMAN, A.M. PASTOR OF THE CHURCH IN GOSHEN, (MASSACHUSETTS.)
[Four lines of Scripture texts.]

Printed at Northampton, (Massachusetts) by William Butler. M,DCC,XCVII.
pp. [31.] 8vo.   AAS. BM. JCB. NYPL. UTS.

33223 WHITTEMORE, JOSEPH
TO THE GENEROUS PATRONS OF JOSEPH WHITTEMORE, AND ENCOURAGERS OF SOBRI-
ETY, HONESTY, AND GOOD-BEHAVIOR: THE FOLLOWING LINES ARE PRESENTED,
WITH THE COMPLIMENTS OF THE SEASON. [Thirty-four lines of verse.]

[Boston: January, 1797.] Broadside. fol.   HSP.

33224   WIELAND, Christoph Martin   1733–1813
Socrates out of his senses: or dialogues of Diogenes of Sinope. [Two lines of Latin.] Translated from the German of Wieland. By mr. Wintersted. Vol. i. [— ii.]

> *Newburgh: Printed by D. Denniston, for self and J. Fellows.*—1797.—2 vols. in one. pp. xvi, [105]; [119]. 12mo.   AAS. JCB.

33225   WILDE, Samuel Sumner   1771–1855
An Oration, delivered at Thomaston, July 4th, 1797. At the request of the Friendly Society, and in commemoration of the anniversary of American independence. By Samuel S. Wise, a. m.

> *Hallowell: Printed by Howard S. Robinson,* 1797. pp. 15. 4to.   AAS.

33226   THE WILKESBARRE Gazette, and Luzerne Advertiser. Vol. i. No. 1. Tuesday, November 28, [— No. 5. Tuesday, December 26, 1797.]

> *Wilkesbarre: Printed by Josiah Wright.* 1797. fol.   NYHS.

Established, as a weekly, by Josiah Wright, and continued by him into December, 1798, when it was published for the Proprietor, Thomas Wright, into April, 1799; and by Joseph Wright, into September, or October, 1799; then again, for the Proprietor, Thomas Wright, and, beginning May 20, 1800, printed by Joseph Wright, With the issue for February 6, 1798, "The" was dropped from the title; and on November 10, 1800, the title was changed to *Wilkesbarre Gazette and Republican Centinel.* In December, 1800, it was sold to Asher Miner, who had married Thomas Wright's daughter, who established, January 5, 1801, in continuation, *The Luzerne County Federalist.*

33227   WILLIAMS, Nehemiah   1748–1796
Twenty four sermons, on various useful subjects. By the reverend Nehemiah Williams, a m. a.a.s. late pastor of the church in Brimfield.

> *Printed at Worcester, by Leonard Worcester.* 1797. pp. 339. 8vo.
>   AAS. JCB. NYPL.

33228   WILLIAMS. Samuel   1743–1817
The Vermont Almanac & Register for the year of our Lord 1798: being the second after leap year, and until July fourth, the twenty-second of the independence of America. Fitted to the latitude and longitude of Rutland: latitude 43° 21′ north. longitude 2 9 east of Philadelphia.

> *Printed [by Josiah Fay] at Rutland, (Vermont.) And sold wholesale and retail, at the Printing-Office.* [1797.] pp. (36). 12mo.   AAS.

Contains, Chronological history to 1794. Roads from Rutland and Windsor to principal towns on the Continent. Stamp Act, passed in Congress, July 6, 1797.

33229   WILLIAMS COLLEGE.
Commencement at Williams College, September 6, 1797. The order of exercises. . . . [Colophon:]

> *[Bennington, Vermont.] O. C. Merrill, Print.* [1797.] Broadside. 4to.   WC.

33230   WILLIAMSON, CHARLES
The LEGISLATURE AT THEIR LAST SESSION, HAVING GRANTED CONSIDERABLE AID TO
IMPROVE THE GREAT ROAD LEADING FROM FORT-SCHUYLER, ON THE MOHAWK-
RIVER, TO THE COUNTY OF ONTARIO, AND APPOINTED A COMMISSIONER TO CARRY
THE LAW INTO EFFECT . . . [Form of subscription for roads in the Ontario
Reservation,] TO BE PAID INTO THE HANDS OF CHARLES WILLIAMSON, ESQ. OR HIS
ORDER, FOR THE PURPOSES AFORESAID.

> *[Albany: Printed by Loring Andrews & Co.? July 4, 1797.* Broadside.
> 4to.   NYPL.

33231   WILLIAMSON, T. G.
The HOBBIES, A FAVORITE SONG, WRITTEN AND SUNG BY MR. WILLIAMSON AT THE
HAYMARKET THEATRE, WITH UNIVERSAL APPLAUSE. IN WHICH ARE INTRODUCED
THE SCOLD'S HOBBY, THE LAWYER'S HOBBY, THE BEAUX HOBBY, THE SAILOR'S
HOBBY, THE SOLDIER'S HOBBY, THE LADIES' HOBBY, AND THE AMERICAN HOBBY.

> *Printed at Boston, by I. Thomas and E. T. Andrews.* 1797.

33232   WILLIS, GEORGE
The ART OF PREVENTING DISEASES AND RESTORING HEALTH, FOUNDED ON RATIONAL
PRINCIPLES, AND ADAPTED TO PERSONS OF EVERY CAPACITY. BY GEORGE WILLIS,
M. D. S. M. S. EDITOR OF THE LAST EDITION OF MOTHERBY'S MEDICAL DICTIONARY,
AND SYNDENHAM'S WORKS, WITH NOTES, &C. [Four lines of verse.]

> *New-York:* 1797.

33233   WILSON, GOODRIDGE
An INAUGURAL DISSERTATION ON ABSORPTION. [SUBMITTED TO THE EXAMINATION
OF THE REV. JOHN EWING, S. T. P. PROVOST; THE TRUSTEES AND MEDICAL PRO-
FESSORS OF THE UNIVERSITY OF PENNSYLVANIA, FOR THE DEGREE OF DOCTOR OF
MEDICINE ON THE TWELFTH DAY OF MAY. 1797.] BY GOODRIDGE WILSON, OF
VIRGINIA. [Two lines of Latin from] OVID.

> *Philadelphia: Printed by E. Oswald, No. 179, South Second-Street.* M,DCC,-
> XCVII. pp. 25. 8vo.   LOC. 8GO.

33234   WISCASSET ARGUS. VOL. I. No. 1. SATURDAY, DECEMBER 23, [— No. 2. SATUR-
DAY, DECEMBER 30, 1797.]

> *Wiscasset, District of Maine. Published by Laughton & Rhoades.* 1797. fol.

Established, as a weekly, by —— Laughton, and —— Rhoades, and
publication continued only for a few months in 1798, when it was discontinued.

33235   THE WISCASSET TELEGRAPH. [Motto.] VOL. I. No. VI. SATURDAY, JANUARY 7,
[—VOL. II. No. 7. FRIDAY, DECEMBER 29, 1797.]

> *Printed and published by J. N. Russell and H. Hoskins, corner of Main and
> Fore-Streets, Wiscasset.* 1797. fol.

In March, "The" was dropped from the title, and the imprint changed
to: From the Press of Russell and Hoskins, corner of Main and Fore-
Streets, Wiscasset, District of Maine. April 1st. Joseph N. Russell withdrew, from ill-health, and publication was continued in the name of
Henry Hoskins, at the same Office, to November, when John W. Scott,
was admitted to partnership as Henry Hoskins & John W. Scott, at
their Office corner of Main & Water Streets.

33236   WITHERSPOON, John   1723–1794
A Series of [four] letters on education.
New-York. 1797. pp. 108. 12mo.

33237   —— A Sermon on the religious education of children.
Putney, Vermont: Printed by C. Sturtevant jun. & Co. 1797.

33238   WOLCOT, John   1738–1819
The Poetical works of Peter Pindar, esq.
Cincinnati: Printed? by S. Freeman and Son. 1797. 2 vols. pp. 200; 200.
12mo.

Proposals for printing the above were made this year.

33239   A WONDERFUL account of the conversion of two young girls.
Rutland: Printed by Josiah Fay. 1797.

33240   A WONDERFUL visit from the dead: or, a conference with an old deceased
friend, soon after his departure from this life.
Windsor: Printed by Alden Spooner. 1797.

33241   WOOD, Benjamin   1772–1849
The Obligation of ministers to dispense faithfully the word of God. A discourse, delivered at Upton, June, 1796, on the Lord's day immediately
succeeding his ordination: by Benjamin Wood, a.b. pastor of a church in
Upton.
*Printed at Worcester, Massachusetts, at the Press of Isaiah Thomas, by Leon-
ard Worcester, for said Thomas.* 1797. pp. 40. 8vo.   AAS. BM. JCB.

33242   WOOD, John
By permission of the Legislature of Vermont. The following Scheme of a
Lottery is presented to the public for the benefit of John Wood, a
sufferer in the service of his country, by the suppression of the royal
party. . . . Elias Buell, John Wood, Stephen Avery, managers. Rutland.
March 9, 1797.
[Rutland: Printed by Josiah Fay. 1797.] Broadside. 4to.

33243   —— To the public. Being engaged in a Lottery, for the recovery of several
sums of money advanced for the benefit of the public, in the year seventeen hundred and seventy-five, the subscriber begs leave to lay before
the public the following relation of the ground and method of his proceedings. . . . John Wood. Pittsford, September 28th, 1797.
[Rutland: Printed by Josiah Fay. 1797.] Broadside. 4to.

33244   WOOD, Samuel   1752–1836
A Discourse, delivered at the ordination of the rev. Benjamin Wood, to the
pastoral care of the church in Upton, June 1, MDCCXCVI. By Samuel Wood,
a.m. pastor of the church in Boscawen.
*Printed at Worcester, Massachusetts, at the Press of Isaiah Thomas, by Leon-
ard Worcester, for said Thomas.* 1797. pp. 31. 8vo.   AAS. BM. JCB.

33245 WOODHOUSE, JAMES 1770–1809
THE YOUNG CHEMIST'S POCKET COMPANION; CONNECTED WITH A PORTABLE LAB-
ORATORY. CONTAINING A PHILOSOPHICAL APPARATUS, AND A GREAT NUMBER OF
CHEMICAL AGENTS; BY WHICH ANY PERSON MAY PERFORM AN ENDLESS VARIETY OF
AMUSING AND INSTRUCTING EXPERIMENTS; INTENDED TO PROMOTE THE CULTIVATION
OF THE SCIENCE OF CHEMISTRY. BY JAMES WOODHOUSE, M. D. PROFESSOR OF CHEM-
ISTRY IN THE UNIVERSITY OF PENNSYLVANIA, &C. [Two lines from] PRIESTLEY
ON AIR.
Philadelphia: Printed by J. H. Oswald, No. 179, South Second-Street. 1797.
pp. 56, (2), plate. 12mo. AAS.
183d Pennsylvania District Copyright, issued to James Woodhouse, as
Author, 15 June, 1797.

33246 WOODS'S NEWARK GAZETTE AND NEW-JERSEY ADVERTISER. No. 35. VOL. VI, NUMB.
295. WEDNESDAY, JANUARY 4, [— No. 26. VOL. VII. NUMB. 338. WEDNESDAY,
NOVEMBER 1, 1797.]
Newark, New-Jersey: Printed by John Woods. . . . 1797. fol.
With the issue for November 8th, a new serial numbering was begun
under the title of *Newark* [cut] *Gazette and New-Jersey Advertiser.*
Printed by John Woods for the Proprietors.

33247 WOODSTOCK. VERMONT. BAPTIST ASSOCIATION.
MINUTES OF THE WOODSTOCK ASSOCIATION, HELD AT CHESTER.
Windsor: Printed by Alden Spooner. 1797.

33248 WOOLMAN, JOHN 1720–1773
A FIRST BOOK FOR CHILDREN, A. B. C. D. &C.
Wilmington: Printed by Peter Brynberg. 1797.

33249 WOUVES, P. R.
TABLEAU SYLLABIQUE ET STÉGANOGRAPHIQUE. ENREGISTRÉ CONFORMÉMENT À LA LOI.
*Philadelphie: De l'Imprimerie de Benjamin Franklin Bache, No. 112, rue
de Marché.* [1797.] pp. [16.] 4to. AAS. LOC.
Second title: A SYLLABICAL AND STEGANOGRAPHICAL TABLE. ENTERED ACCORD-
ING TO LAW.
Philadelphia: Printed by Benjamin Franklin Bache, No. 112, Market-Street.
[1797.]
The French and English texts on opposite columns. 192d Pennsylvania
District Copyright, issued to P. R. Wouves, as Author, 9 November, 1797.

33250 WRIGHT, GEORGE
THE GENTLEMAN'S MISCELLANY: CONSISTING OF ESSAYS, CHARACTERS, NARRATIVES,
ANECDOTES, AND POEMS, MORAL AND ENTERTAINING, CALCULATED FOR THE IMPROVE-
MENT OF GENTLEMEN IN EVERY RELATION IN LIFE. BY GEORGE WRIGHT . . .
FIRST AMERICAN EDITION.
*Exeter: Printed by H. Ranlet for William T. Clap, Boston. Sold by him,
Thomas & Andrews, E. Larkin, D. West, J. White, Wm. P. & L. Blake, and C.
Bingham.* 1797. pp. 216. 12mo. AAS. LOC.

33251 ——— THE LADY'S MISCELLANY; OR PLEASING ESSAYS, POEMS, STORIES, AND EXAMPLES,
FOR THE INSTRUCTION AND ENTERTAINMENT OF THE FEMALE SEX IN GENERAL, IN
EVERY STATION IN LIFE. BY GEORGE WRIGHT, ESQ. AUTHOR OF THE RURAL CHRIS-
TIAN, PLEASING MELANCHOLY, GENTLEMAN'S MISCELLARY. [Two lines of verse.]
*Boston: From the Press in Union-Street. For William T. Clap—Sold by
him, Thomas and Andrews, E. Larkin, D. West, J. White, Wm. P. & L. Blake, and
C. Bingham.* 1797. pp. 225, (2), (1). 12mo. AAS. BM.

33252 WRIGHTEN, Mrs. ——
YOUNG WILLY FOR ME. SUNG WITH GREAT APPLAUSE BY MRS. SEYMOUR AT THE
LADIES CONCERT. PRICE 25 CENTS.

New-York: Printed & sold at J. Hewitt's Musical Repository No. 131 *William Street. Sold also by B. Carr Philadelphia and J. Carr Baltimore.* [1797.]
pp. (2). 4to.   HSP.

33253 YALE COLLEGE.
ILLUSTRISSIMO OLIVERO WOLCOTT, ARM. LL.D. REIPUBLICÆ CONNECTICUTTENSIS GU-
BERNATORI: HONORATISSIMO JONATHANI TRUMBULL, ARM. VICE-GUBERNATORI:
CLARISSIMISQUE PROCERIBUS POLITIÆ NOSTRÆ CIVILIS; REVERENDO PARITER AC
HONORANDO TIMOTHEO DWIGHT, S.T.D. COLLEGII YALENSIS PRÆSIDI, [Five lines.]
HASCE THESES, IN COMITIIS PUBLICIS COLLEGII YALENSIS, DIE 13TIO SEPTEMBRIS
ANNO DOMINI M,DCC,XCVII, PUBLICÉ EXHIBENDAS CANDIDATIS BACCALAUREALES,
[Thirty-seven names.] HUMILLIMÈ DEDICANT. [Three columns.] [Colophon:]

Habita in Comitiis Academicis Novo Portu Connecticutensium, M,DCC,-
XCVII. *E Typis Thomæ et Samuelis Green, Universitatis Typographorum.*
Broadside. fol.   NL. YC.

33254 YATES, WILLIAM
A VIEW OF THE SCIENCE OF LIFE; ON THE PRINCIPLES ESTABLISHED IN THE ELEMENTS
OF MEDICINE, OF THE LATE CELEBRATED JOHN BROWN, M.D. WITH AN ATTEMPT
TO CORRECT SOME IMPORTANT ERRORS OF THAT WORK. AND CASES IN ILLUSTRA-
TION, CHIEFLY SELECTED FROM THE RECORDS OF THEIR PRACTICE, AT THE GENERAL
HOSPITAL, AT CALCUTTA. BY WILLIAM YATES & CHARLES MACLEAN. TO WHICH
IS SUBJOINED, A TREATISE ON THE ACTION OF MERCURY UPON LIVING BODIES, AND
ITS APPLICATION FOR THE CURE OF DISEASES OF INDIRECT DEBILITY. AND A DIS-
SERTATION ON THE SOURCE OF EPIDEMIC AND PESTILENTIAL DISEASES; IN WHICH IS
ATTEMPTED TO PROVE, BY A NUMEROUS INDUCTION OF FACTS, THAT THEY NEVER
ARISE FROM CONTAGION, BUT ARE ALWAYS PRODUCED BY CERTAIN STATES, OR CER-
TAIN VICISSITUDES OF THE ATMOSPHERE. BY CHARLES MACLEAN, OF CALCUTTA.

Whitehall: Printed by William Young, Bookseller, No. 52, *Second-Street,
corner of Chesnut-Street, Philadelphia.* 1797. pp. (2), (2), 4, iii, (17)–(232). 8vo.
AAS. NYPL. SGO.

Second title: A VIEW OF THE SCIENCE OF LIFE; ON THE PRINCIPLES ESTABLISHED
IN THE ELEMENTS OF MEDICINE, OF THE LATE CELEBRATED JOHN BROWN, M.D.
WITH AN ATTEMPT TO CORRECT SOME IMPORTANT ERRORS OF THAT WORK; AND
CASES IN ILLUSTRATION, CHIEFLY SELECTED FROM THE RECORDS OF THEIR PRACTICE,
AT THE GENERAL HOSPITAL, AT CALCUTTA. BY WILLIAM YATES & CHARLES
MACLEAN. [Six lines from] DARWIN'S ZOONOMIA.—PREFACE, p. 2.

Philadelphia: 1797. pp. (29)–152.

Third title: A TREATISE ON THE ACTION OF MERCURY, UPON LIVING BODIES; AND
ITS APPLICATION FOR THE CURE OF DISEASES OF INDIRECT DEBILITY. BY CHARLES
MACLEAN.

Philadelphia: Printed by William Young, Bookseller, No. 52, *Second-Street,
corner of Chesnut-Street.* M,DCC,XCVII. pp. (2), (155)–185.

Fourth title: A DISSERTATION ON THE SOURCE OF EPIDEMIC AND PESTILENTIAL
DISEASES; IN WHICH IS ATTEMPTED TO PROVE, BY A NUMEROUS INDUCTION OF FACTS,
THAT THEY NEVER ARISE FROM CONTAGION, BUT ARE ALWAYS PRODUCED BY CERTAIN
STATES, OR CERTAIN VICISSITUDES OF THE ATMOSPHERE. BY CHARLES MACLEAN.

Whitehall: Printed by William Young, Bookseller, No. 52, *Second-Street, corner of Chesnut-Street., Philadelphia.* 1797. pp. (2), (189)–231.

33255   YOUNG, John   –1797
        A NARRATIVE OF THE LIFE, LAST DYING SPEECH AND CONFESSION OF JOHN YOUNG.
        [Executed in New York City on August 17, 1797, for the murder of Robert
        Berwick.]
            New-York: 1797.

33256   YOUNG, William P.
        PALLADIUM OF KNOWLEDGE: OR, THE CAROLINA AND GEORGIA ALMANAC, FOR THE
        YEAR OF OUR LORD, 1798, AND 22–23 OF AMERICAN INDEPENDENCE. CONTAINING,
        THE CALENDAR.—SUN'S RISING, SETTING, AND DECLINATION—MOON'S RISING, SET-
        TING, AND SOUTHING, AND THE SIGN OF THE ZODIAC SHE IS IN AT NOON — RISING,
        SETTING, AND SOUTHING OF THE PLANETS, ON THE FIRST DAY OF EACH MONTH—
        TIME OF HIGH WATER, EVERY MORNING, AT CHARLESTON HARBOUR; WITH A TIDE
        TABLE OF MOST OF THE EMINENT PLACES IN THE WORLD—ECLIPSES, LUNATIONS,
        CONJUNCTIONS, QUADRATIONS, &c. BESIDES AS GREAT A VARIETY OF OTHER USEFUL
        MATTER AS IS TO BE FOUND IN ANY ALMANAC, OF THE SAME PRICE, IN AMERICA.
            Charleston: Printed by W. P. Young, No. 43, Broad-Street. [1797.] pp.
        (48). 12mo.   AAS. CLS. NYHS.

        Contains, Mrs, Logan's Gardener's Calendar.

33257   THE YOUNG LADIES AND GENTLEMEN'S SPELLING BOOK; CONTAINING A CRITERION OF
        RIGHTLY SPELLING AND PRONOUNCING THE ENGLISH LANGUAGE.
            Providence (Rhode-Island). Printed by Carter & Wilkinson. 1797. 12mo.

33258   THE YOUTH'S NEWS PAPER. NUMBER 1. SATURDAY, SEPTEMBER 30, [—NUMBER 6.
        SATURDAY, NOVEMBER 4, 1797.]
            New-York: Printed by J. S. Mott, for the Editor, and C. Smith, No. 51,
        Maiden Lane. [1797.] pp. 48. 8vo.   NYPL.

        Established, as a weekly, with eight pages to each issue, paged. The
        above six numbers are all that have been located.

33259   YRUJO, Philip Fatis
        LETTERS OF VERUS, ADDRESSED TO THE NATIVE AMERICAN.
            Philadelphia: Printed by Benjamin Franklin Bache. M,DCCXCVII. pp.
        (vi), 75. 8vo.   AAS. JCB. LOC. MHS. NYHS.

33260   —— — LETTRES DE VERUS, ADRESSÉES AU NATIVE AMERICAN.
            [Philadelphie: De l'Imprimerie de Benjamin Franklin Bache.]—1797.—pp.v,
        68. 12mo.   JCB.

33261   ZIMMERMANN, Johann Georg, ritter von   1728–1795
        SOLITUDE CONSIDERED WITH RESPECT TO ITS INFLUENCE UPON THE MIND AND THE
        HEART. WRITTEN ORIGINALLY IN GERMAN BY M. ZIMMERMANN, AULIC COUNSELLOR
        AND PHYSICIAN TO HIS BRITANNIC MAJESTY AT HANOVER. TRANSLATED FROM THE
        FRENCH OF J. B. MERCIER. [Six lines of French from] LA FONTAINE, LE SONGE
        D'UN HABITANT DU MOGOL. L XI. FABLE IV.
            Wilmington: Printed by Johnson & Preston, No. 73, Market-Street. 1797.
        pp. (2), (2), v, 298. 12mo.   AAS. JCB. NYPL. WIPL.

TRENCK, F. VON DER, 1726–1794
  Life   31313
TREZIULNEY, ——
  Letter to Washington   31314
  Same   31315
  Same, Baltimore   32940
TRIMMER, SARAH K., 1741–1810
  Introduction to Nature   31316
TRUE, BENJAMIN
  Almanac, 1798   32941
TRUELOVE, NURSE, pseud.
  Christmas box   31317
TRUMBULL, BENJAMIN, 1735–1820
  History of Connecticut   32942
  Proposals   31318
TRUMBULL, JOHN, 1750–1831
  Progress of dulness   32943
TUCKER, ST. GEORGE, 1752–1827
  Odes of Jonathan Pindar   31320
  Slavery   31319
TURNBULL, ROBERT J., 1775–1833
  Philadelphia Prison   31321
TURNER, NATHANIEL
  Funeral oration, B. French   32944
TURNER, RICHARD, JUN.
  Arts and sciences   31322
TURNER, ROBERT
  Botanosotia   31323
TWAMLEY, JOSIAH
  Cheese-making   31324
TWILIGHT, pseud.
  Orations, on politics   31325
Two babes in the wood   31326
TYLER, JOHN, 1742–1823
  Masonic sermon   31327
TYLER, ROYALL, 1757–1826
  Algerine captive   32945
  The Georgia spec   32946
TYTLER, JAMES, 1747–1805
  Age of reason answered   31328

UNDERWOOD, NATHAN
  Dedication sermon   31240
UNION COLLEGE
  Commencement, 1797   32947
UNITED BAPTIST ASSOCIATION
  Minutes, 1796   31329
UNITED BRETHREN
  Täglichen Loosungen, 1797   31330
  Same, 1798   32948
UNITED CHRISTIAN FRIENDS
  Hymns   32949

UNITED STATES
  Accounts with States   33019
  Acts, 1795–1796   31330
  Same, Richmond   31332
  Acts, 1796–1797   32950
  Acts, 1797   32951
  Same, Philadelphia   32952
  Address to President, 1795   31368
  Same, 1796   32983
  Same, 1797   32961
  Agriculture   33031
  Algiers   31332, 31408, 31410, 33048
  American seamen   31336–31340, 31350, 31382, 31437, 31438, 32989
  Appropriations, 1796   31342, 31444, 31460
  Same, 1797   31446, 33077, 33088
  Same, 1798   33075
  Arrearages   31376
  Arsenals   31394, 31466
  Artillerists   33098
  Articles of confederation   33044
  Bonds for duties   31442
  Business depending   33016, 33017
  City of Washington   31349, 31406, 33029, 33078, 33085, 33086
  Claims not valid   32994, 33006, 33007
  Coinage   32982
  Commerce   33039, 33053
  Compensation   31398, 32984
  Constitution, U. S.   31403–31405, 32536, 32979, 33044
  Contested elections   33027
  Contingent expenses   33051
  Customs   31445, 32959, 33081
  Debates, 5th Cong. 1st sess.   32965
  Declaration of independence   31403, 31404, 33044
  Defence of country   33039
  Domestic debt   31379, 31434, 31447, 31450, 33087
  Drawbacks   33079
  Duties on carriages   31335
  Duties on goods, wares and merchandize   31341, 31362, 33021
  Duties on snuff and sugar   31348
  Duties on spirits   32960
  Duties on stamped vellum, parchment and paper   32699, 32955–32957, 32022, 33228
  Duties on tonnage   31341
  Engineers   33098
  Exports   31439, 31441, 31449, 31457, 32958, 32962, 33080

UNITED STATES, cont.
  Florida boundary   33052
  Foreign debt   31459
  Foreign nations   33054, 33055, 33077
  Forged Washington letters   33072
  Fortification of harbours   31394, 31468, 32988, 33028, 33082, 33097
  France   31365, 31421, 31459, 33048–33050, 33063–33066
  Frontiers   31437
  Georgia   31431, 32968, 33036
  Great Britain   31332, 31352, 31361, 31411, 31417
  Impressment   31382
  Indians   31332, 31347, 31432, 31466, 32980, 32999
  Internal revenue   31451, 33020
  Journal, H of R, 1795–1796   31354
  Same, 1796–1797   32969
  Same, 1797   32970
  Journal, Senate, 1795–1796   31355
  Same, 1796–1797   32971
  Same, 1797   32972
  La Fayette's son   31391
  Lands   31445, 32967, 32987
  Laws. Vol. I–II   31356
  Same. Vol. III   32973
  Same, 1796–1797   32974
  Laws near expiring   33018
  Loans   31392
  Marshals   31461
  Members, H of R, 1796   31357
  Same, 1797   32975
  Members, Senate, 1796   31357
  Same, 1797   32975
  Memorials:
    Stephen Addington, calico printer   33011
    Canadian refugees   33041
    Samuel Fowler   31393
    Compte de Grasse   33040
    John Hobby, marshal for Maine   33061
    Illinois and Wabash Land Company   32976, 32977, 33032
    Manufacturers of chocolate   33010
    Manufacturers of cordage   33011
    Manufacturers of soap and candles   33011
    Philadelphia   31454, 33071
    John Richards   31373
    Savannah   31370
    Joseph Bradley Varnum   31384

ETHICAL THEOLOGY.

30385, 961, 972, 31079, 118,
125, 190, 191, 203, 228, 521,
576, 641, 679, 779, 843, 844,
891, 924, 925, 939, 940, 963,
32002, 043, 057, 072, 217,
249, 250, 295, 315, 317, 327,
358, 457, 645, 741, 747, 776,
821, 828, 844, 929, 938,
33167, 237

ECCLESIASTICAL THEOLOGY.

POLITY and discipline: 31039,
32162, 32492, 32711
CHURCH government: 30992,
31039–31041, 31609, 31769,
32014. 32711
WORSHIP: 30998, 31240, 32458,
32711
PRAYER: 31038, 31819, 31831,
32727, 33165
FASTS and feasts: 30854–855, 899,
31487, 519, 659, 757, 774,
975, 976, 32006. 086, 299,
331, 360, 442, 443, 498, 758,
846, 887, 33046, 120, 121
SINGING: 32021
PSALMODY: 31494, 791, 792, 884,
912, 32351, 363, 416, 468,
547, 818, 33123
HYMNS: 30899, 31206, 714, 766,
793, 810, 816, 899, 32008,
100, 474, 567, 580, 727, 848–
850, 949

PASTORAL THEOLOGY.

THE MINISTRY: 31609, 32394,
32471, 32724, 33241
HOMILETICS: 32408, 32625,
REVIVALS: 32092

ORDINATION SERMONS.

APPLETON, JESSE. By S.
Macclintock   32398
BAKER, JOEL. By J. Emerson 32082
BALL, HEMAN. By J.
Lathrop   32361
BATCHELDER, WILLIAM. By
J. Peak   32641
BEATTIE, ANDREW. By H.
Packard   32625

BLACKSTONE, WILLIAM. By
J. Rogers   31114
BRAMAN, ISAAC. By S. Palmer 32636
BRIGGS, EPHRAIM. By E.
Briggs   31866
BROWN, JOSEPH. By S.
Payson   30965
COTTON, WARD. By C.
Robbins   32772
CUSHMAN, JOSHUA. By K.
Whitman   31629
EDSON, JESSE. By J. Emerson 32083
FISHER, JABEZ P. By R. Page 30939
FISKE, JOHN. By J. Lyman   32394
HAZARD, JOSEPH. By S. Buell 31899
HOWE, PERLEY. By A.
Packard   30935
LOCKWOOD, WILLIAM. By
J. Marsh   32424
M'KEAN, JOSEPH. By J. Eliot 32078
NELSON, STEPHEN SMITH.
By S. Stillman   32882
PEIRCE, JOHN. By T. M.
Harris   32230
PINNEO, BEZALEEL. By T.
Brockway   31872
SMITH, JOHN. By N. Emmons 32087
TOMPKINS, ISAAC. By S. Mead 32458
TUFTS, JAMES. By N.
Emmons   32084
WOOD, BENJAMIN. By S.
Wood   33244

SERMONS—COLLECTIONS.

30899, 31310, 520, 32091,
141, 384, 457, 580, 787, 788,
820, 33111, 144, 217, 218,
227

ELECTION SERMONS—CON-
NECTICUT.

1797 ISAAC LEWIS   32377

ELECTION SERMONS—MASSA-
CHUSETTS.

1797 JOHN MELLEN, JUN.   32462

ELECTION SERMONS—NEW
HAMPSHIRE.

1796 WILLIAM F. ROWLAND 31126
1797 STEPHEN PEABODY   32640

ELECTION SERMONS—VERMONT.

1797 SAMUEL WHITING   32220

CHURCH HISTORY.

ASSOCIATE REFORMED
CHURCH   31755
BOWDOINHAM ASSOCIATION   31858
CONGREGATIONAL
CHURCH   31767–70
DENNIS, MASS. Church   31240
EVANS, J. Denominations   32101
MACHIAS, ME. Church   32406
METHODIST EPISCOPAL
CHURCH   30472–73
MIDWAY, GA. Century
sermon   32192
MOSHEIM, J. L. VON. Ec-
clesiastical history   32513
NEW HAMPSHIRE ASSO-
CIATION   32538
NEW YORK ASSOCIATION   30879,
32565
NEWBURYPORT. Second
Church   31840
NEWTON, J. Ecclesiastical
history   30899, 32580
OTSEGO ASSOCIATION   30932
PHILADELPHIA ASSOCIA-
TION   30997, 32677
PISCATAQUA ASSOCIATION   32397
PLYMOUTH, MASS. Anni-
versary sermon   31111
PRESBYTERIAN CHURCH 31039–41,
32709–11
PRIESTLEY, J. History   32717
PROTESTANT EPISCOPAL
CHURCH   31057–58, 32724–28
REFORMED DUTCH CHURCH 32745
SHAFTSBURY ASSOCIATION   31179,
32824
SOUTH CAROLINA ASSO-
CIATION   31931
STONINGTON ASSOCIATION   31241,
32885
UNITED BAPTIST ASSOCIATION 31329
UNIVERSALISTS. Convention 33106
WARREN ASSOCIATION   31523,
32456, 33146
WARWICK ASSOCIATION   31524,
33147
WATTS, I. Scripture history 32166
WEST SPRINGFIELD, MASS.
Century sermon   32362
WOODSTOCK ASSOCIATION   31656,
33247
MISSIONS: 30883, 31107, 967, 968,
32281, 384, 438, 601, 847
MARTYRS: 32909

PRINTING INSTITUTED IN
CONNECTICUT, 1709, A. D.

CHELSEA LANDING, 1796.
THOMAS HUBBARD, Printer and publisher. 1796–97.

CHESHIRE, 1782.
WILLIAM LAW, Plate printer and Music publisher. 1796.

DANBURY, 1789.
NATHAN DOUGLAS, Printer and publisher. Douglas and Nichols, near the Court House, 1796–1797.
EDWARDS ELY, Printer and publisher. Ely and Nichols, at their Office south of the Court House, 1796.
STILES NICHOLS, Printer. 1. Ely and Nichols, 1796. 2. Douglas and Nichols, 1796–1797.

FAIRFIELD, 1786.

HARTFORD, 1764.
ELISHA BABCOCK, Printer and publisher. 1796–97.
JOHN BABCOCK, Bookseller. 1796–1797.
GEORGE GOODWIN, Printer. Hudson and Goodwin, 1796–1797.
BARZILLAI HUDSON, Printer, publisher and Bookseller. Hudson and Goodwin, at their Book Store, opposite the North Meeting House, 1796–1797.
APOLLOS KINSLEY, Printer and Inventor. 1796.
NATHANIEL PATTEN, Bookseller. 1796–1797,

LITCHFIELD, 1784.
THOMAS COLLIER, Printer and publisher. 1796–97.

MIDDLETOWN, 1785.
TERTIUS DUNNING, Printer and publisher. 1797.
MOSES HAWKINS WOODWARD, Printer and publisher. 1796–1797.

NEWFIELD, 1795.
LAZARUS BEACH, Printer, Bookseller and Stationer. 1. Stratfield Street, one door south from Capt. Warden's, 1796. 2. Opposite Mr. Hinman's Inn. 1797.

NEW HAVEN. 1754.
ISAAC BEERS, Bookseller. 1796–1797.
GEORGE BUNCE, Printer. 1. George Bunce, 1797. 2. Bunce and Spencer, corner of Fleet and George Streets, 1797.
JAMES COCHRAN, Author Bookseller, Chapel Street. 1797.
AMOS DOOLITTLE, Engraver. 1796–1797.
SAMUEL GREEN, Printer. T. and S. Green, 1796–97.
THOMAS GREEN, Printer and publisher. 1. Opposite the Post-Office, 1796–1797. 2. Thomæ et Samuelis Green, Universitatis Typographorum, 1796–1797.

EDWARD O'BRIEN, Printer and publisher. Edward O'Brien and Company, 1796–1797.
—— SPENCER, Printer. Bunce and Spencer, 1797.
MOSES HAWKINS WOODWARD, Bookseller. In State Street, 1797.

NEW LONDON, 1709.
SAMUEL GREEN, Printer, publisher and Bookseller. At his Office, adjoining the Bank, 1796–1797.
THOMAS C. GREEN, Bookseller. South of the Parade, 1796.
CHARLES HOLT, Printer and publisher. 1797.
JAMES SPRINGER, Printer, publisher and Bookseller. Beach Street, opposite the Market, 1796–97.

NORWICH, 1773.
THOMAS HUBBARD, Printer, publisher and Bookseller. 24 rods west of the Meeting House, 1796.
JOHN STERRY, Bookseller. John Sterry and Co. 1796–1797.
JOHN TRUMBULL, Printer, publisher and Bookseller. A few rods west of the Court House, 1796–1797.

SIMSBURY.
OLIVER BROWNSON, Music publisher. 1797.

SUFFIELD, 1797.
HAVILA FARNSWORTH, Printer. H. and O. Farnsworth, 1797.
OLIVER FARNSWORTH, Printer. H. and O. Farnsworth, 1797.

WINDHAM, 1791.
JOHN BYRNE, Printer and publisher. In the lower room of the Court House, 1796–1797.
JAMES HUNTINGTON, Bookseller. 1797.

PRINTING INSTITUTED IN
DELAWARE, 1761, A. D.

NEW-CASTLE, 1796.
JOHN ADAMS, Printer. Samuel and John Adams, 1796–1797.
SAMUEL ADAMS, State Printer. Samuel and John Adams, 1796–1797.

WILMINGTON, 1761.
JAMES ADAMS, Printer and Bookseller. North side of the upper Market House, 1796–1797.
JOHN ADAMS, Printer. S. and J. Adams, 1796–97.
SAMUEL ADAMS, Printer and publisher. S. and J. Adams, corner King and High Streets, 1796–97.
JOHN BOGGS, Travelling Bookseller. 1797.
VINCENT BONSAL, Printer and Bookseller. 1. Bonsal and Starr, 1796. 2. Bonsal and Niles, 1797.
PETER BRYNBERG, Printer, publisher and Bookseller. In Market Street, 1796–1797.
JOSEPH JOHNSON, Printer. 1. Joseph Johnson & Co. No. 73 Market Street, opposite the Bank, 1796. 2. Johnson and Preston, 1797.

WILMINGTON, *continued.*

HEZEKIAH NILES, Printer. Bonsal and Niles, 1796–1797.

—— PRESTON, Printer. Johnson and Preston, 1797.

WILLIAM CATHERWOOD SMYTH, Printer and publisher. Two doors below Mr. Brinton's Tavern, High Street, 1796–1797.

CALEB STARR, Printer. Bonsal and Starr, 1796.

JAMES WILSON, Bookseller and Stationer. At his Book Store, at the Sign of Shakespeare, No. 5, opposite the upper Market, 1796–1797.

PRINTING INSTITUTED IN
DISTRICT OF COLUMBIA, 1795, A. D.

CITY OF WASHINGTON, 1795.

JOHN CROCKER, Printer and publisher. John Crocker and Co. Greenleaf's Point, City of Washington, 1796.

BENJAMIN MORE, Printer and publisher. At the house next west of the Hotel, 1796–1797.

THOMAS WILSON, Printer and Publisher. Greenleaf's Point, 1796.

PRINTING INSTITUTED IN
EAST FLORIDA, 1783, A. D.

ST. AUGUSTINE, 1783.

PRINTING INSTITUTED IN
GEORGIA, 1762, A. D.

AUGUSTA, 1785.

ALEXANDER M'MILLAN, Printer and publisher. Printer to the State, 1796–1797.

JOHN ERDMAN SMITH, Printer and publisher. Printer to the State, 1796–1797.

SAVANNAH, 1762.

NICHOLAS JOHNSTON, Printer and publisher. Nicholas Johnston and Co. Broughton Street, 1797.

TITUS POWERS, Printer and publisher. 1. Powers and Seymour, corner St. Julien Street, opposite the Church, 1796. 2. Powers and Seymour, in Market Square, opposite Mr. Hill's Tavern, 1797.

GURDON I. SEYMOUR, Printer and publisher. 1. Powers and Seymour, 1796–1797. 2. Gurdon I. Seymour, on the Bay, 1797. 3. Seymour and Woolhopter, on the Bay, 1797.

PHILIP D. WOOLHOPTER, Printer. Gurdon I. Seymour and Philip D. Woolhopter. 1797.

PRINTING INSTITUTED IN
KENTUCKY, 1787, A. D.

FRANKFORT, 1795.

BENJAMIN J. BRADFORD, Printer and publisher. At the Capitol, 1796.

LEXINGTON, 1787.

JOHN BRADFORD, Printer and publisher. At his Office, corner of Main and Cross Streets, 1796–97.

JAMES H. STEWART, Printer and publisher. Printer to the Commonwealth, 1796–1797.

PARIS, 1797.

DARIUS MOFFET, Printer and publisher. 1797.

WASHINGTON, 1797.

WILLIAM H. BEAUMONT, Printer and publisher. Hunter and Beaumont, 1797.

WILLIAM HUNTER, Printer and publisher. Hunter and Beaumont. 1797.

PRINTING INSTITUTED IN
LOUISIANA, 1794, A. D.

NEW ORLEANS, 1794.

LOUIS DUCLOT, Printer and publisher. 1796–1797?

PRINTING INSTITUTED IN
DISTRICT OF MAINE, 1785, A. D.

AUGUSTA, 1797.

PETER EDES, Printer, publisher and Bookseller. Near the Court House, 1797.

FALMOUTH, 1785.

HALLOWELL, 1794.

JOHN KELSE BAKER, Printer and publisher. 1. Wait and Baker, 1796. 2. Fish Street, 1796.

NATHANIEL COGSWELL, Bookseller. At the Hallowell Bookstore, 1797.

PETER EDES, Printer, publisher and Bookseller. Near the Court House, 1796–1797.

BENJAMIN POOR, Printer and publisher. At the Hook, 1796–1797.

HOWARD S. ROBINSON, Printer. 1797.

THOMAS BAKER WAIT, Printer and publisher. Wait and Baker, 1796.

HARRINGTON, 1797.

PETER EDES, Printer and publisher. Near the Court House, 1797.

PORTLAND, 1786.

JOHN KELSE BAKER, Printer. 1796–1797.

STEPHEN PATTEN, Bookseller. At the Portland Book Store, 1796–1797.

JOHN RAND, Printer and publisher. At his Office in Middle Street, near the head of Fish Street, 1796–1797.

BENJAMIN TITCOMB, JUNIOR, Printer and publisher. In Middle Street, 1796.

THOMAS BAKER WAIT, Printer. 1797.

WISCASSET, 1796.

HENRY HOSKINS, Printer and publisher. 1. Russell and Hoskins, 1796–1797. 2. Henry Hoskins, 1797. 3. Hoskins and Scott, 1797.

—— LANGTON, Printer and publisher. Langton and Rhoades, 1797.

—— RHOADES, Printer. Langton and Rhoades, 1797.

JOSEPH N. RUSSELL, Printer and publisher. J. N. Russell and H. Hoskins, corner of Main and Fore [Water] Streets, 1796–1797.

JOHN W. SCOTT, Printer. Hoskins and Scott, 1797.

YORK.

DANIEL SEWALL, Almanac maker. At his Office, 1796–1797.

PRINTING INSTITUTED IN
MARYLAND, 1726, A. D.

ANNAPOLIS, 1726.

FREDERICK GREEN, Printer and publisher. 1. Printer to the State, 1796–1797. 2. F. and S. Green, 1796–1797.

SAMUEL GREEN, Printer. F. and S. Green, 1796–97.

BALTIMORE, 1765.

JOHN ADAMS, Printer. S. and J. Adams, 1796.

SAMUEL ADAMS, Printer and Bookseller. S. and J. Adams, 1796.

MATTHEW BROWN, Printer. Yundt and Brown, 1796–1797.

SAMUEL BUTLER, Bookseller. Thomas, Andrews and Butler, 1796–1797.

ISAAC CARR, Music publisher. No. 6 Gay Street, 1796–1797.

THOMAS E. CLAYLAND, Printer and publisher. Clayland, Dobbin and Co. at the New Printing Office, No. 36, corner of Centre Market, Frederick and Market Street, opposite the Vendue Store, 1796–1797.

THOMAS DOBBIN, Printer and publisher. Clayland, Dobbin and Co., 1796–1797.

PHILIP EDWARDS, Printer and publisher. No. 1 Light Street, 1796–1797.

D. FINCHETE FREEBAIRN, Printer and publisher. 1797.

—— HAGERTY, Bookseller. 1796.

JOHN HAYES, Printer. 1796–1797.

GEORGE HILL, Bookseller. 1796–1797.

CHRISTOPHER JACKSON, Printer. No. 67 Market Street, 1796–1797.

GEORGE KEATINGE, Bookseller. In Market Street, No. 149, three doors above Light Lane, 1796–97.

HENRY S. KEATINGE, Printer and Bookseller. 1796–1797.

WILLIAM PECHIN, Printer and publisher. 1. Pechin and Wilmer, No. 15 Baltimore [Market] Street, 1796. 2. Pechin and Co. No. 27 Gay Street, 1796. 3. William Pechin, No. 10, Second Street, 1796–1797.

D. PORTER, Bookseller. At the Observatory, Federal Hill, 1797.

JAMES RICE, Bookseller. J. Rice & Co. Market Street, corner of South Street, 1796–1797.

SAMUEL SAUR [or SOWER], Printer, publisher and Bookseller. In der Fayettestrasse, 1796–1797.

Hrn. SCHULTZ, Vender. 1796.

JAMES SMITH, Bookseller. James Smith and Co. 1796.

JOHN SMITH, Printer and publisher. J. Smith and C. Jackson, 1797.

Hrn. TSCHUDY, Vender. 1796.

ISAIAH THOMAS, Bookseller. Thomas, Andrews and Butler, Market Street, 1796–1797.

JAMES JONES WILMER, Publisher. Pechin and Wilmer, 1796.

LEONARD YUNDT, Printer and publisher. Yundt and Brown, at their Printing Office, No. 3 Calvert Street, between Market Street, near the Court House, 1796–1797.

CHESTERTOWN. 1793.

JAMES ARTHUR, Bookseller. 1796–1797.

EASTON, 1790.

JAMES COWAN, Printer and publisher. 1796–1797.

GREENBURY NEALE, Bookseller. 1796–1797.

ELIZABETH (HAGER'S) TOWN, 1790.

JOHN D. CAREY, Printer and publisher. 1796.

THOMAS GRIEVES, Printer and publisher. Near the Court House, 1797.

JOHANN GRUBER, Printer and publisher. 1797.

PHEBE HERBERT, Printer and publisher. At her Printing Office in the Main Street leading to the western country, 1796–1797.

FREDERICK TOWN, 1779.

MATTHIAS BARTGIS, Printer and publisher. At his English and German Printing Office, the upper end of Market Street, 1796–1797.

JOHN WINTER, Printer and publisher. At his Office in Patrick Street, 1796–1797.

SHARON, MONTGOMERY COUNTY.

ISAAC BRIGGS, Almanac maker. 1797.

PRINTING INSTITUTED IN
MASSACHUSETTS, 1639, A. D.

ATTLEBOROUGH, 1777.

BOLTON.

ASA HOUGHTON, Almanac maker. 1796–1797.

BOSTON, 1675.

THOMAS ADAMS, Printer and publisher. 1. Adams and Larkin, 1796–1797. 2. Thomas Adams, directly opposite the Court House, in Court Street, 1797.

EBENEZER TURELL ANDREWS, Bookseller. Thomas and Andrews, 1796–1797.

JOSEPH BELKNAP, Printer. At the Apollo Press, No. 8 Dock Square, 1796.

FRANCIS BARTODY, Physician, Author Bookseller. Leverett Street, West Boston, third house from the Brewery, 1797.

CALEB BINGHAM, Author Bookseller. At his Book Store, No. 44 Cornhill, 1796–1797.

LEMUEL BLAKE, Bookseller. W. P. and L. Blake, 1796–1797.

WILLIAM P. BLAKE, Bookseller. 1. At the Boston Bookstore, No. 1 Cornhill, 1796–1797. 2. W. P. and L. Blake, 1796–1797.

D. BOWEN, Printer. At the Columbian Museum Press, Head of the Mall, 1797.

JOHN BOYLE, Bookseller. No. 18 Marlborough Street, 1796–1797.

JOSEPH BUMSTEAD, Printer and Bookseller. No. 20 Union Street, 1796–1797.

SETH CHANDLER, Student of Physic. 1797.

WILLIAM T. CLAP, Bookseller and Stationer. Fish Street, at the corner of Proctor's Lane, 1796–97.

SOLOMON COTTON, JUNIOR, Bookseller and Stationer. At his Book Store, No. 51 Marlborough Street, 1796.

JAMES CUTLER, Printer. At the Printing Office, in Quaker Lane, 1796–1797.

BENJAMIN EDES, Printer and publisher. In Kilby Street. 1796–1797.

SAMUEL ETHERIDGE, Printer. At his Printing Office, No. 9 Newbury Street, 1796–1797.

JOHN FLEET, Printer. 1. Thomas and John Fleet, 1796–1797. 2. John and Thomas Fleet, at the Bible and Heart, Cornhill, 1797.

THOMAS FLEET, Printer and Bookseller. Thomas and John Fleet, at the Bible and Heart, in Cornhill, 1796–1797.

THOMAS FLEET, JUNIOR, Printer. At the Bible and Heart, Cornhill, 1796–1797.

JOHN WEST FOLSOM, Printer and Bookseller. No. 30 Union Street, 1796–1797.

PRINCE HALL, Author Bookseller. At his shop, opposite the Quaker Meeting House, Quaker Lane, 1797.

SAMUEL HALL, Printer and Bookseller. No. 35 Cornhill, 1796–1797.

THOMAS HALL, Printer. Head of Water Street, 1796–1797.

JOHN HOMES, Bookseller and Stationer. Opposite the north door of the State House, State Street, 1797.

BENJAMIN LARKIN, Bookseller. No. 46 Cornhill, 1796.

EBENEZER LARKIN, JUNIOR, Bookseller and Stationer. No. 47 Cornhill, 1796–1797.

ISAAC LARKIN, Printer. Adams and Larkin, 1796–97.

JAMES LORING, Printer. Manning and Loring, 1796–1797.

WILLIAM MANNING, Printer and Bookseller. Manning and Loring, Spring Lane, 1796–1797.

ALEXANDER MARTIN, Printer and publisher. No. 71 State Street, opposite the Custom House, 1796–97.

FRANCIS MARRIOTT, Bookseller. 1797.

THOMAS MINNS, Printer. Young and Minns, 1796–1797.

SETH H. MOORE, Printer. 1797.

PAUL JOSEPH GUERARD DE NANCREDE, Bookseller. No. 49 Marlbro' Street, 1796–1797.

FRANCIS NICHOLS, Bookseller. 1797.

WILLIAM NORMAN, Bookseller and Stationer. At his Book Store, No. 75 Newbury Street, nearly opposite the Sign of the Lamb, 1796–1797.

THOMAS PAINE, Editor and publisher. 1796.

WILLIAM PELHAM, Bookseller and Stationer. No. 59 Cornhill, 1796–1797.

BENJAMIN RUSSELL, Printer and publisher. 1. At his Office, State Street, 1796. 2. Printer to the United States, for the Northern States, South side State Street, next to the Coffee House, 1797.

EZEKIEL RUSSELL'S OFFICE, Essex Street, near Liberty-Pole, 1796–1797.

JOHN RUSSELL, Printer and publisher. In Quaker Lane, near State Street, 1796–1797.

WILLIAM SPOTSWOOD, Printer and Bookseller. No. 55 Marlborough Street, 1796–1797.

BENJAMIN SWEETSER, Printer. No. 57 State Street, corner of Wing's Lane, 1796.

ISAIAH THOMAS, Printer, publisher and Bookseller. Isaiah Thomas and Ebenezer T. Andrews, Faust's Statue, No. 45 Newbury Street, 1796–1797.

DAVID WEST, Bookseller. 1. No. 36 Marlborough Street, 1796–1797. 2. No. 56 Cornhill, directly opposite the westerly door of the State-House, 1797.

JOHN WEST, Bookseller and Stationer. No. 75 Cornhill, 1796–1797.

JAMES WHITE, Bookseller and Stationer. At Franklin's Head, opposite the Prison, Court Street, 1793–1797.

JAMES WHITE, Printer. Near Charles River Bridge, 1793–1797.

JOSEPH WHITE, Printer and Bookseller. Next to the Swan Tavern, 1796.

JOSEPH WHITTEMORE, Vender. 1796–1797.

ALEXANDER YOUNG, Printer and publisher. Young and Minns, opposite the north-east corner of the State House, State Street, 1796–1797. Printers to the honourable the General Court of the Commonwealth of Massachusetts, 1796–1797.

BROOKFIELD, 1794.

ELISHA H. WALDO, Printer and publisher. 1796.

BUCKLAND.

ASAPH CHILSON, Bookseller. 1797.

CAMBRIDGE, 1639.

CHARLESTOWN, 1785.

JOHN LAMSON, Printer. At his Office near the Bridge, 1797.

CHELMSFORD, 1775.

CONCORD, 1776.

DEDHAM, 1796.

BENJAMIN HEATON, Printer. N. and B. Heaton, 1796–1797.
NATHANIEL HEATON, Printer and publisher. Nathaniel and Benjamin Heaton, Minerva Press, about 60 rods east of the Court House, 1796–97.
HERMAN MANN, Printer. 1. N. Heaton and H. Mann, 1797. 2. H. Mann, 1797.

GREENFIELD, 1792.

THOMAS DICKMAN, Printer, publisher and Bookseller. 1796–1797.

HAVERHILL, 1790.

LEOMINSTER, 1795.

CHARLES PRENTISS, Printer and publisher. South of the Meeting House, 1796–1797.
JOHN PRENTISS, Printer. John Prentiss and Co. 1797.

MIDDLEBOROUGH, 1787.

NEW BEDFORD, 1792.

JOHN SPOONER, Printer, publisher and Bookseller. Corner of Union and Sixth Streets, 1796–1797.

NEWBURYPORT, 1773.

WILLIAM BARRETT, Printer and publisher. 1. West corner of Market Square, 1796–1797. 2. Barrett and March, 1797.
EDMUND MARCH BLUNT, Printer, publisher and Bookseller. At the Newburyport Book Store, Sign of the Bible, State Street, 1796–1797.
ANGIER MARCH, Printer and publisher. 1. State Street, 1796–1797. 2. Middle Street, 1797. 3. Barrett and March, 1797. 4. Angier March, 1797.
JOHN MYCALL, Printer. 1796.
JONATHAN PLUMMER, JUNIOR. 1796–1797.

NORTHAMPTON, 1786.

WILLIAM BUTLER, Printer and publisher. 1796–97.
DANIEL WRIGHT, Printer. Daniel Wright and Co. 1797.

PITTSFIELD, 1787.

PLYMOUTH, 1785.

REHOBOTH, 1776.

SALEM, 1768.

WILLIAM CARLTON, or CARLETON, Printer, publisher, and Bookseller. At the Bible and Heart, Essex Street, between Washington and Market Streets, 1796–1797.
THOMAS C. CUSHING, Printer and publisher. Essex Street, between Washington and Market Streets, 1796–1797.
JOHN DABNEY, Bookseller. 1796.

SPRINGFIELD, 1782.

EDWARD GRAY, Printer. At the corner of Meeting House Lane, 1796.
JOHN WORTHINGTON HOOKER, Printer and publisher. J. W. Hooker and F. Stebbins, 1796.
FRANCIS STEBBINS, Printer and publisher. 1. Hooker and Stebbins, 1796. 2. Francis Stebbins, 1796–1797.

STERLING.

MOSES SMITH, Town Clerk. 1796.
ROBERT BAILEY THOMAS, Almanac maker, Bookseller and Stationer. 1796–1797.

STOCKBRIDGE, 1789.

LORING ANDREWS, Printer and publisher. 1796–97.
BENJAMIN ROSSETER, Printer and publisher. Rosseter and Willard, 1797.
HERMAN WILLARD, Printer. Rosseter and Willard, 1797.

TAUNTON.

DANIEL BREWER, Bookseller. 1796–1797.

WEST-SPRINGFIELD, 1795.

EDWARD GRAY, Printer and publisher. A few rods west of the Meeting House, 1796–1797.

WORCESTER, 1775.

ALEXANDER THOMAS, Printer. Thomas, Son and Thomas, 1796–1797.
ISAIAH THOMAS, Printer, publisher, Bookseller, Stationer, Binder and Paper Manufacturer. Thomas, Son and Thomas. At the Worcester Bookstore, 1796–1797.
ISAIAH THOMAS, JUNIOR, Printer and Bookseller. 1. At his Bookstore, Sign of Johnson's Head, opposite the Prison, 1796–1797. 2. Isaiah Thomas and Son, at their respective Bookstores, 1796–1797.
LEONARD WORCESTER, Printer and publisher. At his Office near the South Meeting House, 1796–97.

WRENTHAM, 1795.
DAVID HEATON, Bookseller. 1796.
NATHANIEL HEATON, JUNIOR, Printer. 1796–1797.

PRINTING INSTITUTED IN
NEW HAMPSHIRE, 1756, A. D.

AMHERST, 1794.
WILLIAM BIGLOW, Printer. Biglow and Cushing, at their Office, at the Store of Col. Means, 1796.
NATHANIEL COVERLY, Printer and publisher. Nathaniel Coverly and Son, near the Court House, 1796.
NATHANIEL COVERLY, JUNIOR, Printer. Nathaniel Coverly and Son, 1796.
SAMUEL CUSHING, Printer and publisher. 1. Biglow and Cushing, 1796. 2. Samuel Cushing, 1796–97.
SAMUEL PRESTON, Printer and publisher. 1797.

CONCORD, 1789.
MOSES DAVIS, Printer and publisher. 1. Russell and Davis, 1796–1797. 2. Moses Davis, 1797.
GEORGE HOUGH, Printer and publisher. 1796–97.
ELIJAH RUSSELL, Printer and publisher. Russell and Davis, 1796–1797.

DOVER, 1790.
SAMUEL BRAGG, JUNIOR, Printer and publisher, At his Printing Office near the Court House, 1796–1797.

EXETER. 1775.
HENRY RANLET, Printer, publisher and Bookseller. At his Office [Book Store] in Main Street, 1796–1797.
SAMUEL WINSLOW, Printer and publisher. In Main Street, 1796.

HANOVER, 1793.
JOHN MOSELY DUNHAM, Printer and publisher. Dunham and True, 1796–1797.
BENJAMIN TRUE, Printer and publisher. 1. Dunham and True, 1796–1797. 2. Benjamin True, 1797.

HAVERHILL, 1796.
NATHANIEL COVERLY, Printer and publisher. 1. Nathaniel Coverly and Son, near the Court House, 1796. 2. Nathaniel Coverly, directly opposite the Court House, 1796–1797.
NATHANIEL COVERLY, JUNIOR, Printer. N. Coverly and Son, 1796.

HOPKINTON,
FRANCIS MITCHEL, Bookseller. 1797.

KEENE, 1787.
CORNELIUS STURTEVANT, JUNIOR, Printer, publisher and Bookseller. Cornelius Sturtevant, jun. and Co. 1796–1797.

NEWTOWN.
Rev. JOHN PEAK, Pastor, Baptist Church. 1796.

PORTSMOUTH, 1756.
SAMUEL LARKIN, Bookseller and Stationer. At the Portsmouth Book Store, in Market Street, 1796.
JOHN MELCHER, Printer, publisher and Bookseller. At his Office, corner of Market Street, 1796–1797. Printer to the State. 1796–1797.
CHARLES PEIRCE, Printer, publisher and Bookseller. 1. In Court Street, 1796–1797. 2. No. 5 Daniel Street, 1797.

WALPOLE, 1793.
DAVID CARLISLE, JUNIOR, Printer, publisher and Bookseller. 1. I. Thomas and D. Carlisle, jun., in the Main Street, 1796. 2. David Carlisle, jun., 1796–1797. 3. David Carlisle, 1797.
ISAIAH THOMAS, Publisher. I. Thomas and D. Carlisle, jun. in the Main Street, 1796.

PRINTING INSTITUTED IN
NEW JERSEY, 1755, A. D.

BRIDGETOWN, 1795.
ALEXANDER M'KENZIE, Printer and publisher. 1796–1797.

BURLINGTON, 1765.
ISAAC NEALE, Printer. 1796–1797.

CHATHAM, 1779.

ELIZABETH TOWN, 1786.
SHEPARD KOLLOCK, Printer, publisher and Bookseller. At his Printing Office and Book Store, 1796–1797.

MONMOUTH, 1795.

MORRIS TOWN, 1797.
ELIJAH COOPER, Printer and publisher. E. Cooper and Co. 1797.
CALEB RUSSELL, Printer and publisher. 1. E. Cooper and Co. 1797. 2. Caleb Russell, 1797.

MOUNT PLEASANT,
NEAR MIDDLETOWN-POINT, 1794.
PHILIP FRENEAU, Printer. 1797.

NEW BRUNSWICK, 1783.
ABRAHAM BLAUVELT, Printer and publisher. In Albany Street, 1796–1797.

NEWARK, 1776.
DANIEL DODGE, Printer and publisher. 1. Daniel Dodge and Co. 1796–1797. 2. A. Pennington and D. Dodge, 1797.
AARON PENNINGTON, Printer and publisher. Pennington and Dodge, 1797.
JOHN WOODS, Printer and publisher. Near the Episcopal Church, 1796–1797.

NEWTON, 1796.

ELIOT HOPKINS, Printer and publisher. Eliot Hopkins and Co. 1796-1797.

WILLIAM HURTIN, Printer. Hopkins and Hurtin, 1796.

PRINCETON, 1780.

TRENTON, 1778.

MATTHIAS DAY, Printer and publisher. Printer to the State, 1796-1797.

WOODBRIDGE, 1755.

PRINTING INSTITUTED IN
NEW YORK, 1693, A. D.

ALBANY, 1771.

LORING ANDREWS, Printer and publisher. In Maiden Lane, west of Masters' Lodge, 1797.

JOHN BARBER, Printer and publisher. Barber and Southwick, at Faust's Statue, No. 40 State Street, two doors below the Low Dutch Church, 1796-1797. Or at their Book Store, two doors north of the City Hall, in Court Street, 1797.

J. CHESTNEY, Bookseller. 1797.

ABRAHAM ELLISON, Bookseller and Binder. In State Street, 1796-1797.

JOSEPH FRY, Printer. Fry and Southwick, corner of Dock Street and Mark Lane, 1797.

AMOS HAMLIN, Author Bookseller. 1797.

JOHN M'DONALD, Printer and publisher. 1. No. 18 State Street, 1796. 2. John M'Donald and Co. on the east side of Middle Alley, three doors from the corner of State Street, 1797.

OBADIAH PENNIMAN, Bookseller. Thomas, Andrews and Penniman, 1796-1797.

HENRY COLLINS SOUTHWICK, Printer. Fry and Southwick, 1797.

SOLOMON SOUTHWICK, Printer. Barber and Southwick, 1796-1797.

HENRY SPENCER, Binder. At Spencer's Bookstore and Bindery, in Market Street, 1796.

THOMAS SPENCER, Bookseller. Spencer and Webb, Market Street, 1796-1797.

ISAIAH THOMAS, Bookseller. Thomas, And ws and Penniman, 1. State Street, corner of Middle Alley, 1796. 2. Thomas, Andrews and Penniman, at the Albany Book Store, Sign of Franklin's Head, State Street, 1797.

THOMAS SMITH WEBB, Bookseller. Spencer and Webb, 1796-1797.

CHARLES R. WEBSTER, Printer, publisher and Bookseller. Charles R. and George Webster, at their Bookstore, in the White House, on the west corner of State and Pearl Streets, near the English Church and opposite the City Tavern, 1796-1797.

GEORGE WEBSTER, Printer. Charles R. and George Webster, 1796-1797.

BALLSTON.

D. ROGERS, Bookseller. 1797.

BATH, 1796.

JAMES EDIE, Printer. Kersey and Edie, 1796-97.

WILLIAM KERSEY, Printer and publisher. William Kersey and James Edie, 1796-1797.

CANAAN, 1794.

CANANDAIGUA.

SAMUEL COLE, Bookseller. 1796.

CATSKILL, 1792.

MACKAY CROSWELL, Printer and publisher. 1. T. and M. Croswell, 1796. 2. Mackay Croswell and Co. 1796-1797.

COOPERSTOWN, 1795.

ELIHU PHINNEY, Printer and publisher. At his Printing Office, first door south of the Court House, 1796-1797.

FISHKILL, 1776.

GENEVA, 1796.

LUCIUS CARY, Printer and publisher. 1796-1797.

GOSHEN, 1789.

WILLIAM HURTIN, Printer and publisher. 1796-97.

HUDSON, 1785.

ASHBEL STODDARD, Printer, publisher and Bookseller. 1796-1797.

JOHNSTOWN, 1795.

JACOB DOCKSTADER, Printer and publisher. Two doors north of St. Patrick's Lodge, Johnson Street, 1796-1797.

R. DODGE, Bookseller. 1797.

KINGSTON, 1777.

WILLIAM COPP, Printer and publisher. Copp and Freer, 1796-1797.

SAMUEL FREER, Printer. Copp and Freer, 1796-97.

LANSINGBURGH, 1787.

JESSE BUEL, Printer. Robert Moffitt and Co. 1797.

DANIEL CURTIS, JUNIOR, Printer. Luther Pratt and Co. 1796.

ROBERT MOFFITT, Printer and publisher. R. Moffitt and Co. 1797.

LUTHER PRATT, Printer and publisher. Luther Pratt and Co. 1796.

WILLIAM W. WANDS, Printer and publisher. At his Printing Office, 1796-1797.

MOUNT PLEASANT, 1797.

WILLIAM DURELL, Printer and publisher. 1797.

NEW WINDSOR, 1797.

ABRAHAM LOTT, Printer. Schultz and Lott, 1797.
JACOB SCHULTZ, Printer and publisher. Jacob Schultz and Abraham Lott, 1797.

NEW YORK CITY, 1693.

—— ADAM, Bookseller. Fellows and Adam, 1796.
THOMAS ALLEN, Bookseller and Stationer. No. 136 [186] Pearl Street, 1796–1797.
PHILIP ARNOLD, Bookseller. 1797.
NATHANIEL BELL, Bookseller and Stationer. 1796.
JAMES BERRY, Bookseller. Rogers and Berry, 1796.
NATHANIEL BIRDSALL, Printer. 1796.
JOHN BUEL, Printer, publisher and Bookseller. 1. No. 132 [153] Fly-Market, corner of Water Street, 1796–1797. 2. No. 74 William Street, 1797.
JOHN BULL, Printer and publisher. No. 115 Cherry Street, 1796–1797.
GEORGE BUNCE, Printer and publisher. No. 123 Water Street, opposite the Tontine Coffee House. 1796–1797.
THOMAS BURLING, JUNIOR, Printer. Thomas Burling, jun. and Co. 1. No. 33 Oliver Street, 1797. 2. No. 115 Cherry Street, 1797. 3. Tiebout and Burling, 1797.
SAMUEL CAMPBELL, Bookseller and Stationer. No. 124 Pearl Street, 1796–1797.
HOCQUET CARITAT, Bookseller, and Circulating Library. No. 3 Pearl Street, 1797.
BENJAMIN CARR, Music publisher. At his Musical Repository, No. 131 William Street, 1796–1797.
JAMES CHEVALIER, Bookseller, 1797.
FRANCIS CHILDS, Printer. Francis Childs and Co. 1796.
JOHN CHILDS, Printer. For [John Morton] Printer to the State, No. 7 Garden Street, 1796.
JOHN COBBY, Author Bookseller. 1797.
ISAAC COLLINS, Printer. No. 189 Pearl Street. 1796–1797.
JOHN CROOKES, Printer. 1. Crookes and Saunders, 1797. 2. John Crookes, 1797.
CORNELIUS DAVIS, Bookseller and Stationer. 1. No. 212 Water Street, 1796. 2. No. 94 Water Street. 1797.
MATTHEW L. DAVIS, Printer. 1. M. L. and W. A. Davis, 1796. 2. P. Freneau and M. L. Davis, 1797.
WILLIAM A. DAVIS, Printer. 1. No. 438 Pearl Street, 1796–97. 2. No. 26 Moore Street, 1797.
D. DUNHAM, Bookseller. 1796–1797.
THOMAS DUNN, Bookseller. 1796.
TERTIUS DUNNING, Printer. Dunning and Hyer, No. 21 Gold Street, 1796.
WILLIAM DURELL, Printer, publisher and Bookseller. No. 208 Pearl Street, 1796.

EVERT DUYCKINCK, Bookseller and Stationer. Evert Duyckinck and Co. No. 110 Pearl Street. 1796–1797.
HTD. FEINEUER, Bookseller. 1796.
JOHN FELLOWS, Bookseller. 1. Fellows and Adam, No. 131 Water Street, 1796. 2. No. 60 Water Street, 1796–1797. 3. Circulating Library, 1797.
GEORGE FORMAN, Printer. 1. No. 46 Wall Street, opposite the Post Office, 1796–1797. 2. No. 156 Front Street, 1796.
PHILIP FRENEAU, Printer. 1. P. Freneau and A. Menut, No. 89 Beekman Street, 1797. 2. No. 123 Fly Market, 1797. 3. P. Freneau and M. L. Davis, No. 26 Moore Street, near Whitehall, 1797.
HUGH GAINE, Printer, Bookseller and Stationer. At his Book Store and Printing Office, at the Bible, in Hanover Square. 1796–1797.
GEORGE GILFERT, Music publisher. G. Gilfert and Co. at their Musical Magazine, No. 177 Broadway, 1796–1797.
BENJAMIN GOMEZ, Bookseller and Stationer. No. 97 Maiden Lane, 1796–1797.
THOMAS GREENLEAF, Printer, publisher and Bookseller. No. 54 Wall Street—six doors from the Tontine Coffee House, 1796–1797.
JOHN HARRISSON, Printer and Bookseller. At his Book Store and Printing Office, Yorick's Head, No. 3 Peck Slip, 1796–1797.
JAMES HEWITT, Musical Repository. No. 131 William Street, 1797.
ROBERT HODGE, Bookseller. Robert Hodge and Co. 1796.
GEORGE FOLLET HOPKINS, Printer and publisher. 1. Hopkins, Webb and Co. No. 40 Pine Street, 1796–1797. 2. Geo. F. Hopkins, 40 Pine Street, Printer of the Laws of the United States for the District of New York, 1797.
WALTER W. HYER, Printer, Dunning and Hyer. 1796.
JOHN I. JOHNSON, Publisher. 1797. 2. Johnson and Manchester, 1797.
NAPTHALI JUDAH, Bookseller and Stationer. Sign of Paine's Head, No. 47 Water Street, Coentie's Slip, 1796–1797.
THOMAS KIRK, Printer and Editor. 1. 112 Chatham Street, next door to the Tea-Water Pump, 1797. 2. Wilson and Kirk, 1797.
JOHN LANG, Printer. M'Lean and Lang, 1797.
HENRY LEUTHAUER, Bookseller. 1796.
DAVID LONGWORTH, Directory publisher. 1. No. 66 Nassau Street, 1796–1797. 2. No. 11 Park, 1797.
SAMUEL LOUDON, JUNIOR, Printer and publisher. No. 82 Water Street, 1796.
JAMES LYON, Printer. 1. Mott and Lyon, 1796. 2. James Lyon and Co. at Homer's Head, No. 258 Pearl Street, 1796.
ROBERT MACGILL, Bookseller. No. 105 Maiden Lane, 1796–1797.

NEW YORK CITY, *continued.*

ARCHIBALD M'LEAN, Printer and publisher. 1. Franklin's Head, No. 116 Pearl Street, late 41 Hanover Square, nearly opposite the New-York Bank, 1796. 2. M'Lean and Lang, 1797.

—— MANCHESTER, Bookseller. Johnson and Manchester, 1797.

T. R. MAVERICK, Engraver. 1796.

PETER A. MESIER, Bookseller. 1796-1797.

ALEXANDER MENUT, Printer. Freneau and Menut. 1797.

WILLIAM MILNS, Author Bookseller. At the Literary Printing Office, No. 29 Gold Street, 1797.

EDWARD MITCHELL, Bookseller and Stationer. No. 9 Maiden Lane, 1796.

JOHN MORTON, Printer to the State. 1796-1797.

JACOB S. MOTT, Printer, publisher and Bookseller. Mott and Lyon, at their Printing Office, No. 71 Barclay Street, and at their Store, No. 70 Vesey Street, 1796-1797.

EDWARD O'BRIEN, Printer. Tiebout and O'Brien, 1796.

JAMES ORAM, Printer and publisher. No. 33 Liberty Street, 1796-1797.

CLAUDE PARISOT, Printer and publisher. No. 51 Pearl Street, 1796-1797.

JOHN REID, Bookseller and Stationer. No. 106 Water Street, 1796-1797.

JAMES RIVINGTON, Bookseller and Stationer. No. 156 Pearl Street, 1796-1797.

WILLIAM ROBINS, Printer [for John Morton] Printer to the State, at the State Printing Office, No. 71 Pine Street, 1796-1797.

JOHN ROGERS, Bookseller and Stationer. Rogers and Berry, No. 128 Pearl Street, 1796.

ROBERT SAUNDERS, Printer. Crookes and Saunders, 1797.

CHARLES SMITH, Publisher. No. 51 Maiden Lane, 1796-1797.

ALEXANDER SOMERVILLE, Bookseller. 1797.

JAMES SWORDS, Printer. T. and J. Swords,1796-97.

THOMAS SWORDS, Printer, publisher and Bookseller. T. and J. Swords, No. 99 Pearl Street, 1796-97.

JOHN TIEBOUT, Printer. 1. Tiebout and O'Brien, 1796. 2. At Homer's Head, No. 358 Pearl Street, 1796-1797. 3. Tiebout and Burling, 1797.

CORNELIUS C. VAN ALEN, Printer. C. C. Van Alen and Co. No. 60 Wall Street, 1796-1797.

JOSEPH DUDLEY WEBB, Printer. Hopkins, Webb and Co. 1796.

NOAH WEBSTER, JUNIOR, Editor and publisher. Hopkins, Webb and Co. 1796-1797.

ELIJAH WEEDG, Bookseller. 1797.

R. WILSON, Printer and Bookseller. Wilson and Kirk, 299 Broadway, 1797.

NEWBURGH, 1793.

LUCIUS CARY, Printer and publisher. 1796.

DAVID DENNISTON, Printer and publisher. 1796-97.

PHILIP VAN HORNE, Printer and publisher. 1797.

POUGHKEEPSIE, 1777.

NATHAN DOUGLAS, Printer and publisher. Near the Episcopal Church, 1796.

NICHOLAS POWER, Printer and publisher. 1. At the Post Office, 1796-1797. 2. Nicholas Power and Company [Richard Vanderburgh],1796. 3. Nicholas Power, 1797.

RICHARD VAN DER BURGH, Printer and publisher. Richard Van der Burgh and Company, 1796.

SAG HARBOR, 1791.

DAVID FROTHINGHAM, Printer and publisher. 1796-1797.

SALEM, 1794.

ST. JOHN HONEYWOOD, Publisher. W. W. Wands and S. J. Honeywood, 1796-1797.

WILLIAM W. WANDS, Printer and publisher. W.W. Wands and S. J. Honeywood, 1796-1797.

SCHENECTADY, 1794.
(On the Banks of the Mohawk.)

J. SHURTLEFF, Bookseller. 1797.

CORNELIUS P. WYCKOFF, Printer, publisher and Bookseller. Corner of State and Washington Streets, 1796-1797.

STILLWATER, 1794.

TROY, 1795.

DANIEL CURTISS, JUNIOR, Printer. Luther Pratt and Co. 1797.

GEORGE GARDNER, Printer and publisher. A few rods west of the Meeting House, 1796.

LUTHER PRATT, Printer and publisher. Luther Pratt and Co. near the Ferry, 1797.

UPTON, 1794.

WATERFORD, 1797.

JAMES LYON, Printer and publisher. James Lyon and Co. 1797.

WHITESTOWN, 1793.

OLIVER P. EASTON, Printer and publisher. Near the Post Office, 1796-1797.

—— LEWIS. Printer. Lewis and Webb, 1797.

WILLIAM M'LEAN, Printer and publisher. 1. Wells and M'Lean,1796. 2. William M'Lean,1796-97.

—— WEBB, Printer. Lewis and Webb, 1797.

SAMUEL WELLS, Printer and publisher. 1. Opposite the Meeting House, 1796. 2. Wells and M'Lean, 1796.

PRINTING INSTITUTED IN
NORTH CAROLINA, 1751, A. D.

EDENTON, 1788.

HENRY WILLS, Printer and publisher. Joint Printer to the State with A. Hodge, 1796–1797.
JAMES WILLS, Printer and publisher. Joint Printer to the State with A. Hodge, 1797.

FAYETTEVILLE, 1787.

WILLIAM BOYLAN, Printer. Hodge and Boylan, 1796–1797.
ABRAHAM HODGE, Printer and publisher. Hodge and Boylan, 1796–1797.

HALIFAX, 1782.

ABRAHAM HODGE, Printer and publisher. Joint Printer to the State with H. Wills, 1796–1797.

HILLSBOROUGH, 1788.

NEWBERN, 1751.

FRANCOIS XAVIER MARTIN, Printer and publisher. 1796–1797.

WILMINGTON, 1764.

JOHN BELLEW, Printer and publisher. At his Office, corner of Market and Second Streets, 1796.
ALLMAND HALL, Printer and publisher. 1797.

PRINTING INSTITUTED IN
OHIO, 1793, A. D.

CINCINNATI, 1793.

EDMUND FREEMAN, Printer. S. Freeman and Son, 1796–1797.
SAMUEL FREEMAN, Printer and publisher. S. Freeman and Son, 1796–1797.
THOMAS GOUDY, Secretary. At his Office in Front Street, Sign of the three Tons, 1796.
WILLIAM MAXWELL, Printer and publisher. At the corner of Third and Sycamore Streets, 1796.

PRINTING INSTITUTED IN
PENNSYLVANIA, 1685, A. D.

BETHLEHEM.

Hrn. REICH, Vender. 1796.

CARLISLE, 1785.

GEORGE KLINE, Printer, publisher and Bookseller. 1796–1797.
ARCHIBALD LOUDON, Bookseller. 1796–1797.
JOHN S. M'CLEAN, Printer. Steel and M'Clean. 1796.
JAMES STEEL, Printer and publisher. At the Sign of the Printing Press in York Street, 1796.

CHAMBERSBURG, 1790.

ANDREW DOVER, Printer. 1. Dover and Harper, 1796–1797. 2. Andrew Dover, 1797.
ROBERT HARPER, Printer and publisher. 1. Dover and Harper, 1796–1797. 2. Robert Harper, 1797.
—— LANE, Bookseller. Riddle and Lane, 1797.
—— RIDDLE, Bookseller. Riddle and Lane, 1797.

CHESNUT HILL, 1763.

EASTON, 1793.

Herrn. OPP, Booksellers. 1796.
CORNELIUS N. WEYGANDT, Printer. Jacob Weygandt und Sohn, 1796–1797.
JACOB WEYGANDT, Printer and publisher. Jacob Weygandt und Sohn, in der Neuen Buchdruckerey, 1796–1797.

EPHRATA, 1745.

BENJAMIN MAYER, Printer and Bookseller. 1796–97.

FRIEDENSTHAL BEI BETHLEHEM, 1763.

GERMANTOWN, 1738.

MICHAEL BILLMEYER, Printer, publisher and Bookseller. 1796–1797.
PETER LEIBERT, Printer. 1796–1797.

HANOVER, 1793.

WILLIAM DANIEL LEPPER, Printer. Stellingius and Lepper, 1797.
E. STELLINGIUS, Printer. Stellingius and Lepper, 1797.

HARRISBURGH, 1789.

JOHN WYETH, Printer and publisher. At his Office in Mulberry Street, 1796–1797.

HUNTINGDON, 1797.

MICHAEL DUFFEY, Printer and publisher. 1797.

LANCASTER, 1747.

JOHANN ALBRECHT, Printer, publisher and Bookseller. Johann Albrecht und Comp. in der Neuen Buchdruckerey in der Prinz-strasse, das 2te Haus, nordlich vom Gesangniss, 1796–1797.
JACOB BAILEY, Printer and Bookseller. In King Street, 1796–1797.
ROBERT DICKSON, Printer. W. and R. Dickson, 1796–1797.
WILLIAM DICKSON, Printer and Bookseller. 1. W. and R. Dickson, in Kingstreet, 1796–1797. 2. W. and R. Dickson, in Queen-street, north of the Courthouse, 1797.
WILLIAM HAMILTON, Printer, publisher and Bookseller. At Euclid's Head, in King Street, nearly opposite Mr. Stofft's, 1796–1797.
JACOB LAHN, Bookseller. 1797.
Herrn. LAUMANN, ZANZINGER und GRUNDACKER, Booksellers. 1796.

LEBANON.

Hrn. STOVER, Vender. 1796.

LEWISTON, 1796.

MILLERSTOWN.

Hrn. SCHLAUCH, Vender. 1796.

NEU-GERMANTAUN.

Hrn. MILLER, Vender. 1796.

NORTHERN LIBERTIES, 1797.

B. SCHEFFLER. Printer. B. Scheffler and Co. 1797.

NORTHUMBERLAND, 1792.

GEORGE SCHUSLER, Printer and publisher. 1796–97.

PHILADELPHIA, 1685.

JANE AITKEN, Printer. No. 10 North Third Street, 1796–1797.

JOHN AITKEN, Bookseller. No. 173 South Second Street, 1797.

ROBERT AITKEN, Printer and Bookseller. Robert Aitken and Son. No. 22 Makret Street, 1796–97.

BENJAMIN FRANKLIN BACHE, Printer, publisher and Bookseller. No. 112 Market Street, between Third and Fourth Streets, 1796–1797.

FRANCIS BAILEY, Printer and Bookseller. Francis and Robert Bailey, at Yorick's Head, No. 116 High Street, 1796–1797.

ROBERT BAILEY, Printer. F. and R. Bailey, 1796–97.

ARCHIBALD BARTRAM, Printer. Budd and Bartram, 1796–1797.

GOTTFRIED BECKER, Bookseller. Becker und Comp. Buchhändler in der Rees Strasse, No. 59, 1796.

ROBERT BELL, Printer. 1797.

JACOB R. BERRIMAN, Printer. Berriman and Co. No. 149 Chesnut Street, 1796.

JOHN BIOREN, Printer. 1. Bioren and Madan, No. 77 Dock Street, 1796–97. 2. John Bioren, 1797.

WILLIAM YOUNG BIRCH, Publisher. No. 17 South Second Street, 1796–1797.

THOMAS BRADFORD, Printer, publisher, Bookseller and Stationer. The Free and Independent Political and Literary Press, No. 8 South Front Street, 1796–1797.

DANIEL BRAUTIGAM, Bookseller. 1796.

ANDREW BROWN, Printer and publisher. At Washington's Head, in Chesnut Street—No. 29—between Front and Second Streets, 1796–1797.

HENRY [STACY] BUDD, Printer. Budd and Bartram, No. 58 North Second Street, 1796–1797.

ROBERT CAMPBELL, Bookseller. Robert Campbell and Co. No. 40 South Second Street, 1796–1797.

PHILADELPHIA, continued.

JAMES CAREY, Printer and publisher. 1. No. 83 North Second Street, 1796–1797. 2. James Carey and John Markland, 1797.

MATHEW CAREY, Bookseller and Map publisher. No. 118 Market Street, 1796–1797.

BENJAMIN CARR, Music publisher. At his Musical Repository, No. 122 Market Street, 1796–1797.

JOHN CHALK, Circulating Library. No. 75 North Third Street, 1797.

JOSEPH CHARLES, Bookseller. 1797.

FRANCIS CHILDS, Printer of the Laws of the United States, 1796.

CHARLES [CARL] CIST, Printer and Bookseller. 1. No. 104 North Second Street, 1796–1797. 2. Carl Cist, in der Zweyten-strasse, No. 104 nahe am Eck der Rehs-Strasse, 1796–1797.

DAVID C. CLAYPOOLE, Printer and publisher. David C. and Septimus Claypoole, No. 48 Market Street, 1796–1797.

SEPTIMUS CLAYPOOLE, Printer. David C. and Septimus Claypoole, 1796–1797.

WILLIAM COBBETT, Printer, publisher and Bookseller. No. 25 North Second Street, opposite Christ Church, 1796–1797.

ROBERT COCHRAN, Printer. Stewart and Cochran, 1796.

THOMAS CONDIE, Bookseller. No. 20 Carter's Alley, 1796.

EPHRAIM CONRAD, Printer. 1. Ormrod and Conrad, 1796–1797. 2. E. Conrad, No. 100 Fourth, the second door above Race Street, 1796.

JAMES CRUKSHANK, Bookseller. Joseph and James Crukshank, 1797.

JOSEPH CRUKSHANK, Printer and Bookseller. 1. No. 87 High Street, 1796–1797. 2. Joseph and James Crukshank, 1797.

BENJAMIN DAVIES, Bookseller. No. 68 High Street, 1796–1797.

RICHARD DAVISON, Bookseller. 1797.

JAMES JOHNSTON DENOON, Bookseller. No. 34 Carter's Alley, 1796.

G. DECOMBAZ, Bookseller. No. 48 North Third Street, 1797.

JOHN DICKINS, Methodist publications. No. 50 North Second Street, near Arch Street, 1796–97.

THOMAS DOBSON, Printer, Bookseller and Stationer. At the Stone House, No. 41 South Second Street, 1796–1797.

G. DOUGLAS, Bookseller and Stationer. No. 2 South Third Street, 1797.

TERTIUS DUNNING, Printer. Dunning and Hyer, 1796.

JOHN FENNO, Printer and publisher. Printer to the Senate of the United States, No. 119 Chesnut Street, 1796–1797.

PHILADELPHIA, *continued.*

SAMUEL FINLAY, Printer and publisher. No. 16 Chesnut Street, 1796–1797.

RICHARD FOLWELL, Printer. 1. No. 33 Carter's Alley, 1796–1797. 2. No. 33 Mulberry Street, 1796–1797.

JOSEPH GALES, Printer and publisher. No. 145 [126] North Second Street, 1796–1797.

—— GRIFFITHS, Bookseller. Griffiths and Rhees, 177 South Second Street, 1796–1797.

DAVID HALL, Printer and publisher. Hall and Sellers, at the New Printing Office, near the Market, No. 51 Market Street, 1796–1797.

J. HOFF, Printer. J. Hoff and H. Kammerer, jun. 1796.

DAVID HOGAN, Printer. 1797. 2. Hogan and M'Elroy, George Street, third door below South Street, 1797.

DANIEL HUMPHREYS, Printer. No. 48 Spruce Street, 1796–1797.

JAMES HUMPHREYS, Printer and Bookseller. No. 74 Third Street, corner of Cherry Alley, 1797.

WALTER W. HYER, Printer. Dunning and Hyer, 1796.

BENJAMIN JOHNSON, Bookseller. B. and J. Johnson, No. 147 Market Street, 1796–1797.

JACOB JOHNSON, Printer. 1. B. and J. Johnson, 1796. 2. Jacob Johnson and Co. No. 147 High Street, 1796–1797,

HEINRICH KAMMERER, Printer. Steiner und Kammerer, 1796–1797.

HEINRICH KAMMERER, JUN. 1. Neale and Kammerer jun. 1796. 2. Hoff and Kammerer jun. 1796. 3. H. Kammerer jun. 1797. 4. H. Kammerer jun. und Comp, No. 24 in der Dritten Strasse, zwischen der Markt-und Arch-Strasse, 1797.

THOMAS LANG, Printer. Lang and Ustick, No. 79 North Third Street, 1796–1797.

RICHARD LEE, Publisher. 1. No. 84 Mulberry Street, near the corner of Third Street, 1796. 2. No. 131 Chesnut Street, 1797. 3. No. 4 Chesnut Street, near the Wharf, 1797.

SAMUEL LONGCOPE, Bookseller. No. 147 Spruce Street, 1797.

WILLIAM M'CORKLE, Printer. Snowden and M'Corkle, 1796.

JOHN M'CULLOCH, Printer and Bookseller. No. 1 North Third Street, 1796–1797.

WILLIAM M'CULLOCH, Bookseller and Stationer. No. 306 Market Street, 1796.

—— McELROY, Printer. Hogan and McElroy, 1797.

—— MADAN, Printer. Bioren and Madan, 1796–97.

JOHN MARKLAND, Printer. 1. Carey and Markland, 1797. 2. No. 91 South Front Street, 1797.

—— MILLS, Bookseller and Stationer. Young, Mills and Son, 1796–1797.

M. L. E. MOREAU DE ST MERY, Printer and Bookseller, No. 84 corner of Front and Walnut Streets, 1796–1797.

TIMOTHY MOUNTFORD, Printer and publisher. 1797.

ISAAC NEALE, Neale and Kammerer, jun. No. 24 North Third Street, 1796.

JOHN ORMROD, Printer and Bookseller. 1. Ormrod and Conrad, No. 41 Chesnut Street, 1796–1797. 2. J. Ormrod, 1796–1797.

ELIZABETH OSWALD, Printer and publisher. 1. No. 156 Market Street, South, 1796. 2. No. 197 South Second Street, 1797.

J. H. OSWALD, Printer. No. 179 South Second Street, 1797.

JOHN PAGE, Printer. No. 67 Mulberry Street, 1796.

WILLIAM T. PALMER, Printer and publisher. No. 18 North Third Street, 1797.

PIERRE PARENT, Printer and publisher. 1. No. 85 Vine Street, 1796–1797. 2. No. 32 South Fifth Street, 1797.

WILLIAM PECHIN, Printer. Woodruff and Pechin, 1796.

ZACHARIAH POULSON, JUNIOR, Printer and publisher. Number eighty Chesnut Street, eight doors below Third Street, 1796–1797.

MORGAN JOHN RHEES, Bookseller. Griffiths and Rhees, 1796–1797.

HENRY RICE, Bookseller. H. and P. Rice, No. 16 South Second Street, and No. 50 Market Street, 1796–1797.

PATRICK RICE, Bookseller. H. and P. Rice, 1796–97.

WILLIAM ROGERS, Bookseller. 1796.

WILLIAM ROSS, Printer. Congress Hall, 1796–97.

SAMUEL SAMSON, JUNIOR, Printer. No. 21 Mulberry Street, 1796–1797.

DAVID SAUR [or SOWER], Bookbinder and Stationer. No. 66 North Third Street, 1796–1797.

HEINRICH [HENRY] SCHWEITZER [SWEITZER], Printer, publisher and Bookseller. No. 85 in der Rees-strasse, zwischen der Zweiten und Dritten-strasse, 1796–1797.

WILLIAM SELLERS, Printer. Hall and Sellers, 1796–1797.

ABRAHAM SMALL, Printer. 1797.

SAMUEL HARRISON SMITH, Printer and publisher. No. 118 Chesnut Street, 1796–1797.

THOMAS SMITH, Printer. S. H. Smith and Thos. Smith, 1797.

—— SNOWDEN, Printer. Snowden and M'Corkle, No. 47 North Fourth Street, 1796–1797.

MELCHIOR STEINER, Printer, publisher and Bookseller. Steiner und Kammerer, No. 85 in der Rees Strasse, zwischen der Zweyten und Dritten Strasse, 1796–1797.

THOMAS STEPHENS, Bookseller. No. 60 South Second Street, 1796–1797.

PHILADELPHIA, *continued.*

JAMES STEWART, Bookseller. 1. James Stewart and Co. 1797. 2. Stewart and Rowson, No. 9 Cherry Street, 1797.

PETER STEWART, Printer. Stewart and Cochran, No. 34 South Second Street, 1796–1797.

ROBERT STEWART, Travelling Bookseller. 1796.

RAYNOR TAYLOR, Music publisher. No. 96 North Sixth Street, 1797.

JOHN THOMPSON, Printer. No. 34 Carter's Alley, 1796–1797.

HENRY TUCKNISS, Printer. No. 25 Church Alley, 1796–1797.

JOHN TURNER, Printer and publisher. 1. No. 224 Market Street, 1796. 2. Between 72 and 74 Chesnut Street, 1796–1797.

STEPHEN C. USTICK, Printer and Bookseller. 1. Lang and Ustick, 1796–1797. 2. Stephen C. Ustick, No. 79 North Third Street, 1796–1797.

THOMAS USTICK, Bookseller. No. 79 North Third Street, 1796.

JAMES WATTERS, Printer and publisher. 1797.

MASON LOCKE WEEMS, Travelling Bookseller, 1796–1797.

GEORGE WILLIG, Music publisher. At his Musical Magazine, 165 Market Street, 1796–1797.

J. WOODHOUSE, Printer. 1797.

WILLIAM WOODHOUSE, Bookseller and Stationer. No. 6 South Front Street, 1796–1797.

ARCHIBALD WOODRUFF, Printer and publisher. Woodruff and Pechin, No. 224 Market Street, near Seventh Street, 1796.

WILLIAM W. WOODWARD, Printer. No. 36 [17] Franklin's Head, (new Sign) south side of Chesnut Street, 1796–1797.

WILLIAM YOUNG, Printer, Bookseller and Stationer. No. 52 Second Street, the corner of Chesnut Street, 1796–1797. 2. Young, Mills and Son, 1797.

PITTSBURGH, 1786.

JOHN SCULL, Printer, publisher and Bookseller. At his Printing Office in Front Street, next door to the corner of Market Street, 1796–1797.

READING, 1789.

Hrn. DUNDAS, Vender. 1796.

GEORGE GERRISH, Printer. Schneider and Gerrish, 1796–1797.

Hrn. HAHN, Vender. 1796.

GOTTLOB JUNGMANN, Printer and publisher. 1. Jungmann und Gruber, 1796–1797. 2. Jungmann und Comp. in der Deutsch-und Englischen Buchdruckerey, in der Callowhill Strasse, sud von dem Courthaus, 1797.

JACOB SCHNEIDER, Printer and publisher. Schneider und Comp. in der Deutsch-und Englischen Buchdruckerey in der Pennstrasse, 1796–1797.

SHIPPENSBURGH, 1797.

BENJAMIN GRIMLER, Printer. H. and B. Grimler, 1797.

HENRY GRIMLER, Printer and publisher. Henry and Benjamin Grimler, 1797.

SOUTHAMPTON, 1797.

STEPHEN C. USTICK, Printer. 1797.

TULPEHACKEN.

Hrn. SPICKER, Vender. 1796.

VIRGINIEN.

Hrn. STAUFFER, Vender. 1796.

WASHINGTON, 1795.

WILLIAM H. BEAUMONT, Printer. Colerick, Hunter and Beaumont, 1796.

JOHN COLERICK, Printer and publisher. 1. Colerick, Hunter and Beaumont, 1796. 2. John Colerick, 1797.

WILLIAM HUNTER, Printer. Colerick, Hunter and Beaumont, 1796.

WEST CHESTER, 1794.

PHILIP DERRICK, Printer. Derrick and Sharples, 1797.

—— SHARPLES, Printer. Derrick and Sharples, 1797.

WEST LIBERTY.

WILLIAM SKINNER, Vender. 1796.

WILKESBARRE, 1796.

BENAJAH HALL, Printer. 1. M. Johnson and B. Hall, 1796–1797. 2. Benajah Hall, 1797.

MICAH JOHNSON, Printer and publisher. M. Johnson and B. Hall, near the Post Office, 1796–97.

JOSIAH WRIGHT, Printer and publisher. 1797.

YORK, 1777.

JOHN EDIE, Printer and publisher. 1796–1797.

SALOMON MAYER, Printer and publisher. 1796–97.

PRINTING INSTITUTED IN

RHODE ISLAND, 1727, A. D.

NEWPORT, 1727.

HENRY BARBER, Printer and publisher. Near the State House, 1796–1797.

JOSEPH J. TODD, Bookseller. 1797.

PROVIDENCE, 1762.

JOHN CARTER, Printer, publisher, Bookseller and Stationer. Carter and Wilkinson, at the Providence Book Store, opposite the Market, 1796–97.

JOSEPH FRY, Printer and publisher. Directly opposite the Market, 1796.

JOSEPH J. TODD, Bookseller, and Circulating Library. At the Bible and Anchor, 1796–1797.

BENNETT WHEELER, Printer and publisher. 1. At his Office in the Market House Chambers, 1796. 2. No. 1 Westminster Street, a few rods westward of the Great Bridge and directly opposite the Turk's Head, 1796–1797.

WILLIAM WILKINSON, Printer. Carter and Wilkinson, 1796–1797.

WARREN, 1792.

NATHANIEL PHILLIPS, Printer and publisher. Printer to the State, at the Post Office, 1796–1797.

PRINTING INSTITUTED IN
SOUTH CAROLINA, 1732, A. D.

CHARLESTON, 1732.

S. J. ELLIOTT, Printer. No. 47 Bay, 1797.

PETER FRENEAU, Printer and publisher. Freneau and Paine, Printers to the City, No. 47 Bay, 1796–1797.

WILLIAM PRIMROSE HARRISON, Printer and publisher. Harrison and Co. No. 38 Bay, corner of Elliot Street, 1796–1797.

JOHN M'IVER, JUNIOR, Printer. No. 47 Bay, 1796.

WILLIAM MASON, JUNIOR, Printer. Timothy and Mason, 1796–1797.

SETH PAINE, Printer. Freneau and Paine, 1796–97

BENJAMIN FRANKLIN TIMOTHY, Printer and publisher. 1796–1797.

WILLIAM P. YOUNG, Printer and Bookseller. Franklin's Head, No. 43 Broad Street, 1796–1797.

COLUMBIA, 1792.

DANIEL FAUST, Printer and publisher. Young and Faust, 1796–1797.

WILLIAM P. YOUNG, Printer and publisher. W. P. Young and D. Faust, State Printers, 1796.

GEORGETOWN, 1791.

JAMES SMYLIE, Printer and publisher. 1796–1797.

PRINTING INSTITUTED IN
TENNESSEE, 1791, A. D.

KNOXVILLE, 1792.

GEORGE ROULSTONE, Printer and publisher. Printer to the State, 1796–1797.

ROGERSVILLE, 1791.

PRINTING INSTITUTED IN
VERMONT, 1778, A. D.

BENNINGTON, 1783.

ANTHONY HASWELL, Printer and publisher. At his Office, a few rods south of the Court House, 1796–1797.

REUBEN LANGDON, Printer. Merrill and Langdon, 1797.

ORSAMUS C. MERRILL, Printer and publisher. 1. For Anthony Haswell, 1796. 2. Merrill and Langdon, 1797.

BRATTLEBOROUGH, 1797.

THOMAS DICKMAN, Publisher. Dickman and Smead, 1797.

BENJAMIN SMEAD, Printer and publisher. 1. Dickman and Smead, 1797. 2. Benjamin Smead, 1797.

BURLINGTON, 1796.

ROBERT DONNELLY, Printer and publisher. Donnelly and Hill, directly opposite the Court House, 1796–1797.

JAMES HILL, Printer. Donnelly and Hill, 1796–97.

DRESDEN, 1778.

FAIRHAVEN, 1795.

JAMES LYON, Printer. At Voltaire's Head, 1797.

JUDAH P. SPOONER, Printer and publisher. 1796–1797.

NEWBURY, 1793.

NATHANIEL COVERLY, JUNIOR, Printer and publisher. Near the Court House, 1796–1797.

PUTNEY, 1797.

CORNELIUS STURTEVANT, JUNIOR, Printer and publisher. Cornelius Sturtevant, jun. and Co. 1797.

ELIAS STURTEVANT, Printer. Sturtevant and Co. 1797.

ABIJAH WILDER, Printer. Sturtevant and Co. 1797.

RUTLAND, 1792.

JOSIAH FAY, Printer. S. Williams and Co, 1797.

JOHN S. HUTCHINS, Printer. S. Williams and Co. 1796–1797.

JAMES KIRKALDIE, Printer. S. Williams and Co. 1796.

SAMUEL WILLIAMS, Editor and publisher. S. Williams and Co. a few rods north of the State House, 1796–1797.

WESTMINSTER, 1781.

JOHN GOOLD, JUNIOR, Printer and publisher. A few rods south of the Meetinghouse, 1796.

WHITINGHAM.

Amos Taylor, Tutor and Bookseller. At his Book Store, 1796.

WINDSOR, 1783.

Oliver Farnsworth, Printer. Press of A. Spooner, 1797.

Alden Spooner, Printer and publisher. On the west side of the Main Street, 1796-1797.

PRINTING INSTITUTED IN VIRGINIA, 1730, A. D.

ALEXANDRIA, 1782.

Henry Gird, junior, Printer. Price and Gird. 1796-1797.

Ellis Price, Printer and publisher. Price and Gird, at the east end of the Market House, 1796-1797.

John V. Thomas, Printer and publisher. Thomas and Westcott, Royal Street, between the Post Office and Coffee House, 1797.

James D. Westcott, Printer. Thomas and Westcott, 1797.

CHARLOTTESVILLE, 1781.

DUMFRIES, 1791.

James Kempe, Printer and publisher. J. Kempe and T. Thornton, 1796.

Thomas Thornton, Printer and publisher. 1. J. Kempe and T. Thornton, 1796. 2. Thomas Thornton, 1796.

FREDERICKSBURG, 1787.

George Carter, Printer. Mercer and Carter, 1797.

Timothy Green, Printer and publisher. 1796-97.

Robert Mercer, Printer and publisher. Mercer and Carter, 1797.

Lancelot A. Mullin, Printer and publisher. Market Street, west corner of the Upper Tobacco Inspection, 1796-1797.

Mason Locke Weems, Travelling Bookseller. 1797.

GEORGE-TOWN, 1789.

David English, Printer. Green, English and Co. 1796-1797.

Charles D. Green, Printer and publisher. Green, English and Co. 1796-1797.

Samuel Hanson, Printer and publisher. Two doors from the Commissioner's Office, 1796.

Mason Locke Weems, Travelling Bookseller. 1797.

LYNCHBURG, 1793.

Robert Mosby Bransford, Printer and publisher. 1796.

John Davis, Printer and publisher. John Davis and Co. 1797.

MARTINSBURG, 1790.

Nathaniel Willis, Printer and publisher. At his Printing Office, in Burke Street, near the Court House, 1796-1797.

NORFOLK, 1774.

William Davis, Printer and publisher. 1796-97.

Robert Hannah, Bookseller. Rainbow and Hannah, 1795-1797.

James O'Connor, Printer. Willett and O'Connor, 1796-1797.

Thomas Rainbow, Bookseller. Rainbow and Hannah, at the Norfolk Circulating Library, 1795-97.

Charles Willett, Printer and publisher. Willett and O'Connor, near the Market, 1796-1797.

PETERSBURG, 1786.

William Prentis, Printer and publisher 1796-97.

RICHMOND, 1780.

Archibald Currie, Bookseller. 1797.

Augustine Davis, Printer and publisher. Printer for the Public, 1796-1797.

John Dixon, Printer and publisher. Near the Market, 1796-1797.

Thomas Nicolson, Printer and publisher. Two doors above the Eagle Tavern, 1796-1797.

Samuel Pleasants, junior, Printer and publisher. 1. Opposite Bowler's, and next door below the Columbia Tavern, 1796. 2. Near the Vendue Office, 1796-1797.

SHEPHERD'S-TOWN, 1791.

Charles Blagrove, Printer. P. Rootes and C. Blagrove, 1797.

Philip Rootes, Printer and publisher. Rootes and Blagrove, 1797.

STAUNTON, 1793.

—— Adams, Printer. Wise and Adams, 1796-97.

Robert Douthat, Printer and publisher. 1796.

John Wise, Printer and publisher. 1. Wise and Adams, 1796-1797. 2. John Wise, 1797.

WILLIAMSBURG, 1730.

WINCHESTER, 1787.

Richard Bowen, Printer and publisher. Opposite the Episcopal Church in Loudoun Street. 1796-1797.

END OF THE ELEVENTH VOLUME.